American Library

Presented to
American Library
Memorial to the 2nd Air Division
8th Air Force
United States Army Air Forces

by
In memory of all who served in the
2nd Air Division USAAF
Eighth Air Force WWII

Presented by members of the 2nd Air
Division Association,
50th Anniversary Convention, Irvine

RG HEAD, PHD
BRIG. GEN., USAF (RET.)
FOREWORD BY ADM. SCOTT H. SWIFT, USN (RET.)

US ATTACK AVIATION
AIR FORCE/NAVY LIGHT ATTACK
1916 TO THE PRESENT

SCHIFFER MILITARY

4880 Lower Valley Road   Atglen, PA 19310

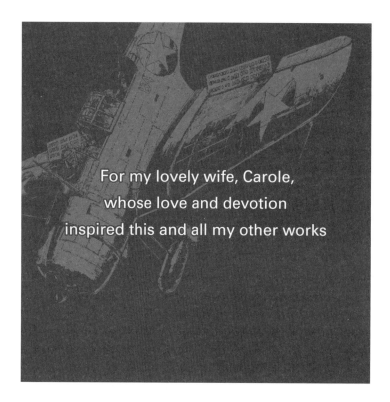

For my lovely wife, Carole,
whose love and devotion
inspired this and all my other works

Cover artwork, *Douglas Dauntless SBD Dive Bomber*, courtesy of the artist, Lucio Perinotto

Copyright © 2022 by RG Head

Library of Congress Control Number: 2021942583

Designed by Justin Watkinson
Type set in Impact/Minion Pro/Univers LT Std

ISBN: 978-0-7643-6356-6
Printed in India

Published by Schiffer Publishing, Ltd.
4880 Lower Valley Road
Atglen, PA 19310
Phone: (610) 593-1777; Fax: (610) 593-2002
Email: Info@schifferbooks.com
Web: www.schifferbooks.com

For our complete selection of fine books on this and related subjects, please visit our website at www. schifferbooks.com. You may also write for a free catalog.

Schiffer Publishing's titles are available at special discounts for bulk purchases for sales promotions or premiums. Special editions, including personalized covers, corporate imprints, and excerpts, can be created in large quantities for special needs. For more information, contact the publisher.

Contents

Acknowledgments

My career in the Air Force was balanced among flying and commanding fighters, air-to-air, air-to-ground, instructing, and policy analysis. But the most-memorable moments were those I spent hurling myself at the ground in close air support—the attack mission. After graduating from the Air Force Academy, I spent three years flying the F-100 Super Sabre and another year flying the A-1E Skyraider in combat, where our dominant mission was close air support. I did not know much about naval air, but when the Air Force sponsored me in graduate school, I was able to write my PhD dissertation on the Vought A-7 Corsair II. My first thanks go to my advisor, Edwin A. Bock, the head of the Inter-University Case Program at Syracuse University. My second and third acknowledgments go to Maj. Gen. Richard Bowman, who guided me through the research on the Air Force A-7 program, and Robert "Bud" McFarlane, with whom I wrote a book while at the National War College.

I am grateful to all of the many officers who helped me throughout my careers in the Air Force and engineering consulting. Two classmates, Generals Ron Yates and Mike Loh, read several sections and provided extensive inputs and advice on the F-16 and F-15 programs. Another classmate, Ken Alnwick, contributed his experiences flying the B-26 in Vietnam. Class of 1959 colonel Ed Montgomery, who preceded me as the operations officer of the 421st Tactical Fighter Squadron in Thailand, contributed his story of night-fighter escort of B-52s in Operation Linebacker II. Gen. Ron Fogelman, former chief of staff (1994–1997), loaned me his monograph on the development of Army ground attack aviation doctrine in the 1920s, from which I drew heavily. Gen. Nordy Schwartz, former chief of staff (2008–2012), read an early draft and contributed his comments.

A lifetime friend, Col. Richard L. Kuiper, was an F-100 pilot, Super Sabre Society member, F-4 instructor pilot, and forward air controller with the 1st Cavalry Division in the Central Highlands. He contributed his textbook on close air support, *Air-Ground Operations*, when we taught and flew F-4s together at Davis Monthan AFB. Dick also read several chapters and provided fatherly guidance and expertise on a wide range of subjects.

This book would not have been possible without the yeoman assistance and advice from Ed Beakley. Ed, call sign "Boris," is a naval aviator with 170 combat missions in Southeast Asia, including 100+ over North Vietnam in Attack Squadron 56 (VA-56). He was qualified in both fighter and attack aircraft, and as a test pilot he flew all USN attack/strike aircraft. He was the program manager / test director and test pilot for all variants of the Tomahawk Cruise Missile and worked on the Harpoon, Walleye, Phoenix, and multiple air launch UAS vehicles. His twenty years of operational service was augmented by thirty-five years of RDT&E (research, development, test, and evaluation) support of Navy weapons and command and control systems. Ed was present at the creation of this research, and he contributed greatly by identifying dozens of other naval aviators with attack stories to tell. His website, Remembered Sky, is the repository of countless adventures told by the participants in naval aviation over the past sixty years. This work is a tribute to the vision, research, writing, and recording of attack aviation issues and history.

Thanks especially to Byron Huckee, fellow A-1 pilot, author, and creator of the website The Skyraiders (www.skyraiders.org) for his several inputs and suggestions. Maj. Gen. Don Shepperd wrote a piece on the Air National Guard and his experiences flying the F-100 FASTFAC and A-7. Fellow F-100 pilot Ralph Wetterhahn contributed his unforgettable story about his experiences as a

Navy exchange officer qualifying for carrier landings and firing the Gatling gun in the A-7E. Lt. Gen. Jack Hudson was one of my protégés when teaching political science at the academy. He had a successful Air Force career and continued his service as head of the National Museum of the US Air Force. Jack enlisted the help of his staff, who provided yeoman support for research and the location of photographs for many of the epic Army Air Corps and USAF attack aircraft pictured in the book. Thanks to Teresa Montgomery, Krista Strider, Bryan Carnes, Andrew Davis, and Michael Smith for their sustaining efforts. Brig. Gen. David Eaglin, 7th Air Force, give us some valuable last-minute guides to current photographs.

Ken Neubeck gave permission to use some of the material from his wonderful book, *A-10 Thunderbolt II*. The story of Linebacker II could not have been told without the input of G. Ray Sullivan, who provided a description of his father's heroic decision while in Strategic Air Command. A special thank-you to Robert P. Dorr, son of Robert F. Dorr, Arlington, Virginia, author of one of the original A-7 volumes, for permission to quote from his father's books. TSgt. Andrew Davis, USAF Public Affairs, gave us some good references. Maureen De Felice, executive director of Daedalians, the premier fellowship of military aviators, provided sustaining support, and Col. Frank Kapp wrote an excellent advance review for the *Daedalian Flyer*.

Ed Beakley introduced me to many of his friends in the A-7 Corsair II Association, including its executive director, Mat Garretson. Their website houses an extensive collection of A-7 material and was a treasure trove of reports and sea stories. I am especially grateful to Adm. Scott H. Swift, who wrote the foreword from his desk at MIT. Adm. Leon "Bud" Edney has been a constant friend and advisor. VAdm. Brent Bennitt read several of the chapters and added two wonderful stories of flying the A-7E.

Many pilots and members of the A-7 Corsair II Association responded with vignettes and advice that gave realism to the narrative and authenticity to the story. They included Adm. Jim Busey, VAdm. Rocky Spane, RAdm. Lew Chatham, and RAdm. W. W. Pickavance Jr. Thanks to Brig. Gen. Keith Connolly, USAF, for his A-7D

story, as well as Mace Gilfrey, Wally Moorhead, Bill Thomas, Terry Wolf, Kevin Miller, Jeff Edwards, and Charlie Dills. Thanks also to John "Rat" Leslie, for sharing quotes from his book, *In My Father's Footsteps: A Story of Father and Son Naval Aviators*. Thanks to Capt. Denny Laack and Ken Sanger, who sent several inputs on the A-4, A-7, and three-ship divisions. Barrett Tillman commented from his excellent book *The Dragon's Jaw*, the story of the Thanh Hoa bridge. Greg Stearns, F/A-18 pilot, read several of the chapters and provided some excellent narrative and advice.

James G. Kidrick, A-7E pilot, and the president of the San Diego Air & Space Museum (SDASM), characterized the A-7D/E avionics as a "breakthrough" technology. His staff, including Katrina Pescadore, Alan Renga, and Melissa Culbertson, at the SDASM library and archives, provided photographs and the manuscript of *The History of Rockwell Field* by Maj. Hap Arnold and loaned me the Bureau of Aeronautics' valuable *Attack Plane Design History*.

The Naval History and Heritage Command (NHHC), led by RAdm. Samuel Cox at the Washington Navy Yard, researched and provided dozens of photographs of early and modern attack aircraft flown by the Navy and Marine Corps. Many thanks to their staff: Patrick Burns, deputy director; Kristina Giannotta, photo archives; John DeLuca, director of communications and outreach; and W. Paul Taylor, David Dull, Jay Thomas, Timothy Francis, Jonathan Roscoe, and Eden Marie Picazo. Hill Goodspeed is especially thanked for his advice and early nomination of the ten most significant attack aircraft, which gave structure to the book.

Three artists, Lucio Perinotto, Peter Chilelli, and David Tipps, gave permission to use their wonderful artwork. Great appreciation to Daniel Holt, assistant historian at the US Senate, for information on the Truman Committee's comments on attack aviation. The Boeing Company's Deborah VanNierop and Heather Anderson contributed images of the early B-17 and the current F/A-18E/F. Defense analyst Pierre Sprey was a key player in the Air Force A-7 program, and his colleague, Lon Ratley, provided valuable reference advice on the German approach to close air support and interdiction.

A special note of thanks to Lucio Perinotto for his magnificent artwork of the Douglas Dauntless SBD. Lucio is a renowned French official aviation artist whose works include a wide range of aircraft, airfield, and aviation scenes. His work is found on numerous magazines, in five volumes of his work, and in multiple other locations. His website is www.lucioperinotto.com.

Thank you to Osprey/Bloomberg for permission to use some of their published material. Mike Hanlon provided some unique references to World War I ground attack, and Cmdr. Jason Ward provided research material. Thanks to Jeff Edwards for his kind words. My brother, Brig. Gen. James Head, contributed valuable expertise in proofreading and commenting on the manuscript. My wife, Carole, was a continuing source of good advice and inspiration, including coordination when we were both self-isolating during the coronavirus pandemic. Finally, at Schiffer Books, I was fortunate to have several wonderful professionals: Carey Massimini, John Stone, and senior editor Bob Biondi.

Preface

The story of Navy and Air Force attack aircraft can be likened to two half brothers. They were sired by the same father (the experience of war). But they were bred by two quite different mothers: the Revolutionary War–era British navy and the US Army Signal Corps in World War I. Jacob and Esau, if you must. They were raised by separate families with unique historical experiences and missions. The elder Navy founded a boarding-school academy on a Maryland river in the nineteenth century—in the days of iron men in wooden ships. The younger Air Force brother found no established school that would have him, so he started with two bicycle repairmen and built his own school in the mountains of Colorado. Both were loved at birth by their parent organizations but were viewed with suspicion, lest they change the established order. The naval child was picked to be cherished and mentored shortly after the aircraft carrier was accepted as a capital ship. He grew healthy and strong as a better means to accomplish an old mission—to attack enemy fleets.

The Army Air Corps attack branch had more difficulty, falling as it did as a low third in mission priority to strategic bombardment and pursuit fighters. Single-engine aircraft in the light-attack role were cherished by the Navy as a fundamental force. But in the face of war, they were rejected by the Army Air Forces in favor of twin-engined bombers. There were literally no successful single-engine, attack-designated aircraft in the Air Force until it borrowed the A-1 from the Navy in the early 1960s and modified the A-7 of the mid-1960s.

Both brothers trained in the same profession—of arms—but interpreted it in dissimilar ways. The brother services respect one another but are hotly competitive—on the friendly fields of strife and in the Pentagon. They both use vehicles of the air, launched from vastly different media—sea and land. They attack the same targets, but from different angles. They are learning to coordinate and cooperate in this era of jointness. They protect us.

Foreword

When Brig. Gen. RG Head asked if I would consider writing the foreword for his book, I was both humbled and honored. I did not know RG personally, but his reputation as a leader, aviator, author, and professor preceded him. After reading the manuscript I was even more enthused by the opportunity to directly support this book.

The challenge with writing this foreword is trying to capture the scope and scale of what RG has described in his book. From a historical perspective alone, there is something here for everyone. From the early genesis of what would become the core capabilities and tenants of attack aviation, to the transformation the community is facing today, the reader is presented with the expansive history of both the Air Force and Navy attack aviation in peacetime and war.

This historical perspective is brought to life by RG's inclusion of the personal remembrances, recollections, and experiences of a broad spectrum of aviators from these two communities of warriors. These are individuals who stood out from a backdrop of a very select group of airmen and naval aviators who successfully completed a rigorous selection and training regimen. Regardless of service, it tested their intellect, ability to focus on the right detail at the right time in crisis, and mental toughness to set fear aside to focus on mission execution and success.

I was struck how RG captured my own journey to becoming a light-attack pilot. I became fascinated with flying during my preteen years. Working odd jobs in high school to pay for flying lessons, I eventually obtained my private pilot's license, as he did.

I wanted to be an airline pilot, but that extensive training was too expensive. I went to college with the goal of joining the military to become a pilot, leaving for the airlines once I completed my initial obligation.

I joined the Navy, went through Aviation Reserve Officer Candidate School, received my commission, and started flight school in 1979. During pilot training, I was drawn to the light-attack community by my admiration of the instructors who had flown the A-7E Corsair in their operational tours. They struck me as an inclusive group, focused on themselves only in the context of ensuring they were contributing their full measure to the team's success. I was lucky enough to be selected for my first choice of both aircraft and location upon graduation and received my wings, flying the A-7E out of NAS Lemoore, California.

Once at VA-122, the Fleet Replacement Squadron, I was even more convinced the light-attack community was where I belonged. I admired and respected the leadership in the community and among my instructors, as well as my fellow students. During this time, I realized I had been transformed by the light-attack community. It was with the mentorship, support, and guidance of the community that I first experienced night qualification in the A-7E on the USS *Lexington*. That said, once I was "winged," it was not lost on me that my service clock began the countdown to the four and a half years until I could resign and pursue my dream of flying for the airlines. I completed my training in the A-7E and joined my first fleet squadron (VA-94) in the last half of their eighteen-month deployment in the Far East. I joined a cadre of pilots at the peak of their game, confident in their abilities to overcome whatever challenges that might come their way. They took me in as a peer and became models for me to emulate. Two of them had extensive experience flying in Vietnam as junior officers, the same point in their career then that I was in mine. There was no slowing down the pace of operations for me. I was forced to address uncertainty, self-doubt, and fear on a daily basis, factors all inherent in the profession I had chosen. A profession I still considered a means to a bigger goal.

After a three-year tour that included three cruises on two carriers, I transitioned back to VA-122 as an instructor. It was in this tour that I completed my initial obligation and began the process of "rushing" the airlines. I quickly realized I had been transformed by the light-attack community I was now a part of.

This reality of being a part of something that was bigger than me came home to me the week before I was on track to leave naval aviation and achieve my dream of flying for the airlines. In that last week the one fear I could not overcome became a reality I could not ignore. I was afraid I would not be able to engender the same relationships outside the Navy that I had within it. So, I decided to take one more tour. And so it went, tour by tour, until a little over forty years after enlisting, it was time to make room for others to serve.

There is a wealth of value I gained in each of those tours, too much to cover in this foreword but well documented by RG in this excellent book. There are a few examples of what I was most grateful to be a part of during my years in this great community of Air Force and Navy attack aviation.

I served during several "technological evolutions." The first was the introduction of digital-computing hardware and software into the cockpit of the A-7E aircraft. When I began flying the Corsair II, the A-7B had been fully phased out by the introduction of the A-7E, with its more advanced weapons system. That said, more-senior aviators in the community were still very much "old school" A-7B diehards, which was not a bad thing. While the new technology made the aircraft much more effective and efficient, our old-school aviators made sure there remained within the community a strong core commitment to staying excellent in the basics, with a deep commitment to the fundamentals of airmanship required to fully realize any advantage new technology might bring. This remains critical today as the F-35 populates our squadrons

and wings, with unmanned technology continuing to mature and grow in capability, at least matching traditionally manned aircraft.

It is also important to note how "baked in" jointness is in the attack community. As a young junior officer in my first tour, interaction both with Air Force and Marine attack squadrons was a norm, not an exception. I participated in numerous training events in Red Flag at Nellis AFB, fully integrated with Air Force units, at NAS Fallon, Nevada, again, with Air Force units. As a deputy air wing commander during Operation Iraqi Freedom, joint operations was the norm rather than the exception. Integration was seamless, "baked in," due to how extensive our basic and advanced training had become. The "baked in" nature of Air Force and Navy attack aviation manifested itself again when I was the deputy commander of US Naval Forces, Central Command. I worked with commanders of our Air Force counterparts such as Gen. Gary "Nordo" North, a preeminent Viper driver. Two tours later I would serve as the PACOM J3 when he was the Pacific Air Forces commander. Of note, he had also served as the PACOM J3, providing me great insights and mentorship to me in that same role.

These are all examples underscoring the fact that through all my years of service, the biggest impact on my life was the community that accepted me in August 1979, and the individuals within it who shaped me into who I was as a naval officer and who I am today. My journey is what RG has captured in his wonderful book. More than that, he makes it clear that my journey is not unique or individual; it is common and shared. While the aircraft the larger attack community flew were a cornerstone to our shared experiences, it was, and is, our fellow aviators who were on the same journey. Even for those of us who flew single-seat aircraft and developed a certain independence of spirit, we were never alone.

If you have a love of history and an appreciation for aviation or are a member of the attack community, you will find your own and your fellow aviators' stories being told with each page you turn. If you have a friend or loved one who served in this community, you will gain a deeper understanding of how this community shaped them and became such a large part of their lives.

As you read this book, there are more pages being written by those serving today. If you are young enough to consider joining them, you have the opportunity to write them yourself.

RG has done a great service by providing us context on the scope and scale of attack aviation in the United States. Regardless of how this book came to be in your hands—as a gift or through your personal interest—each page you turn will be an opportunity to reflect on and experience the same gift all of us have who were a part of this community. Turn the page and join us.

Scott H. Swift, Admiral, USN (Ret.)
Commander, Pacific Fleet, 2015–2018
Westport, MA
2022

Introduction

This is a story about flying. It is told by naval aviators, Air Force fighter pilots, and the men who built the airplanes they flew. All served our country with honor. This narrative on attack aviation is a part of our history, an important link from those who were the pioneers of early aviation. They invented ways to use the airplane, built it, maintained it, extended its range, and made it lethal against America's adversaries.

The Attack Mission and Aircraft

Attack operations in the US Army, Navy, and Marine Corps grew out of combat experience in World War I, but the formal designation of aircraft as "Attack (A)" did not begin until the interwar years. Until World War II, the missions of sea strike, ground attack, interdiction, and close air support tended to be performed by a wide variety of aircraft. The Navy currently uses the mission terms of "strike" and "attack"; the Marine Corps adds "close air support" and the Air Force uses "close air support" and "interdiction."

The best definition of the attack mission is "strike, armed recce [reconnaissance], flak suppression, interdiction, close air support and direct air support."[1]

Ironically, there appears to be no current official Armed Forces definition of "attack" or the "attack mission" in joint publications, but there are definitions of close air support (CAS) and air interdiction.

The same joint document contains a definition of "strike" as "an attack to damage or destroy an objective or a capability."[2] The Tactical Air Forces of the United States are charged with three fundamental missions:

- **Air Superiority**: "That degree of dominance in the air battle of one force over another which permits the conduct of operations . . . without prohibitive interference."

- **Air Interdiction**: "Air operations conducted to destroy, neutralize, or delay the enemy's military potential before it can be brought to bear effectively against friendly forces at such distance from friendly forces that detailed integration . . . is not required."[3]

- **Close Air Support**: "Air action by fixed- and rotary-wing aircraft against hostile targets which are in close proximity to friendly forces and which require detailed integration of each air mission with the fire and movement of those forces."[4]

The "attack" mission combines the capabilities and objectives of air interdiction, close air support strike, and what has come to be known as strategic attack.

Separate Attack Communities

This work focuses on two professional communities: Navy attack pilots and Air Force pilots who fly attack aircraft. It is also a story of many of the engineers who made the machines they flew. The story starts in World War I because that is where the roots of all combat aviation and these two communities lie. It builds through the interwar years, when the characteristics of these groups formed and defined themselves as distinctive entities with different platforms, tactical skills, doctrines, and cultural beliefs.

Naval Attack Pilots

Navy and Marine Corps attack pilots are educated at the Naval Academy and the nation's universities and are taught to fly at Pensacola, Florida.

As soon as they complete basic flying training, they begin to specialize. For those who chose or are directed to attack aviation, they quickly learn the differences among Navy fighter pilots, multiengined pilots, and themselves. They are constantly told that they are not as good as the air-to-air jocks and that they are "attack pukes," but they also learn that they are the indispensable ones—the ones who are the offensive arm of the aircraft carrier. They go to the RAG (replacement air group) on the East or West Coast to qualify in an aircraft. They all are assigned a fleet squadron, where they train to become combat ready. Then, selected fighter jocks refine their art at "TOPGUN." But the attack pilots during the Vietnam War and until 1984 had none of that. Their flying was limited to what the squadron could provide during the Inter-Deployment Training Cycle, which provided a few sorties in the beginning phase and gradually increased in number and intensity until the carrier deploys. Their specialized training is similarly limited to what can be provided on the few bombing and strafing ranges at El Centro, Yuma, Fallon, Cherry Point, Oceana, and Key West.

When the "TOPGUN" training program was initiated at Fallon, Nevada, it was exclusively focused on air-to-air combat. There was no integrated-strike, graduate-level attack training until the Naval Strike Warfare Center was established in 1984, twelve years after Vietnam. When TOPGUN merged with the warfare center, it became the Naval Strike and Air Warfare Center (NWASC).

The Marine Corps focused on attack years earlier. It established the Weapons and Tactics Training Program (WTTP) at Marine Corps Air Station Yuma, Arizona, in 1976. The WTTP developed a Weapons and Tactics Instructor course and in 1978 founded the Marine Aviation Weapons and Tactics Training Squadron One.

Navy squadrons tend to be small, only twelve or so aircraft. They have squadron maintenance, and pilots have their own names on airplanes. Navy and Marine Corps pilots launch off catapults on the deck, have to qualify on carrier landings before every deployment, fly and fight in the air, and return to land on a postage-stamp-size carrier in the dead of night, under drizzling rain. They know that their worth had been certified long

ago—in the skies over the Battle of Midway, where their older brothers sank four Japanese carriers. They continued over the many amphibious landings across the Pacific, providing close air support to Marine Corps and Army ground forces.

Since the F/A-18 Hornet and Super Hornet aircraft are multimission planes, their Navy and Marine Corps aircrews balance their training between air-to-air and air-to-ground missions. F-35 pilots are being similarly trained.

Air Force Fighter Pilots

Air Force pilots are different. Those who fly supersonic jets and specialized attack planes are all "fighter pilots." Some went to the Air Force Academy, others took ROTC, but all trained at a host of Air Force bases across the United States. They learned formation takeoffs in pilot training but did not specialize until after getting their wings. Those who graduated high in their pilot training class got to choose their type of aircraft. But they all knew they would be flying off 10,000-foot runways wherever they had to go. They learned in Red Flag and Cope Thunder, and if they were lucky, they got to attend the USAF Fighter Weapons School. The pilots live in squadrons of twenty-four airplanes, in wings of three or four squadrons, and their airplanes are maintained by separate maintenance and munitions squadrons. They carry similar bombloads to their naval colleagues and fly in the same weather, but their runway doesn't pitch and roll on final approach. The idea of landing on a boat is pretty far from their imagination.

Those who flew "attack" aircraft scarcely remember that the Air Force had terminated all single-engine attack aircraft in 1940. The Air Force performed close air support in Korea with multipurpose aircraft and would not embrace the "attack" designation again until they needed A-1E Skyraiders in 1963. Under external pressure from the Army and political sources, they developed the A-7 in the late 1960s. The Air Force plan was to fly the A-7 for a while, then retire the aircraft to the National Guard as soon as possible. They treated the A-10 a little better, with a longer combat interval, but part of the plan was to assign new A-10s right off the production line to the Guard and Reserve also.

Navy and Air Force attack/fighter pilots specialized in training for the nuclear delivery mission in the 1950s and early 1960s. Conventional weapons training was conducted as a second priority but was not highlighted until the Vietnam War focused their mission. As an academic and flying instructor pilot in an F-4 Phantom II training wing in 1966–68, the author can attest that the shift to convential weapons delivery was immediate and overwhelmingly devoted to attack operations, specifically for North and South Vietnam.[5]

It is interesting that A-10 pilots were so specialized in close air support prior to 1991 that they were surprised to be tasked for battlefield air interdiction and even deep interdiction in Desert Storm.

This is also the story of specialized aircraft versus multipurpose aircraft. The distinction of the Navy's air defense mission and the Air Force's air superiority mission both dictated supersonic aircraft, and supersonic airplanes were produced in large numbers. The Navy continued to be dedicated to the attack mission, and the admirals continued to require subsonic airplanes for the air-to-surface mission. The Air Force, at its heart, believed multipurpose aircraft could do everything. Virtually all Air Force fighter squadrons flying the F-100, F-4, or F-16 were dual tasked with conventional and nuclear weapons delivery qualification.

Attrition in Military Flying

Aircrews in World War I experienced losses from training, combat, and aircraft accidents. Between combat and noncombat losses, the numbers were approximately equal. Aviation has always been a hazardous undertaking. In the 1960s, Navy fliers were calculated to have a 23 percent chance of dying from an aircraft accident.[6] Losses to combat added to this frightful toll. Among the many wartime missions of air operations, none were more hazardous historically than ground and sea attack. The reason is simple: these are the missions that place the aircraft in closest proximity to enemy guns and missiles.

Aviation as Controversy

Naval and Air Force aviation was born in controversy. Battleship admirals and Marine Corps generals ("Every Marine is a rifleman!") saw little use for airplanes. Even after naval aviators proved their worth in World War I, naval aviation faced constant conflict within the Navy and Marine Corps, from the War Department, and from skeptics in the Congress.[7] The Air Force was no different. It was placed strangely in the Signal Corps; early Army aviators struggled with chasing Pancho Villa and flying wood-and-fabric "kites" in combat against the Flying Circus. The interwar years were rife with disputes with the Navy over bombing ships and coastal defense and within the Air Corps between strategic-bombing advocates and fighter pilots. In 1949, strategic deterrence caused the biggest controversy, exemplified by the "Revolt of the Admirals" over the funding of the B-36 and the cancellation of the flush-deck carrier.

Unrecognized at the time, the "culture" of naval aviators and fighter pilots was and is amazingly similar: youth, competitive athletics, mechanical ability, initiative, cheerful, optimistic, "good hands," high-spirited, seldom sedentary, and with a certain swagger.[8] In their respective armed services, they shared the joys of adventurous flying, a high casualty rate,[9] night landings in thunderstorms, higher pay, flying combat with crippling political restrictions, competition within their service, interservice rivalry at the higher levels, and sometimes public scorn.

Case Studies

This story is told using a wide sweep of history over a century, but with concentrations on several case studies that characterize the evolution, technology, and tactics of the time: the SBD Dauntless, the AD Skyraider, the A-4 Skyhawk, the A-7 Corsair II, the A-10 Thunderbolt II, F-16 Falcon, and the F/A-18 Hornet. Each of the cases (including the Dauntless) contains first-person accounts that include a description of its origin, competitive procurement, major attack features, and combat employment told through the eyes of its pilots in first-person accounts. The A-7 story is expanded into several chapters because it explores the details of several of the controversies of attack aviation: Navy vs. Air Force differing requirements in the design of a common aircraft; Army / Air Force controversy over the close-air-support mission; military service disagreements with the Office of the Secretary of Defense, especially Systems Analysis, in the McNamara administration; and internal Air Force disputes over multipurpose vs. specialized aircraft. The heroes in these stories are the aircraft and the young men (and now women), warts and all, who debated, built, flew, and fought with these aircraft.

These are their stories and their history. We owe them our freedom.

CHAPTER 1
The Mission of Attack in World War I

The enemy's aircraft inspired our troops with a feeling of defenselessness against the enemy's mastery of the air.

—General Otto von Below, German army

Aerial Warfare Begins

The combatant powers mobilized their air units alongside infantry, artillery, cavalry, and logistics forces. Since the Germans planned their ground campaign to be one of expeditionary offense, their aircraft had been designed with folding wings so they would fit into the route of march. In prewar maneuver exercises, and in the early days of September–November 1914, the most important mission for aviation was visual reconnaissance (observation). One of the first actions of the war occurred on August 1, 1914, when a German dirigible hovered over a British fleet in the North Sea. Although there was no attack that day, life on the sea and on the land would never be the same. After the initial battles on the western front, the attack mission was inherent in virtually all of the aerial operations of the Great War.

Aerial-Observation Mission

Armies and navies needed to know where their opponents were and what they were doing. Whereas the observation function in armies had been virtually the exclusive mission of the cavalry,

the stagnation of the western front into trenches from Switzerland to the English Channel ended the dominance of cavalry and passed that role to primitive aircraft. Early records of medal awards for aviators talk of flying a certain number of "kilometers behind enemy lines,"[1] a term that was derived from cavalry raids in a land orientation. With the armies engaged in trench warfare, the observation mission rapidly evolved into artillery spotting, with pilots and observers looking for enemy guns and correcting the fall of shot of friendly artillery.

Aerial-Bombing Mission

Bombing became the second aerial mission when a French Voisin III bombed the German airship hangars at Metz-Frascaty on August 14, 1914. Subsequent bombing was almost entirely tactical and was performed by every air force on both sides of the line. The only attacks that could be called "strategic" were the zeppelin raids on Great Britain. By September 1914, air defense became important in England to ward off (not very successfully) German dirigible attacks. Interestingly, it was Winston Churchill, as the First Sea Lord, who established the first policy for air defense using antiaircraft artillery, searchlights, and fighter aircraft.

Fighter/Pursuit Mission

Fighter aviation did not begin until 1915, with the first aircraft specifically designed for air combat. Frenchman Roland Garros led the way when he mounted a machine gun on the forward fuselage to fire through the propeller. Tony Fokker invented the synchronized machine gun and attached it to the top fuselage of a Fokker M5K powered by an 80 hp Oberusel U.0 rotary engine. With this aircraft designated the *Eindecker* E.I monoplane, Oswald Boelcke and Max Immelmann initiated fighter sweeps and were the first German aviators to receive the Pour le Mérite (the famous "Blue Max"), with eight victories each.[2] In August 1916, partially due to the recommendations of their leading ace, Oswald Boelcke, the German Air Service, the *Luftstreitkräfte*, designated the first fighter squadrons, the *Jagdstaffeln*.

Attack Mission

The attack mission was arguably the last of the major airpower missions to evolve in World War

I. At first, aircraft were not armed, and when the aviators began to carry shotguns, rifles, and other assorted weapons, they were mainly interested in defending their own aircraft. No one really wanted to dive down into the cauldron of the front lines to get within range of the thousands of infantrymen with rifles and machine guns. After the invention of synchronized machine guns firing through the propeller and the employment of the aerial gunner, the air machine finally had enough firepower to be of some utility as an airborne firing platform. Some of the first uses of aircraft in ground attack were recorded in the Battle of the Somme (1916), where Lord Trenchard ordered his aircraft to attack German front lines. Their success led to expanded use, but a more complete exploitation of that attack mission was conducted by the German Air Service, first by the development of a "Protection" mission and then by the advent of units dedicated to ground attack.

The Advent of Aerial Photography

With the employment of cameras aboard aircraft, the observation mission changed dramatically. The stagnation of the western front created the requirement for photographs, which became essential in planning any kind of ground movement, attack, or disposition. Thus, the two-seat aircraft with pilot and observer/photographer was thrust into prominence. The observer, who was usually an artillery lieutenant (and in command of the aircraft), became so overwhelmed with photographic and artillery-spotting duties that he had very little time to be looking for enemy aircraft. In 1915–1916, with the advent of armed aircraft and the deployment of specialized pursuit/fighter squadrons, there evolved recognition that the reconnaissance aircraft needed protection.

British Experience at the Battle of the Somme

One of the first British uses of attack was on July 1, 1916, at the Battle of the Somme. The chief of the Royal Flying Corps (RFC), Brig. Gen. Hugh Trenchard, had twenty-seven squadrons with 185 aircraft (some sources say over 400) at his disposal, and the French had 201. The German Air Service could muster only 129 with nineteen scouts. The allocation of fighters from pursuit to ground attack was a relatively easy decision because over the preceding six months the Royal Flying Corps (RFC) and the French Air Force had wrestled air superiority back from the Germans with the introduction of the more advanced DH-2 pusher and the Nieuport 11 "Bebe." Trenchard employed his forces forcefully, with an offensive doctrine. He assigned many squadrons to attack the German front lines in coordination with the infantry offensive. Their orders were to fly low and attack targets of opportunity with machine guns, small (20 lb.) bombs, and hand grenades. Trenchard combined close-air-support attacks on the German front lines, "offensive counter air" bombing of German airfields, and interdiction of German supply lines. The ground offensive was not well planned and resulted in nearly 30,000 casualties the first hour and 60,000 the first day. RFC sorties were highly effective, but the losses were very high. In the five months of the battle, the RFC is reported to have lost 800 aircraft and 252 aircrew killed.[3]

German Reactions to Air Attack in the Battle of the Somme

General Otto von Below, commander of the First German Army, reported the effects of the Royal Flying Corps' success in attacking ground troops in the 1916 Somme offensive:

> The beginning and the first weeks of the Somme battle were marked by a complete inferiority of our own air forces. The enemy's aeroplanes enjoyed complete freedom in carrying out distant reconnaissances. With the aid of aeroplane observation, the hostile artillery neutralized our guns and was able to range with the most extreme accuracy on the trenches occupied by our infantry; the required data for this was provided by undisturbed trench-reconnaissance and photography. By means of bombing and machine-gun attacks from a low height against infantry, battery positions and marching columns, the enemy's aircraft inspired our troops with a feeling of defenselessness against the enemy's mastery of the air.[4]

There were no special aircraft built for the ground attack mission in 1916, but most of the military services could see the need for one. In the meantime, the RFC preferred single-seat pursuit aircraft in a multirole use for frontline attacks, and conventional twin-seat bombers for the airfield attack and deeper missions.

Gen. Trenchard's Priorities

Brig. Gen. Trenchard was the commander of RFC units in France from August 1915 until January 1918, when it separated from the British army and became the Royal Air Force. His time in command was characterized by three priorities. First was the Doctrine of the Offensive Spirit. Trenchard believed, unalterably, that airpower was inherently an offensive weapon, and as such, all missions should be relentlessly offensive. This meant that squadrons should produce a daily high sortie rate. Pilots should fly often and attack enemy aircraft and ground targets over the lines and as deep into enemy territory as possible. It also meant taking risks, attacking against enemy odds and in bad weather. The pilot-training-and-supply system had a hard time keeping up with the operations tempo that Trenchard demanded, and casualties among aircrew were extremely high. Second, the RFC would emphasize ground attack and coordination with army units. While not opposed to strategic bombing, Trenchard in 1916 fought attempts to divert his squadrons to long-range bombing, since he believed the strategic role was less important than army co-operation, and he didn't have enough resources to do both. In January 1918, he was appointed chief of the air staff of the newly formed Air Council and Royal Air Force. He resigned from that position after a long series of acrimonious disputes with the civilian minister for air. In June 1918, Trenchard became the general officer commanding the Independent Air Force. In this new role, he pioneered strategic bombing, primarily of railways, behind the lines and deep into Germany. His favorite aircraft for this mission was the venerable Handley-Page twin-engined bomber, which could carry six 100 lb. bombs and had armor for the crew and engines. When the Americans conducted the St. Mihiel offensive, his bombers provided tactical interdiction of lines of communication and bombing of German airfields. Third, he stressed the importance of morale, which is ironic because his overall emphasis on offensive patrolling and high sortie rates was exceptionally stressful on his men. Hundreds of pilot accounts talk of eyelids twitching, lapses of memory, blurred vision, hands shaking, nightmares, and a deathlike fatalism.[5]

The Origin of Air/Ground Support

The German Air Service reacted to the situation in the air in 1916 with three innovations: the attack mission, organization, and equipment. In December 1916, the chief of the German Air Service disbanded seventy-eight existing field flying sections (*Feldfliegerabteilungen*) and organized forty-eight as long-range reconnaissance (*Flieger Abteilungen-Fl.Abt.*), and the other thirty as artillery flying sections (*Artillerie-Flieger-Abteilungen Fl.Abt.[A]*). The German High Command followed on January 1, 1917, with a general order that redesignated twelve squadrons as *Schutzstaffeln* (*Schusta*) (protection squadrons).[6]

Schusta Organization

Schusta units were assigned six aircraft and were commanded by an officer. He was assigned seventy-nine enlisted men, composed of six pilots, six gunners, one foreman, one top sergeant, one sergeant, one medical officer, seven noncommissioned officers (including three tent maintenance personnel and one for bookkeeping), six primary aircraft maintenance personnel (one for each aircraft), ten privates first class, and thirty-one lower ranks. Each *Staffel* had a support detachment at a local Armee flying park with one pilot, one gunner, and eleven other personnel.[7]

Instructions for the commander included

1. When battle conditions require it, a *Schutzstaffel* will be assigned to a *Flieger Abteilung (A)* [artillery] or *Flieger Abteilung* to protect the artillery aircraft and will be placed under its command with respect to finances and disciplinary measures.

2. The *Staffel* and its component parts will be at the disposal of the commander of the *Flieger Abteilung* with respect to its tactical deployment and its utilization.[8]

The role assigned to the *Schutzstaffeln* was to escort the *Fl.Abt.* and *Fl.Abt. (A)* (reconnaissance and artillery) aircraft and protect them from aerial attack. Thus, during 1917, the reconnaissance aircraft would be accompanied by a "protective" aircraft, the *Schusta* often being stationed at the same airfield as the unit they were designated to escort. British combat reports are filled with instances of their fighter aircraft attacking a pair of two-seaters, with the result that one immediately "flew east," while the other "stayed to fight."[9]

Schusta and *Schlachtflieger* Aircraft

Germany also led with the development of specialized aircraft for the attack mission. There were three phases of aircraft development. The first was merely the assignment of current two-seat models. As squadrons switched over from *Abteilungen* to *Schastas* in 1917, they kept their equipment: Albatros, Roland, and Rumpler C-model, "two-bay" biplanes. (The term "two bay" is a reference to the number of open spaces between the struts. The first bay was the one between the fuselage and the inboard struts, and the second bay was the outer one, between the inboard struts and the outboard struts.) Orders had been made in 1915 for these new aircraft, with the first ones arriving at the western front in 1916. They were powered by 150 hp Benz or 160 hp Mercedes engines. These aircraft had a crew of two: pilot and observer/gunner. Armament consisted of a single, fixed, forward-firing machine gun for the pilot and a ring-mounted, flexible machine gun for the observer. In all respects, they were the same type machines as the aircraft they were escorting.

Replacement aircraft constituted a second generation. They were Aviatik, AEG, DFW, AGO, Albatros, Rumpler, and LVG machines, with the same two-bay construction, but with lighter-weight, more-powerful engines and more armament. They retained the single machine gun for the pilot, but several models gave the gunner twin guns. They also carried lightweight bombs in the cockpit and heavier bombs under the wings. These were deployed to the front in 1917.

Advent of the Two-Seat Fighter/Attack Aircraft

The third generation was truly attack aircraft, two-seat fighters. They were built by Halberstadt, Hannover, and Albatros. Most were single bay, the same design as the fighters, which made them faster and more maneuverable. They were powered by upgraded engines and could carry a heavier payload of bombs. The first were the CL type, standing for light biplanes, usually two-seaters. Two of the best of these were the Halberstadt CL.II and the Hanover CL II/III.

The second category was the J type, a heavily armored two-seater designed for low-level army cooperation. The J types enclosed the crew with armor plate, and the Albatros J.I also added it to the engine compartment. Two of the J types were the A.E.G. JI (860 pounds of armor plate) and the all-metal Junkers JI monoplane, the best example of the specialized type.[10] (This self-protection design with armor would prove to be reintroduced in the design of the Navy AD/A-1 in the late 1940s, and the Air Force A-10 aircraft in the 1970s.) The evolution was clear, from the initial *Schusta* aircraft to the more specialized *Schlachtfliegern*.

Weapons

The armament of the *Schutzfliegern* and *Schlacktfliegern* consisted of the machine guns described earlier, signal flares, and 12.5 kg bombs carried on an internal bomb rack in the gunner's cockpit, with a trap door. Two to four bombs of 50 and 100 kg were also attached under the wings. In the last year of the war, the size of bombs increased to 300 kg and 1,000 kg. The bombs were variously fragmentation, high explosive, and high-explosive demolition (penetration). The bombs could be dropped one at a time or salvoed together. The crews also carried stick hand grenades, and grenade launchers with five or six grenades were frequently attached the side of the fuselage and dropped by the gunner.[11]

Tactics

The attack squadrons developed special tactics, some of which are still used today. First, the aircraft dropped their explosive ordnance, then turned around, reassembled, and rolled in again in an "extended line" formation, reattacking the targets with machine guns. With the attack completed, they reassembled over an agreed-upon point and returned to base. They used basically two types of tactics: line astern, attacking from the east over the heads of the German lines onto the Allied lines, or line abreast, where they penetrated the Allied lines in formation, then made "column-right" or "column-left" turns, following which each aircraft would turn 90 degrees and dive upon the Allied targets simultaneous from the rear, heading toward the German lines.[12]

The reader should note that the German tactics were specifically designed for the target complex they were facing—an extended front line with no discernible end to go around. Major a.D. Hans Arndt described the two sets of tactics:

In line-astern flight the target could be maintained under fire longer. It offered ground defenses only a narrow and more difficult target. In a "line abreast attack" a broader section lay under unified concentrated fire. It had a greater moral[e] effect on friend and foe because of the closed approach in waves; however, it was more intensely subject to ground fire. But it was increasingly chosen because in this closed form one could more easily fend off enemy fighters which now also sought aerial combat at the lower altitudes.[13]

Attack Aircrew Training
Pilots went through one of the many flying schools in Germany or one of the replacement training squadrons. They had three examinations in six months of training and "were required to carry out a certain number of missions over hostile territory before being awarded the *Flugzeugführer Abzeichen* or pilot's badge."[14] Gunners were trained at separate schools and included ground and aerial gunnery, and they too had to complete combat missions before being awarded their aerial rating.

The *Schutzstaffeln* in Combat
The first use of the *Schutzstaffel* aircraft in direct infantry support was recorded on April 24, 1917, in the German defense against the ill-fated French Nivelle Offensive, near Arras. The *Schusta* led in the German counterattack at the Battle of Cambrai

(fall 1917), attacking Allied trench sections, troop concentrations, and artillery battery positions. The *Schlachtflieger* authors noted that

the *Schusta* were so successful in fact that the British convened an official Court of Inquiry on January 21, 1918, at Hesdin to examine the German Success. It lasted a full nine days. The findings recorded the appearance of close-support aircraft in considerable numbers at altitudes lower than 100 feet, firing into both the front line trenches as well as the rear positions. The effect on morale was reported as being very great and facilitated the German success. British infantry seemed at a loss to counteract the performance of these low-flying aircraft.[15]

German losses were reported to be entirely within acceptable limits.

Training the *Schlachtfliegern*
By 1918, the German Air Service had evolved the attack mission to include the new two-seat fighters, the *Schlachtflieger*, originally called the *Halberstädter*. In preparation for the March offensives, the chief of the general staff of the field army issued an order outlining the role and duties of their ground aircraft. This document contains a fascinating picture of the specialized training these units were to perform:

27. Battle flight must make use of every opportunity to carry out *training behind the front* [emphasis in the original] for their difficult task. The most important features of this training should be attacks in close formation, manoeuvre in single combat, observation of the flight leader and rapid concentration for a new attack. Each individual man must be completely master of his weapon: the machine gunners must also be familiar with the use of hand grenades and bombs.

Practice over the enemy's lines, so far as the enemy's anti-aircraft defense permits, offers the best opportunities of training in picking up targets quickly.[16]

The *Schlachtflieger* in Combat, 1918
When the great offensive, Operational Michael, began in March 1918, it included thirty-five

squadrons of attack aircraft, forty-nine squadrons of artillery support, and forty-two fighter squadrons, virtually 50 percent of the German airpower on the western front. The new *Schlachtflieger* aircraft with its single-bay configuration was relatively lightweight and very maneuverable, with a good rate of climb, but was slower than the fighters. Nevertheless, it was a star of the 1918 offensives. Operation Michael surprised the Allies, gaining over 1,200 square miles of territory, but ultimately ground to a halt. Subsequent offensives of Operations Georgette, Blücher, and Gneisenau-Yorck had similar initial success but failed due to the increasing shortages of supplies and the massive infusion of Allied forces led by the American Expeditionary Force.

British Ground Attack in 1917

There were three British battles in 1917 that featured aerial ground attack on the Allied side: Messines in June, the Third Battle of Ypres (Passchendaele) in July/August, and Cambrai in November. In the first, Trenchard ordered his pilots to fly low over the Messines front lines and strafe whatever targets they could see.[17] Trenchard tasked over three hundred aircraft from fourteen squadrons for the Third Battle of Ypres, which included the first massed attack of frontline enemy troops by Sopwith Camels, strafing and dropping four 20 lb. Cooper bombs each. The loss rate of attacking aircraft was recorded as very high.

RFC missions in the Battle of Cambrai were coordinated with a large tank attack (>320 tanks), with more than three hundred aircraft. The RFC performed simultaneous attacks on trenches, supply convoys, and artillery emplacements and cooperated effectively with advancing columns of tanks and infantry. Unfortunately, the German opposition had also improved. German infantry had learned how to fire on low-altitude attackers, and the British lost nearly 30 percent of the aircraft deployed.

In February 1918, British general headquarters issued a memorandum that provided official recognition of the ground attack mission. Paragraph 1, titled "The Necessity of Fighting," notes that

the moral effect produced by an aeroplane is . . . out of all proportion to the material damage which it can inflict, which is in itself considerable, and the mere presence of a hostile machine above them inspires those on the ground with exaggerated forebodings of what it is capable of doing.[18]

And Paragraph 4, "Choice of Objective":

The attack with bombs and machine-gun fire of the enemy's troops, transport, billets, railway stations, rolling stock, and moving trains, ammunition dumps, & c. [sic] on the immediate front in connection with operations on the ground.[19]

On June 18, 1918, the Royal Air Force (RAF), successor to the Royal Flying Corps, ordered large numbers of the two-seat Sopwith TF.2 Salamander, essentially a modified Camel single-seater. The "TF" stood for "Trench Fighter," and the aircraft was designed to attack enemy trenches both with Vickers .303 machine guns and 25 lb. bombs. The aircraft carried 640 pounds of armor plate.[20] Of the thirty-seven Salamanders produced, none reached the western front in time to see combat.

A German instruction, "The Employment of Battle Flights," dated February 20, 1918, described these aircraft as "a powerful weapon which should be employed at the *decisive* point of the attack. They are not to be distributed singly over the whole front of attack but should be concentrated at decisive points."[21] (This dictum is almost identical to one articulated by the US Army Air Service near the end of the war.) The Germans employed these aircraft in formations of four or six. This disciplined approach contrasted sharply with the British habit of assigning small patrols of aircraft to rove freely over the battlefield, looking for targets.[22]

The commander of the German army, General Erich Ludendorff, was a strong advocate of military aviation. He integrated ground attack with his tactic of "infiltration" in the great March offensives of 1918. The mission of the *Schutzstaffeln* was to aid the initial breakthrough of his light, mobile elite troops and to help consolidate their initial gains.[23] Attack aviation was on the march.

The US Enters the Great War: 1917

US aviation was woefully unprepared for war. On the day the US declared war on Germany, April 6, 1917, only a few of the Air Service of the Signal Corps had experience with expeditionary, deployed operations with the 1st Aero Squadron in Mexico. The Signal Corps flew and maintained almost two hundred airplanes, but not one of them was fit for combat in this modern war. Nor were there any capable aircraft being manufactured in the United States.[24]

Gen. John J. Pershing, the commander of the American Expeditionary Force (AEF), wrote in 1917 that "the situation . . . was such that every American ought to feel mortified to hear it [the Air Service] mentioned. Out of the 65 officers and about 1,000 men in the Air Service Section of the Signal Corps, there were only thirty-five who could fly. With the exception of five or six officers, none of them could have met the requirement of modern battle conditions."[25]

One of the first actions of the Aviation Section just before the declaration of war was to send five officers to Europe, three of whom were flying students. Shortly after his appointment by President Wilson to be the commander in chief of the AEF, Gen. Pershing selected Maj. T. F. Dodd as "aviation officer" of the AEF. When Lt. Col. William "Billy" Mitchell arrived in France in July 1917, he was appointed to replace Dodd. Fully aware of the dismal performance and profound discontent within the Signal Corps, Mitchell immediately separated AEF aviation activities from the Signal Corps; they became the Air Service, AEF, placing them well beyond the reach and control of the chief signal officer.[26]

By July 1917, the AEF had developed a general organizational project to provide fifty-nine squadrons to support the AEF's ground forces, which was Gen. Pershing's policy. Soon it was learned that the US government had adopted an Air Service program proposed by the French to provide 4,500 aircraft, or about 260 aero squadrons! In August, the AEF and the French government signed a contract whereby the French would deliver to the Air Service 5,000 airplanes and 8,500 engines by June 1, 1918.[27]

The immediate problem for the Air Service was training.

US Army Aviation Training in Europe

The Army, Navy, and AEF Air Service were in quite different states of training on the declaration of war. The Army had active-duty and National Guard regiments and divisions organized and trained, albeit not trained for trench warfare. Of the Army's small aviation cadre, only the 1st Aero Squadron had experience in looking for Pancho Villa in Mexico and New Mexico. The Navy had active ships and crews with a fledging air force. On May 18, 1917, the US enacted the Selective Service Act to conscript men for the "national army" to expand the ranks. The Air Service was in a unique situation, having so few trained pilots that the Department of War decided that the first priority was to enlist potential pilot candidates and get them to France for training. The flow began slowly in July 1917, with eight officers and successively larger numbers, ending 1917 with 529 officers and 11,719 enlisted. Flying training began by sending student pilots to British, Italian, and French flying schools. The first "Preliminary" training began in Italy, at Foggia with Farman airplanes. It continued there with "Advanced" training but was considered unsatisfactory due to the low quality of the training machines. Britain was different, with the training given by the Royal Air Force in flying, gunnery, bombardment, navigation, and night flying considered to be "invaluable." In France, Preliminary training at Tours and Advanced training at Issoudon began on November 1. Bombardment training was expanded to Clermont-Ferrand, and gunnery at St. Jean de Monts. The most-important training made by the French was the advanced aerial gunnery at Cazaux.[28]

Attrition in Air Service Training

A unique feature of flying training was that it was dangerous. In the time period between the arrival of air officers in July 1917 until Armistice Day, 218 pilots were killed; 169 were students, but forty-eight were instructors! Midair collisions accounted for nineteen deaths. Whereas there was one fatality for every 2,738 hours of flying in Preliminary training, there was one per 1,173 for Advanced, twice as high. Translated another way, AEF statistics showed that there was one fatality for every ninety graduates of Preliminary training, one in about fifty for advanced observation and bombardment, and the rate of fatalities increased to one in nine in advanced pursuit training! The total average appeared to be one death for every eighteen pilots trained, and these were all officers.[29] No parachutes were provided.

Discipline in Aviation Units

AEF senior officers became very aware of the sensitivity of applying regular Army discipline to pilots. The *Final Report* is revealing on this point:

> It must be remembered that in action the pilot is necessarily his own master and that treatment of him as a schoolboy and not as a man during the course of his instruction, though it may save trouble at the time, will tend to produce an irresponsible and worthless officer. The principle should be to give the students, especially when commissioned, such liberty as will tend to let them "find" themselves during their course of instruction and those who are not able to comport themselves properly under such conditions should be eliminated.[30]

The Lafayette Escadrille and Flying Corps

US citizens were inspired by France's defense of Paris, and many of them immediately joined the French Foreign Legion to fight. They were formed into Battalion C, Second Regiment, and a thousand of them marched to the front on September 30, 1914. Other Americans in 1915 had joined the French Service Aeronautique. On April 20, 1916, these pilots were assembled into a single squadron, *l'Escadrille Americane*, official N. 124 (for Nieuport). Commanded by a French captain, Georges Thenault, the squadron was deployed for the defense of Verdun on May 20, 1916, flying the new Nieuport 11 ("Bebe"). When the German ambassador to the United States heard about the unit called "American," he protested to the State Department that this was a violation of US neutrality. The fliers promptly changed the name of the squadron to *l'Escadrille Lafayette*.

Dozens of other American pilots, too numerous to be assigned to the l'Escadrille Lafayette, joined the French air service and were made a part of the Lafayette Flying Corps. After much bureaucratic bungling, the pilots of the *escadrille* were transferred to the US 103rd Pursuit Squadron in January 1918. Some of the Corps pilots joined them, and the rest were assigned to other squadrons.

Air Service AEF Missions

The Army Air Service conducted combat operations in World War I in four categories: observation, pursuit, bombing, and attack. Specialized aircraft were developed for the first three of these missions, but none were developed or optimized for the attack mission. The 1st Aero Squadron arrived in France on September 1, 1917, and entered a period of training with French and English aviators. Their first combat employment was on April 12, 1918, flying the SPAD XI, a two-seat reconnaissance aircraft. Two days later, the 94th Pursuit Squadron in the Toul sector shot down two German aircraft. Three more squadrons joined the next month and formed the 1st Pursuit Group. In July, the group was reassigned to the Marne sector, which was much more active than Toul. There, German aircraft reportedly outnumbered the Americans by a large ratio. US tactics included patrols in a double-tiered barrage: medium and high altitude. It soon became the rule that there would be no medium-altitude patrols unless they were guarded by at least one high-altitude patrol. By this time the engines of opposing aircraft were so powerful that flights above 22,000 feet—without pressurization or oxygen—were quite common.

Day bombardment missions began on May 18, 1918, when the 96th Aero Squadron conducted active operations in the vicinity of St. Mihiel. The 96th Aero had ten Breguet 14 B Z aircraft with giant 300 hp Renault engines.[31]

A Humorous Episode

Billy Mitchell recites a funny but tragic incident when the commander of one of the US bombardment squadrons led his unit on a mission but got lost in the fog and landed behind the German lines. All of the aircraft landed intact, but the entire squadron of pilots and observers was captured. The Germans, appreciating the humor of the situation, sent back a note that was dropped on an American airfield: "We thank you for the fine airplanes and equipment which you have sent us, but what do we do with the major?"[32]

AEF Ground Attack

The American Air Service had its first large-scale ground attack missions during the Battle of St. Mihiel, September 12–15, 1918. Col. Mitchell combined all the air units he could muster (nearly 1,500) to support the 400,000-man ground army in the US offensive. Mitchell outlined three tasks for his aviation: "Provide accurate information for the infantry and adjustment of fire for the artillery; hold off the enemy air forces from interfering; and bomb the back areas so as to stop the supplies for the enemy and hold up any movement along his roads."[33] Mitchell's own words reveal his preference for light attack in "interdiction" behind the lines, over close air support. The Air Service official history reports the American Expeditionary Force used observation, bombing, and pursuit aircraft to conduct "Ground Straffing" [sic] with machine guns and small bombs.[34]

The contribution of pursuit aircraft to the Battle of St. Mihiel was well documented in Air Service records. In the *Final Report of the Chief of the US Air Service*, Maj. Gen. Mason Patrick was quite specific about these aircraft:

On September 11, the day before the battle, and on the next two days, our pursuit pilots showed the value of fast, high-powered, single-seater airplanes for the missions of visual reconnaissance in unfavorable atmospheric conditions. These aircraft could fly at times when it was almost impossible for the biplane machines to take the air, and although the pilots had not been specially trained in observation, they brought back important information of our advancing troops.

These pursuit pilots also attacked ground objectives or engaged in "ground straffing," as this work came to be called.[35]

The *Final Report* continued with a summary paragraph on the effectiveness of "Ground Straffing":

"Ground Straffing" having proved so efficacious this was continued during the Argonne offensive, and the enemy's troops were attacked by our pursuit airplanes with machine guns and light bombs. Our intelligence reports showed that

a much-desired effect was obtained, for the mere sight of any of our airplanes, no matter of what type, caused much confusion among the enemy.[36]

This employment of airpower was so successful that it was repeated in the Meuse-Argonne campaign, September 26–November 11, 1918. One of the aircraft in these ground attacks was the de Havilland DH-4, of which there were 1,087 in France between the British and Americans.[37] One of the DH-4s included armored seats for the two-man crew and was equipped with *eight* machine guns for "ground strafing."

Maj. Gen. Patrick, chief of the Air Service, AEF, was supportive of the attack mission. In his *Final Report*, prepared in 1919, noted that

lacking such specially prepared airplanes, we did employ our pursuit airplanes in this way, and at times even our observation airplanes joined in such attacks on enemy infantry. Just before hostilities ceased it had been decided by the Air Service to organize a number of such battle squadrons and sample airplanes had been equipped and armed for their use.[38]

US Army Air Service
Attack Aircraft and Experience

As the Army Air Service began engaging in flying operations in 1917, AEF intelligence summaries began to record the effectiveness of air attack on ground forces:

Prisoners captured by the British state that losses caused by bombs and machine gun fire from the air have been heavy, and that the moral effect of this method of attack is great. That after an attack on the 22nd March the 109th Body Gren. Regt. relieved the 40th Fus Regt. but were so severely bombed from the air that they had to be again relieved on the following day. A battery of foot artillery was destroyed by bombs at the same time, and its detachment, together with 12 horses killed.[39]

The US Air Service also devised a novel observation mission. Among the pilots it was called "Cavalry reconnaissance." The mission was assigned to observation squadrons, and it was performed by aircraft flying a very low altitude over and behind the lines immediately in front of our own infantry. The mission was to locate the positions of machine gun nests, strongpoints, and other obstacles and drop messages to warn our troops.

During World War I, the US Air Service considered ground attack as just one of the missions of "Tactical Aviation." The division of responsibilities that had more meaning to the Air Service was that between tactical support of the ground army and "Strategical Aviation: or that acting far from troops of other arms and having an independent mission."[40]

Here is a key example of the major difference between the US Navy's experience with the attack mission and that of the Army Air Service. Whereas the Navy experience grew out of finding a new technology to perform an old mission—the finding and attacking of surface ships—the Army Air Service was pulled in two opposed directions, with the attack mission having to compete with the strategic mission of deep bombing attacks on the enemy's homeland. Between these two, airpower advocates recognized early on that only the strategic mission could be viewed as the path to an independent air force.

US Army Air Corps Attack Lessons and Doctrine

The professional air doctrine supporting the attack mission that emerged from World War I for the US Army Air Service included two different beliefs. The first was expressed by Brig. Gen. Billy Mitchell in a provisional manual of the Third Army, AEF. In a section titled "Organization and Employment of Attack Squadrons," he presented the mission of attack aviation as direct support of the infantry.[41] This view was supported by Col. Edgar S. Gorrell, the assistant chief of staff and, later, the chief of staff of the Air Service, AEF. Gorrell recognized the attack mission as essential and required specially trained crews who were highly experienced and trained in air-to-ground gunnery, communications skills, and liaison with ground forces. He wrote the following:

Bombing and its results have heretofore been little understood. The great mobility and speed of airplanes makes it possible to utilize day bombardment tactically to influence an action in progress.[42]

Thus, by mid-1919, virtually all the reports, manuals, and histories prepared by the Air Service reflected the belief that the attack mission was essential, second only to the observation and air superiority missions.

There was a slightly divergent belief that the most-important targets were the enemy's airfields, lines of communication, and supply points *behind* the trench lines, not close air support of engaged forces. This belief is curious since US aircraft made such an outstanding contribution to the victories at St. Mihiel and the Argonne by attacking the front lines. Officers with this belief conceded that attacks on frontline forces were important in special cases and were morale boosting for friendly ground forces, but these attacks were considered highly dangerous, wasteful, and inefficient. They resulted in high loss rates.[43]

It is fascinating to note that both of these beliefs were dominant over the high-altitude bombardment mission, which tended to be discounted because of "a lack of experience and conclusive results but also on ethical grounds."[44] Virtually everyone agreed on the unacceptability of, and that the international rules of war prohibited, the targeting of civilians. But many people, especially those who had not seen the destruction of the World War I battlefields, thought that attacks on military targets far from the front lines, where civilian casualties could occur, were immoral and uncivilized. Many of those thoughts exist today.

The techniques of attack favored in World War I were low-altitude, level, or slightly diving attacks on frontline infantry, and higher-altitude, level bombing of targets behind the lines. The technique of dive-bombing was attempted by some pilots, but it was considered a distinctly inferior tactic due to the small size of the bombs that the aircraft could carry and the high risk from ground fire.

The aiming devices on World War I aircraft were primitive and mechanical. The most famous is the "ring and post" for machine guns. Indeed, the device was called the "gunsight" because that was about the only weapon for which it was useful. The "ring" was metal, of no particular diameter, and was mounted above the chamber of the gun, and the "post" was a small metal ball on top of a short post, mounted near the muzzle. Bomb-dropping sights were even more primitive, varying from an angle device in the rear cockpit to an estimated point on the wing of a biplane.

The Employment of Attack Squadrons

The Air Service introduced into its doctrine the principle of the economy of force, such that attack aviation was a limited resource and should be reserved for only the most-important battles. This is the same point made by the Germans in their doctrine. When Billy Mitchell was commanding the Air Service of the First Army, he pulled together his official procedures for the employment of attack units, and as he moved up to command the Air Service of the entire army group, he issued a bulletin titled "Organization and Employment of Attack Squadrons." The plans in that bulletin formed the basis of his "Provisional Manual of Operations of Air Service Units," which he issued on December 23, 1918. It observed:

> The successful employment of attack squadrons depends upon their concentrated, continuous, uninterrupted engagement at the decisive time and place. This condition limits their use to that particular portion of the battlefront upon which the entire operation depends and prohibits their distribution over relatively unimportant portions of the battle line.
>
> Attack squadrons are to be employed in DECISIVE infantry actions [emphasis in the original]. At other times (when the military situation is such that there is no probability of attack missions being required), attack squadrons may be employed as protection for corps and army observation units.
>
> Attack groups will normally be held under the direct command of the Chief of Air Service of an army or, (in extended operations) of the Chief of Air Service of the Army Group."[45]

The point about using attack aircraft only in "decisive" engagements and holding their use at the highest levels of army command became bedrock elements of US as well as German air doctrine. That is, the USAF insisted in virtually all of its doctrinal debates over the succeeding century that attack and close-air-support sorties were *not* to be parceled out, like so many "penny packets" to army divisions or lower-level units. Mitchell's requirement that attack units be held at chief of Air Service at the "Army" or "Army Group" levels meant that they were so valuable and limited in quantity that they needed to be controlled from a command *two levels above* the Army division (the "Army level") or *three levels above* (the "Army Group level"). Some military officials compare tactical attack aircraft to the Army arms of artillery, which tends to be controlled at higher command levels. The USAF today uses the 1943 Battle of Kasserine Pass in North Africa as an example of the consequences of parceling out air units to individual corps commanders. The German/Italian army under General Rommel initially defeated the American divisions by concentrating their attack with air and armored units. The Army Air Corps units in the sector being attacked were overwhelmed, while other air units sat on the ground, not even participating because they were unaware of the battle.

In writing about the early days of combat aviation, observers tended to highlight the fear, fright, and confusion caused by enemy aircraft. This was probably due to the surprise experienced by troops not accustomed to seeing and hearing attacking aircraft. But the phenomenon was not long lasting, and records of similar reactions in World War II are remarkably few. It is highly likely that the World War I experience influenced those advocates of strategic bombing to predict and claim similar panic reactions among civilian populations who witnessed bombing attacks. These predictions turned out to be correct only in the period of early aircraft. Strategic bombing of London, Germany, and Japan—though terrible—did not result in mass surrenders, but in extensive damage and deepened resistance.

US Army Aviation End Strength on Armistice Day

Seventeen months later, on November 11, 1918, there were 7,738 officers and 70,769 enlisted men, of whom 6,861 (89 percent) of the officers and 51,229 enlisted men (72 percent) were serving in France.[46]

US Naval Experience in World War I

Navy interest in the potential of aircraft began in 1898, when it sent a representative to participate in evaluation of the Samuel Pierpont Langley's efforts to build a flying machine. Eight years after the Wright brothers' first flight, the Navy contracted with Glenn Curtiss for two biplanes, the A-1 and A-2, in 1911, creating the official birth of naval aviation. Two years later, a non-Navy airman, Dedier Masson, flying for the rebel army of Venustiano Carranza, carried out a dramatic one-man attack campaign against Mexican Federal Fleet gunboats by dropping bombs on them.[47]

When the US declared war on the German Empire on April 6, 1917, the Navy had one air station (North Island, which it shared with the Army), forty-eight officers and 239 enlisted men, and fifty-four airplanes. Two months later, on June 5, Lt. Kenneth Whiting led the Navy's First Aeronautical Detachment on board the collier *Jupiter* and landed in France. This ship would achieve universal fame when it was converted to become the first US aircraft carrier, USS *Langley* (CV-1). This detachment was the first US military command to arrive in Europe. One week later, the Navy's first overseas naval air station was established at Dunkirk, France. Later that month, the first R-5 biplane arrived at Pensacola and began torpedo experiments.[48]

On July 27, 1917, the Congress passed Public Law 31 during the sixty-fifth Congress, authorizing President Wilson to take possession of North Island, the northern section of Coronado Island, across the bay from San Diego, for use by the Army and Navy to establish an aviation school, thus creating the "Home of Naval Aviation." The original title of the base was NAS San Diego, and it remained so until 1955, when it was changed to Naval Air Station North Island.

Naval Aviation Missions in World War I

The first combat deployment of an aviation ship was the Imperial Japanese Navy seaplane carrier *Wakamiya*, which arrived off Kiaochow Bay, China, in August 1914 to conduct aerial operations during the siege of the German colony at Tsingtao. Within days, a three-place Farman seaplane from *Wakamiya* conducted a naval attack mission by bombing German fortifications around the city.

On March 25, 1918, Ens. John McNamara, RNAS Portland, England, marked first US attack on an enemy submarine, which was "apparently successful."[49] On October 5, Squadron D of the First Marine Aviation Force arrived in France and was assigned to the Northern Bombing Group. This group of Navy and Marine Corps squadrons prepared a round-the-clock air campaign that was to have been the first strictly American air offensive of the war. Two weeks later, eight DH-4s and DH-9s of Marine Squadron 9 made the first day-bombing raid on German positions near the English Channel. The Navy also employed the Curtiss HS-1 flying boat against German targets in the English Channel and North Sea from bases in Ireland, England, and Brest, northern France.[50]

Lt. j.g. David S. Ingalls became famous by scoring his fifth aerial victory on September 24, 1918, to become the US Navy's first ace. His accomplishment occurred while on a test flight in a Sopwith Camel. In company with another Camel, he sighted an enemy two-seat Rumpler over Nieuport and shot it down.[51]

Navy End Strength on Armistice Day

Navy personnel and aircraft also grew in orders of magnitude after America's entry into the war. At the time of the Armistice, naval aviation listed 2,107 aircraft, fifteen airships, and 215 kite and free balloons. The force contained 6,716 officers and 30,693 enlisted men in the Navy and 282 officers and 2,180 men for the Marine Corps. Of these, about 570 aircraft and 18,000 officers and enlisted men had served abroad. Naval aircraft dropped 155,998 pounds of bombs and made thirty-nine attacks on German submarines.[52] The essential missions of naval aviation were designed and experienced in battle.

US Lessons on the Attack Mission in World War I

There appear to be several important findings from the attack experience in the Great War:

1. Virtually every one of the major air missions were initiated in the First World War: strategic homeland bombing, observation, artillery spotting, tactical interdiction, close air support / attack / battlefield air interdiction, and pursuit/fighter air superiority.

2. Gaining air superiority was important to allow extensive attack upon enemy ground forces and to defend friendly ground forces from hostile air attack.

3. Aviation can make an important contribution to the success of ground and sea battles.

4. Observation of the enemy is a key task.

5. Low-attitude attack aircraft are extremely vulnerable to enemy ground fire. While enemy forces were often very exposed to attack, attacking-force losses ranged as high as 20–30 percent in certain battles.

6. The design of specialized attack aircraft made a significant difference in effectiveness and the reduction of losses.

7. The debate between using multipurpose versus specialized aircraft of the ground attack mission arose in World War I. In general, the Allies frequently used multipurpose fighters for frontline ground attack, while using two-seater bombers for battlefield interdiction and deeper bombing. Germany developed many models of ground attack aircraft and was very satisfied that this specialization was worthwhile.

8. Aircraft designed for the attack mission are best protected by liberal use of armor.

Some of these lessons were never learned, and others became neglected between the wars.

CHAPTER 2
Army Air Force Attack Aircraft, 1920–1960

I guess we considered ourselves a different breed of cat, right there in the beginning. We flew through the air and the other people walked on the ground: it was as simple as that!

—Gen. Carl Spaatz

The Great Debates on the Role of Air Forces in the 1920s

The general debate between the advocates of an independent air force and the traditional general staff became more controversial as it became public in the Roaring Twenties. As World War I grew more distant, the advocates on either side grew, and their arguments became more strident, more political, and less connected to the experience of the war. On the one hand, the Army general staff maintained that aviation was developed and existed to support the established order, the land army. The opposing view of the airpower advocates was that airpower was a completely new venue of warfare, separate from and equal to the other regimes, so that air, land, and water should each have its own, independent arm. The three so-called air prophets were Billy Mitchell, Benjamin Foulois, and Giulio Douhet. Their theme was that long-range bombers would be so powerful they would devastate the enemy homeland, both by causing panic and material destruction.

Former chief of staff of USAF Ron Fogleman had an interesting perspective on this situation. He noted in his master's thesis at Duke University that

the so-called air prophets initially took balanced views of the role [of] the aircraft in the First World War and relied on the experiences of the war to help swell their points of view. As the controversy became more heated [and more political] and they found themselves stymied, they began to speak less of the proven concepts and turned to the projected potential of the airplane for support of their arguments.

The crux of the dispute rested on the fact that the Air Service needed a definite and distinct mission to justify the creation of an independent air force. Missions such as observation and attack which were so closely tied to the operations of ground forces gave more support to the arguments of the [Army] general staff than to those of the airmen.[1]

This debate had a profound effect on the Congress and the public. No fewer than five major commissions convened to examine the proper place of aviation within the US military establishment. Eight separate congressional bills were introduced to create a separate military service for the air force in the 1920s and 1930s. None of these passed into law.

Six Airpower Debates in the Air Corps

The new weapon of aviation was the source of major debates within the War Department and between the War and Navy Departments in the 1920–1940 period:

1. Whether aviation was sufficiently different from ground and naval warfare that it warranted its own, independent military service.

2. Which mission of airpower should be the dominant force: strategic bombing or tactical aviation?

3. Would strategic bombers need the support of pursuit or fighter escort to accomplish their deep-penetration mission?

4. Within tactical aviation, would it be more important to conduct interdiction behind enemy lines to cut the flow of supplies, or in direct attack of frontline troops in close air support?

5. Could the tactical aviation mission best be performed by single-engine aircraft or twin-engined light and medium bombers?

6. What should be the relationship of the Army Air Corps with naval aviation? Many Army advocates maintained an independent "Air Force" should unify Army, Navy, and Marine Corps aviation.

These questions energized the development of air force doctrine and equipment. In addition, there was another debate: whether the invention of the bombing airplane seriously increased the vulnerability of surface ships. The answers to these doctrinal questions evolved during the interwar years until finally a quasi consensus was reached within the Air Service: Yes, the Air Force should be independent from the Army, but in what time period? The most succinct statement of this belief was by Gen. Carl Spaatz: "I guess we considered ourselves a different breed of cat, right there in the beginning. We flew through the air and the other people walked on the ground: it was as simple as that!"[2] The remainder of this chapter addresses the elements that affected those questions.

During World War I and even afterward, the Air Service was considered legally as an adjunct to Army fighting forces, well below that of a combatant arm such as the infantry. In 1920, in response to an overwhelming push by airpower advocates, the Congress passed the National Defense Act of 1920, which granted the Army Air Service status as a combat arm—equal to the infantry, artillery, and cavalry.

The Virginia Capes Tests—Army and Naval Air against the Surface Navy

The question of warship vulnerability was the subject of a series of controversial bombing tests off the Virginia Capes against captured German ships in June–July 1921. Both naval air and Air Service aircraft took part in several test events. The Air Service formed the 1st Provisional Air Brigade at Langley Field, Virginia, to participate, with Billy Mitchell in charge. In the first test, the Navy flew three F-5L flying boats from Naval Air Station Norfolk on June 21, against the German U-boat U-117, and stunned observers by sinking it in only sixteen minutes. On July 13, Air Service pursuit planes strafed the German destroyer G-102, and two waves of Langley bombers sank it with 300 lb. bombs in seventeen minutes. The German cruiser *Frankfort* was the target on July 18 but stubbornly refused to sink after two attacks with 250, 300, and 550 lb. bombs—some of them delivered by Navy torpedo-bombers based at Aviation Field Yorktown. Then, six Langley planes made a final sortie with 600 lb. bombs. The *New York Times* reported, "Two hit cruiser's deck and third, exploding alongside, breaks her back." The concussion of the near miss sent the ship to the bottom in minutes!

The main event didn't take place until July 20 and 21. That test was to evaluate the effect of aerial bombs on the battleship *Ostfriesland*, a 27,000-ton behemoth that had survived eighteen direct hits from heavy British naval guns. Navy and Army planes used 230, 550, and 600 lb. bombs, but the first day's attacks were ineffectual.

On the second day, July 21, Brig. Gen. Mitchell instructed his aviators to drop most of their 2,000 lb. bombs all at one time rather than allow the attack to be interrupted for the Navy's inspections. The huge ship shuddered at the impact of the intentional near misses, which smashed through its hull below the waterline and sent it to the bottom in twenty-two minutes. "We could see her rise 8 to 10 feet between the terrific blows from under the water," said Mitchell, who directed the attacks from his DH-4 biplane, nicknamed "Osprey." "On the fourth bomb, Capt. Street, sitting in the back of my plane, stood up and, waving both arms, shouted, "She is gone!"[3]

Even such conservative observers as the Army ordnance chief, Maj. Gen. C. C. Williams, saw that Langley airmen had scored a landmark triumph. "A bomb was fired today that will be heard around the world," he said. "It is a heavier explosive charge than has ever been delivered against a battleship. Its sinking of the *Ostfriesland* means that the capital ship now faces a new menace that must be guarded against by every possible study and effort."[4]

Langley fliers celebrated their milestone kill with far less reserve, convinced by Mitchell and their own exploits that the airplane was the weapon of the future. They repeated the feat in September, sinking the obsolete US battleship *Alabama* off the Virginia Capes during a multiday series of tests demonstrating the effects of chemical bombs and strafing runs, before concluding with 2,000 lb. demolition bombs. USS *Virginia* and *New Jersey* suffered the same fate in September 1923, providing persuasive evidence of the growing power of aviation.[5]

The Air Corps Act of 1926

Despite operational success and public acclaim, airpower advocates were not satisfied with their status as a combatant arm of the Army. With the establishment of the Morrow Board and its influence on the legislature, the Congress passed the Air Corps Act of 1926, changing the name of the Air Service to the Army Air Corps. The act (44 Stat. 780) created an assistant secretary for air and also established a limit on its aircraft at 1,800. Much to the Navy's displeasure, the law set a ratio of 18:10 between Air Corps and naval aircraft that would not be abolished until more than ten years later.[6]

The Third Attack Group

The 3rd Group and its successor units have served the United States on a continuing basis since the group's activation as the Army Surveillance Group on July 1, 1919. In August, the Air Service organized its first seven groups, and the 3rd became the 1st Surveillance Group. In a functional re-designation of Air Service groups in 1921, the unit was named the 3rd Attack Group. Initially the group used Airco DH-4Bs to patrol the border from Brownsville, Texas, to Nogales, Arizona.

The DH-4 had not been built as an attack aircraft, but with its US-built Liberty engine, it had performed heroically in the Great War. As revolution and disorder broke out in Mexico, the chaotic situation resulted in border violations and the killing of American citizens. The unit participated in maneuvers, tested new equipment, experimented with tactics, flew in aerial reviews, patrolled the United States–Mexico border (1929), and carried airmail (1934) flying a wide variety of biplanes, including DH-4, XB-1A, GA-1, and A-3.

On March 1, 1935, the Army Air Corps formed the first centralized control of its combat striking units within the United States under the General Headquarters Air Force. The 3rd Attack Group moved to Barksdale Field, Louisiana, as part of the 3rd Wing, commanded by Col. Gerald Brant, together with the 20th Pursuit Group. Aircraft assigned to the 3rd Attack Group were the Curtiss A-12 Shrike in 1935 and the Northrop A-17/A-17A Nomad in 1937.[7]

The commander of the 3rd Attack Group, Lt. Col. Horace Meek Hickam, was killed on November 5, 1934, when the A-12 he was piloting crashed while landing at Fort Crockett, Texas (Hickam AFB, Hawaii, was named in his honor). Some A-12s were still at Hickam Field on December 7, 1941, when the Japanese attacked; however, none of the aircraft saw any combat. The A-12 was withdrawn from service soon after.

The A-17s were fairly fast and had heavy forward-firing armament for its time. During the 1938–39 war games, it was deemed to be the most effective ground attack aircraft yet devised. However, the career of the A-17 with the Army was quite brief. After only three years of service with the Army, the A-17As were declared surplus. In 1940, the unit was redesignated as the 3rd Bombardment Group (Light), being reequipped with the Douglas B-18 Bolo and B-12 bombers and moved to Army Air Base, Savannah, Georgia.

The Air Corps Tactical School

In the interwar period, the primary institution for the study and distribution of Air Corps doctrine was the Air Corps Tactical School, first at Langley Field, Virginia, and after 1931 at Maxwell Field, Alabama (the current headquarters of the Air University). The views of Billy Mitchell and his followers in support of strategic bombardment began to dominate, largely on the basis of the belief this was the only track to an independent air force. As bomber technology developed in the 1930s, these advocates argued the long-range bombers would not need fighter escort.

The lessons on tactical air doctrine as were taught at that school stressed the identification of the close-air-support mission with attack aircraft. The principal influence on attack tactics and doctrine was Capt. (later general) George C. Kenney; when he left in 1926, the study and doctrinal development of attack aviation entered a long period of decline.[8] Kenney would retain his interest in close air support and devoted numerous assets to it when he was commander of Far East Air Forces in 1943, and his aircraft were involved in the battles for New Guinea.[9]

The answers to the vigorous debates would be determined not just by the application of doctrine, but by the development of advancing technology. In the 1920s and 1930s, the Navy development of the Norden bombsight and the Air Corps development of the four-engine bomber combined to bolster the arguments for the strategic bombardment mission.

The Army Air Forces also preferred the tactical mission of interdiction, free from close coordination and dependence on ground forces, and as the decade of the 1930 progressed, twin-engined bombers promised better performance in this role than single-engined ones. With Air Corps pilots and planners working with little contact with their Navy counterparts, air force officers were unknowledgeable or unreceptive to Navy advancements in dive-bombing accuracy, with the result that level bombing became the tactic preferred for the Air Corps attack mission. And the attack mission itself declined in importance in the restricted-budget era of the prewar years.

Maj. Ron Fogleman again wrote in his master's thesis:

> After 1926, attack aviation simply became a mission with few aggressive and vocal supporters. Without the demands of a combat situation or realistic maneuvers, the War Department, with no organization charged with the responsibility for developing and preserving concepts such

as the attack mission, allowed that idea to slowly die from a benign sort of neglect.[10]

The close relationship of doctrine to technological progress can be judged by the procurement of aircraft to perform Air Corps missions in the interwar years.

Army Air Corps Attack Aircraft, 1920–1941

The immediate postwar period featured sustained aviation research and development. For example, the engineering division at McCook Field, Ohio, designed and built twenty-seven airplanes of all types between 1919 and 1922. They tested modified DH-4s and many other designs. In 1920, the Air Service requested bids on a specially designed attack aircraft, designated the Ground Attack Experimental (GAX). The Boeing Airplane Company was awarded a contract for 10 GA-1 and a second contract for the GA-2, but only one GA-2 was ever built.

In 1923, government funding for defense was severely reduced, and the research and development of Air Service programs was hard hit. Subsequent development of attack aircraft as a distinctive design was especially slow. Several attack models were developed between the wars, but they were hampered by the low priority of the attack mission and the low-powered engines of the time. With the extreme cutback in the defense budgets of the interwar period, the development of aircraft was a high-risk business and almost exclusively left to private industry. Aviation manufacturers were universally interested in building to market demand, and with the government's lack of funds, they organized to meet civilian needs for air service. The first attack model was the Falcon, a biplane built by Glenn Curtiss.

The Curtiss Falcon A-3

The Curtiss Falcon was a family of military biplanes built by the American aircraft manufacturer Curtiss Aeroplane and Motor Company starting in 1925. With a 426 hp engine, the A-3 Falcon's top speed was 139 mph. The A-3 used a ring-and-post gunsight for the pilot and flexible machine guns for the observer. Most saw service as observation aircraft with the designations O-1 and O-11, but many were designated for attack. The Army bought 338 Falcon aircraft, and the Navy Department purchased 150 for the Navy and Marine Corps. US Navy variants were used initially as fighter-bombers with the designation F8C-1 and F8C-3, then as the first US Marine Corps dive-bombers when redesignated OC-1 and OC-2, with the name Helldiver. Curtiss Falcons fought in the Constitutionalist Revolution of 1932 in Brazil and in other South American countries. The aircraft saw first-line service in the United States in 1934.

The General Aviation / Fokker XA-7

The XA-7 was an experimental aircraft designed in response to a 1928 Air Corps requirement for a replacement for the A-3 Falcon. It was ordered in December 1929 for a competition in 1931 with the Curtiss A-8. The aircraft was a two-place, low-wing monoplane with a 48-foot wingspan, an engine of 625 hp, and a top speed of 184 mph. It carried five .30-caliber machine guns but could carry only 488 pounds of bombs. It had no discernible gunsight. The Curtiss A-8 won the competition.

The Curtiss A-8

The A-8 was the first all-metal, low-wing monoplane purchased for the Army ground attack mission. Powered by the 625 hp Curtiss 1570-23 engine, it had a top speed of nearly 180 mph. The airframe featured several innovations: automatic leading-edge slats to increase maneuverability and trailing-edge flaps to lower takeoff and landing speeds. Only thirteen were produced, but it created quite a sensation when it went into operations with the 3rd Attack Group, Fort Crocket, Texas, in 1932. All the other aircraft at that base were cloth-and-wood or metal biplanes.

Status of Personnel and Squadron Strength in 1932–1933

The 1930s were a hardship time for aviators. There were 1,300 officers and 13,400 enlisted men and 1,800 serviceable planes in the Air Corps. The aviation accident rate had not decreased since World War I. In 1932, fifty aviators were killed, over 2.5 percent of the force. Promotion was stagnant, on the basis of longevity alone. Dwight Eisenhower was a captain for sixteen years; it took him twenty-three years to make major. If an officer volunteered in 1917, he could anticipate being eligible for promotion to that rank in 1940! Enlisted privates were paid $18 per month, while a Civilian Conservation Corps worker was given $30 per month!

The allocation of the fifty tactical squadrons in 1932 was four attack, twelve bombardment, thirteen observation, and twenty-one pursuit. The next year, 1933, reflected the priorities of the nascent Air Corps: the total number of serviceable aircraft had dropped to 1,409. The bombardment force was planned to increase from twelve to fifteen squadrons, with three additional long-range, light bomber units and three long-range amphibious squadrons. The attack force had been increased from four to ten squadrons, observation units dropped from thirteen to ten, and pursuit squadrons were cut from twenty-one to twelve![11]

The Curtiss A-12 Shrike

The A-12 was the second all-metal monoplane produced for the Air Corps. It was like the A-8, but the in-line, liquid-cooled engine was exchanged for an air-cooled radial of 690 hp. It was slow, only 177 mph. Armament was five .30-caliber machine guns, two each in the wheel fairings and one for the gunner. The Air Corps ordered forty-six aircraft, and they served from 1932 to 1941.

Tactical Exercises Demonstrate the Inadequacy of Attack Aircraft

In 1936, the Army held a series of tactical exercises in the Hawaiian Islands to evaluate the progress of attack aviation. The primary aircraft participating was the A-12 Shrike. The tasks involved were low-level navigation, bombing, and strafing. The results of those tests were observed and communicated to the Air Corps Tactical School by Maj. Clayton Bissel, a former instructor there. He wrote that the Curtiss A-12 Shrikes used in the exercise carried no precision bombsights, were capable of hitting only very large area targets with bombs, and were inaccurate with machine gun fire against precision targets.[12] There is no evidence the aircraft used the Navy tactic of high-angle dive-bombing. Units included the 3rd Attack Group and the 8th and 18th Pursuit Groups. Nine A-12 aircraft were on active service at Hickam Field when the Japanese attacked on December 7, 1941, but none of them got airborne.

Northrop Gamma

Jack Northrop and Donald Douglas formed the Northrop Corporation in 1932 and began a series of single-engine monoplanes called "Gamma" for air transport and mail carrying. Soon realizing the plane's performance exceeded that of the Curtiss A-12, Northrop modified the design to meet military specifications in 1933 and called it the Gamma 2C. After testing, the aircraft was modified again and designated the XA-13 (YA-13), but only one was built.

The Chinese government ordered a light-bomber version 1934. In 1935, the aircraft was given a new, more powerful 750 hp engine. That model became the XA-16 for the Army and the A-16 for the Navy. The XA-16 evolved into the popular A-17. In 1937, the Northrop Corporation was dissolved when Jack Northrop left the company, and the El Segundo plant became the foundation of the Douglas Aircraft Corporation. Douglas produced a successful export version as the Douglas 8A.

Internal Air Corps Competition: Strategic versus Tactical Aviation

The competition for resources between tactical and strategic aviation in the Air Corps and Air Force has always been fierce. The lessons of World War I did not resolve the issues. With the extremely limited US investments in national defense between the wars, the development of technology was slow and uneven. The advocates of strategic bombardment were skeptical of the need for attack and pursuit aircraft and were aided by technological advances. In 1921, the Navy began testing on a high-altitude bombsight, the origin of the Norden series. By 1929, Navy tests showed that the Norden Mk. XI bombsight gave 40 percent more hits than earlier ones. In 1934, the Air Corps initiated a competition to replace the 115 mph twin-engined Keystone biplane bombers and the Martin B-10 for the coastal-defense mission. Specifications were

range of at least 1,020 miles
speed of 200 to 250 mph
bombload of 2,000 lbs.

The Saga of the B-17 Flying Fortress

The Boeing Company invested its own money to design its competitor, based on their passenger airliner, the 247. Boeing conducted the first flight of the Model 299, the prototype of the B-17, in 1935. Together with the Norden bombsight, the B-17 gave the strategic bombardment advocates their dream weapon. Early B-17s exceeded 250 mph, and later ones 325 mph. It was faster than many pursuit planes. The Boeing design immediately started breaking records.

In 1935, the prototype B-17 flew nonstop from Seattle to Wright Field, Ohio, a distance of 2,100 miles, in nine hours as an average speed of 232 mph.[13] Unfortunately for Boeing, the entry in the competition crashed, and the contract was awarded to Douglas for the twin-engine B-18 Bolo. Nevertheless, the Army awarded Boeing a small contract, and in 1938 six B-17s flew from Miami, Florida, to Buenos Aires, Argentina, in twenty-eight hours, with only one brief stop in Lima, Peru. Both the southern flight and the return trip made headlines, and the crews were awarded the Mackay Trophy.[14]

The next major event was an audacious stunt by three B-17s to intercept the Italian passenger liner Rex, 700 miles at sea in the Atlantic. The patrol was successful, but the Navy was so incensed it went public to remind everyone that the Army was limited to coastal defense only up to 100 miles offshore.[15] The combination of the Norden bombsight with the B-17 bomber reinforced the doctrine of the strategic-bomber advocates, to the detriment of the attack and fighter communities.

The theory was that the "Flying Fortress" was so heavily armed and fast that it would not need fighter escort. This theory was based on the situation at the time. In the late 1930s, the speed of a typical fighter aircraft, the P-26 Peashooter, was 200 mph, slower than the B-17. But with bigger engines, the P-38, A-36, P-51, and P-47 leaped ahead. By 1942, when the US introduced the B-17 in Europe and began bombing Occupied France and Germany, these aircraft were twice as fast as the B-17—a development missed by the bomber advocates. The theory quickly was disproved on bomber missions deeper into Germany.

Meanwhile, the technology of attack design was proceeding slowly.

Curtiss XA-14

The XA-14, in 1935, was the first multiengine aircraft built for the Army attack mission. Curtiss designated it the Model 76, an all-metal, twin-engine aircraft with two 775 hp engines. At 254 mph, it was faster than the pursuit aircraft of the time. The Army accepted the single experimental aircraft and designated it the XA-14. One test featured the use of a 37 mm cannon in the nose. Only one of the XA-14s was produced, since the Army wanted to wait for the next model, the YA-18. With the shift to twin-engined bombers, gunsights for the pilot and forward-firing machine guns became less common.

Northrop A-17

The A-17 was derived from the Northrop Gamma 2F, the YA-13, and the XA-16 as a single-engine attack bomber. Delivered to the Army Air Corps in 1934, it had fixed landing gear and perforated flaps. Bombs were carried in an internal bomb bay and on external wing racks. An A-17 variant had retractable landing gear. France, Britain, and other countries purchased and flew the aircraft.

The Army purchased 110 of Northrop's single-engine XA-13 design, redesignated the A-17. Its two distinguishing features were split, perforated dive flaps and an internal bomb bay that could carry twenty 30 lb. fragmentation bombs. Four external racks added to the capacity to carry a total of 1,200 lbs. of bombs. The aircraft had four .30-caliber machine guns firing forward and one in the rearward-facing gunner's position. The radial engines of 750 hp (A-17) and 825 hp (A-17A) powered the plane to 206 and 220 mph, respectively, which was fairly fast for the time period.[16] This model replaced the Curtiss A-8 and A-12 aircraft. The Army ordered a total of 411 aircraft, and the A-17 entered Army service in 1935. Three attack groups were operational between 1936 and 1939, and the aircraft was seen as reliable and popular. During the 1938–1939 war games the A-17 was deemed to be the most effective ground attack aircraft yet developed.

Air Corps Continued Doubts about Attack Aviation

With the doctrinal devotion to strategic bombing, the burden was on the proponents of other air missions to demonstrate their worth. Reports were coming in about Legion Condor operations in the Spanish Civil War, with both the Junkers Ju 87 Stuka and light bombers being effective in ground support. Accordingly, the chief of the Air Corps in August 1937 directed the Air Corps Board to study the attack mission and suggested that a light bomber be considered. Despite this and other attempts by the Army-dominated War Department, Air Corps leaders were wary of endorsing attack aircraft, lest it result in an emphasis on ground support for the Army that could threaten the strategic-bombardment mission.[17] Thus, the studies of 1937 produced no conclusive results on the attack issue.

Curtiss A-18 Shrike II

Curtiss modified the twin-engine A-14 by upgrading the engines to 850 hp, but it was no faster than the 252 mph of the A-14. It was designated the Y1A-18, and the Army ordered thirteen and assigned them to the 3rd Attack Group, Barksdale, Louisiana, where the aircraft won the Harmon Trophy in gunnery and bombing accuracy in 1937. However, the aircraft had several weaknesses in its design that revealed themselves with operational use. Its undercarriage was prone to collapsing when landing or taking off, and its engines were underpowered. The Shrike II was operational only a short time since it was replaced by the A-20 Havoc, which seemed to be the aircraft the planners had been looking for in the studies of the late 1930s.

In 1938, the Air Corps began a corporate discussion to make all future attack aircraft multiengine. The A-17 was rendered obsolete. Douglas followed the Army thinking, and one of their first products was the twin-engined B-18 "Bolo," a military modification of their successful airliner, the DC-2. By 1939, the three A-17 groups began getting the B-18. However, Douglas also followed the US Navy's requirements and soon designed the single-engined Dauntless dive-bomber. Jack Northrop had left Douglas but bounced back and, in 1939, formed another Northrop Corporation and continued to produce aircraft until its merger with Grumman in 1994 to form Northrop Grumman.[18]

The US Army Air Corps Rejection of Single-Engine Attack Aircraft

The influence of the advocates of strategic bombardment and the disenchantment with the low-altitude tactic increased the interest in the development of twin-engined light bombers. At the top of the Air Corps command, Gen. Hap Arnold in April 1939 communicated his persisting doubts to Lt. Col. Carl Spaatz, chief of the Plans Section. He wrote that the status of attack aviation was in doubt, and he questioned "what it is, its characteristics, its performance, and its proper place in the scheme of things in the system of national defense."[19]

Lt. Col. Spaatz, in a reply to the request from Gen. Arnold, ventured in 1939 the opinion that the attack aircraft had *not* been proven tactically or experimentally, and that experience might well show that the mission could be better performed by bombers. Spaatz's opinion was reinforced by a report of the Air Corps Board in September 1939 that formally recommended the elimination of the attack and attack-bomber in Air Corps requirements. In their place the board recommended the development of a light bomber to support ground forces. By 1940, the Army Air Forces' decision to switch to light bombers was doctrine. An Air Corps doctrine manual of the time stated this:

> This move was based upon the conclusion of the board that bombs were the most valuable weapons against the usual targets of support aviation and that the proper type of plane would therefore be one built especially for bomb-carrying. The machine gun [.30 cal. at that time] was regarded as of limited effectiveness as a ground attack [weapon] because of the ready dispersion of targets suitable to destruction by that weapon, the ineffectiveness of fire at high aircraft speeds, and the proved vulnerability of aviation in low-altitude attacks. The board believed that light bombers, supported by the necessary pursuit, reconnaissance, and transport aircraft, would best fulfill the mission of ground support.[20]

With the abandonment of the single-engine attack design, the Army Air Corps also terminated use of the dive-bombing tactic since the larger, multiengined aircraft dropped their bombs from level flight.

Regardless of the rationale behind this Air Board decision, in retrospect one can make several observations that were neglected at the time:

1. The denigration of the machine gun was due in part to the small size and extremely light weight of the .30-caliber bullet. Airplanes in the late 1930s as they switched from fabric covering to aluminum were on the verge of having strong-enough airframes that they could support the new .50-caliber machine gun. The difference is significant. The Browning machine gun, of .303 caliber, fired a 150-grain bullet with sixty-eight grains of propellant that could travel at 2,200–2,900 feet per second and had the kinetic energy upon impact of 1,300–3,600 joules. The Browning .50 cal. M2 fired a 650–800-grain bullet at 2,800–3,000 feet per second and impacted with the kinetic energy of 18,000 joules. In other words, a .50 cal. bullet had between five and fourteen times the energy of a .30 caliber. The *cannon*, which was a primary weapon of the German Bf 109, was occasionally mounted in ground attack aircraft and was an order of magnitude even more powerful. The shell alone was thirteen times heavier than the .30 cal. bullet and two and one-half times the mass of the .50 cal. bullet. The British, soon after the start of World War II, shifted the armament of the Spitfire and Hurricane from .30 cal. machine guns to 20 mm cannon.

2. The statement that guns firing at high speeds are "ineffective" is patently false, as any modern F-100, A-7, Air Force F-4E, F-16, F/A-18, or F-35 pilot can affirm. Dispersion is minimized by skill and training to develop accurate and steady pipper placement on the target. Scores of 80–90 percent are common when firing the rotary M-61 gatling gun onto a ground, scored range target.[21]

3. The reported inaccuracy of single-engine attack aircraft in bombing can be attributed to (a) insufficient training in dive-bombing, (b) too-shallow dive angles, which are inherently less accurate in range, (c) a lack of information exchange with Navy attack pilots who won the Battle of Midway with single-engine dive-bombers, or (d) a combination of these.

4. The lack of support for machine guns in attack aircraft and the decline of the dive-bombing tactic in the Army Air Forces led to a discontinuation of research on improved gunsights.

The Doctrinal Shift to Twin-Engined Bombers for Ground Support

Although the Air Corps had received and evaluated a few light bombers previously, the 1938–1940 doctrinal belief altered their military requirements and requests from the aviation industry. The Air Corps doctrine of the light bomber was formalized in the publication of Field Manual FM 1-5,[22] and procurement followed the doctrinal preference.

Interestingly, this doctrine against single-engine aircraft was to remain relatively stable in the face of several official attempts to change it. In June 1941, Robert A. Lovett, assistant secretary of war for air (and later secretary of defense, 1951–1953), advised Gen. Arnold that in his judgment the Air Corps was devoting insufficient attention to ground support. Lovett recommended the Air Corps reconsider its stand on procuring light bombers and purchase instead more attack dive-bombers. Arnold reported that he would assign the matter to a conference of interested War Department agencies. Lovett's attempt was unsuccessful, but it was representative of other War Department efforts to increase the Air Corps priority for the attack mission, but they made little headway against the doctrine and advocates of heavy and light bombardment.[23]

Douglas A-20 Havoc

Jack Northrop, Donald Douglas, and Ed Heinemann had begun designing a Model 7A attack bomber in 1936, due to the Japanese invasion of China and the Spanish Civil War. It was powered by two 450 hp engines with a top speed of 250 mph. When the Army Air Corps issued a new requirement calling for a 1,200-mile range, 1,200 lb. bombload, and at least 200 mph speed, the design team increased the crew from two to three, added engine power with two 1,100 hp engines, narrowed the fuselage, and enlarged the bomb bay. The Model 7A was entered in the Army's design competition of 1938 for a medium bomber against the Martin Model 167F and the North American NA-40. All the prototypes were successful. (The North American design became the B-25 Mitchell, and the Martin entry became the B-26 Marauder.)

The A-20A was the first major production version for the US Army Air Corps. These aircraft were powered by 1,600 hp Wright R-2600-11 engines. Weight was increased 3,750 lbs., self-sealing fuel tanks were installed, and fuel capacity was 394 US gallons. The armament consisted of four .30-caliber machine guns in side-mounted fuselage blisters, twin .30s in an open dorsal position, and one .30 in the ventral position.

The A-20B was powered the same as the A model and had a modified Plexiglas nose. Bomb racks were changed from a vertical to horizontal configuration, and the bomb bay could house a 200-gallon fuel tank for ferrying purposes. Two .50-caliber machine guns were mounted in the forward fuselage, one .50 was placed in the open dorsal position. A field modification replaced the plastic nose with a solid nose that housed four to six .50-caliber machine guns. Six A-20Bs were transferred to the US Navy and designated BD-2s.

The A-20G model was built in greater numbers than any other version. It had a solid nose, which housed a battery of guns. They were powered by two Wright R-2600 engines. Other changes were the addition of carburetor heat, heavier armor plating, and removal of the dual controls in the gunner's compartment. The A-20G-1 nose contained four 20 mm cannon, one .50-caliber machine gun in the dorsal position, one .30-caliber machine gun in the ventral position, and 2,000 lbs. of bombs internally. The A-20G-5 model replaced the nose cannons with six .50-caliber machine guns but were found to be less accurate. Starting with the 751st aircraft in the series, the A-20G-20 replaced the dorsal machine gun with a Martin turret with twin .50 machine guns, and twin .50s were placed in the ventral position. Bomb racks were also added to carry 500 lbs. of bombs on stations beneath the outer wing panels.

Douglas sold the first order for 100 to the French government, which followed up with 270 more. Over 3,600 were purchased by the US government and shipped to the Soviet Union under Lend-Lease. The British made two orders totaling 450 and added major orders for a specific model, called the "Boston III" (DB-7B). These aircraft served in North Africa, Sicily, Italy, and western Europe. The Australian air force bought the A-20 and used it throughout the Pacific campaign. US Air Corps A-20As, Bs, and Gs flew mostly in the Pacific and Australia. Douglas built over 7,000 A-20s, and an additional 380 were built by Boeing.

The Douglas A-24 Banshee

The A-24A was a version of the Douglas Dauntless (SBD-4A). Despite the official decision to abandon single-engine aircraft for the attack mission, elements of the Army Air Corps bought 170 Banshees for use as attack aircraft. When Douglas modified the aircraft to the SBD-5A, the Army bought another 615.[24] The USAAC used the Dauntless in the Louisiana Maneuvers in 1941 and sent two squadrons to the Philippines in the fall of 1941. Before the Philippines fell, the aircraft were flown to Australia.

Gen. Orvil A. Anderson was in charge of the expansion of US Army Air Corps, and he deleted sixteen dive-bomber groups (including A-24s) from the budget and shifted the monies to fighter aircraft. His rationale was that "fighters could dive-bomb, but dive-bombers couldn't fight."[25] Gen. George C. Marshall, Army chief of staff, heard about this and, in an energetic manner, told the staff that *he* had put those aircraft in the budget himself, and who was it who took them out? In fact, Marshall decreed the policy that no aeroplane should have a range greater than the infantry could march in two and one-half days! This policy is reminiscent of the German Imperial Army in 1910–1914, which required all aircraft

to have folding wings so they could be loaded on wagons to accompany the Army on marches. The A-24s and other dive-bombers were quickly restored to the budget.[26] However, before the A-24 groups went into combat, their aircraft had been replaced by P-38s!

Curtiss-Wright A-25 Helldiver/Shrike

In 1940, elements of the Army Air Corps became interested in the Navy XSB2C-1A dive-bomber after the success of the German Stuka in the invasions of Poland and France. The aircraft was a two-place midwing monoplane, powered by a Wright R-2600-8 double-row fourteen-cylinder radial engine. The first Army order was for one hundred, followed by a massive order for three thousand in 1942.[27] Modifications to meet Army requirements included deleting the tail hook and wing folding, and adding underneath armor plate, larger wheels, and a pneumatic tailwheel (the solid rubber tire absorbed heat and shed its rubber on long taxiing, a problem the Navy A-1s had when used on air bases in South Vietnam). Navy versions continued to be produced by Curtiss-Wright's Columbus plant, while the Army's version was to be manufactured in their St. Louis plant. After the Battle of Britain in 1940, the news of the Stuka's poor performance against modern fighters was widespread, and the Army Air Forces became even more disillusioned with dive-bombers. The A-25 was suddenly excess to their needs. A total of 410 were subsequently returned to the Marine Corps, and the rest never saw combat.[28]

Here the difference between the Air Corps and naval aviators could not have been more stark. The Navy had perfected the dive-bombing tactic to attack heavily armored ships. Even those who disparaged the dive-bomber in favor of the torpedo plane did not object to the combined use of the two types and their complementary missions. That was fortunate because the superiority of the dive-bomber would not be proven until the Battle of Midway. Air Corps attack pilots had no such precise target, and they did not practice the high-angle tactics of the Navy. The dive-bombing mission of attacking the enemy fleet was close to the central doctrine of the Navy; it had no responsibility or desire to design aircraft to attack industrial targets in the homeland, *and* the Navy had no Army clamoring for air support of its defensive or advancing ground forces.

Congressional and Army Policy on Dive-Bombers

As the nation was gearing up to produce aircraft for the coming war in early 1941, Senator Harry S. Truman became concerned that there was corruption and graft in the multimillion-dollar procurement contracts being awarded. Elected in 1940 on an anti–New Deal platform, Truman drove his personal car to Fort Leonard Wood, Missouri, and discovered corruption in the housing contract. Motivated, he visited several other military installations and found the same thing. When the Senate convened, he lobbied other senators with his convictions. On March 1, 1941, by unanimous consent, the Senate formed the Committee to Investigate the National Defense Program and made Truman its chairman. As it conducted its investigations throughout the war it drew praise from multiple sources for its success in exposing wrongdoing and saving the government millions of dollars in cost overruns. His committee is credited in saving an estimated $10–15 billion in military spending and saving thousands of lives of US servicemen. The committee's 1943 report is instructive in what it said about Army and Navy dive-bombing programs:

> The airplane has proved to be the most important single weapon in the present war. We have succeeded in building an air industry in the United States which our foes cannot hope to equal.

> *Single-engine dive and attack bombers.*
> The Army has concluded that it will have little need for additional dive bombers for the reason that dive bombers could not be operated unless there is a clear air superiority and then, only when the ground forces are not adequately equipped with antiaircraft equipment.
> The Curtis[s] A-25 is the Army's version of the Navy's SB-2C Helldiver. The Curtis[s] A-25 is manufactured at St. Louis, MO, and the program will be greatly reduced both because of the Army's opinion that the dive bomber is not valuable for most Army purposes and because of the inability of the company to date to produce useable planes.

> *Navy dive bombers.*
> As previously indicated, the Army has concluded that additional dive bombers will not be needed by the Army. The success of Battleship X against an attack by dive bombers, although not conclusive, indicates that dive bombers have very definite limitation even for Navy uses. Skip-bombing may prove to be more satisfactory than dive bombing, but the Navy is till of the opinion that it should proceed with the dive-bomber program.
> This is a question of military tactics on which the decision of the Navy should be final. On the statements of the Navy and Army officials with respect to the dive bomber, it appears clear that great caution should be taken by the Navy to make sure that the program for the construction of dive bombers is not greater than that justified by the Navy's own interpretation of its technical value.

> *The Curtis[s]-Wright SB2C (Helldiver)*
> Production of such [Navy] dive bombers was to have been commenced by Curtis[s]-Wright at Columbus, Ohio, in December 1941. Production did not actually commence until September 1942. It has been hopelessly behind schedule and to date Curtis[s]-Wright has not succeeded in producing a single SB2C which the Navy considers to be usable as a combat airplane.[29]

If the Congress was truly interested in advocating the Navy switch from high-angle dive-bombing to glide bombing, it had only to look at the Marine Corps experience with their Midway-based dive-bombers in the Battle of Midway to see their error. There, shallow-angle dive-bombing had cost the Marine Corps attackers 50 percent of their force.

North American B-25 Mitchell

The second medium bomber in the 1939 multiengine competition was the B-25. The design had originally been prepared to beat the Douglas B-18 Bolo as a medium bomber in 1937, but it was updated and proposed as a twin-engined attack aircraft in 1938. Despite the crash of its earlier competition aircraft, the Army ordered the revised design into production before its first flight.

The B-25 featured two 1,700 hp engines powering it to 328 mph and cruising at 233 mph for 2,500 miles of range. It soon upgraded to multiple .50-caliber machine guns mounted in a top power turret, the tail, the side windows, and the bombardier's nose. Solid-nose versions were produced with six and eight machine guns and even a 75 mm cannon. With a light wing loading and none of the adverse characteristics of the Martin B-26, the Mitchell became a favorite in all theaters. Nearly 9,900 aircraft were produced in nine models. The B-25 became famous in April 1942 as the "Doolittle's Raiders" flew to bomb Tokyo and other Japanese cities from the aircraft carrier USS *Hornet*.

The Martin B-26 Marauder

The Glenn L. Martin Co., in Baltimore, Maryland, produced the B-26 for the 1939 attack competition. The aircraft was very streamlined with a short wingspan, resulting in an extremely high wing loading. Its two 1,850 hp engines powered the aircraft to a blazing maximum speed of 315 mph with cruising at 266 mph. The high wing loading made it unwieldy to maneuver, and the high landing speed of 140 mph made it difficult to land. However, it was the most successful of the competing aircraft. The Army ordered 201 aircraft directly from the plans of the Model 179 in 1939, before the aircraft had even flown. The B-26 suffered high casualties and frequent accidents when employed at low altitude. Despite its speed and other outstanding features, it gained a reputation of being dangerous and difficult to fly. One of its sardonic nicknames was "the Baltimore Vagrant," for its "lack of visible support." A total of 5,200 B-26 aircraft were delivered, and they served with many Allies in all World War II theaters.

One of the notable and little-known missions performed by the Marauder was in the Battle of Midway. On the morning of June 4, 1942, four Army Air Corps B-26s, armed with a single torpedo each, took off from Midway Island with six Navy torpedo bombers to attack the Japanese fleet. The gunners of the B-26s shot down two Japanese Zeros. Two of the aircraft launched torpedoes at the Japanese flagship *Akagi*, which avoided them. The second B-26 then strafed the carrier's flight deck. One of the B-26s was shot down. The pilot of the third B-26 deliberately crashed his crippled aircraft into *Akagi*, narrowly missing the bridge and VAdm. Nagumo. Two of the flight of four returned to Midway, only to crash-land.[30]

Douglas A-26/B-26 Invader

The Invader was built on the success of Douglas's Havoc. Similar in design, it featured a more robust airframe, heavier armament, and more-powerful engines. The A/B-26 was designed to meet a 1940 Army Air Corps requirement for multirole light bombers for low-level and medium-altitude bombing attacks. Three prototypes were ordered, and the first XA-26A flew on October 31, 1941. The A-26B was the first attack version. The original carried six .50-caliber machine guns, which were upgraded to eight. Successive modifications loaded as many as sixteen guns.

In 1947, the newly independent Air Force deleted the Attack category completely but retained the A-26. When the B-26 Marauder was retired in 1948, the Air Force redesignated the A-26 as the B-26, and the aircraft performed through the Korean War and into Vietnam. For Vietnam duty the Air Force retained the B-26 designation and had Douglas upgrade the engines to 2,500 hp. They also installed fourteen forward-firing machine guns. Assigned to the Special Air Warfare's 606th Air Commando Squadron, the B-26 fought valiantly in the advisory role, but in 1963–64 the wings began to come off due to long-term stress of the g-forces in the pullout from dive-bombing. A total of 2,503 Invaders were produced over its thirty-two-year history.

Luftwaffe Experience in the Spanish Civil War and World War II

First World War ace Ernst Udet believed in the dive-bomb tactic on the basis of his flying experience in the Great War. His position and influence in the fast-growing Luftwaffe in 1935 led to the design and development of a specific aircraft, the Junkers Ju 87 Stuka (*Sturzkampfflugzeug*, literally "drop-down fighter"). Two other models, the Junkers Ju 88 and the Dorner Do 217, also were equipped for dive-bombing. In 1936, Adolf Hitler dispatched the Legion Condor to Spain to support the Falange Nationalists of General Franco. Their experience with dive-bombing and low-level attacks tended to validate these tactics with German pilots and officials. The result was the extensive use of the Ju 87 in the 1939 attack on Poland and the 1940 attack on France. The Stuka had several severe deficiencies: it was slow, carried only one bomb on a fuselage trapeze, and had few forward-firing machine guns, only one lightweight rear-firing gun, and no armor. The Stuka did not fare well in the face of Hurricanes and Spitfires in the Battle of Britain, and the type was hurriedly withdrawn from action.

The Use of Attack Aircraft in the German Blitzkrieg

Generaloberst Heinz Guderian is considered the primary advocate of "lightning warfare," the combined arms theory of armored tanks, artillery, and attack aircraft.[31] Guderian was the leader of German forces in the famous penetration of the Argonne Forest in 1940, leading to the fall of France. By the skillful maneuvering of his tanks and the use of Luftwaffe aircraft in attack missions, he pioneered air-ground coordination. Though many students of Guderian have presumed his theory and practice focused on close air support, an Air Force analysis reveals he primarily used attack aircraft in *interdiction*, not CAS. Maj. Ainsworth M. O'Reilly, in an Air University paper, claims Guderian's interpretation of German World War I experience led him to believe that aircraft were a major threat and were best used in the follow-up to the penetration on the frontier, as Guderian wrote:

It was the ground-attack aircraft that became the immediate threat. Germany suffered from the attentions of the enemy aircraft on the Somme and at Ypres, and in the course of 1918 the superiority of the Allies in the air became more tangible still. While enemy air raids against the German homeland were rare and not particularly effective, aircraft intervened to significant purpose in the ground battle, as at Amiens on August 8, 1918. They created disorder in the German rearmost communications, they hindered the movement of reserves, they took

German batteries under actual attack, they laid smokescreens in front of occupied ground, and they reported the progress of the attack.[32]

O'Reilly references Guderian's writings to add a specific focus of his tactics in 1940:

After tanks exploited the breach in enemy lines, Guderian stated that the most pressing issue was to keep enemy reserves from engaging his tanks, and this interdiction focus became his major argument for airpower use.[33]

Everything comes down to delaying the intervention of the enemy anti-tank reserves and tanks. . . . The best way of delaying the intervention of reserves is through aircraft, and this is probably one of their most important contributions to the ground battle.[34]

O'Reilly observes as further evidence of his claim that Guderian only once conferred directly with the commander of the air unit supporting his tanks, and that the Luftwaffe never developed the air-ground liaison or the air-to-ground communications to integrate attacking aircraft to the "detailed integration of each air mission with the fire and movement of those forces,"[35] as is required for close air support.

Soviet Experience in World War II: The *"Shturmovik"*

In 1938, Sergei Ilyushin, the head of the legendary Ilyushin aircraft design bureau, spoke to the Soviet premier, Joseph Stalin, and asked to design a "flying tank." Stalin agreed, and two prototype Il-2s were ordered, with the first flying in October 1939, one month after Germany's invasion of Poland. The Il-2 was originally designed as a two-seater but was changed to a single seat and then changed back again when a pilot wrote to Stalin asking for a gunner to defend against German fighters. The single mission of the Il-2, now called the *"Shturmovik,"* was to attack armored tanks. The aircraft was built of wood and metal and was designed to be manufactured by relatively unskilled labor. Its most distinctive design feature was the forward fuselage, which was composed entirely of a special-alloy armor plate to protect the engine, fuel system, radiators, and crew station. The result was its strength and robustness in combat. The armament was two 20 mm cannon, later upgraded to 23 mm. The heavy armor led the Germans to dub it *Betonflugzeug* (the concrete plane), since it was extremely difficult to shoot down. Although only 249 were built by the time of the German invasion on June 22, 1941, Soviet factories turned out an amazing total of between 31,000 and 36,000 aircraft, making it the most produced aircraft of the Second World War.

One of the close-air-support tactics developed by the Soviet Union was the concept of a "waiting area," airspace close to the scene of an expected ground target, where a flight of attack aircraft would loiter while waiting for the target to be better identified. They also developed a second tactic—separating the flight into a high element for dive-bombing and a low element for strafing the target. Yet a third aerial tactic was practiced: launching simultaneous or near-simultaneous attacks from different directions.[36]

The second of these tactics was extensively adopted by Navy tacticians and employed extremely successfully at the Battles of Midway and Coral Sea and elsewhere in the Pacific war. Similarly, tactics 1 and 3 of the Russian set were reinvented and employed by US attack aircraft in Vietnam. Virtually all aircraft with enough fuel were directed to loiter in holding areas in South Vietnam while forward air controllers refined target types and locations. The author employed the "divergent attack heading" tactic on numerous attacks in his A-1E.

North American A-36 Apache / P-51 Mustang

One exception to the emerging light-bomber doctrine in the late 1930s was the single-engine North American A-36 Apache. Noting the US Army Air Corps' lack of interest in procuring attack aircraft, North American marketed Great Britain. In early 1940, the British asked North American Aviation (NAA) to build P-40s for them under license from Curtiss. NAA responded by proposing to build a fighter from their own design, although this would be their first. The NA-73X initial test flight was October 26, 1940, and the British ordered 320, calling them Mustang Is. This aircraft was built for the attack mission,

with perforated dive brakes and six .50 cal. machine guns. The US government kept two of the aircraft and designated them XP-51. The British ordered another 300 before the US government became interested in the design as a high-speed dive-bomber to be used in ground support missions in the forthcoming North Africa campaign. The Army Air Force contracted for 500 A-36s in April 1942, and the aircraft entered combat in May 1943.[37]

Army captain Charles Dills flew thirty-nine missions in the A-36 between November 1943 and February 1944. The A-36s would begin their dives from approximately 14,000 feet. Capt. Dills describes a typical Army Air Forces dive-bombing run:

As the group neared the target, the leader would waggle his wings. This was the signal to get in trail (single file behind the lead plane). As we got closer to the target, the leader would open his dive brakes and roll upside down. We would follow suit and fly upside down until we were directly over the target. We would then go straight down, until we had a good aim at the target. I've seen some reports that say we released our bombs at 3,000 feet. That's getting a little low. I'd say we dropped the bombs at around 5,000 feet or so. As you were pulling out, you'd shut the dive brakes and it was like getting a kick in the butt. Your speed would jump from 350 mph to about 450, and you'd get the hell out of there. If there was no flak, we'd climb and re-group for whatever we were supposed to do next. If there was a lot of flak, we'd just get out of there as fast as we could and re-group elsewhere.[38]

Sometimes, danger came from one's own squadron mates. Says Dills:

We were attacking some docks, and I had dropped my bombs; I was flying straight down but there were two bombs, right in front of me! They were no more than 30 or 40 feet from me, and I could not pull out of the dive without hitting them! They must've been dropped by the guy behind me, and I had to fly formation with them until they passed me! They were so close that I could read right on the bomb "five hundred, thirty-six pounds, GP (General Purpose)"!

When the need for a long-range escort fighter became apparent due to high losses among the B-17s raiding Germany, the A-36 was modified into an air superiority fighter, the P-51 Mustang. The story of strategic-bomber vulnerability and the subsequent crash development of the P-51 escort fighter is wonderfully told in Maj. Gen. Perry Smith's classic, *The Air Force Plans for Peace*.[39]

Republic P-47 Thunderbolt

The grandfather of the P-47 was the controversial Russian immigrant Alexander de Seversky. Born in Russia in 1894 as Alexander Nicolaiovitch Procofieff-Seversky, the young boy was entered into the Imperial Naval Academy. In 1914, he was commissioned in the Naval Air Service and became a pilot. His bomber was shot down on July 2, 1915, and he lost a leg in the crash. The czarist regime appointed him to a commission to study aircraft production and design in the United States, and he arrived here in 1916–1917 (some reports say he was an assistant naval attaché in the Russian embassy). With the Russian Revolution in October 1917, he decided to remain in the US and applied for citizenship. Within three years he became a test pilot and consulting engineer for the US Army Air Service. One of his duties was to design a bombsight for Brig. Gen. Billy Mitchell. He rose to the rank of major in the Army Reserves. By 1923, he had 364 engineering patent claims.[40]

He founded the Seversky Aero Corporation in 1923 and became a US citizen in 1927. The small corporation did not survive the stock market crash of 1929, but Seversky bounced back and re-formed the corporation in 1931. Two of his first hires were also Russian immigrants, Michael Gregor and Alexander Kartveli. Together the group began designing and building an amphibian seaplane dubbed the SEV-3. The aircraft was a single-engine, metal monoplane with a Wright R-975-ET engine with 350 hp. Its first flight was in 1933. The original engine was soon replaced by a Wright J-6-9E, which developed 420 hp. With this aircraft Seversky established a world record of 179.76 mph over a 3-kilometer course on October 9, 1933.[41]

Seversky was so confident in his ability and the value of his invention that he flew the aircraft with pontoons to Wright Field, Ohio, to obtain a contract from the Army. He was refused, but he dropped the pontoons, reworked the design, and returned some weeks later. This time he was awarded a contract for $878,000 for thirty BT-8 basic trainers. While producing the trainers, in 1937 Seversky took over the Grumman factory at Farmingdale. After tinkering with the design, he delivered the P-35 to the Army.

The P-35A featured an upgraded engine and the elliptical wing form so familiar on P-47s. The aircraft was the Army Air Corps' first production single-seat, all-metal pursuit plane with retractable landing gear and an enclosed cockpit. The Army accepted seventy-six P-35s in 1937–1938 and assigned all but one of them to the 1st Pursuit Group at Selfridge Field, Michigan.[42] Sweden purchased sixty improved aircraft (designated EP-106), and the United States diverted a second Swedish order for sixty to the USAAC in 1940. These aircraft were assigned to the 17th and 20th Pursuit Squadrons in the Philippines, where they all were lost in action early in the war. Ironically, the Japanese navy ordered twenty two-seat versions of the P-35 in 1938, and these became the only American-built planes used operationally by the Japanese during World War II. However, 1937 and 1938 were terrible economic years in the depth of the Depression, and Seversky's attention turned to national air races and export marketing, neither of which produced many sales. At the end of 1938, the Seversky Corporation's board of directors removed de Seversky from his leadership position and elected Alexander Kartveli to vice president. They then changed the name of the firm from Republic Aeronautical Corporation to Republic Aviation. The next year, 1939, Jackie Cochran set a world speed record of 305 mph on September 15, flying a P-35 in California.

Then there were the XP-41, P-43, and P-44. As late as November 1939, the Army turned down offers for the XP-47 and the XP-47A.

The next model, the XP-47B, was the turning point. By small changes, addressing deficiencies one by one, the XP-47B won the approval of Army Air Corps authorities, and a contract was awarded to Republic for production. One XP-47B(RE) prototype was produced, followed by

170 RP-47B(RE)s. Several dozens of P-47Cs were produced, but the big break came with the P-47D. Starting in 1942, the Army Air Forces awarded some thirty-six separate contracts for P-47Ds and twenty contracts for other variations, totaling 15,683 aircraft.

Powered by the eighteen-cylinder Pratt & Whitney R-2800-21 or 59, with 2,300 hp, the aircraft exceeded 410 mph at 20,000 feet and went over 430 mph at 30,000 feet. With its eight .50 cal. machine guns and up to 425 rounds per gun, the firepower was tremendous.

The P-47 gained fame with US and Allied pilots beginning in 1943. No fewer than sixty-four US fighter groups were equipped with Thunderbolts, with an average of three squadrons per group. The most famous were in 8th Air Force (England) with (arguably) the 4th and 56th Fighter Groups. The aircraft was exported to Great Britain, France, the Soviet Union, China, Mexico, Italy, Yugoslavia, Brazil, and several other Latin American countries. Production ended in 1945, but the aircraft remained on active duty until 1949 and in the US Air National Guard until 1953. Though loved by its pilots and ground crew, the big, ugly P-47 could not compete with the sleek P-51 for retention after World War II, and it was the P-51 that remained to fight the Korean War.

US Fighter-Bombers

By May 1944, US aircraft based in England comprised *twice* the total of all German aircraft of all types, in all theaters (12,617 vs. 6,832).[43] As the strategic-bombing campaign continued, and German fighters were losing their fight to defend the Reich, US fighter escort aircraft would descend looking for other German aircraft to attack and then strafe German airfields and other installations. After D-day, while US and British armies were battling across France, P-51s and P-47s were increasingly tasked to attack ground targets. The P-47 was especially effective. P-47 units destroyed 86,000 railway cars, 9,000 locomotives, 6,000 armored fighting vehicles, and 68,000 trucks.[44] While the P-47's eight machine guns were effective against most targets, it also carried 500 and 1,000 lb. bombs. Ground fire inflicted high loss rates on all ground attack aircraft, but

the lesson that tactical and Air Staff planners learned was that these multipurpose fighter aircraft were satisfactory in their fighter-bomber role. That belief in multipurpose aircraft, proven in the caldron of combat both in the European and Pacific theaters, entrenched itself in Air Force doctrine and remains strong even more than seventy-five years after World War II.

US Air Force Postwar Decision on Attack Aircraft

With the development of the light bomber and the attack capabilities of the "fighter-bombers," Air Force planners saw little reason to continue the development of a specialized "attack" airplane. The Air Corps previously had terminated the use of the "attack" designation by single-engine aircraft in 1940, and the attack designation was formally dropped by the independent Air Force in 1948. The A-26 Invader was redesignated the B-26.[45] There was no major Air Force program to buy another attack aircraft until the 1964 purchase of the A-1 Skyraider from the Navy, and no attempt to *modify* another attack aircraft until the A-7 decision in 1965.

USAF Attack Missions in the Korean War

The US Air Force fought the Korean War with the aircraft it had in World War II (P-51, B-26, B-29) plus the F-80 Shooting Star, F-82 Twin Mustang, F-84 Thunderjet, and F-86 Sabre. Far East Air Forces (FEAF) responded, with the 8th Fighter-Bomber Group on Itazuke Air Base, Japan, flying F-80s, being one of the first units to respond to the North Korean invasion on June 25, 1950. The 69th All Weather Fighter Squadron also responded with its F-82 night fighters.

The first contributions of tactical air were to gain air superiority by defeating the North Korean air force and slow the rate of advance of their ground army, which had overrun Seoul in three days and was driving toward Pusan in the South. The Air Force mounted the majority of seven thousand sorties in July with close-air-support and interdiction missions that resulted in slowing the enemy's rate of advance to 2 miles per day.[46] When the F-86 Sabre jets arrived on the peninsula, they constituted about 9 percent of the air forces and flew 12 percent of the sorties in air defense, air superiority, and counter air attacks. Once the Pusan perimeter was established, the USAF ground attack missions were shifted even more to close air support.

The United Nations' counteroffensive was launched on September 15 with the dramatic landing at Inchon, combined with a breakout from Pusan. Within two weeks the US 8th Army and Marines were crossing into North Korea and continued on to the Yalu River. USAF and Navy air had destroyed the enemy air force, and the majority of missions were attack. After the Chinese army invaded across the Yalu and forced the painful retreat, the Chinese introduced the MiG-15, and air-to-air battles over the Yalu began. With the armies stalemated within a few miles, back and forth near the Demilitarized Zone, the air war gained the headlines, but not most missions.

The Air Force order of battle in February 1951 included the following:

Far East Air Force Aircraft	
Type	**Number**
F-51	187
F-80	252
F-84	75
F-86	75
Light bombers B-26	139
Medium bombers B-29	90
Total	**818**

Source: Allan R. Millett, "Korea, 1950–1953," in Benjamin Franklin Cooling, ed., *Case Studies on the Development of Close Air Support* (Washington, DC: US Government Publishing Office, 1990), 355.

The total of CAS and interdiction missions was 313,765, or nearly four times the number of air-to-air sorties. Of course, the dominant mission was combat support, which included troop lift and material supply to UN, Army, and Marine Corps ground units.

One of the issues that remain between the US Army and the US Air Force is the ground-centric and relatively more narrow view that is revealed by Army histories of wars, not just Korea. The typology and nomenclature of Army narratives tend to describe and analyze ground maneuver. Indeed, the symbology of ground combat operations has changed little since the Roman legions conquered Carthage. There were virtually no changes between the Civil War and World War I except to add armored symbols. The small change for World War II battles was to add an Airborne symbol (a pair of bird's wings) and Air Force unit with the infinity symbol.[47] Whether this ground-centric focus is because the special and temporal characteristics are difficult to diagram or there is a genuine neglect of airpower contribution would be a good point to debate.

John Correll makes the point in his 2020 article on the Korean War that "then and later, the Army was reluctant to give the Air Force credit for significant results in Korea. A study for the Army chief of military history in 1966 said that air interdiction had been 'helpful during the early months of the war in assisting the ground forces to overcome the North Korean Army,' but that 'the air interdiction campaign was not a decisive factor in shaping the outcome of the war.'"[48]

The Army also disagreed with the Air Force's targeting of newly arrived B-29s. The Air Force deployed three whole wings of B-29s to bomb North Korea's few strategic and deep-interdiction targets; the Army wanted them used for close-air-support missions. How those high-altitude B-29 missions would have been integrated with the fire and movement of Army ground forces in proximity to US troops is anybody's guess. Even with forward air controllers, the accuracy from level bombing at 25,000 feet would have been questionable.

Air Force–Army Doctrinal Dispute over Close Air Support

The United States entered the Korean War with three air forces: USAF, Navy, and Marine Corps. Each had its separate air control system, and there was no one below Gen. MacArthur who could resolve disputes. MacArthur's chief of staff, Maj. Gen. Edward M. Almond, was especially enamored with the Marine Corps system of decentralized control, and he was critical of the Air Force's centralized system. He and other critics charged the Air Force had not provided adequate close air support for the Army.[49] Gen. J. Lawton Collins, Army chief of staff, in November 1950 filed a formal criticism of close-air-support operations with USAF chief of staff Hoyt Vandenberg.[50] Collins's major complaint was that the Air Force displayed a lack of interest in the ground attack mission. Vandenberg responded that the USAF would not neglect the CAS mission, but that the issue required further study. The major problem was not the aircraft or the operation, but in the allocation of sorties and the centralized tactical control system.

Far East Air Forces continued to believe that the best way to end the war was to attack the North Korean transportation system. The high percentage of interdiction missions was witness to this belief. Heavy artillery support might have lessened the demand for CAS, but the 8th Army had only light artillery support. When Gen. Mark Clark took over as United Nations commander, he proposed a three-phased program: better training on air-ground operations, a limited delegation of air sorties to the Army, and a joint operations center for each corps (with daily sorties). Simultaneously, Gen. Clark asked the Navy Task Force commander to provide a high number of frontline CAS attacks. Air Force general Otto Weyland agreed to many of these positions, but he warned Gen. Clark that the Air Force was losing one aircraft for every 382 CAS sorties, and one in twenty-six were damaged.[51] One of the interesting differences between Air Force and Navy attack participants was that naval aviators were much more willing to conduct CAS rather than interdiction or air superiority. One of the reasons the Navy and Marine Corps did not compete vigorously for the air superiority

mission was that their straight-wing F9F Panther was no match for the swept-wing MiG-15.

The Air Force learned another lesson in Korea. The P-51s were assigned priority for ground attack missions, but they required more maintenance per flight hour than the newer jets. Thus, they were less available for mission tasking. This only added to the USAF preference for multipurpose jet aircraft.

Though the air-ground system was under attack, with justified complaints for its lack of timeliness, the Air Force doctrinal argument prevailed because the theater commanders in 1953 were unwilling to pursue the issue. Similarly, the Joint Chiefs of Staff, still wounded from the acrimony of the interservice disputes over the 1947 Unification Act and the 1949 cancellation of the supercarrier, were unwilling to initiate another doctrinal roles and missions battle.

Post–Korean War, 1950s

The Air Force after Korea developed two major lines of combatant aircraft: the jet bombers, (B-47, B-52) for the strategic-nuclear-deterrence mission, and jet fighters (F-84, F-86, F-100, F-101, F-104) for the tactical air mission. The air-to-air F-86 Sabre was replaced initially with the air-to-air F-100A Super Sabre, but the design was deficient, and only 203 were built. Recognizing that the national strategy had turned to "massive retaliation," the F-100A design was modified to accommodate tactical nuclear weapons with the F-100C and the F-100D, which made it a dual-role fighter-bomber. North American produced 1,254 F-100Ds, and it was deployed in squadrons around the world. The unique feature of the F-100D was its air-refueling capability. The primary mission was nuclear ground alert, with bases in England, Germany, (initially) France, Turkey, and Korea. The secondary mission was tactical—strike, interdiction, and close air support, with an air-to-air capability. The practice of actual close air support was very rare, being limited to a few Army–Air Force exercises, mostly in Europe.

In 1955, Tactical Air Command developed a capability for stateside fighters, with transports, reconnaissance, and tankers to contribute to deter and, if necessary, fight limited wars. The concept was called the "Composite Air Strike

Force" (CASF). It envisioned selected combat-ready continental US squadrons organized with aerial tankers into CASF packages that could deploy on a moment's notice to any limited war location with either conventional or nuclear weapons.[52] There were two major deployments of CASFs in the 1950s: the Lebanon crisis and the Taiwan Straits crisis, both in 1958. The largest was for the Berlin crisis of 1961, which included Air National Guard squadrons.

Smaller, squadron-sized deployments were used to backfill overseas squadrons converting to the F-105 Thunderchief, which had been specifically designed for the nuclear mission by having an internal bomb bay.

This, then, was the Air Force configuration as the decade of the 1950s ended, and the attack force waited for the tumultuous 1960s.

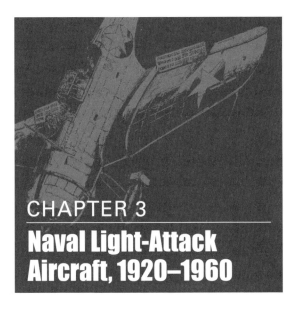

CHAPTER 3
Naval Light-Attack Aircraft, 1920–1960

Scratch one flat top.

—Lt. Cmdr. Robert Dixon

The Aircraft Carrier Controversy in the 1920s

Aircraft carrier advocates had disputes both with the "battleship admirals" and the seaplane sailors in the "Roaring Twenties." These events are not well known among Air Force and Army aviators. There were essentially five controversial issues facing the US Navy following the Great War:

- What was the role of the new air weapon, which threatened to create a new dimension of warfare that challenged traditional concepts and doctrine?

- How was air warfare to be considered in relation to the established "Gun Club" that had reigned in the US Navy since Nelson's victory at the Battle of Trafalgar and the USS *Constitution*'s victory over the HMS *Guerriere* in the War of 1812? The battleship admirals had been trained and believed in the supremacy of the "capital ship," the bearer of the big guns that could fire on an opposing fleet beyond 20 miles. No matter what means were used to determine the location of the enemy, the victory would go to the side with the biggest guns and their most accurate firing.

- How should the Navy respond to the airpower advocates such as Billy Mitchell, who argued for a single, unified air force for the nation?

- If airplanes are important, should the Navy invest in seaplanes or wheeled airplanes?

- How can the Navy best meet the nation's foreign policy of protecting US interests in the Far West Pacific?

A sixth issue was directly between naval aviation and the outspoken advocates of an independent air force—should naval aircraft, especially on land, be under the Department of the Navy or the Air Force?

Navy planners since Alfred Thayer Mahan had always prepared for the big battle at sea between opposing fleets. A smaller number of naval airpower advocates envisioned battles between fleets that were located by airborne reconnaissance and that remained out of range of the big guns. Since both sides agreed that the Great War had proven the value of airborne reconnaissance, the battleship admirals acknowledged the utility of seaplanes—launched and recovered from surface ships—that were under the close control of the Surface Fleet commander. In 1919, the only mission that Navy admirals agreed on for aviation was observation and to spot the fall of shot from the big guns of the battleships.[1]

One of the great advocates of aircraft and seaplanes was Capt. Washington Irving Chambers, USN. He argued that seaplanes could use the sea, "that universal airdrome, the water."[2] This philosophy was reinforced in the early 1920s by the development and success of very fast seaplanes—aircraft with floats that could be launched by cruisers and battleships. The supreme examples were the Supermarine S6 and S6B, which won the Schneider Trophy in 1927 and 1929, respectively, with speeds in excess of 400 mph.

The Royal Navy made the decision in the early 1920s that any victory at sea would have to be preceded by air superiority; the side that had it would prevail. That was a key judgment.

And the only way to win air superiority was to have large numbers of very fast aircraft that could attack the other's air fleet.[3] And the only way to launch large numbers would be off the deck of an aircraft carrier. The US Navy followed the British example of this doctrinal precept.

The theory and tactics of carrier warfare were developed to support this belief. By the end of 1922, "despite games rules which allowed the airplane only modest performance, it was evident, according to Capt. Laning of the War College, that aviation had come to exert 'a decisive influence in all stages of a campaign, and particularly in the battle stage.'"[4]

The next big decision was where to get the aircraft carriers. The only existing one was the USS *Langley*, a slow, converted collier. With the Washington Naval Conference of 1922 setting limits on the number and weight of battleships, one of the unregulated categories was the number of battle cruisers.

On January 4, 1922, the assistant secretary of the Navy, Theodore Roosevelt Jr., proposed an amendment to allow the US to convert two of its battle cruisers to aircraft carriers. The amendment received little opposition and passed.[5] The USS *Lexington* and *Saratoga* were selected. Their conversion did not go smoothly. Initial estimates were for a cost of $23,000,000 each and a schedule of two and a half years. By 1925, the cost estimates were raised to $34 million, and the next year to $40 million each. By the time they were completed in 1927, the cost was almost 90 percent over the original estimate, with a total construction time of five and a half years.[6]

The USS *Lexington* (CV-2) and *Saratoga* (CV-3) proved their worth. The legendary RAdm. Joseph Reeves captained the *Saratoga* task force in the Panama Games, US Fleet Problem Nine, in 1929. The aircraft on the *Saratoga* included Boeing F2B fighters and the Boeing F3B, which were employed both as a fighter and bomber. They were accompanied by Chance Vought O2U-2 Corsair scouts and Martin T4M-1 torpedo bombers. Charles Melhorn tells the story:

The defending screen, which included the *Lexington* as well as the cruisers, was penetrated at night during a high-speed run-in on the

target, and before dawn the first wave of seventy aircraft was on its way. Complete tactical surprise was achieved. Canal locks and Army airfields in the Zone were pummeled with both dive-bombing and low-level strafing attacks. When finally engaged by defending Army aircraft, *Saratoga*'s fighters gave more than they got. Pratt termed the strike and the maneuver that preceded it "the most brilliantly conceived and most effectively executed naval operation in our history."[7]

The attack aircraft carrier had proven its worth in concept and operations.

US Navy Attack Tactics and Aircraft

The basic types of naval aircraft were decided immediately after World War I. In 1919, the chief of naval operations (CNO) described four categories of aircraft needed by the Navy: (1) fighting planes, (2) spotting and short-distance reconnaissance planes, (3) torpedo and bombing planes, and (4) large flying boats.[8] Navy aeronautical engineers, planners, and tacticians produced a steady track of aircraft and tactics development in the interwar years.

One of the most significant achievements was a technical breakthrough that advanced carrier development dramatically. "That breakthrough, which changed the course of carrier aviation, was the appearance of the dive bomber."[9] Until that time in the late 1920s, naval tacticians had considered the torpedo plane the fleet's most powerful offensive strike and the best weapon to sink opposing ships. But the size and weight of the torpedo required a large aircraft, which took up sizable deck space and required a long takeoff run. The dive-bomber, on the other hand, was no larger than a fighter, could carry a diverse set of ordnance, and, due to its speed and angle of attack, stood a much-greater chance of survival against enemy guns. The dive-bomber supported the case for smaller, lighter aircraft carriers that could be built in larger numbers.

Types of Bombing Attacks

From the pilot's point of view, there are at least five types of low-level attacks on land and sea targets, ranging from level to steep:

- The *level attack* is inherently inaccurate, but it can be used when the aircraft is over water or level ground, and the weapon can be aimed directly along this path. Examples are a torpedo drop, skip bomb, or a napalm delivery.

- The *diving* tactic developed in the Great War is more accurate and was most likely 10 to 15 degrees to strafe troops or drop small bombs. This is the regular tactic still taught for air-to-ground or air-to-surface strafing in the USAF and USN today. These angles are steep enough to concentrate the machine gun or cannon fire, usually at very low altitude in a permissive environment. The minimum slant range to the target is usually 1,000 feet, and the pullout is just high enough to avoid flying into one's own ricochets.

- The next-*steeper* tactic is a 30-degree dive, which is routinely used to drop bombs with fins that retard the bomb's speed and is moderately accurate, at least more than at a lower angle.

- The *normal* angle taught for "dive-bombing" in the Air Force is 45 degrees, with a 10,000-foot roll-in and a minimum of 1,000-foot recovery to avoid encountering fragments of one's own bombs. In areas where there are small arms and antiaircraft artillery (AAA), the minimum altitude has been arbitrarily set at 5,000 feet, 10,000 feet, or even higher.

- The Navy in the 1920s developed and preferred a *steep*-angle attack of 70-plus degrees that provided a higher degree of accuracy for hitting ships.

By 1927, the Navy had acknowledged that dive-bombing was more accurate than horizontal bombing. Using the Curtiss F8C, Navy tests showed that aircraft dive-bombing scored a hit record of 67 percent, whereas level bombers averaged only 30 percent.[10]

In combat against an enemy's air defense, all services recognize that a minimum altitude is 4,500 feet to stay above the range of small-arms weapons, primarily the .50-caliber machine gun. With 37 mm and 57 mm cannon and surface-to-air missiles, even higher minimum altitudes are used. Beginning in the latter part of Vietnam War and continuing today is the use of precision-guided weapons, which allow the pilot to remain at much-higher altitude and still deliver bombs on target.

Developing the Dive-Bombing Tactic

The US Army after World War I pursued the attack mission, and on September 13, 1921, the Air Service organized the 3rd Attack Group at Kelly Field, Texas. The assigned aircraft were DH-4Bs.[11] The DH-4 had not been designed as an attack aircraft, but with its US-built Liberty engine, it had performed all kinds of bombing missions in the Great War. The 3rd Attack Group set up an Advanced Flying School at Kelly Field, and in the early 1920s it was training Army, Navy, and Marine Corps aviators.

One of the students was Marine Corps major (later lieutenant general) Ross Rowell, who reported to the school in May 1923. Rowell learned from the Army aviators a tactic of low-altitude attack that Rowell characterized as "dive bombing."[12] The practice bombs weighed less than 25 pounds and were loaded on a new A-3 bomb rack that held five bombs under each wing. The technique the Army aviators taught was to enter a shallow dive at about 1,500 feet, point the nose to the ground, release the practice bomb, and pull out about 600 feet. In the words of Tom Wildenberg:

> Rowell was so impressed with the accuracy of this approach to bombing that he later claimed to have immediately visualized its certainty of "naval employment where accuracy against small moving targets is paramount."[13]

After his time at the Kelly Field school, Maj. Rowell was transferred to the Air Service 1st Pursuit Group at Selfridge Field, Mount Clemens, Michigan. There he met Lt. (later brigadier general) George P. Tourtellot, who had flown with the Army Air Service in France and was one of the participants in the Virginia Capes bombing of surface ships in 1921. Tourtellot had bombed the German battleship *Ostfriesland* by using the very tactic Rowell had been taught at Kelly. Although Tourtellot believed the shallow dive technique was too vulnerable to antiaircraft fire, apparently Rowell saw the potential of a modified technique to be quite devastating. Tourtellot told Rowell that he had learned the tactic from the British while he was flying with them in the Great War.[14] Maj. Rowell's next assignment was command of VO-1M, the Marines' first aviation unit on the West Coast at Naval Air Station (NAS) San Diego, later changed to NAS North Island.

VO-1M was also flying the rugged DH-4, which Rowell soon fitted with miniature bomb racks. Rowell led his squadron on routine training flights to practice dive-bombing, and they put on a series of air shows to demonstrate their prowess and the accuracy of their dive-bombing tactic.

Thomas Wildenberg, the author of *Destined for Glory*, cites 1925 as the beginning year for a study of carrier airpower. That was the year the Navy's first aircraft carrier, USS *Langley* (CV-1), began aircraft operations, and the first airplane unit trained to operate from a carrier, Fighting Squadron 2 (VF-2), reported to *Langley*.[15] The month after VF-2 reported, the squadron and *Langley* participated in that year's Fleet Problem. Wildenberg also nominated Lt. Cmdr. Frank D. Wagner as the first to record the steeper dive-bombing maneuver flying a Curtiss F6F Hawk of VF-2, on October 26, 1926.[16] The Navy History and Heritage Command concurs and records that on that day, Wagner's squadron was the first unit to demonstrate high-angle dive-bombing:

In a display of tactics, VF-2 simulated an attack on the heavy ships of the Pacific Fleet as they sortied from San Pedro, California. The Hawks conducted almost vertical dives from 12,000 feet at the preappointed time, of which the fleet had been forewarned, but nonetheless achieved complete surprise. The general consensus among observers was that the tactic proved operationally effective. This became the first fleet demonstration of dive bombing. Although VF-2 had independently initiated this demonstration, VF-5 on the East Coast

was simultaneously developing similar tactics, indicating the obvious nature of the solution to the problem of effective bomb delivery.

Later, Wagner's VF-2 pilots flying F6C and FB-5s separately made 45-degree dives and dropped 25 lb. fragmentation bombs from 1,000 feet. Tom Wildenberg cites their accuracy:

Out of 105 bombs dropped, they made seventy hits for an average score of sixty-seven percent— more than double the accuracy of conventional aerial bombing, which at best could achieve an accuracy of about thirty percent.[17]

As the need for more accuracy became apparent, the tactic of higher than 45-degree dive-bombing was developed and generally replaced the old concept of horizontal bombing as well as low-angle bombing. An angle of 70 degrees was deemed to be the best choice.

It is noteworthy that the dive-bombing tactic was initially conducted by "fighter" aircraft, the F6C "Hawk," and the implicit belief was that this type possessed a multimission capability. The Air Corps would have agreed with that as doctrine. It was not until 1932 that RAdm. Harry Yarnell, commander, Aircraft Squadrons, Battle Force, observed that "it is becoming increasingly evident that if the performance of fighters is to be improved . . . bombing characteristics of fighters must be made secondary to fighting characteristics."[18] This observation led to the Navy belief in specialized aircraft, as the "Fighter" aircraft were designed for air-to-air combat, and the slower "Attack" aircraft for carrying bombs and torpedoes.

The use of the dive-bombing tactic was given official status in a decision from the top, as Adm. Edward W. Eberle, the chief of naval operations, on May 27, 1927, ordered the Commander-in-Chief Battle Fleet to evaluate the dive-bombing tactic against moving targets. This led directly through the next few years to the formal adoption and training of attack crews in this tactic.

An indication of the US lack of aviation readiness in the 1930s can be derived from the fact that President Herbert Hoover accepted the resignation of the assistant secretary of the Navy for aeronautics, David S. Ingalls, on the first of

June 1932 (for reasons unrecorded), and this critical position was not filled again until 1941!

Naval planners were encouraged when Marine Corps squadron VO-7 conducted dive-bombing and strafing attacks against Nicaraguan bandits in July 1927. The aircraft reportedly were guided by Marines with radios on the ground. The next year, 1928, the Navy issued a contract for the Martin XT5M-1 "diving bomber," which became the BN-1, the first designed to drop 1,000 lb. bombs. Three years later the Navy contracted for twelve BM-1s, the successor to the BN-1. Navy pilots were required to train in night flying, as if flying off an aircraft carrier was not dangerous enough.

One of the Navy's commendable and most useful methods of training was to conduct large-scale exercises at sea to simulate the complexity of modern warfare. Fleet Problem XV was conducted in April 1934, incorporating three separate exercises in the Caribbean. Attack aircraft "sank" *Saratoga* (CV-3) and put *Lexington* (CV-2) out of action, while *Lexington* fighters shot down the rigid airship *Macon* (ZRS-5). The vulnerability of airships and aircraft carriers was affirmed, as well as the need for attack aircraft to carry 500 and 1,000 lb. bombs.

In the 1920s, the Navy tried to build tripurpose aircraft to fulfill the missions of scouting, horizontal bombing, and torpedo bombing. Several aircraft models were built, but the designs did not meet operational needs, and multipurpose aircraft were discontinued.[19] In 1922, Stout Engineering flew the ST-1 twin-engined torpedo plane, which was the Navy's first all-metal aircraft. It was not until 1931 that the keel of the next aircraft carrier was laid; *Ranger* (CV-4), with commissioning in 1934. *Ranger* was the first ship built from the keel up as an aircraft carrier. It was also the first carrier to be equipped with bow and stern arresting gear.

Dive-Bombing Gunsights

The iron sight, composed of a circular ring and a forward post, was adequate for forward-firing machine guns in World War I and for a few years thereafter. The rings were useful, to a degree, in estimating bullet drop in a deflection shot, but they were totally inadequate in estimating the impact of a bomb dropped in a dive. The dive-bomb tactic is a difficult maneuver. The ballistics of a rounded nose and cylindrical shape can be calculated precisely in a no-wind situation, but the physics depend on four critical variables: dive angle, speed, altitude of release, and g-forces on the aircraft. Then, there is always wind drift.

Two improvisations were devised. First was a telescope-type tube mounted on the forward fuselage. In a very steep dive, with the target apparently quasi-motionless, this device provided an approximation of the location of the bomb impact. Still, it did not do a good job in accounting for wind drift of the aircraft, which, of course, was transmitted to the bomb at release.

The second sight was an invention that added a light source near the instrument panel, projecting rays through an image-forming, curved mirror up to a "combining glass," where it was reflected through a 90-degree angle and out to the armored glass windscreen. These were called "reflecting sights." The projected image was like the "ring and post," but now it was easily manipulated to add any number of rings and radial lines intersecting the pipper dot of light. The invention that made it useful for dive-bombing was a calibrated dial from zero to several hundred "mils" of depression. The variability of the "depression" could be set to coincide with the bomb drop at varying degrees of dive angle. Since most bombs were of a slender, streamlined shape, their fall could be represented scientifically by ballistic tables, and these, in turn, could be transferred into mil settings for the gunsight. The pilot, knowing the dive angle he intended to use, could dial in the appropriate mil setting. This "reflective sight" was more useful than the telescope because it could be used to estimate wind drift. Though there were improvements made over the years, the reflective sight was essentially the same after 1935 and continuing into the 1960s. The same principle forms the basis for the heads-up displays on the A-10, F-15, F-16, F/A-18, and F-35.

Top Light-Attack Aircraft before 1960

Hill Goodspeed, historian at the National Naval Aviation Museum, Pensacola, proposed what he called the "Top Navy light attack planes."[20] The author of this volume agreed and added the Republic P-47 and Douglas A-4 to the list as the best attack aircraft before the A-7.

Top Attack Aircraft before 1960	
Aircraft	**Era** [*]
De Havilland DH-4	1917–1932
Martin T3M/T4M	1926–1938
Martin BM	1931–1937
Douglas SBD Dauntless	1940–1950
Grumman TBF/TBM Avenger	1942–1960
Vought F4U Corsair	1942–1953
Republic P-47 Thunderbolt	1942–1953
Curtiss-Wright SB2C Helldiver	1943–1950
Douglas AD/A-1 Skyraider	1946–1972
AF Guardian	1950–1955
Douglas A3D/A-3 Skywarrior	1956–1991
Douglas A4D/A-4 Skyhawk	1956–2003

[*] The dates refer to the period in US military service.
Reference: Hill Goodspeed, historian at the National Naval Aviation Museum, Pensacola.

The de Havilland DH-4 [21]

The DH-4 was designed by Geoffrey de Havilland, a captain in the Royal Flying Corps (RFC), in early 1916, and he was also the test pilot on its first flight in August of that year. Built by the Aircraft Manufacturing Co., it was to perform the roles of reconnaissance and bombing. The aircraft was desperately needed to replace the obsolete British Experimentals (BE) 2C/D/E, which were so slow they were being shot down by the dozens. The DH-4 was a conventional tractor biplane design with a crew of two and a powerful engine. The original engine was a six-cylinder, in-line, water-cooled 160 hp Beardmore with a four-bladed propeller.

The fuselage was of unusual construction because only the section between the observer and the tail was steel framed with fabric covering. The forward and tail sections were of plywood, a lightweight but very strong design pioneered by Albatros in the construction of their D. I through Va series of fighters in 1916. The DH-4 was used by RFC and later RAF squadrons on the western front and in Mesopotamia. It was also built as a float plane and used by the Royal Navy. The British provided DH-4s and plans to the US, and the American factories produced the Liberty engine, a V-12 400 hp monster. Over 1,200 Liberty-powered DH-4 were supplied to the US American Expeditionary Force. The first ones arrived in France in May 1918 and were first used in combat in August. By the end of the war the Air Service had 696 DH-4s, nearly 24 percent of the aviation force.[22] Four combined US Navy and Marine Corps squadrons flew the DH-4 along the Belgian coast. These were used extensively in France for observation, reconnaissance, bombing, and early attack missions.[23] After the war, DH-4s participated in over 2,600 aviation experiments.

Martin T3M/T4M

The Glenn L. Martin Company produced the T3M/T4M as a series of torpedo bombers and reconnaissance biplanes for the Navy in the mid- to late 1920s.[24] The first model was the T3M-1, of which twenty-four were delivered in 1926. The Dash-1 model had the Wright E-3B engine of 575 hp, but the Dash-2 had the upgraded 770 hp Packard 3A-2500 engine.

The T4M-1 fell back on the Pratt & Whitney R-1690-24 engine, which produced only 525 hp, and eight aircraft were delivered to the Navy in 1928. Total production was 252, including the later versions, the TG-1/2. It was designed to carry one torpedo or 1,000 pounds of bombs at a top speed of 99 mph.

Martin BM

Martin also produced the BM torpedo bomber in 1931[25] to meet a Navy / Marine Corps requirement for a special-purpose dive-bomber. The aircraft was a biplane with two crew members and a fixed tailwheel landing gear. The Navy ordered two prototypes: one from Martin, designated the XT5M-1, and one from the Naval Aircraft Factory, designated the XT2N-1. The Martin XT5M-1 was powered by a 525 hp Pratt & Whitney R-1690-22 Hornet radial engine. The Navy ordered sixteen aircraft from Martin with the designation BM-1, which was powered by an upgraded R-1690-44 engine. A further order followed for sixteen for the BM-2. The first squadron was VT-1S on board USS *Lexington*. In 1934, both the BM-1 and BM-2 were used on board USS *Langley* until 1937, when all the aircraft were withdrawn to shore bases.

Douglas TBD Devastator Torpedo Bomber

The Douglas Devastator TBD was the second all-metal, low-wing airplane to be produced for the Navy's attack mission. Ordered in 1934, with first flight in 1935, it completed carrier qualification trials at North Island Naval Air Station aboard USS *Lexington*. When the pilot folded its wings while taxiing, the tower almost called the crash crew!

The first Navy contract produced 114 aircraft, and the first operational squadron was Torpedo 3 aboard *Saratoga* (CV-3) in 1937. The 900 hp engine drove the aircraft to a top speed of 205 mph, but it had to slow down to 115 mph to drop its torpedo. Devastators participated in the first offensive action in World War II by attacking Japanese-held islands. The Battle of the Coral Sea, May 4–8, 1942, provided the TBD its biggest success. VT-2 and VT-5 sank the light carrier *Shoho* and other ships, although some of their torpedoes did not explode.

The Devastator's last show in the Pacific was its epic performance in the Battle of Midway, June 4, 1942. Three squadrons of TBDs totaling forty-one aircraft were aboard VT-3 on *Yorktown* (CV-5), VT-6 on *Enterprise* (CV-6), and VT-8 on *Hornet* (CV-8). On the first day of the battle, all three squadrons launched against four Japanese carriers.

Only one of Torpedo 3's Devastators returned to *Yorktown*. Torpedo 6 lost eleven, and unlucky Torpedo 8 lost every one of its fifteen aircraft. Only four of the forty-one aircraft survived. The torpedo bombers' attack was early and not coordinated with their fighter escort or the dive-bombers. The majority of their losses were to enemy fighters, whose tenacity in attack resulted in the Japanese top cover diving to the surface after the Devastators, thus allowing the follow-on US dive-bombers a clear attack. Within months, the Devastator was withdrawn from service.

There are no surviving Devastators. Hollywood stage crews constructed a mockup for the movie *Midway*, and that model is now displayed on the hangar deck of the USS *Midway* Museum in San Diego Harbor.

The Devastator's replacement, the larger and heavier Grumman TBF Avenger, was also present at Midway Island. Six of the new aircraft were assigned to VT-8 and flew off the island. Five of the six were shot down, and the last one was severely damaged.

Vought SB2U Vindicator

The Navy's Bureau of Aeronautics (BuAer) wrote a requirement for a new scout bomber for carrier use in 1934. The request for proposal (RFP) was issued in two parts, one for a monoplane and one for a biplane. The biplane was considered alongside the monoplane design as a hedge against the US Navy's reluctance to pursue the more modern configuration. Six manufacturers responded. Curtiss and Great Lakes entered biplane designs and were quickly eliminated. Vought submitted designs in both categories, and they were later designated the XSB2U-1 and XSB3U-1. Brewster submitted the XSBA-1, Curtiss the XSBC-3, Great Lakes the XB2G-1, Grumman the XSBF-1, and Northrop the XBT-1. The Navy ordered the Vought monoplane and all but the Great Lakes and Grumman entries for experimentation and production.

The Vought XSBU-1 Vindicator was a low-wing monoplane dive-bomber with pilot and gunner seated in tandem under a long, greenhouse-style canopy. The rear fuselage was covered with fabric, while the folding cantilever wing was all metal. It was powered by a Pratt & Whitney R-1535 Twin-Wasp Junior radial engine, which drove a two-blade constant-speed propeller. The prop was intended to act as a dive brake during steep attack. The aircraft carried a single 1,000 lb. bomb on a swinging trapeze to allow it to clear the propeller in a steep dive, while additional bombs could be carried under the wings to give a maximum bombload of 1,500 lbs. One prototype was ordered on October 15, 1934, and delivered eighteen months later, on April 15, 1936. The prototype crashed later that year, but not before the test program had been completed. The Navy ordered 260 aircraft, and it remained in service until the Battle of Midway.

Brewster XSB2A Buccaneer

Brewster's submission was an ill-fated design, XSB2A, which was a single-engined, midwing monoplane with a gun turret, intended as a scout, dive-bomber, and smoke layer. As the aircraft was being designed in 1940, Brewster received orders from Great Britain and the Netherlands. As the war progressed in Europe the British and Dutch increased their orders for dive-bombers, such that the US Navy order for 411 was the smallest of the three. The result was that as the Brewster Company completely reorganized its engineering department and management, the aircraft design fell behind schedule. The Navy Attack Design Office noted this:

The contractor was very lax in meeting the Navy contract requirements, and the airframe was overweight. From February 1943 on, the history of the SB2A airplane is one of structural failures, modification programs, delays, and poor overall performance of the contractor.

Troubles on the SB2A series had reached such a peak, and delay in correcting these troubles was so long that Contract 76492 was cut back in the fall of 1943 by sixty-two model SB2A-3 airplanes, [and] in June 1944, all SB2A airplanes were stricken from the Navy's list.[26]

British Attack Aircraft in World War II

The British Fleet Air Arm was the first to prove the value of dive-bombing in the Second World War. On April 10, 1940, just before the German invasion of France, Royal Navy dive-bombers sank the German cruiser *Königsberg*, the first major warship ever sunk in wartime from the air.

The Saga of the Dauntless:
From the XBT-1 to the SBD;
A Mini Case Study

The Navy's 1934 requirement for a dive-bombing monoplane contained two specifications: a "bomb displacement gear" to allow the bomb to clear the propeller, and dive brakes. The Navy had been aware of Northrop's capabilities with their Gamma series of aircraft and the XA-14, built for the Army.

Donald Douglas had been the codesigner of the first wind tunnel at Massachusetts Institute of Technology when he was a student there in 1915. By 1934, he owned 51 percent of the stock in the Northrop Corporation. The firm selected one of its young engineers, Ed Heinemann, to lead the design team, and together they developed

the XBT-1 as a low-wing, heavy dive-bomber. With an initial 700 hp engine, it was rapidly upgraded with a 750 hp radial. The BT-1 featured split flaps on the trailing edge of the wings to limit speed in the dive. When tests revealed heavy tail buffeting, Northrop engineers perforated the flaps, and the problem was solved. This was an important feature because it allowed the aircraft to perform a steep (60–80 degree) dive yet control the speed, both of which are important variables in achieving accuracy. The Navy liked the design and ordered fifty-four of the aircraft. The engineers continued improving the aircraft design as the initial models were being produced. The result was the XBT-2, which was a BT-1 modified to incorporate leading-edge slats and an 800 hp radial engine. The XBT-2 first flew on April 25, 1938, and after successful testing the Navy placed an order for 144 aircraft.[27]

In 1939, Donald Douglas bought out the rest of the stock from Jack Northrop, and the plant became the El Segundo division of Douglas Aircraft. The aircraft designation for the BT-2 was changed to the Douglas XSBD-1 (eXperimental Scout Bomber, Douglas). The aircraft was subjected to a rigorous testing program. However, the Navy was concerned the aircraft did not have armor plate for the crew, nor did it have self-sealing gas tanks. In what some say is a repeated pattern, the Navy assigned the production SBD-1s to the Marine Corps.[28] When Douglas took over the program, they replaced the 15-gallon fuel tanks with 65-gallon ones in the outer wing panels, and the last eighty-seven were designated the SBD-2.[29] The resulting 310-gallon fuel supply increased the range from 900 to 1200 miles.

The Navy *Attack Plane Design History* described the environment in 1941:

Taking stock at the situation at the time of this country's entry into the present war, the January 9, 1942 Status Report . . . details the story of the US Navy's dive-bombers in that fateful period. None of the models were modern combat airplanes. As a matter of fact, they were a far cry from being either modern or combat ready. The SBC-4 [Curtiss Helldiver] was obsolescent beyond doubt and few were left in service. The SB2U series [Vought Vindicator] were throwbacks to the SBU-1 and were little better off with their small 825 hp engine and fabric covering on portions of both the fuselage and wings.

This then left the SBD series airplanes with which to engage enemy in offensive combat. The SBD-1 came of good stock being a direct descendant of the BT-1. (In fact, the prototype of the SBD-1 was the SBT-2.) The major changes which were incorporated in the SBD-1 were the installation of the larger, 1,000 hp R1820-32 engine in place of the 750 hp R-1535-94 engine of the BT-1, fully retractable main landing gear and redesigned tail surfaces.[30]

From a pilot's point of view, the instrument panel is interesting. The center instrument on most of the aircraft of that time (and today) is the attitude indicator, the artificial horizon that shows climb, dive, and bank. But the center instrument on the Dauntless was a gyro compass to show heading. With the Dauntless being a clear-air, visual aircraft designed for long, over-water navigation, it makes sense that heading was more important than attitude. Second, the instrumental panel was divided into two sections with a sliding chart table between them.

The SBD-2 was the model of the Dauntless on board the Pacific Fleet carriers during and after Pearl Harbor, with SBD-3 joining the Fleet in the spring of 1942. The SBD-3 started production of 584 aircraft in 1941 and featured armor plate, self-sealing tanks and four machine guns. The SBD-5 was modified to accept a 1,200 hp engine with a larger ammunition capacity. 2,965 of the SBD-5s were built.[31]

The Dauntless had a gross weight of 8,400 lbs., a top speed of 250 mph, and a ceiling of 27,000 feet.[32] Navy test pilots rated the stability and flying characteristics of the Dauntless to be "excellent." Navy and Marine Corps SBDs took part in the battles of Pearl Harbor and Coral Sea before Midway and raids on the Gilbert and Marshall Islands, New Guinea, Rabaul, and Wake and Marcus Islands. Six Navy SBD squadrons, totaling 112 aircraft, participated in the Battle of Midway. VB-3 and VS-5 flew off *Yorktown*, VB-6

and VS-6 off *Enterprise*, and VB-8 and VS-8 from *Hornet*. Together, they were the squadrons that sank the Japanese carriers. Marine squadron VMSB-241 took off from Midway Island with sixteen SBDs but was not as fortunate. The Marines did not train in the Navy's high-angle dive-bombing tactic, so they attempted shallow bombing at 30 degrees. The Navy lost thirty-two out of their 112, and the Marines lost eight of their sixteen.

Douglas produced over five thousand of the aircraft in the war, and, as the Navy judged, "Dauntless airplanes more than paid for themselves in terms of enemy ships sunk and cripples, and shore installations destroyed and damaged, to say nothing of enemy personnel casualties inflicted."[33]

The Adventure of Ens. Hopkins

Lou Hopkins was born in rural Georgia; his family members were poor sharecroppers. He plowed fields, walked two miles to school, and completed his eleventh-grade high school at age fifteen. He worked his way through Berry College in Rome, Georgia, and graduated at nineteen. Hopkins joined the Naval Reserve in the spring of 1940. He served as an apprentice seaman, peeling potatoes, on a cruise to see the World's Fair in New York City. When called to active duty in the fall of 1940, he was told that with his college degree, he could go into flight training, which he jumped at. He graduated in 1941 and had just been assigned to USS *Ranger* at Norfolk, Virginia, when the Japanese bombed Pearl Harbor on December 7. He was immediately transferred to the West Coast before he even had time to qualify for carrier landings.

Shipped to Hawaii, he was stationed at Kaneohe and performed all his field carrier landing practice there, qualifying for carrier operations. When *Enterprise* returned from a raid on Marcos Islands, he joined the ship. Years later, he told his story:

> I remember the first cruise was on the *Enterprise*, and when we left Pearl Harbor, we were heading northwest. Day one northwest, day two northwest, day three northwest, and I thought the only place northwest from here is Japan. So, I was thinking,

here I am on my first combat cruise on the *Enterprise* and we are going to attack Japan. We went up every morning on the flight deck to check our planes and everything, and I look out and see this carrier with B-25s (Mitchell bombers) on it . . . That was April 18, 1942. I was sitting in the cockpit of my plane because as soon as the B-25s were launched, they were going to launch us. I could see the B-25s taking off.

After the Doolittle Raid, the *Hornet* and *Enterprise* kind of traveled together, and we went down to the Southwest Pacific, expecting to join the USS *Lexington* and the USS *Yorktown*. It turns out the Battle of the Coral Sea occurred before we got there. The *Lexington* was sunk, and the *Yorktown* was damaged, but while we were there the ships were ordered back to Pearl Harbor. They took the radios out of our planes so that we could not make any transmissions. If we saw something that we wanted to report back to the ship, we had to fly back, and we had what we called "bean bags." We would write a note and tie it to the bean bag and drop it on the deck, which wasn't easy, by the way. It kind of got to be a game, and every time you came back you were supposed to go through the procedure whether you had a real note to drop or not. . . . Basically, they didn't want any radio transmission because that would tip off the Japanese that the ships were going back to Pearl Harbor for whatever reason. We wanted them to believe that the ships were still down in the Southwest Pacific.[34]

Ens. Hopkins was assigned to Bombing Squadron 6, with Cmdr. Dick Best. Hopkins thought Best was a terrific guy who taught him so much. He took all the new pilots under his wing, teaching them scouting and bombing. They flew generally two flights a day, and Cmdr. Best would go over every dive-bombing flight and dive. They had quite an experienced squadron. There were three lieutenants, four or five junior grades, and the rest of the pilots were ensigns:

On the morning of June 4, there were twenty-nine ensigns flying the mission. There were three squadrons that did the damage: Bomber Squadron 6, Scouting Squadron 6, both from the *Enterprise*,

and Bomber Squadron 3, which was from the *Yorktown*. It all happened in six minutes. From 10:20 to 10:26 a.m. At 10:20, the Japanese carriers had not been touched. At 10:26, three of them were headed for the briny deep.

Ensign Hopkins continued:

We got up about 0100 in the morning and went down and had breakfast of a sort. I don't think anyone was particularly hungry and then we went to the Bomber 6 ready room. . . . There were some sketchy reports coming in but not sufficient to know precisely what was happening. The first very concise report that came in was from a PBY out of Midway reporting Japanese planes coming in on a certain heading to attack Midway [Island]. . . . [F]inally, at 0700 they said, "Pilots man the planes."[35]

The lineup on the deck was Scouting 6 (eighteen planes), Bombing 6 (sixteen). Hopkins's Dauntless was the thirtieth aircraft to take off, carrying a 1,000 lb. bomb. After a circling join up, they climbed to 22,000 feet, breathing oxygen for the first time on a continuous basis. Some of the pilots had a problem, so Cmdr. Best reduced the altitude slightly. When the formation got to the location where the Japanese fleet was supposed to be, they were not there. There was nothing. They were at the point of no return, but the CAG, Cmdr. Wade McCluskey, decided to continue and see if he could find them. McClusky led the formation for about another fifteen minutes, and:

most everybody else knew we didn't have enough fuel to get back. He turned northwest and ran across this destroyer hightailing it back to the rest of the Japanese fleet, and he decided to follow it. We were flying in formation, so we follow. I mentioned how you can be impressed with image, and I remember seeing the Japanese fleet. I am sitting here today, and I can see that Japanese fleet as clear now as I saw it then. It was something else and I was clearly impressed. . . . At almost precisely the same time coming from another direction was Bomber Squadron 3 from the *Yorktown*[,] who had better information about the ships' location at the time they took off. The Japanese were amazed that an attack could be so well coordinated that two attacking forces, approaching almost 180 degrees from each other, could converge upon their fleet at precisely the same time. . . . I was twelfth position in the formation so there were 11 ahead of me in the dive. You see four or five ahead of you in the dive and you see the bombs dropping and they pull out. I went down at a dive of about 60 to 70 degrees. The plane has split flaps and you get 240 knots is about the maximum speed with the split flaps. In those days you had what you call a gun sight that is a tube with cross hairs in it. You look through that, and in the meantime, you are flying the plane and you have to keep it balanced. I put the cross hairs on the leading edge of the carrier [Akagi]. The radioman calls out the altitude, "5,000, 4,000, 3,000, 2,500," because you are looking in the cross hairs you can't see the altimeter. He calls out 2,500 and a Zero coming in from the right. I went ahead and released the bomb and immediately turned into the Zero in a defensive maneuver. I think post analysis showed that I didn't get a hit. [Author's note: But the near misses of the Ostfriesland caved in her bottom, and the same could have happened to the Akagi.]

I got down on the water as close as I could and Anderson, the gunner, says, "Let's get the hell out of here." I said, "What do you think I'm trying to do?" I was joined up by two other planes flown by ensigns, Ens. Green and Ens. Ramsey. We got about forty miles out from the Enterprise and Ens. Green runs out of fuel, and so he has to ditch. There is nothing I can do about it but take note of the location. We get within sight of the carrier and Ens. Ramsey runs out of fuel and so he has to ditch, and I make a note of that. When I get back to the carrier, I found that I am one of five planes [of 34] that made it back to the carrier.[36]

Also, from an article by William Green:

The morning raid had sunk the Akagi, Kaga, and Sōryū. The fourth carrier, Hiryū, was severely damaged in the afternoon attack and had to be scuttled the next morning. The three squadrons of Dauntless that flew in the Battle of Midway made history with the sinking of four Japanese aircraft carriers. The Japanese also lost nearly 300 aircraft and 3,500 men. That made Midway, as military historian John Keegan called it, "the most stunning and decisive blow in the history of naval warfare."[37]

Lou Hopkins went on to participate in other campaigns in the western Pacific and then was assigned back to Cecil Field to train other pilots to dive-bomb. He tested the F4U Corsair in the dive-bombing mode and found it to be "difficult to keep steady." He earned a master's degree in aeronautical engineering, specialized in research and development, went to Vietnam several times, and became the commander of the Naval Air Weapons Center Point Mugu, where he mentored a future A-7 pilot, Ed Beakley.

Grumman Avenger Torpedo Bomber

The Navy selected the Grumman TBF Avenger as the follow-on torpedo bomber in a 1940 competition and ordered two prototypes in April. It was a heavy aircraft, weighing 10,080 lbs. empty and nearly 16,000 lbs. loaded. It could carry a Mk. 13 torpedo, a single 2,000 lb. bomb, or four 500 lb. bombs. Its huge internal fuel capacity gave it a range of 1,200 miles. The 1,700 hp engine drove it to a maximum speed of 271 mph. Over 9,800 were produced between Grumman and General Motors, where they were labeled the TBM. Avengers were major contributors in the battles in the Eastern Solomons, where they sank the light carrier Ryujo and Guadalcanal, and helped sink the battleship Hiei. In June 1943, future president George H. W. Bush flew an Avenger with VT-51 on board USS San Jacinto (CVL-30). He was thought to be the youngest naval aviator at that time. He was shot down on September 2, 1944, over the island of Chichi Jima and rescued. He was awarded the Distinguished Flying Cross. Avengers claimed thirty submarine kills in the Pacific and Atlantic theaters. (Note: Author Barrett Tillman, while he as working at The Hook magazine in the 1980s, found that Chuck Downey was eleven days younger but commissioned a few days after Bush.)

Engine Power: The Key to Speed

Since the Wright Brothers built their own 12 hp engine, the speed and weight capability of aircraft has been limited by engine power. The following table demonstrates the increase in engine power over the decades.

Engine Power Increase: 1914–1945			
Engine	**Power (hp)**	**Era**	**Aircraft**
Obersel Rotary	70	1914–1918	Fokker E series
Curtiss OX-5	90	1910–1920	JN-4
Mercedes	160	1916–1919	Albatros D series
Liberty L-12	400	1917–1930	DH-4
Pratt-Whitney R-1340	410-600	1930s	P-26/Gee Bee
Allison V-1710	1,000–1,600	1930–1945	P-38
Wright R-1820	1,525	1930s	B-17
Rolls-Royce Merlin	1,030–1,290	1933–1945	Spitfire/P-51
Pratt-Whitney R-2800	2,000	1940s	P-47/F4U
Wright R-3350 Double Cyclone	4,000	1944	B-29/F9F

Source: Flying Magazine, March 14, 2014.

The Navy also tested the use of air-cooled radial engines against liquid-cooled in-line engines. Radial engines tended to be lighter and more reliable. For example, the Navy's minimum acceptance standard for water-cooled engines was fifty hours. In 1922, the Navy's first radial, the Lawrence 200 hp J-1, ran for three hundred hours. The Navy also ran a direct comparison using a Chance Vought aircraft:

Comparison of Water-Cooled vs. Air-Cooled Engines				
Aircraft	**Cooling**	**Max. speed (mph)**	**Ceiling (ft.)**	**Range (sq. mi.)**
Vought VE	Water	117	15,000	291
Vought FU	Air	122	26,500	410

Source: Charles M. Melhorn, Two-Block Fox, 99.

Chance Vought F4U Corsair

The Corsair was the Vought entry in the February 1938 Bureau of Aeronautics competition for twin-engined and single-engined fighters. Vought won the single-engine contract for a prototype, and the contract was signed in June 1938. The aircraft was powered by a Pratt & Whitney XR-2800-4, the first of the Double Wasp twin-row, eighteen-cylinder radial engines, rated at 1,805 hp. Because the engine was so powerful, it required a 13-foot propeller. To keep the landing gear a reasonable length, the wing was designed in two sections, with a sharp anhedral (downward sloping) of the stub that gave the Corsair its distinctive "V" shape. The XF4U-1 made its first flight on May 29, 1940, and on October 1 it became the first single-engine US fighter to fly faster than 400 mph (the Army's twin-engine Lockheed P-38 Lightning had flown over 400 mph in January–February 1939).

There were four problems with the initial design of the Corsair, the first three of which were (1) test pilots learned it was impossible to recover from a two-turn spin, (2) the high-powered engine produced a record amount of torque, and (3) the Navy had underestimated the amount of armament needed for a modern war. As a result of this third issue, the Navy changed its requirement for .30 cal. machine guns into .50 cal. and increased the number from four to six, which were to located in the wings. When the designers made the structural changes, the space for fuel tanks in the wings was reduced, and a tank had to be added to the forward fuselage, which in turn required the cockpit to be moved backward 32 inches.[38] This reduced the pilot's visibility over the nose and added problem number 4: great difficulty in landing aboard carriers.

Vought upgraded the engine to the 2,000 hp R-2800 Double Wasp radial as it became available. With these changes made, the Navy began acceptance testing in February 1941 and awarded Vought a production contract for 584 F4U-1 fighters in June 1941. Vought flew the first production aircraft on June 24, 1942. However, carrier qualification trials revealed the most serious issue. In the normal left-hand turn to final approach, the left (low) wing tended to stall abruptly and fall off to port. Adding power swiftly accentuated the problem and could cause a torque roll. Then, upon touchdown, the short oleo struts tended to make the airplane bounce, causing the hook to skip over the landing wires. The restricted forward visibility, early wing stall, and landing bounce combined to delay carrier qualification for nearly two years. In the interval, production F4Us were assigned to Marine Corps squadrons and flown off island runways in the South Pacific. The powerful engine, high speed, high rate of climb, ease of maneuverability, and lethal armament quickly made the Corsair the best naval fighter of the war.

The early-stall issue was not resolved until the engineers added a thin, triangular piece of metal to the right wing's leading edge, causing it to stall a little sooner. The result of the change to the aerodynamics was that both wings tended to stall at about the same time, eliminating the more dangerous asymmetrical effect. The visibility issue was resolved by raising the pilot's seat 9 inches and increasing the size of the semibubble canopy.

The Grumman F6F Hellcat, Republic P-47 Thunderbolt, and Corsair all used the P&W R-2800 engine. The Corsair was faster than the Hellcat, but slower than the Thunderbolt. The performance of the Corsair was so good and the demand so high that the Navy ordered thousands and made Vought share production rights with Goodyear, which built the F4U-4 to the F4U-7 and the FG.

The Corsair also served as a fighter-bomber in the Pacific and the Philippines. Loaded with bombs and rockets, Navy and Marine Corps pilots performed valiantly in close air support during amphibious landings, especially in the battles for the Marshall Islands, Palaus, Iwo Jima, and Okinawa. However, it was not a natural dive-bomber. Hopkins tested the aircraft extensively and reported: "In the dive bombing mode, what you did was put the gear down and put the propeller in low pitch and the plane kind of wobbled around. I was so used to the SBD for it was so steady. The F4U would kind of ramble around and was difficult to keep steady."[39]

Charles Lindbergh flew Corsairs with the Marines as a civilian technical advisor for United Aircraft Corporation. He showed the Marines how to get into the air with 4,000 pounds of bombs, with a 2,000 pounder on the centerline and a 1,000 pounder under each wing.[40]

"US figures compiled at the end of the Second World War indicate that the F4U and FG flew 64,051 operational sorties for the US Marines and Navy through the conflict (44% of total fighter sorties), with only 9,581 sorties (15%) flown from carrier decks."[41] F4U and FG pilots claimed 2,140 air combat victories against 189 losses to enemy aircraft, for an overall kill ratio of more than 11:1.[42]

Goodyear went on to make the F2G-1 with a twenty-eight-cylinder Pratt & Whitney R-4360 of 3,000 hp. The F2G-7 was specifically designed for the French in Indochina. Finally, in 1953, the last of 12,571 Corsairs rolled off the production line, the end of eleven years.

Curtiss SB2C Helldiver

The SB2C was the third of the Curtiss Helldiver series and the most successful. It was a two-place midwing monoplane with a bomb bay designed primarily for dive-bombing. Powered by a Wright R-2600-8 engine with 1,700 hp, the aircraft replaced the aging Douglas Dauntless in the fleet and sank more Japanese ships than any other aircraft. The US Army Air Forces also liked the Helldiver and redesignated it the A-25.

Post–World War II Navy

During the war, naval aircraft performing surface attack or close air support tended to be called scout bombers (SB) or torpedo bombers (TB or BT). The "Attack" mission designator was given more prominence in the Navy and Marine Corps in 1946. After the war, the Navy and Marine Corps renamed the BT2D Skyraider as the AD (Attack-Douglas), and the BTM Mauler as the AM Mauler (Attack-Martin).

Douglas AD Skyraider

The Skyraider was designed in 1944, and the manner of its inception is the stuff of legends. The AD began its history when El Segundo division's chief engineer, Ed Heinemann; his chief designer, Leo Devlin; and the chief aerodynamicist, Gene Root met in Washington, DC, at the Navy Yard to discuss three proposals for the next-generation attack aircraft. The competitors were Martin, with the XBTM Mauler, and Fleetwood, owned by Henry Kaiser, proposing an XTBK. Douglas had been struggling with designing the BTD-1 Destroyer, and the meeting was to help the Navy decide on a winner.

Ed Heinemann reported the meeting was an intense one and lasted well into the day. Sensing the discussion was inconclusive and going nowhere, Heinemann asked permission to address the group. He said this:

> We would like to request that the Navy allow Douglas to cancel the existing contract for the BTD. Instead, we ask permission to use the unexpended funds to build an entirely new bomber, one that I am convinced will do the job for you.
>
> If you agree, I would like thirty days in which to draw up and present the design.[43]

The admiral agreed but told Heinemann he couldn't give him thirty days; he had to have the design to them by 0900 the next day!

Working through the night, Heinemann's design team developed a series of sketches for a large, low-wing, single-seat attack aircraft with nearly a dozen ordnance stations, using the most powerful engine available. It was a "straightforward, uncomplicated design."[44] The Navy was intrigued. It agreed to allow Douglas to submit a formal design proposal for the ongoing competition, but only if the firm could meet the scheduled deadline.

The Douglas XBTD-1 design submitted in July 1944 was for a "single-seat, folding-wing, high-performance general-purpose attack (dive bomber and torpedo) airplane designed around the [Pratt & Whitney] R-3350-4 engine.... Bombs were carried on three stations (bomb ejector on fuselage centerline, one Mk. 51 bomb rack in each wing) and 5-inch HVAR [high-velocity aerial rocket] on eight stations (four Mk. 5-3 launchers on each outer wing panel)."[45] The Navy loved these 5-inch rockets. Unlike the 2.75-inch rocket, the 5-inch flew straight. The engineers at China Lake even designed a heat-seeking warhead for it and produced the AIM-9 Sidewinder in the 1950s, perhaps the most effective air-to-air missile of the 1950s and 1960s.

The Navy accepted the Douglas proposal, designated the design experimental model XBT2D-1, and contracted for fifteen airplanes. The contract was signed on July 21, 1944, and the estimated cost for the fifteen aircraft was $10,400,000.[46] The Navy Attack Design Section continued in its *History*:

> This new dive-bomber was to be procured, like the XBTK-1 and the XBTM-1 airplanes, on an expedited basis. The contractor, wishing to erase the unfavorable reaction to the model BTD-1 airplane, understood this desire for expediting the program and showed it by building a very complete mock-up in some 45 days. . . . The mock-up was very complete and gave an excellent impression.

The unknown author (believed to be Lee Pearson) continued on the same theme:

> With practically the full engineering department of the El Segundo plant working on this project, engineering drawings were released to the shop with an amazing rapidity. On December 31, 1944, a goal set by the contractor, all engineering necessary for the first flight of the airplane had been completed. Besides the rapidity of the engineering releases, another factor should be brought out which was a credit to the contractor. Conscious that the BTD-1 airplane had been very strong but some 3000 lbs. overweight, he adopted a new policy for the design of the XBT2D-1. He decided that instead of building the strength into the airplane immediately and thus avoid static test failures, he would design the structure such that its strength would be as close to the requirements [as necessary] but on the negative side. This policy was evidently one which would cause many static test failures

but the saving in weight, the incorporation of fixes made necessary by the structural test's results, would still be very large and would result in an optimum efficient structure. This sort of thinking proved to be very fruitful, as the underweight of the airplane became larger as the design progressed.[47]

Douglas engineers and machinists had a goal to reduce weight by 750 pounds but were able to save over 1,000 pounds in their weight-reduction effort. The aircraft performed its first flight on March 18, 1945. The flight tests proved to be "highly satisfactory," and the Navy project office concluded the following:

From the viewpoints of

1. capabilities of the airplane,

2. progress of Service Acceptance Trials,

3. status of Preliminary Demonstration, which is almost 100% complete, and

4. speed with which airplanes are being manufactured, *the BT2D program is in better shape than any other dive-bomber project* [emphasis added].[48]

Ed Heinemann's crew paid particular attention to the cockpit. "We 'cleaned it up' compared to preceding planes and left virtually all the plumbing out. For the first time we really concentrated on making the driver's environment a more livable one for the man at the controls. One innovation for the BT2D pilot comprised easy-to-read instruments. Generally, there was a twenty-four-inch distance between the pilot's eye and the panel. So, through an engineering study, we determined that the size of the key digits should be one-quarter of an inch high. Also, the flap and gear handles were formed to look like the system they actuated."[49]

The BT2D became the AD-1 and had the following performance characteristics:

AD-1 Performance Characteristics	
Power plant	R3350-26 WA
Maximum power	2,700 hp
Gross weight	18,029 lbs.
Max. speed at 17,000 ft.	305 knots
Service ceiling	27,000 ft.
Combat range	1,350 nm
Stall speed, power off	80.5 knots

Source: Ed Heinemann, *Combat Airplane Designer*, 136.

First flight was March 18, 1945, which was followed by Navy flight test, and the Navy's "letter of intent" to buy 548 aircraft was signed on May 5, 1945. In April 1946, the Navy changed its designation system for aircraft, and the BT2D-1 became the AD-1. About the same time, the Navy assigned the generic term "Skyxxxxx" for all aircraft Douglas produced.

Ed Heinemann tells a funny story about the armament trials aboard USS *Saipan* in 1948.

An amiable young pilot named Zirkel was selected to test the AD at increasing loads, beginning with a 1,000-pound bomb and increasing it until some part, probably the landing gear or wing, showed signs of failure. Zirkel made landing after landing with ever-increasing loads, each followed by a thorough inspection. He landed repeatedly with three 2,000-pound bombs aboard in an airplane which was originally intended to carry far less.

"Zirkel in a circle," as we had come to call him, finally finished his assigned task. He came up to the ship's CO and said, "Jesus Christ, captain, if you want to bust this airplane you've got to get someone else. My ass won't take any more."[50]

The Korean War

The AD was one of the first aircraft to respond to the North Korean invasion of South Korea in June 1950. The carrier *Valley Forge* was on duty in the Sea of Japan with Attack Squadron 55 (VA-5), with AD-4s aboard. On July 3, the ADs attacked airfields and installations around Pyongyang, and Navy and Marine Corps squadrons continued to fly attack missions for the next three years. It was the Skyraiders that bombed the bridges in North Korea and were the subject in James Michener's *The Bridges at Toko-Ri*. Commanders Malcolm W. Cagle and Frank A. Manson summarized their praise for the AD in their book, *The Sea War in Korea*:

> In particular, the AD Skyraider was to be the most successful airplane of the thirty-seven-month war. Only the Skyraider could carry and successfully deliver the 2,000-pound bomb with dive-bombing precision against the target of interdictors: the bridge abutment or span, the tunnel mouth, and the cave entrance. The AD's versatility and weight-lifting capacity (as much as 5,000 pounds on a carrier mission) made it the war's outstanding performer.[51]

In the late summer of 1950, Lt. Cmdr. Henry Suerstedt was assigned as the AD class desk and project officer in the Bureau of Aeronautics. He had enlisted in the Aviation Cadet program in 1941, been commissioned, earned his gold wings, flew 160 combat missions, and ended the war as the commander of Torpedo Squadron 100, flying the TBM Avenger. As the Korean War intensified, he got reports of ADs suffering extensive battle damage and losses from ground fire in the conduct of their low-level attacks. In his own words:

> At one point in the autumn of 1950 we believed we were going to run out of ADs. We projected that within nine months to a year at the existing attrition rate, the Skyraiders would be nearly gone.[52]

Keeping the AD Line Open

While the "Night" version [the AD-4N] was still in production in 1950, the regular AD-4 line was scheduled to close in fiscal 1951. Suerstedt continues the story:

> It was bold of me as a lieutenant commander, I suppose, but I wrote a letter and forwarded it up the channels to the chief of BuAer. The gist of it was: "In view of the hostilities and significantly high combat losses of ADs in Korea, I urge that immediate action be taken to initiate a new contract for additional AD aircraft."

> My letter was returned bearing the cryptic note which was like a sock to the head: "Zapateros A Tus Zapatos," which is Spanish for "Shoemaker, to your shoes." The memo was signed by a senior plans officer and was his way of telling me to mind my own business.

> But I felt so strongly about keeping the Skyraider alive and minimizing losses that I was really stirred up now.[53]

Suerstadt next wrote to the famous radio host Arthur Godfrey, who had some naval aviators on his show but who had not boasted enough about the virtues of the Skyraider. Then he sent Godfrey a wooden model of the AD with a complete ordnance load and enough data about the aircraft to fill hours of airtime.

Adding Armor Plate

Cmdr. Suerstadt was equally fervent about the need for armor protection:

> If the Navy would not contract for more Skyraiders, maybe they would add defensive armor plate to reduce losses from ground fire.

> I asked [Bob] Canaday [Douglas's Washington representative, and a friend] for assistance, and Bob summoned help from his ordnance and engineering groups. They expeditiously produced a small replica of the AD featuring entry and exit holes that depicted typical damage patterns from anti-aircraft and small-arms fire. Douglas personnel had used battle damage reports to precisely locate common "hit" areas. Lucite rods were planed through the in-and-out holes so that the model took on the likeness of a porcupine.

> Douglas came up a design package whereby sections of armor plate made of steel and duraluminum (an alloy of aluminum, copper, manganese, magnesium, and silicon) in thickness from one-eighth to one-half inch could be strategically placed over the Skyraider's most vulnerable areas as revealed in the "porcupine" model. The sections weighed about 600 pounds, which was acceptable because they did not significantly degrade flying characteristics or performance. There would be only a 1.5 knot decrease in V_{Mas} or maximum velocity.[54]

Author Rosario Rausa relates, "One piece of half-inch[-]thick aluminum was rigged directly behind the pilot's seat to reduce hazard of injury from a six-o'clock hit. Others, a half-inch thick, protected the T-shaped area on the under fuselage beneath the cockpit wing stubs and fuel cell. More pieces were mounted around the engine and fuselage. Some especially vulnerable sections had steel plates inside the duralumin, installed primarily to stop ball-type ammunition."[55]

Aluminum was in short supply because of Korea and the post–World War II economic boom. So Suerstedt called an old friend and fellow aviator who had flown ADs, Lt. Cmdr. Willard "Willy" Nyburg; Nyburg was then the naval staff member and special assistant for military production in the Office of the Secretary of Defense (OSD):

I briefed Willy at a cocktail party. "We need aluminum badly," I told him. "Otherwise we're going to end with zero Skyraiders." Nyburg said, "Where do you want the stuff delivered?"[56]

Less than a month later, a senior Douglas man called Suerstedt from the plant in El Segundo, asking, "I got eight box cars of aluminum sitting out here: What do I do with the stuff?"

"Make armor plate," answered Suerstedt.[57]

The aluminum was turned into armor plate and mounted on Navy and Marine Corps ADs, and the loss rate of Skyraiders in 1952 decreased markedly. [The author and all other AD aviators benefited also in Vietnam, since the armor plate was installed in most subsequent models of the AD, including the A-1E, G and H.] In the same year of 1952, the Bureau of Aeronautics contracted for another set of AD-4s, and the production line was reopened.

When it came time for Harry Suerstedt to rotate out of BuAer in 1953, he was given his choice of commanding a squadron of Panthers, Corsairs, or Skyraiders, but he chose the AD. "Since I'd been the AD class desk officer, I developed a paternal affinity for the plane. It seemed best to stay with what I knew. Plus, I experienced a strong feeling of moral obligation to the aircraft."[58] Thus, Lt. Cmdr. Suerstedt became a squadron commander for the second time in his career—nine years apart. His squadron VA-54 deployed to Korea, had a 93 percent availability, flew some 3,500 combat hours, and dropped nearly 1,800 tons of ordnance. Suerstedt noted that both the AD-4 and 4N were faster than the Corsairs that accompanied them aboard USS *Valley Forge*.[59]

Attack Aircraft in the Cold War

United States strategic doctrine in the 1950s was "Massive Retaliation"—the strategy that held as its central tenet the idea that future wars most likely would be nuclear, intercontinental and total.[60] US policy was designed to deter such war if possible and ensure the survival of the US in case war did occur. The Department of Defense's (DoD) operational implementation of that policy was based on the theory of the decisiveness of strategic bombardment, and units of the strategic forces were given budgetary and organizational priority. The Navy disagreed with this policy, but in the DoD of the mid-1950s, it was powerless to change it. After the Korean War Armistice in 1953, the Navy's proportion of the DoD budget fell dramatically as compared to the Air Force. In fiscal year 1953, the Navy's $12.5 billion in "total obligational authority" was only 27 percent of the DoD total of $46.4, while the Air Force was granted $20.3 billion, or 44 percent. By fiscal year 1957, the Navy share had increased slightly to 29 percent, but the Air Force dominated the DoD budget, with 49 percent. A case study of the Navy's attempt to contribute to the Cold War mission is told in excellent monograph, *The Politics of Innovation: Patterns in Navy Cases*, by Vincent Davis, and his longer work, *The Admirals Lobby*.[61]

One of the measures of this emphasis on nuclear weapons was the number of "lines" or targets a military service could cover in the Single Integrated Operations Plan (the SIOP). Strategic Air Command, of course, held the largest number, but the Tactical Air Forces (composed of Tactical Air Command, Pacific Air Forces, and Air Forces in Europe) covered a large number. With the small attack aircraft inventory coming out of the Korean War, and the short range of its attack aircraft, the Navy was hard pressed to contribute a significant share to this strategy. Two of the results were the arming of the fleet's AD attack aircraft with the capability to deliver nuclear weapons, and the focus on nuclear capability in the development of new aircraft.

The Nuclear AD

In December 1950, the Navy asked Douglas to provide two flying prototypes of a larger, carrier-based night-attack, early-warning, and electronic-countermeasures aircraft. This required the addition of a radar operator / navigator and a radar countermeasures operator, a large radar set, other electronics equipment, and a large fuel load. Douglas modified the successful AD-4 design by adding seats behind the pilot. The added weight and size necessitated a modified ventral fin and increasing the power. One month later, on January 26, 1951, BuAer authorized the modification of the AD-4 to provide a capability to carry a 3,600 lb. store on the centerline bomb rack. This was the first requirement for a single-engine attack airplane to carry and drop a nuclear weapon. The model was designated the AD-5, and it first flew on August 17, 1951. The first delivery to the fleet was April 1953, near the end of the Korean War. The AD Skyraider and other aircraft were modified with electrical wiring to monitor and drop a nuclear weapon from aircraft carriers deployed in the Atlantic and Pacific Oceans. The tactic was an "Over-the-shoulder" or "Loft" delivery, with the AD attacking at low altitude and maximum speed, pulling up with 4 g, releasing the weapon, and diving away to get as far as possible from the blast. At the AD's slow speed, it would not have been very far.

Interestingly, in April 1954 the Navy was so concerned with the survivability of the AD in a planned nuclear weapon attack that CNO directed a project to investigate the increase of AD attacking speed by at least 10 knots to increase safe separation distance. BuAer ordered three hundred AD-5s without the nuclear weapons capability for use by the Marine Corps. The last AD off the production line was in 1956. Overall, of the 3,180 total ADs delivered to the Navy, 670 were AD-5s. The AD retained its nuclear mission until 1965, when Secretary McNamara announced that "carriers will be released from their nuclear mission in fiscal year 1966."[62]

Douglas produced seven major models of the AD, with seemingly countless variations. They spanned the missions of day attack, night attack, submarine search and attack, ASW hunter-killer, transport, ambulance, photoreconnaissance, target towing, and aerial refueling. ADs were purchased and flown by the nations of the United Kingdom, France, and Sweden and were passed on to Afars and Assas, Malagasy Republic, Republic of Chad, Central African Republic, Cambodia, and Vietnam.[63]

North American AJ and Douglas A3D

In 1948, the chief of naval operations issued a requirement for a long-range, carrier-based attack plane that could deliver a 10,000 lb. bomb or a nuclear weapon. The first attack aircraft designed and deployed to meet this requirement was the North American AJ (A-2) Savage. Though not a light-attack aircraft, the Savage and Skywarrior are included here for their 1950s contribution to the attack mission. The AJ had two propeller-driven engines and one jet in the tail. First flight was in 1948, and by 1950 the aircraft was operational in the fleet. It was relatively slow (470K) but had a range of 1,600 nm. The Navy soon was planning for a follow-on aircraft.

The original gross weight specification was 100,000 lbs. for an aircraft to fly off the Navy's newest carrier in development, USS *United States*. But this "supercarrier" funding was locked in a death struggle with the Air Force's B-36 in the post–World War II era of greatly restricted funding.

Ed Heinemann proposed a much-smaller (68,000 lb.), twin-jet, three-man-crew, folding-wing bomber that could fly off the fleet's Essex-class carriers. At first, BuAer officials were openly skeptical, then opposed to such a radical concept. Heinemann and Douglas persisted, and in the 1949 design competition they submitted their proposal for a twin-jet-engined bomber that would deliver a nuclear weapon over a 2,000 nm range.

In April 1949, Secretary of Defense Johnson canceled the construction of USS *United States*, and the Navy was left with limited alternatives for its aviation fleet. Heinemann's instinct had prevailed.

The Navy contract for three prototypes of the A3D was signed on September 29, 1949, and the prototype XA3D-1 first flew on October 28, 1952. The original aircraft was underpowered, and Douglas switched to the Pratt & Whitney J-57, the same engine that powered the F-100 and F8U Crusader. The first operational A3D was delivered in 1956. Its maximum speed was 537K and a range of 2,080 nm. The last production run of 282 was in 1961.

In 1959, an A3D in the aerial tanker version was catapulted off a carrier at a gross eight of 84,000 pounds, the heaviest launch up to that time. Thirty-two Navy squadrons flew the A3 in the missions of attack, reconnaissance, electronic warfare, and aerial tanker until it was finally retired in 1991. The attack squadrons were designated VAH (Heavy).

The Air Force ordered 294 of the aircraft, modified as the B-66 Destroyer. Douglas built and delivered two hundred. They performed virtually the same missions (except tanker) as the Navy. The B-66 served in multiple Air Force squadrons, worldwide in the Cold War.

Douglas A4D Skyhawk

The Skyhawk has another unique backstory to its inception. It seems that Ed Heinemann and his colleagues at Douglas had been worried for some time that there was a disturbing trend in the addition of secondary systems and associated weight in airplane designs. Heinemann had his staff conduct a study in 1951 of this growth factor, and he requested to brief BuAer on his findings. In January 1952, he briefed over fifty Navy officials in a crowded conference room. His pitch:

If this aircraft's gross weight is increased by ten percent due to additions in the form of equipment and performance remains constant, then the wing area, power plant, fuel, and structure must be increased by as much as 100 percent. This is a growth factor of ten.[64]

Navy officials were skeptical but asked Heinemann to work up a concept for a 12,000 lb. attack aircraft in a month. Returning to El Segundo, he challenged his staff to develop, hone, and modify the design. When he returned a month later with the design, the Navy was pleased with the product but increased the required payload to 2,000 pounds (an obvious requirement to carry one nuclear weapon), added the requirement for JP-type fuel, which was 0.5 pound heavier per gallon than aviation gasoline, increased the gross weight limit to 14,600 pounds, and announced it had to cost less than $1 million dollars a copy![65]

The Navy was pleased with the progress on the A4D and in June 1952 awarded Douglas a contract for two prototypes. The evolving operational requirement was for an attack aircraft that would have the same mission profile as the AD Skyraider, nuclear and conventional but with a faster speed that would save flying time and thus reduce airframe fatigue.[66] The contract specified "a lightweight, single-engine, single-place, high-performance, carrier-based, day attack airplane capable of performing dive-bombing, interdiction, and close-support missions."[67] The nuclear mission was unspoken but understood.

Heinemann's weight reduction program paid off, and the aircraft flew its first test flight in June 1954. After working out a few bugs in testing, the first five hundred aircraft were delivered to the Navy, underweight and for $860,000 each.

On October 15, 1955, an A4D broke the world record with an average speed of 695 mph over a 500-kilometer closed course, the first for an attack aircraft!

Terry Wolf, an A-4 pilot and member of the A-7 Corsair II Association, noted that the A-4A and B models had only three ordnance stations: a heavy nuclear weapon on the centerline, with drop tanks on each of the two wing stations. The A-4As and Bs had small speed brakes on either side of the rear fuselage, but not the massive speed brake of the A-1 or A-7.[68]

VA-72 received the first operational aircraft, and within months, all Navy jet light-attack squadrons were flying the A-4. At this time in the late 1950s, there was so much emphasis on the nuclear deterrent mission that there were Navy squadron pilots who reported that they never practiced conventional dive-bombing.[69] Douglas produced 166 A-4As, 542 A-4Bs, and 638 A-4Cs. Modifications included a new engine (J52), adding an improved bomb delivery system, air-to-ground missile delivery, an automated analog navigation computer, a dual hydraulic system, and in-flight refueling, both as a tanker and receiver.

In 1959, US Marines were deployed to Lebanon in one of the first Middle East crises, and the importance of conventional, limited war capabilities became apparent. To meet this new requirement, Douglas added three external "hard points" to carry munitions. The A-4E with the J52 engine could carry 2,000 pounds of bombs over 1,400 miles.[70]

Terry Wolf was one the of the pilots who flew the later models of the A-4. He began by describing the pilot's view:

The cockpit of the A-4 was spartan by modern standards. Simple round dials for engine instruments, a small, seldom-used, radar scope, another smaller well-used scope that was the early version of the SAM warning display, various small boxes added on to the cockpit glare shield and rails that attempted to upgrade or add electronic sensors and a small illuminated gunsight at eye level just inside the windscreen. In addition to the standard "T" layout of instruments, there were bits of magic, such as the angle-of-attack gauge and associated display lights, and the all-attitude gyro which gave you not only pitch and roll, but also heading in one instrument. This instrument made it possible to perform a perfect barrel roll without outside reference.[71]

I flew the Navy's last model of the A-4, the A-4F with the largest engine, the J-52 P408 which produced 11,200 lbs. of thrust. By that time, the basic weight of the aircraft had grown to 11,500 lbs. so the larger engine was a necessity. The first A-4 had an empty weight of 8,200 lbs. so the J-65 engine at the time had plenty of thrust. The A-4F had a radar and much-improved avionics by 1972, when I started flying it.

One other thing you should know, the A-4 was designed as a nuclear delivery platform, not a dive bomber. The A-7 was designed as a dive bomber, meaning a dive angle in excess of sixty degrees. That was why it needed the massive speed brakes. When Vietnam rolled around, they adapted the aircraft very well as a conventional bomber. The book *Scooter* by Tommy Tomason[72] tells that story very well.

Terry Wolf continued:

The only characteristic of the A-4 that I found wanting, at first, was the effect of the uneven extension of the gravity-actuated leading-edge slats in a high G maneuver. The F-9, and later the A-7, were very stable when pulling G loads. If you pulled too many G's with the A-4, the slats would start to extend asymmetrically, causing the A-4 to wing walk, rolling side to side. This took some getting used to and almost caused me to ride a bomb-laden A-4F into the jungle in South Vietnam during a heavy pull off a target when one slat stuck out. I was forced to jam forward stick to get the slat back in and then pull gently, recovering at tree-top level. The slats took a beating on the ship, slamming in and out during catapult and arrestment and occasionally got bent enough to cause a problem. This trait may have contributed to the loss of multiple aircraft over the years. During the years, the A-4 was used by the Blue Angels, the slats were bolted up, resulting in a slightly higher takeoff and landing speed but more predictable handling under G.

We did mostly forty-five-degree bombing, rolling in at 10,000–11,000 feet AGL, pickling at 5,000 and pulling out by 3,000. Delivery of retarded weapons, snake-eye fins on the Mk. 82 500-lb. bomb and the like, was usually done lower and at thirty degrees.

The J-65 was a much more temperamental engine too. *You* were the fuel control and you had to constantly monitor the EGT to avoid an over-temp. The J-52 was a modern engine which could be jam-accelerated without problem.

The A-4 was a very agile bomber. It quickly responded to corrections the entire bomb run. Unlike, I am told, the F-4 which, once you got the nose pointed down, was very hard to move to improve accuracy.[73]

The A-4 and subsequent naval aircraft pioneered the use of the "angle of attack" gauge, a small instrument on the left side if the instrument panel that displayed the exact angle at which the wing was hitting the oncoming air. The beauty of this instrument was that it told the pilot whether he was "On Speed," "Fast," or "Slow," and it was independent of the weight of the aircraft. One can appreciate the value of this instrument if you consider that the final approach speed of the Air Force F-100C was 180 knots *plus* 2 knots for every 1,000 pounds of fuel, a rough calculation at best. The Air Force did not adopt the angle-of-attack gauge until it purchased the F-4 and A-7 aircraft.

Attack Aircraft vs. Fighters

In the last several decades, the rise of the ubiquitous multirole fighter has created some confusion about the difference between attack and fighter aircraft. According to the current US designation system, an attack aircraft (A) is designed primarily to find, attack, and destroy land or sea targets. Only a single aircraft in the USAF's current inventory bears a simple, unmixed "A" designation: the A-10 Thunderbolt II. The fighter category (F) in the USAF incorporates aircraft designed primarily for air-to-air combat, but as multipurpose aircraft they are capable of ground-attack missions. The US Navy combines the roles of fighter and attack in the F/A-18 Hornet, which was designed both for air-to-air and air-to-surface missions such as interdiction and close air support.

CHAPTER 4
USN and USAF Attack Aircraft, 1960–1968

Navy Attack Aircraft in 1960

The Navy entered the 1960s with a stable set of aircraft of high performance. The F4H Phantom II was the fighter of choice, and the A4D was the attack aircraft of the fleet. The AD Skyraider was still operational, but it was being phased out. Both the F4H and A4D were being produced in high numbers. In 1962, Department of Defense reorganized the aircraft designation system. The F4H was redesignated the F-4, the AD became the A-1, the A4D became the A-4, the B-26 became the A-26, and the A2F was relabeled the A-6.

The Kennedy Administration and Limited War

President Kennedy took office on January 21, 1961, with results that would have immense effects on Air Force and naval attack aircraft. Kennedy promised to change the basic course of the country toward the "New Frontier." He had campaigned on the defense issues of a "missile gap" and the need to build up the nation's conventional forces. He chose as his secretary of defense Robert S. McNamara, the former president of Ford Motor Company, and gave him an extreme mandate:

1. Reappraise our entire defense strategy.[1]

2. Develop the force structure necessary to our military requirements without regard to arbitrary or predetermined budget ceilings.

3. Having determined that force structure, procure it at the lowest possible cost.[2]

Arthur Schlesinger, the president's biographer, described Secretary McNamara's method of operation:

McNamara had been fascinated by the intellectual problem of administering large organizations since his days as a student of statistical control in the Harvard Business School and his experience as a junior officer in the Pentagon during the war [World War II]. The quest for control required in his judgment two things: the use of analysis to force alternative programs to the surface and the definition of the "options" in quantitative terms in order to facilitate choice. . . . The computer was his ally in making options precise.[3]

One of Secretary McNamara's first actions was to hire Rhodes scholar Charles J. Hitch to head the Office of the Secretary of Defense (OSD) Comptroller's office, and Alain Enthoven, PhD, to lead its programming section, which came to be labeled Systems Analysis.

Systems Analysis Suggests the Air Force Buy the Navy A-4

In 1961, the Air Force had sixteen wings of F-100s, one wing each of F-104s and F-84s, and two wings of F-105s, which was replacing the F-100. Each wing had seventy-two aircraft. The primary mission of the F-100 squadrons was training and deployments overseas to conduct ground alert for a possible nuclear war. The F-105 contained an internal bomb bay to carry a nuclear weapon, and it was powered for subsonic attack and supersonic fighter missions. McNamara's director of defense research and engineering (DDR&E) was convinced the Air Force needed a lower cost and better aircraft for the attack mission than the F-105. In the June 1961 time frame, the Air Force submitted a set of alternative budgets, with the F-105 in all of them. Systems Analysis entered five wings of Douglas A-4D Skyhawks into the Air Force fighter structure.[4]

The substitution of the subsonic Navy A-4 for the supersonic F-105, and the arbitrary way it was done, caused considerable alarm in the Air Force, especially in the Air Staff and Tactical Air Command. Not only was it a Navy airplane, but it was considered much too slow for the Air Force tactics of low-altitude, high-speed penetration and completely incapable of conducting supersonic air-to-air combat.

The consensus view of Air Force fighter pilots was expressed by triple ace Lt. Gen. Gordon Graham:

> We hadn't bought an attack airplane since World War II. The general doctrine and philosophy in the tactical area is that those [A-4 and later the A-7] aircraft are not the kinds of machines that would survive in a sophisticated environment, and that is the kind of war that we have to be prepared to fight. So, we don't want to encumber ourselves and fill our force structure up with them.[5]

Simultaneously, DDR&E and Systems Analysis were interested in getting the Navy F-4H for the Air Force. DDR&E's staff had asked the Air Force to evaluate the capability of the F-4 in competition with the new F-106 air defense interceptor. In "Project High Speed" the Air Staff found the F-4 to have 25 percent greater radar acquisition and tracking range, and it could carry a heavier load a longer distance.[6]

The Air Staff accepted the F4H into its force structure but wanted to modify the aircraft and start a very slow procurement program. OSD was trying to get them to buy the aircraft *fast*. Dr. Enthoven characterized this as another of the old "strategic" versus "tactical" fights: that the less money spent for Tactical Air Command (TAC), the better, and particularly if TAC was not going to be a nuclear force, because the F-105 was built primarily as a nuclear bomber, and the Navy F-4 had no nuclear capability.

Subsequently, the Air Force made several changes to the Navy production model, including adding nuclear-delivery capability, full aircraft control in the back seat, and an inertial navigation system.

Crises in Europe and Asia

The first international crisis of the Kennedy administration was over Berlin. On August 13, 1961, East German police and army troops occupied all crossing points between East and West Berlin, and four days later they began constructing the infamous "Berlin Wall." US forces in Europe were placed on alert, and reinforcing active-duty and three Air National Guard units were deployed there. President Kennedy and Secretary McNamara were concerned the US did not have *enough* forces in Europe. Among those forces were three wings of older F-84 Thunderjets. When the crisis ended in October 1961, DoD decided to leave the Air National Guard units there and increase the force structure to twenty-one USAF wings. In addition, the Air Force replaced ten squadrons of F-102 air defense fighters with F-4s, and the number of wings increased to twenty-four.

The Laotian insurgency was the second crisis of the Kennedy administration. After the North Vietnamese violated the 1962 Geneva agreement and joined the Pathet Lao in a renewed insurgency, Prime Minister Souvanna Phouma asked the United States for aircraft and supplies for the Royal Laotian Air Force. Deliveries of T-28s began in August 1963, under a code name, Operation Water Pump. Helicopters and light transports came later. These aircraft and others became involved in combat with the Pathet Lao and North Vietnamese that continued throughout the Vietnam War and afterward.

The Navy A-1 Skyraider after 1960

The AD entered the fleet in 1946, fought in the Korean War, and was the primary attack aircraft for the 1950s until the A-4D Skyhawk was deployed in 1956. In 1960, the Navy refurbished twenty-five surplus AD-6 (A-1H) aircraft that had been stockpiled at Litchfield Park, Arizona, and transferred them to the Republic of Vietnam Air Force (VNAF) under the Mutual Defense Assistance Pact to replace their older F8F Bearcats. Navy pilots trained VNAF pilots at Corpus Christi, Texas, and many were assigned as advisors to VNAF squadrons in Vietnam. The Navy continued this transfer and training process, and by 1966 the VNAF had five combat squadrons with 166 A-1Hs.

Navy and Marine Corps attack squadrons continued to fly Skyraider aircraft on worldwide deployments. Navy combat in Vietnam began in 1964, with the "Tonkin Gulf Yacht Club." Navy A-1s gained some distinction in Vietnam in addition to attack sorties. Two A-1H lieutenants, Charles Hartman and Clinton Johnson, of VA-25 off USS *Midway* shared in the shoot-down of a North Vietnamese MiG-17 on June 20, 1965. A year later, Lt. j.g. W. Thomas Patton of A-1 squadron VA-176, from USS *Intrepid*, sent another MiG-17 down in flames near Hanoi on October 9, 1966.

By this time, eleven years after the Korean War, the Navy was no longer using the high-angle-dive delivery. Pilots found that the AD in a 70-degree dive felt as if it was upside down, and the pilot had to corkscrew around the target to keep the pipper on a stationary point. In addition to being a difficult maneuver, this would cause problems when several aircraft were diving on a target in a sequence, since the pullouts would be in different directions and could cause a midair collision. In addition, the widespread introduction of surface-to-air missiles (SAMs) negated this tactic for propeller-driven aircraft that were too slow to outmaneuver the missiles. Instead, the Navy substituted the 30-degree dive method for conventional bombing.

Lt. (later rear admiral) Lewis Chatham recalled that "as the North Vietnamese moved their mobile multibarrel AAA south, we lost the skipper of our A-1 squadron to a flak trap during a day road recce flight. That ended daylight road recce missions for our SPADS."[7]

The major missions for the SPADs in Vietnam were interdiction close air support and Rescue Combat Air Patrol (RESCAP), which had not been taught either to Navy or Air Force attack units. Attack Squadron 25 (VA-25), "Fist of the Fleet," was flying A-1H/Js in 1965 when they were tasked with this new mission. They rapidly developed on-the-job tactics for RESCAP at the same time as Air Force A-1Es were beginning to perform the mission out of Udorn, Thailand.

In 1966, VA-25 pilots deployed on USS *Coral Sea* were instrumental in saving the defenders of a Special Forces camp at Lang Vei. Working under an overcast, the A-1s were bombing and strafing troops and tanks around and on top of an underground bunker. The book *Night of the Silver Stars*, by William R. Phillips, documents that battle from the troops' perspective.

The last Navy A-1H/J was retired in 1968. During this period, the Navy lost sixty-five A-1s to enemy action or operational mishaps.[8]

The Douglas A4D/A-4 Skyhawk after 1960

As the A-1s were phased out of the Navy inventory, the VA squadrons transitioned to the Douglas A-4. One of the first naval aviators to fly the A-4 in Southeast Asia was RAdm. Chatham. Later he recalled:

My early combat was as a lieutenant in deployment December 1964–May 1965 flying A-4Es in VA-216 off USS *Hancock*. I returned in 1971/72/73 flying A-7Bs off USS *Midway*.

My squadron, the "Blue Diamonds," and I went to war as fully qualified nuclear-delivery pilots. That had been our only mission. Most of us had only a few hops at El Centro doing 30-degree daylight pattern bombing. We learned combat tactics—what to do and what not to do—over Vietnam. We flew off Yankee Station in the Gulf of Tonkin with missions of armed reconnaissance over North Vietnam and armed reconnaissance and strike missions in eastern Laos, covering the infiltration routes used by the Communists in Barrel Roll. We also flew in Operation Flaming Dart, the February 1965 reprisal attacks against targets in response to the shelling of an American advisor's compound at Pleiku by the Viet Cong. From March to May 1965 we participated in the Operation Rolling Thunder campaign, against designated military targets in North Vietnam.

The first thing we learned was that multiple runs lost pilots and airplanes. The skipper of our sister A-4 squadron briefed and led (I led the other division) an eight-plane strike against a defended radar site, using a new tactic developed at the Navy Tactical Warfare Center. It was called "low and slow." The skipper was shot down on his second run but made it to water and was rescued by our helo. I gathered my division and climbed to altitude, and we made one more run, dropping all our remaining ordnance. You could not publish the skipper's debrief! Needless to say, that was the first and last "low and slow" mission of the war.

Another thing we learned was that despite the determination and bravery of their crews, antisubmarine warfare helos were not suited for overland recovery of downed pilots.

My first night road recce mission was over the North. I strafed a truck near Vinh and on return to the carrier was chewed out by my carrier air group (the CAG) for not identifying my target!

I personally learned that a low-level entry to a target in a loaded A-4 meant struggling to roll in. You were almost relieved to be able to drop your nose and put your pipper on the target. None of us had ever seen a surface-to-air missile (SAM). Our first SAM warning system was a red (fuzz buster) light mounted on top of the instrument panel.

My toughest flight was returning to the ship and leaving my wingman, Paul Galanti, on a hillside in North Vietnam. [*Author's note*: Paul Galanti's wife would later be one of the organizers of the POW/MIA Wives movement, which became so instrumental in mobilizing American public opinion.]

Operating in the South off *Hancock* presented other problems: I launched many times with only 4 knots excess airspeed off the catapult due to the heavy bombloads we were carrying.

We saved the few Mk. 82 500 lb. bombs we had on board for when we moved north, so we junior officers (JOs) joked that the World War II depth charges we dropped on the trees along Ho Chi's trail exploded in the treetops and provided BBQ monkey to the NVN.

As a final note: VA-216 was blessed with great leadership during those years. We JOs formed bonds that remain to this day.[9]

Starting in 1963, the A-4 became the major Navy attack aircraft for missions in South Vietnam and in Operation Rolling Thunder in the North.

A-4 Skyhawk Missions over Vietnam

During the 1972 cruise, a combat line period would last approximately a month with a week-to-ten-day break in port. The period would usually start with a forward air controller (FAC) close-air-support mission in South Vietnam, with the carrier sitting just east of Danang at what is traditionally known as Dixie Station. Our typical weapons load for these missions would be six 500-pound bombs carried on the wing stations and a 3,000-pound auxiliary fuel tank on the centerline.

Radm. Chatham continued:

At Dixie Station, we would work in two-plane or four-plane groups, rendezvousing overhead the carrier at designated radials and distances and then departing ships control to check in with an airborne controller in a C-130, who would assign us individual FACs to work with. Working with a forward air controller was always rewarding. I have nothing but respect for every aviator who did that job. By the time we arrived, they would have targets ready for us, based on their own searching or in response to calls for help from the ground. They would use various methods, geographic points, or white phosphorus, "Willy-Pete" (WP), rockets, to help us identify the target, warn us of the position of any friendlies, and then clear us to drop. In the south, where there was no AAA threat, we would often make multiple runs on different targets, dropping two bombs per run. Having held over a target watching other aircraft from other services try to hit the target identified by the FAC, I can say honestly that we did a superior job, and the FAC was always glad to see us. This superior level of performance has been confirmed by many infantry troops I have had the pleasure to talk with over the years who used our services.[10]

Lt. Bud Edney (now admiral), USNA '57, also flew the A-4 in strike missions over North Vietnam. His description of missions is illustrative:

I will share with you some personal observations based on my 287 missions over North Vietnam from 1963 through 1973, when the war ended. During this time, I flew the A-4E and A-7 aircraft. Luckily for me, I was hit only once while flying the A-4E. I gather the Air Force never flew this aircraft. The A-4E had a backup fly-by-wire [not electrical, but a mechanical wire] capability if your main control systems were damaged. The A-7A/B did not have this capability, and if I had been hit flying the A-7 over Hanoi, I would have had to eject over North Vietnam. I was able to get the damaged A-4E back to the carrier, and with a long straight approach, I caught a wire. When I got out of the airplane, I could stand up through the hole in the wing."[11]

He continued to outline the distinctive characteristics of naval aviation.

Air Force pilots probably do not keep track of all their landings. Carrier aviation does, and in my career I had 1,280 carrier landings, with 520 of them at night! Day carrier landings in reasonable weather become rather routine. However, *no* night carrier landing is routine!

Air Force runways are 10–12,000 feet. Most Air Force people do not understand the complexity of carrier aviation. It is basically a city at sea, with the runway moving at 20–30 knots. The carrier is 1,000 feet in length, with roughly five thousand officers and sailors on board. Three thousand belong to the ship, two thousand to the Air Wing. In addition to operating the landing and takeoff area, they run a nuclear engineering plant, provide meteorology/weather predictions, operate a fuel farm for aircraft, provide sleeping accommodations, feed five thousand people three meals every day, provide exercise rooms for physical fitness, religious services, intermediate maintenance for shipboard systems and aircraft, and store and move all weapons to and from the flight deck. The aircraft carrier launch aircraft at the same time they are recovering aircraft. Aircraft are launched from a catapult that accelerates high-performance aircraft to 170 mph in three to four seconds. Before the launching aircraft go to

full power on the catapult, a jet blast deflector is raised for the safety of crews on deck and aircraft recovering. Carrier landing area consists of four arresting wires that are 50 feet apart. A recovering F/A-18 lands at 155 mph and is stopped within three to four seconds. When the wheels hit the deck, the pilot goes to full power on the throttles. This is required in case the hook misses the wires so that he can go around. Individual wires are replaced after they have stopped an aircraft a hundred times.[12]

VAdm. Robert "Rocky" Spane attended the Naval Academy and graduated in the class of 1962. His first assignment after naval flight training was an A-4 Skyhawk squadron, where he participated in several cruises. His most eventful cruise was his third, where he flew the A-4 in Vietnam in 1967.

On his first hop he joined up on the wing of Cmdr. "Dutch" Netherland, the CAG (carrier air group commander), and they proceeded at the head of the Alpha Strike Group to Hanoi, Route Package VI Alpha. Their target was the MiG airfield, just southeast of the city. They had a full load of Mk. 82 bombs and refueled en route. They went in high and were going downhill as fast as the A-4 could travel when the CAG's airplane banked sharply left, and a SAM missile impacted in the cockpit area, blowing the aircraft apart. Lt. Spane was left as the strike leader, a position he was surprised to be in. He recalled they dropped their bombs, perhaps not near the target, and exited.[13]

Spane's second most memorable mission was a night road recce in the area of the famous Thanh Hoa bridge. He hit a truck loaded with high explosives, which blew off his two external drop tanks. In his clean airplane he cruised all the way back to the ship, tanking all the way.

Ed Beakley, who flew A-7Bs, reported that his generation who participated in Operation Linebacker years later learned their lessons from the Navy attack guys such as Rocky Spane, who had flown in Operation Rolling Thunder.[14]

Air Force Attack Readiness in the early 1960s

Gen. John P. McConnell, USAF chief of staff, is quoted as saying in 1968, near the end of his tour of duty, that "we did not even start doing anything about tactical aviation until about 1961 or 1962."[15]

This may have been a true observation at the chief's level, but on the flight line, the US had plenty of conventional war capability. The author was an F-100 pilot in 1962–1964, and an A-1 pilot after that. It is true that my two F-100 overseas deployments were in support of nuclear-readiness missions in Japan/Korea and Turkey. We deployed to Japan in the summer of 1963 to pull tactical nuclear alert for the 8th Tactical Fighter Wing's missions while the wing transitioned from the F-100 to the F-105. The wing was in Japan, but we pulled nuclear alert in South Korea. The second deployment in January 1964 was to pull ground alert for planned nuclear missions from a base in Turkey, as part of US Air Forces in Europe contribution to the Single Integrated Operations Plan. However, all tactical fighter squadrons trained in the USA and overseas both for conventional and nuclear missions, and our conventional capability was considerable. In fact, our training combined nonnuclear air-to-ground and nuclear missions. The Navy may have been different. Navy attack squadrons in A-1 Skyraiders, A-3 Skywarriors, A-4 Skyhawks, and A-6 Intruders routinely pulled ready alert for nuclear strike lines when forward-deployed but retained some inherent general-purpose, conventional capabilities.

Gen. McConnell's overall point was that the conventional warfare training took second priority to the nuclear mission, and that it degraded and diminished the US capability for limited war, counterinsurgency, and the ability to contribute to the growing crisis in Vietnam. In addition, the limitations placed on US forces as a result of the political-military situation made a robust tactical response virtually impossible, which is demonstrated by the nature of Air Force and Navy actions during the whole Vietnam War, right up to Linebacker II.

The Grumman A-6 Intruder

The A-6 first flew on April 19, 1960, and virtually dominated the medium/heavy-attack mission from that day and for four decades after. In the late 1950s, the Navy was looking for a jet to replace the heavy-load-carrying AD Skyraider. The initial requirement was written in 1955 and finalized in 1957. The requirement specified a "close air support attack bomber capable of hitting the enemy at any

time." It had to carry either a single bomb or a heavy bombload at low level over a great distance at night and in bad weather. The nuclear requirement was paramount. Eight aerospace firms responded to the RFP with eleven bids. After a tough competition, the Grumman model G-128 was selected as the winner and designated the A2F-1, continuing to use the letter "F" for Grumman.

The design was a subsonic, two-place, twin-engined aircraft with five load-carrying stations: one on the fuselage and four under the wings. The side-by-side seating for the pilot and bombardier/navigator was unconventional but provided for easy crew coordination. The large nose housed a ground-mapping radar for the bomb/nav, with an unusual cathode ray tube that projected a synthetic ground representation on the pilot's windscreen. This was a primitive version of a heads-up display.

The heart of the A-6A was the Digital Integrated Attack Navigation Equipment (DIANE) system, which provided precision navigation and bombing. One of the best examples was a section of two A-6As that attacked a North Vietnamese power plant during a particularly dark and stormy night. The Intruders dropped twenty-six Mk. 82 500 lb. bombs on the target, but the damage was so extensive that the North Vietnamese were convinced that it had been a B-52 strike.[16] Nearly two dozen A-6Bs were modified to carry and fire the AGM-78 Standard ARM and AGM-45 Shrike antiradiation missiles in Iron Hand missions. The A-6s and A-7Es would be used this way in Linebacker also.

A-6s also were flown by a half-dozen Marine Corps all-weather attack squadrons. When expanded capability was needed, the airframe was stretched to accommodate two additional electronic-warfare officers to form the EA-6B Prowler. Another of the valuable modifications of the A-6 was the KA-6, the aerial refueler. These carrier birds could be sent aloft to refuel flights en route to their targets and again when they came out. Or they could orbit the carrier and refuel any aircraft that was short of fuel for the landing pattern.

As the service of the A-6 continued, the Navy had Grumman improve the avionics until the later models were quite different from the earlier ones. Naturally, this complexity translated into more maintenance, and the A-6 was one of the most labor-intensive aircraft on the carrier, resulting in low in-commission rates. One of the squadrons on USS *Midway* in 1972 had twenty aircraft assigned, but seldom more than twelve operationally ready to fly. Naval A-6s flew 35,000 combat missions in Vietnam and lost only eighty-four aircraft. When the A-6 was retired finally in 1997, it had served the fleet for thirty-seven years in multiple roles.

Air Force Early-Attack Experience in Vietnam

The USAF recognized early in the Kennedy administration that general purposes / tactical forces needed to be a policy and budgeting priority. On October 11, 1961, President Kennedy approved National Security Action Memorandum 104, which authorized DoD to introduce an Air Force "Jungle Jim" squadron into Vietnam for the initial purpose of training Vietnamese forces. The unit was officially named Detachment 2 of the 4400th Combat Crew Training Squadron, code-named Farmgate, reporting to the Military Assistance Advisory Group Vietnam and the ambassador. Detachment 2A flew the Douglas B-26 Invader, and Detachment 2B flew the T-28 Trojan. In addition, the Air Force established the Special Air Warfare Center at Hurlburt Field, Eglin Auxiliary No. 9. The center rapidly gained the name "Jungle Jim" for its emphasis on counterinsurgency, Air Commando operations in general, and Vietnam in particular. The Air Force established the 2nd Air Division in October 1962 to manage air operations in Vietnam, and in July 1963 it organized the 34th Tactical Group at Bien Hoa Air Base to continue VNAF training and manage the Farmgate operations as US "advisors."

Simultaneously, the Navy was already flying tactical air missions over Southeast Asia.

1Lt. Andi Biancur, a 1960 graduate of the US Air Force Academy, was one of the first of the B-26 pilots. He began flying missions on May 2, 1963, with his navigator, 2/Lt. Wells T. Jackson. Andi and Wells later recalled the diversity of missions they conducted:

The majority of the Douglas B-26B aircraft were assigned to Detachment 2A, First Air Commando Group, in Vietnam. The two gun

turrets had been removed, along with a significant portion of the original armor plating. The gunner's compartment was stripped of all but a simple seat and safety belt, along with other weight-saving measures, and only very essential equipment remained throughout the aircraft. The cockpit featured a single control yoke for control. The strike model aircraft had four hardpoints under each wing, either six or eight forward-firing .50-caliber machine guns in the nose, a fully usable bomb bay, and a K-19 vertical camera behind the bomb bay. The only communications gear consisted of an eight-button UHF radio and an antiquated ADF navigation system.

The aircraft was unpressurized, with rudimentary heating supplied by the engines and no air-conditioning and little space in the cockpit for any storage whatsoever. The crews wore a sidearm of choice and an improvised survival vest with a radio and a few survival items.

The standard ordnance configuration consisted of six 500 lb. cannisters of napalm, 400 rounds of .50 cal. armor-piercing incendiary (API) ammunition in each gun, twelve 100 lb. general-purpose bombs, and twelve 120 lb. fragmentation cluster bombs, along with a significant reel of camera film. Alternatively, we often carried two 2.75" rocket pods, 750 lb. cans of napalm, and 250 or 500 lb. bombs under the wings, with contact or delayed-fuse general-purpose bombs in the bomb bay. The B-26 carried enough fuel to provide loiter time of five hours over a target.

The cockpit layout was fairly standard to accommodate a pilot, side by side with one crew member, usually a navigator, and a very small jump seat behind the center console. All aircraft controls were easily accessed by the pilot with a removable aluminum table under a small camera control panel in front of the right seat. There was a fixed reticule gunsight in the pilot's windscreen, and a bomb intervalometer just outboard of the pilot's left hip. Ordnance controls were located on an overhead panel between the two halves of the clamshell canopy.

Tactics evolved over time with an increase in skills of the crew and were usually dictated by the terrain. Missions typically consisted of a single B-26 with an occasional two-ship mission when a target demanded, generally to support ground troops in contact.

The missions consisted of interdiction, close air support, air cover, and ground alert response. The first three missions were generally scheduled on a daily "frag order," with alert aircraft being "scrambled" with minimum notice. Mission preparation was standard. Upon reaching the target area, we would establish contact with either the airborne or ground forward air controller (FAC), who was established to determine the exact location and description of the targets. I would plan the attack vectors and proceed with weapons delivery. In most cases, weapons selection would be commanded by me to be selected and armed by the navigator / crew member on each pass. A napalm pass would require low-level approach at 300-plus knots, with weapons delivery initiated by a bomb release button on the control wheel. A bomb pass could be conducted either level at any selected altitude or a medium-angle, high-speed dive (usually 20–35-degree angle at 300–350 knots). In most cases, I would trigger a short burst of machine gun fire to discourage any return fire. The gunsights were generally unreliable and usually augmented by grease pencil marks on the windscreen following the initial weapons pass.

The air cover mission consisted of weaving over and around a truck convoy or train for 3–5 hours at 2,000–5,000 feet altitude, with an occasional low pass over the projected ground route/tracks. The cockpit had no air-conditioning, so it would become nearly unbearable with temperatures well above 130°F.

We flew night missions but only over the southern/flat portions of Vietnam, as most of the country geography was too rugged for safe operation after dark. The crew would proceed to the target area, pick up any visual clues (e.g., fire arrows), establish any ground contact, and attempt to disrupt any ongoing enemy attacks, occasionally supported by a C-123 or C-47 flare aircraft. Otherwise, the most effective tactic was to release one napalm to establish a visible ground reference.[17]

Air Force Combat Experience with the A-1

Since the Geneva Accords of 1954, which separated the two Vietnams, prohibited jet aircraft, the Air Force borrowed two A-1Es from the Navy from August 1962 to January 1963 for evaluation. The test was conducted by Tactical Air Command's Special Air Warfare Center at Hurlburt Field, Florida, to see if the A-1s were suitable for the USAF's new counterinsurgency mission. The two-seated version of the A-1, the A-1E (previously the AD-5), was found to be excellent both for attack and training of VNAF pilots, and about a dozen changes were made to update the aircraft.

Twenty-five A-1Es were delivered to Hurlburt in early 1964, and another forty-eight were sent to Bien Hoa Air Base. The early aircraft were assigned to the 1st Air Commando Squadron (ACS), and the follow-on ones to the 602nd Fighter Squadron (Commando).

I was flying the F-100 out of the 31st Tactical Fighter Wing at Homestead AFB, Florida. I had been on three deployments, including a three-month one with the 306th Tactical Fighter Squadron to Itazuki Air Base, Japan, with nuclear alert at Osan, Korea, in 1962. When we got back, and being a bachelor, I was transferred to the 308th Squadron for another three-month deployment to Cigli AB, Turkey, again for nuclear alert. My roommate, Gary Gulbransen, got to fly his F-100 on the twelve-hour flight from Florida to Turkey, but I rode a KC-135. Upon return from Turkey, we deployed to McChord AFB, Washington State, flying close air support for one of the many exercises, since the services were exercising for conventional war. After that, I saw many pilots being shipped off to be FACs with the Army. So, I volunteered for Vietnam, was accepted, and entered an A-1E checkout class at Hurlburt. With three years in the F-100, I'd had plenty of training in low-level flying, simulated nuclear deliveries, conventional dive-bombing, napalm delivery at 50 feet, firing rockets, and strafing. We practiced some air-to-air combat in the F-100, but not much since this was considered fairly hazardous, and the commanders did not want to lose pilots or airplanes.

When I got to Hurlburt, I found to my satisfaction that I was one of the few fighter pilots in the class. This was a big advantage for the flying we were about to do. Most of the other pilots had come from bombers, transports, or weather reconnaissance aircraft. After hours of "cockpit time" and a few sorties, I was completely comfortable in the aircraft and scored high on the gunnery range. That Christmas I made captain, and I joined the 602nd Fighter Squadron (Commando) in January 1965.

I flew a hundred missions in the first ninety days, training Vietnamese pilots in the finer arts of dive-bombing and strafing and flying attack missions with a Vietnamese observer. After the Viet Cong attack on the US barracks at Pleiku, President Johnson ordered us to remove the Vietnamese markings on our aircraft and replace them with US ones. We flew attack missions daily. In July, the 1st Air Commando Squadron and the 602nd set up the SANDY Combat Search and Rescue mission from Udorn Royal Thai Air Base in northern Thailand. The A-1 was the perfect aircraft to escort helicopters and protect downed airmen for the Sandy missions with its slow speed, long loiter time, and precise weapons delivery accuracy.

In South Vietnam we specialized in saving Army Special Forces camps. We flew missions daily. The squadron kept a flight of four A-1s on ground alert at Bien Hoa, and we scrambled in response to short-notice Vietnamese or US Army requests. Frequently, these were in the middle of the night, since that was the Viet Cong's preferred attack schedule. Those scrambles happened frequently, and in fact I do not recall ever going on alert and not being scrambled. One of those nights was in October 19, 1965.

Successful Close Air Support at Plei Mei

Shortly after midnight on October 20, 1965, a North Vietnamese army division came out of its encampment in Cambodia and launched the first People's Army of Viet Nam (PAVN) offensive campaign. The 33rd Regiment attacked the US Special Forces camp at Plei Mei in the highlands of II Corps. The North Vietnamese army's tactical plan was a traditional "lure and ambush" to "lure" a relief force and then "ambush" it.[18] Within twenty-five minutes

an Air Force C-130 flare ship arrived and began dropping flares and coordinating air support. The author was on ground alert at Bien Hoa when our flight was scrambled to the Army's aid. We got to the scene about forty-five minutes later and dive-bombed just outside the perimeter. We also dropped cluster bomb units and strafed with cannon in the treeline bordering the cleared fire zone. The day after the attack, I deployed with my flight of four to the Army helicopter base at Qui Nhon, where we kept a detachment. From there, I flew in support of the 1st Cavalry Division, which had responded to relieve the Plei Mei garrison and attack the North Vietnamese regiments in the Ia Drang Valley.

Air Force captain (later colonel) Richard Kuiper, a 1st Cavalry Division forward air controller (FAC), tells a story of the next event from his viewpoint as the pilot of an O-1E Bird Dog:

> An A-1 flight out of Qui Nhon responded to support a Cav squad that had ambushed the PAVN at night as they withdrew from Plei Mei up a trail to the west with pack animals and poor (drunk) security. The CAV squad had placed claymores long and short and machine-gunned up and down the trail but misjudged the size of the column and was soon in danger of being overrun. I was the FAC and laid down white phosphorus [rockets] at each end of the PAVN column and got out of the way. The ADs [A-1s] cut them to pieces with napalm on both sides of the trail and saved the CAV squad, which had withdrawn under fire a half mile to the north and tried to hide in the tall grass. There were lots of gray-green tracers . . . and a few cherry-red ones.[19]

Two of the most famous battles in this campaign were those for Landing Zone X-Ray and Albany.[20] In each of these, as in the whole campaign, the role of attack aircraft was critical. Air Force A-1E and Navy A-4s were the principal aircraft of choice, providing close-in close air support day and night.

Over the next seven days, the Air Force and Navy flew 588 close-air-support sorties and dropped over 830 tons of ordnance, an average of six 500 lb. bombs per aircraft, many at night under flares. One of the American soldiers defending Plei Mei is quoted as commenting: "If it hadn't been for air, we would have lost this place. The air chopped them up at the wire. My men had about thirty rounds of ammo left per gun when the attackers were driven off, never having broken the perimeter. They [USAF and Navy attack aircraft] came right down our perimeter with cannon, antipersonnel mines, and then when the enemy began pulling back, they hit them with high-explosive stuff."[21]

A Medal of Honor Mission

The Medal of Honor was awarded in the Vietnam War to an A-1E pilot, Bernie Fisher, 1st Air Commando Squadron. On March 13, 1966, Maj. "Jump" Myers of the 602nd FS (my old wingman) was shot down over the embattled A-Shau airstrip. Major Fisher was flying a follow-on attack mission over A-Shau and saw his friend escape from the fireball that was his aircraft and scurry safely to a ditch. Fisher recognized he was getting good support from the other A-1s on the scene, so he landed amid the holes in the runway, picked up Myers, and took off again, performing one of the more daring rescues of all time. For his gallant action, Fisher was awarded the Medal of Honor.[22]

The F-100 Super Sabre as an Attack Aircraft

The F-100 was designed as an air superiority fighter to follow the highly successful F-86 Sabre of Korean War fame. With the rapid advance of jet engineering after World War II, North American Aviation (NAA) developed a vision to design a supersonic airplane. Starting in 1949, the firm began design studies using a 45-degree sweep of the wings and added the powerful Pratt & Whitney J-57 engine. The result was an unsolicited proposal to the US Air Force for the construction of two prototype Sabre 45s on May 14, 1951. Six months later, the Air Force issued them a letter contract, and nine days after that, NAA had a full mockup. First flight followed on May 25, 1953, with test pilot George Welch in the YF-100A exceeding Mach 1 at 30,000 feet.[23]

The F-100A was a pure air superiority fighter, with four 20 mm cannon in the nose; the next model, the F-100C, added fuel cells in the wing and reinforced hardpoints under the wings to carry ordnance. It had no flaps. The cockpit and the gunsight were optimized for specialized air-to-air combat, but the aircraft was now multipurpose.

The F-100D was redesigned to be a fighter-bomber by adding wing and tail area, an autopilot, in-flight refueling probe, and extensive avionics for weapon delivery, including a Low Altitude Bombing System (LABS) for an over-the-shoulder half loop (or Immelmann) maneuver to drop a nuclear weapon. F-100D production was the largest of the four operational models, with 1,274 of the 2,294 total. F-100Ds were deployed to dozens of squadrons and stood nuclear ground alert in Europe and Asia. In 1962, the Air Force deployed an F-100 squadron to Thailand for the crisis in Laos, and in spring 1965 several wings of F-100Ds were deployed to South Vietnam and began flying close air support.

The Air Force FASTFAC Program

As the war dragged on through 1967, the quality of VC and North Vietnamese air defenses increased, and US air losses mounted. Especially vulnerable were the forward air controllers (FACs) in the South, flying initially the O-1E Bird Dog and later the O-2 Skymaster. The FACs were vulnerable because the aircraft were slow, and their mission required them to mark targets and remain in the local area to perform a poststrike assessment. The areas of Laos and North Vietnam close to the Demilitarized Zone were of particular interest because they were an important link in the supply route to the South.

Air Force veteran fighter pilot Jim Chestnut, while assigned to 7th Air Force, reviewed many battle damage assessment reports and was disturbed by the poor results reported for strikes in Route Pack 1, just north of the DMZ. He took his concerns and an idea to Maj. Gen. Gordon Blood, the deputy commander for operations. He proposed they could get more effectiveness if they used jet fighters as FACs in this area. Gen. William Momyer, 7th AF commander, agreed and initiated a top-secret program, Commando Sabre (call sign Misty), in June 1967 to test whether the F-100's superior speed would produce better results.[24]

The concept was to ask for volunteers from among the F-100 squadrons in South Vietnam and form a new unit flying the two-seat F-100F. The "F" model was chosen because it could hold a pilot and a pilot/observer to locate lucrative targets and guide other jets for attacks. The inboard pylons were removed and a seven-shot rocket pod was mounted on the outboard stations, with white phosphorus marking rocket heads. Missions were from four to six and a half hours, with multiple aerial refuelings.

Capt. Ron Fogleman (later general and USAF chief of staff) was Misty 86, flying eighty combat missions with the unit between December 1968 and April 1969. He described the training for Misty pilots:

We had a very interesting transition training program for new guys. They would get their first five missions in the back seat. And on one of these missions, you got training on "identifying AAA," and believe it or not, we had training aids that we never killed. These were gunners that were *so bad* that we sort of had a truce. Because they couldn't hit us, we would leave them alone. They were very valuable. We would take a guy up on his first day and say, "OK, we're going to show you 23 mm guns." The thing you gotta remember about 23 mm is twin barrels, fires a lot of rounds at you, and about every twenty-five rounds there is an accumulation of cordite in the barrel, and it ignites with a big puff of smoke. So, 23 mm gun sites are "self-marking." Don't waste marking rockets on them because they have this puff of white smoke that comes up every now and then, so you just tell the guy [the new Misty], "See that?" Then you go by and let some guy hammer at you, then pull up and bank to see the site. Then you say, "Let's go see a 37 mm site." A 37 mm fires clips of five, and they kind of look like softballs coming up at you. And that is the way we would go through this and orient people. And sometimes it was very exciting.[25]

Fogleman also commented on targeting:

By 1968, we were still using the handheld 35 mm cameras as our intelligence collecting device. Then we had a night vision camera that weighed about 40 pounds. And the way you survived as a Misty was you never had less than about 4 g on the airplane. So, we were

building some real bodybuilders there in the back seat, trying to hold this thing up.

And we were very successful. This is the kind of stuff that literally led to the development of things like the lantern pod and things of that nature. In my mind, one of the real untold stories coming out of Vietnam is how the Air Force leadership took the lessons we learned in Vietnam, and the lesson from an airpower perspective was that you must deny the enemy sanctuaries. And some of the sanctuaries the enemy had were political, some were night, some were foliage, and some were weather. So, what happened in the late 1960s was that the leadership and the technological base began taking those sanctuaries away. And the greatest sanctuary was an integrated air defense.

Analyst Lawrence Spinetta described the tactical success of the MISTYs:

Despite the dangerous and costly nature of the operation, Commando Sabre would blossom into arguably the most successful air mission of the war. Indeed, F-100 Fast FACs gave Charlie more than a few unpleasant surprises in their day. Two missions in particular—the "Great Truck Massacre" of March 20, 1968, and another that annihilated nearly 1,000 enemy troops caught in the open on the Ho Chi Minh Trail in February 1970—were remarkable feats in the annals of air warfare. Their results would not be surpassed until two decades later, when more sophisticated American fighters found Saddam Hussein's army retreating on the roads from Kuwait City.[26]

But the mission was extremely high risk. There were 157 MISTY pilots who flew in the three-year period June 1967 to May 1970, and thirty-two of them were shot down (22 percent). Two were shot down twice. Those fighters who provided the firepower to the MISTYs also suffered heavily. F-100, A-4, and F-4 pilots claim they suffered the second-highest loss rate in the war.[27]

A Comparison of the A-1 with the A-7

By mid-1967, the USAF was able to acquire single-seat A-1H/Js from the Navy. From then on, A-1Es, Gs, Hs, and Js flew missions together. Over the eight years from 1964 to 1972, the Air Force would lose 201 A-1s in the countries of Southeast Asia.[28] The last A-1s were turned over to the VNAF in 1972, and the Sandy mission transferred to the A-7Ds of the 354th Tactical Fighter Wing.

Since 1972, there has been among Air Force fighter/attack pilots a vigorous debate about the merits of three aircraft for the CAS/Sandy mission: the A-1, the A-7, and the A-10. An anonymous A-1 pilot published a passionate comparison of the first two in an article titled "A-1 versus A-7 in the CAS/SAR Role," in which he made some specific comparisons:

Speed to the [SAR] survivor's area was a plus for the A-7; however, the A-7 flew the orbit similar to the A-1, negating this factor to a degree.

The IAS [indicated airspeed] of the A-7 in the target area was too high to effectively accomplish a good visual search. Pilots had to maintain 300–350 knots to retain maneuvering energy. The On-Scene Commander had to rely more on the survivor's radio than on visual cues.

Keeping the helicopter in sight was another problem due to the A-7's high speed. The A-7 could not stay close enough to the Jolly Green [helicopter] for good coverage and the Jollys felt somewhat naked.

The A-7 did not have the ordnance selections that we had on the A-1. Of course, it is hard to compare here because the A-7 had only six hard points compared to the A-1's fifteen. Two of the six were used for external fuel tanks, whereas the A-1 only needed one.

The navigation and radio equipment aboard the A-7 were excellent. The A-7's tactical computer could store up to eighteen locations, nine pre-set and nine MARKS which could be used for locating/relocating the survivor and other landmarks. . . . The A-7 had UHF and VHF/FM, but no VHF. [The A-1 had all three.] That third radio in the A-1 was a great asset.

Like the A-1 pilot, the Air Force A-7D pilot was well protected by armor around the cockpit areas.

The A-7 did not have the loiter/endurance time of the A-1. The six[-]to[-]seven[-]hour on-station time of the A-1 could not be matched by the A-7 or any other fighter type aircraft for that matter.[29]

The first point, on the slow en route speed of the A-1, was mitigated somewhat by Air Force planning that relocated detachments of the 602nd FS, and the rest of the 1st ACS and 602nd, to Pleiku, Nha Trang, Udorn, and Nakhon Phenom. It was further negated by sending A-1s aloft to orbit in the vicinity of a ground operation and wait to be called in by a FAC.

The last point is correct, but only in part. All the A-7s had aerial-refueling capability that could extend the loiter/endurance time indefinitely, as will be demonstrated in the saga of the rescue of Bobbin 05 in 1972, described later in this volume.

The unknown A-1 author concludes with a two-paragraph comparison of all three aircraft in the CAS/SAR role:

The A-7 is a great machine and well suited for the interdiction type mission. Because of the high maneuvering and delivery speeds it was not the CAS/SAR aircraft needed. The A-7 could never have replaced the A-1 in the CAS/SAR role and, unfortunately, neither will the A-10. The A-10 should do well in the low-and-slow business but will not match all the qualities of the A-1.

The A-10/A-7 flyoff was a mismatch as the aircraft were designed to do different-type jobs. The A-10 is strictly close air support and the A-7 is a strike/interdiction aircraft. The A-7 is not a true close air support aircraft. Ask any Navy A-7 pilot. The A-7 and A-10 should complement each other, similar to the proposed F-15/F-16 roles. What is really needed is a mix of A-10s and A-7s for the CAS/SAR and interdiction roles. The F-15/F-16 would provide air superiority.[30]

The F-105 Thunderchief as an Attack Aircraft

The Republic F-105 was designed in the mid-1950s to meet Air Force requirements for a single-seat, supersonic, fighter-bomber aircraft to carry a nuclear weapon in low-level attack over long distances. Unlike its predecessors—the F-100 and F-104— it was not an adaptation of an air-to-air combat aircraft designed for air superiority. Republic Aviation started the F-105 in 1952 with designer Alexander Kartveli**a** (of P-47 **fame**) as a follow-on to its RF-84F Thunderflash, and the Air Force awarded Republic a contract in 1952 for 199 aircraft. That contract was greatly reduced, and in 1955 the F-105 was in a competition with the F-107 for a larger contract. The North American F-107 was originally designated the F-100B in 1953 but was greatly redesigned with a larger engine to carry a fuselage-mounted nuclear weapon. The F-105 won the competition and was first flown in 1955. It entered Air Force service in 1958.

The F-105 mounted the Pratt & Whitney J-75 engine of 14,300 lbs. thrust (26,500 in afterburner), which gave it a speed of Mach 2+. Ever since the P-47, Republic had a reputation for building heavy fighters, and at 53,000 pounds the F-105 was the heaviest fighter ever built up to that time (it was exceeded by the F-111). The weight and the small wing area gave it a very high wing loading, which the designers intended to give it stability at low altitude and lower drag at high altitudes. Maneuverability was a secondary consideration.[31]

The primary modifications of the F-105 were the F-105D and the F-105F/G Wild Weasel. The F-105D model added an improved radar, an all-weather fire control system, armor plate, terrain-avoidance radar, and expanded hardpoints to carry sixteen 500 lb. bombs. The F-105F was a two-seater version with a lengthened fuselage and dual controls. The F-105F was almost immediately modified to the EF-105 configuration (E = electronic warfare), the initial designation of the Wild Weasel / Defense Suppression aircraft that, when improved, became the F-105G. The Wild Weasel aircraft was equipped with radar-homing-and-warning gear, advanced electronic-warfare sensors, and the AGM-45 Shrike antiradiation missile. A total of 833 aircraft were produced.

In 1962, the Fighter Weapons Wing at Nellis AFB hosted a gunnery competition for Tactical Air Command. Aircraft participating were the F-100, F-104, and F-105 in a series of low-level simulated nuclear strikes, conventional bombing and strafing, and air-to-air firing on the aerial "Dart" target. The F-105 easily won the low-level event, did not do so well at dive-bombing, but totally lost the air-to-air segment, which was based on the elapsed time to hit the Dart. In fact, the aircraft was unique in that the pilot did not turn in the direction of the target but turned the *opposite* way to get into an advantageous firing position.[32] The weapons competition was won by Capt. Gene Toffler's F-104 of the 479th Tactical Fighter Wing at George AFB.

The commander of TAC at that time was Gen. Walter Sweeney, who had been transferred from Strategic Air Command in Gen. LeMay's attempt to "SACemsize" the other major air commands. When Gen. Sweeney was asked what he thought about the competition, he is reported to have said, "Nice event; the wrong airplane won!"

The F-105 Thunderchief in the War in the North

F-105s first engaged in the Vietnam War on a "temporary duty" status from the 18th Tactical Fighter Wing in Okinawa and the 6441st Tactical Fighter Wing, deployed from Yokota Air Base, Japan, to Korat Royal Thai Air Base, Thailand, in 1964. Their targets were in Laos. In early 1965, additional F-105 squadrons were deployed to Korat and Takhli. At the start of Operation Rolling Thunder in March 1965, large numbers of F-105Ds were shipped to these bases to participate in intense bombing missions.

One of those missions is described by Craig White, who flew F-105Ds out of Korat Air Base, Thailand, in October 1967. "The first time I saw the F-105 at Nellis, I was amazed how big it was. The cockpit was sixteen or seventeen feet off the ground, and you could easily walk under the wings without bending down."[33] After five missions over the southern portions of North Vietnam, White was number four in a strike force to attack Bac Mai airfield on the outskirts of Hanoi. He was carrying three 1,000 lb. bombs. After dropping off the KC-135 tanker, the flight headed into North Vietnam at 500 knots. "I don't remember if MiGs tapped us going in or not, but definitely remember the SAMs and intense AAA. When I rolled in to the target, the air below me was filled with small puffs of gray and black, and I thought it would be impossible to fly through that layer without being hit. But somehow, I did, and coming off target at 550 knots and 5 g, I climbed and 'jinked' and tried to find my flight for join up. . . . The expression 'There ain't no way to live through 100 [missions] became clear."[34]

The Air Force would lose 397 F-105s and 446 F-4s over Vietnam and Laos.[35]

Another one of the most famous (infamous) targets of the aircraft was the Thanh Hoa bridge. The story is best told by Stephen Coonts and Barrett Tillman in *Dragon's Jaw: An Epic Story of Courage and Tenacity in Vietnam*.[36]

F-4 Phantom II

The F-4 would turn out to be one of the most remarkable multipurpose fighters in the history of aviation. The original design was derived from the single-seat McDonnell Aircraft F3H Demon as a subsonic attack airplane because the Navy already had the F-8 Crusader for air superiority. McDonnell proposed the aircraft to the Navy in 1953 and received a contract for a mockup. Completed in 1954, the mockup contained eleven hardpoints to carry munitions. The Navy liked the design and ordered two prototypes of the YAH-1 in 1954. Six months later, in May 1955, Navy officers visited the factory with a completely different set of requirements—for a fleet air defense interceptor. The aircraft was to add a radar intercept officer and two GE J-79 engines and carry four Sparrow air-to-air radar-guided missiles. There was no requirement for a gun or for nuclear weapons. Two months later, the Navy ordered two XF4H-1 test aircraft and five YF4H-1 preproduction examples.

First flight was in May 1958, following which the aircraft won a head-to-head competition with the Vought XF8U-3 Crusader III. The Navy contracted for forty-five F4H-1A aircraft, and it performed launch-recovery tests from USS *Independence* in early 1960. The Navy ordered 649 F-4Bs, with the first squadron being VF-121 Pacemakers.

Secretary McNamara's push for a unified fighter resulted in a fly-off, called Operation Highspeed, with the Convair F-106 Delta Dart. Following the competition, the Air Force borrowed two F-4Bs, temporarily designating them F-110A "Spectre" in January 1962, and developed requirements for its own version. Continuing its emphasis on multipurpose aircraft, Air Force requirements specified both air-to-air and air-to-ground attack capability. When DoD unified designations in September 1962, the Navy version became the F-4B, and the Air Force model, the F-4C. The first F-4C flew on May 27, 1963, and exceeded Mach 2.

The Navy continued production of the Phantom II with models of the F-4J, F-4N, and F-4S, totaling 1,264 for Navy and Marine Corps squadrons. The Air Force employed the F-4C, F-4D, and RF-4C in combat and upgraded the F-4E with an internal 20 mm M-61 Gatling gun.[37] The F-4G was redesigned as Wild Weasel SAM Suppression aircraft. Total Air Force production was 2,874, with the aircraft continuing in service until 2016, fifty-eight years after the type's first flight. The aircraft was exported to nearly a dozen foreign countries.[38]

The F-4 Phantom II in the Vietnam War

Air Force F-4s were deployed to Ubon Royal Thai Air Base in Thailand in the summer of 1965, and others were deployed to Udorn, Thailand, and to Cam Rahn Bay in South Vietnam. One of the most famous units was the 8th Tactical Fighter Wing, Ubon, under the command of triple ace Col. Robin Olds. Olds developed and executed Operation Bolo in January 1967, which featured the destruction of seven MiG-21s with no F-4 losses.[39] (In a December 27, 2020, email to this author, author Barrett Tillman told a little-known anecdote about this: "The last one-on-one conversation I had with Robin Olds included Operation Bolo's origins. Beneath that red-meat exterior was an active, agile mind, and he explained how he adapted Hannibal's battle of encirclement [against the Romans] at Cannae into the third dimension.") As F-105 attrition increased, F-4 units performed more and more of the attack missions over the North, until finally in November 1970 the last F-105 unit was withdrawn from combat. Sixteen squadrons of F-4s were deployed permanently to Southeast Asia, and another seventeen served there on temporary assignments. At the time of Linebackers I and II, there were 353 of the aircraft based in Thailand.[40]

Next-Generation Navy Attack Aircraft Planning in the 1960s

By 1963, the Douglas A-1 was aged. And the A-4 was aging. A new attack aircraft was needed. One of the first decisions Robert McNamara made as John F. Kennedy's secretary of defense was to have the military services combine their efforts and develop a single tactical aircraft. The cost savings on such a joint program were expected by McNamara and the Office of the Secretary of Defense (OSD) to be substantial. McNamara's decision to initiate what became known as the TFX (tactical fighter experimental) program was communicated to the services through a memorandum from the director of defense research and engineering (DDR&E), Dr. Herbert F. York, dated February 14, 1961, only days after the inauguration of the new administration on January 20. The response of the Department of the Navy was strong in tone and quick in forming. The assistant secretary of the Navy for research and development, Dr. James H. Wakelin Jr., articulated the Navy position. His letter to OSD of March 9, 1961, not only marked the Navy's opposition to the TFX, but it targeted its opposition to the inability of the TFX to perform the attack/close-air-support mission. He firmly stated the Navy's need to develop a new, lightweight attack plane that eventually became the A-7:

The Navy considers that the TFX is not suitable for Navy use since it has little or no application to Navy or Marine missions. Further, the Army has indicated that the TFX will not meet the close-air-support requirements. The Navy has better aircraft of our purposes in being and in development.

The Navy is interested in RDT&E for light attack / close-air-support aircraft which would incorporate variable-sweep wing design and turbofan engines.

With regard to your referenced memorandum, I agree that the TFX program should be reoriented in order to provide a good light-attack

aircraft to meet the close-air-support requirements of the Army and Marines. We also have in mind interdiction, and reconnaissance—emphasis on limited war missions. In this respect, I commend to you the extensive experience of the Navy in developing light attack / strike / close-air-support aircraft (F-4J, A-4D, A-2F) and suggest that the Navy should be program manager for the RDT&E. program in the event that such a program were established.

I recommend:

Drop the TFX altogether.
Procure A-4D-5's now to meets the requirements of all services for early close air support under visual flight conditions.
Procure A-2F's [later to become the Grumman A-6 Intruder] now to meet all-weather close air support and interdiction.
Procure F-4H's [McDonnell Douglas Phantom II, later the F-4B] to meet the requirements for all services for air superiority aircraft, to be followed by the Eagle Missileer, when available.
[Omitted]
Expand the scope of the planned Navy-Marine RDT&E program, to develop a follow-on light attack aircraft for the A-4D-5, to include Army participation and/or Air Force participation

I am concerned about what appears to be overemphasis on a single aircraft configuration to meet these vital operational national Defense requirements.[41]

The recipients of Secretary Wakelin's letter in OSD almost universally rejected its advice, underestimated the Navy's opposition to the TFX program, and disregarded what turned out to be almost a prescient prophecy. The Navy, for its part, waited patiently and, when the time was right, canceled the Navy version of the TFX, withdrew their financial support from the program, and began development of the F-14.

The "follow-on light attack aircraft" that Secretary Wakelin referred to was in the preliminary stages of "concept formulation" in 1961. It was called the VAX for "aircraft, light attack, experimental"), a much-lighter, smaller, and less costly aircraft that the TFX. The Navy was considering, as Wakelin noted, the use of a swing-wing configuration, powered by nonafterburning turbofan engines to give it the capability for long endurance.

The Navy was also considering in 1961 the alternative of improving the A-4 Skyhawk. There had been many proposals for improving the A-4, mainly by exchanging the nonafterburning turbojet engine for a turbofan, which was a more fuel-efficient engine. The OSD pressure to have the Navy participate in the TFX program brought this alternative to the surface once again. The internal dynamics of one of these proposals was observed by a Navy officer who was to play a major role in the development of the A-7, Capt. Robert F. Doss. Capt. Doss later described how the TFX affected the Navy's plans for the VAX and the proposal for an improved A-4:

> I was the junior member of a TFX-VAX strategy team hurriedly formed in the Chief of Naval Operations Office to deal with the TFX issue (spring 1961). My primary interest was attack—hence VAX. In examining the preliminary VAX requirement—small (under 30,000 pounds), twin-engined, high performance—it was obvious we were a long way away from getting it. There were no engines of the appropriate size in development. I didn't think we could wait. The A-4 as configured would not meet the demands of [the national strategy of] flexible response and conventional warfare. It was primarily a miniature nuclear bomber. It had three bomb racks, but two were always used for external fuel [tanks]. It was underpowered for multiple carriage of conventional ordnance. But there was no other airframe as good. I proposed a gap-filler, a big A-4, using the TF-30 engine which was planned for the Missileer [aircraft]. With encouragement from the team, I called Leo Devlin at Douglas. In one week we three together had a rather respectable airplane proposal for a great thrust-to-weight ratio, enough internal fuel, space for avionics, and five bomb racks. Leo estimated the cost to develop it to be under $25 million. This idea was set aside temporarily because it

would have interfered with the prospect of getting an all-new VAX.[42]

The military services extensively studied the need for the TFX in an attempt to reconcile their widely divergent military "requirements." Many studies were conducted by DDR&E, and Dr. York formed a Committee of Tactical Air to achieve consensus on the issues. However, in May 1961, he left the Department of Defense and was replaced by McNamara's choice of Dr. Harold Brown, who became the new director of DDR&E. The role of this OSD deputy as the technical agency responsive to Secretary McNamara was especially significant on the TFX because of the engineering and design complexity of the new aircraft. The position of DDR&E in the organizational hierarchy was stated by Mr. Blackburn, the head of its tactical air office, to the Congress as part of the TFX hearings in 1963:

> Neither [the Navy nor Air Force] Service wished for the [TFX] program to proceed as a joint development because it would deny them the privilege of autonomously developing their own weapon systems. Moreover, there was a feeling that it would be unwise to have the entire high-performance spectrum for the next generation of tactical aircraft covered by a single development effort. Finally, there was a strong feeling held by many of the "old pros" in the weapons development business that competition between the Air Force and the Navy tends to generate better more effective weapons. Throughout the exercise these points were never formally voiced by the services but rather they chose to argue against the bi-service development program on the grounds of technical infeasibility This was at a time when the Air Force was making a decision to buy into the Navy F-4H program and indeed to supplant much of the F-105 scheduled production with the Navy-developed F-4H. Thus, the outstanding Navy-developed aircraft will be the backbone of both the Air Force and Navy tactical airpower until the introduction of the TFX. The question of technical feasibility is indeed difficult to substantiate under these circumstances particularly when one contem-

plates the very much greater flexibility of operations offered by the incorporation of such TFX innovations as the variable-sweep wing and the afterburning turbofan engine.[43]

The discussion (and controversy) among DDR&E, the Air Force, and the Navy on the TFX issue continued throughout the spring and summer of 1961. The Committee on Tactical Air, chaired by DDR&E, rendered its report on May 19 and recommended the joint development of the TFX *and* a new light-attack aircraft. In the meantime, during the period March–May 1961, all funds for the Navy air-to-air Missileer program were canceled by OSD, and the Navy was faced with the possibility of having no new air defense fighter for the fleet, unless it was to be the TFX.

Several leaders of the Air Force agreed conceptually on having a joint fighter, especially those generals who had served in Strategic Air Command and were partial to large, heavy aircraft. Recall that at this time, starting in about 1958, Gen. LeMay consciously assigned SAC generals to positions in Tactical Air Command and other important USAF command positions. The Navy was less convinced, since its admirals were inclined by tradition to believe the fleet's requirements were unique.

The difficulty for even those who were dedicated to having a joint fighter was to identify what the technical details and specifications should be for the aircraft. On August 22, 1961, the two services reported to Secretary McNamara that it was not considered technically feasible to build a single TFX that would meet both the operational requirements of the Air Force for a long-range interdiction fighter and Navy for an air defense aircraft.

McNamara disagreed with the service chiefs, and he was determined to prevail over them. There was even the feeling among the uniformed personnel of the Pentagon that Robert McNamara and many on his staff did not respect the generals and admirals. This was true not only of the civilian officials in the Department of Defense, but also the White House, where John Kennedy voiced his concern over "military advice" in the wake of the April Bay of Pigs disaster.

A week later, on September 1, McNamara sent the secretaries of the Navy and Air Force a decision memo drafted by Blackburn of DDR&E:

My office has reviewed the most recent positions of the Air Force and Navy with regard to the joint development of a tactical fighter for both services. I believe that the development of a single aircraft of genuine tactical utility to both services in projected time frame is technically feasible.

A single aircraft for both the Air Force tactical mission and the Navy fleet air defense mission will be undertaken. The Air Force shall proceed with the development of such an aircraft.

Changes to the Air Force tactical version of the basic aircraft to achieve the Navy mission shall be held to a minimum.

If the expeditious resolution of differences in specifications cannot be achieved, these differences shall be delineated and presented to the Director of Defense Research and Engineering [Dr. Harold Brown] for solution.[44]

With the order to proceed, OSD entered the number of 876 aircraft in the procurement plan for the TFX, approximately two-thirds of which would go to the USAF and one-third to the Navy. The service chiefs had been overruled! The decision to overrule the Joint Chiefs of Staff, and the way the relationship was allowed to develop caused a controversy that dominated the Pentagon for a decade!

The development and production costs were expected to be high, perhaps as much as seven billion dollars. The cost of this joint program was to be a major factor in DoD decisions for the entire decade of the 1960s. This high cost was driven by two technological factors: (1) the time to design, develop, and test the variable-sweep wing and (2) the simultaneous design of the afterburning turbofan engines. One of the factors that was unknown at the time was the extremely costly development of a completely integrated electronic navigation and bombing system, primarily to meet the needs of the Air Force for a night/all-weather attack aircraft. The Navy already had the A-6 Intruder, so it was not at all interested in paying for a second expensive all-weather attack aircraft. At the beginning of the TFX program, this necessity to develop a technologically advanced bomb/nav system was unknown. It is an example of what later came to be called an "unknown unknown." The first unknown was the uncertainty of the extent of technical details to be solved, and the second unknown was the fact that the very *need* for the new system was unknown and could, therefore, could not be planned and budgeted for.

There was also an unknown interaction; if the TFX development and test phases took longer than planned, the fighter forces would need more aircraft on an interim basis until the TFX was available. If the TFX cost more money than expected, there possibly would be less money to spend on other programs. Of course, these are only some of the possibilities in the acquisition process; there were countless considerations that had to be addressed, and the alternatives were not simple nor easy to forecast.

The decisions in the fields of strategic and tactical aviation involved the selection of weapons systems and changes in the level of US force structure (the numbers of aircraft, personnel, and ships). The TFX began the most expensive acquisition program in the history of the DoD to that time. It would influence virtually every other major program in the Air Force and Navy. The Navy had witnessed the complete cancellation of the Missileer aircraft program. It was allowed to continue with concept formulation of a new attack aircraft, but the future of that program was most uncertain in 1961.

The OSD decisions on tactical fighters created a great deal of anguish and turbulence in the Air Force, Navy, and Marine Corps staffs. First, the production line of the F-105 was terminated. Second, the OSD staff arbitrarily inserted the subsonic A-4 in its place in the Air Force structure. Not long later, OSD became convinced of the merits of the Navy's Mach 2 F-4 Phantom II for the Air Force, and the F-4 replaced the OSD plans for the Air Force A-4.

As the year 1961 ended, the whole picture of the tactical air forces looked completely different than it did a year earlier, and much more controversial. The Navy was now committed to a joint program it never anticipated, or wanted. The Air Force had its newest tactical fighter program terminated (the F-105), and it was forced to buy large numbers of a Navy fighter. The entire decade of the 1960s in the field of tactical airpower would largely be measured by the programs started in 1961—the TFX, the F-4 and the new, unknown attack airplane. And the Vietnam War was yet to come.

The Competition for the TFX Contract

As Robert McNamara was completing his first year as secretary of defense, the Air Force was submitting its request for TFX proposals to industry. Six bids were returned with various proposals to develop the aircraft. The competition for the contract and the evaluation of their evaluation will be only briefly described here.[45]

The source selection process was considered from October 1961 to November 1962. There were four successive source selection evaluations. After the last one, the combined Air Force / Navy Source Selection Board voted unanimously to recommend the Boeing Company as the winner. On November 21, 1962, OSD formally announced that the General Dynamics–Grumman team had been awarded the contract to develop the TFX! The initial fee was $439 million. As the *TFX Decision* book described the source selection,

> McNamara had thus overruled the unanimous recommendation of one Colonel, four major generals, six lieutenant generals, five generals, five rear admirals, and one full admiral.[46]

The McNamara decision on the TFX is not the subject of this study, but it is impossible to omit the controversy for two reasons. First, the decision prompted a congressional investigation by Senator John McClennan, who was second-most-senior member of the Senate and chairman of the Senate Appropriations Committee. Congressional hearings were to dominate the defense environment intensely during the February–November 1963 period and to a lesser degree through the remaining seven years of the decade. Second, many of the participants in OSD and the military services on the TFX decision were to be the actors in decisions on the A-7 and

A-10 programs. The TFX (later the F-111), then, becomes an important part of the environment for the A-7, which in 1962 was wrapped up in Navy proposals for a new attack aircraft. The combination of those factors led to the Sea-Based Air Strike Forces Study and the design competition for the A-7.

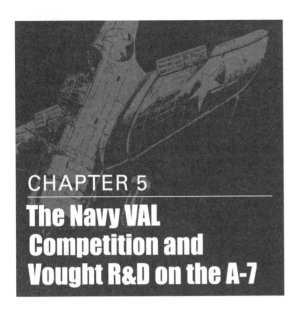

CHAPTER 5

The Navy VAL Competition and Vought R&D on the A-7

The Sea-Based Air Strike Forces Study

The Sea-Based Air Strike Forces Study was a Navy exploratory effort to develop parameters for an attack aircraft to replace the Douglas A-4. It was also in response to a 1962 McNamara request and was run from February to May 1963. The exercise was under the supervision of VAdm. William A. Schoech, the deputy chief of naval operations for air. A steering committee was established and was composed of Dr. Wakelin, Adm. Schoech, VAdm. Ulysses S. G. Grant Sharp (later admiral and commander of Pacific Command), Adm. John B. Colwell, and Maj. Gen. Edward W. Snedeker, USMC. RAdm. Turner E. Caldwell and Dr. Alain Enthoven were ex-officio members.[1] This technique of forming a study group composed mostly of naval and military officers with Systems Analysis representation was to be followed in other studies during the McNamara period. One of the economic principles that Enthoven was interested in emphasizing to the military services was that of "full system cost"—considering the multiyear operating costs as well as the investment costs on any new system. Dr. Enthoven described how he approached the Sea-Based Air Strike Forces Study and its relationship to developing a Navy requirement for a new attack aircraft.

I had felt my office played an important role in that original decision, and the role was in reviewing the Navy's program. We made the point to them that they should think about total system cost to do the job and not just procurement cost of the airplane. If you thought about total system cost you would see that, with the new engines technology would make available, it would be possible to build a plane that in terms of effectiveness relative to cost you would get a big increase. We criticized the A-4 as being not effective enough in relation to cost and encouraged the Navy to come in with a new plane with substantially more payload, although I remember the idea was in part to figure some comparatively cheap way to develop it.[2]

Enthoven was right in recognizing that advancing technology would produce scientific and engineering opportunities for improved performance, but he did not envision the revolutionary performance of digital technology in replacing the conventional analog bombing systems. That was in the not-too-distant future.

Dr. Enthoven did not attend all the meetings, so Mr. Russell Murray and Dr. Dieter Schwebs were the Systems Analysis representatives for most of the exercise. Russ Murray was an aeronautical engineer with a BS and MS from MIT, 1950. He had worked in the Missile Flight Test Analysis Division of Grumman Aircraft Engineering Corp. and spent eight years as the assistant chief of the company's Operations Analysis Group. At the time the study started, he was a consultant to Systems Analysis, but in April 1963 he joined Enthoven's staff full time.

All the Navy members of the study group were hand-picked, and the result was the first of the Navy's large studies in the 1960s directed specifically at systems analysis. The study consisted of two parts: first, an analysis of attack carrier force levels; second, an analysis of the composition of the carrier aircraft wing and the air group (types and numbers of aircraft). The second phase of the study was run by Capt. (later vice admiral) E. P. Aurand, the director of Air Weapon System Analysis staff of the deputy CNO (Air). The only option open to the Phase II Study Group was to change the attack aircraft of the carrier air wing. The panel investigated twenty-seven existing and future aircraft designs in the categories of light, medium, and heavy attack. In addition, fighter aircraft and five versions of VAX were priced and evaluated with 144 different combinations of avionics (aviation electronics), ordnance, and airframe programs. The general decision rule of the panel was to program a minimum number of fighters as well as reconnaissance, light-attack, all-weather-attack, electronic-countermeasures, and antisubmarine airplanes and helicopters to complete the mission and then to maximize the number of attack aircraft without endangering the defense of the fleet.[3]

The portion of the study concerned with the attack mission evaluated, among others, the Douglas A-4, the North American FJ Fury, a modified Grumman A-6, and a Vought Aeronautics proposal. The preliminary proposal from Vought was numbered V-463 and was a subsonic variant of their successful F-8 Crusader. V-463 evolved into the A-7 design. Due to its late submittal, the Vought proposal was not analyzed in as much detail as the others. The mechanics of the study were relatively simple, one of the most critical parameters being a substantial increase in the desired range over the version of the A-4 currently in service. At the long range selected (600–700 miles), it was determined that the aircraft carrier could stay beyond the range of the potential enemy's aircraft and yet cover close to 100 percent of the world's potential limited-war areas.[4] Supersonic flight was still not a requirement.

The cost-effectiveness analysis conducted by George Haering pointed out that the preferred aircraft designs available in 1965 would best be obtained by matching an existing airframe with the Pratt & Whitney TF-30 turbofan, which had been planned for the Missileer and was going into the TFX/F-111. Of the aircraft in the fleet, the analysis showed the F-4 and A-4 lacked the long range inherent to meet this requirement. The follow-on A-4 design submitted by Douglas (similar to the design proposed by Capt. Doss and Douglas's Leo Devlin in 1961) met the specified range, as did the North American FJ Fury design. These two aircraft were indistinguishable in performance, and both designs promised cost-effectiveness factors greater than any of the other proposals. The modified Grumman A-6 was recognizably high in cost. The Vought V-463, although in preliminary form, promised an aircraft of comparable effectiveness with only a slightly higher cost. The previously available VAX design was not favored because of the expected four to five years to develop this wholly new aircraft.

The Sea-Based Air Strike Study was also significant in that it restated the beliefs of naval aviators toward the supersonic/subsonic argument in general and the F-111 in particular. The VAX and the already-approved F-111 were proposals for supersonic, heavy-attack aircraft (in addition to the air defense mission of the F-111). The costs of the VAX were estimated to be so high relative to the A-4 that three light-attack aircraft could be purchased for the price of one VAX. If the supersonic aircraft did not promise a commensurate increase in effectiveness, the study group did not feel justified in recommending the VAX.

The summary and conclusions section of the study stated, "Supersonic performance does not appear to promise an order of magnitude decrease in vulnerability although there is conflicting opinion on this point. In any event, an enormous increase in A-4D-5/FJ-5 attrition would be required to make the F-111 superior in cost/effectiveness to the A-4D-5/FJ-5."[5] Haering ran a sensitivity test to determine the value of supersonic speed for the attack mission. He found the increased effectiveness would not be worth the added cost, and so he briefed it to Secretary McNamara. McNamara agreed.[6]

The result was that the Douglas-modified A-4 design and the North American FJ design tended to dominate the study, but their dominance was not overwhelming. The study group did not consider the small differential in cost-effectiveness (less than 10 percent) to be sufficient to warrant a recommendation to develop a new aircraft. This led the members of the group to include such factors as compatibility with the then-current equipment in the fleet, maintenance, experience, and flight simulators. When viewed in this light, there seemed little reason to recommend anything but another version of the lightweight, low-cost A-4, changed primarily to accommodate the TF-30 turbofan engine. Accordingly, the study recommended purchasing the modified Douglas A-4 with the TF-30.[7] The new light-attack aircraft was given the designation

VAL (fixed-wing, attack, light). The VAX proposal was delayed further and finally canceled altogether. However, since the performance of all current models of the A-4 had been halted by Systems Analysis, the Navy decided it needed the new VAL as soon as possible. Efforts were taken to speed the new proposal through the decision process in minimum time.

The study was signed by Adm. Anderson, the chief of naval operations, dated May 17, 1963, and was sent to Secretary McNamara.[8] *Aviation Week* reported that the Strike Panel Report had "smooth sailing" with OSD largely because of the early and continuous consultation with OSD representatives (Enthoven, Schwebs, and Murray).[9]

What did Systems Analysis think of the VAL, and what effect did the hiring of Russ Murray have on Systems Analysis? Although Murray's education had been in aeronautical engineering and not operations research, his experience with the operations research group at Grumman had convinced him of the importance of asking broader and more-penetrating questions than those engineers usually asked. He was particularly interested in the operation of the new Systems Analysis staff in DoD and was in general agreement with the application of economic principles to the acquisition process as enunciated by Alain Enthoven. Murray was becoming less influenced by his formal education than his working experience in the emerging discipline of systems analysis / operations research. Insight into his influence on the development of the A-7 can be seen from Alain Enthoven's description of him:

Russ Murray was really "Mr. Tactical Air" for the Systems Analysis office; that is, Russ and I tended to divide up the work based largely on background and prior interest. My own background had been in the strategic nuclear business, doing strategic studies for Rand [the corporation, the USAF's federally funded Research and Development Center in Santa Monica, California], and I knew something about and was very interested in NATO. So, I tended to do the nuclear and NATO business. Russ had a background in tactical air, so he was the leading person on tactical air questions in Systems Analysis and worked also on various

other General Purpose Forces questions (Army equipment, Navy ships, etc.).[10]

Since Murray had worked at Grumman, and Grumman had built many Navy attack and fighter aircraft, he was later asked if his studies there had influenced his thinking about the subsonic/supersonic argument for attack airplanes. He answered:

Yes, without a doubt. When you work for a company that's pushing subsonic product (the Grumman A-6 Intruder) there is a natural bias to favor a subsonic machine, and I don't know how much of that I suffered from. But it seemed to me that the arguments were pretty clear. We did some cost work[,] which is hard to do in the industry because your empirical base is so small. You can get data on your own airplanes (and even some of that is hard to get since some of the contract people do not want to tell the engineers what the costs are). We did some work that indicated the supersonic airplane on a cost-per-pound basis was running something like twice the cost of a subsonic airplane, not counting the avionics [which turned out to be a very expensive portion of the total cost, but this was not apparent in 1963]. We also tried to do some work on survivability, and it seemed to us the difference between penetration at .9 Mach and 1.2 Mach was small and might even be negative. . . . At any rate I had an *opinion* that the subsonic would be a better buy, that twice as many subsonic aircraft would be a better buy than half as many supersonic.[11]

The Secretary of Defense Approves the Navy Request to Begin VAL Development

Since Russ Murray had been in almost continuous consultation with the Navy Study Panel on the VAL, he was familiar with the Navy proposal and recommended approval to Enthoven. Dr. Enthoven carried the Systems Analysis recommendation to Secretary of Defense McNamara. McNamara approved the development proposal for the VAL aircraft, and that cleared the Navy to formalize a written military requirement and an RFP to industry. The "Requirement" document was dated the same day as the study was submitted,

May 17, 1963, indicating prior staff work. The speed and efficiency with which the requirement was drafted, approved, and implemented were largely due to the decision to hand-pick the right officers for the study. In particular, the group included Capt. John Fair, the assistant head of the Aviation Requirements Branch of the DCNO (Air). The document was titled the "Specific Operational Requirement (Follow-on Light Attack Aircraft)" and went from the Office of the CNO to the chief of the Bureau of Naval Weapons (BUWEPS), the organization that in 1966 became the current Naval Air Systems Command.[12]

The VAL Requirement

The operational requirement specified the need for a single-seat, single-engine attack aircraft using the Pratt & Whitney TF-30 turbofan. The requirement continued the need for a nuclear delivery as well as conventional weapons. It stated the importance of maintainability and simplicity of operation and stressed the criticality of funding. The principle was reaffirmed that the cost had to be held to a minimum, so large numbers could be bought within a limited budget. The avionics were to be simple: existing Navy equipment was to be used until such time as the Integrated Light Attack Avionics System (ILAAS), which had been under development for some time, was proven ready to be backfitted into the aircraft. The requirement was included for a two-seat version to be used as a trainer.[13]

Capt. Henry Suerstedt, who had been the program manager for the AD and a VA squadron commander in the 1950s, worked on the Sea-Based Air Strike Force Study and was appointed the VAL program manager in BUWEPS. Capt. Suerstedt's charter included this directive: "This program is of the highest priority and greatest importance; . . . He is hereby delegated full authority to direct and control (not simply coordinate) Bureau actions."[14]

Since Capt. Suerstadt had worked for many weeks on the study, he knew intimately what the Navy staff wanted in the VAL aircraft. He coordinated the bureau's activities, and preparations were quickly made to issue a formal RFP from industry. Within a week after the requirement had been received (May 15), the bureau issued a synopsis of the RFP to industry (May 24, 1963).

The decision to open the competition (and not just award a contract to Douglas for a modification of the A-4) was made at the highest levels of the Department of the Navy (the CNO and the Secretariat). There were at least three good reasons for opening the competition. First, the estimated performance of the modified Douglas A-4 had not dominated the Sea-Based Air Strike Force Study or any of the other Navy analyses. North American had done a great deal of work on their proposal to modify the FJ, to the point where it was competitive with the Douglas design. The Vought design was considered a possibility, but at this point it was far behind North American and Douglas.

Douglas was trying to market the improved A-4 as just another modification of the aircraft that could be awarded sole source. Douglas's competitors were, of course, trying to convince Admiral Schoech (DCNO Air) and other DoD officials that the TF-30 engine would require a major structural change to the small A-4 fuselage, so an entirely new aircraft would be required.[15]

The second reason for making the source selection competitive was the general belief that multiple entries would motivate industry to produce a better, higher-performance design at a somewhat lower price than if the award was made to a sole source.

The third reason for opening the competition was the political climate in Washington over weapons system acquisition contracts. The TFX had just gone through extensive source selection procedures, and the Air Force, OSD, and the Navy were in the midst of congressional hearings before the McClellan committee. The VAL contract looked like it was leading to the most important development in attack aviation for several years, and the whole decision-making process was working under the shadow of the TFX.

The exact location of the decision is uncertain at this late date, but several participants in the process indicated Admiral Schoech as the DCNO Air was a central figure. He was heard to remark that it would be politically infeasible to develop the VAL as a modification of the A-4.[16] However, there was widespread belief in industry and DoD that Douglas was the odds-on favorite to win the competition.

The formal RFP was published on June 29. Capt. Suerstedt coordinated the RFP and carefully outlined a series of penalties the contractor would incur if their proposal failed to meet certain guarantees of weight, speed, maintainability, and delivery date.

Bids on the VAL Contract

The VAL contract competition in the summer of 1963 was conducted amid the congressional controversy over the award of the TFX contract to General Dynamics of Fort Worth, Texas. The Chance Vought Corporation became a subsidiary of Ling-Temco-Vought in 1961 and was also a Texas company, located at the Dallas Naval Air Station in a leased Navy facility. The Vought Aeronautics Division had been awaiting the opportunity to bid on another Navy aircraft. By 1963, the Navy F-8 Crusader production line was being cut back and was scheduled to terminate in 1965, when the VAL program would be at its peak. The lead times and the lack of alternatives combined to induce LTV to make an all-out effort to win the VAL contract.

The position of LTV in the competition from the view of the Bureau of Naval Weapons was later related by a civilian aeronautical engineer with one of the most extraordinary reputations in the Navy Department: George Spangenberg. He had graduated from the University of Michigan in 1935 with a BS and an MS in aeronautical engineering. He first went to work for the Naval Aircraft Factory that same year, transferred to the Bureau of Naval Weapons in 1939, and had been involved in design work and aircraft competitions ever since. In 1970, his rank was roughly equivalent to a general officer, per Public Law 313, although there was no specific grade. He had been awarded the Distinguished Civilian Service Medal. Years later he pointed out the strong factor of company desire to win the competition and the contract.

> At that time Vought was running well behind because they hadn't faced up to the problem of doing an honest-to-goodness modification of their F-8. Their studies were built around the J-57 [engine in the F-100 and F-8] and it just did not have the range to do a good attack job. I think the Vought effort was the biggest surprise to the industry as a whole. We were aware of the amount of effort they were putting into it, and they needed the business badly.
>
> One thing that normally happens in this business is the guy that needs the business the worst ends up doing the best job. Sometimes the company that needs it the most gets the award, and then you read in the trade journals that they were awarded the contract *because* they needed the business. It is really the desire and amount of effort the contractor puts into the job.[17]

The tradition of building Navy aircraft at Vought extends as far back as 1917, when the company designed and flew a biplane known as the VE-7. In the 1920s and 1930s, the company produced five different attack aircraft and the O2U-1, the very first Corsair, in 1927. Various dive-bombers and torpedo bombers were produced before and during World War II, but the most famous and successful Vought creation was the F4U Corsair. Corsair pilots established an overall kill ratio of 11 to 1 over Japanese aircraft, and between 1943 and 1953 over 12,000 of the aircraft were produced.

The Navy tradition at Vought was more than a public-relations theme; there was a widespread feeling of "belonging" to the Navy that was reinforced by an unusually high percentage of former naval officers and pilots in the company's management. The president of Vought Aeronautics was Paul Thayer, a World War II Navy ace and formerly an experimental test pilot with the firm.[18]

The nominal decision to incur the substantial expense of identifying a proposal fund, devoting a large proposal team, and preparing a bid on the VAL competition was made by Paul Thayer but was agreed to by James Ling, the chairman of the board of LTV, Inc. Conrad Lau, in concert with Sol Love, the head of the engineering department, set about to organize the company's effort. While LTV's engineering people were designing the proposal to be submitted to the Sea-Based Air Strike Force Study Group, the Marketing Division set about to convince the Navy decision-makers to open the competition to industry—or at least to those companies with aircraft in service that could be modified to the VAL mission. J. W. Lankford, a Navy commander and Dauntless dive-bomber pilot in World War II, worked directly for Conrad Lau at this time and handled much of the marketing activity along with John Allyn, the vice president of LTV's Washington office. Lankford spent about four days a week in Washington and made a major effort to convince Adm. Schoech that Douglas would have to extensively modify their aircraft to accept the larger TF-30 engine.[19] The thrust of the argument was that the opening of the competition would benefit the Navy as well as LTV, in providing a better, cheaper aircraft.

As soon as the RFP was announced, LTV formed a Blue Team and a Purple Team. The Blue Team worked on the LTV design, and the Purple Team forecast what the competitors would do. Sol Love was the program team director and had been associated for the preceding few years with attempts to adapt the F-8 Crusader to carry air-to-ground ordnance, in addition to its de-signed air-superiority mission. He described the competition from his viewpoint:

> In my judgment, the Navy did an excellent job in projecting what their requirements were with respect to carrier-based attack forces and justifying it to DoD.[20] . . . We took a look at it and decided there was one way to win the competition, and that was to optimize the [F-8] airplane for the attack role. With no supersonic requirements, radius, payload, cost, maintainability, and reliability were important. So, we set out to come up with an airplane that used as many common parts of the F-8 as we could. . . . We proposed to the Navy that we'd willing to take pre-negotiated penalties for failure to meet the performance guarantees.[21]

The magnitude of the LTV effort can be gauged from the internal publication *Light Attack Airplane (VA)L Primer*, which was written to summarize the LTV approach to writing the proposal and winning the award. Under a section called the "Name of the Game," it outlined the philosophy of LTV's development, the Navy requirements, the company risk, and the "Size of the Pot," which was estimated to be worth about $500 million to LTV for 600 aircraft.[22]

One of the sections is especially illuminating on the interaction of marketing with design:

> The V-463 design philosophy was established recognizing the existence of several basic facts:
>
> In order to be competitive, CV's [Chance Vought's] entry had to be a member of the F-8 family.
>
> The F-8 maintainability history has not been competitive with that of the strongest VAL competitor, the A4D.
>
> The A4D was the favored airplane for the VAL, was almost procured without a competition, and was the basis for a large part of the VAL type specification.
>
> A cost[-]effectiveness evaluation was to be made and the results of it utilized in the selection of the VAL winner.[23]

The design implications of this industry evaluation were the following:

- To preserve the F-8 family resemblance the V-463 must include at least: single, chin duct inlet; high wing with a planform of the F-8; low horizontal tail.

- It is not possible to compete in weight.

- Maintenance and turnaround character-istics must be greatly improved.

- Dollar cost and spotting factor (size on the aircraft carrier) are to be minimized.[24]

LTV stressed the "experienced, old-line Navy Team" in the proposal, and in the management proposal, LTV went on to discuss the backlog of each company, with the intent of showing how LTV's was the lowest in contract awards of the four competitors, which would ostensibly show how they could give the VAL development im-mediate and continued priority in R&D and production. LTV even went into the total military RDT&E and Prime Contractor awards from 1958 to 1962 by state and showed how Texas had only 6.1 percent in 1958, versus 23.6 percent for California (the home of Douglas Aircraft). In

1962, the balance had shifted further against Texas (3.5 percent) and for California (25 percent). The differences showed California had increased in awards by 41.9 percent in these four years, while Texas had *declined* by 29.9 percent.[25]

An internal LTV cost-effectiveness study influenced the following aspects of the LTV VAL 463 design:

1. Eight external bomb and rocket racks instead of six

2. 10,000 pounds of internal fuel instead of 6,500

   Analysis indicated superior cost-effectiveness would obtain from exceeding specified performance rather than by attempting to cut cost. The physical characteristics of the F-8E precluded extensive cost reduction.

The V-463 analysis showed it to be superior in close air support and multiple missions. However, the problem of commonality with the production F-8 proved to be a problem. When the pieces were laid out, counted, and put on the scale, the tally showed this:

Commonality between Vought's VAL Design and F-8		
Airframe	13.0%	By weight
Airplane systems	58.0%	By weight (component quantity)
Special support eq.	76.0%	Including government-furnished equipment (GFE)
Special support eq.	72.0%	Excluding GFE
Spares	13%	NA
Major tooling	7.6%	NA

Source: VAL Primer.

The proposal tried to put a positive face on the commonality issue:

Although most V-463 airframe parts will be new, their similarity to previously produced F-8 parts affords a kind of commonality not measurable in pounds or numbers of parts.[26]

By aircraft section, the count looked even worse:

Commonality by Aircraft Section			
Section	# Parts	% Identical	% Similar to F-8
Wing	6,543	0	96.0
Nose and midsection	7,663	0.1	98.0
Aft sec & tail	4,326	27.7	67.4

Source: VAL Primer, p. 5.1.2.

This problem of commonality between the V-463 proposal and the F-8, of which it was supposed to be only a modification, was never really resolved. The general subject of commonality was an issue that was to come up again over the 1969 Air Force–Navy modifications to the A-7B. LTV and industry apparently did not know it, but the decision-makers in the bureau and Navy headquarters had already acknowledged that the proposals would have very little production commonality with previous aircraft. The changes in the fuselage to accommodate the larger-diameter TF-30 engine would lead to changes in the wings to carry the heavier load, which, in turn, would require a more robust landing gear, for example, in an iterative process familiar to all aeronautical engineers. The issue is significant, however, because the lack of commonality was a factor in the A-7 congressional appropriations in January 1964, and it formed the basis for later Systems Analysis reservations about the aircraft in comparison with the known A-4.

The contractors had until August 12, 1963, to respond to the Navy's RFP with engineering and management data, and until September 3 with cost figures. Because of the short time period, the contractors were able to convince the Navy to postpone the request for a two-seater version of the aircraft. Four contractors submitted designs. The Douglas A-4F design showed an aircraft outwardly looking like the A-4D Skyhawk, but with wingspan, wing area, and a larger fuselage to hold the TF-30. It had a somewhat shorter range than the competitors on internal fuel but proposed to make up the difference with external tanks. The North American Aviation NA-295 was a modification of the FJ Fury but with a completely redesigned structure.

The Grumman G-12 entry was designed around the A-6 Intruder all-weather attack aircraft, but Grumman proposed to strip it of all the expensive avionics equipment and just manufacture the basic airframe. Even with this effort, the G-12 cost was about $2 million per aircraft. However, it used two J-52 nonturbofan engines instead of the suggested TF-30 power plant. In addition, the Grumman position was weakened by its recent award of part of the TFX contract as half of the General Dynamics / Grumman team.[27]

The Navy Evaluation

Proposals were received by the Bureau of Naval Weapons, which was located on the Washington Mall, just across the Potomac River from the Pentagon. There they were distributed to many offices, one of which was George Spangenberg's Evaluation Division. As director of the division, he organized and supervised the VAL evaluation.

The evaluation was conducted in a two-phase effort: the first runs were to pick the best aircraft design, and the second runs were to test whether the leading proposal would be cost-effective enough to warrant putting it into a new development program. In the first round, the designs were subjected to intensive analysis on their ability to perform three types of attack missions: (1) defense against an enemy air attack, (2) close air support of ground forces, and (3) isolation of the battlefield (interdiction). Instead of the normal ten mission/radius problems, the aircraft designs were evaluated on eighty-five different range/payload combinations, ostensibly to demonstrate to OSD the thoroughness of the Navy's evaluation methods.

George Spangenberg described the results of the design competition:

The way the competition ended up was that technically the North American and Vought

designs were very close from a capabilities standpoint. The capabilities of the North American and Vought designs were virtually the same, with the Douglas design being less capable. Then the cost of the Douglas design and the Vought design were the lowest. Vought had a substantial edge over North American in price.

So, the choice really became even; you took the greatest capability at the least cost. You really didn't have to do much analysis to see the way the thing was going to come out. I think those experienced in the art can really make the determination of what is the most cost-effective without going through all the elaborate process, when you have that clear a case.[28]

Since the best aircraft design was selected, the evaluation continued to determine the cost-effectiveness of the selected system compared with the A-4E, which was then in the fleet. At this time, the costs of the LTV V-463 proposal were about one million dollars per aircraft with the Douglas A-4F proposal, and the A-4E about $800,000.[29]

According to *Aviation Week*, the formal evaluation ended with two conclusions:

- When cost is not a factor, the relative effectiveness of all the designs is substantially superior to the A-4E. The Chance Vought design shades the North American on an overall basis, with both showing superiority to the Grumman and Douglas designs.

- When compared relatively on a fixed dollar expenditure basis, the Chance Vought design shows a clear advantage over the other designs and over the A-4E.[30]

The cost-effectiveness study showed the LTV design to be "clearly superior" to the A-4E. This having been decided, the evaluation was signed by the chief of the Bureau of Naval Weapons in November 1963 and sent to the CNO office, where it was distributed to OPNAV. The secretary of the Navy, Fred Korth, approved it on November 13, 1963, shortly before he resigned. The new secretary was to be Paul H. Nitze, who had been

McNamara's assistant secretary of defense for international security affairs. The VAL decision was in the meantime sent to OSD, where it was examined by Systems Analysis and DDR&E.

Russell Murray was the primary Systems Analysis representative assigned to monitor the evaluation, and his view of the process is enlightening. When asked how Systems Analysis viewed the Bureau of Naval Weapons recommendation, he said, "George Spangenberg did his usual, first-rate, excellent job on the competition."[31]

When asked if he respected Spangenberg's office, he responded philosophically:

It's the only one like it I've ever even heard of. He's just in a class by himself. He is extremely knowledgeable and absolutely the soul of integrity. Unfortunately, he got on McNamara's "list" for what he said about the F-111, but I've known George for a long time, and I have the highest respect for him. He is first rate from a technical sense and with a sense of integrity. He's done a great service for the country. As far an evaluating the competition, Systems Analysis was there really to sort of monitor what the evaluation was. Nobody in our shop was competent and nobody in DDR&E was competent to second-guess George on what the airplane was going to do and how much the contractors' estimates should be changed. From my point of view having known George for a long time, I figured that anything he said was the most knowledgeable, authoritative source on performance. I took that at face value.

Then we ran some relatively simple tests of the airplane to see if it lived up to what the Sea-Based Air Strike Forces Study had claimed such an airplane would. We presented that to McNamara, and he agreed. He said, "Okay, let's go ahead with it," and that was that.[32]

Alain Enthoven commented about the significance of his own position on this decision.

That illustrated a point that I thought was important about the kinds of things the Systems Analysis Office did, and that is, we were not always just looking for a cheaper airplane per copy; we were looking for something that could

do the overall job cheaper, which might mean a more capable plane. . . . We thought the A-7 was a good idea, and the approvals went through pretty quickly. It was clearly a step in the direction we thought we wanted to go.[33]

DDR&E was not intimately involved with the selection of the prime contractor for the VAL (now designated the A-7). The director of DDR&E, Dr. Harold Brown, was consulted on the selection of LTV and approved, but he reported at the time that since high technology was not involved, DDR&E really had no large role.[34] DDR&E did, however, approve an exception to the normal acquisition process by waiving the need for a "contract definition" phase. This sped up the process of getting the development phase underway.

The speed with which the A-7 proposal went through the OSD decision-making process is indicative of the priority and merit attached to it by the Navy and OSD. There is no set time for each of the four phases of the "system acquisition cycle." But concept formulation can nominally take twelve to eighteen months or more, and contract definition often required another twelve to thirteen months to complete. Although there was no formal contract definition phase in DoD in 1962, the TFX took fourteen months (October 1961–November 1962) to complete it, amid extensive controversy.

By way of contrast, the A-7 decision process took only six months from the establishment of the Navy requirement until the contractor was selected. Although DDR&E had just announced in 1963 that the requirement for all future weapons systems was to include a contract definition phase, contract definition on the A-7 was waived by OSD. The reasoning given was that the intent of contract definition had been met by the Navy's evaluation and selection process.

This establishment of the process by which the original A-7 requirement was developed by the Navy, approved by Systems Analysis, designed and marketed by LTV, evaluated by BUWEPS, and agreed to by the Navy and OSD is important to the understanding of the rest of this program. Even though Systems Analysis played a continuing role in many aspects of the process, in retrospect, the decision-making process was little changed from those used by the Navy for years.[35] What *was* different was its dramatic departure from virtually every other acquisition program in DOD, including those with relatively minor modifications. One such study showed that the *average* time to obtain Systems Analysis approval of just a *modification* of a system was 144 days!

Although there was a strong consensus at the time, specific individuals in Systems Analysis later disputed the validity of the A-7/LTV competition because of the commonality issue, and the philosophy of a low cost-per-ton-mile criterion being the basis for the competition. One of those individuals was Mr. Pierre Sprey, who joined System Analysis in 1965. Sprey vehemently objected to the cost-per-ton-mile criterion. He was of the opinion that it might have been better to let Douglas build another modification of the A-4 than to open up the competition. Sprey discussed the relationship of Systems Analysis to the decision to proceed with the VAL/A-7 and the criterion for the decision:

Looking back on what we knew at the that time, it is not clear that we should have built any airplane at all. Looking back to the alternative of improving the A-4 versus building a new airplane, it is not clear there was any justification whatsoever to build a new airplane rather than keep building better A-4s. The Douglas entry [in the VAL competition] was *not* a modified A-4, but a totally new airplane. The Navy convinced Russ Murray that we needed a new airplane, and that the appropriate criterion was to build the cheapest possible airplane to deliver a large amount [of ordnance] ton-miles. This is a *dreadful* criterion for building airplanes, I might add, and it's evident by the way the airplane has turned out. *I think that is the most important institutional factor, because Russ Murray was directly responsible for convincing Alain Enthoven, who, in turn, was directly responsible for convincing McNamara to go ahead with the whole thing.* And, of course, the way they got Enthoven and McNamara to go ahead with this whole idea that they were going to have a *cheap* airplane. That whole competition was just going to be cost to deliver ton-miles. . . . One of the chief reasons LTV did win the

competition was their sales [marketing] department made a basic decision at the beginning of the whole program that they were going to make the airplane look like the F-8, and that was done specifically and intentionally to "buy-in" to the program. The fact of the matter is the A-7 is a totally new airplane, requires completely new tooling, and cannot be built on an F-8 production line.[36]

Once the decision to buy the A-7 was made inside DoD, the question arose of how many were to be purchased. This led Systems Analysis almost immediately to ask, "Why shouldn't the Air Force be in on this?"[37] This philosophy of "jointness" continued. Before this question could be answered, Congress would have to give its approval for funding the A-7 program. With the backing of DDR&E, Systems Analysis, and the Navy Secretariat, Secretary McNamara signed the Navy request to approve the procurement of the A-7 on November 23, 1963, and sent it to the Congress.

Congress Approves the Program

When the A-7 came before the Congress in November 1963, it was in the form of a Department of Defense request to reprogram $34,400,000 of fiscal year 1964 funds.[38] Until the reprogramming was approved, the A-7 program was limited to using unobligated funds from the RDT&E account, and that already had used some $15 million from the DoD emergency funds.[39] The way the law was written, the two Armed Services Committees and the two Appropriations Committees had fifteen days to object to the reprogramming action. If they did not notify the secretary of defense to the contrary in that time period, it could be assumed they approved, and the program could go ahead. If the A-7/VAL request had been the only reprogramming action to come before Congress that year, that is probably what would have happened. However, in the preceding two years, over $7.4 billion dollars had been reprogrammed in the DoD accounts for aircraft, missiles, ships and R&D alone.[40] Congress, feeling the loss of its control over its constitutional appropriation function, held up the A-7 request until hearings could be held on the request in January 1964.[41]

German Halberstadt CL.II, 1916.
National Museum of the US Air Force

Brig. Gen. Billy Mitchell in his Vought VE-7 Bluebird, 1920. *Public domain*

Curtiss A-3 Falcon attack aircraft, 1926. *National Museum of the US Air Force*

Brig. Gen. Billy Mitchell beside his command plane, 1918.
National Museum of the US Air Force

Curtiss A-8 Army ground attack aircraft, 1932. *National Museum of the US Air Force*

Curtiss A-12 Shrike dropping parachutist, 1933. *National Museum of the US Air Force*

Northrop XA-13 Gamma with multiple bomb racks, 1933. *National Museum of the US Air Force*

Northrop A-17 airborne, 1934. *National Museum of the US Air Force*

Curtiss A-18 Shrike II, 1937. *National Museum of the US Air Force*

Douglas A-20G Havoc medium bomber, 1944. *National Archives and Records Administration*

Martin B-26 Marauder with D-day markings, 1944. *Air Force Historical Research Agency*

A-24B Banshee on ramp in Army Air Forces colors. *National Museum of the US Air Force*

A-24B Banshee in flight, Army Air Forces. *National Museum of the US Air Force*

North American B-25 Mitchell. *Air Force Historical Research Agency*

Soviet Ilyushin Il-2 Shturmovik

German Ju 87

North American A-36 Apache in North Africa, 140 combat missions, 1944. *National Archives and Records Administration*

Douglas B-26 Invader night attack aircraft in Korea, 1951. *National Archives and Records Administration*

Republic P-47 Thunderbolt Razorback. *National Archives and Records Administration*

De Havilland DH-4, 1918. *National Museum of the US Air Force*

De Havilland DH-4 in France, 1918. *Public domain*

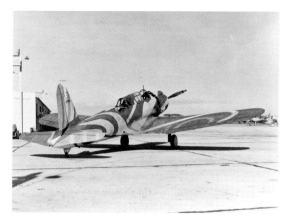

Vought SB2U Vindicator, 1930s. *Naval History and Heritage Command*

Martin BM torpedo bomber. *Naval History and Heritage Command*

Brewster XSB2A Buccaneer scout bomber. *Naval History and Heritage Command*

Douglas TBD-1 Devastator torpedo bomber. *Naval History and Heritage Command*

Northrop BT-1 bombing/torpedo. *Naval History and Heritage Command*

Douglas Dauntless SBD dive-bomber. *Courtesy of the artist Lucio Perinotto*

Martin T4M-1 approaching USS *Saratoga*, 1926. *Naval History and Heritage Command*

Grumman TBF Avenger, "Action in the Pacific." *Courtesy of the artist Peter Chilelli*

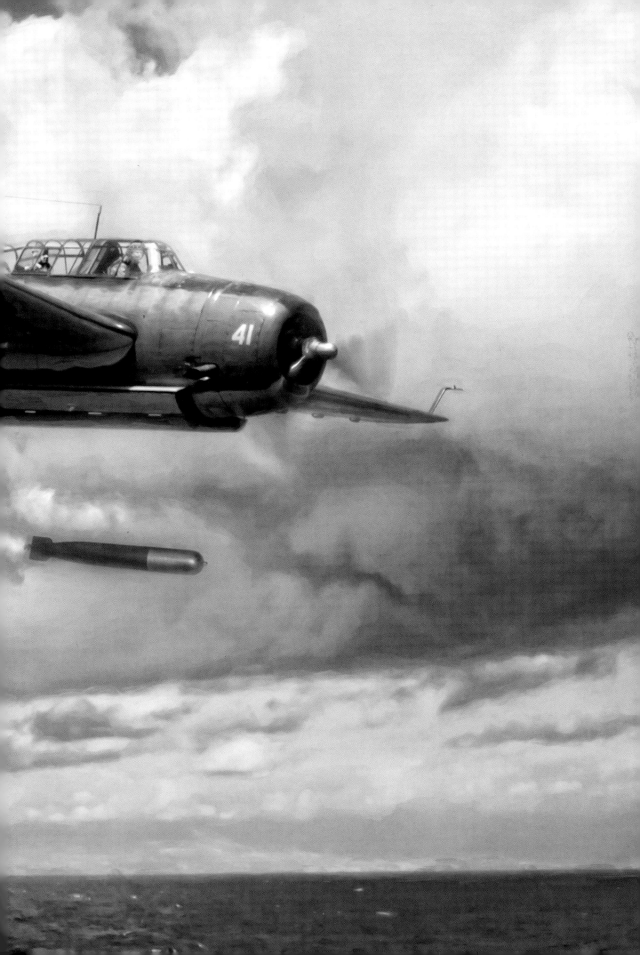

Chance Vought F4U Corsair, 1950. *Naval History and Heritage Command*

Curtiss SB2C Helldiver over China, 1945. *Naval History and Heritage Command*

Curtiss SB2C Helldiver over carrier, 1945. *Naval History and Heritage Command*

Douglas A3D Skywarrior, 1956. *Naval History and Heritage Command*

Douglas A4D-2 Skyhawk, 1957. *Naval History and Heritage Command*

B-26 Invader on mission over South Vietnam. 1963. *National Museum of the US Air Force*

Douglas AD Skyraider VA-702 in the Korean War, off USS *Boxer. Naval History and Heritage Command*

Grumman A-6 Intruder strike, North Vietnam. *Courtesy of Ed Beakley*

The author's Douglas A-1E SPAD, 1965. *National Museum of the US Air Force*

North American F-100F MISTY FASTFAC. *Courtesy of the artist David Tipps*

Republic F-105G Thunderchief "Wild Weasel." 561st Tactical Fighter Squadron, 1972. *National Museum of the US Air Force*

McDonnell Douglas F-4C refueling with bombs en route to North Vietnam. *National Museum of the US Air Force*

Vought A-7A Corsair II prototype test flight, 1965. *A-7 Corsair II Association*

A-7A showing steam ingestion on the catapult. *A-7 Corsair II Association*

The first Fleet A-7A departs the Vought factory in Dallas, bound for VA-174, the East Coast A-7 RAG. Don Ross standing in the cockpit. *A-7 Corsair II Association*

Dr. Harold Brown, secretary of the Air Force, 1965. *National Museum of the US Air Force*

Gen. John P. McConnell, chief of staff USAF, 1965. *Air Force Historical Research Agency*

Northrop F-5A with full bombload, 1965. *National Museum of the US Air Force*

A-7A on catapult for combat, VA-216 Barn Owls, 1967. *A-7 Corsair II Association*

Col. Robert E. Hails, Air Force A-7 deputy program manager, 1966. *National Museum of the US Air Force*

Navy combat division of three A-7s, 1972. *Courtesy of the artist Peter Chilelli*

A-7D Corsair II of the 354th Tactical Fighter Wing en route to North Vietnam target, 1972. *A-7 Corsair II Association*

A-7E of VA-147 aboard USS *Constellation*. *A-7 Corsair II Association*

Ca Chao petroleum-oil-lubricants Alpha strike results. *Courtesy of Ed Beakley*

Cockpit of the A-7H of the Hellenic air force, 1975. *Courtesy of Ed Beakley*

Heads-up-display (HUD) of the F/A-18. *Boeing Company*

Fairchild Republic A-10A. *National Archives and Records Administration*

F-35A Lightning II aircraft of the USAF. *National Museum of the US Air Force*

F/A-18C during Operation Desert Shield, 1990. *Naval History and Heritage Command*

Grumman F-14

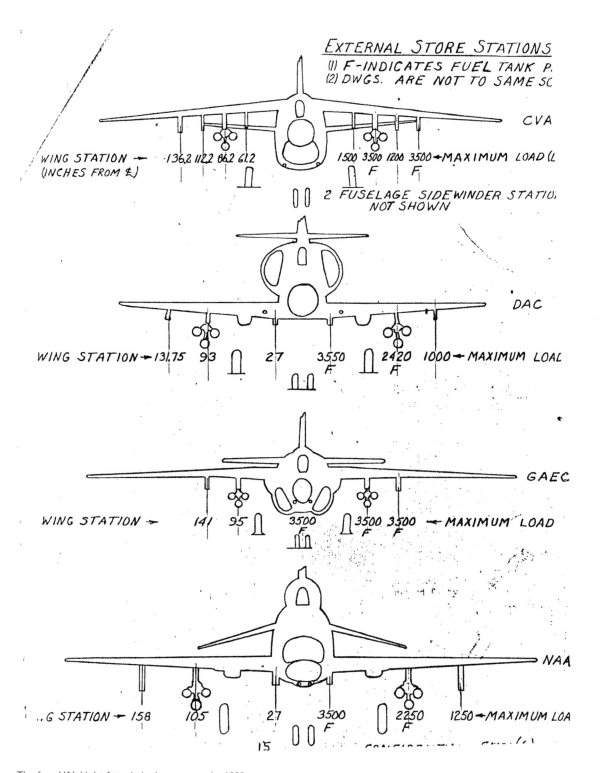

F-16 Fighting Falcon dropping bombs. *US Air Force*

Insight into this issue can be obtained from a House Report in 1965, after another Navy reprogramming request was received, this time on the Douglas TA-4E two-seat trainer. (The Navy had decided to defer the design of a two-seat TA-7 Corsair trainer and to proceed with the TA-4 version.) The House Report noted:

The reprogramming of the VAL and the TA-4E followed a similar pattern. Both programs were presented to the committee as modifications of existing aircraft in the Navy inventory. Both provided for an initial procurement of a few planes, but these relatively small buys opened the door to follow-on procurement of substantially greater quantities of aircraft.

The VAL was more than an ordinary reprogramming action in that [it] initiated development of a major weapons system involving future requirements of airplanes. The VAL procurement was limited to those design/manufacturers who had single[-]engine aircraft in the Navy inventory capable of incorporating a TF-30 turbo fan jet engine. Despite these limitations, the Navy insists that this was a competitive procurement. . . . The Navy presented the VAL as the modification of an aircraft already in the Navy inventory. However, Navy witnesses agreed that the modifications involved a new engine and changes to the fuselage, wing, and avionics.[42]

The intent of the Congress, especially the House Committee on Armed Services, which issued this report, is set forth in their recommendations:

The Secretary of Defense should issue appropriate instructions . . . to insure [sic] that:
 1. Each reprogramming proposal contains all information necessary for its complete and *objective* evaluation by congressional committees concerned.

 2. The reprogramming procedure will not be used as a vehicle to obscure or excuse confusion and delay in decision-making or result in avoidance of the safeguards of competitive bidding.

 3. The military departments will not be allowed to begin a major weapons development program through the reprogramming process."[43]

Although this particular reprogramming report was not written until 1965, these same arguments were heard over the VAL request. Nevertheless, the House Armed Services Committee approved the reprogramming request on January 15, 1964. Representative Otis G. Pike (D-NY), a frequent critic of Defense, opposed the program and was quoted as saying that the "Navy played games with Congress on this procurement. . . . The VAL program is designed to keep some production lines, which were about to be shut down this summer, in operation."[44] He said the VAL was not common with any F-8 version but would be a 90 percent new aircraft, and called it a "brand-new $2 billion program illegitimately conceived and dedicated to the proposition that members of Congress will vote for any military program because they would rather be called soft in the head than soft on Communism."[45] He then proposed an amendment to delete the Navy's A-7 appropriation of $171.5 million in the fiscal year 1965 DoD budget. His amendment was defeated by the House of Representatives on February 20, 1964.

LTV R&D on the A-7

Ling-Temco-Vought (LTV) was announced as the winner of the A-7 competition on February 11, and a fixed-price contract of $24,119,698 was negotiated for the initial R&D of the first three prototypes on March 19. The proposal and design work were conducted by the Vought Aeronautics Division in Dallas, Texas. At that time, the Navy was thinking about buying nearly a thousand A-7s at an average unit cost per weapons system (including support equipment and personnel costs) of $1.7 million.[46] Discounting the cost of government-furnished equipment (GFE) (such as the TF-30 engines, which the Navy would buy separately from Pratt & Whitney), the value of the contract to LTV was estimated to come close to one billion dollars. The Marines also had expressed an interest in buying the A-7 for their forces, but only the boldest optimist could have predicted the Air Force also would be getting the A-7. Meanwhile, and largely unseen by the Navy, developments in the Army and the Congress were beginning to influence Air Force thinking about the close-air-support mission.

LTV Vought Aeronautics Division

Chance Milton Vought learned to fly directly from the Wright brothers in 1910. Seven years later, he and a group of men established a company in Long Island City and built the VE-7 biplane. In 1919, they founded the Lewis and Vought Corporation. In 1922, Lt. V. C. Griffith made the first takeoff from USS *Langley* (CV-1) in the VE-7SF. Chance Vought built and sold the O2U-1 to the Navy, and he named it the "Vought Corsair."[47]

In 1963, Vought brought together the team of Russell Clark, Sol Love, William C., Schoolfield, Paul Hare, and others to transfer the work of the proposal team to the design of the prototypes.[48] Reportedly it was Sol Love who sold the firm on the concept of a Blue Team and Purple Team for the proposal and had a key role in the whole design and development process. Sol was a pilot, administrator, and executive vice president of the Vought Division. The chief designer was Russell Clark, who had designed the firm's F-8 Crusader. The F-8 had established an enviable record in the fleet as a gun-armed air superiority fighter that was easy to maintain. The characteristics of Clark's designs were sturdiness, maintainability, and load-carrying potential. As one colleague put it, designing "the most, best airplanes which do the job superlatively well but would never win a beauty contest."[49] Many pilots would disagree, since the F-8 had the look of a real gunfighter.

The design of V-463 followed the general planform of the F-8 but was shortened. It retained the F-8 canopy and intake-duct design, but the nose was blunted off to save carrier deck space. The fuselage was widened to contain large fuel tanks, and the aft section was uplifted to provide more deck clearance rotation on takeoff and landing. The wings supported three ordnance pylons on each side, and the wings folded just outside the outboard pylon. The vertical fin was chopped off to save hangar space, but this was later negated by the installation of an electronic-countermeasures antenna. One AIM-9 Sidewinder missile rail was installed on each side of the forward fuselage. The starboard side, just under the canopy rail, housed a retractable refueling probe. The cockpit was spacious. The engine was the Pratt & Whitney TF-30-P-6 turbofan, which was a bow toward commonality with the ill-fated Navy F-111. The engine was purchased by the Navy and provided to LTV as government-furnished equipment (GFE).[50]

Barely three months after the award of the development contract, in June 1964, LTV displayed a full-scale mockup of the A-7A with very real-looking bombs on six pylons and two AIM-9 Sidewinder air-to-air missiles on the two fuselage rails. Seven months later, on January 15, 1965, the engineering drawings were completed and prototype construction was begun. President Johnson had just ordered the bombing of North Vietnam in April 1965, so the company was urged to complete the test program as rapidly as possible to get the aircraft operational. Until then, the fleet was waging the war with the A-4 Skyhawk and the old A-1 as its attack aircraft.

First Flight, September 1965

The first aircraft was completed in early September, and taxi trials began on the twentieth. The taxi tests revealed minor problems with the hydraulic system and ejection seat, but these were corrected quickly. A week later, LTV test pilot John W. Konrad made the bird's first flight, on September 27, 1965, twenty-five days ahead of schedule. It was a short flight because just after liftoff from NAS Dallas, the aircraft began to buffet and shake with increasing speed. The chase pilot reported the horizontal tails were vibrating, and the trailing-edge flaps were shaking. Konrad immediately banked into a 90-degree/270-degree turn and landed downwind. No pieces came off, and no one was hurt. The ground crew found that the flap slot tunnels had become obstructed, which caused the flaps to vibrate in the "down" position. The flaps were repaired, and a second test hop was accomplished the same day. The second flight was over an hour and was a complete success.

Flight number 3 was the next day, this time with a full fuel load. The engineers discovered the "engine performance appears to reduce with increasing altitude"; this was the first indication that the aircraft might be underpowered. Flight 4, on September 29, confirmed the engine "rollback." The flight test crew worked on the engine issue while it continued the testing on an accelerated basis. Chief test pilot Konrad said this:

Eighteen days after its first flight, 15258 has been flown seventeen times and had achieved 43,000 feet, a Mach number of 1.025 in a dive and 530 knots level flight speed at 5,000 feet.[51]

Konrad continued:

Thirty-four days after the first flight, flight 36 was flown on a public demonstration of the A-7 Corsair. The aircraft was loaded with twelve 500 lb. bombs on the inboard and missile pylons and six 250 lb. bombs on the outer pylons. Two Sidewinders were also included on the fuselage. The demonstration consisted of low-altitude high-speed passes, 360-degree rolls achieving roll rates of approximately 160 degrees per second and simulated high-angle dive bombing.[52]

The Navy was reportedly very pleased with the aircraft and its performance:

Navy purchasing officials were impressed by the airplane's ease of access and its potential to be quickly returned to the air. Required by contract to demonstrate a maximum of no more than 11.5 maintenance man-hours per flight hour during the test and development program, Sol Love told the Press that this figure would be exceeded. The manufacturer exceeded every requirement of a contract imposing penalties for failure to meet specified goals, except that the A-7A, with its wing strengthened for carrier operations, was about 600 lbs. over design empty weight.[53]

In November 1965, only two months after first flight, the secretary of the Navy, Paul Nitze, announced the Navy would exercise the option for a fourth lot of 140 aircraft for $91 million. The first three lots had been for three, four, and thirty-five aircraft,[54] so this brought the production to 182.

By June 1966, eight aircraft had flown 750 hours in five hundred sorties. There were a few serious accidents, the first of which was with the prototype on March 23, 1966. Vought test pilot John Omvig took off at Edwards and was flying near China Lake when the aircraft developed engine trouble. Omvig ejected at low altitude but landed unhurt. The second occurred on August 18, near Cleburne, Texas, when Lt. Richard Birtwhistle's aircraft suffered a compressor stall, and he ejected safely. Ironically, the aircraft continued straight ahead and landed belly up in a farmer's field. Retrieved, it continued its life as a mockup.[55]

Navy Test and Evaluation at Patuxent River

With the company testing near its end, the Navy took delivery of several A-7A aircraft and began Navy Primary Evaluation (NPE) at Patuxent River, Maryland. NPE tests were also conducted at NAS Dallas, Edwards AFB, and the Naval Weapons Evaluation Center at Kirtland AFB. The aircraft performed admirably at most steps in the process. However, the A-7A was underpowered, and there were early reports that steam ingestion from the catapult could interfere with airflow through the intake duct, but it was not known how serious this situation could be. NAVAIR was anxious to determine the extent of this problem, so the issue was sent to the naval test pilots at Patuxent River. Lt. Brent Bennitt (later vice admiral) was one of those chosen to investigate the problem. Bennitt tells the following non–sea story.

The test was to determine if the steam ingestion issue was significant enough to cause the engine to lose power on takeoff and the duration of that thrust reduction. The test design required a maximum-weight takeoff with a heavy saturation of steam being fed into the intake. The season was winter at Pax River, with ceilings of 300 feet overcast. The test was delayed and delayed, but the unit was under pressure from higher headquarters to determine if this was a serious problem or not. The fleet was demanding an answer.

Finally, it was determined that if the weather was too bad to fly, the test could be conducted by an airfield catapult shot, followed by a high-speed, heavyweight abort down the 9,732-foot runway, with arresting gear at the end. Lt. Bennitt was detailed for the test, which was to include three cat shots and three runway decelerations. It was complicated because the angle of the catapult was several degrees off from the heading of the runway (incidentally, the Navy routinely did not install antiskid brakes on carrier aircraft). As he taxied onto the catapult, the sky was menacing but not raining. In his words:

The cat shot propelled the aircraft to 165 knots, followed by skidding around the angle to the runway, and, using the brakes to their maximum effect, the aircraft slowed down slightly and the hook caught the barrier as planned. Then I taxied back for the second shot, worrying a little about the heated brakes and warm tires. The second shot was the same acceleration, turn, and high-speed run down the runway. However, the third shot was a little more exciting. The cat shot was the same, the skid around the corner was hair-raising, but "bang"—one of the tires blew out! To counter the drag of the flat tire, I blew the other tire and was trying to use nosewheel steering to guide the aircraft to the center of the barrier. No luck. The aircraft veered off to the right, catching the wire near the right end, and the aircraft slowed but careened to the edge of the runway, stopping only feet from the concrete structure of the barrier housing.[56]

The test confirmed that steam ingestion was indeed causing a loss of thrust on takeoff. The result was that the Navy restricted the maximum ordnance load off the carriers' catapult.

Delivery to the Fleet

Cmdr. James C. Hill was the first fleet pilot to fly the A-7A when he visited Dallas on August 2, 1966. He was very pleased with the aircraft and announced on landing that "it was just we are looking for."[57] The Navy's Board of Inspections and Standards (BIS) tests began the next month, in September 1966 at Patuxent River and Kirtland AFB. Cmdr. Don Ross, commanding officer of VA-174, picked up the first fleet A-7A and delivered it to the East Coast Replacement Air Group (RAG) at Cecil Field on October 14.

Cmdr. Fred Hueber flew the seventh A-7A in its initial carrier qualification aboard USS *America* (CVA-66) on November 15, 1966.[58] Cmdr. Scott Smith of VA 122 delivered the West Coast RAG's first airplane to NAS Lemoore on December 10, while carrier qualifications were undergoing in the Atlantic. Carrier qualifications and initial pilot cadre training in the two RAGs continued through early 1967. Finally, the first squadron was ready to deploy. Cmdr. Hill led VA-147 with Air Force crews assigned, on board USS *Ranger* in September 1967 for the first combat deployment. Cmdr. Hill was the ideal leader for the first squadron. He had enlisted in the Navy in 1948, transferred to Aviation Cadets, won his gold wings, flew first with an antisubmarine squadron, then became an attack pilot in A-4 Skyhawks. The squadron's exploits are discussed in chapter 7.

The Navy A-7B

Meanwhile, LTV continued producing A-7As and developing the planned evolution to the next model, the A-7B. The "B" model was virtually the same as the "A," with the upgrade of the engine from the Pratt & Whitney TF-30-P-6 to the P-8 with 12,000 pounds of thrust. It also included variable-position flaps for improved slow-flight characteristics. The first flight of the A-7B was on February 6, 1968. Problems with the second-stage turbine plagued the first batch of fifty aircraft, and all the engines were rejected by the Navy. The problem proved difficult to resolve through 1968, and the first A-7B squadron deployment did not occur until January 1969. Delayed by a huge fire on board USS *Enterprise* (CVAN-65) en route in Hawaii, the two A-7B squadrons did not arrive on Yankee Station until April 1969. As A-7Bs were assigned to new squadrons for subsequent deployments, twenty-four A-7Bs were converted to two-seat TA-7Cs. These aircraft were used for testing and training new pilots in the RAGs and for indoctrination and instrument flights in operational squadrons.

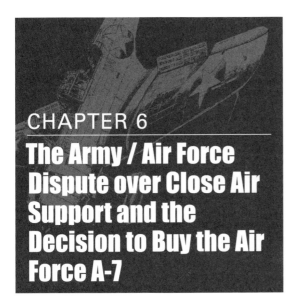

CHAPTER 6

The Army / Air Force Dispute over Close Air Support and the Decision to Buy the Air Force A-7

We hadn't bought an attack airplane since World War II.

—Lt. Gen. Gordon Graham

In the increasingly tense international environment of 1961, the Army made a move to capture from the Air Force the mission of providing close air support for US ground forces.[1] In June, the secretary of the Army, Elvis J. Stahr Jr., let it be known that he was not satisfied with the current "roles and missions" arrangement and desired to extend Army aviation into the performance of the close-air-support mission.[2] Rumors began flying that the Army could be getting as many as eleven squadrons of A-4 aircraft.[3]

Secretary McNamara had decided in October 1961 to buy the F-4 Phantom II for the Air Force rather than more F-105s. He did this to increase jointness, build up tactical forces, and provide a better capability for close air support. In later testimony before the House Armed Services Committee, McNamara said this:

I don't disagree a bit as to the implication that in the past, the Air Force has not directed sufficient attention to Close Air Support for the Army. I think this is absolutely correct. Quite frankly, that is why I ordered the Air Force to procure the F-4 and replace the F-105 with the F-4. It is a better airplane.[4]

The decision on the F-4 coincided with a previous memorandum that McNamara sent to the secretaries of the Army and Air Force, directing the Air Force to study tactical airpower needs and composition of forces. In this memo he referred to a previous letter in which he had expressed a tentative decision that the Air Force should have a large force of tactical aircraft, and that *it should include a specialized close air support aircraft.*[5]

Secretary of the Air Force Eugene Zuckert promptly answered with a request for an increase in the number of tactical fighter wings and recommended the future purchase of a new multipurpose fighter.[6] Within three days, Secretary of the Army Stahr forwarded his comments on Zuckert's memo and stated the Army position *against* multipurpose aircraft. He noted the Army needed "Close Air Support aircraft of a proper type" that would be "under a system of operational control which makes them responsive to Army needs."[7] In addition, Secretary Stahr attached a list of desirable characteristics for close-air-support aircraft. These included (1) rapid response, (2) extensive loiter time, (3) operations at night and in bad weather, and (4) *accurate* delivery of mixed ordnance. (Among these characteristics, the qualities of "extensive loiter time" and "accurate delivery" of ordnance were to play a major role in the Air Force decisions on the A-7.)

In addition to the "roles and missions" debate in the Pentagon, the doctrine of the Army was again pointed out by a 1961 study of close air support conducted by the Army Command and General Staff College, Fort Leavenworth, Kansas, at the request of the Continental Army Command. This study concluded the following:

- Joint Air Force / Army planning should be decentralized to field army–tactical air force level or to the independent corps.

- Enough close-air-support sorties should be allocated to meet requirements.

- Aircraft and units allocated to close air support should be under command of the Army commander.

- Air units designated to support close-air-support tasks must be equipped with aircraft designed for ground attack as a primary mission.[8]

Secretary McNamara was interested in how these doctrinal precepts would translate into requirements and hardware development. Indeed, it seemed at the time, and in retrospect, that he supported and encouraged this "roles and missions" debate since it coincided with his general belief of open and full discussion of all alternatives, supported by quantitative analysis. In a memorandum to Secretary of the Army Stahr in April 1962, he was critical of the Army's conservative approach to developing quantitative and qualitative requirements for new aircraft and helicopters:

I do not believe the Army has fully explored the opportunities offered by aeronautical technology for making a revolutionary break with traditional surface mobility means.[9]

He called for an innovative approach "conducted in an atmosphere divorced from" traditional viewpoints and past policies.[10]

The implications were clear: McNamara did not consider the current Army weapons and transport capability adequate, and he was challenging the Army to investigate the technological advances of helicopter and fixed-wing aircraft mobility. At the same time, McNamara sent another memo to Secretary Zuckert in which he threatened to remove the close air support mission from the Air Force unless it developed a better capability for Army support.[11]

The secretary of the Army in April 1962 orally gave the job of developing "an innovative approach" to Army requirements to the commanding general of the Continental Air Command, Gen. Herbert B. Powell. Powell directed the formation of the US Army Tactical Mobility Requirements Board, with Lt. Gen. Hamilton H. Howze as the chairman. Howze had been the first director of Army aviation and promptly selected seventeen Army generals, other officers, and civilians to form seven working groups.[12] Many of those selected had been identified with Army mobility in the past.

The Howze Board met in May–July 1962 and submitted its informal final report to the secretaries of the Army and Defense in August. The board's recommendations were centered on a broad expansion of Army aviation designed around a new type of army unit—the "air assault" division. The extent of this break with tradition can be measured by reference to the following figure.

Comparison of Howze Board Recommendations
with Previous Army Aircraft per Division

Date	Aircraft per division
1945	10
1957	50
1962	101
Howze Board	459 (air assault only)

Source: Armed Forces Journal, April 25, 1970, 19.

The 459 aircraft were composed of fixed-wing and helicopters and would perform the missions of observation, reconnaissance, air transport, and attack. The attack helicopters would be armed with antitank and antipersonnel weapons such as rockets and machine guns. In addition, the board specifically recommended Army development of a close-air-support fixed-wing aircraft!

The Howze Board also recommended a massive increase in the total number of Army aircraft from the approved level of 4,887 to 10,992 (for fiscal year 1967). The cost of the current level was $1,662 billion, while the Howze Board recommendations for six air assault divisions would cost $3,784 billion.[13] With the formation of any official committee with the scope and mandate given to the Howze Board, it was apparent that a major attack on or a significant modification of the roles and missions agreements of 1947 and 1958 could be expected.

The Air Force had already taken action to implement President Kennedy's decision to set up attack aircraft units in Vietnam. It also had responded promptly to the McNamara challenge in his April 1962 memo by standing up the Special Air Warfare Center at Hurlburt Field, Florida, to provide an increased tactical air capability in counterinsurgency situations. The new center was authorized a thousand men and two squadrons of converted T-28 trainers and B-26 medium bombers for use as close-air-support aircraft.

After informally reviewing the Howze report, the Air Force borrowed two A-1E (AD-5) Skyraiders from the Navy in August 1962 and assigned them to the Special Air Warfare Center. It also established the 2nd Air Division in October 1962 to manage air operations in Vietnam.

The Special Air Warfare Center evaluated the A-1s on the Eglin AFB gunnery ranges from August 1962 until January 1963. USAF then requested the permanent transfer of more A-1Es for training and combat. In the spring of 1963, twenty-five A-1Es were assigned to the 1st Special Operations Wing at Hurlburt for the purpose of training USAF pilots. These first A-1Es had controls only in the left seat, so in their training students the instructor pilots could only sit and watch . . . and yell![14]

In January 1963, the Army pressure increased with the wider dissemination of the Howze Board's recommendations. At the same time, the Air Force increased the manning of the Special Air Warfare Center from one thousand to three thousand and the aircraft from two to six squadrons. One of the most significant aspects of these six squadrons was that they were established *outside* what came to be known as the "tactical fighter force structure." Thus, increases in special air warfare aircraft did not have to come at the expense of F-100, F-4, F-105, or F-111 wings in the OSD-approved five-year DoD plan.

One month later, in February 1963, Secretary McNamara sent another memo to the secretaries of the Army and Air Force, requesting a new series of close air support studies, He noted the following:

Much of the impetus for the Army desire to provide its own close air support, reconnaissance and airlift stems from the low national priority which these missions have enjoyed in recent years. It seems appropriate that this situation will change.[15]

Before the next close-air-support boards could meet, however, another change in direction occurred. The Army chief of staff, Gen. Earle G. Wheeler, recommended in a memo to the secretary of the Army the development of a weapons helicopter. The Army secretary (now Cyrus R. Vance) denied the request, but in doing so he set in motion a program that was to have consequences far outside the bounds of the Army. Vance's memo of March 1963 read as follows:

After most careful review and consideration, I have concluded that the marginal military advantages represented in the attached proposal to initiate a weapons helicopter development program do not warrant the expenditure involved. Accordingly, the proposal as it now stands is disapproved.

At the same time, I want to emphasize that this disapproval is, in essence, a signal to lift the Army's sights in its efforts to provide aircraft for the helicopter escort role. We must now press forward with speed and imagination to develop a more advanced weapons system which will more nearly approximate the optimum.

In view of the foregoing, please have the Staff prepare recommendations aimed at reaching this objective.[16]

The direct result of this memo was the initiation of the Cheyenne (AH-56) program to build a 220-knot attack helicopter to compete for the close-air-support role.

Meanwhile in Vietnam, in July 1963, the Air Force organized the 34th Tactical Group at Bien Hoa Air Base, and in June 1964 the 1st Air Commando Squadron deployed to South Vietnam with forty-eight A-1Es Skyraiders. The pilots were "advisors" to the Vietnamese air force. In October, the Air Force activated the 602nd Fighter Squadron (Commando) and assigned them twenty-four of the A-1Es. The author joined the 602nd in January 1965.

The Army Tries to Interest the Air Force in the A-7

Secretary McNamara requested that the Army and Air Force each establish a close-air-support board, whose purpose was to "determine the Army's quantitative requirements for close air support in the FY 1965–1970 time period" and "to determine improvements that can be made in close air support effectiveness during this time period."[17]

The Army Close Air Support Board formally acknowledged that the Air Force was best qualified to determine what type of aircraft was best suited for close support. However, it stated there were qualities that the Army would like to see in any new weapon system. These features included the ability to carry 4,000 pounds of ordnance, take off from very short fields (1,000 feet in length), loiter for long periods of time, and incorporate all-weather navigation capability. However, the Army only requested "simple, visual target acquisition means." Specifically, the Army Report called for the Air Force to buy an aircraft like the Navy VAL (A-7).

The Air Force Board concluded that improvements were needed in three basic areas: improved survivability, improved target acquisition by the strike pilot (aided visual means), and development of low-level delivered munitions against hard, small targets (the Air Force was later to come under fire from Representative Pike because its conclusions did not include any mention of improving the response time to Army requests).[18]

The fall of 1963, when the close-air-support boards were submitting their reports, was also the time of the Navy VAL competition. By March 1964, the contract to develop the VAL/A-7 had been awarded to LTV. Gen. LeMay, the Air Force chief of staff, was under fire from OSD to at least look at the A-7 as the answer to the Army's complaints. LeMay replied tersely to the A-7 proposition before Congress: "I am very unenthusiastic" about the A-7. "Preliminary investigations that we have made so far indicate, cost-effective-ness-wise, it is not much good."[19]

At this point, Gen. Maxwell D. Taylor, chairman of the Joint Chiefs of Staff, wrote a memo to Secretary McNamara. In it he acknowledged the impasse of the two services on the limits on Army aviation. He recommended the limits be based on design and functional characteristics of the aircraft and be enforced by budgetary decisions on individual vehicles. Essentially, he abrogated the opportunity to provide military judgment and threw the decision over to the OSD-dominated PPBS system. Some of the distinguishing characteristics of Army aviation vehicles that he saw were that they were

- comparatively short range, low performance, independent of prepared airfields

- not designed or equipped to penetrate hostile airspace

- able to carry weapons for self-defense or to conduct their primary mission[20]

The memo was received by the Army chief of staff and with minor changes to the draft by the CNO. However, it drew the ire of Gen. LeMay, the Air Force chief of staff, who wrote a strong rebuttal: "Army and Air Force Responsibilities Regarding the Use of Aerial Vehicles":

Essentially, the fundamental issues reflected in CM-1356-64 evolve from differing Service philosophies on the proper use of aviation. The intrinsic question which these issues pose is whether a single Service requires, in the context of the Unified Command concept, all of the resources necessary to wage war in both the land and air media. The Army position reflects the philosophy that possession of all organic means, including air resources, is necessary for prompt and sustained combat on the ground. . . . In contrast, the Air Force position is based on the premise that no one Service can realistically obtain all the resources needed to fight a war and should not attempt to do so by substantially extending its primary combat functions into other operational media. Each Service contributed the particular forces for which it is expert, and collectively theses forces form a unified, mutually supporting combat team. Specifically, the Chairman's memorandum delineates Army and Air Force responsibilities regarding the use of aerial vehicles in a manner which would provide the basis for development and employment of two separate but parallel tactical air capabilities for support of land combat. . . . The functional alignments prescribed by CM-1356-64 constitute an unnecessarily arbitrary assignment of responsibilities for aviation which ignores the essential considerations of operational and cost-effectiveness. . . . I envision an arrangement which consists of interdependent elements:

- The Air Force would provide, equip, and operate all aerial vehicles required by the Army.

- The Army would revise its organizational plans and arrangements as required to transfer to the Air Force all of its aerial vehicles and associated facilities and personnel.[21]

DDR&E Expresses an Interest in the A-7 for the Air Force

Not only were the Joint Chiefs of Staff unable to agree on the limits of Army aviation, the civilian appointees in OSD were equally at a loss to decide the issue. The director of defense research and engineering, Dr. Harold Brown, wrote McNamara on June 1, 1964, following LeMay's memo. He noted that the Army and Air Force Close Air Support Boards were in fundamental disagreement, and it appeared to him that they could *not* be made compatible by quantitative analysis. Brown indicated that his thoughts were basically that the multipurpose aircraft had advantages, but that there were limits on its utility, and that, at some point, a lower-cost aircraft might improve the quality of the mixed force. He said that this ratio where a lower-cost aircraft might be valuable could be around a 3:1 figure compared to the F-111A.[22]

Dr. Brown was very perceptive of the nature of the differences between the Army and the Air Force over the full range of issues under the general rubric of close air support. Being a physicist by education and training, he developed a feeling for the significance of professional doctrine in the debate over centralized versus decentralized control. He began a later interview by expanding on his memo, predicting that the differences of the Army and Air Force on this issue were not going to be reconcilable by quantitative analysis.

I never really changed my mind about that. It was really an argument between two doctrines. One was that the Army commander had to have control of whatever impacts on him just as he does on his artillery. The Air Force argument is that air is a unity. I'm afraid that neither of these is terribly convincing by itself. The argument, which from the Air Force point of view I always found most convincing, the command ought to be determined on the basis of range, and that the range of the aircraft was 600 miles. And it shouldn't be at the disposal of anybody who didn't control that much of the front. If you give it to the Army, by that time it is already up to such a high level in the Army that it is no good to a guy who's calling in the close air support. To put it at Field Army level is really no better to the battalion commander than to give it to the Air Force. He doesn't really know the difference. The Army headquarters may know the difference, but he [the battalion commander] doesn't know the difference. That's why in the end we always argued, "Give it to the theater commander; he's the man who really is best able to balance demands between elements 600 miles apart." There's nobody in the Army who can, or in the Air Force either.[23]

Although there had been efforts by the Army and OSD Systems Analysis to get the Air Force to look closely at subsonic aircraft for the close-air-support role, Dr. Brown's memo seemed to signify a change in the organizational alignment of decision-making. Until then, DDR&E had not been particularly involved in close air support aircraft issues. After this memo the environment became increasingly receptive to change on this issue. The change was not revolutionary, but incremental. Many individuals in the decision process did not change at all, and Air Force doctrine remained where it consistently had been since the late 1930s—opposed to specialized aircraft for close air support. The major difference expressed in Brown's memo was to move from doctrinal justifications to more-practical rules, based on the technical characteristic of range, and some acceptable ratio of multipurpose to special-purpose aircraft. In 1964–1965, the A-7 repeatedly was nominated as a candidate for purchase by the Air Force.

Air Force Air Battle Analysis

The Air Force in 1964 assigned the director of plans a special assistant for analysis and force plans. This group began to develop analysis techniques for evaluating weapons systems.[24] This office was to run two computer studies that would be of special significance to the A-7 program.

The pressures on the Air Force to reexamine its requirement for close air support were accumulating from the Howze Board's recommendations, the formation of the 11th Air Assault Division, the Army initiation of the attack helicopter program, and Dr. Brown's memo of June 1, 1964. In addition, Systems Analysis was encouraging the Air Force to look at the A-7, and they specifically requested a study of alternative mixes of tactical aircraft during the summer of 1964.

The Bohn Study

By direction of Gen. LeMay, the Directorate of Plans ran a study from August to December 1964 called *Force Options for Tactical Air*. It was begun with the formation of a formal Headquarters USAF Study Group on August 17. With Lt. Col. John W. Bohn as the project officer, the study became known as the "Bohn Study." The basic approach was to review different tactical-force alternatives with various numbers of F-111s, F-105s, and F-4s *and* to include an evaluation of a mix of lower-cost airplanes. The aircraft nominated for the role of lower-cost designs were hypothetical versions of the Northrop F-5 Freedom Fighter (a single-seat version of the T-38 trainer) and the LTV A-7. At that time the costs of the F-5 were estimated to be about $700,000 a copy, and the A-7 was slightly over one million.[25]

Lt. Col. John Boyd, a tactical fighter pilot and instructor at the USAF Fighter Weapons School, Nellis Air Force Base, Nevada, conceptualized a theory called "energy maneuverability."[26] Boyd was a bigger-than-life, cigar-smoking, loud-mouthed fighter pilot. His theory, which became famous, was named "the OODA loop" for Observe, Orient, Decide, Act. The Boyd methodology was adapted for the Bohn Study.

Since the A-7 had already been nominated by some members of Systems Analysis for possible Air Force purchase, there was at least the implicit belief that the A-7 was more than a hypothetical input. Alain Enthoven expressed Systems Analysis' intentions at this time:

> We asked the Air Force to do studies of alternative force mixes, and we in Systems Analysis were

definitely trying to encourage the Air Force to buy the A-7. Why were we trying to do that? Because, first of all, we believed that for the kind of wars the tactical air forces were likely to fight that the A-7 would simply be substantially better. It would have longer range and better payload, and the payload could be translated into all sorts of things. . . . It would be a lot more effective in relation to cost, and in fact, there was even good reason to believe that it was just *more effective*, that a subsonic design would be positively advantageous because it would be more maneuverable; you could have better [steeper] dive angle for bombing[,] which would mean more accuracy and less vulnerability.[27]

The differences between the A-7 and the F-5 were pronounced, but their characteristics were not strictly comparable. The turbofan engine and large fuel capacity of the A-7 gave it great advantages in range and loiter time. With six wing pylons and two fuselage pylons, it could carry a varied, 15,000-pound load of ordnance. The F-5 was generally limited to about 3,000 pounds of ordnance over a short range. Thus, if the decision criterion was a low cost per ton-mile, the A-7 showed a competitive advantage. On the other hand, the twin engines of the F-5 and its small size gave it a high degree of survivability against enemy fighters and ground fire. Its speed gave it definite advantages in air-to-air combat with enemy fighters.[28] The F-5 was supersonic and multipurpose and thus consistent with Air Force doctrine and pilot preferences.

The conclusions of the Bohn Study were that the addition of a lower-cost aircraft would improve the overall effectiveness of the force. Although this study did not specifically choose the F-5 as the winner of the competition, the consensus was that the study could be used to justify a recommendation for F-5s.[29]

The Bohn Study was verbally presented to many officials within the Air Force, up to and including Secretary Zuckert. The study was also briefed to Systems Analysis staffers, Murray, Enthoven, and others. Russ Murray's evaluation of the Bohn Study's conclusions is significant because he was the Systems Analysis director for tactical air programs:

In the first one [the Bohn Study] the Air Force's predilection for supersonic airplanes just came through everything. One of the airplanes that they wanted was the F-5 for an attack airplane. I think this was just generally the feeling of the Air Staff that we should have a supersonic aircraft, and the idea was to look for a little less expensive airplane. They didn't want something big like the F-111 because they already had that.[30]

Systems Analysis was still interested in getting the Air Force to buy the A-7, and Enthoven and Murray recommended that the Air Force run another study, this time with wider participation.

The result was a memorandum from Secretary McNamara to Secretary Zuckert on January 7, 1965, requesting the Air Force conduct another study of tactical aircraft in production and "optimized for close air support."[31] McNamara discussed the need to replace the A-1 Skyraider, in use with the Special Air Warfare Center and in Vietnam. He noted that the supply of Skyraiders was extremely limited and that a new attack aircraft was badly needed for the Air Force, with an "initial operational capability" by 1967. This criterion, he added, indicated that it had to be "acceptable" for the [twenty-four-wing] structure of the tactical fighter force. He stated the use of the new attack aircraft should be considered assuming air superiority or air cover "in all cases." He specifically suggested the consideration of the A-7, the A-6 Intruder, the F-5, or similar types.[32] The first response to McNamara's memo was an Air Force request for two wings of F-5s. The memorandum was routed to Systems Analysis and never answered.

The Army Starts to Develop a Close-Air-Support Helicopter

The Army, on August 1, 1964, issued an open request to the aerospace industry for proposals to build a two-place, compound helicopter with a top speed of 220 miles per hour. The program was called the Advanced Aerial Fire Support System (AAFSS/AH-56) and nicknamed the Cheyenne. It was viewed by Air Force planners as a direct threat to USAF supremacy in the close-air-support mission.[33] The implicit threat

was that if the Air Force did not design or buy a specialized close-air-support aircraft, OSD could justify a redistribution of budgetary allocations to the Army.

Gen. McConnell Becomes USAF Chief of Staff

Gen. John P. McConnell succeeded Gen. LeMay as the Air Force chief of staff on February 1, 1965. The general was a West Point graduate in the Class of 1932 and had flown fighters as a young lieutenant. His most recent assignments were with Strategic Air Command.

Col. Howard Fish, of the Office of Analysis and Force Plans, prepared comments for the Air Force argument to counter the Systems Analysis critique of the Bohn Study. The arguments were then presented in a high-level meeting of Air Force and OSD officials, including Alain Enthoven and Dr. Brown. The results of that meeting were not conclusive regarding the Bohn Study, but a consensus was obtained that a follow-on study would be conducted. The USAF request for F-5s would be held in abeyance until the impending study was complete.

The secretary of defense and OSD were still not convinced the Air Force was making a full effort to develop a true close-air-support capability as envisioned in the national strategy of flexible response.[34] They were, on the other hand, becoming more impressed with recent Army developments. Having followed the Howze Board's recommendations, with the subsequent formation of the 11th Air Assault Division, McNamara was increasingly receptive to Army requests for more helicopters and aviation assets. As a specific example, he approved the redesignation of the 11th Air Assault Division as the 1st Cavalry Division (Airmobile).[35]

The growing US involvement in Vietnam during the spring and summer of 1965 was undoubtedly a factor. In February 1965, there were only 23,000 Americans in South Vietnam. By June there were 51,000, July saw 70,000, and by the end of 1965 the total reached 181,000.[36] The new 1st Cavalry Division was one of the first division-size American units sent to Vietnam that summer.[37]

The Origin of the A-10

With the implicit OSD disapproval of the request for F-5s, and the growing Army pressure, the Air Force was having its alternatives limited. In May, Gen. McConnell sent a formal request to Secretary Zuckert recommending the development of a new attack aircraft. He cited the Bohn Study and its conclusion that within a fixed budget, a mix of lower-cost aircraft with F-4s and F-111s would be more cost-effective than the currently approved five-year force structure. He recognized the attractive features of the A-7 as stated in the study (low cost, high payload), but wondered about its slow speed in a hostile air environment. Accordingly, he recommended R&D for a program of a close-air-support-optimized aircraft, with the source selection by December 1966. The secretary forwarded the memo to the secretary of defense.

The Position of Tactical Air Command

Tactical Air Command (TAC) held a position that was quite clear. TAC pilots wanted more F-4s and F-105s, not A-7s or F-5s. But TAC was being lobbied by Systems Analysis with proposals for the A-7. As Lt. Gen. Gordon Graham, the TAC director of operations, described it:

> In December 1964, Vic Heyman, who was one of the exponents of the A-7 in Systems Analysis, told me personally that we were going to be given that airplane, and I laughed at him. In fact, I didn't really know what it was. That spring of 1965, we got the first specific piece of paper that said, "We are considering giving you the A-7."[38]

The secretary of defense was still dissatisfied with the studies on the close air support issue; his displeasure was expressed by the OSD comptroller, Charles Hitch, who had led the Economics analysis shop at the Rand Corporation from 1948 to 1960 and was assistant secretary of defense between 1961 and 1965. "I just don't think anybody had thought this problem through and come up with the answer for the airplane or mix of airplanes for the whole range of missions which must be performed." He said, "It's a hard problem" because of the mission variety, and "until recently" there has been little combat experience with aircraft in a counterinsurgency situation.[39]

There was a shift in the Systems Analysis section of the comptroller's office after the Bohn Study. An analyst named Patrick J. Parker moved from Navy Tactical Air to head the all-service Tactical Air office. Parker (a GS-16, roughly equivalent to a one-star general) then worked directly for Russell Murray (GS-18, equivalent to a three-star general/admiral), who headed General Purpose Programs. Dr. Heyman noted, "Pat Parker came from the Center for Naval Analysis to Systems Analysis, so he had 'salt water' in his veins and kept the Air Force's nose to the attack business."[40]

The Joint OSD / Air Force Computer Effort: The Fish Study

The study's formal title was the *Joint Air Forces / OSD FX Effort*, but it was widely called "the Fish Study" because Col. Fish was selected to head the Study Group's Air Force Secretariat. One of the methods of the planners was to agree on the inputs and methodology so that there would be no disagreement on the results. The study was conducted amid increasing tension over Vietnam: the deployment of the 1st Cavalry Division and other Army units; increased casualties in Vietnam; the lack of perceived success in the Rolling Thunder campaign on the North, which had begun in March 1965; and the congressional pressure represented by the Pike hearings.

A Policy Group and Steering Group supervised the study. There was a Coordinating and Control Group with four Air Force colonels and three civilian officials. Col. Fish's Secretariat consisted primarily of Air Force officers with some Rand Corporation assistance. The study began with a meeting attended by the four members of the Policy Group on June 4 and ran during the summer and into the late fall of 1965. From the start, the requirement for a lower-cost aircraft had been established: the purpose of this study was "to define the characteristics and select a lower[-]cost aircraft for the tactical fighter force."[41]

Supervision of the Fish Study[42]	
Policy Group	**Organization**
Dr. Harold Brown	DDR&E
Dr. Alain C. Enthoven	OSD Systems Analysis
Lt. Gen. K. K. Compton	DCS / Plans & Operations
Lt. Gen. James Ferguson	DCS / Research & Development
Steering Group	**Organization**
Maj. Gen. Arthur C. Agan	Director of Plans
Maj. Gen. Jack Catton	Director of Operational Requirements
Maj. Gen. Gordon M. Graham	Director of Operations, TAC Hq.
Dr. Thomas P. Cheatham	DDR&E
Mr. Russell Murray	Systems Analysis, Director, GP Programs

Source: DCS / Plans and Operations, Joint Air Forces / OSD Effort, Vol. III, November 1, 1965.

The candidates for the study included the A-7, F-5, A-6, and CL-901, and a stripped F-4. The CL-901 was a version of the Lockheed F-104 that had won the Tactical Air Command Fighter Weapons Meet in the fall of 1962. The stripped F-4 was a McDonnell proposal for a cheaper version of the F-4 Phantom II without avionics. In addition, the study eventually included an improved air-to-air fighter to compensate for a lack of such capability in the lower-cost attack aircraft. This additional entry was represented by proposals for a modified F-4 with an internal 20 mm gun and was called the TSF, for tactical strike fighter. This modification later became the F-4E and was an almost constant companion, with influence on the development of the A-7.[43] With the insistence of the Air Staff and TAC, the study also examined the requirement for a completely new air superiority fighter to meet the expected worldwide threat beyond 1975, ten years hence. This model was known as the FX and eventually became the F-15.

The model used in the Fish Study was a theater-wide war game with essentially the same methodology as the Bohn Study—an evaluation of air-to-air engagements using energy maneuverability to compare aircraft. Then, simulated close-air-support and interdiction missions were run with various bombloads at various distances. Throughout the simulation the inputs had to be approved by the several committees before they could be put into the computers. There was also an attempt to specify the hardness or softness of the data by classifying it according to four categories in an input data matrix: (1) test data, (2) analysis, (3) rationale—"reasonable, logical processes which try to reflect operational, real-life factors, and for which no test or analytically-derived data is available," and (4) hard data.[44]

The capability of each aircraft was figured by using the average number of sorties required to "nominally" destroy each target and the probability of each raid being successful. The cost of each airplane was obtained, and the relative cost-effectiveness of each one was determined.

The characteristics of the A-7 inserted into the computers included the basic Navy A-7A but added a low-cost afterburner to the engine to increase its thrust and improve the total performance of the airplane.[45] (The A-7A was known to be underpowered, with the high gross weight and limited thrust of the TF-30 turbofan. This became more significant when the Air Force later was deciding on a new engine for the aircraft.) The CL-901 was exceptionally fast but lacked both the excellent radar of the F-4 and the long range and heavy payload of the A-7. The study boiled down to another evaluation of the stripped-down F-4 versus the A-7 and F-5, although the F-4 was recognized as being more expensive, even in a stripped-down version.

The supervision of the study was a critical factor since the elaborate hierarchy had been established to approve the inputs. The Policy Group (Brown, Enthoven, Compton, Ferguson) met only twice and generally deferred to their respective subordinates in the Steering Group.[46] The Steering Group (Agan, Catton, Graham, Cheatam, Murray) was intimately involved in the study. The significance of the group and its method of operation were later described by Col. Fish:

Really and truly the Steering Group made the policy, and the Secretariat did the work. We [the Secretariat] prepared briefings and went to the Steering Group [and] sat in session as long as eight and nine hours—and these are pretty high-level guys—eight and nine hours as a session, taking briefings and giving me instructions then to go ahead and make another excursion of this or that sort.[47]

There is an important point lodged in this description of the computer study. By the accounts of everyone interviewed, the methodology was *extremely* complex—so complex that it taxed the abilities of the study members to comprehend it. It should be remembered that this was one of the first attempts to model the air-to-air battle *and* to link it to the air-to-ground situation. The study was a major education for the personnel involved, especially the Steering Group.[48] The difficulty of the Steering Group's job was primarily due to two factors: first, the stakes were very high. The decision they were participating in would affect the Air Force for decades. Second, the level of technical expertise required to understand the computer model was very sophisticated. It was extremely difficult to determine the effect of an input factor on the output of the computer. The magnitude of the problem for the Steering Group was indicated by Russ Murray:

The activity I can remember best is sitting in Harold Brown's conference room, day after day having these meetings with generals and DDR&E. We would have these great discussions. Then the Air Force computer was just going like mad; it was grinding out pages and pages of data. They build this gigantic model which simulated a whole air war. Then the Energy Maneuverability guys were in there attempting to show how a given difference in energy maneuverability would translate into a difference in kill probability.

There was a lot of this [discussion] going on, and I didn't feel we were getting to any particular conclusion. Naturally, Systems Analysis was pushing for an A-7 or an airplane like that. By pushing I mean we were there to see that it at least got a fair shake. The

calculations were not done by us; they were done by the Air Force. But the Air Force model was [extremely complex]. . . . I spend some time running through these pages and pages of data, and I can still recall a couple of things that came out of this war. We had a situation where the F-4 was just shooting down everything in sight! It was wonderful what the F-4 could do.

It was so complicated that nobody could figure out really what was going on in the model; that was the problem. It was a gigantic set-up that put forth reams and reams of data, and there wasn't anybody that could analyze the thing and understand it.[49]

Thus, the Steering Group had been appointed because of the importance of having interorganizational approval of the process, yet the complexity of the model challenged the supervisors' abilities to understand the workings of this new decision-making instrument. The TAC representative, Lt. Gen. Graham, agreed the model was very complex. This exemplifies a classic management problem: the supervision of highly complex, technical work being done by specialists from a level that must, by its very nature, be generalist oriented.

The Secretariat, led by Col. Fish, could not have helped but be pleased by the outcome of the F-4's performance. For his part, Col. Fish had to reconcile many conflicting opinions and viewpoints. His was a potentially controversial position, but he was aided by a chance association. The Systems Analysis official working directly for Russ Murray on the study was Pat Parker. Parker's former association with Navy tactical air could have been a disruptive factor, had it not been for his objectivity and the fact that Parker and Fish had been classmates at the University of Chicago graduate school of business administration. There they had become acquainted, and that respect carried over into the Study Group.[50]

Col. Fish held the central position of monitoring the computer runs and preparing the many briefings for the supervising groups. As the study continued into September and then October, a feeling of urgency pervaded the atmosphere. "Budget season" in Washington was approaching, and many officials were hoping to convert the study's results into a budget request before the window for the annual Defense budget closed. But the complexity of the study resulted in delaying the deadline for its completion. Still, the study dragged on, while the organizations attempted to get a consensus on the inputs.

Two Defense Organizational Changes Affect Systems Analysis and DDR&E

Before the study could be completed, two significant personnel changes occurred. First, Charles J. Hitch, OSD comptroller, returned to private life, and Systems Analysis, which had been in the comptroller's office, was moved out and elevated. Secretary McNamara promoted Dr. Alain Enthoven to the separate organizational position of assistant secretary of defense (Systems Analysis). This move into one of OSD's seven assistant secretary positions prepared the way for an enlargement of the staff from about twenty-five professionals in 1965 to 125 in 1967.[51]

The second major change was the promotion of Dr. Brown from DDR&E to become the secretary of the Air Force. Two weeks after Dr. Enthoven was promoted, Air Force secretary Eugene M. Zuckert retired, leaving that position open. McNamara wasted no time in nominating Dr. Harold Brown to the position. Dr. Brown was a nuclear physicist and, at age thirty-eight, became the youngest Air Force secretary in history. He turned his DDR&E position over to Dr. John S. Foster and assumed his new post on October 1, 1965.[52]

As secretary of the Air Force, one of Harold Brown's first actions was to send a memorandum to the secretary of defense on the progress of the Fish Study. In his memo of October 5, Brown stated that the initial computer runs were being reviewed, that additional sensitivity tests were being run, and that the results should assist in choosing among the competing aircraft. He stated, however, that the study would not say whether the tactical-force structure *should* be increased. That decision, he noted, must rest on a comparison of the effectiveness of an expanded force with the currently approved twenty-four wings of tactical fighters.[53] He attached a memo from the Policy Group.

The Policy Group memo stated that the "entire methodology, programming, costing, and input data for the model were thoroughly reviewed" by the Air Staff, DDR&E, and Systems Analysis. They cautioned that it was "not possible to obtain unqualified agreement on each input but in all cases, the matter as issue was resolved to a degree that all parties accepted the resultant position as a reasonable basis on which to proceed. . . . It is evident from the early results that a powerful tool has been developed for assisting in the determination of optimum tactical aircraft force mixes." They went on to say that the A-6 aircraft had been dropped because of its high cost and that additional analysis was needed to refine the result.[54]

As the study continued, it narrowed the field of candidate aircraft to the A-7, the F-5, and the F-4. Their costs and performance in the model were exhaustively compared among the various missions, and the Study Group prepared to draft its conclusions. Just as in the Bohn Study, the F-5 and A-7 each demonstrated an area of specialization. The F-5 was rated the better air-to-air fighter, while the A-7 could carry a larger bombload to a greater distance.

This capability of the A-7 for long range, which could be converted into long loiter time for close air support, was primarily due to its use of a technological innovation—the turbofan engine—and its larger internal fuel capacity. Another, more subtle factor was its large, relatively spacious fuselage (when compared to the tiny F-5). The combination presented to the research-and-development community an opportunity to incorporate in future models a variety of armament and avionics equipment to achieve greater firepower and accuracy in navigation and dive-bombing. This quality is generally referred to as "growth potential."

The many and varied qualities of the different aircraft were finally brought together by the Study Group, and the factors were arrayed for a decision. However, some of the factors in the study were especially prominent. Lt Gen Graham commented on how the study was concluded, and the salience of the A-7's cost:

Although that study never came out and said, "Buy the A-7," of course, it was used that way. I'll give you another very concrete and specific on why it came out the way it did. The single most important item in that Fish Study was the cost quote on the A-7.... (LTV and Systems Analysis validated the cost, the fly-away cost, at $1.4 million dollars a copy. This made the A-7 come shining because of the price. We had an exact price of the F-4 because of the history of production, but the A-7 was mushy enough that you could call it whatever you wanted and get away with it.... [LTV] people in furnishing the cost came up with this, and the Systems Analysis guys popped on that and insisted that it be used, although we in the panel objected to it because we knew what it involved.[55]

The price of the A-7 referred to by Lt. Gen. Graham was requested from LTV early in the study. In discussing the price, LTV personnel said they were asked for the production cost of the original A-7 after LTV had built a thousand aircraft for the Navy. The price LTV sent to OSD that was subsequently placed in the model was $1.2–1.3 million per aircraft.[56]

With the A-7s performance and its relatively low cost, it appeared to be a real contender. The case for the F-4, however, was strengthened by some aspects of the war game, and many officers (including several generals) thought the F-5 was the better aircraft. While the conclusions and recommendations of the study were being drafted and briefed through the Air Force Board structure, four external events were affecting the environment of the decision.

First, the intensity of the Vietnam War was increasing. The number of US servicemen in country had multiplied, and US units were coming into larger and larger battles with the Vietcong (VC) and the People's Army Vietnam (PAVN) regulars. One of the most significant battles was launched by a large PAVN battalion on the Special Forces camp at Plei Mei in the Highlands of II Corps on October 19, 1965.[57] During the six days that the camp was besieged, the Air Force and Navy flew 516 close-air-support-strike sorties, many at night.[58] The camp held. The commander

of the camp, Army colonel Harold M. Moore, said, "In my opinion, the Air Force has saved this camp ... air strikes outstanding. When the North Vietnamese withdrew to the northwest toward the Chu Phong Masstif on the Cambodian border, the 1st Cavalry Division attacked with two battalions that became heavily engaged. One of the battalions was ambushed, and the second barely survived. US losses were exceptionally heavy. Close air support was critical."

The second set of events was concerned with deployment of the first test squadron of F-5s to South Vietnam. They arrived from the US on October 23 and began flying close-air-support missions in the area around Saigon. This real-life experience with the aircraft immediately began to filter into Headquarters USAF, and several limitations of the F-5 became apparent, primarily its lack of range and load-carrying ability. *Aviation Week* reported the range of the F-5 was limited to 120 miles, while the ordnance load was limited to four 750 lb. bombs (3,000 pounds total).[59]

The First Flight of the A-7

The third event was the first flight of the A-7 at the Dallas plant of Ling-Temco-Vought. The chief test pilot, John Konrad, flew the aircraft for five minutes and again for one hour on September 27, 1965. This event was significant because it proved LTV was one month ahead of even its accelerated schedule in producing the aircraft, and it demonstrated the aircraft's technical feasibility.[60]

The fourth event was in the political process outside the Pentagon, in a set of congressional hearings on close air support by the Special Subcommittee on Tactical Air Support of the House Armed Services Committee under the chairmanship of Congressman Pike. These hearings were begun in September 1965 and ended on October 14, during the conclusive phase of the Fish Study. Representative Pike was critical of the Air Force performance in Vietnam, and he specifically charged the Air Force with neglecting to develop a specialized aircraft for close air support, a charge that he had made earlier and often. He requested testimony from several relatively junior officers and noncommissioned officers who had just returned from Vietnam.

One of these junior officers was an Air Force captain named Alan L. Rennick. Rennick personified the Vietnam version of the young, Air Force fighter pilot of the operations profession. He had flown over three hundred missions in Vietnam, most of them in the A-1E Skyraider. Representative Pike and the members of the committee were especially interested in getting Capt. Rennick's opinion on the need for a new attack aircraft. Rennick's testimony is important because officers in the Air Staff were also interested in what these pilots thought, on the basis of their combat experience. Rennick stated he liked the advantages of speed as represented by the F-100, which he had flown before going to Vietnam, but that the propeller-driven, slow A-1 had several advantages:

Mr. Ichord: "You have a pretty high opinion of the A-1E, even though it is a twenty-year old airplane, as Mr. Wilson put it."

Capt. Rennick: "Yes, sir. I think that in the given set of circumstances, that we have discussed, that it is doing a real fine job. And I don't—it is as good an airplane as we have in the inventory right now for a given set of circumstances."

Mr. Pike: "I can understand why it would drop more bombs [it had fifteen bomb racks]. Why is it more accurate?"

Capt. Rennick: "*Slower release speed*, sir. You can release your ordnance at a lower altitude and effect the recovery in much less distance. Therefore, you can release closer to the target."[61]

This point about the accuracy of the A-1 versus any other airplane because of its *slow* speed was a controversial issue because the committee and the press then openly questioned the Air force position on using multipurpose supersonic tactical fighters for close air support. The committee then asked Rennick what specific qualities a new attack plane should have. He replied as follows:

Capt. Rennick: "Well, I think that any new airplane that we develop specifically for close air support should have a good, large capacity to carry ordnance. It should have a long loiter time and be able to respond rapidly. I would think that these three things would be the most important."[62]

Rennick's testimony came close to specifying the decision criteria for the Fish Study, in addition to the fact that the hearings were an external factor to the decision process.

The Air Force Decision on the A-7

All these factors began to come together in late October 1965 as the Air Force, in conjunction with OSD, prepared to decide on the results of the Fish Study. The Air Staff was split in its opinions. Col. Fish later explained the differences. He answered as follows:

Oh, yes. I think the best way to point that out was the fact that . . . DCS/R&D, including its Requirements [office] was absolutely convinced that we had to continue to press for a multipurpose, supersonic airplane that was the F-5. The Operations people were heavily and strongly for continuing in the supersonic business. Our Requirements people were that way, and the TAC people were that way. But when we finished all of our simulations, I would say the Requirements people . . . had come around very strongly to the fact that it made sense to have some small part of the force able to carry large loads of bombs, like the A-7 showed up in the studies. You couldn't have a *whole lot* of the force doing that, but you would always have some portion of it doing that, close air support.

The Plans position was that we wanted a *decision*! Here's an interesting thing. The Plans positions was that we wanted an airplane that we could put into that force structure and get on with the problem. My immediate boss in those days was [Brig.] Gen. [R. D.] Reinbold, although I worked for [Maj.] Gen. Agan on this problem. Brig. Gen. Reinbold said to me, "I don't care which airplane you all come up with, but your principal job—and you haven't done anything if you don't do it—we need a decision for this next budget cycle which starts really in December. If we're going to do something, we have to have a decision in November." So, the Plans position was whichever airplane comes out best, that's the one we want, but we want a decision.[63]

Finally, the results of the study came into focus. The Secretariat initially pointed out that it thought a stripped-down F-4 would be the best vehicle, but this was not considered feasible because of production schedules and other [unexplained] reasons. Then Col. Fish wrote a paper, circulated it to Generals Agan, Catton, and Graham, in which he said, "Let's buy the A-7 and put bigger engines and a gun in the F-4 to fill in for an air-to-air fighting capability in the near term to compensate for the fact that the A-7 would not have air-to-air fighting capability, and start a crash development program for the FX, the F-15—a superior air-to-air fighting aircraft that would be able to withstand the enemy threat in 1975 plus twenty percent."[64] This paper was not meant to be a recommendation, but only for use as a discussion topic. It did not meet with universal approval, but it formed the basis for what was to follow.

Col. Fish described the events leading up to the critical decision point on November 5, 1965.

I thought it would be better if we didn't come up with "Buy the A-7" or "Buy the F-5." One night about two in the morning I said the way we should present this thing is to list all the characteristics in two columns and say, "Buy the A-7 if you believe these things," and "Buy the F-5 if you believe in these things." Because even within my own group there was a division of opinion as to what we should do; there was no consensus.

We briefed it to the Steering Group, and Gen. Agan said, "Let's take this to the chief." So, they arranged a meeting for the chief of staff [Gen. McConnell], and he said he'd take the briefing with the Secretary [Dr. Brown]. This thing got on a real fast train. I've spent six years on the Air Staff, and I don't think in all the days I've been here that I remember anything like this going quite as fast as this. Zap! We took it on into the chief of staff and the Secretary at about six o'clock at night.

Without there having been any formal announcement that this briefing was to be given to the chief of staff and the Secretary, every three-star [USAF] general in the building showed up in the room, plus some extras. The word was out! This had been a gut issue, and there had been lots of meetings on it.

I gave the briefing, and I ended up with these two slides: "Buy the F-5 if you believe these things," and "Buy the A-7 if you believe these things." One of the Deputy Chiefs of Staff said, "There are a lot of things wrong with that slide on the left" (meaning the A-7), and Gen. McConnell said, "There are a lot of things wrong with that list on the right" (meaning the F-5). And I knew right then where we were. Up to that minute we really didn't know which way the chief of staff was coming down.

The chief of staff said, "I think we ought to buy the A-7" to the Secretary. The Secretary said, "I certainly agree. Let's prepare an appropriate piece of paper for Mr. McNamara." I prepared that letter, and I prepared it immediately the next day. It was *not* coordinated throughout the Air Staff. I prepared it with direct guidance from Gen. McConnell and Secretary Brown.[65]

For his part in the study, Col. Fish received an unusual tribute from OSD. In a letter dated December 13, 1965, and addressed to Gen. McConnell and Maj. Gen. Agan, Russ Murray and Tom Cheatham formally commended Fish for his finesse and competence in the exceptionally difficult job of coordinating the study. They pointed out that Fish had been the "most important single member of the Joint OSD/AF F-X Study Group" and had been the inspiration behind the excellent efforts of the Air Force Secretariat.

The memorandum was dated the same day as the briefing, November 5, 1965. What were Gen. McConnell's thoughts as he listened to the briefing and balanced it off against the other factors he had to consider? McConnell later related his decision to the long history of roles-and-missions disputes between the Air Force and the Army:

Ever since World War II the Air Force began dedicating all its funds gradually towards the buildup of a strategic offensive capability and continental defense capability, and therefore didn't have enough money to go into a tactical air capability the way they should have. But that was the philosophy of the government at that time—Massive Retaliation, at places of our own choosing. So, we got behind the eight-ball in tactical aviation. And naturally the Army attempted to move into the tactical aviation area with organizational [Army] aircraft.

The thing that was pushing [in 1965] was that we *had* to get something to give the Army close air support. First, it was our job. Second, if we didn't do it, somebody else was going to do it for us. Every once in a while, that would come up on the Hill, especially with Representative Pike. Pike wanted to turn the Army into another Marine Corps since he was an old Marine. Senator Symington kept showing charts all the time that he was the last guy to lay down a fighter aircraft when he was Secretary of the Air Force [1947–1950].

The thrust of the whole thing was that if the Air Force was going to meet its responsibilities, it *had to* go to a tactical weapons system that would drop iron bombs in close support and *specialize it* for close air support. That is what drove it.

We didn't pay too much attention to the briefings and the computer study; we knew we had to have an airplane, and this one we thought we were going to get for $1.4 million.[66]

Gen. McConnell and Secretary Brown consulted extensively over the decision. Dr. Brown later reflected on his perspective:

It was perfectly clear by late 1965 and early 1966 that the Air Force was going to put to the test, both by the existence of the Vietnam War and its nature—however representative or unrepresentative they would be of a war somewhere else—and by Congressional interest and by OSD interest in the question of how could the Close Support role—however defined—[be fulfilled] as part of the area intrinsic to the ground battlefield.

The Air Force was going to be put to the test by all these things, and therefore it had to look at the question of close support specifically, and not just say as had been part of doctrine of organizations within the Air Force for many years, that whatever can fight the air battle can then go ahead and do the Close Support role.

I think there was coming an awareness in the Air Force that, as a result of constraints inherent in limited war, you might not be able to fight the air battle. You might be forced to a close support situation where you hadn't won the air battle; you might have complete air superiority, but there might be other constraints as well.[67]

Secretary Brown then discussed the Fish Study and the decision to buy A-7s. He stressed the role of the TAC commander, Gen. Disosway:

It became clear that—depending on how you defined the tasks—it *did* help to have *some* specialized close support aircraft. Providing you has a big enough total force you could devote some to this activity. . . . This, I think, was reinforced by the political view that lacking *some* close support aircraft the Army would inevitably have a better argument for developing its armed helicopters to do the close support role.

It really narrowed down to the F-5 and the A-7. By then enough information had come in from Vietnam on how important it was to have a big payload—both because of the bombs you could carry and because it gave you room to put in all kinds of targeting equipment which would allow you to get accuracy. People didn't yet realize the importance of this, at headquarters at least, but were beginning to. So, a decision was made to go with the A-7. It was really made at the Chief's level and mine, but it *was* recommended by the Air Staff Board and the Air Council, and it was supported, in the end, by TAC. I think that was very important, because it would have been very difficult to overrule Gen. Disosway had he come to a different conclusion."[68]

When asked if the computer study had any effect on his decision, Secretary Brown answered as follows:

The computer was, I think, quite important. What it did was that it showed what I think computers are good for; it showed what's important. Then you go back, and you look at those and make the judgment of how that's likely to be. In other words, it tells you what characteristics and what premises govern the outcome of the study. Then you make a judgment on which of these premises is most likely to be right, and that tells you which is the right answer. It saves you from having to make a judgment of whether the A-7 is better or the F-5 based just on their characteristics, and allows you to make a judgment that the distance you will want to go is so and so far or that the increased accuracy which will require fairly heavy aiming devices is going to be important. You decide that, and then it tells you what your choice should be.[69]

Secretary Brown's articulation of the A-7's "growth potential" to install improved avionics / targeting equipment was especially prescient considering the evolution of the A-7 program. Brown also indicated the significance of having the major air commander (TAC) support the decision. Gen. McConnell was later asked *why* it was so important that Gen. Disosway support the decision:

Because Tactical Air Command was going to employ the aircraft, and he was the commander of Tactical Air Command. If he was going to use it he was supposed to be knowing what he would be required to do with it, and therefore we needed concurrence out of him before you go up to the Hill, and he says, "No, I don't agree with it and never did agree with it." They'll always ask him.[70]

Gen. Disosway's position in 1965 was as the commander of all stateside tactical-fighter forces. He had over 80,000 personnel in his command and included some sixteen Air Force bases. His fighter force had virtually all supersonic aircraft (except for the Special Air Warfare Center's commandos), consisting of F-100s, F-105s, and F-4s. Gen. Disosway described the general assessment of the operations profession before the A-7 decision:

As soon as you get a better machine you can take on all those low performing aircraft [and shoot them down]. You've got historic examples of that that are just as applicable today as when they happened. Look at the German [Ju 87]

Stuka; it was a great airplane [for attacks on ground forces] as long as it didn't run into anything that could shoot it down. As soon as they started using it in the Battle of Britain where British Spitfires and P-40s were available to fight it, it disappeared off the battlefield. The Me 109 and the Fw 190 were a similar example because they set their production on those two aircraft prior to the time we set the production on ours, and ours were superior aircraft. And we beat them. Now if they had come out with the Me 262 [jet fighter] sooner, they would have beaten us. I don't think there is any question about it, in the air-to-air business you've got to have a superior aircraft.[71]

The relation of the A-7 to the German Stuka is one continually made by Air Force fighter people, but ironically *not* Navy pilots. There is a more supportive attitude of the attack mission in the Navy than the Air Force.[72]

Gen. Disosway related how Gen. McConnell called him before the final decision and asked for his position as the TAC commander:

Really, the Air Force didn't want the A-7, but they wanted the F-5 less. McNamara, according to my understanding, gave the Air Force a choice to buy a cheaper aircraft than the F-4 which we were buying, and then if we would buy the cheaper airplane, we could have the F-4E with the gun on it, which was going to cost some extra money. So, the choice was between the A-7 and the F-5. There wasn't any question in my mind as to which aircraft we should have, because the F-5 wasn't as good.

McConnell called me and asked which aircraft I'd pick. I said I'd take the A-7. We really didn't know a lot about the airplane, but once the decision had been made, we got the people together to see what changes needed to be made. TAC's big job to get *any* airplane.[73]

It is significant that TAC wanted *two* outcomes from the Fish Study—*more* tactical fighters and the TSF F-4 with a gun. TAC recommended that if A-7s were to be purchased, the request also should contain TSF F-4s to protect them. The request for A-7s and F-4s was related to

TAC's attempt to increase the twenty-four-wing force structure limit for tactical fighters.

With Gen. Disosway's verbal concurrence, Secretary Brown signed a memo to the secretary of defense to request both TSF F-4s and A-7s:

November 5, 1965
MEMORANDUM FOR THE SECRETARY OF DEFENSE
SUBJECT: Interim Buy Tactical Fighters
My memorandum of October 15, 1965, deferred recommendation on an interim medium-cost aircraft for the tactical fighter force until additional analysis could be accomplished. The computer simulation being used in the joint Air Force / OSD selection effort has been subjected to numerous sensitivity tests. This data thus developed supports some general and some specific conclusions.

The study considered the performance of a variety of alternative equal-cost forces added to the approved basic tactical fighter force.

The cost/effectiveness of the A-7 and F-5 was very close. Review of the results of the analysis, including the numerous sensitivity tests and excursions, shows that under certain conditions the F-5 would be the most cost-effective aircraft, whereas given other conditions, the A-7 would be a better choice. For a given acquisition and ten-year operation cost, the equal-cost forces represent a larger number of F-5s than of A-7s, and they are of near equal effectiveness in the environment considered in the study. This makes important such factors as MAP [Military Assistance Program] compatibility or disposability (favoring the F-5), compatibility with the Navy (favoring the A-7), and providing an increased hot production line (favoring the F-5, which now is planned for a lower rate in MAP than the A-7 is for the Navy).

However, the overriding requirement was to determine what weapons system at comparably low cost would be most capable of carrying out the missions of close air support in a permissive environment. . . . Under such assumptions . . . the A-7 (on the basis of ten-year investment and operating costs) has a probable cost-effectiveness superiority. The added flexibility provided by the payload/range/mission

time advantage appears to make the A-7 a better choice providing air superiority is established by the recommended F-4 force (including the TSF version). Put another way, when added to the F-111/F-4 mixture now approved, the combination of the F-4 (TSF) and A-7 appears to cover the widest range of low- and medium-intensity air-to-air and air-ground situations. The chief of staff and I on the basis of the above factors, recommend such a mixture as an addition to the force.
/s/ Harold Brown[74]

Secretary Brown's memo asked for approval to buy ninety-six F-4 TSFs[75] and 387 A-7s.[76] The A-7 issue also had foreign-policy implications as it lay on McNamara's desk. The situation was aptly described soon thereafter by *Aviation Week* in its "Washington Roundup" column:

Defense Secretary Robert S. McNamara is leaning toward buying the Navy/Ling/ Temco/ Vought A-7A for the Air Force rather than the F-5—a move which had the Canadian Defense Ministry up in arms.

Before placing their order for 125 F-5s last summer Canadian defense officials felt they had assurance the Pentagon would buy some F-5s for the USAF. They were counting on the US to follow through to neutralize criticism at home that the Canadian Defense Ministry was buying a "second-class" aircraft not good enough for the USAF.

Pentagon insiders say the latest plan—always subject to change in last-minute budget conferences—is to buy the A-7A for entry into the USAF inventory in 1968. Canada also had considered buying the A-7A before deciding on the F-5.[77]

Secretary Brown later reflected on his view of the fate of the memorandum as it went to McNamara and then to Systems Analysis:

We sent down this recommendation to the Office of the Secretary of Defense, which was well received at the time, partly because some of the people in Systems Analysis considered this was their airplane.

I'm sure they had some reservations about the question of future growth. They were trying to keep the price down, again because it was their airplane; if you kept the price down, it would look better.[78]

Systems Analysis did receive the request favorably, as had been expected. Enthoven and Murray had been trying to interest the Air Force in the A-7 for over two and a half years. When asked five years later, Dr. Enthoven did not remember the memorandum as such, but he noted, "I would have had the action on that recommendation. If that was the first time the Air Force recommended the A-7, then we would have concurred and recommended approval."[79] In fact, Systems Analysis recommended the Air Force be given *more* A-7s than Brown and McConnell requested.

Meanwhile, the Navy was forging ahead with the A-7 program. In November, Secretary of the Navy Paul Nitze announced the Navy would be exercising the next contract option by ordering 140 more A-7s valued at $91 million.

Secretary McNamara consulted with Systems Analysis and only two weeks later, on November 19, sent his answer. He approved the procurement of 561[80] A-7s for the Air Force and the development of an afterburner. He denied the request of the F-4 TSF with an internal gun because of its development cost and the delayed schedule that would result.[81] (He did not approve the request for the F-4 TSF modification with a cannon and a microminiaturized radar until July 22, 1966.) OSD at this time anticipated the Air Force A-7 would be a virtual copy of the Navy A-7A (plus afterburner) and that initial deliveries of the aircraft would begin two years later, in January 1967. That was wishful thinking.

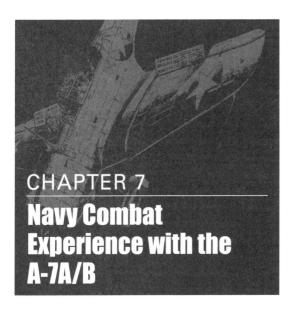

CHAPTER 7

Navy Combat Experience with the A-7A/B

Ling-Temco-Vought delivered the first A-7A to a fleet squadron on October 14, 1966, only three years after the contract was signed. Cmdr. Donald S. Ross, skipper of VA-174, flew the aircraft from NAS Dallas to NAS Cecil Field, Florida, and delivered it to the East Coast Replacement Air Group (RAG). Two months later, Lt. Cmdr. Scott Smith delivered the first West Coast aircraft on December 10, 1966, to VA-122 at NAS Lemoore, California. Lt. Cmdr. Lou Taylor delivered VA-122's second aircraft the next day. VA-174 "Hell Razors" and VA-122 "Flying Eagles" became known as the "Corsair College" at Lemoore.[1]

Carrier Qualification

Simultaneously, the test squadron at Patuxent River initiated carrier qualifications aboard USS *America* (CVA-66) off Norfolk, Virginia; Lt. Cmdr. Fred Hueber took off from Pax River and was the first pilot to land on the carrier. During the following week, two aircraft made seventy-five catapult launches, seventy-nine touch-and-goes, and seventy-three arrested landings. They identified two problems: steam ingestion and low thrust. Steam ingestion occurred while on the catapult, with steam being sucked into the intake, causing a compressor stall. This could be controlled somewhat by the pilot closing the twelfth-stage compressor bleed air valve. The steam problem was mitigated by the squadron limiting

all A-7As on combat operations to a maximum takeoff weight of 38,000 pounds (8,000 pounds of bombs). This limitation was unfortunate because it meant the A-7 could carry only 1,000 pounds more than the A-4 it was replacing. The issue was mitigated further by the A-7B being delivered with the slightly more powerful TF-30-P-8 engine. But the A-7 low-thrust issue would be only partially solved by the P-8 engine and would not be completely resolved until receipt of the Allison Spey engine in the upgraded A-7E.

The first carrier landings with realistic ordnance loads began on February 14, 1967, aboard USS *Independence* (CVA-62), again in the Atlantic. The first shots were loaded with 8,000 pounds of fuel in four 300-gallon external fuel tanks. The aircraft made a total of twenty-eight successful catapult launches.

Flying the Vought A-7 vs. the Vought F-8

Vought made it a marketing point that the A-7 would be similar to the F-8. While we have seen that there was actually very little commonality when the parts were compared, there is an interesting point made by Cmdr. Ed Beakley. Ed was fresh out of flight school and in the Navy pipeline in fall 1968, when President Johnson called a halt to Rolling Thunder, the bombing of North Vietnam. He, therefore, was "stashed" at Point Mugu to get some experience before attending the A-7 RAG. Since all young pilots are itching for flying time, he was fortunate to be introduced to the DF-8 (F-8A), F-8H, and J. As he told it:

A buddy and I were ordered to be prepared for the A-7 RAG when we left, so the test pilots at Point Mugu designed a training program for the two of us in the Crusader—fantastic deal. That eighteen months included almost 300 hours of F-8 flying. When I read that Vought desired to use the F-8 as much as possible in the competition, it brought back a few memories. While the A-7 looked like a little brother to the F-8, not much else wound up being used. While I can't throw numbers at you, when I first got into A-7 at the RAG, I felt really at home. Even with limits on roll rate, thrust, speed, etc., it felt very similar—with one aspect in particular—

going straight vertical. Obviously, the g "egg" was much smaller, but that big tail allowed the same hard rudder rollover to straight down.[2]

Ed spent eighteen months at Point Mugu, thoroughly enjoyed the F-8 flying time, reported to the A-7 RAG at Lemoore, and deployed with VA-56 and -93 on USS *Midway* for Linebacker I and II.

Combat Deployments for Rolling Thunder

Cmdr. James Hill led VA-147 on the first combat deployment on the aircraft carrier USS *Ranger* (CVA-61) from North Island San Diego to Southeast Asia on November 4, 1967. With the squadron was an Air Force contingent, led by Maj. Charles McClarren, who later would become the officer in charge of the A-7 detachment from the 4525th Fighter Weapons Wing at Luke AFB, Arizona. The group consisted of fighter pilots, a maintenance officer, and nineteen enlisted technicians. VA-147 was part of Carrier Air Group 2 (CVW-2), with other squadrons of F-4Bs, A-4s, A-6s, and KA-3 tankers.[3] The wing participated in the last year of Operation Rolling Thunder.

USS *Ranger* arrived on Yankee Station in the Gulf of Tonkin on December 3, 1967, and launched Alpha strikes against Vinh in Route Package I, just north of the DMZ. More Alpha strikes were launched on December 17, with A-4s, A-7s, and A-6s attacking the Hai Duong railway and highway bridge complex between Haiphong and Hanoi. "A typical Alpha Strike combined F-4B Phantoms, A-4 Skyhawks, A-6 Intruders, and A-7 Corsairs, with supporting ECM, tanker and reconnaissance aircraft—24–48 airplanes in all—with a coordinated attack on a single target or closely-clustered set of targets."[4]

Cmdr. Hill's aircraft was an Iron Hand, anti-SAM mission, carrying Shrike antiradiation missiles. Hill was narrowly missed by a SAM, and MiGs scrambled after them. Hill spotted MiGs in the distance, but they did not attack the strike force. Cmdr. Hill related:

> I got a really good shot at a flak site and I'm sure it hasn't fired at anybody since then. I launched a missile at a SAM site shortly after we got in and both my wingman and the strike leader confirmed my shot as a direct hit.[5]

Five days later, on December 22, 1966, an A-7A was hit by ground fire and became the first Corsair lost in combat. The pilot ejected, hit the ground safely, but was captured and spent five years as a prisoner of war. It would be the only A-7 aircraft casualty of the deployment.

Other missions flown included armed reconnaissance with smaller numbers of aircraft—a section of two or a division of four—flying over highways, rivers, and the countryside, looking for targets of opportunity. During the rest of December and early January, the squadron continued dropping bombs and firing rockets at bridges, watercraft, railroad equipment, supply dumps, petroleum concentrations, and vehicle convoys. "The A-7A proved itself relatively free of maintenance problems and pilots were impressed by the comfort they felt in its roomy cockpit while dodging everything the enemy could throw at them."[6]

What the pilots were *not* happy with was the guns. The Mk. 12 cannon on the A-7A were prone to jamming after only a few rounds had been fired. F-8 pilots had complained of the same problem.[7]

Maintenance Issues with the A-7/B

The deployment of a new weapon system to the fleet is always a complicated operation. The normal logistics system is usually not yet set up and stocked with spare parts, and there is no established rate of usage. Thus, the fleet squadron must rely more on the Program Office to provide needed equipment. This was true both with the Atlantic and Pacific Fleet deployments of the A-7A and later the A-7E. Norman Birzer is a naval aviator with combat experience in the A-7E on two deployments with VA-146 aboard USS *America* in 1970 and on *Constellation* in 1971–72. He later teamed with writer Peter Mersky to write *US Navy A-7 Corsair II Units of the Vietnam War*, in which they described several of the maintenance problems with the early A-7s:

> [The] Corsair II evolved into what could arguably be called the most successful jet bomber of the Vietnam War. However, the new aircraft had its share of problems. The "A" and "B" model were underpowered, and there were sporadic engine problems. A chronic shortage of spare

parts also plagued the Corsair II throughout its service life. Yet, its pilots were, by and large, well pleased with what turned out to be Vought's last aircraft.

The A-7 carried much more ordnance than the A-4 and enjoyed one of the greatest flight endurance periods of any major tactical jet aircraft. As the Corsair II carried 80 percent of the payload of a Grumman A-6 Intruder, with considerably more versatility, it was much closer to the medium attack category than the light attack designation exemplified by the A-1 Skyraider and A-4.[8]

Unfortunately, many of these early jets had been hardwired at the factory, which in turn meant that many of their systems could not be replaced easily, did not work, or did not match the schematics of the maintenance manuals supplied with the A-7s. These problems with aircraft availability resulted in less-than-favorable mission capability that hindered training schedules—often fewer than ten jets were available to train the dozens of waiting pilots in the early days of the Corsair II's frontline service.[9]

In late January 1968, the North Koreans captured USS *Pueblo*, and USS *Ranger* was diverted north to the Sea of Japan. CVW-2 flew numerous sorties, but there was no combat while the frustrating situation continued. The aircraft flew in torturous winter conditions for over sixty days, until relieved by USS *Enterprise* (CVAN-65). *Ranger* sailed back to the Gulf of Tonkin to complete its combat deployment. The "Argonauts" of VA-147 resumed flying strikes against targets in North and South Vietnam. The pilots each flew approximately 125 missions.[10]

Cmdr. Jim Hill praised the A-7A for its turbofan engine, whose low fuel consumption was its "most desirable advantage." The "almost unbelievable fuel specifics in terms of previous engine performance" was revolutionary.[11] It allowed the Navy to "double-cycle" the A-7s by having them take off with one jet launch cycle, skip one, and land with the second cycle two hours later.

One of the outcomes of this first deployment was the generation of some one hundred requested changes for follow-on A-7 aircraft, about sixty of which were incorporated.[12]

The second deployment included two A-7A squadrons aboard USS *America* (CVA-66). Despite their embarking from Norfolk, the ship sailed around the Cape of Good Hope and joined Yankee Station on May 31, 1968. Its two squadrons were the VA-82 "Marauders" and VA-86's "Sidewinders." With the arrival of *America* on Yankee Station, *Ranger* was cleared to return home. On their first strike, VA-82's Lt. Ken Fields's aircraft was hit by ground fire, and he ejected near the DMZ. The Navy and Air Force launched a massive rescue operation, and thirty-nine hours later he was picked up by a "Jolly Green" helicopter. Unfortunately, a second A-7A ran out of fuel on the rescue, but the pilot ejected safely and was picked up.

Ben Short of VA-86 summarized the squadron's activities in the summer of 1968:

During this period we were only bombing North Vietnam up to the 19th parallel, so the entire cruise was spent working over the real estate between 18 and 19 degrees north except when the weather was bad and they would send us south to work with Air Force FACs. The Air Force had the territory between the DMZ and the 18th parallel. There were one or two SAM sites around the gunnery school at Vinh Son, and they managed to pick off a couple of other aircraft from the Air Wing [not A-7s] during the course of the cruise.

The normal operations were twelve hours on, noon to midnight, or mid to noon, then twelve off. Every six to ten days we would stand down for twenty-four hours and change the cycle. This played hell with my biological clock. If I had an 0300 hop, I would just get up at that hour. Initially we were carrying twelve Mk. 81s on MERS (multiple ejector racks) on stations one and eight. I was out with a load of twelve 81s (250 lb.) when I picked up a concrete bridge on Route 1 (probably 300–400 feet long) and being new to the game decided to dump the entire load on the bridge. I made a pretty good run cutting across the bridge at a slight angle. As I pulled off, I rolled up on a wing tip after getting my nose well above the horizon to observe the hits. There's a lot of smoke and fire but after the smoke flew away there was no apparent damage to the bridge.[13]

In July 1968, USS *Constellation* (CVA-64) arrived on station, bringing the fourth and fifth A-7A squadrons to the war. They were VA-27, the "Royal Maces," and VA-97, the "Warhawks." Together the five squadrons of A-7As flew missions in North Vietnam and "Steel Tiger" in southern Laos. In October 1968, President Johnson declared a bombing halt and Rolling Thunder ceased. The fleet switched its air missions to South Vietnam, and for four years there was no more bombing of the North.

A-7 Deployments to Yankee and Dixie Stations

The Navy deployed successive A-7A and B squadrons as they became available. Many flew in Rolling Thunder off Yankee Station in the Tonkin Gulf, and others flew in the South off Dixie Station, offshore Cam Ranh Bay in the South China Sea.

As one can see from the following table, the A-7A was first deployed to Southeast Asia (SEA) in late 1967; the A-7B followed fourteen months later, in January 1969, with the improved TF-30-P-8 engine. From then on, the two models were deployed together. The A-7C, which contained all the improvements of A-7E except the Spey engine, was not deployed to SEA until mid-1972, and A-7E squadrons followed.

A-7A/B Squadron Deployments to Southeast Asia				
Squadron	Model	Ship	Air Wing	Dates
VA-147	A-7A	CVA-61	CVW-2	4 Nov 67–25 May 68
VA-86	A-7A	CVA-66	CVW-6	10 Apr–16 Dec 68
VA-27	A-7A	CVA-64	CVW-14	28 May 68–31 Jan 69
VA-97	A-7A	CVA-64	CVW-14	28 May 68–31 Jan 69
VA-105	A-7A	CVA-63	CVW-11	30 Dec 68–4 Sep 69
VA-146	A-7B	CVAN-65	CVW-9	6 Jan–2 Jul 69
VA-215	A-7B	CVAN-65	CVW-9	6 Jan–2 Jul 69
VA-87	A-7B	CVA-14	CVW-16	1 Feb–18 Sep 69
VA-25	A-7B	CVA-14	CVW-16	1 Feb–18 Sep 69
VA-97	A-7A	CVA-64	CVW-14	11 Aug 69–8 May 70
VA-153	A-7A	CVA-34	CVW-19	14 May–10 Dec 70
VA-86	A-7A	CVA-43	CVW-15	23 Sep 69–1 Jul 70
VA-56	A-7B	CVA-61	CVW-2	14 Oct 69–1 Jun 70
VA-93	A-7B	CVA-61	CVW-2	14 Oct 69–1 Jun 70
VA-155	A-7B	CVA-34	CVW-19	14 May–10 Dec 70
VA-215	A-7B	CVA-34	CVW-19	14 May–18 Dec 70
VA-56	A-7B	CVA-41	CVW-5	16 Apr–6 Nov 71
VA-93	A-7B	CVA-41	CVW-5	16 Apr–6 Nov 71
VA-153	A-7A	CVA-34	CVW-19	14 May–18 Dec 71
VA-215	A-7B	CVA-34	CVW-19	14 May–18 Dec 71
VA-56	A-7B	CVA-41	CVW-5	10 Apr 72–3 Mar 73
VA-93	A-7B	CVA-41	CVW-5	10 Apr 72–3 Mar 73

VA-37	A-7A	CVA-60	CVW-3	11 Apr 72–13 Feb 73
VA-105	A-7A	CVA-60	CVW-3	11 Apr 72–13 Feb 73
VA-153	A-7A	CVA-34	CVW-19	5 Jun 72–30 Mar 73
VA-155	A-7B	CVA-34	CVW-19	5 Jun 72–30 Mar 73
VA-215	A-7B	CVA-34	CVW-19	5 Jun 72–30 Mar 73

Source: Britzer & Mersky, *US Navy A-7 Corsair II Units of the Vietnam War*, appendix (Osprey Publishing, by permission).

An Assessment of Operation Rolling Thunder

Gary Ohls, a thirty-five-year Marine Corps veteran and professor of joint maritime operations in the Naval War College program at the Naval Post Graduate School, Monterey, wrote an assessment of Rolling Thunder from the point of view of the Navy:

The execution of Operation Rolling Thunder involved carrier aircraft from Task Force 77 along with land-based Marine Corps and Air Force planes flying from South Vietnam and Thailand. There were many problems with Rolling Thunder, including the fact that the first attacks [were] ... mostly against insignificant targets. Additionally, the missions were initially limited in frequency, placing little or no pressure on North Vietnamese leaders and certainly having no effect on their behavior. Unlike the aggressive, hard-hitting interdiction and strike packages against North Korea during 1950–1953, Rolling Thunder amounted to an ineffective, highly restricted, low-impact effort entirely wanting in its effect.[14]

Tactics Evolution in Combat

There are many instances of Navy pilots learning to adapt tactics in the face of enemy fire. Two involved the A-7. The first had to do with the configuration of ordnance on the aircraft. There was always a limit on the number of hardpoints on the wings where the armorers could hang pylons (4–8). To overcome this limitation and carry more bombs, industry designed triple-ejection racks (TERS) to carry three bombs and multiple-ejection racks (MERS) to carry six. The advantage of course was being able to carry more firepower, but the disadvantage was the weight and drag of the heavy and blunt racks and bombs, which slowed down the airplane and made it difficult to maneuver.

Navy attack squadrons adapted to overcome these problems in combat by going back to a "slick wing" configuration, which meant that only one bomb was loaded on each pylon, without the use of MERS or TERS. As noted by many of the pilots in this book, the Navy's normal Alpha strike configuration was six Mk. 83 1,000 lb. bombs and one Sidewinder missile. This "slick wing" was a lot better than the configuration of MERS and TERS for mission into North Vietnam.[15]

The second instance of adaptation was the change of the basic attack formation. Ever since the invention of the "Finger Four" formation led by Werner Molders in the Spanish Civil War, the basic formation for fighter and attack aircraft had been and continues today to be four aircraft spaced as the shape of the fingers on your hand. That is, the leader and his wing are the first and middle finger on either hand, and the third and fourth members of the flight are the third and little fingers on the other side of the leader. The airborne flight can either be tucked in tight, as in "Close Formation," or several wingspans apart, as in "Spread Formation," or one mile or more apart, as in an air-to-air superiority formation. There are six advantages of this configuration. (1) The flight is composed of two "elements," in Air Force terminology, or two "sections," as in naval language. The elements can take off and land as two two-ship formations, thus compressing the time to get off the ground and join up for a mission. (2) The aircraft can be moved apart to allow maximum visual coverage and mutual support of each other with disciplined, overlapping "lookout" areas for each crew. (3) The two "element leaders" will be more experienced than the "wings." (4) A flight of four fulfills the principle of "mass" taught in the Principles of War. (5) Multiple flights of four can be assembled and tasked together to form a much-larger task force or strike package, which was used both by the Air Force and Navy in Vietnam and elsewhere. (6) There are several recorded instances where an aggressive flight lead has landed on a runway with *all four* aircraft in tight formation.

Navy pilots in attacks on North Vietnam became concerned about the difficulty of maintaining a flight-of-four formation when forced into hard maneuvering to avoid a surface-to-air missile (SAM) or antiaircraft artillery (AAA). There was a strong tendency for no. 4 to be "flung out" as the flight broke away from him. Needless to say, a hard break INTO the element of two was even more hazardous, since TWO aircraft had to avoid the leader as he passed in front of, over, or under them.

One solution developed by the USS *Midway* air wing was to downsize the flight/division to *three* aircraft, which put only one aircraft on each side of the leader. As VA-56 pilot Ed Beakley explained it:

The three-plane division was developed mostly by VA-56 operations officer Lt. Cmdr. Ken "KT" Sanger. KT had multiple combat missions in the A-4 during Rolling Thunder, including a harrowing shoot-down and rescue in Laos. He had resolved that divisions with three versus four aircraft were more maneuverable and safer. The formation provided better tactical separation in a SAM environment and also reduced the probability of "Tail-End Charlie" getting slung out or hung out to dry in hard maneuvering. Big Alpha strikes still mostly used two groups of twelve to fifteen, for a total of twenty-four to thirty bombers. As a new guy, I flew no. 3 quite a few times, and not having to worry about anything on a hard or break turn was great. I didn't have to worry about hitting no. 2. You could cut inside or "yo-yo" high to do whatever was necessary to maintain flight integrity. The attached picture (digital by Peter Chilelli) is my first Alpha strike. The lead was Lt. Wayne Lotsberg, no. 2 was Keith "Floo" LaFlair, and no. 3 was me. Probably depicted a little closer than we actually flew, but we granted him artist leeway to get it in. Also, I would guess it made scheduling easier—

particularly for early Linebacker I missions because we were a really young, first-cruise group. Another advantage was that we could schedule an experienced division-qualified leader with two newbies instead of being forced to have a qualified section leader as no. 3.[16]

RAdm. Pickavance describes his experiences in Linebacker:

We arrived in the Philippines for a few days and then proceeded to Yankee Station, where combat ops started immediately, first down south (An Loc, etc.), and then we moved north, and for the next eleven months stayed mostly up north. I flew my first combat hop the day my son was born! We generally flew three days of "Alpha strikes," big gaggles (like World War II), three days of armed recce noon to midnight, followed by three days of midnight to noon. It really screwed up our sleep, but relief was [available as] we cycled into Cubi/Subic Bay after thirty days on the line. There we let loose after a couple of days of solid sleep!

The A-7B was a great attack jet. We flew it "slick wing" with various combinations of weapons: 4 × 500 lb. Mk. 82 and 2 × 1,000 lb. Mk. 83 or 2 × 2,000 lb. Mk. 84 or four Rockeyes, or four Shrikes with 20 mm cannon. The A-7 mix and match was tactically superb since it could be tailored for the mission. So, thumbs up on load/range/time on station (RESCAP) [Rescue Combat Air Patrol] / survivability / boarding rate (i.e., landing on the boat) / great manual bomber / fairly reliable engine / great acceleration downhill in a bombing run. Distractors: [slow] airspeed when loaded, the engine smoked, [only] two hydraulic systems versus three like in our A-7E aircraft.

There were times when I really wished I had an afterburner, especially when the SAMs were ripple-fired at us. But the A-7B brought me home every time, although my wingman got zapped when we rolled in on some trucks about five miles east of Brandon Bay, NVN. He got a bit sucked in on the roll-in and got hit in the right-wing-root area. He ejected over the water just offshore, and we got him out and back home.[17]

While the Navy was flying combat with the A-7A and B, the Air Force was joining the Navy in the A-7 Program Management Office and trying to figure out how to develop this newly found weapon.

CHAPTER 8
Development of the Air Force A-7D

The "Doctrine of Quality":
"Superior arms favor Victory."

—I. B. Holley Jr.

Air Force Improvements to the Navy A-7

The selection of the A-7 for the Air Force was a traumatic event that rippled through four major organizations: the Air Staff, Tactical Air Command, Air Force Systems Command, and Air Force Logistics Command. The specific responsibility for the development of the aircraft was the Navy Program Management Office (PMO), which had been established in 1963 and had been managing the A-7 for over two years. Before these organizations were finished with the A-7D, they would add three major changes to the aircraft. This chapter is a story of technology and quality.

The military services of the United States share a belief in technology as the fundamental basis of weapons. This belief is most elegantly stated in a British volume in the History of World War II series titled The Design and Development of Weapons.

The Doctrine of Quality

The doctrine of quality, i.e., the view that the power of the RAF depends largely if not wholly, on the perfection of its equipment, was one which the Air Ministry handed down to the Ministry of Aircraft Production and which the Air Staff consistently pressed. It was equally accepted that the sacrifice in the numbers of output and establishment was necessary in order to maintain quality; and it was well understood, both on the Air Staff and in the Supply branches, that perfection of aircraft has to be paid for in term of output.[1]

The historian I. B. Holley stated this doctrine more simply: "Superior arms favor Victory."[2]

The Air Force Selects a Program Manager

Air Force Systems Command nominated, and the secretary of the Air Force approved, Col. Robert Hails as the Air Force program manager. Hails had extensive systems management experience and a feeling for the complexity and sensitivity of interservice, joint development programs. He had an aeronautical engineering degree (BS, 1947) from Auburn and an MS degree in industrial management from Columbia (1950). He had flown B-24 bombers in the Pacific during World War II, but his assignments since then had been generally in R&D / systems management. Prior to his selection, he was working for the assistant secretary of the Air Force (Installations and Logistics; I&L) on the joint F-4 and F-111 programs.

Col. Hails recalled how he was notified he was to be the USAF program manager:

When I was first called into the program, Gen. Schriever was commander, Air Force Systems Command, and Gen. Austin Davis was vice commander. I had previously worked for Davis. They were looking for somebody who had Systems Program Office experience, technical background, and yet understood the difficulties involved in a joint service program, which I had by benefit of three and one-half years in the Secretary's office, working on the F-111 and F-4. I was the Military Assistant for Weapons System Management in the office of the Assistant Secretary (I&L). At the time I went to the A-7 program I had been at Harvard at the Advanced Management program and got back on the 15th of December [1965].

Davis called me, and I might say that I was dumbfounded when I found out the Air Force was going to buy the A-7 because it contradicted everything we had been talking about and doing. We were going to have two motors and two pilots in any future fighter, and it would jolly well be supersonic! So, the A-7, in my *personal* judgment as an Air Force aviator with some knowledge of requirements, was absolutely the wrong airplane at the wrong time for the wrong mission. And I told this to Gen. Davis when he asked me if I'd go over to the Navy to run the program. He said, "Look, that's none of your business; you didn't make the decision to buy it. Your job is to go make it the best airplane that we can get." And that was essentially my entire charge.[3]

Col. Hails became the Air Force deputy under Capt. Carl Cruse. Cruse was working with a small staff because the functional staffs of the Bureau of Aeronautics provided most of the technical expertise for the A-7 (engineering, logistics, contracting, avionics, etc.). Hails was virtually alone in the Air Force section of the office for several months. In January 1966, Capt. Cruse and the PMO staff were following the Navy Primary Evaluation that was underway at the Naval Aviation Test Center Patuxent River.

Tactical Air Command Enters the Scene and Focuses on Changes to the Navy A-7

When the staff of Tactical Air Command at Langley AFB, Virginia, heard about the decision to adopt the Navy A-7A for Air Force use, they were both astounded and unprepared. They had, in 1964, retrieved Navy A-1Es from the boneyard and deployed them to Vietnam. This was followed by being told they were to absorb the Navy F-4 into Air Force operations and now faced yet another Navy-designed aircraft. The A-7A had been test-flown but was not yet combat ready in any Navy squadron, so they had no operational experience to guide them. The TAC staff, together with that of Air Force Systems Command, developed a long list of "required" changes to make it compatible with Air Force equipment. Some of the changes had to do with the fact that the aircraft would be taking off and landing on long, concrete runways. This meant adding "antiskid" features to the landing gear, new brakes, and new

tires. The combination of these reasons led the staffs to want to *change* the A-7 from an *off-the-shelf purchase* to the *development* of an Air Force attack aircraft.

The first big issue was the jet engine. The engine in the Navy A-7A was the Pratt & Whitney TF-30-P-6, a turbofan derivative of the TF-30-P-1 on the F-111. The P-6 engine delivered 11,350 pounds of thrust.[4] With this engine the Navy A-7A was underpowered, as the F-111 before it had been underpowered. Tactical Air Command pilots were worried the aircraft would be hampered by an excessively long takeoff roll with a load of bombs.

The list began with adding an afterburner. The Navy PMO had already been looking at the problem of increasing the thrust of the TF-30 engine. As early as October 6, 1965, LTV, Pratt & Whitney, and the Bureau of Naval Weapons discussed the possibility of putting a low-augmented afterburner on the follow-on TF-30-P-8. The afterburner would have increased the thrust for takeoff from 11,350 to about 15,000 pounds. After this discussion, P&W did some figuring and on November 2 sent the PMO a list of costs and schedules to add the afterburner.

The Dominance of the Cost Factor

The price of the A-7 was to be a continuing issue for the duration of the program. The figure of $1.2–$1.3 million unit flyaway cost per aircraft had been entered into the computer study on the basis of certain assumptions about the Navy buying a thousand aircraft and the Air Force following with 864! As Col. Hails gathered data about the program, he learned that the Navy A-7, and therefore any Air Force version, was going to cost more than $1.2–$1.3 million:

When I came to the program, first, I had to disabuse them that this [$1.2 million] ever existed. That's fantasy. The Navy would have had to buy airplanes out to 1972. . . Who was going to buy these 1,000 airplanes? Somebody had to buy down that learning curve [the reduction in unit cost with increased production]. The facts are that the Navy airplane—when they got through putting all the fixes on it—that $1.2 airplane never existed. The average after they bought 199 A-7As and 200 A-7Bs was more like $2.6 or $2.4 million.

So, the first bad news that I brought over there [to the Pentagon in December 1965] was that the airplane was not going to come as cheap as you people have been led to believe. We made an analysis of what the airplane was capable of as opposed to what had been advertised, and we said, "Here is this information. Do you still want the airplane?" The decision was "Yes, we do."[5]

Initial Air Force Inputs to Change the A-7

One of the organizations that was to play an especially important part in the A-7 was the Directorate of Operational Requirements and Development Plans in the Air Staff. The deputy director of the organization in 1965–66 was Brig. Gen. (later major general) Kenneth C. Dempster. He described the orientation and function of "requirements":

The operational command *always* establishes the "requirement." In the Directorate of Operational Requirements, we really always treated that as an operational group of people. We predominantly were operations people in there; we had some [R&D people] but the majority were operational. We looked for the smartest man we could lay our hands on, but if you look back on it, most of them had an operational background, too [in addition to advanced degrees].

They take the operational requirement as specified by the operational command; they translate that into a RAD [requirements action directive], and then it is handed to the R&D people.[6]

TAC developed a packet that contained thirty-three changes to the Navy (later upgraded to forty-two). TAC requested a two-place aircraft in addition to the single-seat model for use as a trainer, deletion of the 11,500 lb. thrust engine and development of a 15,600 lb. thrust afterburner version, replacement of the Navy mechanical cannon with the standard Air Force M-61 gun, replacement of the Navy's analog weapons release computer by an "aided-visual" analog system, and dozens of other changes to make the A-7D compatible with Air Force logistics.[7]

During this period the Navy had been moving toward a decision on a new engine. Essentially, the Navy staff decided on having P&W modify the TF-30-P-6 to a P-8 version and add an afterburner for takeoff only. The secretary of the Navy on January 6, 1966, sent a memorandum to Secretary McNamara requesting approval for the development of the afterburner engine. Meanwhile, Col. Hails was having engine specialists at Aeronautical Systems Division evaluate the feasibility of the afterburning P&W engine. Their evaluation did not take long, and on January 12 the ASD engineers replied, recommending *against* adding an afterburner to the TF-30 if another method could be found to augment the aircraft's thrust.[8]

Col. Hails immediately began searching for alternatives to the P&W engine. His reconnaissance led him into discussions with LTV, TAC, the Air Staff, DDR&E, the Navy, and several contractors where the subject of the British Spey engine arose. The Rolls-Royce "Spey" was a family of turbofan engines developed in the UK during the early 1960s, primarily for use in civil airliners.

Developing Air Force Requirements for the Avionics System

Col. Hails also was engaged in an effort to examine the avionics / weapons delivery capability of the Navy A-7A. In doing this, he worked with his Navy boss, Capt. Carl Cruse, the Navy project manager, and the avionics specialists in the Bureau of Aeronautics. Capt. Cruse later described the situation in January–February 1966, when Hails was seeking to establish the alternatives for the engine and avionics equipment. His concept of what the A-7A was designed to do provides a base for the avionics changes that were to come:

The A-7A was laid out pretty clearly in the [Sea-Based Air Strike] study that was made by the chief of naval operations. It was to be a simple, not-sophisticated avionics suite, daylight, visual aircraft with long range and large bomb-carrying capability. So, there was never any real question about what the A-7 was supposed to be. Then all this started to change.[9]

Part of the change referred to by Capt. Cruse was influenced by another Navy program—the

Integrated Light Attack Avionics System (ILAAS). A history of the purposes and plans for this component will show its relationship to the A-7.

A Short History of the Integrated Light Attack Avionics System (ILAAS)

When the Navy first conceived the VAL program, the initial A-7A was intended to have a simple avionics suite, but incremental improvement was planned for the A-7B to add the ILAAS. ILAAS was one of the attempts to approach avionics on a "systems" basis and design a total package of components that would be designed and tested as a unit and could, theoretically, be installed in any one of several different aircraft. ILAAS based its advances on digital computer techniques that would provide, for the first time, a "continuous" solution to the communications, navigation, and bombing problems of the pilot. This was especially attractive for single-seat aircraft. ILAAS was to include four digital computers, sensors, several types of radar, and a heads-up display for the pilot.[10]

There were two major problems with ILAAS: (1) it was overly sophisticated and complex, and (2) it was expensive. It was expected to cost from $800,000 to $1.4 million per system, in addition to the cost of the aircraft's airframe and engine.

Establishing the Alternatives for the Air Force Avionics Decision

When Col. Hails reported to the PMO in December 1965, he was confronted with many of the same problems with ILAAS that Capt. Cruse had experienced. But to Hails, the ILAAS was only one of many possibilities in a rapidly changing situation. With the Air force starting a program for a potentially new aircraft, various contractors saw an opportunity to sell their products. On January 10, 1966, the Air Staff received an unsolicited study from North American Autonetics on an improved avionics system. The study was passed around the Air Staff and was forwarded by Maj. Gen. Catton to Harry Davis, deputy assistant secretary of the Air Force (R&D) for special programs. Gen. Catton noted the proposal did not contain any new optical sensor or display elements to improve the pilot's ability to find and destroy visual targets. If close air support

was to be improved, he added, *new* means would be needed to *visually* acquire the target.[11]

Basic Avionics Alternatives

For an understanding of the avionics debate over the next two years, it is important to know something of the equipment being discussed. The purposes of an avionics systems are primarily to achieve accuracy—accuracy in navigating *to* the target and accuracy in delivering weapons *on* the target. If the system is simple and austere, as they were in World War II, Korea, and early Vietnam, the achieved accuracy is largely dependent on the individual pilot's training and ability. As the equipment gets more complex, the degree of accuracy becomes dependent on the pilot's ability to use the equipment, its performance, and its reliability. The arguments over the level of capability desired generally took the form of advocacy of one of three mutually exclusive categories of equipment. These ranged from simple aids for the pilot to complex computers for elaborate computations. The following table sets out the basic differences.

Avionics Alternatives, 1966			
	System I "Basic A-7A"	System II "Improved"	System III "Complex"
Computer	Analog	Improved analog	Digital
Gunsight	Fixed	Servo stabilized	Computer-generated heads-up display
Accuracy	20–40 mils	15–20 mils	10 mils

Source: LTV, *A-7D Tactical Fighter*, 1969, p, 4.

Tactical Air Command (TAC) at this point was requesting a capability represented by System II, with an improved analog computer and a servo-stabilized sight. TAC stated in the letter of January 15 that it recognized the alternatives included the basic Navy system (I) as it stood, an aided visual system (II), or a new system such as that represented by ILAAS (III). TAC's interest in improving the avionics capability was reinforced by opinions at Air Force Systems Command (AFSC). The "Doctrine of Quality" was definitely operating here.

Accordingly, in January 1966, Hails requested that LTV conduct a study to see what would be available as alternatives and what accuracy could be obtained with each option. LTV conducted that study in January and February 1966 and reported that with the selection of the latest computer technology using many of the *concepts* of ILAAS, it would be possible to develop an avionics system with an accuracy of 7 mils.[12] This turned out to be an important benchmark.

Congressional Pressure Increases with the Pike Report on Close Air Support

Congressman Otis Pike published his critical report on Close Air Support on February 1, 1966. The report singled out the issue of a specialized close-air-support aircraft:

It is the official position of the US Army, expounded by the Chief of Staff, that "The Air Force is best qualified to determine what types of aircraft is best suited to support." The Air Force has done exactly that with the results noted above. They have never built an aircraft designed primarily for close air support. They are not actively engaged in developing one at the present time.

When funds are limited, first things must come first. Unfortunately, Close Air Support did not have the urgency of air lift, or interception roles, or strategic bombing in the Air Force planning. Time has been wasted, but there is still time to correct our deficiencies in Army–Air Force Close Air Support operations. We hope this report will serve as a useful prod, and not as a criticism that must be defended or explained.[13]

The *Washington Post* picked up the February 1 Pike Report and printed a column on February 3, 1966, titled, "Pentagon Charged with Delays in Developing Ground Support Plane." The Air Force ignored the admonition and issued a response to Representative Pike's allegations. The

Air Staff paper reaffirmed "that unified strategic direction and unified command of combatant forces is the best way of integrating land, naval and air forces into an efficient team."[14] It went on to note that historically, the development of tactical fighter aircraft in the United States had emphasized high-performance and multipurpose aircraft. While it added that this was still the policy of the Air Force, the paper added that the service was working with OSD officials to jointly select a specialized close-air-support aircraft.

The situation between the Air Staff and the Congress was not eased when the Pike Report published the views of young Air Force pilots [the author included] and Army personnel returning from Vietnam who testified to the need for more propeller-driven aircraft like the A-1 Skyraider. Both in testimony before the Pike committee and in press conferences, some returning officers had been saying the Air Force was delivering excellent close air support, but that it was partially due to the slow speed, long endurance, and high accuracy of the older planes, not to the supersonic jets. Air Force jets in South Vietnam in 1965–66 were F-100 Super Sabres and F-4 Phantom IIs.

Enter A-1 Pilots with Combat Experience

The author returned from flying the A-1 Skyraider in January 1966. Since I was one of the first returning combat pilots, I was directed to the Air Staff to provide an assessment. The event I remember best was a press conference held in the DoD press office. I spoke about the capabilities of the A-1 and the kinds of target we were asked to hit. Then I was asked the reason for the A-1 effectiveness. I explained candidly that the SPAD's low speed allowed us to release our bombs at lower altitude, so much closer to the target that our bombs were more accurate. At that point, the general standing next to me stepped in front, grabbed the microphone, and said, literally, "What the captain meant to say was that the jets had not yet arrived in country." I was so naive I did not realize the politicized environment surrounding the interservice issues and the development of the A-7 at that time.

Alternatives Are Considered by the Air Force Board Structure

Meanwhile, the A-7 alternatives briefing was being prepared to go before the multilayered Air Force Board committees. The initial presentation was made to the Air Staff Board during February 1966 by officers in the Directorate of Requirements, who were of the persuasion that a simple, mechanical fixed sight would be the most cost-effective avionics option. When this briefing was given, the chairman, Maj. Gen. Lavelle, expressed the opinion that the slides showed that for a little more money they could get a more accurate system, and perhaps the problem should be restudied. He directed the formation of an ad hoc group on A-7 requirements.[15]

The ad hoc group reviewed the problem, with the result that the briefing was modified several times in the Tactical Panel, the Requirements office, and the A-7 PMO. Most of the briefings from this point forward were conducted by Col. Hails. His briefings showed that the forty-two proposed changes would result in an increase of 1,600 pounds in weight. The addition of an afterburner would decrease the takeoff roll by 1,400 feet, but it would also decrease the range by 100 miles in radius or would decrease the loiter time by twenty-five minutes. The changes would increase the cost from $1.4 million to approximately $1.7 million for each aircraft.

The Air Force Council meeting on February 26 was chaired by the vice chief of staff, Gen. Blanchard. Before Col. Hails gave his briefing, Gen. Blanchard observed to all present that the chief of staff (Gen. McConnell) had stated to him, "There had better not be a lot of costly changes to that or he would throw out both the changes and the present Council."[16]

Col. Hails recalled the atmosphere in the room:

We went to the Air Council, and the airplane [issue] was extremely emotional! Some people didn't want it because it was subsonic; others didn't want it because it was a Navy airplane; others didn't want it because they felt OSD had some covert objective in mind.[17]

The briefing itself by Col. Hails and Capt. Cruse met with a "well done" from Gen. Blanchard.

Gen. Catton noted, "It's getting to be a pretty expensive investment we're looking at," when he saw the price tag of $1.7 million per plane. However, no firm decision was made.

The deliberations at the AF Council and the whole decision process on the A-7 also were the subject of continued interest at TAC. There existed a high degree of uncertainty about the A-7. Gen. Disosway and Lt. Gen. Graham, in particular, were worried the A-7 might hinder TAC's chances of getting more F-4s. In addition, TAC had very little information on the real capabilities of the existing Navy A-7A. The first flight had just been conducted six months earlier, and no one in the Air Force had flown the few test models in existence.

In an effort to learn more about the A-7, Lt. Gen. Graham, as the deputy commander of TAC for Operations, went to Dallas on March 2 to fly the airplane. He later described the experience and his view of the changes needed for any Air Force version.

With that I went out and flew the airplane to see what kind of merchandise were going to be equipped with. . . . I chose to fly three strike missions. . . . I loaded up with three sets of stores, complete combat profile . . . then I came back and wrote a report that established forty-seven modifications on the aircraft to make it even safe enough to fly. It needed a bigger engine, etc.

Well, we got a good number of those modifications . . . my feelings were let's fix it, but don't make it so expensive that it becomes a monster and we don't get very many. If we are going to get some, we have to have at least [360 aircraft].[18]

When he was asked the TAC position on changing the avionics system and possibly including ILAAS, he answered:

I felt we shouldn't disturb the avionics on the airplane . . . but I felt we desperately needed a digital computer. We got more than we asked for. . . . That ILAAS was an extremely sophisticated and expensive system. We didn't want any part of that.[19]

As the debate over the configuration and avionics equipment went on, Air Force secretary Brown received a memorandum from Secretary of the Navy Nitze. The memo, dated March 9, noted that Secretary McNamara had appeared before Congress on February 11, 1966, and had said the Air Force would be getting its first A-7 in January 1967 (less than a year away), but Nitze said that this schedule was considered infeasible by the Navy. He stated the lead time required for government-furnished equipment (radar, radios, engine, etc.) and support equipment would require more time. Nitze noted that the lack of a firm Air Force configuration prevented any promise of a realistic schedule. While the original schedule worked out by the two services in the December 1965 configuration conference had called for a first delivery in September 1967, Secretary Nitze now estimated that this first delivery would take place in April 1968.[20]

On March 14, the Air Staff Board, with Maj. Gen. Lavelle as chairman, met again with the task of recommending a configuration of the A-7.[21] A colonel from the Requirements office briefed with the assistance of Col. Hails. The briefing officer reported on the progress of the ad hoc group and presented four options with varying levels of accuracy. He recommended and supported a version with maximum capabilities. The Air Staff Board did not agree. It recommended eliminating the bombing computer, radar, radar beacon, Doppler equipment, navigation computer, and navigation roller map. It recommended an engine without the afterburner and also recommended deleting most of the basic A-7A avionics.[22]

This recommendation did not correspond to the desires of TAC. The next day, Gen. Disosway wrote a letter to the chief of staff, stating his need for a weapons system with integrated avionics to perform the night and all-weather close air support mission. He noted this would require a totally new system rather than an incremental change to the Navy A-7A. He stated that TAC needed the A-7, especially amid congressional and OSD pressures on the possible neglect of the close-air-support mission. TAC therefore needed the new A-7 to incorporate these additional features to achieve increased delivery accuracy (with capabilities approximated by System III).[23]

He proposed buying fewer than the 561 aircraft programmed if that was necessary to stay within cost considerations. He strongly stated that such a reduction would have to be augmented by permission to buy the F-4 TSF with an internal gun.[24] In short, the "austere" avionics configuration was unacceptable to TAC!

When the Air Force Council met again on March 31, it had the Air Staff Board recommendation for an "austere" avionics system to consider, as well as Gen. Disosway's forceful letter to the chief. The council debated the issues and equipment and decided on a version close to System II, with only an improved analog computer and a servoed gunsight. Other proposals were recommended to make the aircraft compatible with Air Force ground support equipment, but all options that would increase the cost without making significant improvements in weapons delivery accuracy were rejected. On the subject of the engine, the council recommended buying the TF-30-P-6 without an afterburner until the afterburner performance could be demonstrated.

On March 23, one of the Vought test pilots, John Omvig, was airborne near China Lake in the first A-7A prototype, flying a series of runs simulating complete hydraulic-control-system failure during landing approach. The aircraft lost power and crashed, with Omvig ejecting at the last moment. His parachute took one swing, and he hit the ground.[25]

The Cheyenne Helicopter (AH-56) Continues Development

By 1966, the features of the Cheyenne attack helicopter were becoming better known, and it looked like a fearsome high-technology machine. It was a bold attempt to challenge the Air Force for the close-air-support mission. Lockheed built the aircraft by using design features it had pioneered earlier in its XH-51A test ship. The AH-56 had a long, slim fuselage with retractable landing gear and short wings that spanned almost 27 feet. Power was supplied by a General Electric T64-GE-16 shaft turbine engine with 3,922 horsepower that drove a four-bladed rigid rotor, a small tail rotor for directional stability, and a modest-size *pusher propeller that drove the aircraft at high speed in level flight.* The rotor system was very sophisticated.

In the words of author Robert Dorr, "During vertical and hovering flight all power was applied to the main and anti-torque rotors, while during forward flight all but about 700 shaft horse power was shifted to the pusher propeller. In forward flight, lift was generated by the stub wings and windmilling main rotor. In "clean" configuration the AH-56A was capable of sea-level speeds in excess of 275 miles per hour. Its range was 2,200 nautical miles. The weapons load was formidable. It included a 30 mm cannon in the belly, 40 mm grenade launchers and a 7.62 mm mini-gun. The wings had six hard points for bombs or rockets. "It was a helicopter carrying the kind of weapons you typically found on an Air Force fighter-bomber," said Donald F. Segner, the Lockheed test pilot in a 2003 interview. This was "spectacular" performance for a helicopter.[26]

The 1966 Army–Air Force Agreement on Roles and Missions

The Army chief of staff, Gen. Harold K. Johnson, and the Air Force chief of staff, John P. McConnell, met on April 6 after a series of conferences and signed a new agreement on the roles and missions of the respective services. Each military service gained what appeared to be organizational victories. The Army "agrees to relinquish all claims for CV-28 (Caribou) and CV-2 (Buffalo) aircraft, and for future fixed-wing aircraft designed for tactical airlift."[27] The 140 Caribou and four Buffalo aircraft in the Army inventory were to be transferred to the Air Force. In addition, the Army was to disarm all of its reconnaissance aircraft in Vietnam lest they infringe on the close-air-support mission of the Air Force.

The Air Force, in exchange for the exclusive right to develop all future airlift aircraft, agreed "to relinquish all claims for helicopters and follow-on rotary wing aircraft which are designed and operated for intra-theater movement, fire support, supply and resupply of Army forces and those Air Force control elements assigned."[28] This was seen by Army leaders as a victory and promised them a clear field to develop transport and advanced armed helicopters like the Cheyenne. (The feeling reported in the press was that the Air Force was losing the bureaucratic fight to prevent the development of the armed helicopter

anyway, and this, therefore, was a minor concession.) The Army also gained the right to command certain Air Force units (such as airlift aircraft performing supply, resupply, or troop lift) in case of combat urgency. The significance of this doctrinal innovation was not lost on the Army. One Army general said, "The Air Force has never [before] agreed to be under an Army commander. This is quite a significant step."[29]

The Air Force Decision on a Configuration for the A-7D

In this environment and with the continued development of the armed helicopter, it seemed doubly important to decide on a firm A-7 configuration and get the program moving. The briefings and recommendations of the Air Staff Board and Air Force Council were presented to the Designated Systems Management Group, which included the chief of staff and the secretary of the Air Force. On April 7, 1966, Gen. McConnell and Secretary Brown made a formal decision on the A-7 configuration. The decision was expressed and transmitted in two different documents, directed toward internal (Air Force) and external (OSD) audiences.

The internal document was titled "Chief of Staff Decision" to indicate its significance. It was published on April 8 and signed by the vice chief of staff for Gen. McConnell. The decision document stated that the chief had approved the USAF configuration, and that he directed immediate action to procure the aircraft, "which incorporates only minimum changes from the Navy version essential to insure [sic] compatibility with Air Force equipment, mission requirements, and safety features necessary for the environment in which it will be operating." The document reviewed a list of seven avionics options and indicated the chief's decision had been for the center column, a moderate improvement on the existing Navy A-7. The list specified a servoed gunsight and an improved analog computer, essentially System II. In addition, the decision specified that the improved Pratt & Whitney TF-30-P-8 with afterburner would be developed and produced for the Air Force A-7.

At the same time, Secretary Brown initiated action on a memorandum to the secretary of defense and OSD. The letter was written by the Directorate of Operational Requirements to "inform" OSD of the Air Force decision. It reaffirmed the concept of a "low cost, close air support aircraft" but noted that nineteen changes were in line with that concept. The changes were expected to increase the cost by 10–12 percent and fell into three categories: standardization with Air Force equipment (e.g., cannon), equipping for land-based operations (afterburner), and improvement of the avionics to improve accuracy. It stated, however, that the avionics were recognized as being undefined at this point and that the afterburner installation would be only after its performance was demonstrated. The memo requested $36.2 million of the impounded funds on "OSD hold" to be released for seven Air Force A-7 aircraft and initial spares. A total of $10 million of RDT&E funds were requested for immediate development of the afterburning engine.

A special attachment to the memo listed the ground rules for either a "maximum" or a "normal" effort. Both sets of rules specified May 1, 1966, as a go-ahead and a request for *only* 367 aircraft. The difference between the two efforts was in the development of the new engine.

Secretary Brown followed this memorandum with a letter to Navy secretary Nitze in which he stated the Air Force decision on a firm configuration. He said the Air Force was moving rapidly to implement the decision and had an urgent need to field the A-7. He submitted a proposed schedule that he "strongly desired," with the first aircraft in November 1967, eighteen months away and six months earlier than Nitze's memo envisioned.[30]

During May 1966, the Department of the Navy undertook a large reorganization of its support bureaus. The Bureau of Naval Weapons was redesignated the Naval Air Systems Command (NAVAIR). The A-7 Program Management Office now reported to NAVAIR. In July, Col. Hails's Air Force Project Office began to grow from two people (one officer and one civilian)—although he was authorized fifteen—to nine by December.

The Air Force Requirement Is Published
Finally, after many drafts and revisions, the A-7 Requirements Action Directive (RAD) was finalized and published on August 11, 1966. It provided the following guidance to the Project Office:

Direction/Proposal: This RAD validates the requirement for a tactical attack aircraft to be operational during the 1969–1970 time period. It is based on the A-7A, a US Navy attack aircraft in production. The scope of this RAD is limited to a description of those changes made necessary by Air Force operations and maintenance concepts, and the effects of these changes on the performance/capability of the aircraft. Operational Mission: The aircraft will be used to deliver air-to-surface non-nuclear weapons in visual weather in support of tactical air operations.[31]

The RAD included the phrases "aided visual weapon delivery" and "no canned delivery."[32] These stated "requirements" would have a major effect on the capabilities of the aircraft and the Air Force program manager's insistence on their demonstration and reliability.

The chief of staff and secretary's decision on the configuration had been implemented by the publication of the RAD. The issues were expected to be solved easily by the A-7 R&D process and the Navy PMO. That would prove not to be the case. The issues of the engine, the gun, and the avionics soon developed lives of their own.

The A-7D Gets a New Engine
There were three issues of primary concern to Col. Hails and the Air Force decision-makers during this early period: the engine, the gun, and the avionics (aviation electronics). All three were issues of quality. These were the reasons the Air Force decision was essentially one to *develop* the A-7 rather than just "buy" the Navy A-7 off the shelf.

The A-7A was underpowered. The LTV test pilots knew it on the second flight of the prototype. Lt. Gen. Graham knew it when he flew the aircraft at NAS Dallas in 1966. Naval aviators knew it as soon as it was delivered for testing and to the fleet. The engine in the Navy A-7A was the Pratt & Whitney (P&W) TF-30-P-6 turbofan derivative of the TF-30-P-1 on the F-111. The P-6 engine delivered 11,350 pounds of thrust.[33] The TF-30 was prescribed by the Navy in the VAL aircraft RFPs, and it was government-furnished equipment (GFE), purchased and delivered to the contractor by the Navy. All LTV had to do was design the fuselage around the engine. The low thrust was acceptable to the Navy because its aircraft were launched off a catapult on the aircraft carrier. However, when the aircraft arrived in the fleet, the aircraft bombload had to be restricted because steam ingestion reduced the thrust on launch. The low thrust was considered insufficient for Air Force use because of the extremely long takeoff roll the aircraft would require getting airborne with a load of bombs. However, there were many Navy officers who wanted to see more power in the aircraft if it were available.

The Navy Program Management Office (PMO) had already been looking at the problem of increasing the thrust of the TF-30 engine. As early as October 6, 1965, a discussion took place among LTV, P&W, and the Bureau of Naval Weapons on the possibility of putting a low augmented afterburner on the next version of the engine, the TF-30-P-8.[34] The afterburner would increase the thrust for takeoff from 11,350 to about 15,000 pounds. LTV's managers noted that Pratt & Whitney's response to the request was "less than enthusiastic."[35] P&W's reasons may have been that they were saturated with engine business, making hundreds of engines for Boeing 707s and F-111s. After this discussion, Pratt & Whitney did some figuring and responded to the PMO with costs and a schedule to add the afterburner.

When Secretary Brown and Gen. McConnell made their decision on April 7, 1966, to use the Pratt & Whitney TF-30 on the A-7, one of the stipulations was that the afterburner would have to be proven technically feasible, and this involved a high degree of technical risk. The basic problem for the Air Force was that no other engine seemed to be a viable alternative. (Col. Hails was still gathering data on the Spey engine, but he felt he did not have enough information to bring it to the attention of top officials.) The development costs associated with new engines were high ($30–$40 million), and the Pratt & Whitney TF-30 was already in production for the Navy A-7A.

DDR&E Advice on the Afterburner Engine
The Office of the Defense Director of Research and Engineering had been interested in the development of the Air Force and Navy engines for the A-7 program for some time. The staff office most directly involved was that of Mr. T. C.

Muse, the assistant director for Tactical Aircraft Systems. Muse and his principal deputy on aircraft engines, Raymond Standahar, had never been enthusiastic about afterburners that were limited to use on takeoff only. Such devices had been proposed at various times in the past, but none had been proven feasible, and none had been installed in production aircraft.

DDR&E had advised the Navy against contracting for a takeoff-only afterburner on its new TF-30-P-8. DDR&E and OSD *did* approve the Navy change from the model P-6 to the P-8 *without* afterburner in its response to Secretary Nitze's letter of January 6, 1966. The TF-30-P-8 subsequently was planned for all Navy A-7Bs, but with only 12,200 pounds thrust it was still much less than the Air Force wanted.

After Muse and Standahar had registered their disapproval of the afterburner engine to the Navy, they saw Air Force interest growing for the same engine. Secretary Brown's memorandum of April 9, requesting to develop the P-8 with afterburner, was routed to DDR&E and did not meet with approval.

The secretary of defense responded to Secretary Brown's request the same day as the DDR&E memo was sent out. McNamara wrote to both the secretaries, Air Force and Navy, and approved the plan to proceed with the Air Force A-7. He noted that since the changes from the Navy A-7 were minor, a formal "contract definition" phase, with other contractors invited to bid, was not required. However, he disapproved the takeoff-only afterburner in favor of a nonafterburning engine (TF-30-P-8A) with 13,000 pounds thrust that was under development, he said, by Pratt & Whitney. He stated his reason was that the non-afterburning engine would not provide better takeoff or acceleration capability, but it would be better in all other areas of performance (such as range and loiter time). He then released $10 million in the Air Force RDT&E account for the development of the new engine.[36]

The triple problems of engine, gun, and avionics had been primary issues confronting Col. Hails when he took over the management of the Air Force A-7 program. During the first six months he worked almost single-handedly in the office with the Navy, LTV, Pratt & Whitney, and the Air Staff, attempting to reach a decision on the configuration of the aircraft. He described his early approach in February to the engine problem when the Air Staff had been considering the afterburner as the best solution to the underpowered airplane:

They told me to put an afterburner on it to get the aircraft off the ground, because the thrust was [only] 10,500 pounds. We used to have a joke that the takeoff distance of the A-7 was equal to the radius of action of the F-5! So, Pratt & Whitney came down, and they wanted to put an afterburner on the TF-30-P-6. It would have given a simple fifty percent increase in thrust for takeoff. Well, in my experience with the F-111 program, most of our early problems were from putting an afterburner in back of a by-pass [turbo] fan. This is because when you light the afterburner you get a transient backpressure that comes up through the side ducts and stalls the fan. This is a very sophisticated development, and it has many problems.

So, I looked around to see if I couldn't sound out some other way, and I had heard that the [Rolls-Royce] TF-41 (Spey) engine would fit into the airplane. I discussed it with the contractor, LTV, and they said that hadn't done any studies on it, but they had looked at the TF-41 engine when they were trying to sell the airplane to Canada, and it would fit.

This is a humorous story! I thought that General Electric was the company that was going to build it [under license from Rolls-Royce], so I talked to GE and asked them for some information. They came down here and talked like they knew about the TF-41. They were interested in it, for the business. Two weeks went by, and three weeks went by, and they didn't come back. I had told them when they were here that if they were interested, they had better get their boss to buy a ticket to England and talk to Rolls-Royce and come back. They never did come back, and the Washington representative of GE went to see [Asst.] Secretary Charles (Installations & Logistics) to get him to *direct* GE to look at it. It turned out that General Motors Allison has a working relationship with Rolls, and [GE]

couldn't disturb it. That whole month [of March] they cost me was while they were trying to find some way around the relationship. "When I found out that Allison had something to do with Rolls, I called their Washington office and asked their representative if he knew anything about the Spey engine. He said no, "we don't know anything about that." So, I called the British embassy and got the commercial attaché. I told him who I was and that I wanted to find out if that Rolls-Royce engine would go in my airplane.

He got in touch with the North American representative in Canada, and he called me. We had about three or four meetings, and they asked if they could bring a representative from Allison. I said they could bring their mother because I was stalled out. This Allison guy sat in the corner and said he didn't know if GM was interested in the program. The next morning Roger Keyes, the executive vice president of General Motors, walked in my office and said, "I understand you were wondering if General Motors was interested in this, and I thought if I flew out here from Detroit, you'd get the message." They made a corporate commitment. Then I had my engineers look at it. Then I started the long row to hoe to sell that [to the Air Force Board Structure].[37]

The basic situation, as the Navy program manager, Capt. Cruse, saw it, was that the Navy did not face as critical a problem on the engine as did the Air Force. When asked if the Navy was slower to go the Spey engine, Capt. Cruse answered:

To come round to the idea of *wanting* to go to the Spey, I would say definitely, yes. First, remember the catapult reduced the seriousness of the thrust problem as far as the Navy was concerned. Secondly, the Navy already had committed itself to the [TF-30] P-8 program for the A-7B before the Air Force came in, so we had one improvement out there that we hadn't really seen any benefits from, but we knew we were going to get sometime. I believe the first efforts for the Navy to switch over were based on the desire to have a common airplane. . . . But in general, the Navy was reluctant to go this route because the whole

[Navy] logistics system had been geared for the TF-30.[38]

One of the reasons for LTV's reluctance was their lack of understanding of the Air Force as a customer. They knew a lot about the Navy, about Navy requirements, and about Navy officers—Navy culture. There also was the question of size: naval aviation was about the same size as Tactical Air Command, which was just one of the three combatant commands in the Air Force and only one of the dozen major air commands. LTV did not know very much at all, they readily admitted, about the Tactical Air Command, about the Air Force requirements process, Air Force project management, or Air Force culture.

LTV knew it had only an introductory grasp on what the Air Force needed, because of the reasons reviewed above and because of the elimination of the attack branch of aircraft before World War II. The Air Force's only attack airplanes in the 1960s were propeller aircraft assigned to Special Air Warfare units in Vietnam. LTV engineers and executives knew of the extensive Air Force resistance to the concept of subsonic aircraft and witnessed the Air Force opposition to the A-4 and A-7 when proposed by OSD in 1963–65. From LTV's point of view, Air Force resistance to subsonic aircraft had not diminished measurably after the Air Force decision to buy the A-7 in late 1965. LTV management was reportedly continually afraid the Air Force would cancel the program and use the cost of the change of engines and a new gun (or later, the change in avionics) as an excuse.[39] Using LTV's logic, this line of reasoning was rational and straightforward, and it supported a policy of minimum risk; it almost necessitated a no-risk attitude to avoid further jeopardizing the entire program.

LTV was not assisted, in its attempt to relate to the Air Force way of doing things, by its continued close relationship to the Navy. LTV managers related many incidents where the company's approach to Col. Hails, other program management personnel, and TAC had been unwelcome, ineffective, or unresponsive. A large part of this was due to the LTV failure to perceive that the approach it had developed over years of working closely with the Navy would not be appropriate when applied to the Air Force. One of the most glaring examples was the mistake LTV made in underestimating the authority of the Air Force program manager. The Air Force delegates a great degree of trust and authority to the program manager, and attempts to go over his head to officials in Air Force Systems Command or Headquarters USAF are not welcomed![40]

After sounding out the company on the feasibility and desirability of putting in the Spey engine, Col. Hails took the proposal to the Air Staff. One of the first things he did was to have Allison representatives brief the headquarters staff on the possible use of the Spey engine in the A-7. Allison requested permission to submit a formal proposal by June 8, 1966.

Gen. McConnell directed a detailed study of the TF-41 engine versus the Pratt & Whitney–proposed TF-30-P-14. The two engines were under study in four places during June: the Air Staff, the Project Management Office, the Aeronautical Systems Division of Air Force Systems Command, and DDR&E.

It was quite apparent that once the General Motors / Allison management learned of the real possibility of putting the Rolls-Royce engine in the A-7, they produced a coordinated and effective effort. At the same time, although Pratt & Whitney may have been worried about the new competition, indications were that they did not mount any sort of campaign.[41] This was partially confirmed on July 5, when contracting officials from ASD briefed the Air Staff and noted that if the Air Force did plan to continue with the TF-30 engine, the Pratt & Whitney production rate for Air Force engines would be very slow.[42]

The Air Force Decision on the Spey Engine
With a combination of performance factors, contract guarantees, and foreign-policy considerations, Secretary Brown and Gen. McConnell decided to recommend purchase of the TF-41 Spey engine to the secretary of defense. On July 25, 1966, Secretary Brown sent his decision memo forward, stating both the background and rationale for the recommendation. The background stated that the Navy was not joining in the engine program because of the TF-30 commonality with Navy equipment and logistics, but that the Canadian version

of the A-7 could use the Spey engine. It stated that the delay in Pratt & Whitney production availability had been the determining factor in renewed Air Force interest in another source, and that Allison had joined Rolls-Royce in a concerted effort to design an acceptable engine.

The conclusions were that the Spey engine offered the following:

- better overall performance: more range, more loiter time

- lower costs: $315,000 per engine versus $485,000

- higher production rates: 25 per month versus 20

- earlier operational capability and more-meaningful guarantees

- new competitive engine source

- F-111 / United Kingdom gold flow offset[43]

The secretary of defense approved the Spey engine decision nine days later, on August 3, 1966. He noted, however, that the Air Force was to be restrained from putting the Air Force M-61 cannon in the A-7 until a joint Air Force / Navy program could be developed for its use.[44]

McNamara later gave these reasons for changing his earlier decision on the engine:

Two considerations caused us first to delay and then to change this decision. First, it appeared desirable, if possible, to find a new engine production source rather than add to the already crowded schedule of one of our principal engine manufacturers. Second, if a different, more powerful engine could be used, the load-carrying capacity of the A-7 would not have to be penalized by several hundred pounds of dead weight which the afterburner would involve. Such an engine, the Rolls-Royce's "Spey" proved to be obtainable from Allison, who will produce it in the United States under license from the British firm.[45]

During August, President Johnson discussed the use of the Rolls-Royce engine with Prime Minister Wilson while discussing the proposed British purchase of F-111s. Sir Deming Pearson, deputy chairman and chief executive of Rolls-Royce, said that confirmation was "expected shortly" and "I regard it as the biggest breakthrough Rolls-Royce has ever had."[46]

The Air Force agreement with Rolls-Royce/Allison was written on August 31, 1966, and finalized into a fixed-price incentive fee contract on December 30, 1966. The contract called for the development and production of five hundred Spey engines with options for 1,500 more. The cost of the research and development phase was $28 million, and the production phase was for $227,283,619, with an average unit cost of $342,904.[47] Two and a half years later, in June 1968, Allison made the first test run of the prototype TF-41 only one week behind schedule, and it produced almost 15,000 pounds of thrust. The Navy immediately became very interested in the TF-41 engine for its new version of the A-7, the A-7E.

Systems Analysis experienced a change in its views. Before the data on the lower cost of the Spey were available, they had expressed the view that any change to the engine would be undesirable. However, once the analysts learned the Spey would not increase the cost, they did not really involve themselves deeply in the decision. Russ Murray noted:

The Spey was a good idea; it was cheaper than the TF-30 to begin with. We appreciated the fact that it [the A-7A] could use more power. It was a pretty sluggish machine and who can be against having more power? The thing we were a little bit scared about though, was the cost of the TF-30, so when the Spey came up, that looked very promising. So said, "Great, let's go ahead and get the Spey."[48]

Even with the lower costs of the Spey, Systems Analysis was a little wary of the uncertainties of its development. Again, Russ Murray noted a degree of lingering doubt:

So, at that [the engine change] was almost the start of "hard times," but not quite, but that was one of the little chinks in the system.[49]

The result was that the Spey decision went through the government's decision process with exceptional speed, from May 25 to August 3, and with little dissent. As one experienced Air Staff officer commented, "It emerged so fast; it was just such a timely thing. I had never seen anything win approval so fast as did the Spey engine over the Pratt & Whitney."[50]

The Doctrine of Quality had prevailed.

Pilot Report on the New Engine

Greg Stearns is a naval aviator who flew the A-7A, B, and C; the TA-7C; and the A-7E. He provided some observations on the power of the new engine:

The thrust was noticeably different from the TF-30 to the TF-41. The TF-30-P-6 was a real dog compared to the TF-41. Although "gas mileage" was great, we spent most of our time flying low since it took so long to climb to altitude. I flew a few hops in the A-7C with the TF-30-P-408, and that was a great engine . . . powerful and responsive. Although it had less thrust than the TF-41, the responsiveness made up for the thrust difference.

Both the TF-30 and the TF-41 were responsive to the throttle while on the ball [light device that guided the pilot onto the correct flight path to land on the carrier] . . . unless you pulled too much power off. My memory is that the TF-41 took a little longer to spool back up if you made a large power reduction. When the cockpit got real quiet on a dark night inside three-quarters of a mile [from the boat] (other than the landing signal officer screaming, "Power, power, power"), you knew that you had overcorrected and that the rest of the trip to the deck was going to be really exciting (assuming the LSOs did not give you the "Waveoff" lights).[51]

The A-7D Gets a New Gun

The second of the three issues identified in the April 1966 decision was the gun in the airplane. The Navy installed two of its standard 20 mm Mk. 12 cannon in the A-7A and A-7B. The Colt Mk. 12 was a derivative of the World War II Hispano HS 404, which was used in many British and some American fighters. It was a conventional mechanical slide cannon where the receiver was cycled by exhaust gases from the projectile, and the round was mechanically activated by a firing pin. This procedure limited the rate of fire to a thousand rounds per minute. The muzzle velocity was 3,300 feet per second. These parameters were both acceptable to the Navy, and the gun was the basic armament of the F-8 Crusader, the F-11 Tiger, and the A-4 Skyhawk. There were two operational problems with the gun that were being reported by the fleet. It was inaccurate and frequently unreliable, especially after heavy maneuvering, resulting in jams and stoppages.

The Air Force Requirement for the M-61 Gun

One of the problems with the A-7 for the Air Force was that the slide cannon had been replaced long ago, in the 1950s, by a rotary cannon. The General Electric M-61 Gatling was a superior weapon. It fired a similar 20 mm round electronically through six rotating barrels at a rate of six thousand rounds per minute. The muzzle velocity was 3,080 feet per second, virtually the same as the Mk. 12, but it was much more reliable. The two Mk. 12s on the A-7A/B carried 650 rounds, whereas the M-61 had a thousand. The gun was the standard armament in the F-104 Starfighter, the F-105 Thunderchief, the F-111 Aardvark, and the AC-130 gunship. It was a better weapon, and it was high on the list of required changes in the USAF Requirements Action Directive.

The Air Force had never agreed with the Navy decision in the 1950s to rely only on air-to-air missiles for air defense and air superiority missions when they designed the F-4 Phantom. The F-4 radar could detect an enemy aircraft well beyond 30 miles. Its Raytheon AIM-7 missiles could kill an enemy aircraft "beyond visual range." The problem as the Air Force saw it was that most Rules of Engagement required visual identification, so that by the time an approaching jet fighter was within that short distance, he was within gun range. In addition, guns were virtually 100 percent reliable, unlike problematic missiles. The approval was *very* significant also to the A-7 program, because it was the gun version of the Air Force

F-4 that was increasingly seen as the competitor for A-7 funds and force structure.

Secretary McNamara Approves the Tactical Strike Fighter with an Internal Gun

While the new engine was being considered for the A-7, the secretary of defense finally decided in favor of letting the Air Force go ahead with plans to put a cannon in the nose of the F-4 Phantom II, as requested by Secretary Brown in the original A-7 decision memorandum of November 1965 and again on May 25, 1966. Brown's May memo used the following statement:

You will recall that our earlier studies of cost/effectiveness of the F-4 in air-ground operations indicated the improved cost/effectiveness which would result with an internally mounted gun. Recent air actions in North Vietnam have also clearly indicated the desirability of an internally mounted gun for air-to-air combat.

Finally, you will recall that when I recommended inclusion of the A-7 in the force (reference my memorandum to you dated November 5, 1965, Subject: Interim Buy Tactical Fighters), I indicated that the studies which supported this recommendation showed the need for a very high-quality air superiority aircraft in such a mixed force. Making future F-4 buys in the TSF configuration, in addition to being cost/effective itself with respect to both air-to-air and air/ground missions, will support the planned mixture of lower-cost tactical aircraft in the USAF inventory.

I request your approval to substitute procurement of the TSF version of the F-4 for the previously approved FY1966 procurement of the ninety-nine F-4Es without internal guns. Simultaneously the TSF should be redesignated the F-4E.[52]

Secretary McNamara approved Dr. Brown's request on July 22, 1966.[53] This was a landmark decision as far as the Air Force was concerned because of combat experience, Air Force doctrine, and the amount of effort that had gone into the F-4 gun program.

Congressional Pressure Continues to Insist on Better Close Air Support

Representative Otis Pike continued to publicize issues that affected the A-7. His Armed Services subcommittee on tactical air capabilities was holding hearings again in September 1966, with the stated intention to focus more attention on the accelerated production of tactical aircraft, and particularly counterinsurgency aircraft. Pike was quoted as saying that "greater efforts should be visible to make up the ground we lost when we favored strategic aircraft almost to the exclusion of any-thing else. . . . I haven't seen any evidence of it. With the present lead time, we ought to be pushing like mad and we're not."[54]

The Caissons Go Rolling Along

The Army was continuing to move into a position to claim part of the close-air-support mission by acquiring armed helicopters and organizing "air mobile" units. Its actions were being followed closely by the Air Staff. On September 8, 1966, Gen. McConnell sent out a formal Chief of Staff Decision letter titled "Analysis of Close Air Support Operations" that directed:

The Air Force study and incrementally take steps to reflect in official USAF doctrine, tactics and procedures, publications, methods for accomplishing missions for which the armed helicopter is being provided, and which the Air Force considers part of the Close Air Support function.[55]

McNamara Directs a Common Gun for the Air Force and Navy A-7s

During September 1966, the secretary of defense was again involved in deciding what should go into the Air Force configuration for the A-7. The Navy A-7A and A-7B had been approved and produced with two Mk. 12 cannons installed. Secretary Brown in his April memorandum had requested permission to replace the two Navy guns with one M-61 cannon. McNamara's answer to the gun request, in July and again when he approved the Spey engine in August, had been negative until a program for the gun's joint use could be devised. Accordingly, he requested the secretaries of the Navy and Air Force to develop a plan to standardize the use of the Air Force M-61 gun in both versions of the A-7. The Air Force and Navy staffs had discussed and debated the merits of the two guns' performance and their different logistics chains but had subsequently come to an impasse on resolving the issue.[56]

When the issue was brought again to the attention of Secretary McNamara in September 1966, he wasted no time in issuing a directive stating that the gun decision of the two military services would needlessly produce more non-standard aircraft. Observers will recall that standardization was one of the guiding principles of Robert McNamara since he was president of Ford Motor Company, and *the* driving factor in directing the joint Air Force / Navy development of the TFX (F-111). He ordered, on September 21, 1966, "You are to proceed with the incorporation of the M-61 gun into both Air Force and Navy versions of the A-7."[57]

In this case, the "Doctrine of Quality" was reinforced by the policy of standardization. Since the issue of the M-61 gun had risen to the OSD level, Systems Analysis had a prime opportunity to make its views known on the subject. The office was in favor of letting the Air Force use the M-61 gun, but they continued to be staunchly against any efforts to incorporate a complex avionics system. One of the primary views of Systems Analysis was expressed by Russ Murray:

> You can't hardly argue that the Air Force has to use the Navy gun. The M-61 clearly had to go in. We agreed with that. There were a few little changes here and a few little changes there. As a matter of fact, the Air Force put in some things we thought the Navy should have [such as FM radios] to talk to the ground troops. We wondered why the Navy didn't have that; it seems to make pretty good sense.
>
> Well, we were *deeply* involved in it; we were a little distressed to see the price going up as much as it was. The *big* problem came with the fancy avionics. . . . The Navy [and the Air Force] wanted to . . . take our nice, simple, inexpensive, easily maintained A-7 and put one of the *dreadfully* complicated systems in it that we doubted would work.[58]

Until this time, there had been no major changes to the basic configuration of the Navy A-7A or A-7B. The engine change from the A to the B was only a minor upgrade of the P&W TF-30 from the P-6 to the P-8, both of which fit in the same fuselage space and did not require any significant structural changes. The direct order to put the M-61 gun in all future A-7s would be the second major change to the Air Force A-7, but it would require the first major fuselage change in the Navy versions.

The A-7D Gets New Avionics

The April 1966 Air Force command guidance on the avionics issue was to develop "an 'improved' system" with individual components upgraded from the Navy equipment: improved *analog* [emphasis added] navigation computer, a servoed sight, and a separate analog weapons delivery computer with 15–20 mils of accuracy (System II). The decision memorandum specified several of the individual components that were to be installed in the Air Force A-7D. The option of including a *digital* computer had been specifically rejected.

The Air Force RAD was even more specific than the decision memo. Its guidance to the Program Office was to

1. delete Fixed Optical Sight

2. provide Stabilized [servoed] sight

3. delete CP-741 [analog] Weapons Release Computer

4. provide Analog Bombing Computer

Not specifically called out, it also required a separate analog navigation computer.

The Navy Receives the Air Force Requirement

Capt. Cruse was still the head of the Navy Program Management Office. He had been anticipating a changed avionics system with Col. Hails. Both officers were wondering if very accurate weapon delivery could ever be achieved on a regular basis with the limitations of the specified analog computer, even in an improved version. Later, Capt. Cruse was asked if the move to an improved avionics system was partially due to reports coming back from Vietnam that showed the need for increased bombing accuracy. Capt. Cruse said:

Yes, it was that plus we were learning more about the CP-741 [analog] bombing computer; we could see that while we were going to get improvements, but we were not going to get quantum jumps in improvements [from an analog computer], and our accuracy would still be something to be sought. It was about at this point that Bob Doss came on the scene and relieved me of the Navy part of the program and became the Navy Deputy. Bob was something of an expert in this area, having been out at China Lake [Naval Ordnance Test Center] and worked closely with efforts out there to improve bombing accuracy. So, he had a large influence on what happened after that. That's about the only way I know to express it, that Bob had a large influence on how the A-7E turned out to be configured.[59]

This turned out to be the understatement of the year.

The Navy Gets a
New Deputy Program Manager
Robert F. Doss, commander, USN (already selected for captain), was assigned to the A-7 program as the Navy deputy program manager in July 1966. Previously he had served in Capt. Cruse's Carrier Attack Group and in various positions related to attack aviation and the development of avionics equipment. He had just come from a Vietnam tour as the operations officer of the aircraft carrier USS *Ranger*, and his assignment had reportedly been at the request of Capt. Cruse.[60]

Capt. Doss was regarded as an exceptionally innovative and dynamic officer. He had been one of the youngest Navy pilots to fly the McDonnell F2H Banshee in the Korean War and had accumulated a wealth of attack experience since that time. He had been an A-4 squadron commander and had spent a tour of duty at China Lake in VX-5, the Navy's Air Development Squadron testing attack weapons. He had been selected for captain well ahead of his contemporaries and was

regarded as having an excellent chance of making rear admiral. His professional qualifications included a BS in aeronautical engineering from Georgia Institute of Technology and a graduate "professional degree" in aeronautical engineering from California Institute of Technology. Doss had, in addition, completed the Naval Postgraduate School and the Naval War College. He could be called an innovation advocate.

The Innovation Advocate in Navy Cases
Vincent Davis, the Nimitz Chair of National Security and Foreign Affairs at the Naval War College, studied officers who successfully advocated major changes in Navy policy and technology projects. His observations led him to develop a model of those he called "innovation advocates." He is a "man in the broad middle ranks (lieutenant commander, commander, captain). He is seldom the inventor of the innovation that he is promoting, but he possesses a uniquely advanced technological knowledge pertinent to the innovation that is not generally shared within the Navy. He is a passionate zealot. . . . He does not suffer fools gladly. He seldom pays any attention whatever to the way in which his crusading efforts may influence his personal career in the Navy or elsewhere. His first step is usually to try to enlist supporters from among friends and colleagues at his own rank level. His second step is usually to recruit supporters in key positions of authority and power at higher levels. The pro-innovation coalition seldom seeks to sell its idea in terms of new conceptions of international politics, military strategy or tactics."[61]

The Situation in the Program Office
Capt. Doss later described his entry into the Navy Program Management Office:

Bob Hails was there six months ahead of me, . . . and I reported July 1, 1966. He'd gone through all the rat race of not getting any help out of Pratt & Whitney for an engine and not getting much in the way of studies, getting no money and no people. When I got there, there was just him. In fact, there were just about he and I and a few attached people and Carl [Cruse] and Bob Little, who was a GS-13 and the assistant deputy for the Navy, my assistant. Hails had a few people but not many, . . . but we started to grow.

Then in the early fall we got together on the configuration; we started that effort in earnest. I don't know exactly why, but the Navy had the A-7A and B, which was put together in a hurry with off-the-shelf avionics of the 1950s. We *had* everything; we had a computer and we had a gunsight, we had a two-gyro platform . . . etc. We had an analog navigation computer, but the computer read out digitally, and you don't fly that way.

If you're going to pay for all this stuff, you need to integrate it and make it produce as assistance to the pilot—or else you've got to provide a second crewman. Our concept, being a single-place airplane, was to see what we could do with a few hundred pounds of avionics to lessen the workload on the pilot.[62]

Capt. Doss was driven by the need to improve the navigation and weapons delivery of the A-7. He wanted the system to be more integrated with better displays. Now that he was in the Program Office, he was determined to make the weapons system better, and he set out to do this.

One of Capt. Doss's Navy colleagues offered a view of his character:

I think that Bob Doss has always visualized something [such as an integrated avionics capability]; he's been great in the air-to-ground business. He was in VX-5 at China Lake, which is the attack development squadron for the Navy, and he had his own A-4 squadron. He was always insisting on the avionics equipment in his aircraft being updated and working all the time. In doing so, he was able to improve on the weapons systems that were given to us. To us, I mean to the people who were flying aircraft. . . . I think this avionics suite belongs to Bob Doss primarily, because he was the one who insisted and pounded day and night that this was what we had to have in order to get the accuracy out of the weapons that we wanted to . . . I think you're going to have to blame Bob Doss for the avionics on the A-7. It's his fault.[63]

Capt. Doss described his appraisal of the situation and related the approach he saw in respect to the ongoing Navy ILAAS program and Col. Hails's Air Force requirement:

He had his RAD, which was a system that wouldn't work, *and he knew it*. His requirement when it came from the Air Staff was crazy. Basically, you couldn't get the kind of CEP [circular error probable] they wanted with the equipment specified. . . . It had a servoed sight, but you don't need a servoed sight without inertial velocity inputs—why servo it?

The way I looked at the situation was this; the Air Force were going to come in and make a *major* change to the airplane. There were going to put the M-61 gun in it, a different engine, and probably about a 33–50 percent fuselage change. They were going to change the avionics rather extensively. I looked at his RAD, and it sized up to me to be a loser. It wasn't going to produce; we were going to spend all the money, but we weren't going to get the capability the RAD called out, nor the capability that we wanted.

We had 230 A-7Bs (which is the same as the A-7A except for a little more thrust) in the Fiscal '67 budget, which now in July 1966 that's the thing you're aiming toward. It has 240 Bs in the Fiscal 1968 budget. It appeared to me that we were going to lose a number of those airplanes. When you sit down and look at the force structure—the number of Air Wings and carriers we've got—and you see that the attrition is nothing like we had projected, you know somebody's going to cut way back on the numbers of airplanes.

The Air Force was going to make this big change, and there wasn't a chance in hell of us ever doing things with ILAAS in the A-7 or some portions of ILAAS in the A-7 after the Air Force makes their changes. It was too much to ask the taxpayer to go through that twice. The important thing to do was to get the Air Force to buy the basic objectives of ILAAS[,] which was an integrated digital system.[64]

Col. Hails was equally interested in getting the Navy and Capt. Doss to go along with *his* avionics improvements. He noted:

I was desperately interested in the Navy coming in because we already had an agreement that we would share the non-recurring development costs on a 50–50 basis. Up to that point I was carrying the whole bag on the Air Force program, and I was dedicated to get the improved performance on the airplane.[65]

Relationship to the ILAAS Program

The Navy had planned for the ILAAS integrated avionics system to be installed in the A-7, but there was never a decision about the timing or the logistics. The PMO's first priority was to get the A-7A developed and into combat. The urgency of the upgraded engine was a second priority. There had never been a study or plan to identify and address the numerous interface and integration issues that were inevitable with ILAAS. There were two problems with ILAAS: (1) the program continued to fall behind schedule, and (2) it was expected to cost from $800,000 to $1.4 million *per system* in addition to the cost of the airplane and the engine.

An Addition to Personnel in Systems Analysis

Herbert Rosenzweig joined Systems Analysis as the head of Tactical Air. Whereas both Murray and Parker had held the A-7, and Navy attack airplanes in general, in high esteem, the attitude in the office was likely to be different. Rosenzweig had just come from the Rand Corporation in Santa Monica, California, where he coauthored with G. H. Fisher and S. Wildhorn a study titled *A Comparison of Alternative Mixes of Land-Based and Sea-Based Tactical Aircraft* (RM-4444, February 1965). Mr. Rosenzweig's views were widely known within DoD to be in favor of land-based as opposed to sea-based tactical aircraft, and in favor of the F-4 as compared to the A-7 in particular. It was the opinion of many individuals in the A-7 program that the numbers of A-7s in future budgets would be scrutinized and, if possible, reduced by Systems Analysis.

The effect of the personnel shift was reinforced also by a change in attitude toward tactical air of the assistant secretary of defense for systems analysis, Dr. Alain Enthoven, who said this:

We were spending about $16 billion a year on tactical air forces and really didn't know why. There was just no good analytical, logical basis for why we should be spending so much. We had just kind of started down that road of sending more on tactical air because we all believed in it, and we had never figured out when and where to cut it off.[66]

Not only was Systems Analysis developing a general attitude that the level of spending was too high, they were developing a specific attitude toward avionics development. The attitude was expressed by Russ Murray when he was asked why he thought proposals were made continually for improvements in avionics:

Gadgeteers. Gadgeteers. I think it is gadgeteers; it is what happens to every airplane. . . . My image of a new system is that they make the program manager walk down a hallway in the middle of the Systems Command pulling a little red wagon, and as he passes each of the other program offices, they throw on their pet project. Pretty soon your simple little airplane has everyone's favorite gadget on it, and the cost is doubled; how did that happen? Well, it's all this junk that keeps getting put on there.

Now it's not all junk, but the difficulty is that people have high hopes for their latest invention. So instead of taking it out and testing it and demonstrating that it really will work under realistic conditions and then putting it in, they say, "No, that'd take too long; we'd miss half of the production. We'd better put it in at the beginning." And that's what happens.[67]

This statement by Russ Murray is a classic articulation of a fundamental, enduring issue in weapons acquisition: the tension between developing advancing technology and experimenting with it in Development Test and Evaluation (DT&E) and Operational Test and Evaluation (OT&E) so there is high confidence in its performance, versus inserting it into a systems *program* where the success of the overall program is dependent on the performance of this system.

Being convinced that an improvement in the Navy and Air Force avionics systems could be jointly worked out, Capt. Doss described how he and Col. Hails approached the contractors who possessed the best avionics engineers:

Bob and I started around the country going to all the well-known contractors—Sperry, North American, Hughes, IBM, and LTV. We were having trouble with LTV, and we started right out to tell the primes [contractors] that we talked to—the avionics primes—that we were seriously considering an associate contractor to do the avionics and to provide the avionics GFE [government-furnished equipment] to LTV to incorporate in the airplane.

We told LTV that they were going to have to compete, that we were not going to take what they said in this single-source arrangement. We were going to keep competitive pressure on them, and if they were going to do it, they were going to have to show us that they had a winner. Well, we had to back down off of that later, but not altogether, and *we got LTV's attention*, which is a *very* important part of program management when you are in a single-source selection.[68]

The Navy Gets a New Program Manager

Capt. Cruse was reassigned in his normal rotation in September, and the new program manager was Capt. Thomas J. Gallagher. Capt. Gallagher described his concept of his role in the office:

The A-7A and B program was my objective at the time. I could *not* be concerned in the D and E . . . because my objective was to get the A-7A deployed on schedule in November 1967. So therefore, my two deputies, Capt. Doss and Col. Hails, were configuring the D and E together.[69]

In December 1966, the crucial event was the carrier qualification of the A-7A, which was being conducted in the Atlantic Ocean off Norfolk. To prepare the selected aircraft for this test, the PMO was supervising a series of engineering changes to the aircraft, as well as supplying a host of spare parts directly to the deploying squadron.

The Program Management Office Initiates a New Series of Avionics Studies

Capt. Doss and Col. Hails initiated a new round of avionics studies by agencies within the government and industry. These studies were in addition to the first series conducted by LTV in January–April 1966, but were in much more detail. Now they were designing a system! Because of contractual procedures the PMO was required to divide the LTV effort into two studies—one for each military service. They decided to have LTV first do a trade-off study of the avionics on the Air Force version of the A-7. This study was one of the items included in the first official Air Force contract with LTV, signed October 31, 1966. The letter contract was for $19 million and included instructions for additional design effort, tool fabrication, long-lead-time materials, and a study of alternatives for avionics. OSD Public Affairs put out a news release that also envisioned the delivery of the first A-7 in 1968, with a full Air Force wing of seventy-two aircraft in operational service in 1969.[70]

The LTV avionics studies were later described by the Vought vice president / program manager, Sol Love. He began by describing the initial study (January–April) and carried on to the later studies:

There was about a year where we were doing considerable trade-off studies in avionics, and Bob Hails started getting involved. The trade studies were fairly straight forward with a pretty direct objective. The Air Force position—and I support it—was "OK, we're going to get a ground attack airplane." . . . They established some requirements, which were "If I'm going to go into the ground support business, I want an airplane that can deliver a bomb on target, and a target I've preselected. So, we want some accuracy for bomb delivery. You [LTV] tell me that you have a 20 mil system in the A-7A; that's not good enough for us. What we want to look at in terms of what can we get for what cost?"

So we started a long series of trade studies, looking at different types of systems from the A-7A simple analog, to a more sophisticated analog, to a digital system, and eventually to a heads-up display from the point of pilot training and what it might do to increase accuracy for a novice pilot to do, just as good as a top-notch pilot.[71]

There was an initial misunderstanding between LTV and the Air Force over the avionics improvement. The following interview demonstrates the difference between Air Force and Navy program management. This difference was highlighted when Col. Hails went to Dallas in the fall of 1966 with his RAD for increased accuracy. LTV tried to talk Hails out of changing the avionics in the A-7A, since they underestimated the importance of the Air Force written requirement. Col. Hails emphasized:

> I think this is important. LTV thought they were selling the *Navy* an airplane for the Air Force instead of selling the Air Force an airplane for itself. They had done business with the Navy for 25 or 30 years [actually, 50] and never had a major Air Force program.
>
> They had no philosophical understanding of the way we go about establishing requirements, and how we buy airplanes, and who has what authority in the Air Force.[72]

Similarly, one of the LTV program managers said:

> It took us awhile to see what Hails and Doss were working for in an improved avionics system.[73]

In addition to LTV, Doss and Hails went to the ILAAS contractor, Sperry, and had the engineers there do two or three studies. Then Capt. Doss had the Naval Ordnance Test Center at China Lake and the Naval Air Development Center at Johnsville, Pennsylvania, begin independent avionics studies.[74]

An Industry Shift in Aviation Skills: The Rise of Computers

At this point in the A-7 acquisition process, LTV underwent a change of philosophy about weapons system management that is significant. Interviews at LTV revealed that their firm in 1966 was similar to others in the aviation industry, where the dominant business mantra was designing and selling "pounds of aluminum." That is, the aircraft was seen as an aeronautical-engineering vehicle built primarily from lightweight aluminum. It was designed to hold one or more engines and some electronic equipment, much of it instruments and communications radios, supplied by the government for reasons of standardization and commonality. Similarly, the firms that specialized in the manufacture of these electronic items were *not* involved in aircraft production. Their electronic boxes and systems were *purchased* from vendors by the prime contractors, who found it cheaper to *buy* the systems, rather than *make* them. This tended to keep electronic systems at the state of the art, rather than push their development into higher technology. Thus, the top management of LTV and other aerospace firms tended to be test pilots and aeronautical engineers—not electrical or electronics engineers. Interviewees implied that LTV's current management was not capable of understanding or envisioning the power of an integrated avionics system in improving weapon performance.

The result of this tension within the firm was top management's decision to adjust their thinking and reorganize its A-7 development office. To do this, they reviewed their staff inside the firm and picked several top avionics specialists. Chief among them was Mr. Robert Buzard. They sought his opinions and installed him and his colleagues in new and higher positions of authority. These professionals were more sympathetic to Col. Hails's and Capt. Doss's entreaties, and they tackled the avionics system issue with vigor.

The avionics studies being supervised by the PMO were the subject of continued interest in the Air Staff, TAC, and the Office of the Secretary of the Air Force. Gen. Disosway, the commander of TAC, wrote to Gen. McConnell on November 17 and stated TAC's request again for an adverse-weather, night attack capability in the A-7D.[75] Gen. Disosway elaborated in an interview: "Yes, we figured if we were going to get a ground support airplane, then we should get one that was right up to the state of the art. . . . The A-7 in our opinion was bought to do close air support and interdiction, and you needed avionics to do that job, period!"[76]

Gen. McConnell did not agree with Gen. Disosway, and his reply was dated December 6, 1966. He went over the reasons for the April 1966 decision to include only an "improved avionics" system on the A-7 configuration and noted, "This decision was necessary so that we could hold the cost as low as practicable in consonance with the cost/effectiveness studies."[77] The letter noted that other forms of radar equipment were available to perform part of the all-weather weapons delivery mission and that the F-4 was a prime candidate for the incorporation of more-sophisticated avionics.[78] This letter confirmed that the chief of staff was primarily interested in getting an airplane he could use to demonstrate to the Army that his service was taking the close-air-support mission seriously and was buying an airplane specialized for the job. He was not interested in improvements that would make it more expensive.

DDR&E Enters the Avionics Development Process

Previously, DDR&E had not indicated any significant interest in the A-7 program. They supported the Spey engine change, but the avionics equipment in the A-7A and B used almost no advanced technology.[79] However, in December 1966, Mr. Charles A Fowler, the deputy director for tactical warfare programs, initiated a series of actions that were to have far-reaching effects on the eventual decision to incorporate an improved avionics system. He had replaced Dr. Thomas Cheatham on October 1. Fowler had a BS in engineering physics and had specialized in electronics in industry before coming to DDR&E in 1966. He had previously served on one of the panels of the President's Science Advisory Committee that had looked into the advanced Mark II avionics for the F-111. Fowler and the panel had recommended the incorporation of the Mark II system in the upgraded F-111D. Fowler's belief system on avionics was attested to by his article in the *Armed Forces Journal* in 1970. "When I came to the Pentagon I placed 'integrated systems' just below God and Country and well above motherhood."[80]

In early November, Fowler and Dr. Foster took a trip to (among other places) Sperry and North American Autonetics. But as he looked at the number of integrated systems with high costs and long development times, he began to modify his position toward a more critical one. Understanding the possibility of developing a sample version, he drafted a memorandum for the director of DDR&E, Dr. John H. Foster Jr. The memorandum went out from Dr. Foster's office on December 23, addressed to the assistant secretaries of the Air Force and Navy for R&D. The central thrust of the memo was this:

> Recent advances in avionics technology permit major improvements to be made in the accuracy of navigation and weapons delivery, ease of system operation and flexibility of attack and re-attack. Such a capability is significant in a single place aircraft. The technique of built-in-test, combined with the inherent reliability of micro-electronics[,] offers a high probability of reduced total cost of ownership that is particularly attractive, as well as increasing the mission success rate. This quantum improvement can be obtained at a relatively modest increase in initial unit cost.[81]

The memorandum directed the Air Force and Navy to conduct a *joint* study of avionics improvements and their cost and schedule implications. The study was to specifically include developments from ILAAS. The memo had the effect of preempting the Air Force from continuing with an avionics systems management plan solely for the A-7D. Now a joint program would have to be worked out with the Navy before either of the A-7D or A-7E programs could continue. Of course, this is exactly what Capt. Doss and Col. Hails wanted.

On January 16, 1967, Gen. McConnell made jointness an official Air Force policy. In a message to Air Force Systems Command, McConnell quoted Fowler's memo and directed that the DDR&E objectives be included in the avionics study underway by the A-7 Program Management Office.[82] But Gen. McConnell was also interested in addressing the Army's roles-and-missions concerns directly in the near term by the Air Force developing its own close-air-support airplane.

The Origin of the
A-X Close-Air-Support Aircraft

The A-7 program was not operating in a vacuum; indeed, it had been adopted by the Air Force to perform the close-air-support mission under direct pressure from the Army. The A-7 was continually affected by developments in Army aviation and other programs of tactical air. Although the A-7 met many of the Army's requirements for a specialized close-air-support aircraft,[83] it was both heavier and more expensive than what Gen. McConnell envisioned as an optimum Army support aircraft. The concept of a new, armored, propeller-driven, heavy-load-carrying aircraft had been incubating for some time. This concept was essentially what Gen. McConnell had unsuccessfully proposed to Secretary of the Air Force Zuckert and Secretary McNamara in May 1965. Now it was given additional backing and named provisionally the A-X (Attack Experimental). Gen. McConnell mobilized support for it to become an Air Force acquisition program by sending a letter to the Air Staff on January 4, 1967. He stated the Air Force had a growing need for a specialized close-air-support aircraft, which would be "more suitable and less expensive than the A-7." He noted:

I am requesting your full support in the endeavor to expedite the development and procurement of the A-X, if the concept formulation indicates that a replacement for the A-1, more suitable and less expensive that the A-7 can, in fact, be produced.[84]

Gen. McConnell went one step further than supporting the A-X to the Air Staff. He wrote to the Army chief of staff, Gen. Harold Johnson, and stated the Air Force intent to develop the A-X. He stressed that the A-X would be especially designed to meet Army needs for close air support, and asked Gen. Johnson for Army assistance in the development of the aircraft. This is the aircraft that turned out to be the A-10 Thunderbolt II.

The Program Managers Propose
an Improved Avionics System

Capt. Doss and Col. Hails had been working on a new avionics system since about September. They had personally visited or had written communications with Sperry, North American Autonetics, Hughes, IBM, Litton, General Precision, General Motors, Elliot of England, and, of course, LTV.

Col. Hails went on to describe what he interpreted the A-7 RAD to specify:

The RAD didn't address the thing, as I remember the words in it, to say it would be a low-cost airplane. It may have implied that in the way it was expressed, but I didn't think the RAD said that. It said the airplane would be capable of doing this, that, and the other. It was the first time, the only time to my knowledge, that we committed ourselves to buy an airplane without a [previous] requirement. The requirement was clear in Dr. Brown's mind, I think, that the A-7 was going to do for him the mission that the A-1 was doing effectively out there [Vietnam].[85]

The A-7D portion of the LTV avionics study was received on January 4 and was immediately studied by the PMO and the Air Staff. The A-7E study was still underway. The essence of the A-7D study was that a "best estimate" accuracy of 7–8 mils could be achieved if the equipment selected for the aircraft included a central digital computer, a heads-up display, and various other components.[86] The cost was estimated to be about $220,000 per aircraft.[87] The cost of the A-7 at that time was $1.47 million unit flyaway cost.[88]

Briefing the Initial Avionics Study
to the Air Staff

Col. Hails now had to take a briefing on the LTV study of avionics for the A-7D to the Air Force Board Structure to get a formal decision. He started with the Tactical Panel and then, on January 17, 1967, to the Air Staff Board.

Col. Hails described his concept for the briefing:

Once I got the thing sized, and it was about a $2.2 million airplane, it seemed the height of folly to me not to go for ten percent more investment to make the *total* worthwhile. By pouring in another $200,000 you really made an airplane that would effectively do the mission you had alleged to have bought it for. That was the thesis that I sold the Air Staff on. I said, "Look, you're going to buy $2.2 million worth of airplane, but it won't do anything for you. From a cost/effectiveness point of view this last ten percent of investment would make the airplane. And you're going to get them." I said, "Look, McNamara and all of them are committed; we're going to own A-7s on some Air Force base at some time, so why don't we make it where it will at least be an effective airplane."[89]

The reaction of the Air Staff Board was negative. Col. Hails's next step was to brief the Designated Systems Management Group, which included the chief of staff. At this session Gen. McConnell reportedly displayed much displeasure with Hails's approach to the avionics issue. Col. Hails's notes described his idea being for a simple, low-performance avionics system.[90] However, no decision was made at that time.

Gen. McConnell and Secretary Brown Again Appear before Congress

The chief and the secretary had more to worry about on the A-7 program than avionics. They were repeatedly forced to consider the force structure implications of the number of A-7 aircraft. On February 2, Brown and McConnell appeared before the Senate Armed Services and Appropriations Committees. At this point in 1967 the official DoD Five-Year Plan called for a total force of 614 A-7s versus the 387 requested by Secretary Brown in his November 1965 letter.

Senator Margaret Chase Smith was particularly interested in the number of A-7 aircraft and wings and OSD influence on the number. She asked Secretary Brown and Gen. McConnell about OSD acquiring more A-7s than the Air Force thought desirable. Secretary Brown was forceful in his support for three wings of A-7s.[91]

Gen. McConnell reaffirmed his reason for choosing the A-7: "When we first made the proposal, I personally proposed to the Secretary of Defense that we get some A-7s for the main purpose—practically the sole purpose—of giving better close air support to the ground forces. At that time, I asked for three wings, and at that time three wings were all that I thought we should have."[92]

Joint Air Force / Navy Action on the Avionics

Capt. Doss and Col. Hails had been working as innovation advocates for the past six months, researching a wide range of avionics equipment and capabilities. They had visited all the major avionics developers, gained their trust, and received a great deal of encouragement and assistance. They commissioned at least four separate studies, each focused on providing the best avionics suite for the two A-7 models. Doss and Hails had begun by contracting two studies with LTV: one for the Air Force A-7D and one the Navy A-7E. Capt. Doss explained and summarized his activities and tactics to monitor and guide all the studies:

> But we didn't let it stay at that by just letting the prime contractor do the studies; with Bob Hails' concurrence I went to the Naval Air Weapons Center at China Lake and gave them a Weapons Task Study. However, the ILAAS system had been run by the Naval Air Development Center at Johnsville, Pennsylvania, . . . so I integrated a Johnsville team into the China Lake Team. The purpose here was to have an independent avionics configuration study. I met with them nearly every week, either in Johnsville or Washington or at China Lake, California, and I ran the study myself. We had LTV membership in the team so that we had a totally integrated, multiple[-]thrust study effort. I knew exactly what I wanted for the airplane. I wanted to settle all the debate in-house and to leave no issue for the DoD [OSD] staffs to pick on. And it turned out to be extremely effective, because when it came time to present it, we just said, "Study A says that; Study B says that; Study C says that; we all say that; OPNAV agrees, and the Air Staff agrees." What could they do?[93]

[As an aside, one can note Capt. Doss's reference to the Office of the Secretary of Defense as the *whole* of DOD. This represents an attitude, common at that time, that many naval personnel considered that the Unification Act of 1947 unfairly imposed DoD as an unwanted, higher authority on the Navy, demoting one of the most revered institutions in the country.]

LTV sent the study on the application of the Air Force A-7D avionics to the Navy A-7E to the program office in early February. The two deputies added the A-7E study to LTV's January one on the A-7D. Then the results and rationale of each study were integrated and formed the basis of a briefing for each of the two services.

With the several studies consolidated and the briefings smoothed down, they gathered support from their colleagues and prepared to brief the decision chain again. Col. Hails took the briefing to the Board Structure in February. He briefed the Tactical Panel, then the Air Staff Board on February 17. Gen. Catton was again the chairman. Col. Hails conducted the briefing, which consisted of a series of view graphs that built up to the decision climax.

The highlights of the briefing were the following:

- Navy test flights in the A-7A acceptance program had shown the weapons delivery accuracy to be insufficient: 20–40 mils.

- The Air Force requirement stated in the RAD was difficult without an improved avionics system.

- A range of five avionics options was presented.[94]

The PMO had commissioned several studies to survey the technology available and to recommend a solution.

Avionics Options and Costs, 1967

Option	Computer	Sight	Accuracy	Unit cost* (in millions)
I	Analog	Servoed	23 mils	$1.50
II	Analog + radar	Servoed	14 mils	$1.53
III	Digital	Servoed	14 mils	$1.59
IV	Digital + radar	Heads-up display	10 mils	$1.65
V	Digital + radar + map display	Heads-up display	10 mils	$1.74

* Unit Flyaway Cost: An estimate of the price of each aircraft averaged over a total buy of some 1,200 avionics sets (800 Navy and 400 Air Force)

Source: A-7D Program Management Office Viewgraph, undated, unclassified.

Col. Hails, Capt. Doss, and the Program Management Office recommended Option IV, a system with 10-mil accuracy.

The avionics briefing was subsequently given to the Air Force Council and the Defense Systems Management Group. Col. Hails described the briefing process:

We had two "dog and pony" shows; I went with them to present theirs to Admiral Connolly . . . and I took it up through the Air Force channels. By then we had a complete change in the guard in the Air [Force] Council. The whole cell had changed when I went back through there in 1967. Their attitude this time around, when the Air Staff said they thought that we should go this route if we were going to invest in the airplane. (They gave me hell every time I went in there [in 1966] because the price had gone up.) I gave them outside limits on the price, and there were no real ardent or vocal antagonists for the airplane at that point in time.[95]

Secretary Brown discussed his view of the avionics changes and Col. Hails presentation:

The avionics . . . seemed important because by that time I think we were beginning to realize that it wasn't how much you dropped, but how well you dropped it. I had the impression at that meeting of a well-thought-out series of avionics design changes which would make a very much better aircraft.

There were some more arguments about the avionics, but again they didn't seem to be major. It was really an Air Force package versus a Navy package, and there were some wrinkles on the Air Force package, but there didn't seem to be much argument—even from my own [Secretariat] staff, which always did question Air Staff suggestions to make certain that the cost implications had been considered.[96]

Gen. McConnell and Secretary Brown approved the avionics improvement as briefed by Col. Hails. Gen. McConnell later discussed his decision on the issue. He was asked what made him decide the increased avionics would be worth the additional cost, when he previously had been so strong on the need to keep the cost down. He replied:

Because nobody could deny then that we would be able, if they worked out like they were supposed to work, no one would be able to deny that we weren't meeting our responsibilities to be able to support them [Army] day and night under any kind of conditions right up next to the FEBA [forward edge of the battle area].[97]

The result of the briefing to the Air Force Board Structure was that the new avionics configuration was approved formally within the Air Force. In the meantime, Capt. Doss had briefed the Office of the Chief of Naval Operations (OPNAV). VAdm. Tom Connolly, the deputy chief of naval operations for air, approved the configuration and praised the two deputy program managers—Doss and Hails—for taking the initiative on the avionics improvement. He said:

Actually, Capt. Doss and Col. Hails . . . I think, were the two principal architects of the A-7D and E. It was a lot of their thinking mixed with what they got from contractors and what they got from all the technical people. . . . But that's where the real initiative lay. This is the way it really is. It's a combination of the contractor . . . and our own people who want to bring along good airplanes.

About the time the A-7 came into being, so did Southeast Asia. It didn't take very long to realize that a good light-attack airplane needed a more accurate weapons delivery system. Furthermore, advances in stable platforms and computer technology avionics—showed this could be done. It would be possible to greatly improve the weapon delivery accuracy. This is a very efficient thing to be attempting to do. At the same time, the prospect of head-up display became something real, that we could get ahold of. And also the fact that the Air Force began to take an interest in the A-7, it looked as though by combining our efforts and combining some of our financial assets, maybe together we could make a real valuable improvement in the A-7 together.[98]

It was clear that Adm. Connolly had a vision of the importance of adapting aircraft design to the rapid changes that were occurring in data management and integrated systems that were, in turn, creating a new generation of aircraft.

The Final Briefing to OSD

The deputy program managers took their final briefing to representatives of the Office of the Secretary of Defense: Systems Analysis, DDR&E, Comptroller, Installations and Logistics, etc. The Systems Analysis representative was Herb Rosenzweig. Capt. Doss expected the March 1, 1967, briefing would be a confrontation with Systems Analysis:

We had lots and lots of these kinds of briefing. He [Hails] was always briefing in the Air Staff, and I was briefing in Naval Air Systems Command and OPNAV. But the critical one was where we finally came together, and we had the Navy and Air Force in agreement, and we went to DoD [OSD] to say, "This is what we want to do, and this is why." DDR&E bought it lock, stock, and barrel and supported us against Systems Analysis. At the end of the briefing, I said, "This study says this, and this study says this," and what could they do? Rosenzweig got up and left the briefing!

System Analysis [afterward] turned some people to studying it. I went over, tried to talk to them and cooperate with them, but they were hopeless.

We had more systems analysis / cost effectiveness in our series of studies than they could have produced in six months, which is about the time we had applied to it. We had all kinds of efforts—North American, [Sperry, LTV, IBM, Litton, General Precision, General Motors, Teledyne, etc.].[99]

Although the presentation went very well, and the technical changes were favorably received, only an implicit concurrence was given by DDR&E to the detailed configuration. Approval to proceed with contracting the avionics was to be contingent on additional study of technical and funding details.[100]

The major decisions having been rendered, the program managers went to Naval Air Systems Command to work out the details of funding, schedules, and the selection of subcontractors in conjunction with LTV.

Systems Analysis was beginning to fill Doss's prophesy of applying new, lower Vietnam aircraft attrition rates into aircraft programs. On April 10, they sent a memorandum to the secretary of the Air Force, suggesting a revision in the number of A-7s programmed to maintain the force structure. The reason given was the reduced attrition in fighter/attack aircraft over Vietnam. The result was to reduce the planned A-7 buy in fiscal year 1967 from twenty to twelve, and in fiscal year 1968 from 181 to 100.[101]

Even though the number of projected A-7s was being reduced, the program managers continued to work with LTV and the avionics contractors and the management responsibility for its integration. The PMO, it will be remembered, was keeping the pressure on LTV by having companies bid on the avionics integration role. This meant there were two types of competition going on. First, there was a competition to see which of the avionics corporations would supply the equipment to the avionics integrator. Second, there was a less formal competition to see whether LTV or one of the avionics firms would get the "avionics integrator" responsibility. Capt. Doss explained the thrust of both competitions:

We got unsolicited proposals, and meant to do it, meant to bring other industry on support equipment . . . as a means of keeping competition alive in a single-source procurement., That's how these companies really get you, you see. We had five lots of airplanes out of LTV before we got into the A-7E, and then we were no longer protected. The minute we lost the protection [of a fixed-price contract] the cost began to go up. On LTV's side we were beginning to get inflationary factors. When they bid on the airplane there was no General Dynamic F-111 effort in the Fort Worth / Dallas areas, and labor was very available. It was not our intent to not recognize those factors. We did not want them to lose money; we just simply wanted to represent the public's interest and keep it under control.

It looked to us like it was going to be a two-way competition. Sperry was very strong, and Hughes looked very strong. North American finally said, "We're not going to continue. We have enough trouble ourselves." We did everything we could to keep IBM alive in this thing. . . . I wanted to keep a three-way competition on these guys, because when there's just two, there's just too much visibility.[102]

LTV was in the process during the spring of 1967 of modifying its management team for the A-7 program. Vought Aeronautics made a major effort to convince the Air Force and Navy that it could handle the avionics integration job and do it effectively. Robert S. Buzard was put in charge of the A-7 avionics section (and later, the LTV A-7 program office). Under his leadership the LTV avionics capability increased. As a result, the commander of Naval Air Systems Command decided that whoever the avionics contractor was going to be—Sperry, Hughes, or IBM—it would supply the equipment to LTV for final installation. The concept of having an associate prime contractor was discarded when LTV agreed to support the configuration and to provide an avionics integrator as a subcontractor. The contractor/PMO combination worked out the details on schedules, costs, and performance, and the plans were submitted to Secretary Brown.

The Air Force and Navy Secretaries Ratify the Improved Avionics

Secretary Brown sent a formal memorandum to Secretary McNamara on May 5, 1967, requesting permission to install the improved avionics in the A-7. A selection from that memo gives the rationale:

Flight test results to date have revealed the need to improve the weapon delivery capability of the A-7. The Air Force and the Navy have jointly studied the problem and have agreed on a common weapon delivery avionics configuration that included a digital computer, heads-up display, and inertial measurement unit. The cost increases associated with these changes will vary somewhat between the two Service programs and will be contingent upon Navy and Air Force sharing of common non-recurring costs. Air Force cost and funding implications are discussed herein. Expected visual delivery accuracies will be comparable to or better than the F-4 and A-6 aircraft. We are agreed that the recommended changes are necessary and desirable from a cost-worth viewpoint.[103]

In one respect, Secretary Brown's memo was misleading. The F-4 and A-6 did not have and *never* developed the accuracy of the A-7D and -E.

The Honorable Paul Nitze recommended approval of the Navy A-7E avionics to OSD on May 11, 1967, noting:

Southeast Asia experience has shown that high weapon delivery accuracies are needed in our light jet attack aircraft. No single improvement factor can make a greater contribution to cost and effectiveness than a marked improvement in Circular Error Probable (CEP).[104]

The next day, May 12, McNamara wrote to the assistant secretary of defense for installations and logistics. He stated he understood the Air Force and Navy were considering an avionics improvement and desired to move the production schedule back. Such a slippage was approved, he wrote, but no approval for the avionics change was mentioned.[105]

The same day that Secretary Nitze forwarded his decision memo to Secretary McNamara, LTV was making recommendations to the Program Office on the selection of avionics subcontractors. The finalists for the major portion of the contract were Hughes, Sperry, and IBM. When LTV management and the program managers agreed on IBM, the two groups briefed the commander of Naval Air Systems Command and then Dr. Frosch and Dr. Flax, the two assistant secretaries for R&D.

Delay in Obtaining an OSD Decision

The formal answer to the requests of Secretaries Brown and Nitze was rendered by DDR&E. On May 17, Dr. Foster replied to the two assistant secretaries of the services (R&D) with approval of the concept of improved avionics. However, only implicit approval was given to the actual configuration. Final approval to let the contractor proceed would have to be contingent on a resubmission of the two services' Joint Development Plan, the selection of subcontractors, and "schedules, etc."[106]

This information was discouraging to the program office and LTV because they had expected the Pentagon decision process to take only about two or three months. Capt. Doss explained the PMO's dilemma:

We underestimated badly on how fast we could get our decision out of DOD. We got all kinds of assurances. We walked over there right after the first of the year, having studied the hell out of this thing, had a solid case that Navy and Air Force were backing, and yet we didn't get our money for seven or eight months. And until you get the money [you can't put it on the contract]. The prime contractor thinks that the minute you get the money you're going to roll it down there in a wheelbarrow. We were fighting for our prime so hard that he thought that as soon as we broke it loose, he'd get a go-ahead. Well, hell no, we had to make this guy [LTV] negotiate with us for guarantees.[107]

One incident of brightness was the flight of a section of two A-7As from Maryland to Paris in May 1971, which gave all the people associated with the aircraft a sense of pride. The nonstop flight of 3,900 miles had been made many times by commercial airliners and larger military aircraft, but the A-7s achieved the distinctions of becoming some of the few single-seat aircraft to make the flight without aerial refueling. This accomplishment pointed out the advantages of the turbofan engine for tactical aircraft.

The summer of 1967 dragged on, hot and muggy, with the program management people working on revised schedules and development plans. Various letters flew back and forth among the services, their secretaries, and OSD, most of them recommending approval of the avionics change. The Navy was especially concerned over the lack of approval because without the OSD go-ahead, it had no A-7 program in the budget.

With additional information and joint development plans for the A-7D and E, the services again put forward requests for approval of the avionics. On July 20, 1967, the Air Force wrote OSD and compared the incremental costs of the new system with the previously approved avionics. The recommendation for the new system was that it would pay for itself in the increased accuracy of the bombing system, which would require fewer sorties to accomplish a mission. The added avionics would cost about $183 million out of a total program investment cost of $1,263 million.[108] The unit flyaway cost of the A-7D was expected to increase to about $1.8 million.

The OSD answer was partially supplied by DDR&E, when on July 28 the deputy director wrote to Dr. Flax and Dr. Frosch. The memorandum stated concurrence in the belief that the performance, cost, and reliability targets would be met, and the schedule risks would be acceptable. DDR&E formally complimented the outstanding interservice cooperation on the program.[109] At this point the avionics decision had apparently been finalized. The OSD decision, however, was not to be as uniform as it appeared. Formal approval was still required.

Systems Analysis Reduces the A-7 Force by 20 Percent

When Paul Nitze was secretary of the Navy, he had signed the Navy request for approval of avionics improvements. On July 1, 1967, he moved to a position as the deputy secretary of

defense, directly under Robert McNamara. The Air Force and Navy requests and Nitze's position were later commented on by Russ Murray:

The Navy came up, and at that time Paul Nitze was still Secretary of the Navy. He wrote a letter that said, "NADC Johnsville has done the analysis, and they show that each one of these airplanes will be three times as effective with the new system as it would be with the old system. We [Systems Analysis] were skeptical of such claims [but] we were unable to stop that particular one [the A-7 upgrade]."

When we approved this thing, begrudgingly—when McNamara approved it—we got into an interesting discussion there which I think probably created a lot of ill will and resulted in a reduction of the force. The thought was that we would pay for the increased cost of the fancy avionics system by having a smaller number of airplanes. We reduced the force by twenty percent. . . . The idea there wasn't really to be nasty; the idea was to hopefully get the guys who were making these decisions to consider whether they really believed what they were writing. If they honestly believed it was three times as good, then that's one thing, but giving them the option of sticking with the old force or accepting a force twenty percent smaller would make them stop and think, we hoped.

We weren't just trying to be budget cutters there. What we really wanted to do was to make sure that the "operators"—the guys that would be stuck with this thing—aren't just trapped by what the *research and development community* is thinking up. We thought that was the case with the A-7. You couldn't argue that the Soviet threat had gone up. It may have incidentally gone up, but the only thing that happened was that the United States R&D community—independent of anything else that was going on in the world—had thought up a new "gadget." You could really say that with a new gadget that's all that more effective, all we have to do—since McNamara believed the effectiveness of the force was high enough to begin with—is to maintain that same effectiveness and take it all out in saving.[110]

This consideration of the real worth of the avionics improvement on a cost-effectiveness basis was also a primary concern of Dr. Enthoven:

There were some very glowing letters. I think the one we got from the Navy said something about it offered two to ten times the cost/effectiveness of the other plane [A-7A]. They pushed for it very hard. Instead of fighting it because we felt that if you could better accuracy . . . if you really could cut the miss distance in half, that would be worth a lot of money. We thought it was probably right, provided that the claims were true. We proposed that the way to pay for it would be, in the case of the Air Force, to go from five wings to four. . . . The Navy said two to ten times as effective, and we make some equal-cost trade with them. . . . The argument, which was one that I think the Services really have got to learn to understand and accept, is that if the thing costs twenty percent more and it is much more than that effective, then they ought to expect that they'll buy twenty percent fewer. . . . We could have argued that if one new A-7 is as good as two old A-7s, we'll just buy half as many of the new kind.

I recalled that trade, but I thought at the time that was going to raise the cost from $1.2 to 1.4 million. . . . I recall to my horror finding it had gone up to $1.8 million. Then the whole question of the Air Force A-7 started to be called into question. Certainly, an important part of the case for it was that it was a lot cheaper [than the F-111 and F-4].[111]

The OSD Decision
The OSD decision memorandum was approved and signed and sent to the services on August 7, 1967. It formally approved the avionics change, but in a separate action, Systems Analysis, which was the OSD keeper of the force structure program, reduced the number of Air Force A-7 wings from five to four, and the total number of tactical fighter wings from twenty-four to twenty-three. A similar reduction was made in the Navy's A-7 force. While Gen. McConnell and the Air Staff had stated many times that they wanted only three wings of A-7s, they never envisioned a reduction in the twenty-four-wing

fighter force structure. Every one of the twenty-four wings was needed, the Air Force stated, for either F-4s or F-111s.

With the formal OSD approval, LTV and the two program managers briefed Dr. Foster at DDR&E on August 9. The subject was the selection of the avionics subcontractor. Dr. Foster concurred with LTV's recommendation, and LTV was given approval to select IBM as the winner.[112] LTV announced that IBM was "technically equal to Sperry, but that Sperry the early popular leader in the contest was 'substantially higher in price.'"[113] IBM received the largest contract of the six subcontractors—$168 million—to build and test the central digital computer

Avionics in the A-7C, A-7D, and A-7E
With the approval of the new avionics, the major innovations in the A-7 program were complete, but now the deputy program managers had to translate the decision into formal contract changes with LTV. The Air Force and Navy immediately began to negotiate contracts for the development and production of this new version. This took several months. The Navigation / Weapon Delivery System as implemented in the A-7D and E consisted of eight components: the nav / weapons delivery tactical computer, inertial measurement set, Doppler radar set, forward-looking radar, air-data computer, head-up display, armament station control unit, and projected map display set.[114] The projected map display was not in the original A-7D but was added later. The digital tactical computer was the heart of the system. It calculated navigation solutions at a rate of five times per second and weapons delivery solutions at thirty times per second.[115]

The program managers' faith in the integrated navigation and weapons delivery system was later justified when the aircraft were delivered to RDT&E units and operational squadrons. Col. Erv Ethell, 354th Tactical Fighter Wing, verified the accuracy of the system:

I still firmly believe that the A-7 is the best close air support aircraft flying today. The A-7D was manufactured with a 10-mil error or less. That was part of the specs. LTV met those specs and more. The pilot average was better than that, including flying combat in Southeast Asia. The accuracy was closer to 7 mils.[116]

Turbulent Road to Full Production

The OSD approval of the new avionics was received with relief, but the reduction in the number of fighter wings was a surprise and a shock. Secretary Brown notified his staff on August 9, 1967, only two days after OSD approved the avionics and tried to reverse the reduction decision. The attempt was to prove futile.

The Air Force Contracting Dispute with LTV Vought Aeronautics

Col. Hails had been in discussions with LTV for several months over the issues of weapons accuracy, reliability, and the correction of defects. As soon as the OSD decision was final, Hails notified his superiors at Air Force Systems Command that he could not resolve this problem at his level. He stated the contractor's proposed performance and guarantees were not acceptable.[117]

This was actually the tip of an iceberg-sized area of disagreement that had been growing between LTV and the Air Force for some time. It dated back to 1966, when Col. Hails and Capt. Doss were examining alternatives for more accuracy. When asked if LTV was in favor of the avionics improvement, Col. Hails said:

They were opposed to the route that we went. It was tough. [LTV said,] "You don't need that." Later, I made them eat their words that we paid [them to do]. When we finally got the Air Staff commitment to go that route, we went through this tremendous donnybrook with their management on a head-to-head basis. We said, "Look we're not buying 'promises,' 'best effort.' You came in here with that study that I paid you to do, saying the airplane would do that. That's all I'm asking you for, but I want you to give me a contractual commitment, a guarantee for that." They didn't want to do that. The Navy had never made them do that before; they would come in with goals and give them whatever came out the pipe.[118]

LTV's study had concluded that with all the right components integrated, the aircraft could achieve a weapon's accuracy at 7–8 mils. Hails and Doss had rounded this off to 10 mils. LTV subsequently characterized this number as a "best estimate," but Hails wanted a guarantee. LTV, viewing the development risk with the integration of six subcontractors' equipment, was naturally reluctant and reportedly offered to guarantee 14–15 mils, but not 10.[119]

There also was disagreement over how the accuracy was to be measured. The RAD had called for "unconstrained weapon delivery," which meant the accuracy was to be achieved over a wide range of dive angles, airspeeds, and slant ranges out to a certain classified limit. LTV offered to satisfy the requirement at four specific points. Col. Hails was holding out for more.

The issue of the accuracy guarantee was resolved through negotiation, with LTV accepting responsibility for guaranteeing 10-mil accuracy and for twelve points of testing. The LTV project manager, Robert S. Buzard, noted that Hails had, in fact, made LTV guarantee its "best estimate."[120] The issue of reliability guarantees and latent defects proved more difficult for the Air Force to accept. LTV had proposed a 20 percent premium over their costs, and Col. Hails was opposed to any premium.[121] The two sides were at an impasse.

Col. Hails communicated his difficulties with LTV Aerospace to Assistant Secretary Charles, who spoke with Dr. Brown. Dr. Brown sent a strong letter to Mr. Clyde Skeen, president of LTV, Inc., the parent company of LTV Aerospace, on October 18, 1967. Dr. Brown stated the Air Force concern over the delay in the program and the possible impact it might have on the cost. It was imperative, he stated, to reach agreement in order to avoid a stop-work order on the contract.[122]

Mr. Skeen replied to Secretary Brown on October 20 and noted that LTV would cooperate in every way. In addition, he referred to a continuing factor in joint service programs—different requirements and cultures:

I acknowledge with regret that we should have realized sooner than the system requirements and operational philosophies differ in some respects between the Air Force and Navy and this undoubtedly contributed in part to the impression in some quarters in the Air Force that we, as a contractor, were unresponsive and non-cooperative.[123]

The result of the letter exchange was a meeting on the same day, October 20, of representatives of the three organizations: Mr. Paul Thayer, president of LTV Aerospace; RAdm. R. L. Townsend, commander of Naval Air Systems Command; and Maj. Gen. Thomas S. Jeffrey, Air Force director of production and programming. This high-level group resolved most of the outstanding differences. Gen. Ferguson, commander of Air Force Systems Command, formally recommended a contractual go-ahead to the chief of staff on November 27, 1967.

In the meantime, the Navy accepted LTV's "final, best offer" on October 4, 1967, and issued a formal go-ahead for the A-7E program.

Survivability/Vulnerability Changes to the A-7D

One of the lessons from World War I, reinforced in World War II, had been that attack aircraft needed armor because they were so susceptible to ground fire. No sooner had Col. Hails concluded the difficult negotiations with LTV over the contract in 1967 than the survivability issue arose. The survivability of attack aircraft had been registered as a concern by the Air Staff Board most recently in 1963, during the Army / Air Force discussions over close air support. The only current aircraft that incorporated defensive armor was the A-1, designed in the mid-1940s. Reports back from Vietnam confirmed that this was a vital issue and accelerated its addressal. The Air Force had formalized a requirement for new aircraft to have features to reduce their vulnerability and increase their survivability in a hostile environment.[124] Secretary McNamara directed the Air Force to conduct the study, which was delegated to AFSC. In late November 1967, AFSC presented its results to Headquarters USAF and recommended the incorporation of foam-filled fuel tanks, three separate (triple redundant) flight control systems, and extensive ceramic and steel armor for vital systems. The cost of the changes was estimated to be $70,000 for each aircraft, with $32 million for the A-7D fleet.

The Navy program managers incorporated the added flight control system so the A-7E had three independent fight control systems, but they did not see the same urgency to incorporate the rest of the survivability changes to the A-7E. The A-7D and A-7E had already diverged from commonality by having different engines, cockpits, wheels, brakes, refueling systems, antennas, lights, oxygen systems, ejection seats, radios, engine starters, and many other components. LTV personnel later noted they "were at a complete loss to reconcile the Air Force and Navy differences" over the survivability changes.[125]

The survivability/vulnerability features were another change in the military requirement for the A-7 that were to increase its cost, but their value was difficult to debate. As Col. Hails put it:

> From a redundancy and hostile-fire point of view, it had poor survivability characteristics. For us to be buying a new airplane in 1967 without deliberate consideration to install features that would give it a high survivability. ... We lost so many airplanes out there in North Vietnam because the rudder would get shot up, and the pilot would eject because he didn't have redundancy to get him home. We introduced them into the Air Force airplane as a deliberate design intention.[126]

The Air Force Issues a Formal Program Go-Ahead

Although the Air Force was almost finished in definitizing the LTV contract, no approval had yet been issued to proceed. After multiple briefings and recommendations, Gen. McConnell gave approval on December 13, 1967. In his decision letter, he noted the cost had risen from $1.4 to $1.95 million per unit flyaway and that the survivability changes would cost another $100,000. The plan at this time was for five wings, with 517 operational aircraft.

Gen. McConnell explained his thinking about this decision:

> The main factor is that we *had something*, and God knows when we would ever get an A-X. I don't know whether we'll ever get one yet [1970]; I wouldn't put much money down on it. It was getting to the point that. ... The Army says the F-4 is not a close air support aircraft. Well, it

wasn't built for that, but it did pretty well. And it can fight its way in and out, and it can drop its bombs and run.[127]

The high-speed performance of the F-4 was still a detriment in the Army's view, and the demand for a specialized close-air-support aircraft had not diminished. The Army's hope for the development of the Cheyenne armed helicopter was reinforced in January 1968, when the Army staff placed an initial production order for 375 aircraft!

The Cost of the Avionics Ground Equipment Soars

In November 1967, LTV had estimated the cost of the entire avionics upgrade would be $32 million. As the engineers got into the details of this complicated automatized equipment, they recognized that estimate was unrealistic, and in February 1968 they submitted a request for $107.7 million. This would increase the cost of each aircraft about $150,000. This shocked the PMO and the service staffs, and it almost caused the Air Force program to be canceled, but the details were not known, and the program continued.

Robert S. McNamara Leaves the Department of Defense

McNamara had been the secretary of defense since 1961, longer than any other man in that position. He submitted his resignation to President Johnson and left DoD to accept a position as president of the World Bank on February 29, 1968. The president nominated Clark M. Clifford as his successor.[128]

The Navy Changes from the TF-30 to the TF-41 for the A-7E

The Navy switch from the Pratt & Whitney TF-30 to the General Motors / Allison TF-41 followed the Air Force decision by six months. The decision is significant because it demonstrated once again the scheduling difficulties in a joint program.

When the first Spey engine was test run in November 1967 and demonstrated nearly 15,000 pounds of thrust, the Navy interest in the engine peaked. However, by this time, Pratt & Whitney had a proposal for a 15,000-pound-thrust engine, called the TF-30-P-18. On March 18, 1968 Secretary

of the Navy Paul R. Ignatius sent a memorandum to Secretary Clifford outlining a proposal to obtain the performance of a 15,000-pound-thrust engine. Ignatius reported he was leaning toward the Spey but that the Allison engine was unproven. He requested $4 million to develop the TF-30-P-18 as a "backup" engine.

The first A-7D was accepted from LTV in April 1968, with a TF-30 engine temporarily installed as the TF-41 not yet ready. The initial Spey engine would not be delivered for testing until four months later, in August 1968. On September 26, 1968, it was successfully test-flown at Edwards Air Force Base. Early-production A-7Ds that had been accepted with TF-30s were later retrofitted with the TF-41. On the other hand, the Navy's first set of A-7E aircraft was produced with the TF-30-P-8, and these aircraft were given the designation A-7C. The first A-7D with the Spey engine was #3, accepted in August 1968. The first A-7D with the new avionics was #5, accepted on December 11, 1968. Aircraft #27 and subsequent also had the survivability/vulnerability changes incorporated.[129]

Senate Tactical-Airpower Hearings of 1968

The A-7D received particular attention in the Senate Armed Services Committee during the program's entire life. The cost had risen from the $1.2 million per aircraft that had been inserted into the Fish Study, to $1.47 after the Spey engine decision, and to $1.8 after the avionics decision. At the time of the 1968 congressional hearings, the unit cost was $2.1 million, and the total program cost, including R&D, was $2.3 million.[130] The senators were also skeptical of the influence that Systems Analysis had applied to the program.

Senator Stennis opened the proceedings by questioning Dr. Enthoven on his lack of any military experience and that his staff had made significant reductions in military requests for tactical aircraft. Senator Symington continued that line of questioning, adding that Herb Rozensweig had only a mechanical-engineering degree and had stated to the staff that there was no need to modernize the aircraft in the Guard or Reserve. The whole question of the relationship of Systems Analysis with the A-7 program and the tactical-fighter-force level was very much in evidence throughout these hearings.

In addition, the committee was also worried about the organizational forces and personalities behind the Air Force decision to buy the A-7. Senator Symington asked, "Was the A-7 foisted on the Air Force before its time?" Gen. McConnell responded, "No, sir. I asked for the A-7, Senator, because we needed something to give close air support to the ground forces. We did not have any." Senator Symington was not the only person who worried about the cost of the A-7. After Senator Cannon listed the types of aircraft in the fighter inventory, Gen. McConnell added, "Yes, sir, and the A-7 should also be added to the fighter inventory unless the price of it keeps on going up. If the price of it goes up much more, we cannot afford it."

The Election of 1968 and
Changes of Command in DOD

The presidential election of 1968 brought Richard M. Nixon to the White House as president and commander in chief, and a new lineup of politically appointed officials in the Department of Defense. The position of secretary of defense was filled by Representative Melvin R. Laird, while Dr. Robert C. Seamans Jr. became the secretary of the Air Force. Dr. Harold Brown retired to become the president of the California Institute of Technology. Dr. Alain Enthoven also left and accepted a vice presidency of Litton Industries. Murray, Rosenzweig, and Heyman were to leave within eighteen months.

The A-7 program continued to move along in 1969, and finally, on February 19, the Air Force signed a definitized contract with LTV. The PMO had been negotiating with LTV on this contract since the first letter contract in October 1966. The many configurations, the engine, avionics, survivability changes, and total force levels had been significant factors in delaying any agreement. The multiyear contract defined firm ceiling prices on all items.

The Senate Armed Services Committee
in 1969 Again Questions the A-7D

The DoD budget for fiscal year 1970 contained $374.7 million for procurement of 128 Air Force A-7Ds. The prices of the A-7D in the budget were $2.4 million per unit flyaway and $2.8 million

per unit program cost.[131] On April 16, Senator Goldwater again questioned Gen. McConnell:

Senator Goldwater: "We were discussing the A-7 versus the 111. I don't believe the A-7 is an airplane the Air Force particularly wanted; am I right in that? Is there anything wrong with the idea of forgetting about the A-7 and putting the money into the 111, although it is a more costly airplane? Would you rather have that?"

Gen. McConnell: "I personally would rather have the F-111 and the F-4."

Roles and Missions:
Army Problems with the Cheyenne

At the same time as the Air Force and LTV achieved agreement on the A-7, the Army was having increasing issues with the development of its new armed helicopter. The AH-56 Cheyenne had first flown in September 1967. Full production was approved by the Army in January 1968, and $429 million was requested in the fiscal year 1970 budget before the Congress. The aircraft had technical problems, including rotor instability, inadequate directional control, and excessive control difficulty in maneuvering. After a series of incidents, Lockheed's chief test pilot was killed, and a Cheyenne was completely destroyed in an accident on March 12, 1969. The secretary of the Army, Stanley R. Resor, sent a notice to Lockheed to demonstrate plans to correct the "failure to make satisfactory progress towards Cheyenne production and delivery."[132] Lockheed was given until April 25, 1969—barely three weeks—to produce a plan to correct all of the aircraft's deficiencies or have the contract canceled. In May, the secretary of the Army canceled the entire Cheyenne program.

The Senate Armed Services Committee
Again Calls Gen. McConnell

The committee called the Air Force chief of staff on the morning of June 25, 1969, and requested he appear before the committee in executive session. He responded and later described the discussion:

We had $374 million in the 1970 budget, and I was asked point blank if I'd rather spend that money for F-4Es or spend it on A-7s. And I said considering the fact that you could buy only six less F-4Es than you could buy A-7s for the money, and the F-4E had already demonstrated that it could do the close tactical air support—I would prefer to take that money and put it on F-4Es. . . . But I had a provision in there. I said *provided* that we can dispose economically of the seventy-four [A-7Ds] that we've got.

I reneged on my support for the A-7 and said we'll just have to use the F-4 and wait for the A-X. Because by that the time the AAFSS [Cheyenne] had been killed, so we had a little waiting period. We could support the Army with these F-4s.[133]

The Senate Armed Services Committee Cancels A-7D Funds

Immediately after the executive session with Gen. McConnell, the Senate committee began their markup of their report to the Senate on the fiscal year 1970 DoD budget. The report was filed on July 2, 1969, and it read as follows:

The bill as presented to the Committee contained a procurement request of $348.2 million with an additional $26.5 million for A-7D tactical type fighter aircraft. The committee is recommending that the procurement of the A-7 aircraft be cancelled and that the same funds be used for the procurement of F-4E aircraft.

When originally conceived the A-7 was to have been a relatively inexpensive, subsonic aircraft optimized for close air support of ground forces. It is no longer cheap. There have been many changes to the aircraft as well as many schedule slips. As a result, the costs have more than doubled. For roughly the same costs in the fiscal year 1970 budget the Air Force can procure the more versatile F-4E aircraft presently in Air Force inventories.[134]

The Air Force Asks the Navy for Cancellation Costs

It was generally assumed by everyone outside LTV and the project office that the Air Force A-7D and the Navy A-7E were virtually identical, especially since they had the same Spey engine and the same gun, and the avionics effort had been a joint effort. Gen. McConnell approached Adm. Moorer, the chief of naval operations, to find out how much it would cost to convert the seventy-four A-7Ds to Navy carrier configuration.

When the staffs and the project management office finished with the analysis, it appeared that the two aircraft had amazingly little production commonality. In addition to the major items, the two aircraft had different aircraft cockpits, instruments, oxygen systems, survival kits, radios, wheels, tires, brakes, starters, plumbing and wiring, and survivability features throughout the airframe. For example, Capt. Doss developed an instrument and weapons panel that conveniently arranged the weapons switches around the glare shield. Col. Hails was not able to take this approach because he inherited an Air Force standard instrument and weapons panel layout. But the primary issue was the military services' two completely different logistics systems. Upon analysis, it appeared that the two models were only about 30–40 percent common in the production line.

Seventeen of the seventy-four aircraft already contracted for were considered uneconomical to modify. The remaining fifty-seven were estimated to cost $73.2 million to modify to the Navy configuration. In addition, the disruption of the LTV production line and the conversion of 128 Spey engines were estimated to cost $111.5 million, for a total conversion cost of $184.7 million.[135] The potential loss to LTV was even more; the bill eliminated the entire 1970 Navy procurement of twenty-seven A-7Es, the loss of another $104 million to LTV.

When the total conversion cost of $184.7 million was subtracted from the original $374.7 million, the result was only $190.0 million that could be used to purchase F-4s. The actual price of the F-4E in 1969 was $3.108 million each.[136] The result would have been that only sixty-one F-4Es could be purchased if the 128 A-7Ds were canceled.

The Air Force Presents a Reclama to the Senate Action

When all the factors were considered, it was decided that the only viable alternative was to reclama the Senate action and request reinstatement of the A-7D funds. The reclama was prepared and presented by Gen. McConnell to Senator Cannon. It read, in part:

The Air Force has now discussed the problem with the Navy, and it is estimated that modifying the Air Force version of the A-7 to Navy version would cost from $800,000 to $1,000,000 per aircraft. This cost together with the cancellation costs and increased unit cost for the Navy aircraft would reduce the budgeted $374.7 million to such an extent that it is most likely the Air Force buy of F-4 aircraft would be on the order of 50–60 aircraft instead of the previously contemplated 120 aircraft. This would reduce the total Air Force tactical fighter inventory below minimum acceptable levels.

Therefore, the Air Force has submitted to this Committee a reclama of the Committee's action to prohibit the procurement of additional A-7 aircraft. The Air Force now requests that the $374.7 million be restored for the acquisition of three wings of A-7s.[137]

Gen. McConnell met personally with Senator Cannon and presented the reclama. The Senator thanked McConnell but, upon some reflection, notified the Air Force he would not change the committee's report.[138] The reclama would have to be worked out in the joint Senate/House conference.[139]

Gen. McConnell Prepares to Retire and Gen. Ryan Faces a Hearing

Gen. McConnell was commissioned in the Army Air Corps after graduation from West Point in 1932 and by 1969 had served over thirty-seven years. He had been the chief since August 1, 1965, and was scheduled to retire on July 31, 1969. His successor was to be Gen. John D. Ryan, previously the vice chief of staff. Gen. Ryan appeared before the Senate Armed Services Committee on July 24 for a hearing on his confirmation. The committee questioned him on procurement, national defense strategy, and, noting he had spent one-half of his career on bombers, the need for a new manned bomber. Chairman Stennis closed with an oblique reference to the A-7D and congressional decision-making:

We do the best we can, general, around this table to write up a bill, and consider the testimony before us, and everything. But then when we do write it up and send it to the floor of the Senate it is the committee's bill, and it is our responsibility. And it is up to us to handle it the best way we can.

I don't think it is time then to see changes, for any of the services to see changes—I just mention this to you now for your information—unless there are some extraordinary circumstances. There are ways within the legislative channels, as you know, to have changes made. A big bill like the authorization bill, for instance, where you have $20 billion involved in many of the items in there, is hotly contested. The committee cannot go up and change its position or change its mind on the same set of facts. I just mention that for your information.[140]

The hearing lasted only twenty-five minutes, and Gen. Ryan was subsequently confirmed by the Senate on July 25. Gen. McConnell made one final appearance before the Senate Appropriations Committee two days before his retirement. He rejected his previous opinion of canceling the A-7 and stated it was "necessary and advantageous" to continue with the A-7 program.[141]

Secretary of Defense Melvin Laird sent a reclama to Representative Rivers, chairman of the House Armed Services Committee, and requested restoration of $986.8 million cut by the Senate. Among these funds, he specifically requested the $374.7 million for procurement of 128 A-7D for the Air Force.[142] Subsequently, the Congress appropriated the full amount for the A-7D on December 29, 1969.

The new chief of staff, Gen. Ryan, in an attempt to clarify the position of the Air Force and to build internal unity, issued a statement on the A-7D as a headline in the September 1 issue of the *Air Force Policy Letter for Commanders*:

It should be clearly understood that we need the A-7D. In the close air support role, it is superior to any other aircraft available today. We need it to replace the aging F-100s. The planned A-7D force will provide a significant increase in the capability of our strike force in the 1970s.[143]

In January 1970, the Air Staff submitted a budget request for $242.7 million for the procurement of an additional eighty-eight A-7Ds. This number brought the total Air Force buy to 290 aircraft, completing the second tactical air wing and starting the third. In March 1970, the Air Force announced to Congress that the ultimate force planned for the A-7D had been reduced to three wings.[144]

The final production for the A-7D was 459 aircraft delivered and accepted by the Air Force for three wings. The total cost over the nine years of funding was $1.582 billion, which averages out to a $3.448 million program cost per aircraft.

Review of the A-7 Program by Model

Navy A-7A: The Navy selected the A-7 to replace the venerable Douglas A-4, which it did by carrying twice as much ordnance with double the loiter time. The first flight was on September 27, 1965, and the first combat mission was on December 4, 1967. Production totaled 199 aircraft.

Navy A-7B: The A-7B carried an upgraded engine, the P&W TF-30-P-8, and first flew on February 6, 1968. A total of 196 aircraft were produced, with twenty-four converted to two-seat TA-7Cs. Several were converted to A-7Ps for the Portuguese air force.

A-7C: This was a hybrid model consisting of the first sixty-seven A-7Es, but with the older TF-30-P-8 engine. It added the third hydraulic flight control system and carried most of the features of the advanced navigation / weapons delivery system. Two Navy squadrons flew it in Vietnam.

TA-7C: LTV produced this two-seat model for the Navy by converting twenty-four A-7Bs and thirty-six A-7Cs. The aircraft was used for upgrade and instrument training. Seven more were added, for a total of sixty-seven.

Air Force A-7D: The first five aircraft destined for the US Air Force were designated YA-7D. The first flight was on April 6, 1968, with the TF-30-P-6 installed. The third aircraft's first flight was on September 26, 1968, with the Allison TF-41-A21. This test flight reached a speed of Mach 0.94 at 20,000 feet.[145] A-7D number 5 was the first one with the full avionics systems. Production A-7Ds began to be delivered on December 1, 1969, to the 4525th Fighter Weapons Wing at Luke AFB, Arizona. The first operational unit was the 354th Tactical Fighter Wing, Myrtle Beach, South Carolina. LTV produced 459 A-7Ds.[146]

Navy A-7E: Following the deployment of the A-7C, the first operational delivery of the A-7E was to the West Coast RAG on October 8, 1969. The first deployment cruise featured two squadrons when USS *Ranger* sailed for the Tonkin Gulf on October 27, 1970. There were 535 A-7Es produced.[147] There were thirty-eight Navy squadrons that flew versions of the A-7.

TA-7K: The Air Force version of the two-place aircraft was the TA-7K. It had all the features of the A-7D in both cockpits and was used by each of the Air National Guard squadrons. It was produced late in the series and was never flown by the active force. The aircraft were distributed to each Air National Guard unit. Thirty were produced.

CHAPTER 9
Combat in Linebackers I and II, and Beyond

From the Far East I send you one single thought, one sole idea—
written in red on every beachhead from Australia to Tokyo—
"There is no substitute for victory."

—Gen. Douglas MacArthur

Air Force Initial Training in the A-7D

The first flight of the Air Force A-7D took place from Edwards AFB on September 26, 1968, three years after the USAF's decision to buy the aircraft. The first production batch was delivered to the 4525th Fighter Weapons Wing at Luke AFB on December 1, 1969.

Maj. Charles W. McClarren, a veteran of Cmdr. Hill's first combat deployment of the A-7A, was the squadron commander. In January 1970, Lt. Col. Robert M. Bond (later lieutenant general) transitioned from the F-100 to the A-7D and became the commander of the 310th Tactical Fighter Training Squadron, 58th Fighter Weapons Training Wing. He led the new pilots in the A-7 air-to-ground gunnery training that Luke AFB was so famous for.

Although it was not widely known, the pilots were also trained in defensive air-to-air tactics, showing that the tight-turning and Sidewinder-equipped aircraft was very difficult to shoot down.

Late in November 1970, the squadron lost its first aircraft in a crash at the Gila Bend (now Goldwater) Training Range. The aircraft was practicing precautionary landings when it departed controlled flight and crashed upside down.

Col. Bond became famous in the A-7 community. He went on to become the director of operations for the 58th Wing, and in 1972 he was assigned as vice commander of the 23rd Tactical Fighter Wing as it transitioned from the F-100 to the A-7D at England AFB, Louisiana. As a colonel, he flew combat missions in the A-7D while on temporary duty in Thailand in 1972.

Weapons Accuracy in the A-7D/E versus the A-7A/B

The weapons delivery computer in the A-7A and B was the analog CP-741, which had been used previously in the A-4 Skyhawk. It provided assistance to the pilot in dive angle but made no compensation for wind. The upgrade to the digital tactical computer and the other components was revolutionary, since the system made virtually all the calculations the pilot needed. The CP-741 was reportedly difficult to maintain. It worked fine in the early years but degraded until at the end, one pilot reported, "The A-7A's that I flew had been rode hard and put up wet, so about the only things that worked were the master arm, the gunsight, and the bomb pickle" button.[1] Greg Stearns assessment of the A-7E was as follows:

> The bombing system in the E took all of that guesswork out of the situation. When you rolled in, you put the aiming diamond on the target, hit the pickle, and then pulled up the azimuth steering line. You did not have to worry about dive angle, airspeed, release altitude, or winds because the computer figured out when to release your bombs. Routinely, pilots would record a "Shack" or would have a CEP of less than 25'. An excellent CEP in the A/B was 50', with most CEPs much greater.[2]

Terry Wolf had flown the A-4L in combat in Vietnam and the A-7D with the South Dakota Air National Guard. He commented on the avionics systems:

The A-7D and E were the first light-attack aircraft to have a good inertial platform and computerized weapons delivery system that I flew. The A-7 system was so good that it was not uncommon for a four-ship of A-7Ds to go to the range with six bombs each and return with twenty-four bull's-eyes. A bull's-eye in the A-4 was earned the hard way. When the Air Force built the F-117 stealth fighter, they used the A-7 weapons delivery system.[3]

The 354th Tactical Fighter Wing

As newer aircraft came off the production line in November 1970, they were assigned to the 354th Tactical Fighter Wing at Myrtle Beach AFB, South Carolina. The 354th Wing had been reactivated on June 15, 1970, by absorbing the resources of the 4554th TFW at Myrtle Beach. The 355th TFS, which had flown F-100s and F-4s in Vietnam, was reactivated on November 1, 1970, and was assigned to the 354th TFW. When the 356th TFS returned from Misawa AB, Japan, on May 15, 1971, it was also was reassigned to the 354 TFW. Two months later, the 353rd TFS returned from Torrejon AB, Spain, and completed the wing's complement.

The 354th Wing was commanded by Col. Evan W. Rosencrans. Col. Rosencrans was a West Point graduate and had flown 133 combat missions in Korea, where he had shot down a MiG-15. In 1969, he flew 132 combat missions in the F-100 in South Vietnam. The initial cadre of pilots was a mixture of experienced F-100 pilots and new graduates of the combat crew training at Luke. With the first aircraft arriving on November 19, the training was intense and exciting. Col. Rosencrans was amazed at the stability of the A-7 and how difficult it was to get into a spin. He was quoted as saying, "You had to work at it," and "how beautifully it handled."[4]

While the wing was working up qualifying its pilots and maintenance crews in the gunnery qualification and technical intricacies of the aircraft, Colonel Rosencrans selected two pilots for a long journey. Captains James Read and Robert Dewey took off for a nonstop flight on May 21, 1971, to the Paris Air Show.[5] (These two pilots were later to demonstrate the A-7D to the Swiss air force.)

The A-7D Becomes Operational

The 355th TFS was the first Myrtle Beach squadron to be equipped with A-7Ds. Nine months after the 354th was reactivated, the wing sent the 355th with nineteen A-7Ds to Bergstrom AFB, Texas, to participate in Exercise Gallant Hand 72, an Army / Air Force joint war game with Fort Hood's 2nd Armored Division. The squadron deployed on March 17, 1972, and two days later they were flying close-air-support missions with tank battalions and other Army units.

Unfortunately, on March 20, the 354th Wing back at Myrtle Beach suffered an aircraft accident, with one of its pilots ejecting from a disabled A-7D that crashed in a wooded area 16 miles northwest of the base. With an initial indication that the crash was caused by some malfunction of the engine, the Air Force grounded all A-7D aircraft and began inspections of the fleet.

After the exhaustive accident investigation and its formal report, the Air Force determined the accident did not reveal any mechanical or structural flaw in the airframe, and the A-7Ds were released to fly.

On March 30, 1972, the North Vietnamese army, the Viet Minh, invaded South Vietnam with regular units in a massive offensive to conquer the southern republic. One week later, on April 6, President Nixon initiated Operation Linebacker I, resuming the bombing of North Vietnam that had been halted in November 1968. With the A-7s of the 354th Wing operationally ready, the wing was alerted for deployment to Southeast Asia.

In September, the staff at 7th Air Force headquarters in Saigon determined that the remaining A-1 Skyraiders (mostly "H" models) were best reassigned to the Vietnamese air force for their own defense under the Vietnamization program. With the A-1s going away, the A-7 354th Wing would have to pick up the search-and-rescue (SAR) mission when they arrived.

The First A-7D Deployment to Southeast Asia

The deployment of the 354th Tactical Fighter Wing began in September 1972, and by October 16 the 353rd and 355th Squadrons were in place at Korat Royal Thai Airbase, Thailand, on temporary duty with seventy-two A-7Ds. During their stay at Korat, the 354th TFW was augmented with the 354th, 74th, and 358th TFSs.

The wing's squadrons flew deep interdiction missions over North Vietnam and interdiction and close air support in South Vietnam, Laos, and Cambodia and escorted surface ship convoys up the Mekong River to Phnom Penh, Cambodia. Shortly afterward, the commander put out a call for volunteers to fly SAR missions. Most of the A-7 pilots had flown the F-100 and a few the A-1, but very few had flown the Sandy mission. The volunteers began training for the SAR mission under the supervision of A-1 pilots remaining in theater. The A-1 pilots organized and monitored the flying training from helicopters hovering overhead. On November 7, 1972, the A-1 Skyraider flew its last Sandy mission. The mission was transferred to the A-7 pilots. During Linebacker II, the A-7 Sandys would rescue twenty-two downed American airmen, while the wing flew four thousand combat sorties.

The Rescue of Bobbin 05

On November 16, 1972, an F-105G Wild Weasel was shot down while conducting an Iron Hand, SAM suppression mission in support of a B-52 Arc Light high-altitude, night-bombing of a target 60 miles south of Hanoi, near the famous Thanh Hoa bridge.[6] As soon as the sun came up, A-7Ds from the 354th Wing started searching for the crew and located them by one of their transmitter beacons. But they were in deep jungle, and the weather was too bad to begin a rescue mission. The rescue was planned for the next day. Maj. "Arnie" Clarke volunteered and was selected to be the mission commander.

Maj. Colin "Arnie" Clarke

Born in 1935, Arnie Clarke was commissioned in the Air Force from Officer Training School in August 1960. Arnie and I were in the same pilot-training class, and we went to Luke together to fly the F-100. After graduation he was assigned to the 522nd Tactical Fighter Squadron (TFS) at Cannon AFB, New Mexico. While there, he deployed to Southeast Asia twice, being shot down once and flying twenty-seven combat missions. After a brief assignment flying F-100s in England, he was transferred to the 352nd TFS

in 1968, where he flew the F-100, O-1 Bird Dog, OV-10 Bronco, and OH-6 Cayuse with the Army. In January 1969, he volunteered and became Misty 89, flying FASTFAC F-100s. By July 1969, he had flown another 285 combat missions.

He was promoted to major and served his next tour as an air liaison officer with the Army's 82nd Airborne Division at Fort Bragg, North Carolina. He then completed A-7 Corsair II combat crew training and was assigned to the 356th TFS of the 354th TFW in May 1971, where he became a flight commander. One of his flight members was Capt. Douglas de Vlaming, who recalled:

> Arnie was small in stature, but a giant in all other aspects. He was a fighter pilot's fighter pilot. He was courageous, aggressive, tenacious, and highly skilled at flying fighter aircraft. Arnie was born to led men in combat. He was my flight commander, and I wanted to be just like him.[7]

The Mission

The Bobbin 05 rescue force consisted of sixty aircraft: A-7Ds from Korat, Jolly Green (HH-53C) helicopters from Nakon Phanom, F-4D Phantom IIs for MiGCAP, F-105s for SAM suppression, an HC-130P Kingbird (mission coordinator), and KC-135 aerial tankers. Arnie was Sandy 1 as his A-7D flight took off at 0430 on the morning of November 18, 1972. By 0530 he led the rescue package to the vicinity of the downed airmen, but the ground was overcast below 8,500 feet, with mountains all around. The Jolly Greens kept radioing, "We can't get in," and "We can't find our way down into that stuff." There was no hole for them to let down to get beneath the clouds and find the two crew members. Clark descended through the clouds several times, using his projected map display and radar altimeter until the radar warnings went off, and then he climbed back up to the clear air above the clouds. One time he broke out below the clouds, but he was in a valley too narrow to maneuver.

At one point the first two Jolly Green helicopters called Bingo (low) fuel and had to return to base. A second pair joined the search but still could not penetrate. The aircraft were still receiving radio signals from the downed crew, but there was no way to reach them. Red Crown, the surveillance aircraft off the coast, called and recommended an attempt from the beach side. Clarke flew out to the Gulf of Tonkin, descended, and tracked inbound to the survivors, flying through clouds until right over them, noting the men's exact position on his moving map display. Reversing course, he flew the reciprocal course to the water and tried for another pass. This time explosions blew all around him as the AAA guns on the mountainsides and ridgelines opened up. Approaching from the east was not a good plan.

With fuel running low, six and a half hours after takeoff, Clarke and his wingman descended again into the cloud. They broke out into clear air beneath the mist, but in the wrong valley. In fact, they flew directly across the Thanh Hoa bridge, one of the most heavily defended targets in North Vietnam. Tracers and 57 mm shells burst all round them. Suddenly, one of the HH-53s penetrated the overcast and found the right valley and called Sandy 1 to join them. Then, the Jolly Green called, "We're at Bingo!" Clarke ordered the two helicopters to return to base, and he and his wingman pulled up on top of the clouds again. He radioed, "We're not going home. We're going to cycle to the tanker."

It was 11:45 a.m. He and his wingman climbed out to northern Thailand, searching for the KC-135 tanker in its racetrack pattern. Seeing the tanker first on radar and then visually, Sandy 1 went in, hooked up, and refueled. Sandy 2 followed, and the pair were ready to make another try.[8] Other aircraft in the rescue had previously refueled, as necessary, and were ready to go back.

This time the rescuers received good voice communication from the airmen, and the two A-7s led the two Jolly Greens and then a third down though a gap in the soup. They descended into the right valley, leveled off about 800 feet above the ground, and found just enough room for them to maneuver. Other A-7s with smoke cannisters let down over the Gulf of Tonkin and laid their smoke to protect the helicopters. At 150 knots, the helos were hard to escort, so Clarke and his wingman flew S turns and circles around them as they searched for the airmen. Heavy antiaircraft fire now opened up on the quintet. Then Clarke got a strobe warning of a SAM site locking in on them. The signal faded, but the

AAA fire continued. Arnie briefed the downed airmen and the helos and then called down his other A-7s in the flight. "Time to start hitting them back." Clarke set up the A-7s in a rotating chain, each aircraft diving on and strafing the AAA gun positions on the slope just above the downed crew:

Amid much noise and confusion, the Jolly Green crew, unaware of the gun positions, swooped in and touched down. In a few remarkable seconds, the helicopter picked up both F-105G fliers, sprang aloft, and headed west.

Pulling away from a strafing attack, Arnie Clarke felt a sudden jolt and heard a clattering sound, like tin pans banging together. It was the noise and concussion associated with a direct hit by AAA fire. At the same time, his warning receiver told him that a SAM site was locking on again.

Smoke gushed from his starboard wing. "I'm hit!" In the soup now, Clarke lost all instruments! He was blind, with no reference to his own altitude, with ridgelines all around him, and a SAM was locked on, ready to fire.[9]

The missile never came:

Climbing out, still losing fuel, Clarke's A-7 diverted to Da Nang air base, escorted by two other A-7Ds. With no operating instruments, his two wingmen talked him into a straight-in approach, and he touched town safely just after 1:30 p.m., logging nine hours since takeoff that morning. The longest mission was over. The AAA fire that hit his aircraft turned out to be a 7.62 round, but the damage it caused was immense. The aircraft could not be repaired in theater, and it was eventually flown back to the United States with the landing gear locked down. That A-7D is now on display at the National Museum of the US Air Force in Dayton, Ohio.[10]

Maj. Arnie Clarke was awarded the Air Force Cross, the nation's second-highest medal for bravery. The citation to accompany the award read, in part:

For extraordinary heroism in military operations against an opposing armed force as pilot of an A-7 aircraft of the 354th Tactical Fighter Squadron, 355th Tactical Fighter Wing, Korat Royal Thai Air Base, Thailand, in action as On-Scene Commander for search and rescue operations over North Vietnam, on November 18, 1972. On that date, Maj. Clarke directed an extremely complex mission that resulted in the successful recovery of two downed airmen despite adverse weather, mountainous terrain, and intense hostile ground fire. Disregarding these hazards, his own safety, and battle damage to his aircraft, he personally guided the rescue helicopter to the survivors' location, suppressed hostile defenses, and continued to direct rescue efforts even though he sustained additional damage to his aircraft.[11]

Lt. Col. Arnie Clarke retired in 1981 after twenty-seven years of service.

Post-Linebacker Operations

After the end of American combat involvement Vietnam (January 1973), the wing flew combat missions in Laos until February 22, and in Cambodia until August 15. At that point, PACAF wanted to keep one of the A-7 squadrons transferred to its own control. Aircraft and pilots from the two squadrons were selected and assigned to the 3rd Tactical Fighter Squadron, under the 388th TFW at Korat. The 3rd Squadron flew close air support for the rescue of the crew of the US-flagged freighter *Mayaguez* in May 1975.[12]

Flying the A-7D through a "Departure"

Air Force major Keith Connolly (later brigadier general) tells a fascinating story about training pilots to fly the A-7D. In the 1970s, he was selected to be an instructor pilot in the A-7D at Davis Monthan AFB, which was then the "schoolhouse" for the aircraft. As the wing chief of Standardization/Evaluation, one of his jobs was to conduct "final elimination rides" to pilots who were having difficulties learning how to fly the A-7. His story:

On one of these elimination rides, the pilot I was chasing was having difficulty in being "aggressive" with turning the A-7 in a dogfight,

which is considered an essential survival maneuver. During our ground briefing, I discussed with the student the necessity to "pull maximum Gs" to keep a bad guy off your tail. The young captain assured me that he understood the reason for this survival maneuver, combined with the need to pull maximum Gs. We also discussed at length the fact that when you hurriedly placed heavy Gs on an A-7, particularly in a turn, you must remain in coordinated flight or the airplane can "depart controlled flight." This maneuver was known as a "departure" and is somewhat unique to the A-7. The takeoff and trip to the training area were uneventful as we climbed to 20,000 feet.

I placed the student into the "lead" of the flight while I took separation from him to act like an enemy aggressor. As I closed into attacking position, the student pulled the control stick full aft, which placed max Gs on the airplane, causing it to fully depart. I have seen many departures, and ridden through some myself, but I have never seen this resulting maneuver. The airplane flipped end over end—nose over tail—four times, totally out of control pulling max Gs. I was so shocked that all I could do was to transmit—"RELEASE THE CONTROLS . . . RELEASE THE CONTROLS!"

Luckily, the student followed my directions and the aircraft recovered. There was a long silence and the student transmitted, "Sir, I'd like to return to the base now!" We had an uneventful recovery, but during the debriefing, the student stated, "Sir, I don't want to be a fighter pilot, and I sure don't ever want to go through that maneuver again." He was given the opportunity to transfer into multiengine aircraft. For myself, I learned a new respect for the A-7.[13]

Navy Combat Experience with the A-7C and A-7E

The first flight of the A-7E was on March 9, 1969, and one year later the first squadron deployed. On April 10, 1970, squadrons VA-146 and VA-147 in Carrier Air Wing 9 deployed on USS *America* (CVA-66) for Southeast Asia. The two squadrons, the "Blue Diamonds" and the "Argonauts," were originally equipped with the early A-7Cs with the old TF-30-P-8 engine but soon converted to the TF-41 models as production of the engines increased. The carrier headed south and east out of Norfolk, passing the Cape of Good Hope, and arrived on station on May 26.[14] On May 26, 1970, Lt (j.g.) Dave Lichetermann of VA-146 was catapulted from *America*'s deck to be the first A-7E pilot in combat.[15] Since the bombing halt of North Vietnam was still in place, *America*'s combat sorties were accomplished dropping bombs and strafing Vietcong targets in South Vietnam and the Pathet Lao and NVA in Laos. VA-147 was similarly employed, with the distinction of having been the first A-7A squadron in combat three years earlier.

An Air Force Gunner

When VA-146 arrived on Yankee Station on May 26, 1970, it had an Air Force exchange officer on board who was an experienced fighter pilot. Capt. Ralph Wetterhahn, flying an F-4, had shot down a MiG during Col. Robin Olds's "Operation Bolo." With the high minimum-altitude restrictions placed on attack missions in heavily defended area, few Navy pilots bothered to use the new M-61 cannon in the A-7E. Wetterhahn, having been without a gun in the F-4C, looked forward to strafing. He fired the cannon as often as he had the opportunity. One of the characteristics of the M-61 was the large amount of carbon dispersion when the gun fired. Of course, it was the plane captain (crew chief) who had to clean this residue after each flight.

One night at a bar in Olongapo, Philippines, Wetterhahn was accosted by that plane captain. Wetterhahn tells the story:

We all got merrily inebriated and one white hat laid into me, calling me "Capt. Messerschmidt." I thought it had to do with my German name. "Not exactly," says he, maintaining that it was actually my nickname among the "mechs" because whenever I flew, I brought the plane back filthy from shooting the gun. I usually did fire the M61, particularly at night. On one occasion, maintenance wanted the ammo can emptied for some reason, and boy did I accommodate. All 1,000 rounds . . . "zzziiip!" The cordite would stick to the belly, and being corrosive, it had to be cleaned off before salt spray got to it.

I had figured out a way to drop bombs, then open up with the Gatling gun during pullout—a tactic designed to keep AAA heads low while I cleared the area. Truth is, I just loved to shoot the gun.

The plane captain said, "It's a real pain, Capt. Messerschmidt."[16]

"Fine," I told him. "Next time I fly, I'll clean the damn thing myself."[17]

Two weeks later, Ralph flew again with a full load of bombs and ammo. Sure enough, he came back with the bottom black. As he sees the plane captain looking at it with disgust, Wetterhahn says, "Don't touch it. Get what you need to clean it at dawn and wait for me." He went on to debrief, got about two hours' sleep, and came back to the plane to see what must have been two hundred sailors gathered around. Wetterhahn grabbed the can of gunk and a pile of old rags, slid under the fuselage, and began cleaning. Cameras flashed like a fashion show. Ralph reported that he was halfway to the tail when the plane captain slid in beside him and took the rags. "Never thought I'd ever see an officer do this. I'll take over—and another thing. Shoot the gun any time." Capt. Wetterhahn went on to complete the deployment, volunteering for a third combat tour flying F-4s at Korat. After the war, he became quite a famous author.[18]

Eight successive A-7 squadrons deployed to the South China Sea and flew missions over South Vietnam between 1970 and March 1972. VA-165, the "Dam Busters" (so named for their daring exploits in attacking North Korean dams in the Korean War while flying AD Skyraiders), was aboard USS *Kitty Hawk* (CVA-63) in the Philippine Sea when the invasion occurred. Together with VA-192, they headed for Yankee Station and participated in the early attacks, resuming the bombing of North Vietnam in March and April. VA-165 lost its squadron commander, Cmdr. Don Hall, on March 6, when his aircraft disappeared from the glide path on a night approach and crashed into the sea.

Adm. Busey's Thoughts on Attack Carriers

Ed Beakley was assigned in 1971 to the Replacement Air Group at NAS Lemoore, California, to qualify in the A-7A/B before deploying to Southeast

Asia. His squadron commanding officer was Capt. Jim Busey. Busey had two combat tours (189 missions) in Vietnam under his belt in the A-4 Skyhawk and was the recipient of the Navy Cross and three Distinguished Flying Crosses. He would go on to be vice chief of naval operations and head the FAA. Ed's story begins:

I had all of twenty hours in the A-7 and had flown my first flight with Capt. Busey on my wing as the instructor pilot only a few weeks before. Four months later, on April 30, 1972, as a new aviator in the VA-56 "Champs," I would be night carrier landing qualified with 100 Corsair hours and fly my first combat mission in Vietnam.

On an afternoon in mid-December, Capt. Busey called an "all pilots" meeting, including the experienced instructors and the young aviators in training—mostly on their way to a first operational squadron. He began by noting that aircraft carriers were ships designated as CVAs and not CVFs.

This was not the stuff of officer club wrangling between F-4 or F-8 fighter pilots and A-4/A-7/A-6 "attack" pilots; rather, it was serious underpinning that the reason that carriers were CVAs—meaning attack carriers—was the simple fact that aircraft carriers and Navy air's reason for being was to carry home attack to America's enemies. He indicated he meant no disrespect to the fighter community—and indeed they got loaded with bombs often enough—but their role as air-to-air mission squadrons was to ensure that the attack aircraft got to the target and got out safely. We, the attack guys, were the reason everything else was there. This wasn't a "rah rah, win one for the Gipper" talk; Busey was dead serious and straight to the point. When it was over, the puzzled looks indicated that none of us quite understood why the talk and the emphasis. Months later, with multiple combat missions into North Vietnam under my belt, I surmised that in his position, Capt. Busey knew a hell of a lot more about what was going on and would probably occur in Southeast Asia in a fairly short time than the news or any of us had any idea.

Busey's experience included the USS *Oriskany* (CVA-34) war cruise in 1967–68. During that combat tour, CVW-16 suffered the highest loss rate of any naval air wing during the Vietnam conflict, losing half of assigned planes—twenty-nine to combat damage and another ten to operational causes. The wing had twenty pilots killed and another nine taken prisoner. The POWs included the air wing commander, James Bond Stockdale; his VA-163 squadron CO, Harry Jenkins; and squadron mate, John McCain. Busey knew what a restart of bombing missions up north would mean, and I'm guessing he saw it as his duty to give us a heads-up as best he could.[19]

Three months later—March 30, 1972—North Vietnamese army units invaded South Vietnam in mass—the Easter Offensive.

Operation Linebacker I
On May 9, President Nixon initiated Operation Linebacker I with an order to enlarge the air war against North Vietnam and mine the harbors at Haiphong. Cmdr. Hill's replacement in VA-165 was Lt. Cmdr. Maso "Mace" Gilfry, who had an eventful mission in his first month as skipper. Gilfry, who was on his third combat cruise, was leading a strike against the heavily defended Dong Hoi target when his A-7E was hit by a SAM. He recalled:

I successively dodged the first two SAMs and had put my aircraft into full power when I heard the CAG in the number three slot alert me with "Here comes another one, Mace," so I rolled into a hard turn, saw it, and it was too late. My engine and tail were on fire and I began to lose power.

As I was coasting out, heading for the water, I pickled off my bombs and hit a storage area which was known to have about sixty-five guns, and continued coasting out my aircraft to an area about 2 miles out to sea before the airplane became uncontrollable. [He ejected.]

Three or four SAMs passed me as I was floating down. I could hear big coastal guns clacking away at their target, which I assumed was me since the shells, at least thirty of them, splashed into the sea below me.[20]

Lt. Cmdr. Gilfry landed safely in the water and was picked up by Lt. Frank Lockett of Helicopter 7 in an HH-3A. Gilfry went on to complete his tour in command of VA-195.

RAdm. W. W. "Bear" Pickavance Jr. tells of his 1972 deployment where he flew the A-7B and participated in both Linebacker I and Linebacker II:

I received my wings in May of 1971. I specifically requested the A-7 Corsair on the West Coast (NAS Lemoore) because that was where the action was. I received orders to the A-7A/B Replacement Air Group (the RAG) for combat training. At completion, I was assigned to VA-93 flying the A-7B, assigned to Air Group 5, embarked in USS *Midway* (CVA-41). We left immediately for NAS Fallon, Nevada, and air wing integration training preparing for a deployment in July–August 1972. After the Fallon deployment, we prepared for embarked training in Southern California in March 1972. I was one of the lucky ones to fly out to *Midway* vs. walking aboard in Alameda. When we arrived overhead the ship, she was at warp speed headed north. After landing, I was taxied forward, and we all were shut down. When we got to our ready room, we were told that we were leaving in two days for Vietnam—eight weeks early. We went back to Lemoore, packed up, said our goodbyes, and headed back to Alameda and left.[21]

An Alpha Strike in Linebacker I

On July 22, 1972, "Schoolboy" (USS *Midway*, CVA-41) launched a major, thirty-four-plane Alpha strike against the Ca Chau buried petroleum facility just across the river from Hanoi. Here is the story as told by Lt. Ed Beakley from the A-7 side and Lt. Dave Kelly from the A-6 perspective:

MIDWAY / CAG 5's operations, like most other CVs and air wings during Linebacker I and II, consisted of three types of strike missions. During daylight, the Navy executed two-to-four-plane strikes flown by F-4s, A-7s, and A-6s into Route Packages (RP) II, III, and IV. At night, A-7s frequented these same regions and prosecuted targets along the coast in RP VI A. (RP VI B belonged to the Air Force.)

These ops were either against prebriefed specific targets, or they were armed reconnaissance missions looking for movers (trucks and trains) transporting goods south. The so-called medium-attack bomber, A-6, could carry more ordnance than any other carrier-based aircraft and flew these missions, as well as their design bread-and-butter mission, the low-level, single-plane night strikes into VIA and B.

The third type of strike and most-effective raids into the heartland of the north in 1972 were the large multiplane missions launched by both the Air Force and the Navy. And since these missions had many aircraft flying in a formation, they were all daylight missions. These missions were the Alpha strikes.

A-7s, F-4s, and A-6s all participated in these Alpha strikes. They were designed to put as much ordnance as possible on a high-valued target in the shortest possible time and with the least amount of risk. Alpha strike targets included airfields, power plants, factory complexes, POL, air defense staging areas, and other parts of the enemy's war-fighting infrastructure. The missions were quite demanding on the aircrews and the maintenance personnel, and the ship's supply system was also pressed to keep replenishing the tons and tons of ordnance that the Alpha strikes consumed. Given these demands, the carriers tasked with Alpha strikes could handle only two or three daylight launches of the big strikes per day

Launching multiple strike and support aircraft, joining them up, tanking, and getting them to the beach, and then finally getting them in and off target in a high-threat area, took an incredible amount of aerial choreography. This was made even more difficult for USS *Midway*, having only two bow catapults (the more modern carriers in the fleet had four catapults: two on the bow and two waist cats on the angle deck). The plan for the Alpha needed to limit unnecessary exposure to AAA and SAMs, protect the strike aircraft from MiGs, assure the most effective use of ECM/jamming, provide suppression of the surface-to-air missile launches, avoid midair collisions, and assure the success of the mission (i.e., bombs on target).

All the aircraft were launched as quickly as possible and climbed to the rendezvous altitude directly over the ship. Each strike element took off together and then conducted a running rendezvous while spiraling up to the Alpha formation. If this all worked properly, the lead element would be in position and stabilized in a rendezvous turn, circling the ship at a level altitude as each of the other three- or four-plane elements joined and slid into its respective position in the formation.

Since the planes had been launched in sequence, all that was required was for each element to join expeditiously and then proceed to the rendezvous circle and get into position. The result was a very crowded sky with up to forty aircraft jockeying to get into their respective positions.

F-4 elements typically needed to refuel after taking off and climbing all the way to altitude, so they rendezvoused with the tanker and began getting topped off. Depending on the timing for the strike, the flight leader might call for the Alpha to head out prior to the F-4s getting into position. The in-route portion of the flight for the strike group was normally conducted at 20,000 feet and around 475 knots. This was in deference to the A-6s, who were carrying almost the same load as three of the other planes.

Protection for the Alpha included two sections of A-7 Iron Hand elements and multiple F-4 MIGCAP elements. The Iron Hand aircraft were normally configured with four antiradiation (Shrike) missiles to counter the SAM threat. They would monitor their ECM gear, looking for signs of Fansong radar activity (SAM acquisition and guidance radar). If a site launched a missile or acted like it was preparing to launch a missile, the Iron Hand would respond by launching a faster radiation-seeking missile. The idea of this was to destroy the Fansong radar associated with the SAM site or force the site to stop transmitting guidance commands to the airborne SAM. Without the guidance commands, the SAM turned into a Mach 1.5 unguided rocket instead of a radar-guided weapon.

The F-4s set up a barrier between the strike group and likely MiG threat airfields. Both elements went over the coast ("feet dry") 10–20 miles ahead of the strike group. As the strike formation approached "feet dry," the leader would push the throttles up and descend to the roll-in altitude, typically around 15,000 feet, and the ECM warning equipment would start to light up. The audio cacophony would continue and increase for the last 10 or 40 miles to the roll-in point for the attack. At the strike leader's command, the individual divisions of the strike would initiate a formation roll-in and attack their designated aim point in the target area, drop their bombs, jink coming off the target, then level off at about 3,500 feet above the ground and exit at the highest speed possible.

The SAM threat was greatest during the ingress, AAA was worst in the target area, and enemy fighters and random AAA were the menaces during egress. MiGs flying low to avoid the MiGCAP would try to pick off the strike aircraft as they dashed to the water.

For the Ca Chau buried petroleum facility, Cmdr. Neil Harvey, commanding officer of the VA-56 "Champs," was the strike leader, flying an A-7B. Lt. Cmdr. Smokey Tolbert and I were his wingmen.

This was going to be a large strike by *Midway* standards, with the lead formation consisting of three divisions in a fingertip formation followed by a second formation of four divisions. As per CAG Five doctrine, the individual elements were three plane divisions, and per VA-56 A-7 doctrine, we carried six Mk. 83 1,000 lb. bombs on the wing racks (i.e., "slick wing"). The A-6s carried sixteen Mk. 82s (500 lb. bombs) on MERS. The basic approach was as defined previously.

As it turned out, good friend Dave "Snako" Kelly, from the A-6 squadron (VA-115), and I were both on this strike. Dave's story of his first division lead for a major Alpha strike is reflected in his book, *Not on My Watch*, and was an additional source for this story. Our memories coincide pretty closely, but as in all combat, each participant sees and recalls things differently. What is certain was the effect. As can be seen in the picture in the photo section and as noted by Dave, this strike created a huge cloud, visible even from *Midway*'s location at sea, giving the hardworking flight deck crew a view of what their efforts were supporting in the war.[22]

This is Dave Kelly's telling of his story:

We needed a few more Division Leaders to support the Alpha Strikes. Lt. Cmdr. Craig deep selected us for this new qualification. This strike was my qualification flight as a Division Lead. Cmdr. Harvey, the CO of the VA-56 A-7 squadron the CAG, would be leading the strike. The A-6s were in the lead element on CAG's right wing.

The Alpha joined up over the ship at 20,000 feet. The various elements joining the strike from the inside of the rendezvous-turn, then slid into their respective positions. The F-4s in the flight needed to be topped-off on their way in, so with everyone pretty much in position and ready for battle, we turned toward the coast aiming at an area just north of the hourglass which was a lightly defended area at the bottom RP VIB.

I had anticipated this, and since this was my "trial" as a Division Lead, I wanted to show my element that I could "hack it." With Lt. Cmdr. Craig on one wing, and the new skipper, Cmdr. Barrish, on the other, I was determined to maintain my position in the formation no matter what.

The strategy of the strike was good, the Alpha was going to proceed in bound toward Nam Dinh, a heavily defended area. Short of the city we would turn north toward Hanoi. The strategy was to confuse the defenses with this "feint" at Nam Dinh, then boldly head for Hanoi, only to roll-in to the left seven or eight miles short of the city. Since the target was south of that city, we would be flying directly into the high threat SAM zone. Providing we didn't stir-up anything nasty, we would be roll[ing] in to port in a classic fan on the POL giving each division a good steep dive from the roll-in, and then just continue in the turn to the southeast and "feet wet."

The ECM gear had started chattering before we had reached the turn at Nam Dinh. As we approached Hanoi more and more sites joined in the course. The greater Hanoi area was well-defended with AAA and SAMs. Our strike group of aircraft had gotten their attention, and they were certainly going to take a shot at us, if at all possible. Cmdr. Harvey was forced to begin medium-hard maneuvering based on the ECM indications and the initial AAA fired. The APR-27 [radar homing and warning] low warble indicating a SAM was eminent just as the first elements started their roll-in. By the time we reached our roll-in, the warble went to high, meaning that someone in our part of the sky was a "target."

It was then that I realized I had forgotten one rather important thing. Despite leading and flying a near perfect flight, I had failed to turn on the gunsight. So there we were going downhill very fast with Shylock [my bombardier/navigator] calling out the passing altitudes, and I'm fumbling around on the center console trying to locate the switch for the gunsight. Passing something like 7,500 feet I decided to give up on the gunsight and took a look through the windscreen at the ground rushing up at us.

We had fused the bombs for a medium fuse delay, so the bombs would penetrate some of the soil before they exploded. The bombs hitting the ground were sending up plumes of fire as they touched-off the buried POL. By the time I reached our pickle altitude all I could see in the gunsight was a huge fireball as the bombs from the preceding elements hit their mark. I couldn't have missed, even without the gunsight; this must have been a huge cache of fuel.

We followed a direct route to feet-wet attempting to egress at about the same point as we had ingressed. During the flight toward the coast we could see the smoke rising nearly vertically from the target area. Our flight of A-6s joined up, reported feet wet to "Red Crown," looked each other over for any battle damage, and switched to *Midway* Approach Control.

Our traps were uneventful, but by the time we had parked the aircraft and deplaned, the smoke from the target area was visible from the deck of the carrier. *Midway* at this time was at the North Yankee Station around sixty nautical miles off the coast. The target was sixty miles inland, so from about 120 nautical we were able to share the result of the strike with our plane captains and the *Midway*'s flight deck personnel.

These guys were contributing to the war effort, working sixteen-hour days for weeks on end and sleeping in four-high racks in poorly air-conditioned spaces. They very seldom saw any of the effects of their labor. That day was different, we could point at the vertical column of smoke, and they could see their direct contribution to the war effort.

And I had passed my test as a Division Flight Leader and was now qualified to actually lead a division in an Alpha Strike."[23]

Beakley added, "Due to the nature of the layout of the storage area, each striker had a different aim point. After the flight, Smokey told me that as the third plane down, he observed my bombs to be the ones that started the initial explosions. Of all the Alphas I was on, this is one of the three or so I recall most vividly. Ca Chau was just on the other side of "downtown" Hanoi in a bend in the Red River. I never saw a bomb plume like that one. It must have been eye watering from a bicycle on the streets of Hanoi."[24]

Operation Linebacker II

Linebacker II was the largest and most intensive bombing campaign of the Vietnam War. Also known as the Christmas Bombing, the objective of the multiple and continuous strikes was no less than the termination of the war—to force the North Vietnamese leadership into serious peace negotiations. This was most likely the largest attack mission in history, using B-52 as a "Very Heavy Attack." President Nixon believed the North Vietnamese were close to agreeing on a truce to end the Vietnam War. In October, Henry Kissinger announced, "Peace is at hand!" He was wrong, and the White House soon knew it.

Kissinger returned from Paris on December 14. Later in the day, Nixon ordered the reseeding of North Vietnamese ports with air-dropped naval mines and ordered the Joint Chiefs of Staff to direct the Air Force to begin planning for a three-day "maximum effort" bombing campaign that could begin within seventy-two hours.[25] On

December 16, the talks broke down and Linebacker II was launched on December 18, 1972.

With one command from the president, the commander in chief, every aircraft in Thailand, the South China Sea, and the island of Guam became part of the attack mission. Each of the more than two thousand sorties was either a bomb dropper or a support aircraft. For the first time in the history of warfare, multiple wings of B-52s were tasked with high-altitude strikes on the industrial and military facilities in the heart of North Vietnam—in Hanoi and Haiphong—on airfields, SAM sites, port facilities, command and control posts, communications, supply depots, and troop concentrations.

RAdm. Chatham continued his recollections, switching now to his experience flying the A-7C on board USS *Midway* in Linebackers I and II:

There is no greater reward for a warrior than to lead his unit into combat. My finest tour was first to be the XO and then CO of VA-56. My greatest challenge as XO was to keep my JOs out of trouble with the skipper. I perfected my "rug dance" on their behalf. "Moneymaker" can explain further if you want to know more details.

The A-7 was far superior to the A-4 in so many ways. In spite of its limitations, its power meant SPEED. We flew slick wing unless special ordnance required otherwise. (Speed was life.) No one launched without a full load. (There was no reason to go fly unless you could do maximum damage.)

The 1972–73 cruise was a long one for the squadron and for our families. We embarked on June 5, 1972, and were extended to complete Linebacker II and did not arrive back in the States until March 24, 1973. I will never forget the night of October 24, 1972. I was blessed with the opportunity to lead the finest group of men that ever went to war.[26]

The Eleven Days of Christmas Bombing

Strategic Air Command (SAC) was determined to plan and control all the B-52 missions from its headquarters in Omaha, Nebraska. HQ SAC selected the units, the mission, the targets, the routes, the refuelings, the formations and spacing, and the egress routes. This was despite the fact that they had no operations plan to attack Hanoi. It appears they did not ask the SAC Air Division, wings, or squadrons on Guam or in Thailand or 7th Air Force for inputs or comments.

Day 1, December 18, consisted of 129 B-52s in three waves, four hours apart. The first wave consisted of forty-eight aircraft in sixteen cells of three B-52s each, with one minute between cells. The aircraft were directed to attack from the west with a single initial point, on the same attack course, at the same altitude, same airspeed, with an identical post-target turn of 60 degrees bank to the right, egressing toward Thailand. Air Force and Navy sent thirty-nine tactical aircraft in support, but because the attacking B-52s were divided into three waves, 7th Air Force and Task Force 17 had to divide their sorties accordingly, severely limiting the number of chaff aircraft and Iron Hand missile suppression to eight each.

On Day 1, the strike force lost three B-52s and one F-111, and two B-52s were severely damaged. One of the B-52s struck by a SAM was hit in the post-target turn, flying into a 100-knot headwind and blanking some of its own jamming waves. The 7th Air Force in Thailand immediately called SAC's 8th Air Force in Guam and objected to the tactics.

Day 2 used the same exact tactics, with ninety-three B-52s striking Hanoi from bases in Guam and U-Tapao, Thailand. There were no losses, but one of the B-52 pilots, Capt. Don Craig, wrote a friend:

> We knew there were big planning flaws, starting with the long lines of bombers coming in the same route . . . and it was straight down Thud Ridge, for God's sake, . . . It looked very much like ducks in a shooting gallery.[27]

Day 3. When the B-52 crews saw the routes for Day 3, there were "emotions from serious concern to outright disgust."[28] The mission was a disaster. Six of the ninety-nine B-52s were shot down, and another was severely damaged. Four of the six were hit by missiles while belly up in the post-target turn. SAC's worst possible prediction of losses was estimated at 3 percent; on the night of December 20, they were 6 percent!

Reassessment and Changed Tactics

The massive losses on Days 1 and 3 of the bombing campaign were devastating to the president, the Joint Chiefs of Staff (JCS), Strategic Air Command, the B-52 crews, and all the support personnel involved in the operation. The chairman of JCS, Adm. Thomas Moorer, called Gen. John C. Meyer, CINCSAC, and reportedly said, "They're setting their God-damned watches by the timing of your bombing runs!"[29]

The SAC commander at 17th Air Division, U-Tapao, was Brig. Gen. Glenn Sullivan, and he took a courageous action. "Things were just not going too well. I said that enough is enough, let's make some changes, we've got to get rid of these tactics, so let's get some crew members in here and let's figure out the best way to do this."[30] On the morning of December 21, Brig. Gen. Sullivan sent a message directly to the commander of SAC. In his own words:

> I sent the message to Gen. J. C. Meyer, the commander of SAC, and just sent an information copy to my boss at Eighth Air Force, [Lt.] Gen. Gerald W. Johnson. A lot of people told me this was probably not a very good thing to do, but I wanted to get to where we could get some action, and I didn't want to have to go through Gen. Johnson and have him say, "I have to check on this" before he sent it to SAC.[31]

Sullivan told a friend, "The post-target turn was the murder point."[32] He reportedly declared, "I'm not going to launch any more bombers out of U-Tapao until the tactics are changed."

Day 4. The result was immediate. SAC headquarters delegated subsequent planning to the crews in Guam at 8th Air Force, and the tactics were changed. The first effects were to reduce the size of the B-52 force to thirty aircraft in one wave for Days 4, 5, and 6, while the revised tactics could be planned and distributed. The strikes were diverted from Hanoi to other targets in Route Package 6, principally Haiphong. Despite the change in targets, two more B-52s were shot down on December 21.

President Nixon ordered the JCS to take a bombing halt on Christmas Day, which gave the planners an extra day to revise the tactics and get target folders to the crews. Many of the crews were upset because the pause also gave the North Vietnamese time to replenish their stocks of SAM missiles and AAA ammunition.

Day 8 was a massive effort, using 120 B-52s and 113 fighters supported. F-4s created a wide chaff corridor, with F-105s and A-7E Iron Hand providing SAM suppression. The ratio for bombers to support aircraft continued to be about 1:1.3.[33] The result, by consolidating the chaff aircraft and compressing the bombers into a single twenty-two-minute attack window and varying the attack headings, was that 85 percent of the B-52s were able to remain inside the chaff cloud, as opposed to 5 percent on the earlier missions. The force still lost two B-52s, but the mission was considered a tremendous success. The next day the North Vietnamese sent a message to the US, offering to restart negotiations. The bombing continued for three more days, but the strategic mission had been accomplished. Negotiation resumed, the air war stopped, the prisoners came home, and the Vietnam War came to an end.

Linebacker II consisted of 729 B-52 sorties against thirty-four targets. The North Vietnamese fired 884 SA-2 SAMs and scored twenty-eight hits, resulting in fifteen B-52s being shot down, four being heavily damaged, and five suffering medium damage. Forty-three crew members were killed and forty-nine were taken prisoner; two F-111s were lost, along with four A-6s, two USAF F-4Es, one Navy F-4J, one EB-66, one RA-5C, one A-7D, and one Navy A-7C.[34]

Brig. Gen. Sullivan was transferred to command the Aerospace Rescue and Recovery Service in Military Airlift Command, but his career was over. He retired the next year and died in 1998. He never wrote and seldom spoke about his experience, even to his son, Ray. Ray Sullivan has made a valiant contribution to the historical record by establishing a website, Linebacker II (http://www.linebacker2.com), and a documentary video, *PAC 6: A General's Decision*, which are highly recommended.

An Air Force MiGCAP Mission

Ed Montgomery, Class of 1959 from the Air Force Academy, flew F-4s from the 432nd Wing at Udorn during Linebacker:

My flight on Linebacker II was my fifth sortie. It was December 28th (just before the end of the campaign), we were flying two-ships at night as a MiGCAP for the Buffs, and as a "new guy" I was the wingman. We were on Red Crown's frequency and, as I recall, at about FL 200, and we were just coming in from "feet wet" when I saw two white flashes from directly ahead of us and slightly above us. I was wondering what that was all about when there was a huge explosion in the same area ahead of us, and an Air Force pilot came up on frequency and said, "Thanks for my MiG, Red Crown." Obviously the two flashes I had seen were the two AIM-7s he had fired.

From a MiGCAP viewpoint, the rest of the flight was very quiet, and we had always heard that the North Vietnamese didn't fly much at night. That didn't mean that we weren't busy, however, as we had ten SAMs fired in our direction, and four of them were clearly locked onto us. One big advantage of flying at night in that environment is that you can see the flame of every SAM that is launched and can easily follow its route of flight to see if it is tracking you. If it was, we would go burner and gently nose over straight ahead at zero-G so we could accelerate with very little drag. As we began to descend, we would watch the SAM nose over as well, and it would have to aim lower because it needed to pull lead on us. Once we saw it with its nose buried, then we would break hard up and into it and the stubby wings of the SAM-2 couldn't make the turn; it would explode harmlessly below and behind us. We dodged the four SAMs tracking us that way, and once we saw that the maneuver really worked, then it was almost fun.

The challenge to a wingman at night, of course, is to stay with his lead through all the maneuvering being done. When lead is in "burner" he's not hard to see, but otherwise it is a challenge and requires staying almost in close formation. Happily, I was able to hang on to Nick and we came back as a two-ship. (I didn't have to buy beer for anyone.)[35]

The Navy in Linebacker II

Lt. John Leslie provides some background and context for the Navy contribution to Linebacker II. He spent his first seagoing tour as an A-7E Corsair II pilot in VA-97 and was embarked in USS *Enterprise* (CVAN-65) from mid-September 1972 to mid-May 1973. (John retired as a commander after twenty-two years of active duty, including command of two F/A-18 squadrons.):

We were en route from Hong Kong to Yankee Station, so did not conduct flight operations until the following day, December 19. We had six aircraft carriers available to conduct day Alpha Strikes and night cyclic operations in support of the B-52 raids, which were all conducted during hours of darkness. On the nineteenth. I flew an armed reconnaissance (recce) flight on an early launch. Now that I was a designated "Combat Section Leader" I was able to lead a few daytime and then night armed recce flights as a part of Linebacker II. One such night I was out with another junior officer, Lt. j.g. Hank Davison, in the vicinity of Vinh (RP-3) where numerous truck movements had been reported. There were several billowing Cumulonimbus (CBs) clouds in the vicinity, and the moon was like a million[-] watt light bulb—just as big and bright as it could possibly be.

We were weaving around the clouds, searching for a clear area to make our runs. We each rolled in from slightly different headings, and the sky lit up pretty much with AAA, most of it pointed in Hank's direction. When we got back to the ship and in the ready room, Hank was heard to say: "You know that old saying about rolling in out of the sun to blind the shooters? Well, tonight I rolled in out of the moon, and they shot the shit out of me!" That one was entered in our squadron's "Quotable Quotes Log" for sure.

The Linebacker II B-52 raids continued each night, with no losses on the nineteenth but suffering six losses on the night of December 20. I was scheduled for an Alpha Strike into the Hanoi area the next day, and I figured I would be just one of the many bomb-droppers in the middle of a thirty-plane gaggle over the target area. About an hour prior to our scheduled strike brief, I was notified that I would be wingman to Lt. Tom "T-Mac" McClelland, and that we would drop out of the strike formation at the coast-in point when it made a turn to the north to head to Hanoi, and we were to continue as a section straight ahead and each drop a Walleye II glide weapon on the Phu Ly bridge. The Walleye II is a 2,000 lb. glide weapon controlled by four large wings with trailing-edge control surfaces with an optical tracking system that transmits its image to a screen in the cockpit. Once the pilot acquires the target on the screen, he "designates" or "locks" the image, after which the Walleye system tracks its current image with the locked one and corrects its course accordingly. Sounds easy, right? Bullshit! This version of the Walleye was fairly new, and only a few of us in the squadron were able to get one training mission with it prior to departing on cruise. Also, since it tracks "contrast," anything with a long line of uninterrupted contrast, such as a railroad track, or a column of rising smoke, would cause the tracker to just continue tracking along that line—usually away from the intended target.

We were counting on the diversion of the main strike group turning away from our target to add an element of surprise to the enemy during our ingress to the target, which was defended primarily by AAA, but there was always the threat of the infrared tracking SAM-7s in any area in Vietnam. We needed to each lock on to our assigned area of the bridge on the initial ingress, conduct the Walleye delivery, and then egress as a section—if at all possible. It didn't work that way. Neither one of us was able to acquire the target and get a suitable lock on a good aim point during our initial run. The gunners were awake by now and started shooting at us. I was in position to roll-in on one of the AAA sites and begin a strafe attack to suppress it so T-Mac could conduct his attack with his Walleye. That was fun, dueling with a AAA site. It was quite soon when the ground troops lit fires on both ends of the bridge. T-Mac got his Walleye off on his end of the bridge and began to set up to support my attempt to get mine on target as well. I was able to get a good lock and release, and then began my egress to "feet wet" and hopefully regain sight of my flight leader, who was also heading toward the beach. I looked back toward the bridge in my maneuvering and saw a large cloud of smoke and dirt but did not know if it was a good hit or not at that point. We had to wait a couple of days for a photo-reconnaissance flight to gather the "bomb damage assessment" (BDA) on the bridge, which confirmed it had been hit at each end.[36]

Altogether, the six aircraft carriers of Task Force 17 flew thirteen squadrons of A-7s in attacks on petroleum, oil, and lubricant storage facilities in North Vietnam and other targets in South Vietnam during Linebacker II. Navy A-7 aircraft participated in over five years of the Vietnam War, losing forty-five aircraft to hostile fire and another forty-four in operational accidents.[37] The Navy continued to deploy A-7E squadrons with the fleet through Desert Shield / Desert Storm into the 1990s.

Air Force A-7D Events Post-Linebacker

After the Christmas bombing was terminated on December 29, Pacific Air Forces renewed its request to have A-7 squadrons assigned to it permanently. At that point the 3rd Tactical Fighter Squadron was formed under Lt. Col. "Moose" Skowron. The 3rd Squadron's and the 354th Wing's A-7s continued to fly combat in Cambodia until August 1973, and for the next two years they remained in theater, standing alert, propping up the Saigon government until the end. One Air Force officer recalled the mood of the times:

Because there were so few A-7D pilots in the Air Force at the time, a TDY [temporary duty] rotation was started, bringing in both 354th and 355th TFW crews [the latter from Davis-Monthan AFB, Arizona]. At one time in August 1973, I counted over seventy-five A-7Ds on the ramp at Korat, both JH [3rd Squadron] and MB [354th TFW] tail codes. There were some problems with all those TDY A-7D types—they flew by TAC rules, not PACAF. At any given time, five to eight of them were without engines as the TF41 was having blade problems and was in short supply.

Also, every ninety days a new group came in and had to learn the ropes all over again—ROE [Rules of Engagement], area familiarization, and so on. The SANDY role was not one to turn over to a new guy. So PACAF—with good justification, I believe—pressed hard for an A-7D unit of its own. So, the 3rd TFS under the 388th TFW was born in February 1973. The 3rd TFS became the sole A-7D unit [in theater] when the 354th departed in 1974.[38]

A-7D Missions in Cambodia and in the *Mayaguez* Crisis

On May 4, 1975, one of the 3rd TFS's A-7Ds, flown by Lt. Tom Dickens, was pulling off a Cambodian close-air-support target when it was hit by ground fire. The engine seized and Lt. Dickens ejected. The wing launched a SAR mission, and he was picked up shortly thereafter by a Jolly Green helicopter.

The next week, on May 12, 1975, the US-registered cargo ship SS *Mayaguez* was boarded and seized by Cambodian naval forces and was being towed to a Cambodian port. President Ford convened the National Security Council, and over the next four days the A-7Ds from the 3rd TFS flew reconnaissance, air cover, and close-air-support missions to extract the crew. The crisis ended on May 15, when the crew was released, and US helos extracted about two hundred Marines from Koh Tang island. The mission was rife with difficulties, but that is another story.[39]

The final A-7D combat mission, which was also the final American combat mission in Southeast Asia, was flown on August 15, 1975. Two pilots of the 374th Wing dropped the last bombs and fired the last cannon shells in Cambodia about noon of that day, ending more than twelve years of war. The US lost five A-7Ds to combat action and one noncombat operational loss in the nearly three years these Air Force aircraft had been in Asia.

Follow-On A-7D Activities

One of the postwar highlights of the Air Force A-7Ds was participation in the Royal Air Force Tactical Bombing Competition at Lossiemouth, Scotland, in October 1977. A-7Ds from the 23rd Tactical Fighter Wing at England AFB deployed to Lossiemouth and flew against the RAF's new SEPECAT Jaguar aircraft. The A-7Ds won the competition with their digital weapon delivery system and heads-up display and brought the trophies back to England AFB to show for it.

Later that year, the Air Force began a program to fit two late-model production aircraft with automatic maneuvering flaps, which increased the slow-speed maneuvering capability of the aircraft. The rest of the fleet was later retrofitted with the design.

The A-7D Is Reassigned to the Air National Guard

Maj. Don Shepperd (Air Force Academy graduate and later major general, and director of the Air National Guard) tells the story of his experience with the aircraft:

It is always exciting for a pilot to contemplate flying a "new" aircraft. My first fighter was the F-100, and as Ernest Hemingway wrote, "You love a lot of things if you live around them, but there isn't any woman, and there isn't any horse, nor any before nor any after, that is as lovely as great airplane, and men who love them are faithful to them even though they leave them for others. A man has only one virginity to lose in fighters, and if it is a lovely plane he loses it to, there his heart will ever be." So, though I shed my fighter virginity to the "Hun," I was still eager to fly the A-7D, but my eagerness was tempered. How can you truly love something that is ugly?

I was trading a beautiful, sleek, swept-wing, supersonic, afterburning, first of the Century Series fighters for a short, ugly, swept-wing dwarf of an airplane with NO afterburner. First impression—it's going to be hard impressing Mom and Dad when I taxi this airplane in on a cross-country. It looked like an airplane that had been driven into the side of a hanger—a pug-nosed fighter with a sinus problem.

I had flown the F-100 for thirteen years, including a tour in Germany in the nuke alert days and as a Misty FASTFAC over North Vietnam. When the A-7 conversion was imminent, I was an instructor pilot with the 162nd Fighter Group, the Tucson Guard unit that trained all Air National Guard pilots in the F-100. Post-Vietnam, the active-duty Air Force was rapidly converting to the F-4 and shedding all its F-100s to the Guard.

The A-7 was never a welcome addition to the USAF, and in 1975 the actives began to transfer the A-7 to Guard F-100 units. The first Guard squadron to receive A-7Ds was the 188th TFS in New Mexico. Others followed until there were fifteen Air National Guard squadrons flying the A-7D. The Guard pulled the Panama alert rotation with A-7s, deploying and keeping four fighters at Howard AFB for almost ten years, starting in the early 1980s. All Guard A-7 units shared the commitment. In December 1989, the Ohio Air National Guard's 180th TFS deployed A-7Ds to support the invasion of Panama to capture Manuel Noriega. Noriega had been indicted in the US for trafficking drugs and posing a threat to US citizens. This was the only use of the A-7 in combat by the Air National Guard.

The active duty willingly shed their A-7s to the Guard as F-15s and F-16s began to enter the force. I loved the Hun but was also reminded of its limitations. It was a stalwart in Vietnam, the war we lost, but I was ready for a change, and the conversion training was just across town at Davis-Monthan AFB.

When academics started, the opening joke was "We may be ugly, but we're slow." The A-7 instructors at DM were, for the most part, our buddies with whom we had flown in Vietnam. It was an easy and professional transition. Several things were immediately obvious: *first*, good simulators, much improved with visualization over the Hun days; *second*, it was cool to make your first takeoff in a new aircraft SOLO (there were no two-seaters; the two-seat A-7K would come later); *third*, roomy cockpit; *fourth*, good air-conditioning; *fifth*, responsive and sensitive controls (every aircraft has its own "feel," and the A-7D felt good); *sixth*, the greatest invention ever, the PMDS (Projected Map Display System): fighter pilots now knew where they were at all times, a first for many; *seventh*, a HUD (heads-up display), old hat for Navy jocks but magic for the USAF—you could see everything you were doing wrong, displayed right in front of you; *eight*, an INS (Inertial

Navigation System) that improved navigation and weapons delivery accuracy; *finally*, the airplane was simply one accurate bomber and strafer, and the radios didn't quit when the guns shook the airframe. Three auto-ranging bombing modes, forward-looking radar (FLR), barometric and radar altimeter, and a stable strafing platform made this aircraft a veritable warfare beast that could do what we could not do in the F-100—be assured of hitting the target on every pass in combat. We finally had to admit it: technology was overcoming macho.

The aircraft had two nasty habits: departures (from controlled flight) and canopy cracks. The canopy cracking could lead to uncommanded ejection if the canopy departed and the wind caught and activated the upper ejection face screen mechanism behind the pilot's helmet. The active duty had several departure accidents and a couple of cracked canopies. When the Guard received the aircraft, we got permission from Tactical Air Command to include departure training in the syllabus. On instructional flights, students intentionally stalled and departed the aircraft and were taught all they had to do was release the controls, the aircraft recovered itself, and the pilot simply recovered smoothly from the unusual attitude, a no-brainer that saved many aircraft and it was a confidence-builder. The later addition of automatic-maneuvering leading-edge flaps further reduced departures.

I was leading a flight of four on a night refueling mission, and we were late for takeoff, climbing at 400 kts. in route formation. Passing through about 12,000 ft., I saw a flash on my left, heard a "POP!," and my left wingman came diving under the formation. We soon heard his parachute beeper, and he went down in the dark in the rugged, jagged rocky peaks just east of Tucson, a pilot's nightmare. His canopy had cracked, departed the aircraft, and the wind stream activated his upper ejection face screen. This was, of course, an uncommanded and unanticipated ejection. The pilot was severely injured from the ejection and landing amongst the rocks and lost his under-seat survival pack. He had only a small beacon light on his parachute harness that he was able to retrieve and turn on with his teeth. It saved his life, as a civilian rescue helicopter was able to find and pick him up for medical care. The upper face curtain was removed from USAF A-7s after this accident.

The Guard later received the A-7K two-seat aircraft for training. The glamour of a first flight with no instructor vanished, but training likely improved. The A-7 replaced the F-100 as the primary Air Guard tactical fighter from 1976 to 1986, until the arrival of the F-16. The F-16 improved another of the A-7 shortcomings: even equipped with AIM-9 missiles, the A-7 was not an air-to-air machine for modern air combat. The final Guard A-7s phased out in 1993.

We learn early in life: "Beauty is only skin deep." The F-100 was a beauty. Early in my career I dated her, and she captured my virginity. The A-7 was only an ugly step-cousin, but when it came to performing the mission for which it was designed, tactical weapons employment in combat, the A-7 was clearly the superior platform.[40]

The Final Days of Vought Aerospace

Ling-Temco-Vought, Vought Aeronautics, hung on for several years with production of the two-seat A-7K, all of which were assigned directly to National Guard squadrons. There was a brief period in 1990 when there appeared to be an opportunity for an improved version, the A-7F, to be considered for the CAS role. Vought developed the A-7F as a supersonic fighter with a lengthened fuselage, enhanced avionics, and a much more powerful engine. They called it the Strikefighter and marketed it as an interim solution for the CAS and interdiction missions as a lower-cost alternative to the F-16.[41] The Air Force never responded with a contract.

The A-7E in the Navy Attack Mission

The A-7E with As, Bs, and Cs continued to perform the attack/strike mission in the Navy for the rest of the 1970s and 1980s, through the first Gulf War. Navy A-7s from the Atlantic Fleet also participated in the US invasion of Grenada that began on October 25, 1983. The US formed a coalition of six Caribbean nations to attack the island nation of Grenada, 100 miles north of Venezuela, in Operation Urgent Fury.

The A-7E in the Gulf War

When the US began the deployment of forces in 1990 under Operation Desert Shield, the last two A-7E squadrons were flying on board USS *John F. Kennedy* (CV-67). They were VA-46 "Clansmen" and VA-72 "Blue Hawks." The Navy already had them on a schedule for retiring the Corsair IIs and transforming them into strike fighter squadrons with the F/A-18A/B Hornet. Pilots believed the A-7E had a better heads-up display and computer system than the F/A-18A/B Hornet, which would replace it, but they were less enthusiastic about the A-7E's power plant. "We all considered the A-7E to be somewhat underpowered, but we also believed it was the first true precision weapon and it could deliver ordnance with remarkable accuracy," said Cmdr. (later, admiral) Mark P. "Lobster" Fitzgerald, skipper of VA-46.[42]

On the first night of the war, January 17, 1991, VA-72 was assigned to follow the F-117s in and take out air defense radar stations. Armament crews took off two of the A-7's pylons and loaded HARM, antiradiation missiles. En route they saw Iraqi MiG-25s in the air ahead of them, including the one that shot down F/A-18C pilot Lt. Scott Speicher. But they were unopposed when they fired their missiles at the radar sites.

On a later mission, Lt. Dan Wise described his attack on a western Iraqi airfield, carrying seven Mk. 20 Rockeye cluster bombs:

> We could see the field in the bright moonlight, but eight LUU-2 parachute flares (two million candlepower each, four-minute descent time) turned night into day over the runways. Lt. Cmdr. Bud Warfield and his wingman rolled in, each of their Rockeyes filled with 247 armor-piercing bomblets. When they hit, it looked like popcorn bursting off all around several MiGs in the open. As my wingman and I approached roll-in, my worst nightmare turned to reality. Some of that popcorn was muzzle flashes! Within seconds, the entire airfield erupted with AAA. Mixed in with the AAA were numerous SAMs that flew past us and fizzled out several thousand feet above. We dumped chaff continuously until the containers were empty. It was as if we were suspended in the middle of the grand finale of a Fourth of July fireworks display.[43]

The two A-7E squadrons flew 722 missions in Desert Storm and did not lose one aircraft. In May 1991, the Navy retired these two squadrons.

The A-7's retirement left the attack mission to the A-6 Intruder. In the mid-1990s the Navy assigned attack as a secondary mission of the F-14. The A-7 was better than the F-14 at the attack mission because its digital navigation / weapons delivery was superior. The F/A-18 was designed from the beginning as a dual-role fighter, and all versions of the Hornet and Super Hornet have been strike fighters.[44]

Navy Pilots' Comments on the A-7E

RAdm. Jerry C. Breast was executive officer of VA-82, flying A-7Cs (with A-7E avionics) aboard USS *America* in 1972, and was selected to command the squadron in 1973. Previously, he had flown A-4s with VA-163 in the 1967–1968 Rolling Thunder campaign and was in a good position to compare the two combat aircraft:

> One of the greatest differences between the A-4 and the A-7 in my combat tours was the advent of the sophisticated weapons system in the A-7C and A-7E. As a 2,000-hour lieutenant commander flying A-4s, I was much better at dive bombing than the junior officers (JO) in our Skyhawk squadron. However, when I was a 3,000–hour XO and CO, most of our JOs were as accurate as the "heavies." After they became comfortable flying the A-7 (usually after around 350–500 hours on type), their dive-bombing skills using the system could usually match ours.
>
> In my estimation, the engineers, test pilots and aircraft development managers who put the Corsair II and its systems together were the real "Faircuts." They deserve lots of credit, and not only for that early system, but for what came later and is now the forerunner of the F/A-18 Hornet.[45]

One of the key features of the advanced avionics system on the A-7D and E was the heads-up display. Fighter and attack pilots had always looked out the front windscreen in visual weather conditions, through some sort of gunsight, to their target. However, the gunsights were either manually positioned or driven by an air-to-air radar. The innovation of Doss and Hails's digital navigation / weapons delivery system was that the outputs of heading, angle off, airspeed, dive angle and target-aiming point were projected up through the combining glass onto the windscreen.

VAdm. Brent Bennitt, former COMNAVAIRPAC, flew the A-7E in the early 1970s and had these comments about its performance:

When I arrived at the Navy's A-7E Fleet Replacement Squadron in 1971, I was a young lieutenant commander, light-attack pilot with two combat tours flying the venerable A-4C/E, and four years of flight test operations in the US and UK under my belt. I was excited about the opportunity to transition to the "next generation" of the Navy's light-attack "technology" before I joined VA-83 for a deployment to the Med. Both the aircraft and the new, integrated navigation / weapons delivery system were considered to be "giant leaps forward" for our carrier air wings. During my transition training and subsequent operational deployments, I became a "true believer" in the Corsair II's "revolutionary" capabilities.

Until the introduction of the A-7E, with its inertially based navigation / weapons delivery system, its navigation and air-to-ground radar, and its heads-up display (HUD), we light-attack "warriors" were navigating and bombing with World War II technology. In the A-4 we used a manual weapons release based on a precalculated, fixed-mil setting on our gunsight and our ability to fly to a fixed weapons delivery point in the sky at a specific airspeed and dive angle. Under combat conditions, our accuracy was problematic, at best. The A-7E combat system was a true "game changer"—an "order of magnitude" improvement in our ability to deliver "dumb weapons" on target.

That said, I'll focus on two of the A-7E system elements that stand out in my mind, although it was the totality of the integrated "weapons system" that made the Corsair II a real winner. The first element was the "heart" of the system, the digitally controlled inertial platform and the weapons system computer. This combination allowed the pilot to preprogram navigation and weapons delivery information, dramatically reducing pilot workload and exponentially improving "dumb" weapons' flexibility and accuracy.

In the weapons delivery mode, the pilot could "designate" a target, using the symbology on the heads-up display or on the radar display. Then the system would compute a delivery solution and provide the pilot with visual delivery solution cues and release the weapon(s). It was a whole new world for Navy light-attack warriors.

The second element is the heads-up display or HUD, itself. The capability to display essential/critical flight and weapons delivery information directly in the pilot's heads-up line of sight was one of the A-7E "game changers," especially for a single-seat aircraft. The HUD dramatically improved situational awareness, aircraft energy management, weapons delivery accuracy/flexibility, and carrier-landing performance. The HUD also reduced pilot workload significantly.

One aspect of the HUD that doesn't get too much attention was the presentation of a "flight path marker" (FPM) on the display. This was highly beneficial during several piloting tasks, but none more so than in the demanding carrier-landing environment. During carrier approaches and landings, the FPM symbol projected the aircraft velocity vector on the HUD, and that symbol allowed the pilot to "see" the aircraft's projected touchdown point superimposed on the moving/pitching/rolling carrier deck and to make small, precise corrections before getting too far off the glide path. As a senior naval officer, I can tell you that carrier-landing safety improved dramatically.

I was fortunate to participate in one other event during my tour with VA-83 that encapsulates what the A-7E brought to the table. It occurred on the first day of the NATO SOUTH bombing competition in Turkey in 1972. The US Navy was invited to enter the competition as "guest competitors." We were only "guests" because our A-7E integrated weapons delivery system made a head-to-head competition unfair. We flew a thirty-five-minute low level route to the gunnery range. On my first weapons drop, I popped up to 8,500 feet, rolled in on the target, and released a Mk. 76, 25 lb. inert practice bomb at 3,000 feet. The bomb flew straight to the center of the target, scoring a "bull's-eye." That evening at the opening ceremonies, our Turkish hosts presented our team with a huge 300-gallon fuel drop tank. Why a drop tank? It was the tank that marked the bull's-eye at the target, and the tank had my Mk. 76 imbedded in its side—a real "bull's-eye"! A fitting testament to the Vought engineers who delivered a "game changer" to our fleet.[46]

Navy Attack after Desert Storm

The Navy and Marine Corps have been consistent with their commitment to the attack mission. The Grumman F-14 was produced from 1970 until 1992, and it flew in the fleet until 2006. With the retirement of the A-7E, and the impending retirement of the A-6, the Navy modified some of the F-14Bs to enhance their air-to-ground capability. The service added the Low-Altitude Navigation and Targeting Infrared for Night (LANTIRN) pod and precision-guided weapons, including JDAM, which gave the aircraft considerable effectiveness. However, the workhorse of the fleet in the twenty-first century has been the F/A-18.

CHAPTER 10
The A-10 Attack Aircraft

I take back all the bad things I have ever said about the A-10. I love them. They're saving our asses!

—Lt. Gen. Charles Horner, Tactical Air Control Center, Riyadh, January 18, 1991

The Origins of the A-10 Aircraft

The case of the A-10 is an example of the whole USAF dilemma about attack aircraft and close air support. Its development was literally concurrent with the evolution of the F-16 and the F/A-18. This chapter will describe the Air Force / Army continued dispute over the close-air-support mission and the development of the A-X/A-10 aircraft to conduct that mission. The following chapter will describe the parallel development of Air Force and Navy fighter/attack/strike aircraft.

The close-air-support mission had been allocated to the US Air Force in the National Security Act of 1947, which created the Department of the Air Force and unified the armed services under the new Department of Defense. With the renewed emphasis on conventional war and counterinsurgency and the growing foreign-policy commitment to South Vietnam in the Kennedy administration, the Army got very aggressive in pleading for increased authority to field aircraft, primarily helicopters, that could provide responsive direct fire under its own command.

The Air Corps had abandoned the "attack" designation in 1940 in favor of light bombers, but in November 1965, Air Force leadership, including the chief of staff and the secretary, had become convinced by circumstances beyond their control to buy the Navy's A-7 Corsair II and develop it for the attack/close-air-support mission. That decision had been forced by the Vietnam War, the Army's insistence that it was not being adequately supported, and the lack of an inexpensive aircraft that would have been more suitable to Tactical Air Command and the fighter community. The Army's R&D program to develop an Advanced Aerial Fire Support System (AAFSS), the Lockheed AH-56 Cheyenne, became a direct threat to the Air Force CAS mission.[1]

The A-7 decision did not end the close-air-support controversy, so Gen. McConnell attempted more negotiations.

The Army–Air Force 1966 Roles and Missions Agreement

Gen. McConnell met with Army chief of staff Harold Johnson in the early spring of 1966 to negotiate the issues. They and their staffs worked out a formal agreement, signed on April 6, that shifted the issue of service responsibility for aircraft from "type" to "weight." Thus, the Army's heavy, fixed-wing transports were to be transferred to the Air Force, but it retained some light, fixed-wing aircraft for observation and liaison, but not fire support. In return, the Army was allowed to continue to develop helicopters for direct-fire support. The agreement was seen by Army leaders as a victory and promised them a clear field to develop transport and advanced armed helicopters such as the Cheyenne. The Air Staff office that supported Gen. McConnell in this action was the Directorate of Doctrine, Concepts, and Objectives, under the three-star deputy chief of staff for plans and operations. The Doctrine office was led by Maj. Gen. Richard Yudkin. His action officer was Col. Avery Kay.

Two months later, in June 1966, Lockheed unveiled a mockup of the AH-56 that revealed its impressive firepower package. Bell Helicopter was also in production with its armed AH-1 Cobra. In response, Gen. McConnell directed, and the Concepts directorate conducted, a study to determine what CAS roles were not being fulfilled to the satisfaction of the Army. Col. Kay and his action officers, including three A-1 pilots who had just returned from Vietnam, found that the Army was generally satisfied with USAF CAS, but it asserted that Air Force aircraft lacked the capabilities to perform the helicopter escort and suppressive-fire roles.[2] The action officers discussed their analysis with Maj. Gen. Yudkin, who decided the Air Force needed a hardware response, despite its "inevitable controversy." In August, Yudkin briefed the chief and recommended that the Air Force "should take immediate and positive steps to obtain a specialized close air support aircraft, simpler and cheaper than the A-7, with equal or greater characteristics than the A-1."

McConnell pondered Yudkin's recommendation for a month and then issued a decision paper, "Analysis of Close Air Support Operations," on September 8, which directed the Air Force to "study and incrementally take steps to reflect in official USAF doctrine, tactics and procedures, publications, methods for accomplishing missions for which the armed helicopter is being provided, and which the Air Force considers part of the Close Air Support function" and develop a specialized CAS aircraft simpler and cheaper than the A-7 and equal or better than the A-1.[3]

Meanwhile, internal Air Force opposition to the large size, weight and complexity of the initial F-X designs resulted in the coalescence of a group of fighter pilots, analysts, and supporters that later became known as the "Fighter Mafia." This small, but zealous group was led by an Air Force maverick named John Boyd.

John Boyd, Advocate of "Energy-Maneuverability"

John Boyd was born in 1927; enlisted in the Army Air Forces in 1945; graduated from the University of Iowa; flew F-86s in the Korean War; attended and instructed at the Fighter Weapons School, Nellis AFB, Nevada; and gained the reputation as one of the best fighter pilots in the world. In 1963, he graduated with a second BS from the Georgia Institute of Technology.[4] While stationed at Eglin AFB, Florida, he developed, with Tom Christie, a revolutionary concept called "Energy-Maneuverability" (E-M).[5] Energy-Maneuverability

theory is a model that relates engine thrust, aerodynamic drag, weight, wing area, and other factors in an equation that predicts aircraft performance in air combat. The argument of John Boyd and his followers was that air superiority fighters should be developed using the most-powerful engines with the largest amount of thrust, and the aircraft should be designed with a minimum amount of aerodynamic drag and weight. They emphasized the need for a high thrust-to-weight ratio, ideally 1:1 or greater.

In 1966, Boyd was transferred from Eglin to Headquarters USAF (the Air Staff) in the office of Fighter Requirements. At this early stage in its concept development, the F-X was a twin-engined, 60,000-pound, swing-wing design. One of the Fighter Mafia acolytes, Col. Jim Burton, relates what happened next:

> By this time, Maj. Boyd and his theories were well known to many senior Air Force officials, and he was highly sought after as lecturer on fighter tactics. . . . Boyd's new boss, Maj. Gen. K. C. Dempster, gave him two weeks to study the F-X design and then summoned him to his office. Dempster asked, "Well, major, what do you think of our F-X design?" He [Boyd] responded in typical Boyd fashion, "Hell, I've never even designed an airplane before, but I could f@@k it up and still do better than this."[6]

The general was not happy.

OSD Analyst Pierre Sprey Joins John Boyd

In an unrelated event, Secretary McNamara had asked Systems Analysis to conduct a review of airlift requirements in Europe for inclusion in a draft presidential memorandum. The chief of the office was Col. Lyle Cameron, a senior USAF airlift pilot, and one of the OSD analysts who worked on that study was a mechanical engineer named Pierre Sprey. After extensive analysis, Sprey recommended the number of 1,500 C-130s be cut in half, and the remainder upgraded to improved short/rough-field capabilities. This recommendation led him to become very unpopular with Air Force officials, but worse was yet to come.

Sprey transferred to the OSD NATO Group studying USAF tactical aircraft to defend against a one-hundred-division Soviet invasion, and his analysis showed that the five thousand NATO fighters, most of whom were assigned deep interdiction missions, would be ineffective in slowing down a Soviet invasion for even thirty days! Further, he recommended interdiction missions be reduced and the aircraft reallocated to battlefield close air support! Systems Analysis and McNamara agreed with this conclusion. When McNamara passed the study to Air Force chief of staff John McConnell, Sprey instantly became the Air Force's Public Enemy No. 1.[7]

The air staff assigned the job of debunking the Sprey study to Col. Howard Fish, the division chief who had led the Fish Study on the A-7. Fish asked for the foremost air tactician in the Air Staff and was told it was John Boyd. Fish introduced Boyd to Pierre Sprey and left them alone. Unexpectedly, Boyd became impressed with Sprey's knowledge of math, statistics, air combat, fighter aces, and combat history. The two became fast friends and the F-X became as much a part of Sprey's life as it had Boyd's.[8] In 1969, Col. Everest Riccioni, a flamboyant fighter pilot colleague of John Boyd's from Fighter Weapons School days, reported to the Development Plans office and suggested the group call themselves the "Fighter Mafia." The name stuck.

Fighter Mafia / Military Reform Members

The "Fighter Mafia" expanded to include Tom Christie, Boyd's colleague from Eglin AFB; Chuck Spinney, initially a captain at Eglin; Chuck Myers; and Jim Burton. In the 1980s it expanded into the "Military Reform movement" with Bill Lind, Senator Gary Hart, Ray Leopold, and Dina Rasor. Bill Lind introduced John Boyd to James Fallows, the editor of the *Atlantic Monthly*, who had been a speechwriter for President Jimmy Carter. Fallows wrote an uncritically favorable article on the reform movement, "Muscle-Bound Super Power: The State of America's Defense," in the October 1979 issue, and an influential book, *National Defense*, in 1981.[9] The reform movement's message was simple: "The American national defense strategy was flawed because the military leadership was incompetent, the weapons acquisition process corrupt, high defense budgets were linked to high inflation, and what America needed was new strategy that embraced a much-greater number of simple, reliable, and less expensive systems," especially tactical airplanes.[10]

John Boyd was the acknowledged leader of the Mafia; his brilliance, personality, and drive gave the members motivation and direction. John Correll, formerly editor in chief of *Air Force Magazine*, and now contributing editor, wrote in an article on the Reformers and John Boyd:

> The Movement soon became a political and news media sensation. Without question, Boyd was enormously capable and intelligent but also, by all accounts, sarcastic, arrogant, intolerant, and profane. In "Genghis John," an article for the *Naval Institute's Proceedings*, [Chuck] Spinney described Boyd as "wildly gesticulating, loud, and irrepressible, an in-your-face type of guy, who smoked long thin stogies and blew smoke in your face, while he shouted and sprayed saliva at you in a head-on attack, from two inches, nose to nose."[11]

The A-X Requirement

The R&D Requirements Directorate led the drafting of the A-X Requirements Action Directive (RAD), but they were assisted (by direction of the chief) by Maj. Gen. Yudkin's Doctrine office because the A-X was doctrinally important and opposed by many elements of the Air Staff, like the A-7 before it. Colonel Kay had been the Doctrine lead on the dispute with Army over the CAS mission, and he, "without authorization, and outside the chain of command, approached Pierre Sprey [who was still in OSD / Systems Analysis] to see if he would help with the technical aspects of launching the CAS airplane." Sprey was an outspoken advocate of close air support. He believed in the effectiveness of the German Ju 87 Stuka dive-bomber in killing tanks and other CAS missions in World War II. Together, Kay and Sprey arranged for a quasi-secret think tank office at the Analytical Services (ANSER) Corporation, and they began discussing how to shape the new A-X concept. "Sprey now had two jobs, 9 to 5 working for McNamara and 6 to midnight for Col. Kay."[12] Sprey frequently discussed his ideas of a simple, low-technology, ground attack aircraft with John Boyd, and he incorporated many of Boyd's Energy-Maneuverability concepts into the design. In later interviews, Sprey said that his discussions with the A-1 pilots in the Doctrine office convinced him of the importance of a CAS aircraft having characteristics of slow speed, loiter time, maneuverability, heavy ordnance, multiple armament stations, and an FM radio to talk directly to the Army. Since one of its missions would ostensibly be to kill tanks, among other targets, it also would require a heavy gun.

The A-X RAD called for a single-place aircraft with a speed of 450–500 knots, a minimum maneuvering speed of 120–150 knots, and a payload of 6,000–8,000 pounds. "It also added consideration for a large-caliber semiautomatic recoilless rifle," state-of-the-art engines, and maximum survivability.[13] It called for only a simple, depressible-reticle, fixed optical sight. The RAD was approved and distributed on December 22, 1966.[14] (As a comparative note, one can observe that this decision for a simple, fixed sight was consistent with the Air Staff's view for the A-7D, which was in development at the same time.)

Ironically, AF Systems Command assigned the task of implementing the RAD to the F-X (future F-15) System Program Office (SPO), and its engineers prepared and released a request for proposals (RFP) to industry for trade-off studies in March 1967. Sprey and the Doctrine group had argued hard for a streamlined, twenty-page RFP, but the final version was several times that. Two months later, the SPO issued four study contracts to McDonnell Douglas, Northrop, Grumman, and General Dynamics. All four contractors responded with designs and data.

Meanwhile, the Air Force Armaments Laboratory was becoming very interested in adding a modification of the smaller, but proven, M-61 20 mm gun, rebarreled to fire the 30 mm round. The Air Staff issued a RAD for an Air-to-Ground Gun System for CAS on January 5, 1968, sixteen months after Secretary McNamara had directed the Air Force and Navy to jointly incorporate the M-61 gun in the A-7.[15]

The A-X Working Group analyzed the four contractor studies on the aircraft design and new information on the gun and began work on a concept formulation package (CFP). Pierre Sprey was intent on making the A-X far more lethal and survivable than the A-1 Skyraider, and he reached out to John Boyd to better understand and use Boyd's Energy-Maneuverability design trade-off techniques in close air support attack profiles.

Pierre used the EM approach for re-attack profiles to keep ground targets within sight and minimize rearming and reattack times. Low wing loading and good thrust-to-weight to enable high G roll-ins and pull-outs with quick maneuvering climb-outs were key tenets for the new aircraft. All of this was folded into the performance and armament requirements for the final A-X Concept Formulation Package.[16]

Sprey also insisted on the inclusion of a 30 mm cannon, which was designed to kill tanks, among an array of targets in the close-air-support mission. He was committed to a large-bore cannon on the basis of his research into air support by German pilots, notably Hans Ulrich Rudel, who flew 2,530 combat missions and destroyed a record of 512 tanks on the Eastern Front in World War II.[17] Rudel's Stuka fired two pod-mounted 37 mm cannon with six rounds each. Sprey and the A-1 pilots in the Doctrine shop argued that the A-X needed to have capabilities beyond Vietnam's jungle war, and the other major threat was in a massed Soviet tank assault of western Europe.

The Air Staff issued the CFP on March 1, 1968, and revised it in May.[18] The CFP used the same basic description of the A-X as the RAD, but it added four required criteria for development: lethality, simplicity, survivability, and responsiveness.[19] The lethality criterion was implemented by a requirement for ten underwing pylons, ordnance capability of 16,000 pounds, and the antitank gun. The gun requirement was for a 30 mm cannon with a 4,000-rounds-per-minute firing rate and a 1,200-round magazine, enough for ten passes![20]

Secretary Brown approved the package and submitted it to the secretary of defense on June 17, 1968. The proposal was not approved!

Dr. John Foster, DDR&E, a product of the McNamara regime, knowing of OSD's opposition to new weapons programs, recommended the studies be continued. Specifically, he waited six months before answering the request, then he questioned the survivability of the A-X against heavier defenses and wanted to wait for results of A-37, OV-10, and A-7 testing. He stated, "The proposed aircraft seems to be too large, and has too much range/payload at this stage. It is so similar to the A-7 that it is hard to justify when we already have A-7. A smaller, less costly, quick reaction aircraft seems more appropriate."[21]

The Air Staff and Air Force Systems Command were not deterred. The Air Staff expanded the CFP into a development concept paper (DCP), the next step in the R&D process, and submitted it to OSD on December 11, 1968.[22]

OSD Approves the A-X Concept

The A-X program benefited from the support of the deputy secretary of defense, David Packard, who assumed office in the Nixon administration under Secretary Melvin Laird on January 24, 1969. In one of his first initiatives, Packard established the Defense System Acquisition Review Council (DSARC) and designated three panels to study cost growth. The DSARC was a new committee that included the RDT&E heads of the services as well as the vice chairman of the JCS and the service chiefs. This was a much more balanced approach to the review of new weapons systems than had been the case under Robert McNamara.

The deputy secretary of defense moved the A-X system along by approving $12 million in the FY70 budget for Contract Definition. However, he required the Air Force to develop three supplemental studies: (1) the size and weight of the A-X, (2) survivability of the aircraft in the anticipated threat environment, and (3) methods to improve night and adverse-weather capability. While these studies were to slow down the decision process, there was strong support for the program in OSD. Systems Analysis had two outspoken proponents of the A-X: Pierre Sprey and Dieter Schwebs. Both analysts were known as advocates of attack aircraft like the Luftwaffe's Junkers Ju 87 Stuka.

However, the high cost of the tactical-force mix had become even more troubling to OSD since the A-7D/E, F-4E, and F-111 were all in production, with the F-111 taking close to one-half of the USAF's annual tactical-fighter funding. Also, the Air Force had just issued a large development contract to McDonnell Douglas for the F-15, and Grumman was in development with the F-14, all of which made it difficult to justify funding for a new, specialized aircraft.

In this new atmosphere, the Air Force revised the Development Concept Paper DCP-23 again in mid-1969 and forwarded the three supplemental studies to OSD on September 22. DDR&E reviewed the package and issued yet another revision in December 1969. The DSARC met on December 19 but raised only a few questions on cost estimates. The Army expressed concern about the affordability of yet another major tactical-aircraft program and the capability of the A-X to fulfill night and all-weather missions. Dr. Foster issued tasks to resolve the few remaining issues, and the paper was relabeled DCP-23A.

Another reason for delay as the development concept paper proceeded was the introduction of the concept of competitive prototyping. The idea of awarding Defense contracts to two or more aerospace contractors to build test models had been anathema in the McNamara administration's search for cost-effectiveness and cost reduction. David Packard, like McNamara, was a product of American industry, but he was more open minded and believed in the benefits of such competition.

Gen. James Ferguson, commander of Air Force Systems Command, was also a supporter of competitive prototyping, and he influenced the OSD and Air Force to incorporate it into the A-X competition. While it was understood that contracting for hardware would necessarily take more time and increase RDT&E costs, there was an expected payoff in the reduction of technical risk and the lowering of costs in the long term.

Packard's panels on cost growth in weapons acquisition advised that an increase in competition by hardware demonstrations would reduce dependence on paper analysis and benefit the department. Accordingly, the A-X DCP-23A was revised again to include three alternative recommendations on contracting: the first alternative was to use a conventional Contract Definition phase, the second included a competitive prototype fly-off, and the third was to disapprove of the A-X development. The decision package was forwarded to the deputy secretary on March 16, 1970.[23] On April 6, 1970, Packard approved Alternative Two, with competitive prototyping.

Since the flight of the Wright Flyer, the first flight of any new airplane has always been a major achievement and a visible indication of capability. The move to prototyping was viewed with great anticipation by aerospace manufacturers, who were always eager to produce hardware.

The Air Force received a go-ahead for the A-X program on April 10, 1970, and immediately released an RFP for competitive prototypes to twelve companies on May 8, 1970. In the meantime, Republic Aviation had financial difficulties following the last production of the F-105 Thunderchief in 1965, and the firm had been purchased by Fairchild Hiller. The Republic Aviation Division of Fairchild Hiller had difficulty recovering from the loss of the F-15 contract to McDonnell Douglas, and as a result the division was renamed Fairchild Republic in 1969.

Six aerospace firms responded to the A-X RFP and submitted proposals. Northrop and Fairchild Republic were selected on December 18, 1970, for fixed-price contracts to develop prototypes.[24] The Northrop design was designated the YA-9A, and the Fairchild Republic one, the YA-10A. Each of the two prototype designs had the airplane built around the 30 mm gun. In a parallel effort, the Air Force released an RFP for the competitive procurement of the CAS gun system in April 1971, with GE and Philco Ford winning the two prototype contracts.

Congressional Concern over Multiple CAS Programs

In 1968, the Senate Armed Services Committee had questioned DoD's need for the A-X when it already had the A-4, A-6, A-7, A-37, OV-10, and gunships, and the Army was developing the Cheyenne. Antiwar politicians also charged that the A-X would support limited wars such as the unpopular one in Vietnam. The next year, the House Armed Services Committee suspended A-X funding when some members objected to a turboprop design that did not present enough of a technical advance. In 1969, the Marine Corps entered the fray by proposing to buy the British AV-8A Harrier. "The

Marine Corps move was the last straw for the Congress, whose commentary on its Fiscal Year 1971 budget intoned, 'There is a serious question as to whether or not future Defense budgets can support the development and/or procurement of three separate aircraft weapons systems to perform essentially the same mission.'"[25]

In October 1970, the House Appropriations Committee directed OSD to reevaluate the roles and missions and aircraft relative to close air support and determine which of these planes was most suitable.[26]

Deputy Secretary of Defense Packard replied in June 1971 that all three aircraft were needed to fulfill the complex close-air-support mission. The Senate Armed Services' Tactical Airpower Subcommittee attempted to resolve this dilemma but failed. In defense of Packard's submission, the chairman of the Joint Chiefs of Staff, Adm. Thomas Moorer, made a cogent argument by pointing out the Navy did not buy only one type of ship. With the hearings almost complete, the Navy also praised the capabilities of the A-7E, which had just completed a year of combat operations in Vietnam.

The Northrop / Fairchild Republic Fly-Off Competition

Seventeen months after contract award, the YA-10's first flight occurred on May 10, 1972, and the YA-9A ten days later. The contractors were required to deliver two flyable prototypes and, with Pierre Sprey's insistence, one nonflyable airframe that was to be used for survivability analysis. The fly-off between the two was conducted at Edwards AFB between October and December. There was little difference between the prototypes in aircraft handling, performance, and weapons delivery. Air Force officials believed that the YA-10 had a simpler design and was closer to production, and test pilots had commented that they preferred the A-10 for combat operations.[27] In Pierre Sprey's words, "Vulnerability was the key factor in determining the superiority of the YA-10 versus the YA-9. Northrop had not taken the survivability requirements very seriously and they had lost control of the weight."[28] The YA-10 also scored higher in survivability because their engines were armored and mounted high and away from the fuselage, where the flammable fuel was stored.

The Air Force awarded Fairchild a $160 million "cost plus incentive fee" contract on March 1, 1973, for full-scale development. GE was simultaneously awarded a contract for $28 million to develop the TF34 jet engine. Three months later, GE was awarded a $24 million contract to develop the GAU-8/A 30 mm gun.[29]

Managing the A-10 Program

Delivering on the promise to build the CAS airplane was not easy. The system program director was Brig. Gen. Tom McMullen, and the director of the A-10 test program was Lt. Col. Ron Yates. They and their small staffs in the A-10 SPO had a challenging situation. The contract with Fairchild was "cost plus," which is the right type for an R&D effort, but OSD imposed a new "design to cost" policy that required both the contractor and the Air Force to adhere to the initial cost estimate, which was a low ceiling. Right from the beginning, the Air Force program managers found Fairchild resistant to any change, even those required for safety. For example, Fairchild recommended only twelve flights be allocated for the "departure from controlled flight" tests. The Air Force and its contractors had not designed an attack airplane since before World War II. Their aerodynamic experience in the 1970s was with thin wings and narrow airfoils. The A-X required a thick, heavily curved airfoil for high lift at low speed, and it necessarily would have high drag. The Fairchild design featured twin engines mounted high on the aft fuselage. When the aircraft entered flight test, the airflow over the wings and fuselage tended to disrupt the airflow into the engines and onto the tail, and the combination could cause the airplane to depart controlled flight. In the end, the departure test program required 120 flights.[30]

Lt. Col. Ron Yates also related that no one in the Air Force wanted the airplane—almost identical to the attitudes Col. Hails had experienced on the A-7D program. For example, Yates's only contacts for support with the administration were in OSD. The Air Staff had not appointed anyone to support the SPO, and neither had Tactical Air Command. He told an anecdote to

the author that characterized the situation. He attended a staff meeting in 1974 called by Gen. Robert Dixon (commander of TAC, 1973–1976). At one point in the briefing, someone mentioned the A-10, and Gen. Dixon asked if anyone in the room had flown it. Yates held up his hand, and Gen. Dixon asked, "Who are you?" "I'm Lt. Col. Ron Yates, and I'm the A-10 test director." Gen. Dixon turned to Lt. Gen. Charles Gabriel, his deputy chief of staff for operations, and said, "Charley, I don't want this to ever happen again. Here we have an airplane that I am buying for the TAC troops, and we don't have anyone in my command who has flown it!"[31]

Ron Yates had two other conclusions that came out of the test program:

> We really didn't resolve the "night and all-weather" concerns [that the Army was insisting on for a CAS airplane]. Basically, I visualized operating under flares as we did in Vietnam. In that case, the A-10 would be a vast improvement over any competitor due to its low-altitude/low-speed maneuverability and survivability. Of course, the problem was solved with GPS weapons.
>
> Second, we did not meet the specification on reattack due to having more drag than anticipated, along with the engine thrust coming in a bit short. However, we did argue that a flight of four A-10s armed with 500-pound bombs could put a bomb on target every 30 seconds for 20 minutes. That was an awesome improvement that impressed the Army![32]

A-7D vs. the A-10 Fly-Off

The A-7 got injected into the A-X development program in 1972. After the YA-10 won the fly-off against the YA-9, Senator Cannon, the chair of the Tactical Air Subcommittee of the Armed Services Committee, asked the Air Force to conduct a second fly-off. His request was to evaluate whether the new YA-10 was sufficiently better than the A-7D to warrant its production. That competition was conducted at Fort Riley, Kansas, in April and May 1974 "under combat conditions." The competition was a bit uneven because the A-7D had a combat-proven record and, after 1967, was designed with a heads-up display and the most accurate navigation/bombing system in the US inventory. The new YA-10 had only a rudimentary avionics system and no heads-up display and used the same M-61 cannon as the A-7 in the competition, since the 30 mm one was not yet ready. A second major difference between the aircraft was the A-7's higher speed, which in many observers' opinion would make it superior and less susceptible to enemy fire. Others (including Pierre Sprey) argued that the slow speed of the A-10 gave it greater advantages in attack and reattack of a specific target. Test pilots reported the A-7D was faster and superior in good weather conditions, but the A-10, with its slower speed and higher maneuverability, was more effective under low ceilings and restricted visibility. Third, the 20 mm M-61 in the A-7D was unable to penetrate the heavy armor of Soviet tanks. The A-7's advanced avionics system and superior weapons accuracy were negated somewhat by the A-10's closer slant range and the competition's rules that required continuous, high-g maneuvering with only several seconds of stabilized flight time prior to weapons firing. Ron Yates later said the critical factor was the A-10's ability to perform high-g maneuvers at 200 knots, which gave it a high degree of survivability.[33] The A-10 again won the competition.[34] Later in 1974, the A-10 was subjected for a third time to more political opposition, since some congressmen were pushing for the Piper Enforcer (a heavily modified version of the P-51) as a replacement.

Fairchild Republic's production capability had been based on Republic's facilities during the era of the F-105. However, when that line closed in 1965, nine years earlier, the equipment was allowed to age, and investments in modernization were very limited. There also were disputes among members of the board of directors as to control of the firm. Fairchild Republic faced increasingly difficult questions regarding its ability to produce the A-10. In an ironic move, the Air Force appointed Lt. Gen. Robert Hails, previously the A-7D program manager and now vice commander of Tactical Air Command, to review Fairchild's capability. His report was very critical of Fairchild's production capability and its management's competence. Finally, after many difficult changes, DoD approved Fairchild Republic for low-rate production, and

the first A-10 aircraft was delivered to Tactical Air Command in March 1976.

The Subsonic vs. Supersonic Debate Revisited

Since the development of supersonic aircraft in the 1950s, the Air Force developed a preference for that capability in its multipurpose aircraft. The Navy developed supersonic aircraft for naval fighter forces but saw no requirement for their attack forces. The Air Force debate centered on the need for speeds beyond Mach 1.3. The "higher, faster" advocates pushed for much-higher speeds, above Mach 2, often citing the Russian MiG-25 and others with that capability. On the other hand, air combat advocates argued that most air combat would be subsonic, with transonic flight being needed to engage an opponent quicker, to achieve a better position for the fight, or to disengage from an air battle. The capability for acceleration was needed to achieve about Mach 1.6, but not higher. To quote Gen. Mike Loh:

There has been no need to fly faster than Mach 1.2–1.6. Then [the pilot needs to] get out of afterburner to save fuel. That's why, in the LWF [Lightweight Fighter] and ACT [Air Combat Tactics] competitions, we only measured acceleration time from 0.9 to 1.6 Mach and insisted on no top-speed requirement.[35]

Gen. Ron Yates, later F-16 program director and commander, Air Force Systems Command, provided separate views on the subsonic vs supersonic debate:

We learned a lot from Vietnam! The outgrowth of that war was we needed to tailor the aircraft to fight the air war and ground war. Thus, in later years, we developed the A-10 for ground attack and the F-15 for air war. The F-16 was to do both tasks, but neither was done as well as the tailored aircraft. The new F-35 is a dual-role aircraft that creates an entirely new domain and outclasses the previous aircraft by light-years. Frankly, the entire debate has been overcome by the new weapons carried by aircraft. GPS [global positioning system] bombs, carried internally, essentially don't miss the target . . . even if it is moving. Stealth accompanied by jamming greatly reduces penetration losses. For all the wars we have fought in the Middle East over the last fifteen years, our fighter loses can be counted on one hand. So, I think the tables of subsonic versus supersonic aircraft lost in Vietnam were relevant to the doctrinal debate at that time, but the argument is not germane in today's world.[36]

The Famous 30 mm Cannon

It is not possible to proceed further in the development of the A-10 without a brief description of the weapon that made the A-10 so distinctive. Pierre Sprey had been instrumental in getting the requirement for the 30 mm cannon in each of the A-X requirements documents and the request for proposals. The gun's characteristics contributed to the technical, tactical, operational, bureaucratic, and even political benefits of the A-10. First, it was technically the most powerful gun on any attack aircraft in the world. Second, it was tactically important to have a weapon that was instantaneously available to the pilot after jinking wildly before firing. Third, it was operationally useful to have a weapon that could be rapidly loaded for the next sortie. Fourth, it was bureaucratically helpful to have a weapon that was distinctive to the Air Force and the attack community, to differentiate it from other programs that claimed a CAS capability. Finally, it was politically important to show the administration, the Army, the Congress, and the public that the Air Force was taking seriously the needs of the Army and its soldiers in providing a low-cost, capable, and responsive aircraft for the CAS mission.

Col. Robert Dilger, an F-4 fighter pilot with 160 missions in Vietnam, was the program manager for GAU-8 (Gun, Aircraft Unit) development in the A-10 System Program Office (SPO) at Aeronautical Systems Division. They had many obstacles. The Gun and Rocket Division at Eglin AFB objected to the 30 mm gun and wanted to modify the 20 mm M-61.[37] The Army's Ballistics Research Lab at Aberdeen was not cooperative because they feared demonstrating the 30 mm's ability to kill tanks might imperil the Army's purchase of the M-1 main battle tank. Dilger managed the competition and development of the gun and implemented several innovations in the gun system. He also set up several live-fire tests at Nellis test ranges against actual Soviet tanks loaded with fuel and weapons.[38] In one of the early tests in 1979, the A-10s "made twenty passes against fifteen tanks, immobilizing all fifteen and destroying eight."[39]

> The results were spectacularly successful, and Dilger, who was the live-fire project manager, made sure that they were filmed.[40]

The films were shown at Defense Systems Acquisition Review Council (DSARC) meetings and other, multiple locations in DoD. They emphatically eliminated any remaining doubts about the lethality of the GAU-8 gun.

The A-10 Becomes Operational

The first production A-10A Thunderbolt II was delivered to the 333d TFS, 355th Tactical Fighter Wing, at Davis Monthan AFB, Arizona, on March 2, 1976. The first squadron to become became operational was the 356th TFS of the 354th TFW at Myrtle Beach, South Carolina, on October 15, 1977. The 356th squadron deployed to RED FLAG on November 5, 1977, and the wing achieved initial operational capability in January 1978.[41] The 81st TFW at Bentwaters, United Kingdom, became operational in 1979.[42] With the aircraft being assigned to three active-duty wings (the same as the A-7D previously), the next assignments were to the Air National Guard: first, the 103d Tactical Fighter Group at Bradley Field, Connecticut, in May 1979, then, successively, the 174th at Syracuse, New York, and the 104th at Barnes Field, Massachusetts, in June and July 1979. Two Air Force Reserve squadrons rounded out the initial deployments in 1982.

Production continued with periodic upgrades that included an inertial navigation system, weapons delivery computer, better avionics, and a heads-up display. In the 1980s, the Air Force approved an observation-and-reconnaissance version, called the OA-10.

In the early 1980s, the A-10 faced increasing competition from the F-16, which was flying successfully and was appealing with its performance and low-cost history. In fact, in 1982, the Congress voted to cease all funding for the A-10 in the fiscal year 1983 budget and provided production terminations costs of $29 million to Fairchild. The final aircraft rolled off the production line in 1984.[43] A total of 713 A-10 aircraft had been produced.[44]

The Demise of Fairchild

Fairchild followed the A-10 production with a bid for the Air Force's next-generation trainer, and the firm won that contract to build the T-46A. However, the company had cut pricing to the bone and failed a series of USAF inspections in 1985. The Air Force terminated the contract on March 13, 1987. Subsequently, Grumman purchased the A-10 program from Fairchild.[45] Fairchild declared bankruptcy under Chapter 11 in 1990. In 1994, Grumman was purchased by Northrop to form the Northrop Grumman Corporation.

A-10 Sets Sortie Records

In the Air Force, Navy, and Marine Corps, one of the critical capabilities of a operational wing or squadron has always been its performance in producing the maximum number of sorties in a single day, since this is a measure of merit of the entire organization and its personnel. The A-10 was built to fly and be turned around in short order. In 1977, two A-10s in a surge exercise flew thirty-four ordnance-dropping sorties (seventeen each) in an eleven-hour period![46] As A-10 squadrons and wings became operational, they began to demonstrate how reliable the aircraft was, so that large numbers could turn from one sortie to others in a single twenty-four-hour period. On April 22, 1981, the 81st Tactical Fighter Wing at RAF Bentwaters, United Kingdom, set a US Air Force record by generating 533 sorties in a single day.[47]

AirLand Battle, the F-16 vs. the A-10, and the Aborted A-16

In 1982, the Army and Air Force began to focus again on the threat of a European war. Vietnam was in the past, and the Yom Kippur War of 1973 had demonstrated the lethality of modern weapons. The Army's Training and Doctrine Command under Gen. Don Starry rejected a defensive strategy for NATO and developed a doctrine of AirLand Battle, which envisioned maneuver

warfare and offensive thrusts. The new strategy was published in Field Manual 100-5, *Operations*. Gen. Starry's concept was that the Air Force would provide extended attacks on Soviet rear areas to disrupt and destroy forces en route to the battlefield. Air Force planners were delighted with this new emphasis on interdiction, as opposed to close air support, which reinforced the service's preferences dating back to Billy Mitchell. In 1984, the Air Force and Army ratified the doctrine with the publication of "31 Initiatives," which implemented the strategy. The F-16 was now the darling of the fighter community, and as the cheaper of the multirole aircraft, it seemed the best choice for the interdiction portion of the attack mission. At the same time, the Air Force was developing the Fighter Roadmap, but it did not include buying more A-10s. The official Air Force position was that the A-10 was too vulnerable for the deep-interdiction mission, and AirLand Battle required a faster, more maneuverable aircraft. Of course, some modifications would have to be made, and the resulting aircraft was to be called the A-16. The standard argument was that the higher speed of the A-16 would make it more difficult to be hit by ground fire. These proponents chose to forget that the A-10 had won the A-7/A-10 fly-off because it was *slower* and could turn tighter over a target and under the weather. One can understand that the old "subsonic versus supersonic" debate was history, and the more relevant one was "fast versus slow."

Once again, some armament folks said they could match the 30 mm cannon in the A-10 with a pod-mounted cannon for the A-16, just like the apologists argued for the missile-only F-4D that could be augmented with a pod-mounted M-61 20 mm Gatling gun.

The Military Reform Movement Adds to the Controversy

The issue of aircraft procurement got very public throughout the 1980s. Three of the movement's unifying themes were (1) that the F-16 was not the right airplane for the close-air-support mission, (2) the CAS mission was being neglected in the Air Force's current war-fighting doctrine, and (3) the A-10 was exactly the right airplane for the mission. The group was labeled by some as being "anti-F-16." One of the original Fighter Mafia members, Tom Christie, became exasperated with some of this rhetoric, and he remarked, "Suddenly, we who had pushed the F-16 were viewed as being anti-F-16. . . . We weren't anti-F-16. We were just saying that's not the airplane that was going to do close air support well."[48]

In 1989, the argument against close air support was bolstered by the fall of the Berlin Wall, which allowed the A-10's opponents to argue that the diminished armor threat in Europe should result in a decrease in the number of A-10 units. Congress once again intervened and barred the Air Force from spending 1990 money on F-16 production until a new study of more alternatives was conducted. Congress also required a report on the advisability of moving the CAS mission to the Army—the old issue![49]

Near the end of 1990, the Air Force announced it was dropping the idea of modifying part of the F-16 fleet into the A-16. But the service maintained that the F-16 would take over the CAS role in the near future. Meanwhile, after the cancellation of the Cheyenne, the Army developed the AH-64 Apache to replace the AH-1 Cobra. The Apache was a much-heavier, much-faster, and more heavily armed helo than the Cobra and even featured a 30 mm chain gun. It began service in 1986, and a more advanced version, the AH-64D Longbow, was delivered in 1997 and continues in service.

A-10s in the Gulf War[50]

When Saddam Hussein invaded Kuwait in the summer of 1990, the US launched a massive coalition mobilization and deployment operation named "Desert Shield." Among the deploying units were seven squadrons of A-10As that flew to Saudi Arabia and joined the 14th Air Division, 354th Tactical Fighter Wing (Provisional). Six were from active-duty squadrons, and one was from the Louisiana Air National Guard. Their number totaled between 152 and 170 aircraft.[51]

One of the lasting accomplishments of the Gulf War was the designation of an air component commander in charge of all aircraft that were not organic to specific units, such as Army helicopters. A second major innovation was the development of a single, integrated air-tasking order (ATO) that

used the unique capabilities of each type of aircraft to develop missions and targets for each squadron. The F-15s would provide air cover, the F-16s and F-111s would strike deep-interdiction targets, the AV-8 Harrier would attack targets close to the front. A-10 commanders were concerned that the Army wanted them to be *withheld* from the early attacks because they were so closely identified with the close-air-support mission, and there was to be no immediate ground offensive. The thought that they would have NO mission was paralyzing for the A-10 folks! They knew that the majority of air planners considered them to be a force dedicated to Army close air support, and that they might be omitted from the ATO. Some planners were worried about their survivability against the ZSU-23-4 quad cannons of the Iraqi army; some were of the opinion they needed to be held back to support the Army until ground operations began. In fact, the Army commanders had asked Lt. Gen. Charles Horner, the air component commander, to stand down the A-10s because they were concerned about an Iraqi armor attack. One of the A-10 planners is quoted as saying, "The doctrine was that the Hog stayed within twenty miles or so of the ground forces and did CAS, period."[52] Such was the inferiority complex voiced by many in the A-10 community.

Lt. Gen. Horner disagreed and reportedly said this to the Army commanders:

> Baloney; those guys can carry six Mk. 82s, four Mavericks, 1,150 rounds of 30 mm. They can beat the crap out of that artillery and that armor that you are so damned worried about. Let's work them in; we'll work them at the borders and increasingly deeper.[53]

The result was that the A-10s were given three missions on Day 1 of the air war: ground alert for close air support, battlefield air interdiction (BAI), and deeper counter air attacks against Iraqi ground-controlled intercept (radar) sites. Some were assigned to ground alert for combat search-and-rescue (CSAR) missions, the old A-1 Skyraider and A-7 "SANDY" role.

The A-10 pilots were experts at the first mission, flying close air support, but had seldom (never?) practiced interdiction, where their slow airplanes would be exposed to hours of cruising over hostile territory. For the BAI tasking, flight leaders initially received little more than latitude and longitude coordinates. It was helpful that they were assigned to 30-by-30-nautical-mile (nm) "boxes" on their maps. That, at least, limited their search area.

The standard A-10 weapons load-out for the first day, January 17, 1991, was six Mk. 82 bombs or six cluster bomb unit cannisters, two Mavericks, two AIM-9s, ECM and flare pods, and 1,150 rounds of 30 mm, totaling 46,000 pounds. The results of that day's action were that the A-10s destroyed 95 percent of the Iraqi ground-controlled intercept sites and got the other five the next day. Twenty-six sites had been eliminated, and ninety-six radars destroyed. The F-15 Eagle guys were ecstatic because they now could enter and roam over Iraq without fear. The BAI crews were also successful in finding and destroying multiple artillery, ammunition, and armored vehicles. Some pilots flew three sorties a day, and others flew nine- or ten-hour missions, refueling and going deep across the border. Their priority targets were first, artillery; second, armored vehicles.

On the second day, the Iraqis started firing SCUD missiles, mostly at Israel. Several A-10 flights were tasked to fly 500 nm west to locate and attack SCUD sites. They took off, flew to western Saudi Arabia, landed, refueled, and took off again, navigating only to a set of coordinates. One flight flew into heavy weather, popped out and saw three missile launchers, attacked them, and then went farther and found another seven SCUDs.

Later that day, January 18, 1991, the commanders of air units were informally debriefing the assembled staff officers in the Tactical Air Control Center (TACC) in Riyadh. Captain Mike Isherwood was one of the A-10 pilots in the crowd, and he summarized one of the key elements of the discussion:

The low-ranking generals spoke first, summarizing the day's accomplishments and adding their personal cheerleading touches to the presentations. Then the three-star [Lt.] General Horner walked to the front. He looked physically beat, as he often did during the war, but the achievements of the air campaign had been spectacular so far and he energized to the occasion with compliments to the aircraft communities represented in the room. When he came to the A-10s, he hesitated slightly, apparently searching for the right words. Then, in just ten seconds he made a comment that has literally reverberated around the world—a comment that virtually every Hog driver alive today—whether in Korea, Alaska, or in the cockpit of a Delta jet—can quote word for word.

General Horner said: "I take back all the bad things I have ever said about the A-10. I love them. They're saving our asses!"[54]

Now it is a shock of earthquake proportions when the guys at the dance openly state their admiration for the performance of the ugly girl. But it is a shock wave of about ten orders of magnitude greater when one of her vociferous critics openly confesses that love has blossomed. After all, this was the same man (so it is rumored) who said jokingly, when his own son opted to fly the A-10 out of pilot training, "Oh, I don't think I have a son anymore; I think he died of brain damage."[55]

Day and night the A-10 attacks continued. Some of the CSAR flights were very deep, just west of Baghdad on SANDY missions to rescue downed pilots. On Day 11, the A-10 squadrons learned that their taskings were going to change: that they would be going much deeper to hit the Republican Guard divisions 75 to 125 miles behind the lines. The ATO came down two days later, to attack the Tawakalna Division. The A-10 pounded that division for three solid hours, with 154 aircraft participating in the mission, dropping and firing everything they had. When satellites and high-speed RF-4Cs could not get photographs that were detailed enough, the A-10s were even tasked with armed reconnaissance to verify the bomb damage assessment.[56] Upon landing, the pilots went to Wing Headquarters, spread out their 1:50,000 maps, and described the burned-out hulks and convinced the planners that the division had been reduced to 50 percent effective—the Army objective.

The Reconnaissance-Fighter-Observation-Attack-10 (RFOA-10G)

The A-10 pilots by now were getting many different missions thrown at them: reconnaissance, fighter, observation, attack, and SAM suppression. In true fighter/attack pilot fashion, they informally relabeled their aircraft the RFOA-10G. Their story begins:

On February 15, they [the air planners] increased the ante. Basically, they said, "Okay, Warthogs and Wartweasels, you have done a great job so far. You have taken out the western GCI sites, found and killed SCUDs, obliterated artillery and armor in the KTO [Kuwait theater of operations] kill boxes, destroyed SAMs that would have been a threat to the ground war, made an air-to-air kill [actually two], and attrited the Tawakalna Division of the Republican Guard by at least fifty percent. Congratulations. Now we have a new tasking for you."

"We want you to go eighty miles past the Tawakalnas, to the Medina [Luminous] Division of the Republican Guard. They have lots of arty and armor up there and we need to start attriting them before the ground guys move in. You'll have to tanker [refuel] going in so you'll have some playtime. Good luck and check six."[57]

On the first mission of the ground offensive, February 24, four A-10s received severe battle damage, and two were shot down. Compared to the thousands of sorties being flown, the loss rate was not bad. With these losses, the planners pulled the A-10s back from the deep BAI missions, and some squadrons were even prohibited from strafing, except in dire cases. But the crews still had their AGM-65D Maverick, an imaging infrared guided missile with a 126-pound shaped-charge warhead. The A-10s flew missions twenty-four hours a day, killing hundreds of tanks and armored personnel carriers. One pilot set the record for one-day tank kills, with twenty-three destroyed and ten damaged.[58]

The biggest close-air-support battle was at the village of Khafji, when the Iraqis attacked with armored tanks and artillery. There the A-10s wreaked havoc on the attacking forces, using both the Maverick guided missile and the 30 mm cannon.

A Gulf War Assessment of the A-10

An Army Seventh Corps debriefing of a high-ranking Iraqi prisoner of war reads as follows:

The single most recognizable, and feared[,] aircraft was the A-10. This black-colored jet was deadly accurate, rarely missing its target. Seen conducting bombing raids three to four times a day, the A-10 was a seemingly ubiquitous threat. Although the actual bomb run was terrifying, the aircraft's loitering around the target prior to target acquisition caused as much, if not more, anxiety since the Iraqi soldiers were unsure of the chosen target.[59]

On the US side, "There is one estimate with which the A-10 commanders feel the most comfortable. It is one that credits the A-10 for at least half of the artillery and armor that was destroyed during the war. And that is more of a consensus statement than somebody's official tabulation." The Pentagon is slightly less conservative. In a "White Paper" published in April 1991, their analysts said, "Although flying only thirty percent of the sorties, A-10s achieved over half the confirmed bomb damage assessment (BDA)."[60]

A-10 Official Air Force Kills in Desert Storm	
Target	Number Destroyed
Tanks	997
Artillery pieces	926
Armored personnel carriers	500
Trucks	1,106
Radars	96
SCUD launchers	51
SAM missile sites	9
Aircraft airborne	2
Aircraft on ground	12
Helicopters in air	2

Source: US DoD, *Conduct of the Persian Gulf War, Statistical Compendium*, 323, reprinted in Ken Neubeck, *A-10 Thunderbolt*, 70.

The combat performance of targets killed verified one of the A-10 designers' criteria: lethality. Brig. Gen. Robert Scale's official Army history of the war, *Certain Victory*, praised the "tenacity and skill" of fixed-wing CAS pilots and described the A-10 as a "devastating weapon."[61] The Aircraft Battle Damage Repair (ABDR) group verified a second criterion: survivability. "ABDR crews repaired in-theater all but one of the estimated seventy A-10s damaged during the war—and of those, twenty suffered significant damage."[62] A third criterion—responsiveness—was verified by the A-10 ground crews, who launched 8,000 sorties in the war, with a mission-capable rate of 95–97 percent, 5 percent higher than their peacetime rate.

Postwar Congressional Hearings

In April 1991, congressional committees conducted several hearings to assess the effectiveness of US weapons systems. One of their witnesses was Pierre Sprey, the former OSD systems analyst who had opposed the Navy (and Air Force) decision to develop the A-7 attack aircraft on the grounds that the determining criterion was cost per ton-miles. He would have preferred to continue the production of the A-4 Skyhawk. Sprey was also known for his strong support for the A-10 and F-16. He testified to a congressional committee that

> initially the USAF and General Horner resisted deploying any A-10s in support of Desert Shield," and that "it was a tribute to Gen. Horner's character and dedication to combat that he informed his staff and higher headquarters that he was wrong about the A-10 and that it "saved" his campaign.

Ken Neubeck, author of *A-10 Thunderbolt II*, quoted Pierre Sprey as saying that the idea of replacing the A-10 with the F-16 was "one of the most monumentally fraudulent ideas that the Air Force has ever perpetrated."

> Sprey noted that the A-10 was the real hero of the war, even though it represented only one-twelfth of the fighter force, yet it flew over one-third of the sorties and accounted for two-thirds of the tank kills claimed, as well as 90 percent of the artillery kills. He noted that the A-10 was the only aircraft tough enough

at surviving AAA fire, while the F-111 and F-16 were too vulnerable to ground fire to be useful in the ground support role.[63]

Before the Gulf War, the Air Force planned to retire all 650 A-10s and disband the squadrons in the 1990s. As a result of their performance, Headquarters USAF decided to retain 390 of the aircraft and upgrade them with a new safety and target improvement system that would serve the force until 2018.[64]

A-10 Modifications and Enhancements

One of the most significant modifications to the A-10 aircraft was the Low Altitude Safety and Targeting Enhancement (LASTE) system. Installed immediately after Desert Storm in 1991, it was intended to be its last modification before retirement, but that was wishful thinking. The need for an improved targeting was described by Lt. Col. James Marks in a 2015 publication:

> When I flew the A-10A in Europe back in the 1980s, you were lucky if the old inertial navigation system (INS) fitted in the jet got you to within a couple of miles of the target due to its propensity for drifting. That was where you made your money as an A-10 pilot, employing effective clock-to-map-to-ground [pilotage] skills. You knew the terrain, which meant that the INS was just a reference point that might get you close to the target. It would get you to the ballpark, but it wouldn't get you to home plate. You had to become very adept at knowing the roads, hills and valleys. INS gave you some corrections for weapons delivery but not a computed bombsight. LASTE gave us computed bombing, a radar altimeter and autopilot. The A-10 became quite precise as the "death dot" in the HUD (heads-up display) made things a lot easier.[65]

The LASTE system included ground collision avoidance, a low-altitude autopilot, and a computed weapons delivery system. LASTE was an engineering and operational success, and its improvements were much appreciated by A-10 pilots and operations planners.

The 1991 Air Force Air-to-Ground Gunnery Competition

The Air Force capped 1991 after Desert Storm by sponsoring its biennial fighter competition, the Worldwide Fighter Gunnery Meet "Gunsmoke 1991" at Nellis AFB. US fighter and attack squadrons from fourteen active-duty, Reserve, and Air National Guard units all over the world were invited, flying five types of aircraft: F-15E, F-16, F-111, A-7, and A-10. The F-16 units had previously dominated this competition for years. After days of multiple navigation and weapons delivery events, involving over seventy aircraft, the winning squadron was the Maryland ANG's 175th Tactical Fighter Group, using their brand-new LASTE system to win the overall meet. Lt. Col. Roger Disrun of the AF Reserve's 442d Tactical Fighter Wing also flew a LASTE-equipped A-10 to win the individual trophy. A-10s won five of the Individual Top Gun events, with F-16s winning two.[66]

Continued A-10 Modernization

R&D engineers in the Air Force and industry continued to develop the A-10's weapons delivery systems, and in 1997 they proposed what was to become the most significant modification of the aircraft. Lockheed Martin was awarded a contract to be the prime contractor and systems integrator for the Precision Engagement (PE) system. Four years later, the firm was awarded a follow-on contract for the PE's engineering and manufacturing development. Lockheed began installation in 2005. This modification was so significant that it resulted in the redesignation of these aircraft as the A-10C.

The PE mod replaced the single television monitor in the cockpit with two 5-by-5-inch color multifunction displays. It installed new computers and additional controls on the stick and throttle. It added an improved power system and a new electronic data bus that controlled the GPS-guided Joint Direct Attack Munition (JDAM) the Air Force had been working on for years. Final additions included a current-generation targeting pod and a data link. The result was that the A-10C was among the most technologically advanced aircraft in the Air Force.[67] In response to reported cracks in the wings, the Air Force also asked Northrop Grumman in 1998 to inspect

the aircraft and conduct a structure enhancement program. This led to the "HOG UP" program, to sustain the aircraft to its design life of 16,000 hours and extend the life of the wings to 2028.[68]

Starting in 1999, the Air Force upgraded the aircraft with combined GPS/INS, and minor improvements have been made since then.

A-10 Operations over Kosovo

A-10s participated in three operations in the Balkans after Desert Storm: Operation Deny Flight, in Bosnia (1993); Deliberate Force, in Bosnia (1994); and Allied Force, over Kosovo (1999). Kosovo was the most intense.

Following the breakup of Yugoslavia in the early 1990s, Kosovo was left as a land-locked province of Serbia. Its official title was the Socialist Autonomous Republic of Kosovo and Metohija. The region was conflicted between Serbian Orthodox Christians and Muslim Albanians, and there had been violence between the factions. When Slobodan Milošević became president of Serbia, he began to reduce the autonomy of Kosovo and introduce cultural oppression of the ethnic Albanian population. He outlawed Albanian news media and transferred ownership of Albanian enterprises to Serbian control. In response, Kosovo Albanians began nonviolent protest, which turned violent, and formed the Kosovo Liberation Army (KLA), a paramilitary group that conducted guerrilla attacks against the Serbian police and the (Serbian) Yugoslav army. Slobodan Milošević's ethnic cleansing resulted in several internationally publicized massacres and the Kosovo War.

In 1998, international pressure produced a ceasefire and a withdrawal of Serbian forces that was to be monitored by the Organization for Security and Co-operation in Europe. The ceasefire did not hold, and organized attacks resumed in December 1998. Diplomatic negotiations failed when Serbia would not agree with draft language, and NATO intervened in March with air attacks against the Serbian army.

A-10 involvement began with six aircraft from the 81st Fighter Squadron deploying from Spangdahlem, Germany, to Aviano, Italy, to set up a combat search-and-rescue capability on January 7, 1998. With the outbreak of open hostilities, the US contributed to the NATO-led Kosovo

Force (KFOR) with A-10s, F-16s, and F-117s under Operation Allied Force on March 24. Three days later, the Serbs shot down an F-117, and A-10s from the 81st led the successful rescue of the pilot. Two weeks later, the 81st Expeditionary Fighter Squadron redeployed to the southern Italy airbase of Gioia del Colle and formed the core of the 40th Expeditionary Operations Group.[69] They were joined by other active-duty A-10 units and three Air National Guard squadrons. The squadron returned to Aviano in January–March 1999.

Squadron officers quickly worked out plans to have A-10 Airborne FACS (AFACs) lead flights in daytime, and F-16 AFACs at night. A-10 FACs used two unique target-acquisition devices—hand-carried, gyrostabilized, 12- and 15-power binoculars and the PAVE PENNY laser-spot tracker. This mission, leading a large force package with multiple-type aircraft, was new to the A-10 crews and had never been tried in combat. The combined force consisted of dozens of units of nine NATO countries from fifteen bases and three aircraft carriers. A-10s were chosen for their leadership of this complex force because their Cold War mission in Europe had been to find and destroy green-painted vehicles in green fields and forests.

Targeting Technology

The 1968 decision to install a "Lean" avionics package in the A-10 resulted in the aircraft not having a digital navigation and target acquisition system and initially no heads-up display (HUD). Although there had been some improvements over the years, the aircraft in Desert Storm and Kosovo were essentially limited in target acquisition. This resulted in AFAC pilots having to communicate targets to striking fighters in the following manner:

- Find the general target area on a large-scale map (1:250,000) that had markings for each of the smaller-scale maps (1:50,000).

- Determine which 1:50 to use.

- Find the correct 1:50 among the stack of sixteen such maps [in the cockpit].

- Study the terrain, roads, forests, power lines, and houses marked on the map to match the target area on the ground.

- Read the coordinates, in Universal Transverse Mercator (UTM) format, from the scale on the map.

- Write these coordinates on the inside of the A-10s canopy in grease pencil.

- Go back to the 1:50, follow the contour lines to determine the target elevation in meters, and write that on the canopy.

- Use the inertial navigation system to convert UTM coordinates to latitude and longitude, and write those on the canopy.

- Use the HUD to convert the elevation in meters to feet, and write that on the canopy.

- Finally, read the target information to the incoming fighters over the radio.[70]

A fighter pilot could conclude, humorously, that the most important device to communicate target information was the canopy!

By contrast, F-16CG and F-14 FACs with targeting pods could simply point their laser designators at a target to determine its relative range, direction, and elevation.[71]

Tactical Innovation

One of the interesting tactics the A-10 pilots in Kosovo developed was the ability to cooperate with unmanned aerial vehicles in the search for targets. Normally, it was difficult to work with the Predator because the UAV's field of view was narrow, like looking through a soda straw. The Combined Air Operations Center (in Italy) would have a target, precisely located by a Predator, but the UAV operator's description would be so localized that it could not be found by the A-10 pilot looking through his binoculars from 20,000 feet. By adding a laser designator to the Predator, this deficiency was overcome. Lt. Col. Chris Have described the action:

> Capt. Larry "LD" Card, one of our weapons officers, flew a test sortie on the Albanian coast to validate the concept. The Predator marked a simulated target using its onboard laser. That spot was visible to LD [the pilot] using his Hog's laser-spot-tracking pod, which proved that the Predators and Hogs could operate efficiently together. The Predator's laser could nail down a target location very quickly and avoid the lengthy talk-ons.[72]

Kosovo Rules of Engagement

Unlike Cold War Soviet armor, the most urgent requirement in Kosovo was target identification. Extensive sets of Rules of Engagement (ROE) were devised to avoid civilian casualties and neighboring-states overflight. There were three types of ROE: minimum altitudes, restricted areas, and rules to avoid collateral damage. Minimum-altitude restrictions included attacks no lower than 15,000 feet above ground level. At other times, the minimum altitude was lowered to 10,000 feet, then to 5,000 feet for AFACs and 8,000 feet for attackers. Restricted areas included no-fly zones, no-drop zones, and other areas where headquarters authority was required before attacking. One of the original no-attack zones was within 10 miles of the Macedonian border. To lower the risk of collateral damage, there were restrictions on weapons (no use of cluster bombs), restrictions on distance to civilian structures, and limits on the type of targets ("no white busses"). In many, many cases, identified targets could not be attacked until higher headquarters granted approval. This approval was always time consuming, and sometimes too late, and frequently resulted in frustration in the cockpit. A single quote from one of the authors of *A-10s over Kosovo* will be sufficient to describe the situation: "The delay and tactical direction were absurd and a clear violation of the principle of 'centralized control and decentralized execution.'"[73]

Despite restrictive ROE and lots of bad weather, A-10s and other Allied aircraft directly attacked and destroyed thousands of targets, hundreds of tanks and armored personnel carriers, artillery pieces, radars, and surface-to-air missile sites. The result was the defeat of the Third Serbian Army in the field by June 10, 1999, without the exposure of Allied ground forces—a clear-cut, first victory for airpower in this environment.

BRAC 1995 and the A-10+

In 1995, the Congress passed, and President Clinton signed, the Base Realignment and Closure Act, which was to have a significant impact on the country in general and the A-10 program specifically. One of the installations tagged for closure was McClellan Air Force Base, Sacramento, California, a major logistics center and the home of the A-10 System Program Office (SPO). McClellan had housed the A-10 SPO since 1976, and its (primarily civilian) workforce had increased its engineering expertise over the years. When the base finally closed in 2001, the SPO organization moved to Hill AFB, Utah, but the majority of the workforce did not. The result was a major break in the continuity of the Precision Engagement upgrade and increasing frustration in the SPO.[74]

The Air National Guard Bureau and the Air Force Reserve addressed the logistics crisis by launching the A-10A+ (Plus) in 2002 as an interim program to bridge the gap between the older A-10A and newer A-10C models. The A-10+ program was to provide some, but not all, of the capability of the Precision Engagement mods and to field it much sooner. Chief among the needed capabilities was a targeting pod. A proof of concept was completed quickly, in order to get the modified aircraft ready for a deployment to Iraq in 2003 under Operation Iraqi Freedom. With Lockheed Martin and TRW Aeronautical Systems declining to work on the program, the Guard and Reserve turned to Raytheon Indianapolis. Raytheon mounted the operational targeting pod on the bird and added a moving map display to the cockpit. The A-10A's Maverick television monitor was then replaced with a higher-quality projection.

The A-10A+ was flight tested in late 2007, and around a hundred A-10As were modified. The Pennsylvania and Idaho ANG units were deployed to Iraq with the modified A-10+ configuration. The PE modification was not far behind. The Michigan ANG squadron arrived in Iraq with the first A-10C in September 2007.

Operation Enduring Freedom (OEF)

OEF was the official name given to the Global War on Terrorism declared by President George W. Bush on October 7, 2001, in response to the attacks on September 11. Strikes were originally targeted on al Qaeda and Taliban targets in Afghanistan. In the following years, twelve of the A-10 squadrons would participate in the campaign, each being deployed for about six months. Since the enemy in Afghanistan had no tanks and few fighting vehicles, the main missions there were providing fire support to Army, Navy (SEALS), and Marine Corps ground forces.

The capability to drop the 500 lb. JDAM proved to be one of the most valuable features of the A-10C, and it quickly became the weapon of choice. Capt. Eric White described one JDAM attack in Enduring Freedom:

Another memorable mission commenced in the late afternoon and stretched into the evening, during which time we were able to support two different elements. The first was a unit of US Army engineers who, while trying to build a bridge, started taking fire from a small hut in the middle of a whole string of dirt dwellings. As it was going to be a hard target to identify correctly, we fired a couple of rockets and the JTAC confirmed that our aim was accurate. We lined up and came in low at 500 feet for a low-angle strafe. We made two passes, shooting from a slant range of between 4,000 and 5,000 feet. Minutes later, ground forces passed along some "intel" that indicated that the enemy inside were still communicating with outside elements. We simply climbed to 15,000 feet, put our flight in the right position and dropped a 500 lb. GBU-38 JDAM on the hut to stop its occupants from communicating with fellow Talaban. And they did.[75]

One Final (?) A-10 Improvement

During the last year of Enduring Freedom in Afghanistan, there was another modification that turned out to be extremely effective. It was the Scorpion Helmet-Mounted Integrated Targeting (HMIT) system. Lt. Col. Michael Curley, director of operations for the 74th Expeditionary Fighter Squadron, described what he said was the single most important improvement in targeting:

We didn't have access to such [GPS] information in the A-model, and that slowed things down. In the A-10C we had the information, but it was presented via the "four-by-four" [multifunction display] screens. This meant that we had to match the data on the screens with what we were looking at outside the cockpit on the ground. A lot of that work was through the HUD, as that was where the target projections for the weaponry were displayed. With the HMIT, I received information about where the targeting pod was looking, or where my wingman was looking, and I could see it displayed forward of the wing. No matter where I looked, I could see that information.

• • •

The biggest advantage of the helmet for me is that I just put the crosshairs on my target, pull one of the switches down for a second and the pod focusses directly on the spot I am looking at. It's so much quicker and more efficient than how we previously worked. The helmet display is all-color, so all the symbols we see are coded. That helps provide awareness of the things you're looking at. There's so much faster prioritization, and if someone else puts out a threat call, such as AWACS, and places it on my data link, it'll automatically appear on my display.[76]

Continuing A-10 Operations

The Air National Guard in 2021 provided 40 percent of the total A-10 fleet. The aircraft have had a near-continuous presence in Operations Allied Force, Enduring Freedom, Iraqi Freedom, and Inherent Resolve over the past thirty years. A-10 missions continue at the time of this writing, with operations in Iraq/Afghanistan, but the aircraft lives on the edge of the Air Force structure and is always in danger of being retired.

Air Force A-10 Retirement Plans

The Air Force again proposed retiring the A-10 fleet—then down to 281 aircraft—in 2015 and in 2016.[77] An Air Force study estimated that the service could save $4.2 billion over five years by retiring the A-10. Air combat commander Gen.

Mike Hostage said the following in a 2014 interview with *Defense News*:

> I would dearly love to continue [with the A-10] in the inventory because there are tactical problems out there that would be perfectly suited for the A-10. [But] I have other ways to solve that tactical problem. It may not be as elegant as the A-10, but I can still get the job done.[78]

He was talking about the F-16, which itself has been sustained in the force with multiple life-extension modifications. The Air Force rationale cites the same reasons—cost savings, the sequestration of funds, and the availability of other aircraft. But the Congress has been doggedly determined to retain the aircraft in light of its proven and continued performance in the war on terror in the Middle East and its contribution to local economic welfare. In 2014, journalist Tyler Rogoway wrote on the Foxtrot Alpha website, "Regardless of the Warthog's undeniable effectiveness on the battlefield, the aircraft has always been the unwanted straight-winged stepchild of the USAF."

Representative Martha McSally (later, senator in 2019–2020), a Republican from Arizona, had some credentials on the subject of the A-10. She was a decorated combat A-10 pilot and squadron commander. She said in a press statement on January 13, 2018, "It appears the Administration is finally coming to its senses and recognizing the importance of A-10s to our troops' lives and national security."[79] She continued, "With A-10s deployed in the Middle East to fight ISIS, in Europe to deter Russian aggression, and along the Korean Peninsula, administration officials can no longer deny how invaluable these planes are to our arsenal and military capabilities."[80]

The Congress in 2018, 2019, and 2020 blocked the move to retire the A-10 and inserted language into the Defense Authorization Bill that required the Air Force to retain the aircraft. On January 25, 2018, Valerie Insinna reported in *Defense News*:

> Rest easy, Warthog fans. In the fiscal 2019 budget request, the Air Force will be asking for more [aircraft] wings needed to sustain the life of the beloved A-10 Thunderbolt II, but

how many squadrons the service will retain long term is still up in the air, the head of Air Combat Command said.

The Air Force confirmed in 2019 that it could have to retire as many as three of its nine A-10 squadrons unless Congress funded new wings for about 109 aircraft. Congressional committees have been supportive of a $103 million unfunded requirement to start a new A-10 wing line and purchase four wing sets.

"The service will request even more money in the fiscal 2019 budget to continue the re-winging effort," Gen. Mike Holmes, head of Air Combat Command, said at the Brookings Institution.

"In the '19 program that we're working, we also buy more wings, and so we move forward to address the wings of the A-10," he said. "As far as exactly how many of the 280 or so A-10s that we have that we'll maintain forever, I'm not sure. That will depend on a Department of Defense decision and our work with Congress, but we plan to maintain the A-10 into the 2030s at least."[81]

In 2019, David Axe also wrote in *Defense News*, "The US Air Force has all but given up on retiring the A-10 Warthog close-air-support jet. Instead, the flying branch is upgrading the tough ground-attackers so they can fight and survive in high-intensity combat."[82]

Valerie Insinna later in 2019 reported at *Defense News*:

> Acting Air Force Secretary Matt Donovan stoked speculation that the service will retire the A-10 after announcing that its FY21 budget request will include "controversial changes" such as the divestment of legacy aircraft.
>
> But speaking at the conference later that day, Lt. Gen. Timothy Fay, deputy chief of staff for strategy, integration and requirements, confirmed that the A-10 is not one of the aircraft under consideration for divestment and will stay in service until the 2030s. "Short answer: No," Fay said, when asked whether the Warthog is on the cutting block. "I will tell you; I wish the response had been that the Air Force is actually bold enough to get after the threats that we're facing."[83]

The fiscal year 2021 DoD Budget requested to retire forty-four of the 281 remaining A-10s left in the Air Force, but Congress again refused and mandated in the fiscal year 2021 National Defense Authorization Act that all the A-10s be retained. As the Center for Strategic and International Affairs reported in December 2020, "The Air Force has surrendered to the will of Congress (and to real-world operations) by re-winging the A-10 fleet and extending fleet life into the late-2030s rather than retiring the fleet in the near term."[84]

In 2020, Brian Boeding wrote in *Breaking Defense*, "The A-10 may be the closest thing to a religious relic in the US military's weapons inventory. . . . Anyone who's been around ground combat knows F-35s, F-22s and legacy fast jets are far too fast and lack the close in maneuverability to be able to detect camouflaged threats to our troops or to separate friend from foe in a highly fluid firefight."[85] Boeding argued that achieving survivability is more than avoiding or withstanding enemy threats. Survivability has three components: (1) low *susceptibility*, (2) low *vulnerability*, and (3) high *recoverability*. He acknowledged that fast jets have lower susceptibility to air defense threats while in the target area but share with all other aircraft the susceptibility of their airfields and runways to devastation. Second, the A-10 is much less *vulnerable* to ground fire than is a "blowtorch surrounded by fuel."[86] The A-10 is less vulnerable because its design features: separation of fuel from engines; fire suppression in every tank; redundant and manual, widely spaced cable flight controls; titanium bathtub pilot and engine armor; and redundant main spars. Finally, it has amazing *recoverability*. Dozens of Warthogs have received massive hits but returned to base and landed safely. Repairing the damage is relatively easy. He points out that "the average fix time for battle damaged Warthogs in Desert Storm was four hours."[87]

Air Force Requests Proposals for Light-Attack Aircraft

The Air Force released RFPs on October 24, 2019, for a limited number of Beechcraft Textron Aviation's AT-6 "Wolverine" and Sierra Nevada Corporation / Embraer Defense & Security A-29 "Super Tucano" aircraft. The plan was to buy two or three prototypes from each manufacturer to test allies' capacity, capability, and interoperability in training and testing. Secretary of the Air Force Barbara Barrett was quoted as saying:

> Over the last two years, I watched as the Air Force experimented with light-attack aircraft to discover alternate, cost-effective options to deliver airpower and build partner capacity around the globe. I look forward to this next phase.[88]

The AT-6 Wolverine was slated for Air Combat Command at Davis Monthan and Nellis AFBs. The plan was to use Nellis AFB for continued testing and development of operational tactics and standards for exportable, tactical networks. The A-29 Super Tucanos will be tested by Air Force Special Operations Command at Hurlburt, the home of the 1960s Air Commandos, to develop an instructor pilot program for the Combat Aviation Advisory mission.

Neither of these aircraft will replace the A-10.

The Future of Close Air Support

The US has had the benefit of a capable, light-attack aircraft for the past eighty years. The SBD, A-1, A-4, A-7, and A-10 string of aircraft and pilots has served the nation well in a nearly unbroken series of wars, insurgencies, and terrorist actions. The A-10, as the inheritor of this legacy, has had a successful career as the most capable aircraft for close air support for the past forty years. But it is running out of longevity, and the extensive efforts to extend its structural life may succeed only for a few more years. There appears to be no replacement on the horizon. Multirole aircraft in the current and planned forces have excellent performance, but they also have limitations that preclude their accomplishment of the more rigorous close-air-support missions. There is concern in the Fighter / Attack / Strike Warfare community that when that happens, the US will find itself with a gap in mission capability for the nation's defense.

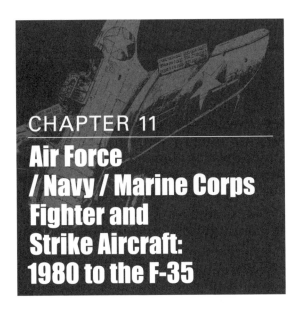

CHAPTER 11
Air Force / Navy / Marine Corps Fighter and Strike Aircraft: 1980 to the F-35

Air to air is what you do going into and coming off the target.

—Maj. Ed Rasimus, coauthor, *Fighter Pilot: The Memoirs of Legendary Ace Robin Olds*

The Innovation Advocate is a passionate zealot. He seldom pays any attention to the ways in which his crusading efforts may influence his personal career.

—Vincent Davis, *The Politics of Innovation: Patterns in Navy Cases*

The US in the 1980s was developing and producing a fleet of fighter/attack aircraft that would dominate the aviation landscape for forty-plus years. In 1966, when Gen. McConnell decided the Air Force needed to buy and improve the Navy's A-7 Corsair II, he included a request to develop a new air superiority fighter, the F-X that became the F-15 Eagle. This chapter includes a case study of the derivation of the lightweight fighter in the wake of the F-X and a description of the other Air Force and Navy fighter/strike aircraft in this period.

John Boyd and the F-X
The previous chapter described how Maj. John Boyd and Pierre Sprey joined forces to attempt

to change how the Air Force designed aircraft, and their effect on the A-10 Thunderbolt II. The A-10 was more Sprey's project than Boyd's, but Boyd's Energy-Maneuverability (E-M) theory supported everything they did. Boyd's assignment on the Air Staff—and his first passion—was to redesign the F-X. The existing F-X design had inherited the swing-wing concept, the twin-engine configuration, and a high-bypass engine (much like the TF-30) from the TFX/F-111 program.

When Maj. John Boyd was an action officer in the Fighter Requirements office of the Air Staff, he worked on the F-X design. In the words of Boyd's biographer Robert Coram:

> Boyd wanted a far smaller aircraft, a high-performance hot rod of an airplane with a thrust-to-weight ratio that would make it the purest air-to-air machine the world had ever seen, an airplane that could dump and regain energy faster than any aircraft ever known, a fighter so maneuverable it could, in Boyd's less than elegant but highly descriptive phrase, "fly up its own [tailpipe]." Boyd did not care about Bigger-Higher-Faster-Farther. He wanted only one thing: a fighter that would dominate the skies for decades.[1]

In 1967, the F-X design weighed about 62,500 pounds, but Boyd's E-M trade-offs allowed him to configure a much more agile fighter design of 32,000–33,000 pounds with a larger wing area, a higher-thrust engine with a much-lower bypass ratio, and a smaller radar dish.[2] This configuration was presented for validation to Wright-Patterson's Aeronautical Systems Division—the authors of the 62,500-pound version—as the RDQ recommendation. The ASD hierarchy did not accept Boyd's austere configuration and added back five tons of weight by increasing the specifications and avionics systems. Boyd's chain of command accepted the revised design, much to Boyd's despair.

Recognizing the situation, Boyd, with Sprey assisting on the weight details, designed a stripped-down, 33,000-pound alternative. They called their version the "Red Bird." Boyd, in secrecy, sent a letter on July 18, 1968, directly to Gen. James Ferguson, commander of Air Force Systems Command, with a twenty-three-page attachment of technical recommendations to lighten the F-X.[3] When Boyd and Sprey briefed Gen. Ferguson, the general reportedly liked the plans for the Red Bird and ended the meeting, agreeing that it was "clearly superior" to the F-X. But over the next few weeks, it became clear that he would not support changes to the heavier F-X his ASD engineers preferred.[4] Although there was a lot of respect for Boyd's E-M theory, the Air Staff, Tactical Air Command, and AFSC were fully committed to the ASD version of the F-X, and no one above Boyd was willing to challenge it.

The Origin of the "Fighter Mafia"

Everett Riccioni had joined the Army Air Forces in 1943, flew transport missions "over the hump" into Burma, and became a test pilot for production aircraft. After the war he earned a bachelor's degree in aeronautics and a master's in applied mathematics. His follow-on assignment was as a test pilot student and then instructor at the USAF Flight Test Center, Edwards AFB. He was flamboyant and passionate about the small size and hot acceleration of the Lockheed F-104, and a devoted advocate of innovation in air-to-air tactics. While at Edwards he spent six weeks at the Fighter Weapons School at Nellis, where he met John Boyd, who was an instructor there. Riccioni had written a controversial paper on fighter tactics, "Double Attack," in which he criticized the USAF "finger four" and Navy "division" tactical formations and introduced "slashing attacks" as more effective. By nature, Riccioni was combative, and he debated the paper with everyone, including John Boyd, who was skeptical of it. But when Riccioni and his paper were harshly criticized by other pilots and senior officers, Boyd defended him and praised his devotion to the art of fighter tactics.[5] Recognizing that flight-testing fighters did not transform him into a "competent operational fighter pilot," Riccioni's applied for and received an assignment to the 36th Day Fighter Wing in Germany, flying F-86Fs and F-100Cs.[6]

Following the tour in Europe, Riccioni was selected to attend MIT for a doctoral program. He completed his course work but left before writing a dissertation. His mandatory follow-on assignment was to the faculty of the Air Force Academy, where he taught one of the first high-level astronautics courses. Two years later, he reported to head Development Plans (RDQD), the parallel office to Operational Requirements in the Operational Requirements and Development Plans Directorate, led by Maj. Gen. Bill Moore, AFRDQ, DCS/R&D. Riccioni's job was to work on research and development planning in aeronautics. Riccioni's office worked directly with the engineering staffs and System Program Offices at Aeronautical Systems Division, Wright Patterson AFB. The two offices (Requirements and Development Plans) were side by side in the Pentagon. When Riccioni arrived in the building, he looked up John Boyd, and they renewed their friendship. Boyd and Sprey told Riccioni how the F-X was overweight and would not outperform new threats, but that they had an alternative approach for a smaller, much-hotter air-to-air fighter. Riccioni, with his advanced mathematical, flight test, and operational experience, was immediately convinced. Recognizing the revolutionary, underground nature of their approach, Riccioni bonded with Boyd and Sprey and suggested the three call themselves the "Fighter Mafia."[7]

The "F-XX" Briefing: Prelude to the Lightweight Fighter

When John Boyd realized that even four-star general Ferguson could not change the momentum of the accepted version of the F-X design, he and Pierre Sprey became very discouraged. More in frustration than anything else, Sprey, with Boyd's help, put together a paper proposing an exceptionally lightweight (20,000-pound), no-frills fighter that he called the F-XX (F-X Squared). The audience was the annual meeting of the American Institute of Aeronautics and Astronautics.[8] The paper traced the history of what Sprey called "A Quarter Century of Fighters," in which he outlined the characteristics of those few aircraft that had been successful in air-to-air, starting with the F-86. Riccioni read a copy of the paper and became enchanted with the concept. When next he met Boyd and Sprey, he shocked them by saying,

We can make this airplane; this is doable! Forget relying on Sprey's all-new F-XX engine; we'll simply wrap the smallest airframe around an already-paid-for engine like the F-Xs.[9]

According to Pierre Sprey, Riccioni became unstoppable in his enthusiasm. The group immediately turned to refining the design and the many trade-offs they had been analyzing for the F-X critique.

The Beginnings of the Lightweight Fighter

Digging into his staff's aeronautical R&D budget, Riccioni quickly came up with $149,000 to fund new contractor preliminary designs of the small, agile planes the Fighter Mafia had in mind. To keep the real purpose of the study secret, the effort was titled "Study to Evaluate the Integration of Advanced Energy-Maneuverability Theory with Trade Off Analysis."[10]

This was the first breakthrough—receiving authorization to expend funds for industry to develop preliminary designs for a lightweight fighter put aerospace firms on notice that the Air Force was considering another fighter procurement that could eventually mean a multibillion-dollar contract. With this incentive and a written contract from the Air Force, the major firms would be able use the money and invest their own independent R&D funds to produce serious design efforts.

Enter Mike Loh. Capt. John Michael Loh finished high in the second class from the Air Force Academy in 1960, flew F-102s, graduated from the Fighter Weapons School and USAF Test Pilot School, and flew F-4s at Eglin AFB. There he met John Boyd, who was developing his theory of Energy-Maneuverability. Mike Loh was one of the pilots who listened to Boyd's briefings and became an advocate of his findings.[11] Loh left Eglin for Da Nang, South Vietnam, flying F-4Cs, but kept in touch with Boyd. At the end of his tour at Da Nang, having flown 204 combat missions over North and South Vietnam, he volunteered for a Pentagon assignment in the Fighter Requirements shop so he could help define the requirements for a new, post-Vietnam fighter force. There, as a captain (selected for major below the zone) in 1969, he rejoined with John Boyd and was destined to be closely involved in the inception of the Lightweight Fighter program.

Mike Loh explained that in the 1970s, the F-14 and F-15 were just beginning development, and many in the Pentagon and Congress were concerned over their high projected unit cost. The cost of a fighter had increased significantly from the first operational jet fighters.

Jet Fighter Aircraft Generations	
Generation	Aircraft
1st	F-80, F-84, F-86
2nd	F-100, F-8, F-101, F-102. F-104, F-105
3rd	F-4, A-7
4th	F-14, F-15, F-16, F/A-18
5th	F-22, F-35

Loh related:

In this period the fourth generation (F-14 and F-15) promised to be even more expensive. So, a small group formed at the Pentagon, including Boyd, Pierre Sprey, Tom Christie, Col. Everest Riccione, and me. Christie had come to the Pentagon with Boyd from Eglin. He ran the computer labs at Eglin that cranked out the EM diagrams. This small group and I started thinking about developing a lower-cost, high-maneuverable fighter using EM theory as the design tool. I started work at the Pentagon in the Fighter Requirements directorate in November 1969 and began working directly and daily with Boyd on the LWF. Riccioni got a $149,000 budget with a very innocent title to conduct studies on the LWF designs! We began talking to the designers from industry, most notably, Harry Hillaker from General Dynamics, John Patierno from Northrop, and Kelly Johnson from Lockheed's Skunk Works.[12]

Many of these meetings were at night and on weekends in motels around the Pentagon. As a result of their seed money from the grant, the industry executives were investing their own firms' money in exploring the many new designs. Loh continued his narrative:

We reviewed the results of the EM-funded study and exchanged ideas on LWF design parameters, using EM theory as the fundamental design tool. We worked very quietly because the Air

Force leadership was opposed to any other fighter work that would get in the way of the F-15. The Air Force leadership knew about Boyd's work but dismissed LWF as a short-range, day fighter, paper design that could not fulfill a serious Air Force fighter role. But Boyd and I knew better. The LWF designs could outmaneuver the F-15 on paper and had greater range on internal fuel. So, we continued to encourage the fighter industry to invest more in LWF designs and think about building some prototypes.[13]

Pierre Sprey adds his insight:

Based on the resulting industry design studies, we applied Boyd's new energy maneuverability trade-off techniques to refine performance, range, armament, and avionics requirements for a small, highly maneuverable air-to-air fighter in the 20,000-pound class, using either one F-X engine or two smaller competing engines from GE. Weapons were the latest-model Sidewinder IR [infrared] missile together with the 20 mm cannon and a ranging radar.

All this would have remained an interesting paper study except for the arrival of a new deputy secretary of defense, Dave Packard, a self-made electronics engineer who was a committed enthusiast for prototyping.[14]

Packard put up a $200 million budget for encouraging prototypes across all the military services. The Air Force immediately formed a prototype board to select two Air Force candidates to compete for a significant piece of that budget. Because the Fighter Mafia already had a thoroughly refined concept-and-requirements package ready to go, their lightweight fighter emerged as the Air Force's number one candidate submitted for the Packard prototype competition.

The backstory is even more interesting. When the Air Force heard there was going to be a competition for aviation grants, they established an Air Force Prototype Board at Aeronautical Systems Division, Wright Patterson AFB. The board chairman was Col. Lyle Cameron, the same officer who had been Pierre Sprey's boss during the Airlift Study in OSD Systems Analysis. Sprey immediately made contact with Col. Cameron

and informed him they would be bidding on one of the grants. The LWF team in Requirements not only wrote a proposal to fund a competitive prototype project for fighters but included proposed rules for the fly-off! The Air Force won both of the OSD awards, one for the lightweight fighter and the other for a tactical airlift aircraft, the C-X.

That was the second breakthrough. With the prototype funds ensured, the Requirements office rapidly expanded their existing requirements package into an innovative request for proposals (RFP). Unique in the history of USAF prototyping, the RFP called for *two competing, fully armed prototypes* to be delivered for a head-to-head dogfighting fly-off competition, with ground rules for the fly-off incorporated into the RFP.[15]

Loh continues the case study:

The LWF prototype program was initiated in 1971, and we began the source selection to pick two designs for competitive, flying prototypes. Boyd and I worked day and night to develop the RFP for LWF. We used EM theory to force the designers to propose highly maneuverable fighter designs. We required high Ps ["specific excess energy"] in the air combat arena, which we defined as 15,000 to 30,000 feet in altitude, and 0.6 to 1.6 in Mach number. To ensure we had sufficient range and combat fuel, we required a radius of 500 nm and a set of combat tasks that included three sustained 360-degree turns at 0.9 Mach / 30,000 ft., two sustained turns at 1.6 Mach / 30,000 ft., and one acceleration from 0.9 to 1.6 Mach at 30,000 ft. We wanted to make sure the LWF had more range and maneuverability than the F-15![16]

The RFP was released on January 6, 1972, calling for a 20,000-pound-class air-to-air day fighter with a good turn rate, acceleration, and range, and optimized for combat at speeds of Mach 0.6–1.6 and altitudes of 30,000–40,000 feet. The small group of true believers reviewed the contractors' submissions and planned for a formal R&D solicitation. Mike Loh continues the story:

John Boyd and I participated in the source selection of the prototypes. We had five proposals, from General Dynamics (GD), Northrop, Lockheed, Boeing, and Vought. [Northrop's was a twin-engine design.] Lockheed and Vought were barely acceptable. GD and Northrop were selected. Boeing had a great design, but it was too small and had much-higher technical risk than GD or Northrop. GD had a better-performing design than Northrop, but we were encouraged to pick one twin-engine design if it met all the basic criteria. We completed the source selection and awarded contracts in early 1972 to GD for the YF-16 and Northrop for the YF-17. I was the first LWF prototype program manager/monitor in the Pentagon. That meant I was the Air Force advocate for the program and had to fight to obtain and retain funding in the DoD budget for the program.[17]

In June 1972, Mike Loh received a Daedalian Fellowship to attend Massachusetts Institute of Technology, where he was promoted to lieutenant colonel below the zone. He received a master's in aeronautical engineering with a thesis titled "The Design of a Fully Fly by Wire Flight Control System for Fighter Aircraft." In what must have been an extremely insightful decision, the Air Force personnel system then assigned Maj. Loh to the LWF Prototype System Program Office at Wright-Patterson AFB as the project manager for YF-16 and YF-17!

As an aside, in 1973, Col. Riccioni's relationship with John Boyd became seriously strained. Riccioni objected to Boyd's habit of interrupting office business with his intrusive manners and even following him into the restroom to insist on a point.[18] For his part, Boyd repeatedly warned the members of the Mafia to *never* present the LWF/F-16 as a better airplane and replacement for the F-15—despite the fact that they all believed privately the YF-16 configuration with its super-hot 1.2:1 thrust to weight to be vastly more effective than the F-15 in any air-to-air scenario. Despite this prudent warning, Col. Riccioni reportedly announced and insisted to a senior Air Force general that the F-16 was far better than the F-15.[19] Boyd lectured Riccioni severely for this outburst, but it was too late. The event with the senior officer got Riccioni banished from the

Air Staff and transferred to Korea. After another tour of duty, Riccioni retired in 1976 and joined the Northrop Corporation.[20]

The Lightweight Fighter to the Air Combat Fighter / F-16 Program

As the project manager at Aeronautical Systems Division, Maj. Mike Loh managed the development of the YF-16 and YF-17 prototypes. General Dynamics was awarded $37.9 million to build the YF-16, and Northrop was given $39.8 million for the YF-17 prototype. The General Dynamics design team was led by Robert H. Widmer, and the YF-16's first full flight was February 2, 1974. The Northrop YF-17's first flight followed on June 9. There were two major technological innovations in the YF-16. The first was the design and installation of the first all fly-by-wire flight control system with no mechanical backup. In Mike Loh's words, this "allowed for a much more flexible and maneuverable design" with no constraints on the location of the center of gravity in relation to the center of pressure. In other words, this innovation allowed the aircraft to have "relaxed stability," which let the aircraft generate g-force more quickly and have higher maneuverability.

Mike Loh's classmate at USAFA, Ron Yates, also a USAF Test Pilot School graduate, worked directly on the F-16 program in 1977, and in 1983 he became the F-16 program manager. In Yates's words,

The most significant risk undertaken by the YF-16 developers (General Dynamics) was the fly-by-wire flight control system.[21] A fly-by-wire system had been demonstrated by the Air Force Flight Dynamics Lab and flown on an F-4 test bed. However, moving the system to the YF-16 was a huge risk . . . but with high payoff. Because the system was all electronic, the aircraft was designed to be aerodynamically unstable. The stability was maintained by the flight control system, not inherent to the airframe. This allowed weight reductions in ballast, actuators (electronic, not hydraulic), and structure. This design resulted in huge YF-16 performance improvements, including moving the envelope to 9 G's vs. the old 7.33 and greatly increased agility.[22]

This innovation was aided by the revolution in miniaturization of electronics that was happening in industry.

Mike Loh elaborated on the second innovation (and risk), which was to adopt the new Pratt & Whitney F100 engine that was being developed for the F-15. The F100 was designed to be a twin-engine installation, so it did not have a secondary engine control. It had other teething problems as well, of reliability, compressor stalls, and "hard" afterburner lighting. All these were high-risk factors for a single-engine aircraft such as the F-16. In addition, there was a bureaucratic issue of coordination between competing programs. Loh related, "It took a great deal of pressure and urging on my part and the part of the commander of Aeronautical Systems Division to force the F100 engine program office, under control of the F-15 program, to pay attention to our needs. . . . These problems were not fully solved for the F-16 until the aircraft reached production in 1977," five years later.[23]

Northrop's YF-17

The YF-17 was developed by Northrop from their F-5E, the single-seat fighter version of their successful T-38 trainer, despite its loss to Vought's A-7. The F-5 was selling well internationally, and Northrop had continually tried to get the US government interested in buying it. The internal Northrop design was labeled the N-300, with a longer fuselage, small leading-edge root extensions, and more-powerful GE15-J1A1 turbojets, rated at 9,000 pounds of thrust each. The N-300 further evolved into the P-530, which was upgraded to the 13,000-pound GE15-J1A5 engines. The wing featured leading-edge root extensions that tapered into the fuselage, giving it a resemblance to the head of a cobra; hence the nickname "Cobra." Northrop modified the P-530 into the P-600 design, which became designated YF-17A in competition with General Dynamics YF-16.

F-16s for NATO

Several NATO countries had been following the Lightweight Fighter development since they needed to replace their F-104Gs, which were performing primarily ground attack missions. These countries declared that if the US would commit to producing the LWF, they would buy the aircraft also. They prevailed with Secretary of Defense Schlesinger, and in April 1974 he announced that the Lightweight Fighter program would be changed to the Air Combat Fighter, and that it would not be a pure air superiority fighter, but multirole. Secretary Schlesinger and Air Force chief of staff George Brown negotiated a deal that in exchange for the USAF accepting the F-16, the number of Air Force fighter wings could increase to twenty-six, and that any DoD order of LWF/F-16s would be *in addition* to the F-15. This established the concept of the "high/low" fighter mix. This decision extinguished much of the official Air Force opposition to the LWF/ACF. On September 11, 1974, the Air Force confirmed plans to order the winning ACF design to equip five tactical-fighter wings!

Mike Loh continued his story.

The competitive prototyping program was a big success. Both the YF-16 and YF-17 demonstrated remarkable maneuverability and fighter tasks. Boyd and I were directly involved in the source selection. GD won with the YF-16. The F-16 performed better than the F-17 and cost less to produce, about two-thirds the cost of the F-15. I briefed the source selection results to the secretary of the Air Force, chief of staff, and commander of TAC. All were impressed with the potential of the Lightweight Fighter.[24]

Air Force secretary John L. McLucas announced the YF-16 as the winner of the LWF competition on January 13, 1975.

F-16 Evolution from Air Combat Fighter to Multipurpose Aircraft

The decision to expand the YF-16 mission from air superiority to multipurpose had already been made by the secretary of defense and the USAF chief of staff. Lt. Col. Loh's job as the project manager was to missionize it to perform these tasks. Mike Loh described his task.

Because of my fighter operational background, as well as aero engineering, my job was to make the F-16 into an operational fighter. I was sensitive to the radius of action, or range, of the fighter because of the constant criticism that "these pure fighters are short-legged and can't go anywhere." We were told never to put a radar-guided missile on the LWF because then it would compete with the F-15. So we had the 20 mm cannon and Sidewinders. We needed a modern radar, despite Boyd and others who wanted only a day-only, clear-air VFR [visual flight rules] fighter. I conducted the studies on equipping the YFs with a look-down, shoot-down radar, and I ran the prototype radar selection. The goal was to keep the cost low so the Air Force could buy them in quantity, fill the 26-wing tactical fighter force structure, and put into effect the "high/low" mix of F-15s with greater numbers of F-16s. The miniaturi-zation of electronics and look-down radars made internal space less important than in the F-15. When the technical and industrial defense communities saw how great a fighter the F-16A was becoming, they all wanted to put their favorite new system on the aircraft and applied considerable pressure on me and the SPO to include them in the baseline configuration. I resisted vigorously, and the Air Force chief, General Jones, recognized we needed support in rejecting these add-ons. He created the F-16 Configuration Steering Group (CSG), headed by Maj. Gen. Al Slay, RDQ, to keep control of configuration and cost. I was the executive secretary. I listened to all the petitioners, from the labs, from industry, from TAC, and from other field units requesting their "widget" be added to the F-16. Then, I would conduct cost versus benefit analyses. In every case, the answer was "NO!" I reviewed these analyses with General Slay before every quarterly meeting, and we ran the CSG with iron discipline. But that is what it took to maintain strict cost and configuration control of the F-16A from the beginning.[25]

The result was the F-16 fuselage was lengthened by 10 inches, and the radome by 16 inches, the tail fin height was decreased, the ventral fins were enlarged, two more stores stations were added (for a total of nine), the wing area was increased by 20 ft.^{2}, and the weight was increased by 25 percent. John Boyd and the Fighter Mafia advocates were opposed to the majority of these changes, especially the weight growth. They made their views known to Loh and the Configuration Steering Group. but they were powerless to prevent the changes. The Air Staff and the Program Office were implementing the SECDEF's guidance to make the aircraft multipurpose.

As Gen. Yates later commented:

This made the aircraft dual-mission capable of dominance in the air and also performing the air-to-ground fighter [attack] mission. These changes enabled the F-16 to replace all the other fighters in the Air Force inventory at the time, with the exception of the F-15 ("not a pound for air-to-ground" was the motto), and the A-10 CAS mission. Operational readiness was a real problem for the Air Force in those days, as maintainability was not designed into the aircraft. However, that was not the case for the F-16. While design maturation was necessary, the reliability and maintainability of the aircraft and avionics was greatly improved. In later years, this was a focus of the continuing development program, and with the F-16C/D, Mission Capable rates were maintained at above 90% worldwide. This was unmatched in Air Force history![26]

The F-16 was so successful in its development that it was purchased and flown by more than twenty-four countries. Over 4,600 F-16s were produced, making it one of the most successful aircraft development programs in history.

Yates was promoted to major general in the F-16 position and later, as a four-star, to be the commander of Air Force Systems Command. As a final exclamation point, he remarked that the F-16 won every bombing competition in which it competed (until the Air Force gunnery competition in 1991, when the A-10 won five out of seven events).

The F-16's Future in Foreign Sales
In 2020, the Air Force awarded a contract to Lockheed Martin to build F-16s for foreign military sales (FMS). The first two examples were Taiwan's agreement to buy sixty-six aircraft and Morocco's for twenty-four. The total amount for these ninety aircraft in a ten-year contract was

$4.94 billion. With sales to the other two dozen foreign countries that have purchased or are interested in purchasing future F-16s, the total contract is potentially worth $62 billion.[27]

The F-14 Tomcat

The Navy and Air Force aircraft research-and-development programs are both governed by DoD instructions, but the cultures are quite different. The differences derive from distinct historical experiences, varying missions, different infrastructure, and personnel cultures. The Navy's development of both the F-14 and F/A-18 derived from the Navy Fighter Attack Experimental (VFAX) projects. There were actually *two* VFAXs. The first was a Navy reaction to Secretary McNamara's insistence that all the services buy the TFX/F-111. The second was the Navy's search for an alternative to the Air Force's Lightweight Fighter program.

The Navy's needs in 1961 contrasted remarkably from those of the Air Force. The USAF wanted primarily a long-range-interdiction aircraft to replace the F-100 and F-105; the Navy wanted a fleet defense interceptor to replace the F-4 and the F-8. The Navy's need was for a long-range, high-endurance interceptor to defend its carrier battle groups from long-range antiship missiles launched from Soviet jet bombers such as the Tu-16 Badger.

The Navy's opposition to the joint TFX was registered from the beginning by Assistant Secretary (Dr.) James Wakelin's letter of March 9, 1961, and NAVAIR's George Spangenberg (see chapter 4 for more details). The marriage of the two sets of requirements was a disaster from the beginning. Air Force requirements dominated the McNamara specifications. The joint military source selection panel picked the Boeing proposal, but McNamara overruled and selected General Dynamics (GD) to produce the F-111A for the Air Force and the F-111B for the Navy. Both models were to use the new technologies of the variable-sweep wing and the turbofan engine. One can imagine the anguish in the Navy over GD's lack of Navy R&D experience. GD added Grumman to the contract for the F-111B, but that was not enough to overcome the divide. As the program developed in the 1960s, the Navy grew more and more distraught over the contrasting requirements, the design's weight growth, and its high cost. VAdm. Thomas Hayward flew the developmental F-111 and reported it had difficulty going supersonic because of its high drag, and it had poor carrier-landing characteristics. By 1965, when the Air Force decided to adopt the Navy A-7, the Air Force's higher priority was to fund the development of an F-X air superiority fighter. The VFX specification was the Navy's 1966 counterpart to the Air Force F-X.

Grumman was intimately aware of Navy needs for a VFX, and some observers say it secretly diverted some of the F-111 funds to investigate designs for a separate fleet defense aircraft. The Navy awarded Grumman a contract to begin studying advanced fighter designs. The Long Island–based firm already had a 303 design that it refined and marketed to the Navy in 1967. Grumman's VFX design transplanted the F-111B's use of the TF-30 turbofan, the swing-wing technology, and the AIM-54 Phoenix missile into a lighter, more agile fighter.

In May 1968, Congress terminated funding for the F-111B, and in July NAVAIR issued an RFP for the VAX. Grumman won the contract and was allowed to skip the prototype stage, and it jumped directly to full-scale development. The F-14 Tomcat (reportedly named for Tom Hayward) first flew on December 21, 1970, and the first squadrons, VF-1 "Wolfpack" and VF-2 "Bounty Hunters," aboard USS *Enterprise*, were operational in 1974. Grumman produced a total of 712 F-14s. The Marine Corps was initially interested in the F-14 as a replacement for its aging F-4s, but it backed out when NAVAIR declined to add a weapons store's management system for attack missions.

In the late 1970s, the Navy developed the Tactical Airborne Reconnaissance Pod System (TARPS), and sixty-five F-14As were modified for the recce mission. The F-14 was the heaviest and most expensive fighter of the 1980s, and these features precluded its being competitive for the VFAX, Lightweight Fighter programs.

A Lieutenant's Adventure with the Tomcat

Lt. j.g. Paul Nickell was an F-14 pilot with VF-24 "Renegades" when he had an exciting adventure with the TF-30s of his Tomcat on a routine training mission out of NAS Miramar. As the reader may recall, Col. Hails and Maj. Loh had already expressed their concern over putting an afterburner on the high-bypass TF-30 engine in the A-7 and the F-111. Lt. Nickell's adventure is an example of what can happen with twin jet engines in an emergency.

In October of 1984, we manned up for an afternoon flight [from Miramar] to the warning area off of San Diego. I don't remember exactly what our mission was, but we were the flight lead for a section of two Tomcats.

We were taking off from the shorter Runway 24 Left. In VF-24 we did not do section takeoffs, where both aircraft rolled down the runway together in a tight formation. The wingman normally waited about 10 seconds after the lead started rolling, before commencing his roll. I was centered halfway between the left edge of the runway and the centerline, and my wingman was on the right half. I was in minimum burner, and as I hit about 135 knots and was starting to ease back on the stick, there was a huge boom from my right side, and the aircraft immediately started to pull right. I countered with left rudder and kept it on my half of the runway as I slowly continued to rotate the aircraft.

Slowly lifting off, I added more burner and carefully monitored the angle-of-attack gauge, keeping it below fourteen units. Early in the life of the F-14, aircraft had been lost because of getting to a higher angle of attack with the large thrust asymmetry associated with an engine failure. Another problem in the early F-14 days was an uncontained catastrophic engine failure where the aircraft was damaged so badly by the engine coming apart that the crews had to eject. Fortunately for us, each engine was now encased in a 1,000-pound titanium sleeve to contain engine failures.

The one other thing that had been added to the aircraft to try to prevent flat spins was an engine stall warning system. It consisted of flashing amber lights up on the sides of the windscreen, and an aural annunciation of something to the effect of "right engine stall" repeatedly. The aural annunciation began immediately after the boom and would not

stop! Intercom communication between myself and my RIO [radar intercept officer], and radio communications with Air Traffic Control (ATC) were almost impossible for me to hear.

Our wingman joined up as I flew the departure and limped the jet out over the water. Eventually we got our volumes up and were able to hear each other and also ATC over the stall warnings. We circled back to the east and flew a single-engine approach to Miramar. After taxiing back to our ramp and shutting the remaining engine down, we got out and looked into the right engine burner can. It was full of mangled turbine blades. My biggest regret was that I didn't grab a few blades as souvenirs. After our wingman returned to land, we debriefed our short flight. They informed us that when the engine blew, there was a huge cloud of smoke that temporarily obscured our jet on the takeoff roll. I had survived another close call but not the closest.[28]

Ironically, Lt. Nickell had previously experienced virtually the same compressor stall emergency on his first flight in the Tomcat three years earlier.

Bombs for the F-14

Despite the F-14's "Fighter" designation, Grumman carried out trials with live bombs in the 1980s, and in 1992 the Navy certified the airframe for dive-bombing. At the same time, the Low Altitude Navigation and Targeting Infrared for Night (LANTIRN) pod was developed, and the F-14D began ground attack missions. Finally, the Navy added an attack stores management system in the 1990s. The F-14 was retired from service in 2006.

F/A-18 Hornet

With the subject of this book turning to the Navy's iconic F/A-18 Hornet, we can take some time to delineate its ancestry. If one takes the long view, you could say that the F/A-18 started back in the late 1930s. Jack Northrop began as a young draftsman with Lockheed in 1912 and joined Douglas in 1923 to become an engineer. He founded three companies, beginning with the Avion Corporation in 1928, Northrop Corporation with Donald Douglas in 1931, and a second Northrop Corporation in 1939. In 1942, Northrop built the P-61 Black Widow night fighter and followed with the YB-49 experimental flying wing bombers, the F-89 Scorpion interceptor, and the SM-62 Snark intercontinental cruise missile. The XB-49 design formed the foundation for the Northrop Grumman B-2.

Meanwhile, Edgar Schmued, a junior engineer for North American Aviation (NAA), had designed the A-36 Apache for the British. With a slight redesign that aircraft became the famous P-51 Mustang. While at NAA, Schmued also designed the F-86 Sabrejet and the F-100 Super Sabre. Schmued left North American in August 1952 and became vice president of engineering for the Northrop Corporation. At Northrop he recruited a top engineering team and, like Ed Heinemann before him with the A4D, developed a lighter, high-performance, lower-cost jet aircraft designated the N-156. There were two versions: a two-seat advanced trainer, designated as N-156T, and a single-seat fighter, designated as N-156F.[29] Ironically, Northrop marketed the N-156 for the Navy's jeep carrier fleet, but that requirement evaporated with the retirement of those small decks. The Air Force purchased the N-156T in 1956, and it became the long-flying T-38 Talon trainer, replacing the T-33. The Kennedy administration in 1962 selected the N-156F as the winner of (another) "F-X" competition for a low-cost export fighter, and hundreds were sold overseas as the F-5A.[30] As described in chapter 6, the F-5 was the major competitor of the A-7 both in the Air Force Bohn Study and the Fish Study, which led to the Air Force purchase of the A-7. Northrop was very successful in marketing the aircraft overseas, and thirty-two countries flew models of the F-5.

Five years later, in 1970, Northrop won the International Fighter Aircraft competition to replace the F-5A. The aircraft had been upgraded with the more powerful General Electric J-85-21 engines, as well as a radar, and it featured enlarged leading-edge extensions for increased wing area and maneuverability. The design was relabeled the F-5E, and it first flew in August 1972.[31]

When Northrop owners and engineers, including John Patierno, heard of John Boyd, his Energy-Maneuverability theories, the "Fighter Mafia," and the DoD interest in a lightweight fighter, they were delighted and immediately set to work to redesign their successful F-5E. The evolution began with the N-300 design, next the P-530 Cobra, and finally the P-600, which became the prototype YF-17.

The Navy's Second VFAX/NACF Competition

Even before the Air Force Lightweight Fighter fly-off competition in 1974, Northrop's marketing and engineering department turned to the Navy and were ready in 1973 when the Navy started to develop the elements of a second VFAX program, this one to develop a multirole aircraft to replace the A-7 Corsair II and the F-4 Phantom II and to complement the F-14's air defense capability.[32] The Congress mandated it have a lower cost than the F-14. Secretary of Defense Schlesinger directed the Navy to evaluate the competitors in the Air Force's Lightweight Fighter program, where GD and Northrop were developing prototypes. In May 1974, Congress redirected $34 million from the VFAX program to a new effort, the Navy Air Combat Fighter (NACF). The CNO released a formal VFAX/NACF operational requirements on August 28, 1974, that directed NAVAIR to "perform solicitation and full-scale development."

That summer, the Air Force conducted the now-famous competitive fly-off between the GD YF-16 and the Northrop YF-17. Meanwhile, the Navy was continuing the NACF competition but was concerned about both GD's and Northrop's lack of Navy experience. NAVAIR resolved that issue by asking each firm to partner with a company that had carrier-aircraft experience. GD negotiated a teaming arrangement with LTV Vought, and Northrop partnered with McDonnell Douglas (MDC), both on October 2, 1974.[33] MDC contributed its own design, Model 267, and it was merged with the YF-17. GD/LTV's design was the Vought model 1600/1601, based on the F-16 Block 10 with a single, upgraded General Electric engine. The GD/LTV proposal stressed that it better met the RFP's requirement for commonality with the lightweight fighter. Both firms submitted preliminary designs in December 1974 and complete ones on January 13, 1975.

On the same day, the secretary of the Air Force announced General Dynamics as the winner of the Lightweight Fighter competition. Lt. Col. Mike Loh briefed the two competing designs to the deputy secretary of defense, the secretary of the

Navy, the CNO, and OPNAV's director of naval air requirements. Deputy Secretary Clements was pulling for the F-16, but the Navy officials' inclination clearly was to separate the Navy from dependence on an Air Force program. Their argument was that the F-16 did not meet the Navy's requirements for carrier operations, the landing gear was too narrow, and it had only one engine.

The Navy promptly declared both contractors' designs to be unacceptable for carrier use but entered discussions with each firm to correct the deficiencies. GD/LTV resubmitted its proposal in March with a 1602 design, which was the most common with the F-16. "Best and Final" offers were submitted on April 15, 1975. Two weeks later, on May 2, 1975, the Navy announced the selection of MDC and awarded the firm a $4.4 million contract and one for $2 million to develop the engines.[34]

GD/LTV protested the Navy's decision, with the rationale that only their proposal met the criterion of maximum commonality with the lightweight fighter, but the protest was denied.

Developing the F/A-18 Hornet

The new aircraft was to be produced in two versions: the F-18 for the air defense mission, and the A-18 for attack; the aircraft differed only in their avionics. However, McDonnell Douglas engineers soon developed a more capable integrated design, and in 1980 the new aircraft was dubbed the F/A-18 Hornet. The aircraft differed greatly from the YF-17, similar to the full-scale development process with the F-16. The major issues were the requirements for heavy ordnance loads, carrier suitability, and increased range. The McDonnell Douglas / Northrop development included structural strengthening and a new landing-gear design. The final design featured advanced aerodynamics, increased fuel capacity, quadruple-redundant fly-by-wire flight controls, and the first multifunctional displays in the cockpit.

The first production aircraft flew in April 1980, and 380 F/A-18As were delivered. In September 1987, the firm made a block upgrade to the F/A-18C. As the retirement for the A-6 and A-7 approached, the Navy recognized the need for improving the attack capabilities of the F/A-18 aircraft, and it contracted for a two-seat model

with more fuel and better navigation and targeting systems. The F/A-18D was welcomed especially by the Marine Corps for its attack capability. The single-seat F/A-18Cs saw their last operational deployment in 2018, and the aircraft was retired in 2019. The Corps is not buying the Super Hornet, and its F/A-18A/B/C/Ds have been upgraded to last until their F-35B arrives.[35]

One Pilot's Comparisons of the A-7 to the F/A-18

Greg Stearns flew nearly all the versions of the A-7, ending with the A-7E and its advanced avionics. He then transitioned to the F/A-18. He provided these observations:

> Besides my A-7 time, I logged over 1,500 hours in the F/A-18A and the F/A-18C. The good news about the F/A-18 is that McDonnell Douglas (MacAir) grabbed a bunch of A-7 guys and asked them to help design the cockpit. MacAir also looked at the A-7 HUD and PMDS [projected map display system] and made them a lot better in the Hornet when they developed the "glass" cockpit. My opinion is that the input from the A-7 community was a very positive influence on taking a multimission aircraft (F/A-18) and making it easy to use by a single pilot. The A-7E had a great bombing system, but a bunch of smart guys made it better in the F/A-18. The A-7E had a very usable inertial navigation system … but the F/A-18 was better. Obviously, evolving technology enabled that, but the A-7E set the system standard until the F/A-18 used the A-7E technology as a starting point and then upped that standard significantly. I will say that having an air-to-air radar was a thing of beauty, and the addition of increased thrust and maneuverability really set the F/A-18 apart from the A-7E. The only downside to the F/A-18 was the "gas mileage." We were able to work longer carrier deck cycles with the A-7E than with the F/A-18 and still had to refuel in the F/A-18 when airborne just to make the shorter deck cycle.[36]

Comparing the Operational F/A-18 to the F-16

The F/A-18 is often closely compared to the Air Force F-16, since they are similar in performance. Some pilots, including naval exchange officers who have flown both aircraft, prefer the F-16 for its performance capabilities, including maneuverability, acceleration, sustained g-force, g-onset rate, and much-greater range. However, with the later design time of the F/A-18, its avionics engineers were able to integrate the aircraft cockpit controls and the navigation and weapons delivery systems to a higher degree, and other pilots who have flown both aircraft tend to prefer the F/A-18 because of its multifunctional displays in the cockpit.

The F/A-18 first saw combat in 1986 over Libya, flying off USS *Coral Sea*. Navy F/A-18As and Cs and Marine Corps F/A-18A/C/D flew both air-to-air and air-to-ground missions, sometimes on the same sortie in Desert Storm. They were also used over Kosovo and in attacks in Iraq, Afghanistan, and Syria.

The F/A-18A/B/C/D produced 1,850 aircraft from 1980 to 2000.

The F-22 Raptor

In 1981, the US Air Force identified a requirement for an advanced tactical fighter (ATF) to replace the F-15 Eagle and F-16 Fighting Falcon. This was one of the first air superiority aircraft to make extensive use of stealth technology to avoid detection. For example, the supersonic jet's radar cross section is only 0.0001 m^2, less than that of a hummingbird![37] The F-22 was built by Lockheed Martin, and the original plan was for 750 ATFs, but in 2009 the program was cut to 187 operational production aircraft due to high costs, a lack of clear air-to-air missions, and development of the impending F-35. The last F-22 was delivered in 2012. Though the requirement was for an air superiority fighter, the F-22 has considerable capability for the attack mission. It can carry two 1,000-pound GBU-32 Joint Direct Attack Munitions internally and has been upgraded to carry up to eight small-diameter bombs.

The F-22 also drew the ire of the Military Reform movement. Everett Riccioni said at a press briefing in 2000 that the F-22 was "conceived for a mission that no longer exists, and is totally irrelevant to modern warfare." In a POGO blog in 2005, Riccioni also said the F-22 "represents no progress over the thirty-year-old F-15C."[38]

The Aborted A-12 Avenger II

The Navy started an Advanced Tactical Aircraft program in 1983 to develop a replacement for the A-6 Intruder, using stealth technology. The A-7 Corsair II had taken over the mission of light attack from the A-4, and the F/A-18 was being developed as a multipurpose aircraft, but neither of those could accomplish the night and all-weather heavy attack that was the mission of the A-6. The Navy awarded two design contracts to industry teams: McDonnell Douglas / General Dynamics and Northrop/Grumman/Vought in 1984 and again in 1986. The McDonnell Douglas / General Dynamics team was awarded a development contract in 1988, when the opposing team declined to bid. Within two years, the program revealed delays and cost increases, due primarily to complications with composite materials. There were accusations and controversy over mismanagement on the part of the contractor, the Program Office, and senior Navy officials. The lid blew off when McDonnell Douglas officials came to Washington and asked for reimbursement of expenses. The issues became heated and public. Finally, Secretary of Defense Cheney issued a show-cause order in December 1990, and on January 7, 1991, he canceled the program. The reimbursement issues continued and were not resolved until 2014.[39]

New Tactics / New Techniques

Tactics and techniques for attack operations continued to evolve after Desert Storm. One of the examples was Operation Desert Fox, a series of airstrikes into Iraq in December 1998. Carriers *Enterprise* (CVN 65) and *Carl Vinson* (CVN 70) participated. Desert Fox was intense and represented a transitional bridge to today's precision and command and control connectivity that were among the lessons learned from Desert Storm.

Capt. Kevin Miller, a veteran of A-7E and F/A-18 flying, related the attack community's learning in that decade:

> For carrier aviation, DESERT STORM was characterized by high-dive deliveries of iron bombs and the use of paper tasking. While stand-off precision weapons were employed and to good effect, naval aviation lagged behind

the US Air Force in precision-guided munitions (PGMs) and sensors to deliver them. The strike-fighter concept was proved early when two VFA-81 "SUNLINER" F/A-18s downed two Iraqi MiGs before delivering their bombs on target. However, shortfalls in positive identification hindered the use and effectiveness of the F-14. Meanwhile, S-3 Vikings from each carrier had to fly daily trips to the beach to pick up and deliver the ponderous Air Tasking Order back aboard ship, where strike leads dissected the tasking. With limited ability to query the sometimes-ambiguous tasking, and strike planning with imagery that was not the latest, aviators did the best they could.[40]

By 1998, the fleet's attack squadrons had "Cat Eyes" night vision goggles, Hornets modified to the "Night Strike" capability, upgraded laser "targeting forward-looking infrared" pod, and improvements in inertial navigational system and color displays. Operation Desert Fox attacks were conducted at night and led to the slogan "We own the night." The US had taken away another of the "sanctuaries" that General Fogleman had discussed in the Vietnam War. All the attacking aircraft had laser-targeting capability, and laser-guided bombs had a success rate of over 80 percent, unheard of seven years earlier. The F-14 had LANTIRN pods, and the GPS-guided Joint Direct Attack Munitions were the preferred weapon.

Even before Desert Storm, the US had adopted stealth as a technological breakthrough. The US applied it vigorously to the F-117 and the B-2 and also to the F-16 in the 1980s. Since then, the US bet the farm on stealth and designed it into our most important weapons systems. One of the lessons we have learned is that stealth technology is hard to maintain; its coating needs careful and expensive care.

Training was also improved. Navy, Marine Corps, and Air Force pilots began an intensive effort to exchange idea with seminars, joint exercises, and revised techniques, tactics, and procedures. Exchange tours of aircrews were increased, and junior tactical aviators were put in other services' squadron environments, developing cross-pollination that led to training standardization and new ideas.

Aerial refueling also improved. The Air Force developed for the KC-135 the Wing Aerial Refueling Pod, which reeled out one hose with a basket from each wing for Navy refueling, while retaining the boom for USAF aircraft with their fuselage receptacle.

In summary, the Navy and Air Force forces had made many improvements to attack aviation in the twenty-year span between Vietnam and the First Gulf War, and there were game-changers ten years later in Desert Fox. There were notable improvements in training and readiness in the 1980s, but in Kevin Miller's words, "They were not like night vision goggles and precision laser-guidance in every strike cockpit, joint command and control coordination at the embarked strike-lead level, reliable encrypted communications and digital mission planning."[41]

The Enhanced Super Hornet

The original F/A-18 was very successful in accomplishing fighter and attack missions and simplifying somewhat the logistics systems on aircraft carriers. With the F/A-18 aircraft well into production, McDonnell Douglas developed a new design, "Hornet 2000," with a larger wing, more-powerful engines, and a longer fuselage to carry more fuel. They lengthened the fuselage by 4 feet and added 25 percent more wing area and an enhanced avionics suite. The result added 7,000 pounds to the empty weight and 15,000 pounds heavier maximum weight. Its designation is the F/A-18E/F Super Hornet or "Rhino." The shorter F/A-18E is the single-seat model, and the F/A-18F has two seats, with a naval flight officer in the rear position. The F/A-18F was also modified into the EA-18G "Growler" to replace the older EA-6B electronic-warfare aircraft.

In the late 1980s, the fleet's primary air superiority was still the F-14, and Grumman was marketing DoD and the Navy with the F-14D. Secretary of Defense Cheney was concerned the F-14 was outdated, with 1960s technology. In 1989, he drastically cut back F-14D production and then in 1991 canceled it altogether, with the intent of buying the enhanced F/A-18E/F. This decision to terminate the F-14 was very controversial, and it was opposed by many Navy officials, but it was irreversible. The Navy canceled the planned Navy Advanced Tactical Fighter (NATF) program in 1992 and contracted for production of F/A-18E/Fs. The NATF, had it been completed, would have been a navalized version of the Air Force's F-22. Grumman had proposed an improved F-14, but it too was rejected as too expensive.

The Super Hornet first flew on November 29, 1995, and production began later that year. First fleet deliveries were in 1999, and its initial operational capability was two years later. The first fully equipped unit was Strike Fighter Squadron 115 (VFA-115) at Naval Air Station Lemoore.[42]

Meanwhile, Boeing was growing and purchased North American Aviation. With its commercial success and deep pockets, it forced a merger with McDonnell Douglas, which had been weakened by the failure of the A-12 program. In 1996, Boeing took over production of the Hornet. The amalgamated corporation continued to develop the Super Hornet design in Blocks II and III in 2008.

With the retirement of the F-14 in 2006, the Navy finally reached a goal of having an all-Hornet carrier air wing, which would have simplified onboard logistics and maintenance, except that the original and enhanced Hornets are largely different aircraft. The Super Hornet replaced the F-14, A-6, S-3, and KA-6D. An electronic-warfare variant replaced the EA-6B.

In 2013, aviation industry giants Boeing and Grumman self-funded a prototype of an Advanced Super Hornet incorporating advanced stealth technology, conformal fuel tanks, and 26,400-pound-thrust engines. In 2019, the Navy issued Boeing a $4 billion contract to deliver Block III Super Hornets through 2033.

In 2020 the Navy requested to end the F/A-18E/F Super Hornet production after 2021 so Boeing could convert the line from building new aircraft to overhauling older ones at a rate of forty per year. This Service Life Modification program added thousands of flying hours to the airframe and also upgraded it to the Block III. That change also added stealth, range, weapons-carrying capacity, and advanced data communications. In 2020, there were thirty-two Navy squadrons flying the Super Hornet. This conversion was proposed to reduce the Navy's shortfall of strike fighter aircraft as the F-35 comes online.[43]

Flying the Hornet vs. the Super Hornet

Although the aircraft look similar, and the Super Hornet was pitched as merely an evolution of the original, it is largely a new aircraft. It is 4 feet longer and 5 feet wider, has 25 percent more wing area, and weighs 13,000+ pounds more in the fighter configuration.[44] An anonymous experienced pilot, who was also a landing signal officer, provided the following comparisons of the two aircraft:

The "Rhino"

- has full-color cockpit displays;

- has much more power on takeoff, is airborne in nearly 1,000 feet less distance, and is 20 knots slower;

- has "SO MUCH MORE GAS," "especially true around the boat";

- lands 10 knots slower;

- has the ability to land with unexpended ordnance;

- has a "larger radar [that] is truly phenomenal";

- is not quite as good as the Hornet in air combat maneuvering;

- has a better ground-mapping radar, air-to-surface, but is a little sluggish on roll-ins for weapons delivery;

- has advanced defensive measures that make it better for strike missions in a nonpermissive environment; and

- has aerial-tanker capability.

Overall, the Hornet was my first love. I'll always look back fondly on flying the F/A-18C and oftentimes I miss it. However, there is no doubt the Rhino is the jet I want to fly off the boat into combat.[45]

The F-35 Lightning II Joint Strike Fighter

The Department of Defense conducted a competition for the joint strike fighter in 2001. The two main entrants were the Lockheed Martin X-35 and the Boeing X-32. Lockheed Martin won the competition with a design that is being produced in three variants. The Air Force version is the F-35A, built for conventional runway takeoff and landing. It has an internal bomb bay for weapons carriage, a variety of missiles, and a 25 mm internal cannon. The Marine Corps flies the F-35B, which is built for short takeoff and vertical landing and carries much the same armament as the Air Force version, except it has no internal gun. There was literally no room for a gun with the larger fan engines. The USMC plans to use an external, pod cannon. The Navy flies the F-35C for carrier operations with the same armament, but no gun.

The extensive incorporation of the most advanced stealth technology, avionics, sensors, and data integration produced what is known as the fifth-generation fighter. Capable of air superiority and attack missions, the aircraft's main contribution is its data fusion and ability to work in conjunction with other aircraft, manned and unmanned.[46]

The F-35B and F-35C provide stealthy all-weather strike fighter and air superiority capabilities. The Navy in 2019–2021 is investing heavily in incremental improvements, embedded as the aircraft come off the production line.

John Venable, a USAF Fighter Weapons Instructor Course graduate and F-16 pilot, is an advocate of the F-35, and he wrote:

> The F-35 Lightning II is now the world's most dominant multi-role fighter. Its detection range, geolocation, threat identification, and system response capabilities allow the jet to detect, find, precisely fix, and destroy the world's most advanced threats, including every element within the layered Russian SA-20 surface-to-air missile (SAM) system. While it still has several rough edges, the F-35 has crossed several thresholds that make it the most lethal and cost-effective fighter in or nearing production within the NATO Alliance.[47]

The first combat F-35A wing in the US Air Force at Hill Air Force Base received the last of its full complement of seventy-eight stealth fighters and began combat deployments to the Middle East in 2019.[48]

"Mission capable" (MC) rates for the F-35 rose considerably over the past year but are still below the 80 percent threshold set for the fleet by the secretary of defense in 2018. According to Lt. Gen. Eric Fick, director of the F-35 Joint Program Office (JPO), the MC rate increased from 55 percent in 2018 to 73.2 percent in 2019. With priority for parts, forward-deployed F-35 combat squadrons were able to sustain an 89 percent MC rate.[49]

Some advocates maintain that the F-35 can perform all the missions of air-to-air and air-to-surface, including close air support. When asked about this proposition, Gen. Mike Loh asked why in the world would one ever want to use the F-35 in close air support if it had to get down in the low-altitude regime, where it would be exposed to intense ground fire. That is the mission of the A-10.[50]

The F-35B entered service with the US Marine Corps in July 2015, followed by the US Air Force F-35A in August 2016 and the US Navy F-35C in February 2019. The Navy's first F-35C squadron was VFA-147, "the Argonauts," which achieved its initial operational capability in February 2019.[51] The first Marine Corps F-35B Fighter Attack Squadron was VFMA-314 in July 2015. The Marine Corps deployed a contingent of F-35Bs to join Royal Air Force F-35s aboard HMS *Queen Elizabeth* for its maiden voyage in 2021. The F-35 was first used in combat in 2018 by the Israeli air force. The US plans to buy 2,443 F-35s through 2037.

Multidomain Attack Operations

With renewed emphasis on joint operations, initiated by the Goldwater-Nichols DoD Reorganization Act of 1986, the joint commands have accelerated coordinating the intelligence, space, land, air, and sea elements into powerful attack forces.[52] For example, in May 2020, DoD integrated the efforts of four joint commands to create a multidomain data-sharing test off the East Coast of the United States. Led by Northern Command, the test linked the real-time data of US Space Command, Transportation Command, and Strategic Command with the Navy's Second Fleet. These forces were arrayed against the penetration by a B-1B bomber attempting to enter US airspace. The defensive force included Canadian CF-18s, US F-15s, and US F/A-18s from USS *Harry Truman*, all refueled by KC-135 Stratotankers. The mechanism of the data integration was Link 16, an improved tactical data system.[53]

In a similar test, the Air Force is exploring the feasibility of arming cargo aircraft by loading semiautonomous long-range weapons for all-domain operations. The Navy has for decades armed its long-range, reconnaissance aircraft (e.g., P2V), but this is a new concept for the Air Force. The idea is to mount standoff, air-to-surface cruise missiles on cargo pallets and load these on C-17, C-130, and MC-130J aircraft. The tests are being conducted by the Air Force Research Laboratory and Air Force Special Operations Command, which dropped these Cargo Launch Expendable Air Vehicles with Extended Range (CLEAVER) cruise missiles during three airdrops at Dugway Proving Ground, Utah, on January 28, 2020.[54] The expansion of the battle space and the flexibility of data-driven missions are likely to revolutionize attack operations.

CHAPTER 12
The Attack Mission in Retrospect

The scope of this study has been broad. We have reviewed the history, achievements, and cultures of naval and Air Force attack professions for over a century. The Navy and the Air Force are very different organizations. They were organized centuries apart and extend from completely different cultures. They operate in different media. Attempts to compare them need to respect their distinctive characteristics. Both services are working to improve their joint capabilities.

The Navy Attack Mission
Nothing describes the cultural differences between the US Air Force and US Navy more than the history of the attack mission. Honored and respected by naval officers, attack aircraft, units, and personnel are organized, trained, and equipped with high-quality machines and personnel to conduct a priority mission.

Attack Culture in the Navy
There is a naval attack culture that extends back to the 1920s, when its pilots began dive-bombing. Navy A-7 pilot Greg Stearns commented on the different communities living on an aircraft carrier:

My time came just after Vietnam, so my opinion of the fighter pukes may differ from my mentors. On the USS *Midway*, we had a bunch of F-4 Phantom II crews. Some of them simply viewed

us as another tanker asset since some of our A-7s flew aerial tanker missions. Some of them looked down their noses at us because we did just air-to-mud, and that was not the "romantic" mission (after all, all the chicks dug the "fighter pilots"). We attack-pukes, on the other hand, felt that the single-seat aircraft told the true story, that we were better pilots because we did not need someone sitting in the back seat reminding us of our fuel state, altitude, airspeed, or where to go. With all that said, there was always the chest jabbing, chest puffing, and back-and-forth claims about who was better, but in the end, we all knew that we were on the same team, supporting the same mission, and that framed our professionalism.[1]

Navy "Attack" and "Fighter" Communities
An A-6 pilot and author, Dave Kelly, also commented on tribalism among Navy pilots and aircrews:

There has always been strife between the attack and fighter communities within naval aviation. The fighter pilots have their inflated self-image, as "cold-blooded, steely-eyed killers." They feel their purpose in life is to kill MiGs, and anything that prevents them from fulfilling that destiny is a "senseless activity." Unfortunately, in the real world, people periodically put heavy, high-drag bombs on their planes and make them fly attack missions. This is probably the last thing they ever want to do, but it comes with the territory.

We used to joke that as soon as those bombs left their planes, the 125-mil ballistics drop (the setting entered into the gunsight to drop bombs) would immediately reset to 35 mils, the trajectory drop for a Sidewinder Air-to-Air Missile. (I may be wrong here; rather than "immediately," they may have waited until they had actually pulled out of the dive before they reset the gunsight.)

The attack community has a mission to "disrupt the enemy and deny him of his treasures." We felt that this was somehow a "higher purpose." The enemy wasn't going to end the war because we shot down all his MiGs, but if we denied him of his lines of communication, supplies, personnel support, etc., we felt that we could make a difference. We also could harass him by flying around his country at high speed and low altitude all hours of the day or night, dropping bombs on his industrial facilities, commerce on his highways, or boats moving up and down his coast and waterways.[2]

Attack Pilots' and Fighter Pilots' Tasks

One of the contrasts between attack pilots and their contemporary Red Barons is the difference in the number of their training tasks. Fighter pilots train to remain proficient in aerial refueling, various tactical formations, day and night intercepts, radar and visual, electronic warfare (EW), and a multitude of air combat tactics. Attack pilots require proficiency in the same aerial refueling, three (now only two) types of nuclear delivery, all kinds of dive-bombing, strafing, Iron Hand SAM suppression, delivery tactics for a wide variety of weapons (each with their own parameters), laser designation, low-level flying, combat rescue support, etc. While the attack pilot's list of tasks seems longer, a quick review of Bob Shaw's *Fighter Combat: Tactics and Maneuvers* (Naval Institute Press, 1985) could lead to a spirited debate.

Navy and Air Force Squadrons

The author was in eleven squadrons in my flying career. Air Force squadrons are large, usually twenty-four aircraft and twenty-eight or so pilots in four flights in a wing with four squadrons. Squadrons with weapons systems officers are twice as large. In the early 1960s, Tactical Air Command was in the process of being taken over by bomber generals from Strategic Air Command. Flight call signs were computer generated. Protocol was more formal. It was against regulations for a pilot to wear a flight suit to traverse the 100 yards to Wing Headquarters or to stop at 7-Eleven on the way home for a loaf of bread. One of the most significant results was the death of squadron maintenance and the consolidation of all the aircraft into one big unit, as it was being done in Strategic Air Command. Pilots lost contact with crew chiefs. Crew chiefs were assigned different aircraft daily; they lost contact with their machines *and* their pilots. Each squadron had to be combat ready at all times, so flying time was averaged out over the year, and we didn't have much of it. Fourteen to sixteen hours

a month was about it. Training was standardized, according to Command "training squares" to be filled. We had to be good at everything: air-to-ground, air-to-air, and aerial refueling. Young pilots got less time because we couldn't fly alone. If the lead aborted, we had to go back and land. Getting enough time to be designated an element lead seemed like forever. No one had his name on an airplane, and in fact, all the F-100s had a standardized paint job. Our wing was distinctive because we were allowed a red fin flash from the Cuban Missile Crisis.

Overseas deployments to support the nuclear SIOP were great because we were away from the wing and had our own maintenance, and flying time was more available—except for nuclear alert. We even had a red-colored tablecloth on "our" table at the officers' club in Japan, and our own flight surgeon. The tradition was continued with fighter squadrons in Thailand when Vietnam began. Ironically, it did not develop in-country.

Navy squadrons, as I understand them, are smaller, twelve to thirteen aircraft and seventeen to nineteen pilots. Flying-time priority was determined by what used to be called the inter-deployment training cycle (IDTC). That is, a phased set of training periods determined by the proximity of the next deployment of the fleet. Upon return from a deployment, the squadron would enter a period of leave, individual training, schools, aircraft maintenance, inspections, and reassignment, and the squadron relaxed to a non-combat-ready status. Six months or so before the next deployment, the squadron would concentrate on basic flying skills, leading up to increased flying time for intermediate mission training and requalification for landing on the ship. The last three months would include advanced, higher-intensity training, deployment to NAS Fallon for Strike Warfare, and an at-sea Joint Task Force exercise. The association of officer pilots and enlisted maintenance crews was closer. Pilots and crew chiefs had their names on individual aircraft. Kevin Miller has a cute story:

The day I reported to VA-82 at NAS Cecil Field, Florida, I stepped into the hangar bay before I reported to the Ready Room. There was an A-7 with my name already stenciled under the canopy rail: "LT. KEVIN MILLER."[3]

The Lack of an Attack Culture in the Air Force

The Air Force really does not have an "attack" distinction. It *does* have a strong "fighter" culture. Nellis AFB, Nevada, is known as the "Home of the Fighter Pilot." In the early 1960s, there was a "Tori" gate at the threshold of the flight line that read, "6,000 miles to MiG Alley," which was a replica of the one in South Korea a decade earlier. Those men and women who fly fighters and attack aircraft universally call themselves "fighter pilots." The author was a fighter pilot before he was an attack pilot. Then he went back to fighters and had three more flying assignments in fighters. Yet, there *is* an "attack" cadre among current and retired Air Force personnel. It is mainly composed of those who flew the A-1 Skyraider in Vietnam, the few who flew A-7s, and the larger number who have flown the A-10.

Air Superiority, Air Defense, and Air Attack

The concept of "air superiority" was conceived a year into the experience of World War I. When Oswald Boelcke and Max Immelmann started shooting down Allied airplanes in 1915, they knew they were pursuing a new mission—one that could make a difference in the war. Their first efforts were to attack enemy aircraft that were observing the German side of the lines for reconnaissance or artillery spotting. This was also consistent with the German Air Service dictum to stay on their own side of the lines. As his prowess increased, Boelcke began to cross the lines to seek his opponents, and he took a wingman for protection. He recommended that the Air Service be more offensive. Boelcke also recognized that air superiority was not an end in itself but was a necessary precursor to winning the ground war.[4]

British field marshal Bernard Montgomery in 1943 said, "First of all, you must win the battle of the air. That must come before you start a single land or sea engagement."[5] Sir Winston Churchill echoed the thought in a speech on March 31, 1949. "For good or for ill, air mastery is today the supreme expression of military power, and fleets and armies, however vital and important, must accept a subordinate rank. This is a memorable milestone in the march of man."[6]

I believe the Air Force has taken upon itself the mission of providing air superiority for the Army. Its officers believed the Navy would be "out there" providing its own air cover. There are many written allusions to Navy fighters being for "defense of the Fleet." The Air Force provides air defense for its bases, but it primarily has this larger mission of protecting the Army in addition to strategic attack.

Lessons on Aviation in World War I

There appear to be several important findings from the attack and close-air-support experience in the Great War that have influenced airpower doctrine and practice through the decades:

- Gaining air superiority is important to allow extensive attack upon the enemy ground forces and to defend friendly ground forces from hostile air attack.

- Aviation can make an important contribution to the success of the ground battle.

- The Army Air Service demonstrated the capability to conduct interdiction bombing, but ground commanders were reluctant to allow aircraft to venture far from the edge of the battlefield.

- Low-attitude attack aircraft are extremely vulnerable to enemy ground fire. While enemy forces were often very exposed to attack, attacking-force losses range as high as 20–30 percent in certain battles.

- Aircraft designed for the attack mission are best protected by liberal use of armor.

The Virginia Capes Tests: 1921

The Navy and the Army Air Service engaged in bombing exercises against surface ships in controversial and meaningful tests in the waters off the Virginia Capes. Though few agreed at the time, the lessons that emerged included the value of aviation attacking ships at sea, and the vulnerability of the ships to air attack. The lessons were important for the surface Navy, the emerging naval aerial attack forces, and the Army Air Service, which was developing both strategic and tactical air aviation. As is dramatically shown in chapters 1–3, the success of tactical bombers to attack and sink large warships, including battleships, outlined a mission for naval air to focus, develop, and train dive- and torpedo bombers for the coming war. The exercises were also important for the infant Air Service, but since the targets were not on land, it had less of an effect, and there was less motivation for the Air Corps (after the 1926 Act) to develop light-attack aircraft.

The Marine Corps Champions Close Air Support

The Marine Corps mantra is that "every Marine is a rifleman!" Marine pilots attend a yearlong infantry officer school before they get to attend flying training at Pensacola, Florida. Of all the military services, the Marines are the most distinctive, with the tightest culture. They are a small service, well trained, and exceptionally well disciplined and have had to fight for their role among the armed services. Their purpose became more focused when the Corps carved out the amphibious landing mission in the last several years of the 1930s. The Army was and is consistently envious of the existence and missions of the Marine Corps, and Marine leaders feel a strong motivation to fight for resources from their parent Department of the Navy. To attain mobility, their divisions are heavy in infantry and light in artillery. They depend on Marine Air to make up for this planned shortage, so they naturally adopted the close air support mission from their experiences in Latin America in the 1920s. They would like to have more support from Navy Air, but the Navy's tactical doctrine for many decades was that fleet assets operated under Navy command and were "in support of" whatever operation was underway. The Marine Corps and Army became painfully aware in World War II that Navy carriers and surface ships could always sail away in search of a higher-priority target and leave the Marines and Army on the beach.

The Dominance of Aerial Doctrine

Tom Wildenberg, in his wonderful history of naval dive-bombing, *Destined for Glory*, concludes, "Prior works discussing the events surrounding the Battle of Midway have largely ignored the importance of aerial doctrine developed by the Navy during the interwar period."[7] He is certainly correct. This was not an overnight undertaking. Initial attempts at high-angle dive-bombing in the 1923–1927 period seemed fruitful, and over the next fifteen years the Navy invested in the aircraft, weapons, and training to make the tactic "the central component of its aerial doctrine." In current language, they developed the tactics, techniques, and procedures to implement the attack. Wildenberg is also right on the mark when he concludes, "Not enough credence is given to the Dauntless SBD dive bomber."[8] The characteristics of the aircraft and pilots that made it capable of fulfilling the doctrinal precept were (1) sufficient speed and (2) range to find the target and defend itself, (3) maneuverability to conduct the tactic, and (4) stability in the dive to achieve accuracy and TRAINING to put all this together.

But one needs to be careful when touting doctrine as policy, since unexamined doctrine can often lead to a stagnant organizational "culture"—the "way things are done around here." The Army Air Corps doctrine of strategic bombing, with its concurrent insistence that "the bombers will always get through," had a major fault. The fact that the planners had an organizational priority—to establish the branch as an independent service—fostered a larger blind spot to a realistic assessment of the situation. In their excessive enthusiasm, the bomber advocates insisted they did not need fighter escort to defend against enemy interceptors. They were wrong and narrowly avoided disaster in 1943. If the Merlin-powered A-36 had not been developed and converted into the P-51 in a timely fashion, the bombers would have been naked and unable to sustain the loss rates they absorbed over Schweinfurt and other deep targets. The lesson was that bombers alone could not defeat the enemy and could not by themselves achieve air superiority. It was the overwhelming mass of high-performance P-51s and P-47s and well-trained pilots that delivered dominant air superiority over the Reich and paved the way for the successful ground campaign on the Continent. The success of the multirole fighter led to its own doctrine.

The Army Air Corps 1940 Decision to Terminate the Single-Seat Attack Airplane

Army and Navy attack pilots of the interwar years had different views of their missions to support the next war. After the Virginia Capes exercises, Navy dive-bomber and torpedo pilots *knew* their mission was to sink large surface ships—battleships and aircraft carriers. This gave them a target that was of great size and slow moving. They practiced at great length on this small number of targets with simulated, practice, and live bombs. Air Corps pilots anticipated a variety of ground targets: tanks, trains, trucks, artillery pieces, and infantry in the field. By comparison, these targets were numerous, small, and well dispersed, and some were swift moving. Precision seemed less important than the ability to carry large numbers of bombs and rockets. In this context, it is understandable to see why the Air Corps could prefer light bombers, which not only could carry multiple bombs but were just smaller versions of the strategic bombers that were at the heart of its doctrine.

The Air Force Experience with Multipurpose Aircraft

The Japanese invasion of China in 1936 is now accepted as the beginning of World War II. The switch from single- or two-seat attack aircraft to multiengine, medium bombers occurred just after that. The North American B-25, the Douglas A-20 Havoc, and the two B-26s (the Martin Marauder and the Douglas Invader) performed valiant work both in the European and Pacific theaters. Although they undoubtedly contributed to the ground campaign through interdiction bombing and strafing, they were not used extensively in close air support (CAS) because of their level-bombing inaccuracy. It was Navy Air and Army Air Force fighters and attack aircraft that provided CAS in the Pacific. The CAS mission was used in North Africa and in Europe after the D-day invasion. Fortunately, by

May 1944 the US strategic-bombing campaign and the rapid production, deployment, and employment of P-51 and P-47 fighters had achieved virtual air superiority. With the decline of attacks on heavy-bomber raids, during their posttarget runs home, many of the fighters had enough fuel to peel off and seek targets of opportunity. A fighter kill on the ground was as good as one in the air, and FW-190s on the tarmac did not fire back. However, the AAA fire from machine gun pits and flak towers was murderous, and many attackers were lost. The experience reinforced the belief that ground attack aircraft needed to be armored, but no attempt was made to armor them. Attackers' vulnerability did not change the dominant policy that multipurpose aircraft were capable of performing the attack mission. They were "good enough." When jet fighters entered the force in the 1950s, it was only natural for the Air Force to focus first on building them for air superiority, providing fighter escort of early jet bombers, followed by altering development to produce multipurpose, nuclear-capable fighters with some conventional capability. The insistence that all future fighter aircraft should be multirole was fine until we had to fight limited wars in Korea, Vietnam, and the Middle East, where we had complete air superiority but needed some specialized attack aircraft to handle the full requirements of the ground battle. Even the requirements of the Vietnam battlefield might not have been enough to motivate the Air Force to build or buy a specialized attack aircraft if it had not been for the Army's top-level bureaucratic offensive on the close-air-support mission with a fleet of attack helicopters.

We might also add that for a considerable time, Air Force doctrine implied manned aircraft, and we somewhat neglected the role of unmanned reconnaissance, surveillance, and attack aerial vehicles.

Lessons on Attack Aircraft from World War II

- Gaining air superiority is still the first priority of air forces, and it is a prerequisite for success in the ground battle.

- Strategic bombing is a vital component of an offensive campaign, both to interrupt and destroy the opponent's industrial output and to support gaining air superiority.

- Ground attack in the missions of interdiction and close air support is an indispensable component of the land campaign. The tools to do this are an effective air-ground system, with personnel, equipment, and training.

- Multipurpose fighter aircraft can be used in ground attack, but with their lack of armor, they are very vulnerable to ground fire.

- The most-devastating attacks on enemy ships were from dive-bombing attack aircraft and submarines.

On the Value of Specialized Aircraft

Alain Enthoven expressed Systems Analysis's professional opinion on specialized aircraft, which has a lot of resonance:

We asked the Air Force to do studies of alternative force mixes, and we in Systems Analysis were definitely trying to encourage the Air Force to buy the A-7. Why were we trying to do that? Because, first of all, we believed that for the kind of wars the tactical air forces were likely to fight that the A-7 would simply be substantially better. It would have longer range and better payload, and the payload could be translated into all sorts of things. . . . It would be a lot more effective in relation to cost, and in fact, there was even good reason to believe that it was just *more effective*, that a subsonic design would be positively advantageous because it would be more maneuverable; you could have better [steeper] dive angle for bombing, which would mean more accuracy and less vulnerability.[9]

Dr. Brown also believed in the value of a mixed force. He told the author in his 1970 interview that multipurpose aircraft had advantages, but that there were limits on its utility. Given the types of wars the US was having to face (and certainly in the wars on terrorism), it made sense to have a lower-cost, specialized aircraft. You couldn't have the whole force that way, but at some ratio, having a specialized aircraft would improve the overall quality of the force.[10]

The "subsonic versus supersonic" fighter debate was relevant when the bombs were "dumb,"

and the accuracy of their delivery was dependent on the pilot in the airplane. In the last thirty years, technology has reversed this role; now the highest degree of accuracy is built into the precision bomb, and it is less dependent on the airframe. To repeat the wisdom of Gen. Ron Yates:

We learned a lot from Vietnam! The outgrowth of that war was we needed to tailor the aircraft to fight the air war and ground war. Thus, in later years, we developed the A-10 for ground attack and the F-15 for air war. The F-16 was to do both tasks, but neither was done as well as the tailored aircraft. The new F-35 is a dual-role aircraft that creates an entirely new domain and outclasses the previous aircraft by light-years. Frankly, the entire debate has been overcome by the new weapons carried by aircraft. GPS bombs, carried internally, essentially don't miss the target . . . even if it is moving. Stealth accompanied by jamming greatly reduces penetration losses. For all the wars we have fought in the Middle East over the last fifteen years, our fighter loses can be counted on one hand.[11]

The Gun

The Air Force switched from machine guns to cannon in the early 1950s, and from fixed cannons to the rotary-barreled M-61 "Vulcan" Gatling gun in the late 1950s with the Lockheed F-104 Starfighter. The M-61 became the Air Force standard cannon, and it was continued in the F-105 Thunderchief and the B-52, F-14, F-15, F-16. F/A-18, and F-35. The Navy had not recognized the value of this new cannon in the original development of the A-7A. The reason is not clear, but part of it may have been the lack of communication between Navy and Air Force R&D personnel and their contractors.

The change to adopt the M-61 Gatling gun did not occur until the remodel of the A-7B into the A-7D and E. It was continued in follow-on naval aircraft. The 30 mm GAU-8/A may be the ultimate rotary cannon for the attack mission. Mounted in the A-10, it is the distinctive feature of the aircraft and a devastating weapon in close air support. Precisely accurate and devastatingly effective, it is often the preferred weapon of both the pilot and the ground forces.

General Dynamics introduced the prototype of the M-61 to the Navy in 1973. When it generated widespread support, the Navy conducted an operational test of the gun for close-in defense. The test was completed in 1977 and was successful. It was named the Phalanx, and the Navy ordered production for twenty-three combatant ships and fourteen foreign systems. The first ship to be thus equipped was the USS *Coral Sea* in 1980.

Gunsights

The evolution of sighting devices is a fascinating subject. Beginning with the iron post of the Spandau's and Vicker's machine guns, early gunsights evolved into sights with mechanical rings, and in the 1940s to a lighted "pipper" and circular rings. The gunsight of the A-1 Skyraider was perhaps the epitome of this evolution, with its pipper depressible over a wide range, concentric rings, and angular guidelines. Its large barrel dial allowed adjustment by increments of 1 mil to 350, and the aircraft was very stable in the dive.

The gunsight in the F-100 was built for air-to-air, and the pipper was surrounded by a circle of diamonds, the diameter of which was adjustable to the wingspan of an opposing aircraft by a large lever at the base of the sight in front of the pilot. When they went from the F-100A to the F-100C and included air-to-ground capability, the depression selection lever was placed on the left console, at the extreme rear so the pilot had to turn his head sharply left and down to see it. Then the rotary switch was limited to about 200 mils of arc, with ⅛ inch being about 20 mils!

The F-4 put the depression control back up on the gunsight itself, but the tiny, ½-inch knob had increments of 5–10 mils. And the aircraft, with its extreme sensitivity to power settings, was not very stable in a dive, as I recall.

All the A-7 sights were superior to any of these, and the digitally controlled computing sight on the heads-up display of the A-7D/E was the best. Its "continuously computed impact point" became the standard for many aircraft. The A-10, F-16, and F/A-18 made additional improvements, and subsequent aircraft have followed suit. The shift to the helmet-mounted sight may be the ultimate sighting device for aircraft-controlled accuracy.

The Air Force / Army Dispute over the Control of CAS Assets

Army officers are trained in the employment of combined arms—armor, artillery, infantry. In their thinking and training, the Army should have control over all the weapons that directly affect the war on the ground. Close air support has always been an issue because it is firepower that is not under their control, and they point to many examples where it was not timely. The Air Force argument was most ably stated by Secretary of the Air Force Harold Brown in 1965. Brown's observation is repeated here because it represents reflective wisdom:

> I never really changed my mind about that. It was really an argument between two doctrines. One was that the Army commander had to have control of whatever impacts on him just as he does on his artillery. The Air Force argument is that air is a unity. I'm afraid that neither of these is terribly convincing by itself. The argument, which from the Air Force point of view, I always found most convincing, the command ought to be determined on the basis of range, and that the range of the aircraft was 600 miles. And it shouldn't be at the disposal of anybody who didn't control that much of the front. If you give it to the Army, by that time it is already up to such a high level in the Army that it is no good to the guy who's calling in the close air support. To put it at Field Army level is really no better to the battalion commander than to give it to the Air Force. He doesn't really know the difference. The Army headquarters may know the difference, but he [the company or battalion commander] doesn't know the difference. That's why in the end we always argued, "Give it to the theater commander; he's the man who really is best able to balance demands between elements 600 miles apart." There's nobody in the Army who can, or in the Air Force either.[12]

Aircraft Acquisition Is Technology Development

Weapons acquisition is a process of managing performance, schedule, and cost. Users develop requirements from a projected threat, projected technology, and need, realizing that they will not get a product until much later. Most military aircraft programs after 1960 have taken about fifteen years from concept to an initial operational capability. The A-7 was much less because the performance and cost were constrained. As F-16 program manager Ron Yates said, "All aircraft systems are in a continuous state of development throughout their life cycle. We cannot be chagrined that new inventions come along to enrich the aircraft; we should be thankful. The issue is how we manage their incorporation into the aircraft."[13] Some officers in the Navy and many in the Air Force and OSD were critical of changing the gun and the improved navigation / weapon delivery upgrade in the A-7. Those changes delayed the schedule and increased the cost. Yet, many of those same officers participated in the decisions that led to those changes. It was relatively easy to see the benefits of changing from a slide mechanical cannon to the electric rotary cannon, which has now been standard on US fighter/attack aircraft and surface ships for forty-five years. It was harder at the time to see the revolutionary increase in performance from the IBM digitized navigation / weapons delivery system, which moved the whole weapons acquisition process to a higher level. We are the beneficiaries of that vision.

Program Management Innovation

Through this history of attack aircraft, we have seen the role of imaginative and forceful designers and program managers. Ed Heinemann at Douglas is probably the leading example of the designer with vision, boldness, tenacity, and salesmanship. The Navy class desk officer Lt. Cmdr. Hank Suerstadt was also a visionary, keeping the AD line open to increase production and adding armor plate to protect the aircraft in Korea. Twelve years later, he was the program manager for the A-7A, and B. Capt. Bob Doss and Col. Bob Hails shared the same vision to increase the capability and effectiveness of the A-7 aircraft by fostering and pushing the common gun and advanced navigation / weapons delivery system through the bureaucracies. All of these individuals were "innovation advocates" in the finest sense of the phrase. They faced the slings and arrows

of the arena and sometimes paid the price in their individual careers. The results were the A-7D and A-7E, which have been called "breakthrough aircraft" in the words of Jim Kitrick, A-7E pilot and CEO of the San Diego Air & Space Museum. The A-10, F-15, F-16, F/A-18, and F-35 program managers are similarly to be praised for taking the risks and championing the higher performance of their systems.

On Decision-Making with Computers

Our story spans the period in US history when aircraft design and mission analysis were more works of art than products of precise calculation. Calculators and slide rules were important to the aeronautical engineer, but there was little precision in comparing one aircraft to another in tactical situations. Test pilots were essential to verify or refute a given theory of design, but this essential community was not equipped to test tactics and techniques and procedures above the battlefield. In the 1960s, computers had progressed to the degree that they were becoming useful in sorting out many of the complexities both of the air-to-air battle and the tactical air-ground situation. Although each of the military and naval services had begun to incorporate computers into tactical analysis, what OSD Systems Analysis really did was to drive them to reinvent their analysis techniques and apply them to the complex issues of weapon system design and selection. By the end of the 1960s, the services were quite proficient in using this new tool, and their expertise has only increased since then. Now we have artificial intelligence that is aiding the design and production systems to higher and better outputs.

Computers can be thought of like a navigation aid. The first lesson is that all navigation is based on dead reckoning. *All* "navigation aids," such as GPS or radar, are devices to refine dead reckoning! All decision-making is human instinct to define the problem, while computers can eliminate unlikely outcomes and identify better solutions.

Dr. Brown, in another of his prophetic remarks, said it pretty well:

The computer was, I think, quite important. What it did was that it showed what I think computers are good for; it showed what's important. Then you go back, and you look at those and make the judgment on how that's likely to be. In other words, it tells you what characteristics and what premises govern the outcome of the study. Then you make a judgment on which of these premises is most likely to be right, and that tells you which is the right answer. It saves you from having to make a judgment of whether the A-7 is better than the F-5 based just on their characteristics or beauty, and allows you to make a judgment that the distance you will want to go is so and so far or that the increased accuracy which will require having aiming devices is going to be important. You decide that, and then it tells you what your choice should be.[14]

The "Doctrine of Quality"

It is a truism that Americans are in love with technology. And why not? At first, it was owning land that gave power, then it was capital, and now it is technology. The British were right when they identified the design and development of high quality as a key factor in military engagements. The high quality of Navy dive-bombing developed before World War II enabled Midway to be a victory. The high quality of American bombers in the 1930s was a precursor for the successful strategic-bombing campaign on Germany and Japan. The high quality of American fighter aircraft peaked after the bomber technology, but it was necessary to let the bombers proceed without unacceptable losses, and it provided air superiority over the Reich. Faster and tougher American fighters in the Pacific led to victory in battle after battle, virtually eliminating the Japanese air force.

Occasionally, there are attempts to limit technology to obtain a solution as merely "good enough." This is admirable and often the most prudent decision. Higher quality is expensive and slower to develop. In World War II, Charles Lindbergh was asked to tour B-24 factories and give his advice. He left the owners with a long list of improvements he said the bomber needed. Virtually none of them were implemented! It would have slowed up the production line!

The Navy and Douglas Aircraft designed the highest quality into the A-1 Skyraider. It had the best reciprocating engine in the world, a well-designed cockpit, the best guns and gunsight of the time, the most ordnance-carrying stations, and the best armor.

Conversely, the Navy did not design the A-7A to include the best technology. It did not have the best jet engine; it had only the best that Pratt & Whitney was then producing. It did not have the best guns. The Navy settled for a low-technology navigation / weapons delivery system, but it was "good enough" for an airplane that was already better, with longer range and a large bombload than its predecessor, the A-4.

The A-7D/E was a wake-up call for the Navy and the attack community. The Air Force, for a variety of reasons–not all of them supportive of the airplane—added a long list of quality improvements to the A-7B design in already production. Many were due to the unique operational venue of the Air Force (long, land-based runways that need drag chutes and antiskid brakes). Many others were due to differences in operations and logistics (refueling systems, a standardized instrument panel among fighters, M-61 cannon, armor, etc.). But others were the result of seeking higher quality: the higher-thrust Spey engine and the integrated digital computer. The Air Force did not want to settle for "good enough." This caused friction in program management, higher costs, and a lack of standardization between the A-7D and A-7E.

Ironically, when the Air Force got the chance to develop its own close-air-support/attack airplane—the A-10—it initially settled for a primitive navigation / weapons delivery system, which was recognized early in test and evaluation and led to a long and expensive set of upgrades to meet evolving operational requirements.

Attack Aircraft: The A-1 Skyraider

The Douglas A-1 has gained legendary status as the supreme close-air-support aircraft. It was the culmination of a long series of single-seat, load-carrying, reciprocating-engined aircraft. Barely missing World War II, it performed herculean missions in Korea and Vietnam. With fifteen stations for ordnance and four 20 mm cannons, it was built for ground and sea attack. Its weapons accuracy and extensive armor plate fulfilled all the lessons of attack from World Wars I and II and Korea. Its design, size, and power gave it a diversity of capabilities that allowed the armed services to assign the widest variety of missions, including CSAR. Air Force A-1 pilots pioneered the SANDY mission of escorting rescue helicopters and providing them close air support during the extraction phase. Later in the war, the A-7D took on this role. The A-1 provided four decades of service to the Navy, Marine Corps, and Air Force.

The A-4 Skyhawk

The Douglas A-4 began life as a carrier-based, nuclear-weapon-delivery vehicle. It had an easy conversion to conventional attack. The design's simplicity, small size, and low cost made it a very desirable follow-on to the A-1, especially to a Navy constrained with its budgets in the 1950s. It and the A-7A/B became the darling of the light-attack community as the last of the completely manual, accurate, dive-bombing machines of the fleet. The Marine Corps adopted the A-4 immediately and retained it, rather than switching to the A-7 in the mid-1960s.

The A-7 Corsair II

The A-7A was produced and deployed fleet-wide and played an important role in Southeast Asia beginning in 1967. The "A" was underpowered and was only marginally improved with the "B." The Air Force bought into the program in 1965 but almost immediately decided to *upgrade* the airplane. This resulted in a new engine, a new gun, and a completely new avionics / weapons delivery system with a heads-up display. That set of changes was a watershed in the history of aircraft development. For the first time, the power of personal computing was applied to airplanes, and the change was continued and improved on with subsequent types. The A-7D and E performed valiantly in Southeast Asia and continued in the Navy through Desert Storm. Unfortunately, it had a shorter active-duty life in the Air Force, and all squadrons were transferred to the Air National Guard by 1980.

The A-10 Thunderbolt II / Warthog

The A-10 was a little better liked because it was an Air Force idea. The A-10 might have been destined to a short life cycle like the A-7D, but it kept being needed to fight a whole series of regional wars, culminating in Desert Storm, the war on terror, and its lead-in to the wars in Iraq and Afghanistan. Nevertheless, a sizable portion of the A-10 force was reassigned to the Air National Guard. Despite frequent attempts to retire the Hog, it looks like the A-10 will be in the Air Force inventory through 2030. We should see in the decade of the 2020s whether there is a requirement and development program for a replacement. The role of the A-10 in the era of the F-35 is unclear, but its cheaper cost and unique capability have many supporters.

F-16 Lightweight Fighter / Viper

The F-16 was initially designed as an air-to-air fighter and was first flown in 1974. With its high maneuverability and low cost, the aircraft was easily modified to be an all-weather fighter and attack veteran, with over a dozen versions produced for more than a dozen countries around the world. It remains in 2020 the backbone of AF squadrons with attack capability.

F/A-18 Hornet

The Navy's development of the F/A-18 after the Lightweight Fighter competition is one of the marvels of aircraft improvement. Contrary to popular opinion, the F/A-18 was developed from but is not a copy of the YF-17. Northrup Grumman took an additional two years to advance the development of the airframe, engines, and avionics to a remarkable degree. The new aircraft improved performance with an advanced navigation / weapons delivery system and an integrated cockpit and produced air-to-air and air-to-ground capability. Harnessing advances in technology allowed the Navy to integrate fighter with attack missions and make dual-capable squadrons.

Since its introduction in 1983, the Hornet has performed remarkable well and is now entering its thirty-seventh year of operations. The original service life of 6,000 flight hours of the F/A-18C is being extended by the Marine Corps to 10,000 hours, and the Navy has modified the aircraft to the F/A-18 E/F Super Hornet. The weakness of the original Hornet was limited range. The Super Hornet mitigates that to a degree, but it still does not match the major feature of the Dauntless or the A-7 in this regard.

F-35 Lightning II

The Tri-Service F-35 marks the transition to the fifth-generation fighter, integrating the most-advanced sensor and data-computing capabilities into a versatile airframe. The combination of airframe, engine, and avionics allows the aircraft to operate like a weaponized mini-AWACS (Airborne Warning and Control System). Whether the cost allows a sufficient number to be produced and deployed remains to be seen. Similarly, will the high value and small numbers of this aircraft make it available for close air support?

Unmanned Aerial Vehicles

This book would not be complete if we neglected to discuss the contribution of unmanned aerial vehicles (UAVs) to the attack mission. They are all over the modern battlefield and our cities. But the UAV was an unlikely weapon in the 1960s. This now-potent system required breakthroughs in several technologies that were not mature in the 1960s: small, powerful engines; miniaturized electronics; precision guidance; command and control systems that would operate over long distances; and the global positioning system of satellites.

Many analysts and planners thought the next weapon after the airplane would be a missile. In 1956, the F-104 Starfighter was foolishly called "the Missile with a Man in It." Predictions abounded that missiles would replace manned aircraft in the air forces of the world. Nothing could have been more wrong. Not only did missiles *not* replace men, but the reliance on a missile-only fighter led to the poor performance of US F-4s in the early part of the Vietnam War. The accuracy and reliability of the gun and the firepower of the cannon increased in the 1970s, resulting in the 30 mm GAU-8 of the A-10. Missile refinement continued in both air-to-air and air-to-ground, leading to precision weapons, but none of them replaced the pilot.

It was left to unmanned aerial vehicles to, first, contribute to battlefield reconnaissance. Then it was modified to fire weapons, using the precision of the previously developed air-to-ground missiles. It continues to evolve to accept new missions.

The primary vehicles used by the US include the Predator MQ-1, Global Hawk RQ-4, Fire Scout R/MQ-8, Shadow RQ-7B, Raven RQ-11B, and larger Predator Reaper MQ-9. They all are assigned the letter "Q" as identifier. The original Predator was the MQ-1, which operated as early as 1995 in Bosnia. The Hellfire missile was added in 2001, and the UAV became a strike machine. In this configuration it was extremely successful in attacking Al-Qaeda and Taliban targets in Afghanistan, Yemen, and Iraq. In 2007, the Air Force stood up the 42nd Attack Squadron at Creech AFB, Nevada, primarily with pilots as controllers. Since then, nonrated officers and enlisted men also have been trained in this new specialty.

When it was realized that the F-35A Lightning II stealth fighter would have a limited range of 600 nm, the Air Force Research Laboratory and Kratos Defense Security Solutions started developing the XQ-58A Valkyrie, a low-cost UAV with a 1,500 nm combat radius. The XQ-58 could be flown independently or as a loyal wingman alongside manned aircraft. It also could be used in a "swarm" of hundreds of UAVs attacking a coastline or complex of targets.[15]

The Predator B (MQ-9; "Reaper") is the follow-on to the original. Produced by General Atomics, it flies at 240 knots and cruises up to 50,000 feet for twenty-seven hours. The total payload is 3,849 pounds. It carries a multitude of sensors and external payload of 3,000 pounds. Ordnance includes Hellfire missiles, GBU-12 Paveway II laser-guided 500-pound bombs, and the Joint Direct Attack Munition (JDAM). The USAF operated 195 MQ-9 Reapers as of September 2016 and plans to keep the MQ-9 in service into the 2030s.[16]

The Defense Advanced Research Projects Agency (DARPA), in coordination with the Air Force and Navy, sponsored research into an unmanned combat air vehicle (UCAV). The Air Force explored the Boeing X-45 to conduct the missions of suppression of enemy air defenses and electronic attack. The Navy contracted with Northrop Grumman to prototype the X-47, primarily for surveillance. The programs have now been combined into a single, joint UCAV program.

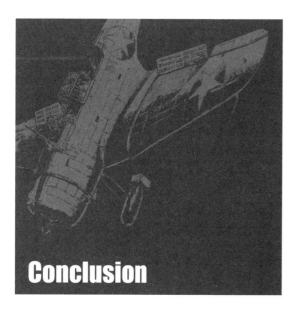

Conclusion

A erial warfare has changed dramatically over the last century. We have seen the design of aircraft evolve on the basis of the power of engines and the needs of the naval and military services. However, the missions that evolved out of World War I have been amazingly stable. The designs of the Air Force F-16 and the Navy F/A-18 were the first to truly combine the characteristics of fighter and attack aviation. The F-35 ushers in a whole new era of aircraft performance. It is ironic that the Navy was the strongest proponent of specialized attack aircraft but was also the first to merge the fighter and attack designation onto a single airframe, the F/A-18. I include the F-16 because it led this integration a couple of years earlier. The F-16 is a wonderful multirole fighter with an exceptionally long service life, but the F-16 is not the aircraft of choice for the close-air-support mission. That role belongs to the A-10. It will be interesting to see whether the Air Force continues specialization with a follow-on aircraft or relies more on UAVs. In any case, ground forces, special operations units, and specialized targets will continue to demand some kind of close-in attack capability.

Endnotes

INTRODUCTION

1. Department of Defense, US Joint Chiefs of Staff, *DoD Dictionary of Military and Associated Terms*, Joint Publication 1-02, updated February 15, 2013, 42.

2. Ibid. Online version, no page numbers.

3. Ibid.

4. Ibid.

5. The author instructed pilots and weapons systems officers in Navigation and Night Attack, and my colleague taught Air-Ground Operations. See Capt. Richard L. Kuiper, Air-Ground Operations (AGO), 4453rd Combat Crew Training Wing Replacement Training Unit Weapons School, 1966.

6. Tom Wolfe, *The Right Stuff* (New York: Picador, 1979), 13.

7. John Lehman, secretary of the Navy, "Is Naval Aviation Culture Dead?," *Proceedings*, September 2011.

8. T. S. Rippon (MD, MRCS, LRCP London, captain, RAMC; attached to Royal Air Force) and Lt. E. G. Manuel, RAF, "The Essential Characteristics of Successful and Unsuccessful Aviators," *The Lancet* 192, no. 4961 (September 28, 1918): 411.

9. In the period 1953–1957, hundreds of naval aviators were killed in 1,500 crashes per year, and those entering had less than a 25 percent probability of finishing twenty years. Lehman, "Is Naval Aviation Culture Dead?"

CHAPTER 1

1. Oswald Boelcke's brother, Wilhelm, was awarded the Iron Cross First Class in 1914 for "covering a total distance of 6,500 kilometers over the enemy's soil, while I have covered 3,400." Oswald Boelcke, *An Aviator's Field Book: The Memoirs of a 40 Victory Ace* (Gotha, Germany: Friedrich Andreas, 1917), translated by Robert Reynold Hirsch and reprinted (Nashville: Battery, 1991), 43.

2. This story is told in RG Head, *Oswald Boelcke: Germany's First Fighter Ace and Father of Air Combat* (London: Grub Street, 2016).

3. See Royal Flying Corps in https://en.wikipedia.org/wiki/Royal FlyingCorps#Origin_and_early years.

4. As quoted in H. A. Jones, *The War in the Air: Being the Part Played by the Royal Air Force*, vol. 2 (Oxford: Claredon, 1922–1937), 271–72; and in Head, *Oswald Boelcke*, 104–05.

5. For Trenchard's priorities, see Royal Flying Corps in Wikipedia. For an excellent primer on pilot training, combat, and psychological stress, see Denis Winter, *The First of the Few: Fighter Pilots of the First World War* (Athens: University of Georgia Press, 1982), especially chapter 13, "Physical Strain"; and Ian Mackersey, *No Empty Chairs* (London: Orion, 2012).

6. Rick Duiven and Dan-San Abbott, *Schlachtflieger! Germany and the Origins of Air/Ground Support* (Atglen, PA: Schiffer Military History, 2006), 15.

7. Ibid., 15.

8. Ibid.

9. Ibid., 19.

10. Ibid., 25. The Junkers JI also is described in Jack Herris and Bob Pearson, *Aircraft of World War I: 1914–1918* (London: Amber Books, 2010).

11. Ibid., "Weapons," 171–74.

12. Ibid., "Infantry Support," 25–33.

13. Major a.D. Hans Arndt, quoted in Friedrich Sesselberg, *Der Stellungskrieg, 1914–1918*; cited in Duiven and Abbott, *Schlachtflieger!*, 25.

14. Duiven and Abbott, *Schlachtflieger!*, 367.

15. Ibid., 38.

16. Ibid., 45–46.

17. The First World War Forum, "The War in the Air," Firstworldwar.com/airwr/groundattack htm.

18. Cited by Maj. (later general) Ron Fogleman, USAF chief of staff, "The Development of Ground Attack Aviation in the United States Army Air Arm: Evolution of a Doctrine, 1908–1926" (MA thesis, Duke University, 1971), 48. This portion was derived from Walter Raleigh and H. A. Jones, *The War in the Air: Being the Story of the Part Played in the Great War by the Royal Air Force* (Sussex, UK: Naval & Military Press, 2002), 4:323–27. The entire memo is reprinted in the appendixes in Fogleman, "The Development of Ground Attack Aviation," 92. Fogleman was a 1962 graduate of the US Air Force Academy, became a fighter pilot, flew two F-100 tours in Vietnam, and was a captain, just promoted to major when he was awarded his master's degree from Duke, en route to teaching history at the academy.

19. Ibid.

20. Lee Kennett, "Developments to 1939," in Benjamin Franklin Cooling, ed., *Case Studies in the Development of Close Air Support* (Washington, DC: USGPO, 1990), 23–24.

21. Kennett, "Developments to 1939," 19, which in turn cites Jones, *The War in the Air*, appendixes XII and IV, 433–38.

22. Kennett, "Developments to 1939," 19.

23. "The War in the Air," firstworldwar.com/airwar/groundattack.htm, 1.

24. Maurer Mauer, ed., *The US Air Service in World War I*, vol. 1, *The Final Report and a Tactical History* (Maxwell AFB, AL: Albert F. Simpson Historical Research Center, 1978), 51. This series of four volumes is the most authoritative

history of the Air Service in the Great War. Available from the Office of Air Force History, Headquarters USAF, Washington, DC.

25. Cited by Herbert Molloy Mason Jr., *The Lafayette Escadrille* (New York: Random House, 1964), 230.

26. *Final Report of the Chief of Air Service*, as taken from Air Service Information Circular (Aviation), vol. II, no. 180, 15 February 1921, known as the "Gorrell's History of the Air Service, AEF," or simply "Gorrell's History." The final report is reprinted in Maurer, *The US Air Service in World War I*, 1:15–163. Gorrell's description of Maj. Dodd and Lt. Col. Mitchell is in Maurer, *The US Air Service in World War I*,1:51–52. For a more detailed view of the breadth and intensity of the dispute between Air Service officers and the Signal Corps, see Dwight R. Messimer, *An Incipient Mutiny: The Story of the US Army Signal Corps Pilot Revolt* (Lincoln: University of Nebraska Press, 2020).

27. Ibid., 54.

28. Maurer, *The US Air Service in World War I*, 1:101.

29. Ibid., 1:110.

30. Ibid., 1:113.

31. Ibid., 1:357–58.

32. Brig. Gen. William Mitchell, *Memoirs of World War I: From Start to Finish of Our Greatest War* (New York: Random House, 1960), originally copyrighted in 1928, 241–42.

33. Ibid., 240.

34. Maurer, *The US Air Service in World War I*, vol. 3, *The Battle of St. Mihiel*; and Maurer, *The US Air Service in World War I*, 1:43–49.

35. Ibid., 1:38–39.

36. Ibid., 1:43.

37. Ibid., 1:117.

38. Ibid., published as Air Service Information Circular, lI, no. 180 (Washington, DC: USGPO, 1921), 21, as cited in Fogleman, "The Development of Ground Attack Aviation," 57.

39. "Air Intelligence, Summary," April 4, 1918, cited in Fogleman, "The Development of Ground Attack Aviation," 84.

40. Ibid., 119.

41. Third Army, AEF, *Provisional Manual of Operations for Air Service Units*, 23 December 1918, 32–34, cited in Fogleman, "The Development of Ground Attack Aviation," 62.

42. Col. E. S. Gorrell, "Notes on Employment of the Air Service from the General Staff Viewpoint," cited in Fogleman, "The Development of Ground Attack Aviation," 64.

43. US Air Force Air University, *The Development of Air Doctrine in the Army Air Arm, 1917–1941* (Gunter Air Force Base, AL: Extension Course Institute, 1961), 39.

44. Fogleman, "The Development of Ground Attack Aviation," 64–65.

45. William Mitchell, brigadier general, USA, Army Air Service commander, Third Army, American Expeditionary Forces, Coblenz, Germany, December 23, 1918. Reprinted in Maurer, *The US Air Service in World War I*, 2:267, 291.

46. Maurer, *The US Air Service in World War I*, 1:51.

47. *New York Times*, May 31, 1913; June 22, 1913; and July 26, 29, and 30, 1913.

48. Mark L. Evans and Roy A. Grossnick, *United States Naval Aviation: 1910–2010*, vol. 1, *Chronology*, 5th ed.

(Washington, DC: Naval History and Heritage Command, 2015), 35.

49. Ibid., 1:46.

50. "US-Built Naval Aircraft in Action," *Roads to the Great War*, March 9, 2020.

51. Evans and Grossnick, *United States Naval Aviation: 1910–2010*, 1:55.

52. Ibid., 1:59.

CHAPTER 2

1. Fogleman, "The Development of Ground Attack Aviation," 65–66.

2. Gen. Carl Spaatz quote from RG Head, ed., *Contrails: The Air Force Cadet Handbook* (Colorado Springs, CO: US Air Force Academy, 1960), 195.

3. Mark St. John Erickson, "Battleship Bombings of July 1921 Marked Milestone Step in Development of Air Power," *Daily Press* (Newport News, VA), July 20, 2018.

4. Ibid.

5. Ibid.

6. James P. Tate, *The Army and Its Air Corps Policy toward Aviation, 1919–1941* (Maxwell AFB, AL: Air University Press, June 1998), 141.

7. Wikipedia, "History of the 3rd Group."

8. Kennett, "Developments to 1939," 46–47.

9. Joe Gray Taylor, "American Experience in the Southwest Pacific," In Cooling, *Case Studies in the Development of Close Air Support*, 310–12.

10. Fogleman, "The Development of Ground Attack Aviation," 84.

11. John F. Shiner, *Foulois and the US Army Air Corps: 1931–1935* (Washington, DC: Office of Air Force History, 1983), 108–22.

12. Thomas H. Greer, *The Development of Air Doctrine in the Army Air Arm: 1917–1941* (Washington, DC: Office of Air Force History, 1955), 87.

13. Kenneth Munson, *Bombers between the Wars, 1919–1939* (New York: Macmillan, 1970), 160.

14. Online Aviation History Museum, www.Theonline aviationhistorymuseum.org.

15. Ibid.

16. J. Rickard, "Northrop A-17," http://www.historyofwar. org/articles/weapons_Northrop_A-17.html, October 6, 2008.

17. Greer, *The Development of Air Doctrine in the Army Air Arm*, 87.

18. Merton Peck and Frederic M. Scherer, *The Weapons Acquisition Process: An Economic Analysis* (Cambridge, MA: Harvard Business School, 1962), 619.

19. Greer, *The Development of Air Doctrine in the Army Air Arm*, 87.

20. Ibid., 122, "Air Board Report," September 15, 1939, tab D, 1–2.

21. The author held the top gun award for strafing in his F-4E 90th TFS.

22. Greer, *The Development of Air Doctrine in the Army Air Arm*, 111, 113–115.

23. Ibid., 122.

24. David Mondey, *The Concise Guide to American Aircraft of World War II* (London: Chancellor, 1996).

25. David Brazelton, "The Douglas SBD Dauntless," *Profile Publications* 94 (Leatherhead, UK: Profile Publications, 1966), 5–6.

26. Ibid.

27. US Navy, Bureau of Aeronautics, *Attack Plane Design History: US Navy to 1957* (Washington, DC: Bureau of Aeronautics, 1957), 77. Attributed to Lee Pearson. Copy available at the San Diego Air & Space Museum Library.

28. J. Rickard, "Curtiss A-25 Shrike," http://www.historyofwar.org/articles/weapons_A-25.html, June 15, 2007.

29. US Congress, Special Committee to Investigate the National Defense Program, *Investigation of the National Defense Program, Additional Report*, 78th Congress, 1st Session, July 10, 1943, also known as the Truman Committee, 1, 7–9, 14.

30. Remarks by RAdm. Sam Cox, director, Naval History and Heritage Command, on Midway Island, June 5, 2017.

31. B. H. Liddell Hart, *History of the Second World War* (New York: Putnam & Sons, 1970), 12.

32. Heinz W. Guderian, *Achtung-Panzer! The Development of Armoured Forces, Their Tactics and Operational Potential* (London: Arms and Armour, 1992), 198; originally published as *Achtung-Panzer! Die Entwicklung der Panzerwaffe, ihre Kampftaktik und ihre operativen Möglichkeiten* (Stuttgart: Union Deutsche Verlagsgesellschaft, 1937), as cited in Maj. Ainsworth H. O'Reilly, *The Better Blitzkrieg: A Comparison of Tactical Airpower Use by Guderian and Patton* (Maxwell AFB, AL: Air University, Air Command and Staff College, April 2010), 3.

33. O'Reilly, *The Better Blitzkrieg*, 4.

34. Guderian, *Achtung-Panzer!*, 128.

35. "Definition of Close Air Support," in Department of Defense, US Joint Chiefs of Staff, *DoD Dictionary of Military and Associated Terms*, Joint Publication 1-02, 42.

36. Kennett, "Developments to 1939," 32–33.

37. Robert W. Gruenhagen, *Mustang: The Story of the P-51 Fighter* (New York: Arco, 1969), 54–61.

38. Scott Schwartz, "A-36 Apache," Online Aviation History Museum, http://www.aviation-history.com/north-american/a36.html.

39. Perry Smith, *The Air Force Plans for Peace: 1943–1945* (Baltimore: Johns Hopkins University Press, 1970). See also Ray Wagner and Edgar Schmued, *Designing the P-51* (New York: Orion, 1990).

40. Warren M. Bodie, *Republic P-47 Thunderbolt: From Seversky to Victory* (Haiesville, GA: Widewing, 1994), 5.

41. Ibid., 7.

42. National Museum of the US Air Force.

43. Cited in W. A. Jacobs, "Operation Overlord," in Benjamin Franklin Cooling, *Case Studies in the Achievement of Air Superiority* (Washington, DC: Air Force History and Museums Program, 1994), 273; extracted from the RAF Historical Branch, "Luftwaffe Strength and Serviceability Tables, 1938–1945," USAF Historical Research Center (AFHRC) K5002, fr 0432-5.

44. "Republic P-47D-30-RA Thunderbolt (Long Description)." Smithsonian National Air and Space Museum.

45. F. G. Swanborough, *United States Military Aircraft since 1919* (New York: Putnam, 1963), 239.

46. John T. Correll, "The Difference in Korea," *Air Force Magazine*, April 2020, 57

47. Col. Vincent J. Esposito, ed., *The West Point Atlas of American Wars*, vol. 2 (New York: Frederick A. Praeger, 1959), x1, following map 71 and following map, p. 168.

48. Correll, "The Difference in Korea," 58.

49. Brig. Gen. Henry P. Viccellio, commander Nineteenth Air Force, "Composite Air Strike Force," *Air University Review* 9, no. 1 (Winter 1956–57): 27–38.

50. Allan R. Millett, "Korea, 1950–1953," in Cooling, *Case Studies on the Development of Close Air Support*, 371.

51. Ibid., 388–89.

CHAPTER 3

1. Charles M. Melhorn, *Two-Block Fox: The Rise of the Aircraft Carrier, 1911–1929* (Annapolis, MD: Naval Institute Press, 1974), 107.

2. Ibid., 9.

3. Ibid., 33.

4. Ibid., 90.

5. Ibid., 84.

6. Ibid., 94.

7. Ibid., 114. The identification of the aircraft in the strike was provided by Hill Goodspeed, curator of the National Naval Aviation Museum, Pensacola, Florida, in a communication to the author, November 30, 2019. The author is indebted to him for many other insights into naval aviation.

8. Letter, US Naval Department, Office of Naval Operations, Washington, "Future Policy Governing Development of Air Service for the United States Navy," to "the Solicitor," August 28, 1919. National Archives, R.G.-80, Secretary of the Navy General Files, 1897–1925, file 11158-71.

9. Melhorn, *Two-Block Fox*, 110.

10. Ibid., 111.

11. Maj. Burwell, commanding officer, in testimony before the Morrow Board, in Fogleman, "The Development of Ground Attack Aviation," 82, citing John H. Jouett, *A History of the Third Attack Group Attack Section* (Department of Air Tactics and Strategy, Air Corps Tactical School, 1923–1941), 48, 55.

12. Thomas Wildenberg, *Destined for Glory: Dive Bombing, Midway, and the Evolution of Carrier Airpower* (Annapolis, MD: Naval Institute Press, 1998), 12.

13. Ibid., 13.

14. Ibid., 13–14.

15. Ibid., xiv.

16. Ibid., 110. Wildenberg's reference for this is Wagner's letter to Commander Dater, December 30, 1948, National Museum of Naval Aviation. VF-2 had only six F6Cs at that time.

17. Wildenberg, *Destined for Glory*, 16. Note: Evans and Grossnick wrote that the area was only 100 by 45 feet and that Wagner's flight hit with nineteen out of forty-five bombs. Evans and Grossnick, *United States Naval Aviation: 1910–2010*, 96.

18. Hill Goodspeed, "Foundation for Victory: US Navy Aircraft Development, 1922–1945," in Douglas V. Smith, ed., *One Hundred Years of US Navy Air Power* (Annapolis, MD: Naval Institute Press, 2010), 205; Goodspeed cites Wildenberg, *Destined for Glory*, 114.

19. Interviews with Navy and Marine Corps pilots; and Capt. C. O. Holmquist's excellent portrayal, "Developments and Problems in Carrier-Based Attack Aircraft," in *Naval Review: 1969*, ed. Frank Uhlig Jr. (Annapolis, MD: Naval Institute Press, 1969), 195–215.

20. The selection of the Navy's top attack aircraft before 1961 was made by Hill Goodspeed, National Naval Aviation Museum, Pensacola, Florida, and sent to the author on August 20, 2019. Hill's list included the SBD Dauntless, SB2C Helldiver, TBF/TBM Avenger, AD/A-1 Skyraider, AF Guardian, A3D Skywarrior, T3M/T4M, F4U Corsair, De Havilland DH-4, and BM. The author added the P-47 Thunderbolt and the A-4D/A-4 to this list to bring it to a dozen.

21. J. M. Bruce, *The de Havilland D.H.4*, Profile Publications 26 (Leatherhead, UK: Profile Publications, n.d.), 3.

22. The Final Report of the Chief of the Air Service [Maj. Gen. Mason M. Patrick], informally known as "Gorrell's History," in Maurer, *The US Air Service in World War I*, 1:25.

23. The author was commander of the 90th Tactical Fighter Squadron, which derived its heritage from the 90th Aero Squadron that flew the DH-4 as part of the American Expeditionary Force in France.

24. http://www.navypedia.org/arms/usa/us_air_t3m.htm.

25. "Martin BM," https://military.wikia.org/wiki/Martin_BM.

26. US Navy, Bureau of Aeronautics, *Attack Plane Design History*, 60. Copy available at the San Diego Air & Space Museum Library.

27. David Brazelton, "The Douglas SBD Dauntless," 2–3.

28. David Doyle, *SBD Dauntless: Douglas's US Navy and Marine Corps Dive-Bomber in World War II* (Atglen, PA: Schiffer Military, 2019), 8.

29. Ibid.

30. US Navy, Bureau of Aeronautics, *Attack Plane Design History*, 16.

31. Ibid., 51.

32. Ibid.

33. Ibid.

34. Interview with RAdm. Lewis R. Hopkins (USN, Ret.), Center for Pacific War Studies, Admiral Nimitz Historic Site–National Museum of the Pacific War, Fredericksburg, Texas, January 28, 2004, 10–11.

35. Ibid., 14–16.

36. Ibid., 18–20.

37. Cited in Ed Beakley's *1942: The Year of the Aircraft Carrier*, part 5—Midway Trilogy (1 of 3), Blown Slick series 13, on The Remembered Sky website, posted on June 4, 2018.

38. William Green, "Vought F4U-1, F4U-4 (FG-1 Corsair)," in *War Planes of the Second World War*, vol. 4, *Fighters* (Garden City, NY: Doubleday, 1973), 188.

39. RAdm. Lewis R. Hopkins interview, January 28, 2004, 27.

40. Edward Jablonski, *Airwar* (New York: Doubleday, 1979).

41. S. B. Barber, *Naval Aviation Combat Statistics: World War II*, OPNAV-P-23V no. A129 (Washington, DC: Air Branch, Office of Naval Intelligence, 1946), table 1, as cited in Vought F4U Corsair, Military Wiki.

42. Ibid., table 2.

43. Edward H. Heinemann and Rosario Rausa, *Ed Heinemann, Combat Aircraft Designer* (Annapolis, MD: Naval Institute Press, 1988), 104.

44. Rosario Rausa, *Skyraider: The Douglas A-1 "Flying Dump Truck"* (Cambridge, UK: Patrick Stevens, 1982).

45. US Navy, Bureau of Aeronautics, *Attack Plane Design History*, 47.

46. Ibid.

47. Ibid., 50.

48. Ibid., 61.

49. Heinemann and Rausa, *Ed Heinemann, Combat Aircraft Designer*, 129.

50. Ibid., 199.

51. As cited in Harry Gann, *The Douglas Skyraider*, Profile Publications 60 (Leatherhead, UK: Profile Productions, 1965), 8.

52. Rausa, *Skyraider*, 89.

53. Ibid., 91.

54. Ibid., 91–92.

55. Ibid., 92.

56. Ibid.

57. Ibid.

58. Ibid., 95.

59. Gann, *The Douglas Skyraider*, 8.

60. Although the policy of "Massive Retaliation" is commonly attributed to Secretary of State John Foster Dulles, it was actually part of the "New Look" strategy that was developed by the Eisenhower administration in 1953. For an in-depth analysis of this national strategy, see Glenn H. Snyder, "The 'New Look' of 1953," in Warren R. Schilling, Paul Y. Hammond, and Glenn H. Snyder, *Strategy, Politics and Defense Budgets* (New York: Columbia University Press, 1962), 379–524.

61. Vincent Davis, *The Politics of Innovation: Patterns in Navy Cases*, Social Science Foundation and Graduate School of International Studies, Monograph Series in World Affairs 4.3 (Denver, CO: University of Denver: 1966–67).

62. Cited in Lt. Cmdr. A. Dodge McFall, "Farewell to Spads," *US Naval Institute Proceedings*, April 1965, 56.

63. Rausa, *Skyraider*, 219–23.

64. Heinemann and Rausa, *Ed Heinemann, Combat Aircraft Designer*, 218.

65. Ibid., 220.

66. Harry Gann, *The Douglas A-4 Skyhawk*, Profile Publications 102 (Leatherhead, UK: Profile Publications, 1966.

67. Ibid., 13.

68. Terry Wolf email to the author, August 2019.

69. Ed Beakley, personnel communication to the author, March 14, 2020.

70. Gann, *The Douglas A-4 Skyhawk*, 4–5.

71. Terry Wolf, letter to the author, August 23, 2019.

72. Tommy Thompson, *Scooter: The Story of the A-4 Skyhawk* (Manchester, UK: Crecy, 2011).

73. Correspondence with the author, August 2019.

CHAPTER 4

1. John F. Kennedy, State of the Union address, January 30, 1961.

2. Robert S. McNamara, statement before the House Committee on Armed Services Committee, Hearings on Military Posture, House of Representatives, 1962, 3, 162.

3. Arthur M. Schlesinger Jr., *A Thousand Days* (New York: Fawcett Crest, 1965), 293–94.

4. Author's interview with Victor Heyman, Systems Analysis, March 12, 1970.

5. Interview with Lt. Gen Graham, vice commander, Tactical Air Command, February 11, 1970.

6. Green, *The World's Fighting Planes*, 193.

7. RAdm. Chatham, personal correspondence with the author, March 16, 2020.

8. Chris Hobson and David Lovelady, Vietnam Air Losses: United States Air Force, Navy, and Marine Corps Fixed-Wing Aircraft Losses in Southeast Asia: 1961–1973 (database on the internet).

9. RAdm. Chatham, personal correspondence with the author, March 16, 2020.

10. Personal correspondence with the author, August 2019.

11. Adm. Edney, personal communication to the author, March 11, 2020.

12. Ibid.

13. VAdm. Spane interview, March 6, 2020. The Cmdr. Netherland story is told in the *Coronado Eagle and Journal* 86, no. 4 (January 26, 1996).

14. Personal correspondence to the author, March 9, 2020.

15. Cited by John J. Sbrega in his case study of "Southeast Asia" in Cooling, *Case Studies in the Development of Close Air Support*, 411. Sbrega cites file K239.034-4, 65/01/01-68/01/01, 33, in the USAF Historical Research Center.

16. Bill Walton, "Six Things You Probably Never Knew about the Mighty A-6 Intruder," Avgeekery.com, April 18, 2017.

17. Andi Biancur, email to the author, November 13, 2019.

18. Lt. Gen. Harry W. O. Kinnard, commander, 1st Cavalry Division (Airmobile), "A Victory in the Ia Drang: The Triumph of a Concept," *Army* magazine, September 1967, as reprinted in Capt. Richard L. Kuiper, Air-Ground Operations (AGO), 4453rd Combat Crew Training Wing Replacement Training Unit Weapons School, 1966, 10-4.

19. Col. Richard L. Kuiper, USAF (ret.), personal correspondence to the author, March 10, 2020.

20. The fight for these two battles is wondrously told in Lt. Col. (later lieutenant general) Hal Moore and Joseph L. Galloway's book *We Were Soldiers Once . . . and Young* (New York: Random House, 1992) and the movie of the same name, starring Mel Gibson. In the battle for LZ Albany, Capt. Kuiper credited the author for shooting a NVA sniper out of a tree, 20 meters in front of US troops.

21. Sbrega, "Southeast Asia," 451.

22. There are multiple tellings of this story. This is the short version as related by Byron Hukee, *USAF and VNAF A-1 Skyraider Units of the Vietnam War* (Oxford: Osprey, 2013), 41–42.

23. Thomas E. Gardner, *F-100 Super Sabre at War* (St. Paul, MN: Zenith, 2007), 35–36. For stories of the F-100 in the Vietnam War, see David A. Anderton, *North American F-100 Super Sabre* (London: Osprey, 1987).

24. Lawrence Spinetta, "Misty Fast FACs," *Aviation History*, July 2009.

25. Gen. Ron Fogleman, videotape, Misty Fast FAC Pilots Panel, part 4, *Air Force Association Blog*, https://www.youtube.com/watch?v=SZVGx4lNeho.

26. Spinetta, "Misty Fast FACs."

27. Ibid. For more complete documentaries of the Mistys, see Don Shepperd, *"Misty": First Person Stories of the F-100 Misty Fast FACs in the Vietnam War, by the Misty FACs Themselves* (Bloomington, IN: AuthorHouse, 2003); and Don Shepperd and Rick Newman, *Bury Us Upside Down: The Misty Pilots and the Secret Battle for the Ho Chi Minh Trail* (New York: Random House, 2006).

28. Hobson and Lovelady, Vietnam Air Losses.

29. "A-1 versus A-7 CAS/SAR Role," *A-1 Skyraider Association Newsletter*, August 1975, 2.

30. Ibid.

31. Wikipedia.

32. Author's information from other pilots at the event.

33. Craig White, "Korat Thud Tour, 1967," in Col. Dennis M. Ridnouer, ed., *The Vietnam Air War: From the Cockpit* (North Charleston, SC: CreateSpace, 2017), 93–94.

34. Ibid.

35. https://vietnamairlosses.com/index/statistics/usaf-losses.

36. De Capo Press, Lebanon, Indiana, 2019.

37. The author flew the F-4C, F-4D, and F-4E models. See "Yankee Phantom Flyer on Three Continents," in Richard Pike, *Phantom Boys*, vol. 2 (London: Grub Street, 2017), 159–168.

38. Wikipedia.

39. Brig. Gen. Robin Olds, Christina Olds, and Ed Rasimus, *Fighter Pilot: The Memoirs of Legendary Ace Robin Olds* (New York: St. Martin's Griffin, 2010).

40. John T. Correll, "The Vietnam War Almanac," *Air Force Magazine*, September 2004.

41. US Congress, Senate Committee on Government Operations, TFX C+ Investigation, hearing before the Permanent Subcommittee on Investigations of the Committee on Government Operations, 88th Congress., 1st Session, Part 3, p. 1462 (hereafter referred to as the TFX Hearings).

42. Letter, Capt. Doss to the author, October 25, 1970.

43. Memorandum for the Record, March 1, 1963, prepared by Mr. Blackburn to summarize the TFX decision process after he heard of the Senate investigation of the contract award. Blackburn had been intimately associated with the TFX since its inception in the previous administration in 1959. Memorandum reprinted in the TFX Hearings, Part 5, p. 1203.

44. Exhibit 42 in TFX Hearings, Part 6, pp. 1513–1514.

45. The competition and award of the TFX contract are extensively covered in the TFX Hearings and developed in narrative in Robert J. Art, *The TFX Decision* (Boston: Little, Brown & Co., 1968).

46. Ibid., 78.

CHAPTER 5

1. *Aviation Week and Space Technology*, April 15, 1963, 37.

2. Alain C. Enthoven interview, April 8, 1970.

3. *Aviation Week and Space Technology*, June 15, 1964, 110. Interview with Mr. George Hearing, Office of the CNO, April 29, 1970. Hearing at the time (1963) was employed by the Operations Evaluation Group, which evolved into the current Center for Naval Analysis (CNA), a federally funded research-and-development center (FFRDC) nonprofit corporation. Hearing was the air attack task leader and wrote the "Gross Offensive Cost Effectiveness, Tab A," in the final report. In addition, he briefed Secretary of the Navy Fred Korth, Dr. Enthoven, and Secretary McNamara on the study.

4. *Flight International*, June 18, 1964, reported that the range requirement for the study was 600–700 miles (p. 1025). *Aviation Week and Space Technology*, June 15, 1964, quoted the combat radius as 621 nautical miles and gave the "close to 100 percent" figure (p. 112).

5. Chief of Naval Operations, *Sea-Based Air Strike Forces Study for the Secretary of Defense* (U), May 17, 1963, Part II, p. A-7. Unclassified extract cited by Mr. Hearing, interview, August 13, 1970. The cost relationship of three light-attack aircraft to one VAX was cited in *Aviation Week and Space Technology*, June 15, 1964, 12.

6. Hearing interview.

7. Ibid.

8. Chief of Naval Operations, *Sea-Based Air Strike Forces Study for the Secretary of Defense* (U), May 17, 1963; and *Aviation Week and Space Technology*, June 10, 1963, 25.

9. *Aviation Week and Space Technology*, April 15, 1963, 37.

10. Alain C. Enthoven interview, April 8, 1970.

11. Interview with Mr. Murray, April 28, 1970.

12. Specific Operational Requirement No. W11-26 (Follow-on Light Attack Aircraft) (U), May 17, 1993.

13. *Aviation Week and Space Technology*, August 12, 1963, 26.

14. Memorandum from the chief, Bureau of Naval Weapons, to all assistant chiefs, May 15, 1963. Project Master Plan, vol. 1, June 30, 1968, 1-5-1.

15. Interview with Mr. J. W. Langford, Vought Aeronautics director of marketing, April 1, 1970.

16. Hearing interview, August 13, 1970; and Murray interview, April 28, 1970.

17. Interview with George Spangenberg, August 17, 1970.

18. LYV advertisements often carried the boast "Thayer's organization has a higher ratio of ex–fighter pilots in management and engineering than any other company." Until 1968, when the company became deeply concerned with its image among Air Force officials, it was almost completely Navy oriented. Between 1968 and 1970, many Air Force pilots were hired by the company, including Gen. Gabriel Disosway, former commander, Tactical Air Command.

19. Interview with Mr. Langford, April 1, 1970, at Vought, where he was promoted to be the director of marketing.

20. Sol Love's reference to the Office of the Secretary of Defense (OSD) as DoD is interesting. The author found this characterization common among Navy and Navy-oriented officials, merging the secretary's office as representing the whole of the Department of Defense and associating the entire organization as being something outside the Navy. Of course, DoD is unique among federal governmental organizations in that the Department of Defense houses in itself the Departments of the Army, Navy, and Air Force. Indeed, the history of the Navy's opposition to the creation of DoD during and after World War II is a matter of record. It was not until the passage of the National Security Act of 1947 that this controversy was officially decided and DoD was created. In the author's service in the Pentagon, 1978–1983, as the assistant to the director of the Joint Staff for Joint Matters, he was the director's action officer for the proposals to elevate the chairman of the Joint Chiefs of Staff to a position slightly higher than the other chiefs and make him the principal military advisor to the secretary of defense, the National Security Council, and the president and to give him a four-star deputy vice chairman who would rank number two in the chiefs hierarchy. After years of additional controversy in which the Navy's view was repeatedly in opposition, the argument was partially settled by the passage of the Goldwater-Nichols Department of Defense Reorganization Act of 1986. See Gordon Lederman, *Reorganizing the Joint Chiefs of Staff: The Goldwater-Nichols Act of 1986*, Contributions in Military Studies 182 (Westport, CT: Greenwood, 1999); and James R. Locher III, *Victory on the Potomac: The Goldwater-Nichols Act Unifies the Pentagon* (College Station: Texas A&M University Press, 2002).

21. Interview with Sol Love, April 2, 1970. His reference to the validity of the Navy requirements will take on more meaning when it is contrasted with the LTV view of the AF requirements process later in the study.

22. LTV, V-463 Light Attack Airplane (VA)L Primer (U), undated [1963]. Hereafter referred to as the VAL Primer.

23. Ibid., 2.2.2.

24. Ibid.

25. Ibid., 5.1.2.

26. Ibid.

27. Interview with Pierre Sprey. Grumman was to perform essentially the Navy portion of the TFX development program.

28. Interview with George Spangenberg, August 17, 1970.

29. *Aviation Week and Space Technology*, March 10, 1964, 17.

30. Bureau of Naval Weapons memorandum RAEV:GS of November 4, 1963, as cited in Cmdr. Leroy B. Keely, *Evolution of the A-7 Attack Aircraft* (Fort Belvoir, VA: Defense Systems Management School, May 20, 1972), 8.

31. Murray interview, April 28, 1970.

32. Ibid. For George Spangenberg's position on the Navy F-111B, see TFX Hearings, Part 2, pp. 423–525.

33. Enthoven interview, April 8, 1970.

34. Interview with Dr. Brown at California Institute of Technology, April 8, 1970.

35. The evidence for this characterization is based on many views of the decision process and was stated clearly by Russ Murray in an interview on April 28, 1970. "The Navy 1963 decision would have gone that way even if Systems Analysis had not been there." Similarly, Victor Heyman supported this view in his interview, March 12, 1970: "The decision to buy the [LTV] A-7 as against any other VAL was a Navy decision. It was not at all an OSD decision."

36. It should be understood by the reader that Pierre Sprey is an acknowledged iconoclast and was one of OSD's resident critics. At the time of the competition in 1963, he was not in Systems Analysis but was working for Grumman as a research scientist. He had a BE in mechanical engineering and an MS in statistics and was an "all but dissertation" (ABD) PhD. His view was not that Grumman should have won the competition, but that Douglas should have. His views are important because they represent a continuing Systems Analysis position of a hard and critical look at military requirements and a preference for low-cost, simple aircraft, which persisted through 1970 and can be distinguished by the office's pressure on the F-15/F-16 programs and their support for the emergent AX. Interviews with Pierre Sprey, October 1969 and March 1970.

37. Confirmed by the person who asked the question, Victor Heyman, interview, March 12, 1970.

38. Reprogramming is covered by DoD Directive No. 7250.5, March 4, 1963, and DoD Instruction 7250.10, March 5, 1963. The latter document reads, "Reprogramming actions are defined as changes in the application of financial resources

from the purposes originally contemplated and budgeted for, testified to, and described in the justification submitted to the Congressional Committees in support of fund authorization and budget requests."

39. US Congress, House of Representatives Committee on Armed Services, *Department of Defense Reprogramming of Appropriated Funds: A Case Study*, report of the Subcommittee for Special investigations of the Committee on Armed Services, 89th Congress, 1st Session, July 8, 1965, 12 (hereafter called the Reprogramming Report).

40. Ibid., 32.

41. *Aviation Week*, December 23, 1963.

42. Reprogramming Report, 13, 14.

43. Ibid., 3–4.

44. *Aviation Week*, March 30, 1964, 16.

45. Ibid.

46. Ibid.

47. Robert F. Dorr, *Vought A-7 Corsair II* (London: Osprey,1985), 28

48. This section draws heavily on the writing of Robert F. Dorr in his *Vought A-7 Corsair II* and his chapter "Devil's Advocate" in *Dallas: Design, Development and Flight Test*. By permission of Dorr's son, Robert Porter Dorr. See 34ff.

49. Ibid., 35.

50. Ibid., 36.

51. Ibid., 43.

52. Ibid.

53. Ibid., 43–44.

54. Ibid., 44.

55. Ibid., 49–50.

56. Personal communication with the author, March 15, 2020.

57. Robert F. Dorr, 50.

58. Gallery Books. *The World's Great Attack Aircraft* (New York: Gallery Books, 1988), 80.

CHAPTER 6

1. The Air Force view of the close-air-support issue in the 1960s time period is well presented in Sbrega, "Southeast Asia," 411–90.

2. "Roles and Missions Get New Review," *Army–Navy–Air Force Journal*, June 3, 1961, 1–6.

3. *Army Times*, November 11, 1961.

4. Reported in *Army Times*, June 15, 1966.

5. Memorandum, "Secretary of Defense to Secretaries of the Air Force and Army," October 9, 1961. Secretary of the Air Force file on Close Air Support, Research and Analysis Library, Headquarters USAF. The other letter referred to by McNamara was unavailable for research.

6. Memorandum, Secretary of the Air Force to the Secretary of Defense," November 1, 1961, "Close Air Support File."

7. US Army Close Air Support Requirements Board, Close Air Support, Fort Meade, Maryland, 1963, Annex A, pp. 62–64.

8. Cited in US Army, Combat Developments Command, Institute of Special Studies, *A Short History of Close Air Support Issues* (Fort Belvoir, VA: US Army Combat Development Command, July 1968), 56.

9. Secretary of Defense memorandum to the secretary of the Army, April 19, 1962. See *Aviation Week*, June 25, 1962, 26.

10. Ibid.

11. *Aviation Week*, January 14, 1963, 27.

12. Membership on the Howze Board's many panels is listed in *Aviation Week*, June 25, 1962, 26–27.

13. *Aviation Week*, May 27, 1963, 30.

14. Bryan Hukee, email on Spadnet, the network of the A-1 Skyraider Association, and recorded in A-1skyraider combatjournal.com, October 17, 2019.

15. Report of the Close Air Support Board, 1963, vol. 1, Headquarters USAF, AFXDOD.

16. Memorandum from the secretary of the Army to the chief of staff, March 27, 1963. The entirety of the memo is reprinted in the *Armed Forces Journal*, December 14, 1968, 7. Vance had succeeded Elvis J. Stahr Jr., as secretary of the Army on May 21, 1962.

17. USAF-US Army, Final Report, CAS Boards, August 1963, vol. V, Annex H, p. 1.

18. Ibid. Conclusions of the boards were published in the US Congress, House of Representatives Committee on Armed Services, Close Air Support, *Report of the Special Subcommittee on Tactical Air Support of the Committee of Armed Services*, 89th Congress, 2nd Session, February 1, 1966, 4867. No. 44, 4122. The Army and Air Force conclusions also appeared in the *Armed Forces Journal*, February 12, 1966, 15. The Air Force desire for improved methods of target acquisition for the pilot will become more significant later, when we describe the 1967 decision to improve the avionics/bombing system in the A-7.

19. Reported in *Aviation Week*, March 23, 1964, under the title "USAF Snubs VAL."

20. Memorandum, "JCS Chairman to the Secretary of Defense," May 13, 1964, CM-1356-64. Reprinted in *A Short History of CAS Issues*, 71–72.

21. Memorandum to JCS from chief of staff, USAF, May 12, 1964, reprinted in *A Short History*, 72–73.

22. Memorandum, DDR&E to the secretary of defense, June 1,1964.

23. Interview with Dr. Brown, April 8, 1970.

24. Interview the Col. E. A. Chavarrie, DCS / Plans and Operations, August 18, 1970.

25. *Aviation Week*, September 21, 1964, 21.

26. John Boyd's career and contribution to the theory of air combat is published in Robert Coram, *Boyd: The Fighter Pilot Who Changed the Art of War* (New York: Little, Brown, 2002).

27. Enthoven interview, April 8, 1970.

28. The F-5 had been the subject of many aviation articles. For a discussion of its performance characteristics, see "The Northrop F-5-21: Study of a Fighter in Evolution," *Interavia* 7 (August 1969). For an excellent summary of how a study can compare aircraft, see "Cost-Effectiveness Analysis of a Ground Attack Mission," *Interavia* 8 (August 1968).

29. Interviews with multiple officers who worked on the study, February 9 and 25, 1970.

30. Murray interview, April 28, 1970.

31. Memorandum, secretary of defense to the secretary of the Air Force, January 7, 1965.

32. Ibid.

33. *Aviation Week*, November 9, 1964, 92.

34. Letter, Dr. Brown to the author, September 9, 1970.

35. Prior to July 1965, the 1st Air Cavalry Division was stationed with the 8th Army in Korea. A change of colors

traded the titles of the 1st Air Cavalry with the 2nd Infantry Division at Fort Benning, Georgia. The 11th Air Assault retained all its air assets and absorbed eight of the maneuver battalions of the 2d Infantry, becoming the 1st Cavalry Division (Airmobile), while the former 1st Cavalry in Korea became the 2nd Infantry.

36. *Aviation Week*, June 14, 1965, 73; and *Aviation Week*, January 3, 1966, 16.

37. Memorandum, "Close Support and Special Air Warfare Aircraft," chief of staff to secretary of the Air Force, May 10, 1965, The secretary forwarded the memo to OSD on June 14, 1965.

38. The author's interview with Lt. Gen. Gordon Graham, vice commander of TAC, February 11, 1970.

39. Quoted in *Aviation Week*, July 19, 1965, 15.

40. Heyman interview, March 12, 1970.

41. Ibid., 1:1.

42. Joint Air Forces / OSD Effort, vol. 3, December 1, 1965.

43. There was a sharp distinction between the F-4B/C, flying in the Navy and Air Force with no internal cannon, and the TSF/F-4E, which was a formal attempt to get the rotary cannon into the aircraft in addition to its missile armament. The design philosophy in the 1950s, when the original F-4H was designed, was that the increased speed of the jet aircraft and advances in heat-seeking and radar missile technology had rendered air-to-air cannon obsolete. When this vaunted missile radar technology did not prove capable of solving all the complex problems of close-in air-to-air battles in Vietnam, a major part of the Air Staff's effort in 1965–66 was spent in establishing a military requirement for an internal gun in the Air Force F-4. Systems Analysis had been resisting any change in the F-4's configuration until it was firmly established that the gun would not disturb the radar in the nose of the aircraft and that the radar could be satisfactorily modified. The placement in the lower part of the nose section was going to require extensive miniaturization of the radar set. Dr. Enthoven stated that he was skeptical of the TSF for this reason. Many officers in the Air Staff and TAC, however, were willing to get the F-4 TSF with NO radar if they could get a gun in the nose. A clear statement of the fighter pilots' position was stated by Maj. (later lieutenant general) Thomas G. McInerney in the *USAF Fighter Weapons Newsletter*, March 1969: "Despite arguments to the contrary, supported by volumes of cost analysis data, the need for an internal gun in fighter aircraft has long been the consensus among fighter pilots," 30.

44. FX Effort, 1:1–2.

45. An "afterburner" is an auxiliary combustion chamber attached to the tailpipe of a jet engine to increase its power or thrust. It involves a process of spraying jet fuel into the hot but unburned oxygen and exhaust gases of the engine to burn and thus increase the temperature and density of the gases as they leave the tailpipe. The afterburner consumes great amounts of fuel, so it is usually used only on takeoff and during short periods (seconds or a minute) of flight when additional acceleration is needed. The afterburner usually increases the thrust of the engine about 50 percent.

46. Interview with Col. Fish, August 15, 1970.

47. Ibid.

48. Ibid.

49. Murray interview, April 28, 1970.

50. Fish interview.

51. Brig. Gen. Arnold W. Braswell, *The Role of the Systems Analysis Staff in Defense Decision Making*, unpublished master's thesis (Washington, DC: George Washington University, 1967), 21. Enthoven was confirmed by the Senate on July 16, 1965, and sworn in by the secretary on September 10, 1965. The official establishment of the new office was in DoD Directive 5141.1, September 17, 1965. McNamara did not create an additional assistant secretary position; the deputy director of DDR&E had just left DoD, so McNamara took this opportunity to demote that position to the deputy assistant secretary level and upgrade Enthoven's.

52. "McNamara Team Extending Sphere into Top Operation Service Posts," *Aviation Week*, July 19, 1965, 24.

53. Memorandum, secretary of the Air Force to the secretary of defense, "USAF Tactical Fighter Forces," October 15, 1965.

54. Ibid., attachment.

55. Graham interview, February 11, 1970. There is some confusion about where the actual A-7 price quote came from. Normally, Air Force Systems Command would get the cost estimate from the contractor and then check it for accuracy. Lt. Gen. Graham indicated that this probably happened, but he couldn't be certain. However, Col. Robert E. Hails had occasion to research this after he was appointed the Air Force program manager. He learned this particular cost quote did not go through the normal channel but was supplied directly from LTV to OSD Systems Analysis.

56. Interview with Mr. Whitney McCormack, LTV A-7 program manager, April 1, 1970. McCormack sent the quote of $1.2–$1.3 million to OSD in the fall of 1965. This figure represented the cost of the A-7A after the Navy had paid for all the development work, with the production facilities and tooling already in place. The only addition the Air Force planners made to the LTV cost quote was to add an afterburner to the jet engine and raise the cost about $50,000. The total cost was based on the Navy buying 1,000 A-7As and the Air Force buying 864 A-7As. The FY1966 unit cost from LTV was $1.421 million for the Navy aircraft, but this cost would decrease with volume purchase, so that the average would be $1.249 million per new A-7.

57. The author was scrambled off ground alert at Bien Hoa to fly night close air support for Plei Mei on the first night of the attack. He also flew close air support for the 1st Cavalry Division when the PAVN units attacked out of the Chu Phong Mastiff onto the cavalry.

58. Cited in "Supplement to the Air Force Policy Letter for Commanders," December 1965, 24.

59. "F-5 Combat Trials Pinpoint Advantages, Limitations," *Aviation Week*, January 17, 1966, 28–30.

60. *Aviation Week*, October 4, 1965, 29. The first flight of any new aircraft is a significant achievement. The degree of its importance is attested to by Robert L. Perry of the RAND Corporation: "A convincing feasibility demonstration would appreciably enhance confidence in the predicted worth of whatever was being evaluated. Indeed, it is difficult to conceive of any single event that could so markedly change the value of the entire equation, particularly if doubt about the technical feasibility of the innovation had been prevalent earlier" (*Innovation and Military Requirements: A Comparative*

Study, RM-5182PR [Santa Monica: CA: RAND, 1967), 9). It is, course, recognized that the A-7 represented far less than a revolutionary technique or vehicle. There was very little debate about its technical feasibility. Still, the very fact that it had successfully flown was a mark in its favor, and it certainly represented a reduction in the uncertainty surrounding the new airplane, an uncertainly that had been particularly high in the Air Force.

61. US Congress, House of Representatives, Committee on Armed Services, Close Air Support Hearings, before the Special Subcommittee on Tactical Air support of the Committee on Armed Services, 89th Congress, 1st Session, September 23, 1965, 4689.

62. Ibid., 4695.

63. Fish interview. The placement of the "Requirements" office both in R&D and Operations will be discussed more below, when the Air Force drafts a requirement for the A-7.

64. Fish interview.

65. Ibid.

66. Interview with Gen. John P. McConnell (USAF, ret.), May 6, 1970. Gen. McConnell retired on July 31, 1969.

67. Interview with Dr. Harold Brown when he was the president of California Institute of Technology, April 8, 1970.

68. Ibid.

69. Ibid.

70. McConnell interview, May 6, 1970.

71. Interview with Gen. Disosway, April 3, 1970.

72. See Col. William F. Scott, "The Rise and Fall of the Stuka Dive Bomber," *Air University Review*, May–June 1966, 46–63; written only weeks after the USAF A-7 decision.

73. Disosway interview, April 3, 1970.

74. The unspoken assumptions of the decision had reportedly been that (1) the F-4 was needed in the gun version for air superiority, (2) the A-7 was the most cost-effective of the low-cost candidates, (3) only minimal changes would be necessary to meet Air Force needs, (4) it would be possible to divert part of the early Navy production to the Air Force, (5) the A-7 would be available to participate in the Vietnam War, and (6) the cost of the A-7 would be about $1.4 million per aircraft. These assumptions are the results of research conducted by Lt. Col. Don McClelland, USAF, in the Office of the Secretary of the Air Force.

75. Graham interview.

76. US Congress, Senate Committee on Appropriations, DoD Appropriations FY1970, hearings before the Subcommittee of the Committee on Appropriations, 91st Congress, 1st Session, July 1969, Part 45, p. 34. Testimony of Secretary of the Air Force Seamans.

77. *Aviation Week*, December 6, 1965, 25. The press lagged the decision process by some weeks, and when they did catch up, they oversimplified the reasons for the decision to the change in service secretaries ("Air Force Retreat on Supersonic Aircraft Traced to New Secretary," *Aviation Daily*, December 13, 1965). This consideration of foreign military sales is certainly an important factor in certain situations. See Richard E. Neustadt, *Alliance Politics* (New York: Columbia University Press, 1970).

78. Brown interview.

79. Enthoven interview.

80. DoD Appropriations, FY1970, Senate, 34.

81. Memorandum, secretary of defense to the secretary of the Air Force, November 18, 1965, "FY 1966 and 1967 USAF Tactical Air Procurement and Utilization Rates (U)." The F-4 TSF decision is recorded in the *History of the Tactical Division, Directorate of Operational Requirements and Development Plans*, DCS/R&D, July 1–December 21, 1966, 6.

CHAPTER 7

1. Robert F. Dorr, *Vought A-7 Corsair II*, 55. This chapter draws extensively from Dorr's work, with permission of his son, Robert P. Dorr.

2. Ed Beakley, communication to the author, March 15, 2020.

3. Dorr, *Vought A-7 Corsair II*, 59.

4. Ibid., 62.

5. Ibid., 60.

6. Ibid., 62.

7. Norman Birzer and Peter Mersky, *US Navy A-7 Corsair II Units of the Vietnam War* (Oxford: Osprey, 2004), 14.

8. Ibid., 11.

9. Ibid., 11, 12.

10. Ibid., 13.

11. Dorr, *Vought A-7 Corsair II*, 73.

12. Interview with Lt. Col. Charles W. McClarren, the leader of the USAF cadre in VA-146.

13. Ben Short, captain, USN (ret.), in Dorr, *Vought A-7 Corsair II*, 64, 71.

14. Gary J. Ohls, "Naval Aviation in the Korean and Vietnam Wars," in *One Hundred Years of U.S. Navy Air Power*, ed. Douglas Smith (Annapolis, MD: Naval Institute Press, 2010), 204.

15. Ed Beakley, personal communication to the author, March 16, 2020.

16. Ibid.

17. RAdm. Pickavance, personal communication to the author, March 15, 2020.

CHAPTER 8

1. M. M. Postan, D. Hay, and J. D. Scott, *Design and Development of Weapons: Studies in Government and Industrial Organization* (London: Her Majesty's Stationary Office, 1964), 2.

2. I. B. Holley, *Ideas and Weapons* (New Haven, CT: Yale University Press, 1953).

3. Hails interview, March 30, 1970. Col. Hails was promoted to brigadier general after he left the A-7 program in August 1968. When interviewed, he was a major general and the assistant deputy chief of staff for maintenance engineering at Hq, AF Logistics Command. He was subsequently promoted to lieutenant general.

4. LTV, *A-7D Tactical Fighter Report*, 4.

5. Hails interview, March 30, 1970.

6. Interview with Maj. Gen. Kenneth C. Dempster, deputy director for general purpose and airlift forces, Directorate of Operational Requirements and Development Plans, DCD/R&D, August 17, 1970.

7. Letter, "Justification of A-7A Configuration Changes," from director of operational requirements, TAC, to Headquarters USAF, director of operational requirements and development plans, January 15, 1966.

8. LTV, "Engine History A-7D Program," in *A-7D Project Master Plan*.

9. Interview with Capt. Carl M. Cruse, A-7 program manager, Naval Air Systems Command.

10. Interview with Mr. Donald R. Spencer, chief, Avionics and Guidance Division, DDR&E, April 29, 1970. He was a naval reserve officer with experience in Naval Air Systems Command and a registered professional engineer. He related how he worked to get ILAAS identified as the avionics system on the A-7 and followed the program closely. Also see *Aviation Week and Space Technology*, June 15, 1964, 109–10.

11. Letter, MG Catton to Harry Davis, SAF-RD. Subject: "Technical Proposal Summary for USAF Avionics (U)," February 21, 1966. MG Catton's thoughts on the type of avionics desired are significant, since he was to become the chairman of the Air Staff Board, which would recommend the final avionics decision.

12. Interviews with Col. Hails and LTV personnel.

13. US Congress, House of Representatives Committee on Armed Services. *Close Air Support*, report of the Special Subcommittee on Tactical Air Support of the Committee on Armed Services, 89th Congress, 2nd Session, February 1, 1966, 4867, 4870, and 4873. The Pike Report is discussed in US Army, Combat Developments Command, Institute of Special Studies, *A Short History of Close Air Support Issues*, 1968; and *Aviation Week and Space Technology*, February 7, 1966, 21.

14. *Armed Forces Journal*, February 19, 1966, 15.

15. Interview with Lt. Col. Richard Haggren, Tactical Division of Requirements. The Air Staff Board briefing was given by Col. William Ritchie.

16. A-7 Program Report, February 26, 1966, written by Col. Hails.

17. Interview with Col. Hails, March 30, 1970.

18. Interview with Lt. Gen. Graham. His flights at Dallas Naval Air Station, the home of LTV's Vought Aeronautics Division, took place March 2–5, 1966.

19. Ibid.

20. Memorandum, secretary of the Navy to the secretary of the Air Force, March 9, 1966. Subject: "Delivery Schedule of the Air Force A-7 Aircraft."

21. Unclassified talking paper on A-7 configuration and status, Directorate of Requirements (AFRDQ), March 23, 1966, 2.

22. PMO, Weekly Management Summary, March 14, 1966, written by Col. Hails.

23. Letter, commander of TAC to chief of staff, March 15, 1966, "A-7 Configuration."

24. Unclassified talking paper on A-7 configuration and status, Directorate of Requirements (AFRDQ), March 31, 1966, 2.

25. Dorr, *Vought A-7 Corsair II*, 49.

26. Robert Dorr, "The Lockheed AH-56 Cheyenne Attack Helicopter Might Have Been a Formidable Weapon," *Defense Media Network*, November 1, 2011.

27. *Aviation Week*, April 25, 1966, 26.

28. Ibid.

29. Ibid.

30. Memorandum, secretary of the Air Force to the secretary of the Navy, April 22, 1966. Subject: "Procurement of Air Force A-7 Aircraft."

31. USAF, Requirements Action Directive RD-7-11-(1) A-7D, August 11, 1966. Unclassified portions.

32. Unclassified page 16 of Briefing in "talking papers," file 17-3-1-1, Tactical Division, Directorate of Operational Requirements and Development Plans, DCS/R&D.

33. LTV, *A-7D Tactical Fighter Report*, 4.

34. LTV, "Engine History A-7D Program," in *A-7D Project Master Plan*.

35. Interview with Mr. J. W. Lankford, LTV, April 1, 1970.

36. Memorandum, secretary of defense to the secretaries of the Air Force and Navy, April 29, 1966.

37. Hails interview.

38. Cruse interview.

39. Multiple interviews at LTV.

40. Hails interview.

41. Confirmed by J. E. Martin Jr., vice president of Vought Aeronautics for engineering and logistics, interview, April 6, 1970.

42. Engine Contracting Office, ASD, briefing to the Air Staff, July 5, 1966 (LTV, *A-7D Project Master Plan*).

43. Memorandum, secretary of the Air Force to the secretary of defense, July 22, 1966. Subject: "Engine for the Air Force A-7 Aircraft." The August 8 issue of *Aviation Week* confirmed the backlog problem of Pratt & Whitney and said they could have made delivery of the initial engine only after thirty-seven months. The Spey gold flow offset was estimated at $100 million. A lengthy description of the decision followed (*Aviation Week*, August 8, 1966, 33).

44. LTV, "Engine History A-7D Program," in *A-7D Project Master Plan*.

45. US Congress, House Committee on Armed Services, hearings on military posture, FY-1968, 90th Congress, 1st Session, March 22, 1967, 926.

46. LTV, *A-7D Project Master Plan*; and *Flight International*, August 4, 1966, 168.

47. *Aviation Week and Space Technology*, January 16, 1967, 30.

48. Murray interview, April 28, 1970.

49. Ibid.

50. Interview with Col. James R. Hildreth, Requirements Directorate, DCS/R&D, February 9, 1970.

51. Greg Stearns, communication to the author, March 15, 2020.

52. Secretary of the Air Force Memorandum, May 25, 1966.

53. History of the Tactical Division, Operational Requirements and Development Plans, DCS/R&D, July 1–December 21, 1966.

54. *Aviation Week*, September 26, 1966, 28.

55. Letter, chief of staff decision (U) September 8, 1966, "Analysis of Close Air Support Operations," signed by Lt. Gen. Hewitt T. Wheless, assistant vice chief of staff.

56. Memorandum from Hugh E. Witt, deputy for supply and maintenance, Office of the Secretary of the Air Force, to his boss, Robert B. Charles, assistant secretary of the Air Force, installations and logistics, August 8, 1966. Subject: "20 mm gun for the A-7 Aircraft."

57. Memorandum, secretary of defense to secretaries of the Air Force, Army, and Navy, September 21, 1966.

58. Murray interview.

59. Cruse interview.

60. Interview with Captain Doss, October 25, 1970.

61. Davis, *The Politics of Innovation*.

62. Doss interview.

63. Interview, February 1970.

64. Doss interview.

65. Hails interview.

66. Enthoven interview.

67. Murray interview.

68. Doss interview.

69. Interview with Captain Gallagher, February 27, 1970.

70. OSD (Public Affairs) news release, no. 923-66, October 31, 1966; and *Air Force and Space Digest*, December 1966, 22.

71. Interview with Sol Love, LTV, April 2, 1970.

72. Hails interview.

73. LTV interview.

74. The second LTV study for the A-7D ran from October to December 1966, and its study for the Navy A-7E from December 1966 to February 1967. The China Lake and Johnsville studies were from November 1966 to January 1967. Undated, unclassified PMO briefing notes; and Doss interview.

75. Letter, commander of TAC to chief of staff, November 17, 1966.

76. Disosway interview.

77. Letter, chief of staff to commander of TAC, December 6, 1966.

78. Ibid.

79. Interview with Dr. Harold Brown, reflecting on his opinion when he was director of DDR&E, 1961–1965.

80. *Armed Forces Journal*, July 25, 1970, 24–28; quote from p. 26.

81. Memorandum, "A-7 Aircraft Avionics," to the assistant secretaries of the Air Force and Navy (R&D), December 23, 1966, signed by Finn Larson for Dr. Foster.

82. Message, chief of staff, USAF to AFSC, January 16, 1967.

83. Letter, chief of staff, USAF, to chief of staff, US Army, January 23, 1967.

84. Letter, chief of staff, USAF, to staff: "Specialized Close Air Support Aircraft A-X (U)," January 4, 1967.

85. Hails interview.

86. Interviews at LTV, April 1–5, 1970; verified the 7–8-mil estimate.

87. PMO briefing, undated, unclassified, "Avionics."

88. Hanson Baldwin, *New York Times*, April 17, 1967. The term "unit flyaway cost" denotes the lowest of the many terms that can be used to describe the cost of a weapons system. The "unit flyaway cost" is the recurring cost of parts that physically are installed in the aircraft; the cost to produce a single airplane. The other important cost figure is the "program unit cost," which includes all the costs of the research and development in addition to production, divided by the number of aircraft to be produced. This "program" cost includes the recurring flyaway cost plus such things as ground equipment, spare parts, and the large development costs. For instance, while the unit flyaway cost in early 1967 was only $1.47 million, the program cost was about $2.0–$2.2 million per aircraft.

89. Hails interview. He was referring to the program cost.

90. Col. Hails, "Briefing Notes" of the January 24, 1967, DSMG meeting, AFSC File 4-30-1.

91. US Congress, Senate Committee on Armed Services, Military Procurement Authorizations for Fiscal Year 1968, *Hearings before the Committee on Armed Services and a Subcommittee on Department of Defense of the Committee on Appropriations*, US Senate, 90th Congress, 1st Session, February 2, 1967, 881. Hereafter called the *DoD Authorization FY1968*.

92. McConnell interview.

93. Doss interview.

94. A-7D Program Management Office viewgraph, undated, unclassified.

95. Hails interview.

96. Brown interview.

97. McConnell interview.

98. Interview with VAdm. Connolly.

99. Doss interview. The intense organizational interest in avionics within DDR&E can be seen reflected by a statement Dr. Foster made to Congress in 1967, very shortly after the A-7 presentation. Dr. Foster testified that the immediate goals for DDR&E for the coming year were to be "improved accuracy ordnance and bomb delivery systems to reduce the required number of sorties" and "better all-weather navigation and ground-directed bomb delivery systems." US Congress, House Committee on Armed Services, Hearings on Military Posture, House of Representatives, 90th Congress, 1st Session, April 17, 1967, 1405.

100. Directorate of Production and Programming, "A-7 Program Element Monitor, History," January 1, 1967–June 30, 1967, 6.

101. "A-7D Attack Fighter, Cost Estimate Tract," 32. Also detailed in *Aviation Week*, July 10, 1967, 30–31; and *Aviation Daily*, July 18, 1967.

102. Doss interview, March 13, 1970.

103. Unclassified paragraph of memorandum, secretary of defense, "A-7 Program (U)," May 5, 1967. SAF File 448-67.

104. Memorandum, secretary of the Navy to secretary of defense, "A-7 Aircraft Avionics Improvement (U)," May 11, 1967. SAF File 448-67.

105. Memorandum, secretary of defense to assistant secretary of defense (I&L), May 12, 1967. SPD File 67-2592-A-7.

106. Memorandum, DDR&E to assistant secretaries of the Navy and Air Force (R&D), May 17, 1967. SPD History.

107. Doss interview.

108. "A-7D Cost Estimate Track," 32.

109. Memorandum, DDR&E to assistant secretaries of the Air Force and Navy, (R&D), July 28, 1967. History of the Tactical Division, RDQ.

110. Murray interview. Emphasis added.

111. Enthoven interview.

112. PMO, *Semi-Annual Historical Report*, July 1–December 31, 1967.

113. *Aviation Daily*, September 14, 1967, 5.

114. Vought Aeronautics, "Nav / Weapon Delivery System," undated. Also see Lt. Frank Wagner, Naval Test Center, Patuxent River, Maryland, "A-7E Attack Systems," in *Naval Aviation News*, March 1969, 31. Both of these documents are located in the archives of the A-7 Corsair II Association.

115. Dorr, *Vought A-7 Corsair II*, 143.

116. Ibid., 145.

117. PMO, *Top Management Information Report (Rainbow)*, August 25, 1967.

118. Hail interview, March 30, 1970.

119. Interview with Lt. Col. John R. Albright, engineer in the A-7D PMO, May 8, 1970.

120. Interview with Mr. Buzard, LTV vice president, A-7 programs, April 3, 1970.

121. Briefing, "Talking Papers," RDQ, File 17-3-1-3.

122. Letter, secretary of the Air Force to the president of LTV, October 18, 1967.

123. Letter, president of LTV to the secretary of the Air Force, October 20, 1967.

124. The document was the Southeast Asia Operational Requirement (SEAOR) #76.

125. Interviews at LTV, April 2, 1970.

126. Hails interview.

127. McConnell interview.

128. *New York Times*, January 20, 1968, 1; and *New York Times*, March 2, 1968, 3:2.

129. PMO, *Top Management Information Report (Rainbow)*, December 1968.

130. A-7D Program Management Office Chart, 1970, updated with DoD Appropriations FY1975.

131. US Congress, Senate Committee on Armed Services, Authorization for Military Procurement, Research, and Development, FT1970, and Reserve Strength, hearings before the Committee on Armed Services, 91st Congress, 1st Session, on S.1192 and S. 2307, Part 2, April 29, 1969, 1519.

132. Cited in *Armed Forces Journal*, April 16, 1969, and April 25, 1970, 25.

133. McConnell interview.

134. US Senate, Report No. 91-290I, to accompany S. 2546, July 3, 1969.

135. Insert for the Record, Senate Armed Services Committee, Subcommittee on Tactical Air Power, February 17, 1970, 507, line 10. Originally prepared July 23, 1969, and inserted into the record of Senate Appropriations Committee, Defense Subcommittee.

136. DoD Appropriations FY1970, 454.

137. Headquarters USAF, unclassified summary statement, undated, probably July 9, 1969.

138. US Congress, Senate, Congressional Record, July 10, 1969, S87861.

139. Office of the Secretary of the Air Force, Memorandum for the Record, A-7D Program, July 15, 1969, 1.

140. US Congress, Senate Committee on Armed Services, Gen. John D. Ryan, chief of staff, US Air Force, hearing before the Committee on Armed Services, 91st Congress, 1st Session, July 24, 1969, 9.

141. Senate Appropriations Committee, DoD Appropriations 1970, 126.

142. Letter, August 2, 1969. See *Aviation Week*, September 15, 1969, 26–27.

143. Office of the Secretary of the Air Force, Air Force Policy Letter for Commanders, September 1, 1969, 1.

144. Testimony by Gen. James Ferguson, commander of AFSC, before the House Armed Services Committee, hearings on RDT&E, March 16, 1970, 8186.

145. Dorr, *Vought A-7 Corsair II*, 91.

146. Ibid., 95.

147. Ibid., 97.

CHAPTER 9

1. Email from Greg Stearns to the author, August 19, 2020.

2. Ibid.

3. Ibid.

4. Dorr, *Vought A-7 Corsair II*, 102.

5. Ibid.

6. Douglas de Vlaming, "The Rescue of Bobbin 05," *Daedalus Flyer*, Summer 2015, 38–39.

7. Ibid.

8. Dorr, *Vought A-7 Corsair II*, 125–30.

9. Ibid., 129.

10. De Vlaming, "The Rescue of Bobbin 05," 39.

11. Veteran Tributes: Honoring Those Who Served, "Colin Arnold Clarke," http://veterantributes.org/TributeDetail.php?recordID=467.

12. The story of the Mayaguez crisis is told in Richard G. Head, Frisco W. Short, and Robert C. McFarlane, *Crisis Resolution: Presidential Decision Making in the Mayaguez and Korean Confrontations* (Boulder, CO: Westview, 1978).

13. Brig. Gen. Keith Connolly, message to the author, April 18, 2020.

14. Birzer and Mersky, *US Navy A-7 Corsair II Units of the Vietnam War*, 27.

15. Dorr, *Vought A-7 Corsair II*, 161.

16. Wetterhahn quote from Birzer and Mersky, *US Navy A-7 Corsair II Units of the Vietnam War*, 27–28.

17. Ibid.

18. Some of Ralph F. Wetterhan's books include *The Last Battle: The Mayaguez Incident and the End of the Vietnam War*; *The Early Air War in the Pacific: Ten Months That Changed the Course of World War II*; *The Last Flight of Bomber 31: Harrowing Tales of American and Japanese Pilots Who Fought In World War II's Arctic Air Campaign*; and *Shadowmakers: A Novel*.

19. Ed Beakley, email to the author, April 13, 2020.

20. As told by Ed Beakley, ibid., 163.

21. RAdm. Pickavance, email to the author, April 2020.

22. Ed Beakley, private correspondence with the author.

23. David Kelly, *Not on My Watch* (self-published by Blurb, 2014).

24. Ed Beakley, op. cit.

25. Earl H. Tilford, *Setup: What the Air Force Did in Vietnam and Why* (Maxwell Air Force Base, AL: Air University Press, 1991), 254.

26. RAdm. Chatham, remarks continued from chapter III, in correspondence, March 16, 2020.

27. Cited in Robert O. Harder's article "The 11-Day War," *Aviation History*, January 2013.

28. A direct quotation from one of the SAC briefing officers, cited in Marshall L. Michel III, *Operation Linebacker II, 1972: The B-52s Are Sent to Hanoi* (Oxford: Osprey, 2018), 63.

29. Ed Beakley, Remembered Sky, http://rememberedsky.com/?page_id=51, posted November 11, 2017.

30. Michel, *Operation Linebacker II, 1972*, 67.

31. Ibid.

32. Harder, "The 11-Day War," 4. G. Ray Sullivan Jr. discovered and recorded his father's contribution and developed it into a website, http://www.linebacker2.com, and two videos, *Triumph and Tragedy at 30,000 Feet* and *PAC 6: A General's Decision*.

33. Brig. Gen. James R. McCarthy and Lt. Col. George B. Allison, *Linebacker II: A View from the Rock* (Washington, DC: Smithsonian Press, 2018; originally published as a USAF Southeast Asia Monograph, vol. VI, monograph 8 (Washington, DC: Office of Air Force History, 1979), 140.

34. "Linebacker II 12/72: Day by Day: A Record of All Air Crews Lost during Linebacker II; December 18–29, 1972," www.linebacker 2.com/Page_2_59Bl.html.

35. Email communication from Ed Montgomery to the author, November 18, 2019. Ed became the operations officer of the 421st Fighter Squadron at Udorn, and the author followed him in that position in October 1973.

36. Jack Leslie and John Leslie, extract from their book *In My Father's Footsteps: A Story of Father and Son Naval Aviators* (Jacksonville, FL: OnLine Binding, 2015), chapter 18, "The Mighty Warhawks."

37. Birzer and Mersky, *US Navy A-7 Corsair II Units of the Vietnam War*, 79.

38. Dorr, *Vought A-7 Corsair II*, 132.

39. For a case study of the SS *Mayaguez* capture and US combat operations, see Richard G. Head, Frisco W. Short, and Robert C. McFarlane, "The Mayaguez Crisis: Piracy on the High Seas," in *Crisis Resolution: Presidential Decision Making in the Mayaguez and Korean Confrontations* (Boulder, CO: Westview, 1978), 101–48.

40. Letter to the author, August 12, 2020.

41. "Prospects of A-7F in Air Support Role Appear Dim," *Defense News*, January 8, 1990, 29.

42. Robert F. Dorr, "Gulf War: Desert Storm Was an Heroic Moment for A-7E Corsair II," Defense Media Network, January 25, 2011.

43. Ibid.

44. Cmdr. David "Bio" Baranek, "TOPGUN: The Navy's First Center of Excellence," *Proceedings*, September 2019, 25.

45. Quoted in Birzer and Mersky, *US Navy A-7 Corsair II Units of the Vietnam War*, 82.

46. VAdm. Brent Bennitt, written communication with the author, December 10, 2019.

CHAPTER 10

1. The author's interview with Gen. McConnell, May 6, 1970.

2. Lt. Col. David R. Jacques and Dennis D. Strouble, *A-10 Thunderbolt II (Warthog) Systems Engineering Case Study* (Wright Patterson AFB, OH: Air Force Center for Systems Engineering, Air Force Institute of Technology, 2010), 19. Jacques and Strouble cite two RAND studies that recorded the conduct and results of the studies: Alfred Goldberg and Donald Smith, RAND Reports C/GDS-83, "The Close Support Issue (U)", 33; and R-906-PR, "Army-Air Force Relations: The Close Air Support Issue (U)," October 1971, 33. The latter study is cited by Douglas N. Campbell, *The Warthog and the Close Air Support Debate* (Annapolis, MD: Naval Institute Press, 2003), 64. The Jacques and Strouble volume is also notable and useful for its extensive set of A-10 references.

3. Letter, Chief of Staff Decision (U), September 8, 1966, "Analysis of Close Air Support Operations (U)." signed by Lt. Gen. Hewitt T. Wheless, assistant vice chief of staff.

4. Chris Turner, "Fighter Mafia: Colonel John Boyd, the Brain behind Fighter Dominance," Avgeekery.com, June 23, 2020, 1.

5. Chris Turner, "Fighter Mafia Part 3: Thomas P. "Tom" Christie, Wizard behind the Curtain," Avgeekery.com, October 31, 2020, 1.

6. Col. James G. Burton, *The Pentagon Wars: Reformers Challenge the Old Guard* (Annapolis, MD: Naval Institute Press, 1993), 14. This version of Boyd's first encounter with Pentagon politics is confirmed in essence by Boyd's authorized biographer, Robert Coram. See Coram, *Boyd: The Fighter Pilot Who Changed the Art of War*, 194–95. The Free Library wrote a review of Burton's book in 1993, which is available at https://www.thefreelibrary.com/The+Pentagon+Wars%3a+Reformers+Challenge+the+Old+Guard.-a014236433.

7. Chris Turner, "Fighter Mafia Part 2: Pierre Sprey, A-10 Close Air Support Aircraft Developer," Avgeekery.com, August 23, 2020, 2–4; and author's interviews with Pierre Sprey, October 7–8 and November 18, 2020.

8. Coram, *Boyd: The Fighter Pilot Who Changed the Art of War*, 196–201.

9. John Correll, "The Reformers," *Air Force Magazine*, February 1, 2008; and Burton, *The Pentagon Wars*, 47, 71, 93, 98. Fallows's article was in the *Atlantic Monthly*, October 1979, 59–78.

10. Marshal L. Michel, "The Revolt of the Majors: How the Air Force Changed after Vietnam," a dissertation submitted to the graduate faculty of Auburn University in partial fulfillment of the requirements for the degree of doctor of philosophy, December 15, 2006, 9–10. Also see Correll, "The Reformers."

11. Note that this paragraph is a quote from Correll's article "The Reformers" (*Air Force Magazine*, February 1, 2008), but that the interior quotation is Franklin C. "Chuck" Spinney's, from his article in *Naval Institute Proceedings* 123, no. 7 (July 1997).

12. Turner, "Fighter Mafia Part 2; and author's interview with Pierre Sprey, October 9, 2020.

13. Jacques and Strouble, *A-10 Thunderbolt II (Warthog)*, 19.

14. AF Form 71, Requirements Action Directive RAD 7-69 (1), "Requirements for a Specialized Close Air Support Aircraft (A-X), December 22, 1966, cited by Jacques and Strouble, *A-10 Thunderbolt II (Warthog)*, 18.

15. See chapter 6 of the current work. The RAD for the gun system is described in Jacques and Strouble, *A-10 Thunderbolt II (Warthog)*, 20–21.

16. Turner, "Fighter Mafia Part 2," 8.

17. Hans Ulrich Rudel, *Stuka Pilot* (New York: Ballantine Books, 1958).

18. Jacques and Strouble, *A-10 Thunderbolt II (Warthog)*, 23.

19. Campbell, *Warthog and the Close Air Support Debate*, 69.

20. Ibid.

21. Jacques and Strouble, *A-10 Thunderbolt II (Warthog)*, 30; and Campbell, *Warthog and the Close Air Support Debate*, 73. Dr. Foster's memo was dated December 14, 1968.

22. Jacques and Strouble, *A-10 Thunderbolt II (Warthog)*, 9.

23. Ibid., 30.

24. Ibid., 33–34.

25. Campbell, *Warthog and the Close Air Support Debate*, 83.

26. Ibid.

27. Jacques and Strouble, *A-10 Thunderbolt II (Warthog)*, 40.

28. Pierre Sprey's interview with the author, October 7, 2020.

29. Jacques and Strouble, *A-10 Thunderbolt II (Warthog)*, 41. The contract was signed June 21, 1973.

30. Gen. Ron Yates, at that time the A-10 test director; interview, October 23, 2020.

31. Direct quote Yates interview, October 23, 2020.

32. Yates email to the author, October 27, 2020.

33. Ron Yates interview, October 23, 2020.

34. Jacques and Strouble, *A-10 Thunderbolt II (Warthog)*, 42–44.

35. Mike Loh, personal communication to the author, November 4, 2020.

36. Ron Yates, personal communication to the author, February 12, 2020.

37. Campbell, *Warthog and the Close Air Support Debate*, 70.

38. There are several sources for more information about Col. Dilger and his role in the GAU-8 development and testing. The source for the first test is Douglas Campbell's *Warthog and the Close Air Support Debate*, 114–15. The second test was in autumn 1975, against Soviet T-62 tanks supplied by the Israelis. The third and most detailed report is Russel H. S. Stolfi, J. E. Clemens, and R. R. McEachin, "Combat Damage Assessment Team A-10/GAU-8 Low Angle Firings versus Individual Soviet Tanks" (February–March 1978) (Monterey, CA: Naval Postgraduate School, 1979), downloaded from Calhoun Institutional Archive, DSpace Repository, 1979-08, http://hdl.handle.net/10945/29216. Another is George E. Kontis, PE, "The Development of the GAU-8 Avenger System: One Burst One Kill, *Small Arms Review* 15, no. 5 (February 2012). The fourth is a telephone interview with Col. Dilger in 1978, transcribed at https://soundcloud.com/audio-oddities/a10-warthog.

39. Campbell, *Warthog and the Close Air Support Debate*, 115. The quotation is from the author's endnote 17 on his page 229, for text, pp. 114–17.

40. Ibid.

41. 2Lt. Paige N. Skinner, "A-10A Initial Operational Capability," Air Combat Command, email to the author, October 15, 2020.

42. Ken Neubeck, *A-10 Thunderbolt II: Fairchild Republic's Warthog at War* (Atglen, PA: Schiffer Military, 2019), 39.

43. The details of the Air Force's difficulties with Fairchild are described in Jacques and Strouble, *A-10 Thunderbolt II (Warthog)*, 47–54.

44. John T. Correll, "The Ups and Downs of Close Air Support," *Air Force Magazine*, December 2019, 60.

45. Neubeck, *A-10 Thunderbolt II*, 61.

46. Brian Boeding, "A-10: Hey Air Force, There's More to Survival than Hiding, *Breaking Defense*, June 26, 2020, 5.

47. Daedalians, "Airpower Blog for the Military Aviation Professional," *Airpower Blog*, April 20, 2020.

48. Quoted by Doug Campbell in *Warthog and the Close Air Support Debate*, 141.

49. Ibid., 61–62.

50. William L. Smallwood, *Warthog: Flying the A-10 in the Gulf War I* (London: Brassey's, 1993).

51. The numbers differ slightly according to different references. Smallwood cites 131; Ken Neubeck says initially 144, but 152 with replacements, while his table on p. 67 notes totals for each of seven squadrons to equal 170 aircraft.

52. Smallwood, *Warthog: Flying the A-10 in the Gulf War I*. This statement was from Capt. Mike Isherwood, but it was refuted by Maj. Gen. Buster Glosson, US Central Command director of campaign plans, who said the A-10s were in from the very beginning.

53. Smallwood, *Warthog: Flying the A-10 in the Gulf War I*, 67. Lt. Gen. Charles Horner was the air component commander.

54. Ibid., 96. Direct quote, cited by Capt. Isherwook, by Lt. Gen. Charles Horner at the Tactical Air Control Center, Riyadh, on the second day of the war. Also quoted by Campbell in *Warthog and the Close Air Support Debate*, 179.

55. Smallwood, *Warthog: Flying the A-10 in the Gulf War I*, 96; Lt. Gen. Horner.

56. Ibid., 126.

57. Ibid., 173.

58. Ibid., 196.

59. Ibid., 203.

60. Ibid., 206.

61. Brig. Gen. Robert Scales, *Certain Victory* (Washington, DC: Office of the Chief of Staff, US Army, 1993), 369–71, as cited in Campbell, *Warthog and the Close Air Support Debate*, 184.

62. Campbell, *Warthog and the Close Air Support Debate*, 179.

63. Neubeck, *A-10 Thunderbolt II*, 70.

64. Gary Wetzel, *A-10 Thunderbolt II Units of Operation Enduring Freedom, 2008–14* (Oxford: Osprey, 2015), 7.

65. Ibid., 7–8.

66. Frank Oliveri, "The Warthog Round at Gunsmoke," *Air Force Magazine*, March 1992, 37.

67. Wetzel, *A-10 Thunderbolt II Units of Operation Enduring Freedom*, 8.

68. Neubeck, *A-10 Thunderbolt II*, 84–85.

69. Col. Christopher E. Haave and Lt. Col. Phil M. Haun, *A-10s over Kosovo* (Maxwell AFB, AL: Air University Press, 2003), 19.

70. Ibid., 210.

71. Ibid.

72. Ibid., 211–12.

73. Ibid., 147.

74. Ibid.

75. Ibid., 20.

76. Ibid., 82–83

77. David Axe, "Instead of Being Retired, the A-10 Warthog Is Getting Even Deadlier," *Defense News*, December 15, 2019.

78. Quoted by Sarah Sicard in "How the A-10 Warthog Avoided Retirement and Went to War Again," *Task and Purpose*, November 10, 2018, 1.

79. Ibid.

80. Ibid.

81. Valerie Insinna, "Air Force to Order More A-10 Wings in FY19 Budget Request," *Defense News*, January 25, 2018.

82. David Axe, "Instead of Being Retired, the A-10 Warthog Is Getting Even Deadlier," *Defense News*, December 15, 2019, reprinted in the *National Interest*, October 30, 2021, 1.

83. Valerie Insinna, "US Air Force To Keep A-10 Off the Chopping Block in Next Budget Cycle," *Defense News*, September 4, 2019, 1.

84. Mark F. Cancian, "US Military Forces in FY 2021: Air Force," Center for Strategic and International Studies, December 3, 2020, 10, citing Stephen Losey, "A-10 re-winging completed, will keep Warthog in the air until late 2030s," *Air Force Times*, August 13, 1019.

85. Boeding, "A-10: Hey Air Force, There's More to Survival than Hiding," 1–2.

86. Ibid., 2.

87. Ibid.

88. Secretary of the Air Force Public Affairs, October 25, 2019, Arlington, VA (AFNS).

CHAPTER 11

1. Coram, *Boyd: The Fighter Pilot Who Changed the Art of War*, 194.

2. Ibid., 225.

3. Ibid., 228.

4. Ibid.

5. Interview with Pierre Sprey, November 18, 2020.

6. Everest E. Riccioni, USAF, "Brief Summary of My Background and Major Accomplishments," September 8, 2014. Center for Defense Information, Project on Government Oversight (POGO), 2020. Also see Project on Government Oversight (POGO), "Member of Fighter Mafia Passes," Colonel Everest Riccioni, May 6, 2015.

7. Coram, *Boyd: The Fighter Pilot Who Changed the Art of War*, 240.

8. The title of the paper was "F-XX and VF-XX Feasible High Performance Low Cost Fighter Alternatives," delivered in St. Louis at the 1969 AIAA conference. Source: Email from Sprey to the author, November 18, 2020.

9. Pierre Sprey, direct quote, interview, November 18, 2020.

10. At this distant date, there is still some question about the source of these funds. Most of the participants are gone. Some sources say Riccioni applied for a grant from his superiors; others say the funds were already a line item in the office's budget. However, there is widespread agreement on the amount, $149,000, and the title, which confirmed by Coram in *Boyd: The Fighter Pilot Who Changed the Art of War*, 239, 245; by Burton in *The Pentagon Wars*, 17; and by Bob Cox in "F-16's Developer, Harry J. Hillaker, Dies at 89" (*F-16 Fighting Falcon News*, February 10, 2009, 2). There is also universal agreement on the dispersion of the funds to General Dynamics and Northrop, the intent of the study, and the results of the effort in energizing industry to produce preliminary designs that met the goals of the Fighter Mafia officers.

11. Gen. Mike Loh, p. 1 of "Personal Notes on the Beginning and Early Years in the F-16 Program," a letter to his grandson, Michael John, on October 14, 2013, and provided to the author.

12. Incidentally, Boyd already knew Harry Hillaker from his days at Eglin AFB. An example of the coordination between the Air Staff members and industry executives is found in Bob Cox's article on Harry Hillaker, "F-16's Developer, Harry J. Hillaker, Dies at 89," 2. "Mr. Hillaker, who since getting to know Boyd had quietly guided some internal lightweight fighter design work, was General Dynamics' point man for the program. On numerous occasions over the next two years, he secretly flew to Washington and met with Boyd, Sprey and a few others to hash out theories and share data and design concepts. "We used to stay up all night arguing about performance and trade-offs," [Pierre] Sprey said. "He gave us a lot of insights both into design and General Dynamics internal politics. He was committed to doing it right."

13. Loh, "Personal Notes," 1.

14. Pierre Sprey, letter to the author, November 20, 2020, 4. Packard's interest in prototyping was not surprising. After all, that was the way he got started on the road to founding Hewlett Packard. He handbuilt electronic prototypes in his garage, failed often, and succeeded with enough to begin and grow a multimillion-dollar company.

15. Ibid., 4–5.

16. Loh, "Personal Notes."

17. Ibid.

18. Coram, in *Boyd*, wrote, "Riccioni was close to Boyd for a while, but he never was one of the Acolytes." Coram goes on to relate instances where Boyd's habit of interrupting Riccioni and following him around while expounding his grievances became bothersome.

19. The recipient of Riccioni's immoderate assertion was rumored to have been Gen. J. C. Meyer, the vice chief of staff. This was never confirmed, but the result of the interaction is a matter of record.

20. Riccioni, "Brief Summary," 2.

21. Harry J. Hillaker, "Technology and the F-16 Fighting Falcon Jet Fighter," *Centennial of Aviation* 34, no. 1 (March 1, 2004), 3; from National Academy of Engineering website.

22. Gen. Ron Yates, "F-16 Development Thoughts," a paper provided to the author, April 22, 2020.

23. Loh, "Personal Notes," 3.

24. Ibid.

25. Ibid.

26. Yates, "F-16 Development Thoughts," 1.

27. Ed Adamczyk, "Lockheed Martin to Build F-16s in Potential $62 Billion Contract," *Defense News*, August 17, 2020, 1.

28. Paul Nickell and Tyler Rogoway, "Taking the F-14A Tomcat on Cruise for My First Time," *War Zone*, April 4, 2017, www.thedrive.com/the-war-zone.

29. Gerard Paloque, *Northrop F-5 Freedom Fighter and Tiger II* (Paris: Historie & Collections, 2013).

30. The author was flying A-1s at Bien Hoa in June 1965 when the F-5A "Skoshi Tiger" unit was there, demonstrating for the Vietnamese air force. We were all pretty skeptical of its small bombload and minimal radius of action. The Vietnamese subsequently purchased and flew the F-5A/B and E.

31. Jon Lake and Richard Hewson, "Northrop F-5," *World Air Power Journal* 25 (Summer 1996): 46–109.

32. Orr Kelly, *Hornet: The Inside Story of the F/A-18* (Novato, CA: Presidio, 1990).

33. Global Security, "VFAX/NACF-Navy Air Combat Fighter," Globalsecurity.org, n.d., 1–2.

34. Ibid., 3–4.

35. John Pike, "F/A-18 Service Life," Globalsecurity.org, July 2, 2017.

36. Greg Stearns, personal communication to the author, March 15, 2020.

37. Colin Riksick, "F-22 Raptor vs F-35 Lightning II," *Military Machine*, February 28, 2020, 1.

38. Cited by John Correll in "The Reformers.", 8.

39. One version of the A-12 story is told in an appendix, "Case Study: The Navy Runs Aground," in Burton, *The Pentagon Wars*, 213–32.

40. Kevin Miller, "The Legacy of Operation Desert Fox," *Hook Magazine*, Fall 2018.

41. Ibid.

42. LCmdr. Rick Burgess, "Flying Eagles Return to Fly Super Hornets," *Naval Aviation News* 81, no. 3 (March–April 1999): 30.

43. Megan Eckstein, "Navy Says Ending Super Hornet Line Frees Up Resources for Life Extension Work," *Defense News*, March 10, 2020.

44. Global Security, "VFAX/NACF-Navy Air Combat Fighter," 4.

45. "G.M.," SOFREP website, posted November 6, 2020, 8:34:15 a.m.

46. Jeffrey W. Hamstra, ed., *The F-35 Lightning II: From Concept to Cockpit* (Washington, DC: American Institute of Aeronautics and Astronautics, 2019).

47. John Venable, "The F-35A Is the World's Most Dominant, Cost-Effective Fighter: The Air Force Needs to Accelerate Its Acquisition Now," *Defense*, March 2, 2020.

48. "US Air Force's Hill Base Receives Final F-35 Lightning II Fighter," Air Force Technology, December 20, 2019.

49. Eric T. Fick, "F-35 PEO End of Year Message to Ms. Lord and Senior Department Leadership," December 19, 2019; and Lt. Gen. Eric Fick, program executive officer, "F-35 Lightning II Program, Statement on F-35 Program Update: Sustainment, Production, and Affordability Challenges," before the Readiness and Tactical Air Land Forces Subcommittees of the Committee on Armed Services, US House of Representatives, November 13, 2019.

50. Loh interview, October 12, 2020.

51. Capt. Thomas "Jethro" Bodine and Cmdr. Gus "Bus" Snodgrass, "Naval Aviation and Weapons in Review," *US Naval Institute Proceedings*, May 2020, 83.

52. The Goldwater-Nichols Act is Public Law 99-433, October 1, 1986. See Locher, *Victory on the Potomac*.

53. Paul McLeary, BreakingDefense.com, May 29, 2020.

54. Garrett Reim, FlightGlobal.com, May 28, 2020.

CHAPTER 12

1. Greg Stearns, personal communication to the author, March 15, 2020.

2. Dave Kelly, input from Ed Beakley to the author, May 15, 2020, excerpt from *Not on My Watch*.

3. Kevin Miller, personal correspondence to the author, March 17, 2020.

4. See Head, *Oswald Boelcke*, on offense (pp. 89–93) and to protect the ground observation and attack aircraft (p. 139).

5. USAF Academy, *Contrails*, 1960, 208.

6. Ibid., 210.

7. Wildenberg, *Destined for Glory*, 214.

8. Ibid., 215.

9. Enthoven interview, April 8, 1970.

10. Interview with Dr. Brown, April 8, 1970.

11. Gen. Ronald Yates, email message to the author, August 19, 2020.

12. Brown interview, April 8, 1970.

13. Gen. Ronald Yates, email message to the author, August 19, 2020.

14. Interview with Dr. Brown, April 8, 1970.

15. James Drew, "USAF's Small UAS Roadmap Calls for Swarming 'Kamikaze' Drones," FlightGlobal.com, May 4, 2016.

16. "The Air Force's Newest MQ-9 Reaper Drone Is Now Hunting ISIS," archived July 7, 2017, at the Wayback Machine, Defensetech.org, June 30, 2017.

Glossary

A

A	attack
AAA	antiaircraft artillery
ACC	Air Combat Command, air component commander
ACT	air combat tactics
AD	Attack Douglas/A-1 Skyraider
ADM	admiral (four stars)
AEF	American Expeditionary Force
AFAC	airborne forward air controller
AFB	Air Force base
AFHRA	Air Force Historical Research Agency
AFSC	Air Force Systems Command
AGL	above ground level
AH-56	Cheyenne, Army armed helicopter
AIM	aerial intercept missile
Alpha Strike	large attack by carrier air wing
ATF	advanced tactical fighter
ATO	air tasking order
AWACS	Airborne Warning and Control System Aircraft

B

B	Boeing Company, Brewster, bomber
BAI	battlefield air interdiction
BDA	bomb damage assessment
BE	British Experimental
brigadier	a one-star general in the Army, Air Force, or Marine Corps
BUAIR	Bureau of Aeronautics
BUWEPS	Bureau of Naval Weapons

C

C	Curtiss aircraft
CAS	close air support
CASF	Composite Air Strike Force
Cmdr.	commander (Navy)
CFP	concept formulation package
CM	chief's memorandum
CNO	chief of naval operations
COAC	Combined Air Operations Center
CSG	Configuration Steering Group, USAF
CV/CVA/CVAN	Fleet aircraft carrier / aircraft carrier attack / nuclear powered
CVL	fleet aircraft carrier light

D

D	Douglas Aircraft Corporation
DAC	Douglas Aircraft Corporation
DCNO	deputy chief of naval operations
DCP	development concept paper
DCS/Ops	deputy chief of staff / plans and operations (USAF)
DCS/R&D	deputy chief of staff / research & development
DDR&E	director, Defense Research & Engineering
DH	de Havilland
DMZ	demilitarized zone
DOD	Department of Defense
DSARC	Defense Systems Acquisition Council

E

ECM	electronic countermeasures
EGT	exhaust gas temperature

F

F	fighter, Grumman Aircraft Engineering Company
F/A	fighter/attack
FAC	forward air controller
FAC(A)	forward air controller airborne
FEAF	Far East Air Forces
FLIR	forward-looking infrared
FPM	flight path marker
F-X	Fighter Experimental

G

G	Goodyear
GA	ground attack
GAEC	Grumman Aircraft Engineering Company
GAU-8	Gun Aircraft Unit-8 (A-10)
GAX	ground attack experimental
GBU	glide bomb unit
GD	General Dynamics
GFE	government-furnished equipment
GPS	global positioning system

H

HARM	high-speed antiradiation missile
HMS	Her/His Majesty's Ship (UK)
HUD	heads-up display
HVAR	high-velocity aerial rocket

I

INS	Inertial Navigation System

J

J	jet engine
JAOC	Joint Air Operations Center
JDAM	Joint Direct Attack Munition
JTAC	joint tactical air controller

K

K	knots, nautical miles per hour
KFOR	NATO-led Kosovo Force
KLA	Kosovo Land Area

L

LASTE	low-altitude safety and targeting enhancement
LCmdr.	lieutenant commander
Lt.	lieutenant (USN)
Lt j.g.	lieutenant junior grade
Lt. Gen.	lieutenant general (three stars)
LTV	Ling-Temco-Vought
LWF	lightweight fighter

M

MacAir	McDonnell Douglas
Maj. Gen.	major general (two stars)
MDC	McDonnell Douglas Corporation
MERS	multiple ejection rack
Mk. 82/83/84	500, 1,000, and 2,000 bombs
Mph	statute miles per hour

N

NA	North American
NAA	North American Aviation
NAS	naval air station
NASNI	Naval Air Station North Island
NAVAIR	Naval Air Systems Command
NAWCAD	Naval Air Warfare Center Aircraft Division, Patauxent River, MD
NAWCWD	Naval Air Warfare Center Weapons Division, Point Mugu / China Lake, CA
NPE	naval primary evaluation
NSAWC	Naval Strike & Air Warfare Center

O

O	observation
OPNAV	Office of the Chief of Naval Operations
OSD	office of the secretary of defense

P

P	pursuit
PAVN	People's Army of North Vietnam
PBY	patrol bomber consolidated
PE	precision engagement

PMO	Program Management Office (Navy)
POL	petroleum, oil, and lubricants

R

R	radial reciprocating engine
RAD	requirements action directive
RAdm.	rear admiral (two stars)
RAF	Royal Air Force (UK)
RAD	requirements action directive
RAG	replacement air group
RFC	Royal Flying Corps (UK)
R&D	research and development
RDQ	operational requirements and development plans, USAF
RDT&E	research, development, test & evaluation
RESCAP	Rescue Combat Air Patrol
RFP	request for proposals
RIO	radar intercept officer
RNAS	Royal Naval Air Service (UK)
ROE	Rules of Engagement

S

SAM	surface-to-air missile
SBD	Scout Bomber Douglas
Schlachtflieger	ground attack squadron
SECDEF	secretary of defense
SIOP	single integrated operations plan
Slick Wing	ordnance configuration with only one bomb per pylon
SPAD	AD or A-1 Skyraider
SPO	System Program Office (USAF)

T

T	torpedo, trainer
TAC	Tactical Air Command
TB	torpedo bomber
TBM	Torpedo Bomber Martin
TER	triple ejection rack
TF-30	the jet engine in the A-7A/B/C

TF-41	the jet engine in the A-7D/E
TFX	Tactical Fighter Experimental
TSF	tactical strike fighter

U

U	utility aircraft, Chance Vought
UCAV	unmanned combat air vehicle
USAAC	US Army Air Corps
USAAF	US Army Air Forces
USAAS	US Army Air Service
USN	US Navy
USS	United States Navy Ship

V

V	fixed wing
VA	fixed-wing aircraft, light attack
VAC	Vought Aircraft Corporation
VAdm.	vice admiral (three stars)
VAH	fixed-wing aircraft, heavy attack
VAL	Fixed-Wing Light-Attack Competition
VB	fixed-wing bomber
VC	Vietcong
VF	fixed-wing fighter (squadron)
VFR	visual flight rules
VFX	Fighter Aircraft Experimental
VNAF	Vietnamese air force
VS	fixed-wing scout
VT	fixed-wing aircraft training
VO	fixed-wing observation

W

WP	white phosphorus
WTTP	Weapons and Tactics Training Program

X

X	experimental

Y

Y	prototype, preproduction

Z

Z	lighter-than-air airship

Bibliography

Unpublished Government Sources

Bureau of Naval Weapons. "VAL Competition, Analysis and Recommendations." November 4, 1963.

Chief of Naval Operations. *Sea-Based Air Strike Forces Study for the Secretary of Defense* (U). Office of the Chief of Naval Operations, May 17, 1963.

Defense Director of Research and Engineering. Close-air-support files.

Headquarters, A-7D Office Files.
  A-7D Program Management Office. Office files.
  A-7D Historical Reports.
  Top Management Information Reports.

Naval Air Systems Command, A-7 Program Management Office. Office files.

Secretary of the Air Force. Office files.
  Office of Legislative Liaison. Research branch files.
  Research and Analysis Library. Files.

US Air Force, Air Force Systems Command.

US Air Force Headquarters, the Air Staff.
  Director of Aerospace Programs. Office files.
  Directorate of Operations. Office files.
  Directorate of Operational Requirements and Development Plans. Office files.
  Directorate of Plans. Office files.
  Directorate of Production and Programming, A-7D Program Element Monitor. Office files.

US Air Force, Tactical Air Command.
  "Cost Effectiveness of Close Air Support." Operations Analysis Working Paper No. 119 (TAC OA WP-119, April 1965).
  Directorate of Requirements. Office files.
  History of the Tactical Air Command: 1964–1969. Historical files.

US Navy, Bureau of Aeronautics. *Attack Plane Design History: US Navy to 1957*. Lee Pearson, reported author.

US Navy, Office of the Chief of Naval Operations.
  A-7 Program Management Office. Office files.

Published Government Sources

Cooling, Benjamin Franklin, ed. *Case Studies in the Development of Close Air Support*. Washington, DC: USGPO, 1990.

———. *Case Studies in the Achievement of Air Superiority*. Washington, DC: Air Force History and Museums Program, 1994.

Department of Defense, US Joint Chiefs of Staff. *DoD Dictionary of Military and Associated Terms*. Joint Publication 1-02. Updated January 2020.

Evans, Mark I., and Roy A. Grossnick. *United States Naval Aviation: 1910–2010*. Vol. 1, *Chronology*. 5th ed. Washington, DC: Naval History and Heritage Command, 2015.

Greer, Thomas H. *The Development of Air Doctrine in the Army Air Arm: 1917–1941*. Washington, DC: Office of Air Force History, 1955.

Maurer, Maurer, ed. *The US Air Service in World War I*. 4 vols. Maxwell AFB, AL: Albert F. Simpson Historical Research Center, 1978.

Shiner, John F. *Foulois and the US Army Air Corps: 1931–1935*. Washington, DC: Office of Air Force History, 1983.

Tate, James P. *The Army and Its Air Corps Policy toward Aviation, 1919–1941*. Maxwell AFB, AL: Air University Press, 1998.

US Air Force Air University. *The Development of Air Doctrine in the Army Air Arm, 1917–1941*. Gunter Air Force Base, AL: Extension Course Institute, 1961.

US Air Force, Tactical Air Command. *Tactical Bombardment Manual*, 51-1, 1957.

US Air Force–US Army. *Final Report, Close Air Support Boards*, August 1963.

US Army, Close Air Support Requirements Board. *Close Air Support*. Fort Meade, Maryland, 1963.

US Army, Combat Developments Command, Institute of Special Studies. *A Short History of Close Air Support Issues*, 1968.

US Congress, House of Representatives Committee on Appropriations and Committee on Armed Services. Multiple *Reports of Hearings*.

US Congress, Senate Committee on Appropriations and Committee on Armed Services. Multiple *Reports of Hearings*.

US Congress, Special Committee to Investigate the National Defense Program. *Investigation of the National Defense Program, Additional Report*. 78th Congress, 1st Session, July 10, 1943, also known as the Truman Committee.

Books

Anderton, David A. *North American F-100 Super Sabre*. London: Osprey, 1987.

Art, Robert J., *The TFX Decision: McNamara and the Military*. Boston: Little, Brown & Co.: 1968.

Birzer, Norman, and Peter Mersky. *US Navy A-7 Corsair II Units of the Vietnam War*. Oxford: Osprey, 2004.

Bodie, Warren M. *Republic P-47 Thunderbolt: From Seversky to Victory*. Haiesville, GA: Widewing, 1994.

Braswell, Arnold W. Brig. Gen. (later Lt. Gen.). *The Role of the Systems Analysis Staff in Defense Decision Making*, unpublished master's thesis. Washington, DC: George Washington University, 1967.

Burton, Col. James G. *The Pentagon Wars: Reformers Challenge the Old Guard.* Annapolis, MD: Naval Institute Press, 1993.

Campbell, Douglas N. *The Warthog and the Close Air Support Debate.* Annapolis: MD: Naval Institute Press, 2003.

Coonts, Stephen, and Barrett Tillman. *Dragon's Jaw: An Epic Story of Courage and Tenacity in Vietnam.* Lebanon, IN: DeCapo, 2019.

Coram, Robert. *Boyd: The Fighter Pilot Who Changed the Art of War.* New York: Little, Brown, 2002.

Davies, Steve. *Fairchild Republic A-10 Thunderbolt II: 1972 to Date (All Marks)—Owners Workshop Manual.* Somerset, UK: Haynes, 2017.

Davis, Vincent. *The Admirals Lobby.* Chapel Hill: University of North Carolina Press, 1967.

———. *The Politics of Innovation: Patterns in Navy Cases.* Social Science Foundation and Graduate School of International Studies Monograph Series in World Affairs 4.3. Denver. CO: University of Denver, 1966–67.

Dial, Jay Frank. *The Chance Vought F4U-1 and F4U-2 Corsair.* Profile Publications 47. Leatherhead, UK: Profile Publications, n.d.

———. *The Chance Vought F4U-4 to F4U-7 Corsair.* Profile Publications 150. Leatherhead, UK: Profile Publications, n.d.

Dorr, Robert F. "Gulf War: Desert Storm Was an Heroic Moment for A-7E Corsair II." Defense Media Network, January 25, 2011.

———. *Skyraider: The Illustrated History of the Vietnam War.* New York: Bantam Books. 1988.

———. *Vought A-7 Corsair II.* London: Osprey, 1985.

Doyle, David. *SBD Dauntless: Douglas's US Navy and Marine Corps Dive-Bomber in World War II.* Atglen, PA: Schiffer, 2019.

Duiven, Rick, and Dan-San Abbott. *Schlachtflieger! Germany and the Origins of Air/Ground Support, 1916–-1918.* Atglen, PA: Schiffer Military History, 2006.

Evans, Mark L., and Roy A. Grossnick. *United States Naval Aviation: 1910–2010.* Vol. 1, *Chronology.* 5th ed. Washington, DC: Naval History and Heritage Command, 2015.

Gallery Books. *The World's Great Attack Aircraft.* New York: Gallery Books, 1988.

Gann, Harry. *The Douglas A-4 Skyhawk.* Profile Publications 102. Leatherhead, UK: Profile Publications, 1966.

———. *The Douglas Skyraider.* Profile Publications 60. Leatherhead, UK: Profile Publication, 1965.

Gardner, Thomas E. *F-100 Super Sabre at War.* St. Paul, MN: Zenith, 2007.

Green, William. *The World's Fighting Planes.* Garden City, NY: Doubleday, 1963.

Gruenhagen, Robert W. *Mustang: The Story of the P-51 Fighter.* New York: Arco, 1969.

Guderian, Heinz W. *Achtung-Panzer! The Development of Armoured Forces, Their Tactics and Operational Potential.* London: Arms and Armour, 1992.

———. *Panzer Leader.* New York: Dutton, 1952.

Hampton. Dan. *Lords of the Sky: Fighter Pilots and Air Combat, from the Red Baron to the F-16.* New York: HarperCollins, 2014.

———. *Viper Pilot: A Memoir of Combat.* New York: HarperCollins, 2012.

Hart, G. H. Liddell. *History of the Second World War.* New York: Putnam & Sons, 1970.

Have, Christopher E. (col., USAF), and Phil M. Haun (lt. col., USAF). *A-10s over Kosovo.* Maxwell AFB, AL: Air University Press, 2003.

Head, RG. *Oswald Boelcke: Germany's First Fighter Ace and Father of Air Combat.* London: Grub Street, 2016.

Head, RG, and Ervin Rokke, eds. *American Defense Policy.* 3rd ed. Baltimore: Johns Hopkins University Press, 1973.

Heinemann, Edward H., and Rosario Rausa. *Ed Heinemann, Combat Aircraft Designer.* Annapolis, MD: Naval Institute Press, 1980.

Heinemann, Edward H., Rosario Rausa, and K. E. Van Every. *Aircraft Design.* Mount Pleasant, SC: Nautical & Aviation Publishing, 1985.

Hobson, Chris, and Dave Lovelady. Vietnam Air Losses: USAF, Navy, and Marine Corps Fixed Wing Aircraft Losses in Southeast Asia; 1961–1973 (searchable database). https://www.vietnamairlosses.com (UK, 2001).

Holley, I. B. *Ideas and Weapons.* New Haven, CT: Yale University Press, 1953.

Hoskins, Tony. *Douglas A-1 Skyraider.* Somerset, UK: Haynes, 2017.

Hozzel, Paul-Werner, brigadier general (ret.), German air force. *Recollections and Experiences of a Stuka Pilot: 1931–1945.* Pine Mountain, GA: Ohio Battelle Institute, 1978.

Hukee, Byron. *USAF and VNAF A-1 Skyraider Units of the Vietnam War.* Oxford: Osprey, 2013.

Jablonski, Edward. *Airwar.* New York: Doubleday, 1979.

Jones, H. A. *The War in the Air: Being the Part Played by the Royal Air Force.* Vol. 2. Oxford: Claredon, 1922–1937.

Kelly, David. *Not on My Watch.* Self-published by Blurb, 2014. Portion on Remembered Sky website.

Kelly, Orr. *Hornet: The Inside Story of the F/A-18.* Novato, CA: Presidio, 1990.

Lambeth, Benjamin S. *Combat Pair: The Evolution of Air Force-Navy Integration in Strike Warfare.* Santa Monica, CA: RAND, 2007.

Laslie, Brian. *The Air Force Way of War; US Tactics and Training after Vietnam.* Lexington, KY: University Press of Kentucky, 2015.

Leslie, Jack, and John Leslie. *In My Father's Footsteps: A Story of Father and Son Naval Aviators.* Jacksonville, FL: OnLine Binding, 2015.

Locher, James R., III. *Victory on the Potomac: The Goldwater-Nichols Act Unifies the Pentagon.* College Station: Texas A&M University Press, 2002.

LTV. *A-7D Project Master Plan.* 1965.

Manson, Frank A., and Malcolm W. Cagle. *The Sea War in Korea.* Annapolis, MD: Naval Institute Press, 1957.

Marrett, George J. *Cheating Death: Combat Air Rescues in Vietnam and Laos.* Washington, DC: Smithsonian Books, 2003.

Mason, Herbert Molloy, Jr. *The Lafayette Escadrille.* New York: Random House, 1964.

McCarthy, Brig. Gen. James R., and Lt. Col. George B. Allison. *Linebacker II: A View from the Rock.* Washington, DC: Smithsonian Press, 2018. Originally published as a USAF Southeast Asia Monograph, Vol. VI, Monograph 8. Washington, DC: Office of Air Force History, 1979.

McCullough, David. *The Wright Brothers*. New York: Simon & Schuster, 2015.

Melhorn, Charles M. *Two-Block Fox: The Rise of the Aircraft Carrier*. Annapolis, MD: Naval Institute Press, 1974.

Messimer, Dwight R. *An Incipient Mutiny: The Story of the US Army Signal Corps Pilot Revolt*. Lincoln: University of Nebraska Press, 2020.

Michel, Marshall L., III. *Operation Linebacker II, 1972: The B-52s Are Sent to Hanoi*. Oxford: Osprey, 2018.

Michener, James. *The Bridges at Toko Ri*. New York: Random House, 1953.

Miller, Kevin. *Fight Fight*. The third novel of his Raven One trilogy. San Diego, CA: Braveship Books, 2018.

———. *The Silver Waterfall: A Novel of the Battle of Midway*. San Diego, CA: Braveship Books, 2020.

Mitchell, Brig. Gen. William. *Memoirs of World War I: From Start to Finish of Our Greatest War*. New York: Random House, 1960. Originally copyrighted in 1928.

Mondey, David. *The Concise Guide to American Aircraft of World War II*. London: Chancellor, 1966.

Munson, Kenneth. *Bombers between the Wars, 1919–1939*. New York: Macmillan, 1970.

Neubeck, Ken. *A-10 Thunderbolt II: Fairchild Republic's Warthog at War*. Atglen, PA: Schiffer, 2019.

Olds, Brig. Gen. Robin, Christina Olds, and Ed Rasimus. *Fighter Pilot: The Memoirs of Legendary Ace Robin Olds*. New York: St. Martin's Griffin, 2010.

Peck, Merton, and Frederic M. Scherer. *The Weapons Acquisition Process: An Economic Analysis*. Cambridge, MA: Harvard Business School, 1962.

Pederson, Tom. *Top Gun: An American Story*. New York: Hachette Books, 2019.

Postan, M. M., D. Hay, and J. D. Scott. *Design and Development of Weapons: Studies in Government and Industrial Organization*. London: Her Majesty's Stationary Office, 1964.

Rausa, Rosario. *Skyraider: The Douglas A-1 "Flying Dump Truck."* Cambridge, UK: Patrick Stevens, 1982.

Renshaw, Andy, and Andy Evans. *The Douglas A-1 Skyraider: A Comprehensive Guide*. Bedford, UK: HobbyZone, 2016.

Ridnouer, Col. Dennis M., ed. *The Vietnam Air War: From the Cockpit*. North Charleston, SC: CreateSpace, 2017. See pp. 328–34.

Rudel, Hans Ulrich. *Stuka Pilot*. New York: Ballantine Books, 1958.

Schlesinger, Arthur M., Jr. *A Thousand Days*. New York: Fawcett Crest, 1965.

Shepperd, Don. *"Misty": First Person Stories of the F-100 Misty Fast FACs in the Vietnam War, by the Misty FACs Themselves*. Bloomington, IN: AuthorHouse, 2003.

Shepperd, Don, and Rick Newman. *Bury Us Upside Down: The Misty Pilots and the Secret Battle for the Ho Chi Minh Trail*. New York: Random House, 2006.

Smallwood, William L. *Warthog: Flying the A-10 in the Gulf War*. London: Brassey's, 1993.

Smith, Perry. *The Air Force Plans for Peace: 1943–1945*. Baltimore: Johns Hopkins University Press, 1970.

Swanborough, F. G. *United States Military Aircraft since 1919*. New York: Putnam, 1963.

Thompson, Tommy. *Scooter: The Story of the A-4 Skyhawk*. Manchester, UK: Crecy, 2011.

Tilford, Earl H. *Setup: What the Air Force Did in Vietnam and Why*. Maxwell Air Force Base, AL: Air University Press, 1991.

Wagner, Ray, and Edgar Schmued. *Designing the P-51*. New York: Orion, 1990.

Wetterhahn, Ralph F. *The Last Battle: The Mayaguez Incident and the End of the Vietnam War*. New York: Penguin, 2002.

Wetzel, Gary. *A-10 Thunderbolt II Units of Operation Enduring Freedom, 2008–14*. Oxford: Osprey, 2015.

———. *Vought A-7 Corsair II*. London: Osprey Air Combat, 1985.

Wildenberg, Thomas. *Destined for Glory: Dive Bombing, Midway, and the Evolution of Carrier Airpower*. Annapolis, MD: Naval Institute Press, 1998.

Winter, Denis. *The First of the Few: Fighter Pilots of the First World War*. Athens: University of Georgia Press, 1982.

Wolfe, Tom. *The Right Stuff*. New York: Picador, 1979.

Monographs

Arnold, Henry H. "Hap." *The History of Rockwell Field*. 1923. Prepublication manuscript edited by Michael Aten, San Diego Air & Space Museum, 2005. Available at either SDASM or the Coronado Historical Association, Coronado, CA, 2020.

Fogleman, Ronald R. "The Development of Ground Attack Aviation in the United States Army Air Arm: Evolution of a Doctrine, 1908–1926." MA thesis, Duke University, 1971.

Jacques, David R., and Dennis D. Strouble. *A-10 Thunderbolt II (Warthog) Systems Engineering Case Study*. Wright-Patterson AFB, OH: Air Force Center for Systems Engineering, Air Force Institute of Technology, 2010.

Keely, Leroy B. *Evolution of the A-7 Attack Aircraft*. Fort Belvoir, VA: Defense Systems Management School, May 20, 1972.

Kuiper, Richard L. "Close Air Support: Concepts and Doctrine, 1954–1968." Unpublished MA thesis, Auburn University, 1969.

Ratley, Lonnie Otis. "A Comparison of the USAF Projected A-10 Employment in Europe and the Luftwaffe *Schlachtgeschwader* Experience on the Eastern Front in World War Two." Thesis, Naval Postgraduate School, Monterey, California, 1977.

———. Antitank Warfare Seminar. Transcript. Washington, DC, October 14–15, 1976.

Rippon, T. S. (MRCS, LRCP, London, captain, RAMC; attached to RAF), and E. G. Manuel, lieutenant, RAF. "The Essential Characteristics of Successful and Unsuccessful Aviators." *The Lancet* 192, no. 4961 (September 28, 1918): 411–15.

Periodicals

"A-1 versus A-7 CAS/SAR Role." *A-1 Skyraider Association Newsletter*, August 1975, 2.

Adamczyk, Ed. "Lockheed Martin to Build F-16s in Potential $62 Billion Contract." *Defense News*, August 17, 2020.

Anonymous F/A-18 pilot, landing signal officer. "The 'Rhino.'"

Arndt, Major a.D. Hans. Quoted in Friedrich Sesselberg, *Der Stellungskrieg, 1914–1918*. Cited in Duiven and Abbott 2006, 25.

Boeding, Brian. "A-10: Hey Air Force, There's More to Survival than Hiding." *Breaking Defense*, June 26, 2020.

Boyne, Walter U. "Linebacker II." *Air Force Magazine*, July 19, 2008.

Brazelton, David. "The Douglas SBD Dauntless." Profile Publications 94. Leatherhead, UK: Profile Publications, 1966.

Brown, Harold. "Deterrence without Destabilization." *Air Force and Space Digest*, September 1968, 56–60.

Bruce, J. M. *The de Havilland D.H.4.* Profile Publications 26. Leatherhead, UK: Profile Publications, n.d.

Correll, John T. "The Difference in Korea." *Air Force Magazine*, April 2020, 56–60.

———. "The Reformers." *Air Force Magazine*, February 1, 2008.

———. "The Ups and Downs of Close Air Support." *Air Force Magazine*, December 2019, 56–61.

Cox, Bob. "F-16's Developer, Harry J. Hillaker, Dies at 89." *F-16 Fighting Falcon News*, February 10, 2009.

de Vlaming, Douglas. "The Rescue of Bobbin 05." *Daedalus Flyer*, Summer 2015.

Eckstein, Megan. "Navy Says Ending Super Hornet Line Frees Up Resources for Life Extension Work." *Defense News*, March 10, 2020.

Enthoven, Alain C. "Choosing Strategies and Selecting Weapon Systems." Address before the Naval War College, Newport, RI, on June 6, 1963. In *A Modern Design for Defense Decision: A McNamara-Hitch-Enthoven Anthology*. Edited by Samuel A. Tucker, 133–48. Washington, DC: Industrial College of the Armed Forces, 1966.

Erickson, Mark St. John. "Battleship Bombings of July 1921 Marked Milestone Step in Development of Air Power." *Daily Press* (Newport News, VA), July 20, 2018.

Esposito, Col. Vincent J., ed. *The West Point Atlas of American Wars*. Vol. 2. New York: Frederick A. Praeger, 1959.

Gallery Books. "A-7 Corsair II: Super SLUF." In *The World's Great Attack Aircraft*. By Gallery Books, 80–90. New York: Gallery Books, 1988.

Gann, Harry. *The Douglas Skyraider*. Profile Publications 60. Leatherhead, UK: Profile Publications, 1965.

Goodspeed, Hill. "Foundation for Victory: US Navy Aircraft Development, 1922–1945." In *One Hundred Years of US Navy Air Power*. Edited by Douglas V. Smith, 199–219. Annapolis, MD: Naval Institute Press, 2010.

Gorrell, Col. E. S. "Notes on Employment of the Air Service from the General Staff Viewpoint." Cited in Fogleman 1971, 64.

Green, William. "Vought F4U-1, F4U-4 (FG-1 Corsair)." In *War Planes of the Second World War*. Vol. 4, *Fighters*. By William Green, 188–94. Garden City, NY: Doubleday, 1973.

Harder, Robert O. "The 11-Day War." *Aviation History*, January 2013.

Head, RG. "The Air Force A-7 Decision: The Politics of Close Air Support." *Aerospace Historian*, Winter 1974, 224–26.

———. "Doctrinal Innovation and the A-7 Attack Aircraft Decisions." In *American Defense Policy*. 3rd ed. Edited by RG Head and Ervin Rokke, 431–45. Baltimore: John Hopkins University Press, 1973.

Hillaker, Harry J. "Technology and the F-16 Fighting Falcon Jet Fighter." *Centennial of Aviation* 34, no. 1 (March 1, 2004). National Academy of Engineering website. http://www.nae.edu/7447/ TechnologyandtheF-16FightingFalconJetFighter.

Holmquist, C. O. "Developments and Problems in Carrier-Based Attack Aircraft." In *Naval Review: 1969*. Edited by Frank Uhlig Jr., 195–215. Annapolis, MD: Naval Institute Press, 1969.

Judson, Jen. "Lockheed and Bell Will Compete Head-to-Head to Build US Army's Future Attack Recon Aircraft." *Defense News*, March 25, 2020.

Kennett, Lee. "Developments to 1939." In *Case Studies in the Development of Close Air Support*. Edited by Benjamin Franklin Cooling, 13–70. Washington, DC, USGPO, 1990.

Larrison, John. "How the SANDYs Got Started: The Day the First A-1s Went to Thailand." *Daedalus Flyer*, Winter 1999, 13–18.

Lehman, John, secretary of the Navy. "Is Naval Aviation Culture Dead?" *Proceedings*, September 2011.

McFall, Lt. Cmdr. A. Dodge. "Farewell to Spads." *US Naval Institute Proceedings*, April 1965.

Miller, Kevin. "The Legacy of Operation Desert Fox." *Hook Magazine*, Fall 2018.

Nickell, Paul, and Tyler Rogoway. "Taking the F-14A Tomcat on Cruise for My First Time." *War Zone*, April 4, 2017. www.thedrive.com/the-war-zone.

Oliveri, Frank. "The Warthog Round at Gunsmoke." *Air Force Magazine*, March 1992, 32–37.

Project on Government Oversight (POGO), 2020. "Member of Fighter Mafia Passes." Colonel Everest Riccioni, May 6, 2015.

Riccioni, Colonel Everest, USAF. "Brief Summary of My Background and Major Accomplishments." September 8, 2014. Center for Defense Information, Project on Government Oversight (POGO), 2020.

Riksick, Colin. "F-22 Raptor vs F-35 Lightning II." *Military Machine*, February 28, 2020.

Rippon, T. S. (MD, MRCS, LRCP, London, captain, RAMC; attached to Royal Air Force), and Lt. E. G. Manuel, RAF. "The Essential Characteristics of Successful and Unsuccessful Aviators." *The Lancet* 192, no. 4961 (September 28, 1918): 411.

Stolfi, Russel H. S., J. E. Clemens, and R. R. McEachin. "Combat Damage Assessment Team A-10/GAU-8 Low Angle Firings versus Individual Soviet Tanks." Monterey, CA: Naval Postgraduate School, Calhoun Institutional Archive, DSpace Repository, 1979-08. http://hdl.handle.net/10945/29216.

Turner, Chris. "Fighter Mafia: Colonel John Boyd, the Brain behind Fighter Dominance." Avgeekery.com, June 23, 2020.

———. "Fighter Mafia Part 2: Pierre Sprey, A-10 Close Air Support Aircraft Developer." Avgeekery.com, October 9, 2020.

———. "Fighter Mafia Part 3: Thomas P. "Tom" Christie, Wizard behind the Curtain." Avgeekery.com, October 31, 2020.

Viccellio, Brig. Gen. Henry P., commander, Nineteenth Air Force. "Composite Air Strike Force." *Air University Review* 9, no. 1 (Winter 1956–57).

Internet and Videos

Beakley, Ed. *1942—the Year of the Aircraft Carrier*. 30 parts. Blown Slick series 13. The Remembered Sky website, 2019.

———. *Air War Vietnam: Remembrance at Forty Years—All Days Come from One Day.* The Remembered Sky website, 2012.

———. *Alpha Strike.* 3 parts. The Remembered Sky website, 2012.

———. *The Mission of "Attack."* Blown Slick series 1. The Remembered Sky website, 2015.

Fogleman, General Ronald. MISTY Pilots Panel. *Air Force Association Blog.*

Jacob, Joachim. Warthog News. warthognews@ymail.com.

Sullivan, G. Ray. *PAC 6: A General's Decision; A Film about Linebacker II.* Atlanta: Peachtree Films, 2016.

Interviews

Col. R. C. Allen (USAF. Ret.), manager, A-7D requirements, Vought Aeronautics Division, LTV.

Mr. John B. Allyn, vice president, LTV Washington Operations.

VAdm. Brent Bennitt, commander, Naval Air Forces.

Dr. Harold Brown, director, DDR&E; secretary of the Air Force; president, Cal Tech.

Mr. Robert S. Buzzard, vice president of A-7 programs, Vought Aeronautics Division, LTV.

Col. Edward A. Chavarrie, staff officer in DCS / plans and operations, Air Staff.

VAdm. Thomas F. Connolly, deputy chief of naval operations for air, OPNAV.

Capt. Carl M. Cruse, A-7 program manager, Naval Air Systems Command.

Mr. Edwin F. Cvetko, vice president for manufacturing and formerly A-7A/B program director, Vought Aeronautics Division, LTV.

Mr. Harry Davis, deputy assistant secretary of the Air Force for special programs.

Maj. Gen. Kenneth C. Dempster, deputy director of operational requirements for general purpose and airlift forces, Air Staff.

VAdm. Vincent P. De Poix, deputy director of DDR&E for administration, evaluation, and management, OSD.

Gen. Gabriel P. Disosway, commander, Tactical Air Command.

Mr. Lee E. Dolan, Air Force Office of Operations Analysis, Air Staff.

Capt. Robert F. Doss, A-7 deputy program manager, Naval Air Systems Command.

LCmdr. Charles M. Earnest, OSD Systems Analysis.

Col. William R. Edgar, director of information, Tactical Air Command.

Dr. Alain C. Enthoven, assistant secretary of defense for systems analysis, OSD, Litton Industries.

Col. Howard M. Fish, special assistant for analysis and force plans to the director for plans and operations, Air Staff.

Mr. Charles A. Fowler, deputy director for tactical warfare programs, DDR&E, OSD.

Lt. Col. Leo J. Gagnon, A-7 and F-4 program element monitor, Directorate of Production and Programming, Air Staff.

Capt. Thomas J. Gallagher, A-7 program manager, Naval Air Systems Command.

Mr. Ben Gilleas, director of investigations, Preparedness Investigating Subcommittee of the Senate Committee on Armed Services.

Mr. Edward M. Glass, assistant director for laboratory management, DDR&E, OSD.

Lt. Gen. Gordon M. Graham, vice commander, Tactical Air Command.

Mr. George Haering, Systems Analysis Division of the Office of the Chief of Naval Operations, OPNAV.

Lt. Col. Richard A. Haggren, Directorate of Operational Requirements and Development Plans, Air Staff.

Lt. Gen. Robert E. Hails, A-7D deputy program manager, Naval Air Systems Command.

Mr. Paul Hare, A-7D program director, Vought Aeronautics Division, LTV.

Dr. Victor K. Heyman, Office of Systems Analysis, OSD.

Col. (later Major General) James R. Hildreth, Directorate of Operational Requirements and Development Plans, Air Staff.

Col. Claude G. Horne, deputy director of requirements, Tactical Air Command.

Mr. F. C. Horton, staff assistant to the assistant director for land warfare, DDR&E, OSD.

Mr. Bernard Kornhauser, Air Force Office of Operations Analysis, Air Staff.

Mr. J. K. Langford, director of marketing, Vought Aeronautics Division, LTV.

Gen. John Michael Loh, commander Air Combat Command.

Mr. Sol Love, president, Vought Aeronautics Division, LTV.

Mr. Burt Marshall Jr., Air Force requirements manager, Vought Aeronautics Division, LTV.

Mr. James E. Martin, vice president, engineering and logistics, Vought Aeronautics Division, LTV.

Lt. Col. Charles W. McClarren, commander, Detachment 1, 57th Fighter Weapons Wing (A-7D Category III Test and Evaluation).

Gen. John P. McConnell, chief of staff, US Air Force.

Mr. Whitney McCormack, A-7D program director, Vought Aeronautics Division, LTV.

Mr. Russell Murray II, principal deputy assistant, secretary of defense; later assistant secretary, systems analysis, OSD.

Mr. Thomas C. Muse, assistant director, Tactical Air Programs, DDR&E, OSD.

Dr. William A. Niskanen Jr., deputy director for special studies, systems analysis, OSD.

Col. John E. Pitts Jr., Tactical Division, deputy chief of staff, plans and operations.

Col. Royce W. Priest (USAF, Ret.), A-7D program element monitor, Air Staff; later assistant A-7D program manager, Vought Aeronautics Division, LTV.

Col. William Ritchie, Directorate of Operational Requirements and Development Plans, Air Staff.

Dr. Dieter Schwebs, Office of the Assistant Secretary of Defense, Systems Analysis, OSD.

Mr. George W. Sickle, assistant chief, Office of Operations Analysis, Tactical Air Command.

VAdm. Robert J. Spane, commander, Naval Air Force US Pacific Fleet.

Mr. George A. Spangenberg, director, Evaluation Division, Naval Air Systems Command.

Mr. Donald F. Spencer, Office of the Director Defense Research & Engineering, OSD.

Mr. Pierre Sprey, Tactical Air Division, Office of the Assistant Secretary of Defense, Systems Analysis, OSD.

Mr. Raymond M. Standahar, Office of Tactical Air Systems, DDR&E, OSD.

Col. Harold W. Stoneberger, A-7D deputy program manager, Naval Air Systems Command.

Gen. Ronald Yates, commander, Air Force Systems Command.

Index

Boldface indicates table.

General

1960 election, 68
1962 Geneva Accords, 69, 75
1968 election, 159
2.75-inch rocket pods, 74
30 mm cannon, (*also see* GAU-8), 133, 186, 191–192, 195, 224, 229, 248

ANSER Corporation, 185
A-X, A-10, 80–81, 87, 183, 189, 205
A-7D/A-10 Flyoff, 190
A-10 RAD, 128, 134, 139, 141, 143, 146, 148, 150, 156, 185–186
retirement plans, 203
sortie record, 193
ADF navigation, 75
Advanced Aerial Fire Support System (AAFSS/AH-56), 107, 183
Aeronautical Systems Division (ASD), 203–204
afterburning turbofan engine, 39, 84
Akagi, Japanese aircraft carrier, 57
Agan, Arthur C., Maj. Gen., 109–110, 113–114
AIM-9 Sidewinder, 60, 98, 179, 194
aircraft generations, **205**
Air Corps Tactical School, 30, 32
air cover, 75, 107, 177, 193, 221
air defense fighters, 69
Air:
    Interdiction (*see* interdiction)
    National Guard Bureau, 199
    Staff Board, 115, 131–133, 148–150, 157

superiority, 11, 13, 16, 24, 27, 38, 42–45, 47, 77, 79–82, 92, 98, 107, 109, 115, 117, 123, 139, 140, 184, 203, 208, 210, 214–215, 217, 221–223, 227
    tasking order, 193, 215, 247
air/land battle, 192
Air Force:
    Academy, 4, 12, 74, 175, 178, 180, 204–205
    Close Air Support Board, 105
    Reserve, 191, 199
Air Service Final Report, 22, 23
Alabama, US battleship, 30
Allyn, John, 92
Almond, Edward M., Maj. Gen., 45
Alpha Strike Group, 72, 170–171, 173
American Expeditionary Force (AEF), 21–24
Anderson, George, Adm., CNO, 82
Anderson, Orvil A., Gen., 37
anti-aircraft artillery (AAA), 78, 81, 124, 166, 168, 170–172, 175–176, 180, 196, 223
antiskid brakes, 100, 227
Anti-submarine Warfare (ASW), 64
Argonne Offensive, 23–24, 40
Armed Reconnaissance, 11, 70, 120, 170, 176, 194
Armed Services Committees, 97, 101, 112, 158–161, 188, 189
Armistice Day, 21, 26
armor, 18
armor-piercing shell, 180
Army:
    Air Corps, 24, 25, 29–31, 34–37, 39, 41–42, 161, 222–223

Air Forces, 7, 31, 35–37, 41, 43, 59, 184, 204
Air Service, 20, 20–24, 29, 42, 49, 221, 222
Close Air Support Board, 104
Command and General Staff College, 101
conservative approach, 102
Special Forces camps, 76
Arnold, Henry "Hap," Gen., 5, 35, 36
arresting wire, 72
artillery spotting, 15–16, 19, 23, 27, 221
A-Shau Valley, 77
attack and fighter communities, 8, 9, 169, 183, 191–192, 219, 227, 228
Attack Carrier force level analysis, 87
attack culture, Air Force, 221
attack culture, Navy/USMC, 219
attack helicopter, 103, 106, 132
Attack Plane Design History, 5, 54
attrition, 13, 21, 62, 81, 88, 143, 152
Aurand, E. P., VAdm., 87
aviation cadets, 100
Aviation Requirements Branch, 90
Aviation Week, 89, 94, 112, 117
avionics ground equipment, 158

backlog, 92
Balkans, 197
Barrel Roll zone, Laos, 70
basic attack formation, 123
Battle of Britain, 37, 40, 116
Battle of Midway (*see* Midway)
Battle of the Somme (*see* Somme)
battlefield air interdiction (*see* interdiction)
battleship admirals, 13, 47
Bay of Pigs, 84
Beakley, Ed., 4, 5, 57, 72, 119, 124, 168, 170, 173
Below, Otto von, Gen., 15, 16
Bennitt, Brent, VAdm., 5, 99, 181
Berlin crisis, 46
Berlin Wall, 69, 193
Biancur, Andy, 74
Bien Hoa, 74–76, 103
"BINGO" fuel, 165–166
Birdwhistle, Richard, Lt., 99
Birzer, Norman, 120
Bissel, Clayton, 32
Blackburn, Mr., 83–84
Blood, Gordon, Maj. Gen., 77
Blue/Purple Teams (LTV), 92, 98
Boeing Company, 5, 31, 33, 37, 48, 77, 85, 135, 207, 210, 216, 217, 229
Boelcke, Oswald, 15, 221
Bohn, John W., Lt. Col., 106, 109–111, 212

dive-bombing, accuracy, 16, 31, 34, 44, 49–50, 54, 66, 106, 111, 113, 115–116, 129, **129**, 130, 132, 134, 141–148, **150**–151, 153–156, 163, 179–181, 190, 197

division, of four aircraft, USN, 124, 171–173

Dixie Station, 71, 122

Dixon, Robert, Lt. Cmdr., 47

Dixon, Robert, Gen., 189

doctrine, strategic, tactical air, 4, 11, 16–17, 24–25, 29–31, 33, 35–37, 41, 43, 47, 50, 63, 69, 101, 105–106, 115, 136, 139, 140–141, 171, 183–186, 192–193, 221–223, 225, 227

"Doctrine of the Offensive Spirit," 17

"Doctrine of Quality," 126, 130, 139

Dodd, T. F., Maj., 21

Donovan, Matt, 201

Doolittle Raid, 56

Doss, Robert F., Capt., 83, 88, 142–153, 156, 160, 181, 226

double cycle, 121

"double attack," 204

Douglas Corporation, 33, 248

Douglas, Donald, 33, 36, 54, 211

East German police, 69

Eberle, Edward W., Adm., 50

economy of force, 25

Edney, Leon A. "Bud," Adm., 5, 71

ejection seat, 98, 157, 179

electronic countermeasures (ECM), 64, 88, 98, 247

element, of aircraft, USAF, 41, 123–124, 171, 172, 220

enemy sanctuaries, 78, 215

energy maneuverability (E-M), 79, 109–110, 181, 184, 186, 203, 205–206, 212

engine "rollback," 99

England, UK, 15, 26, 43, 45, 136, 148, 163, 165, 177

Enthoven, Dr. Alain, 68–69, 87, 89, 95–96, 106–107, **109**, 111, 118, 144, 155, 158–159, 224

Fair, John, Capt., 92

Fairchild/Republic, 188–190, 192

Fallows, James, 185

FASTFAC, 4, 77, 178

Ferguson, James, Gen., **109**, 157, 187, 203–204

Field Manual 1-5, Army, 36

Field Manual 100–5, 192

"Fighter Mafia," 184–185, 193, 204–207, 209, 212

Fighter Weapons School, USAF, 12, 106, 184–185, 204–205

"finger four" formation, 123, 204

fire arrow, 75

first Corsair II lost in combat, 120

first flight, A-7, 112, 131, 162

first test run of the TF-41, 138

Fish, Howard, Col. / Fish Study, 107–**109**, 110–116, 158, 185, 212

Fisher, Bernie, Maj., 77

fixed-price incentive fee contract, 138

Flaming Dart, 70

flareship, 75, 76, 194

Fleet air defense interceptor, 81, 210

Flexible Response, strategy, 83, 107

flight, of four aircraft, USAF, 39, 41, 76

flight deck, 39, 56, 72, 172, 173

Flight Path Marker, A-7E, 181, 248

Fogleman, Ronald, Gen., CSAF, 28, 31, 78, 215

Fokker, Tony, 15

Force Options for Tactical Air, 106

force structure, 68–69, 85, 103, 107–108, 111, 113, 117, 140, 143, 149, 152, 155, 200, 209

Ford, Gerald, President, 177

Ford Motor Company, 68, 141

Fort Bragg, North Carolina, 165

Fort Crockett, Texas, 30, 32

Fort Hood, Texas, 164

Fort Leavenworth, Kansas, 101

Fort Leonard Wood, Missouri, 38

Fort Riley, Kansas, 189

Fort Worth, Texas, 91, 152

Foster, John H., Jr., Dr., 147, 153, 155, 187

fragmentation bomb, 18, 34, 50, 74

fragmentation (frag) order, 75

French air force, 16, 21, 22, 59

French Foreign Legion, 22

full system cost, 87

Galanti, Paul, 71

Gallagher, Thomas J., Capt., 145

Garros, Roland, 15

GAU-8/A 30 mm cannon, 189, 191, 224, 229

General Dynamics, 85, 91, 94, 186, 205, 207–208, 210, 212, 214, 225, 248

General Dynamics / Grumman, 85, 94, 186, 192, 210, 215, 216

General Electric J-79 engine, 81

General Electric M-61 gatling gun (*see* M-61 cannon)

general purpose bomb (GP), 41, 74

general purpose forces, 73, 89, 108

German Air Service, 15–17, 19, 221

Gilfry, Lt. Cmdr. Maso, 169, 170

Global War on Terrorism, 200

Godfrey, Arthur, 62

Goldwater, Barry, Senator, 159, 163, 217

Goodspeed, Hill, 51,52

Goodyear, 59, 248

Graham, Gordon, Lt. Gen., 110–112, 114, 131, 134

Great Lakes, 53

"Great Truck Massacre," 78

Gregor, Michael, 42

Griffith, V. C., Lt., 98

ground alert, 45, 68–69, 73, 75–77, 177–178, 193, 220

ground straffing (*see* Strafing)

growth potential, 111, 116, 118

Grumman Aircraft Engineering Corp., 34, 42, 52–53, 57, 59, 73, 82, 85, 87–89, 94, 121, 182, 186–187, 192

Guadalcanal, 57

Guderian, Heinz, Col. Gen., 40

Gulbransen, Gary, 1Lt., 75

"Gun Club," 47

gun sights, 51, 57, 129, 131, 141, 143, **150**, 186, 225

Gunsmoke "1991," 197

Haering, George, 88

Hal Duong railway, 120

Hails, Lt. Gen. Robert, 126–132, 134–137, 141–151, 156–157, 160, 189, 190, 211, 226

Haiphong, 120, 169, 173

Hanoi, 120, 165, 170, 172–174, 176

Hare, Paul, 98

Hart, Gary, 185

Hartman, Charles, Lt., 70

Harvey, Neil, Cmdr., 171

Have, Chris, Lt. Col., 199

heavyweight abort test, 99

Heinemann, Ed, 36, 54, 60–61, 64–65, 212, 226

Helmet-Mounted Integrated Targeting system, 200, 225

Heyman, Vic, 108, 159

"high/low" mix, fighters, 208, 209

Hill, James C., Cmdr., 100, 120–121

Hillaker, Harry, 205

Hiryu, Japanese aircraft carrier, 57

Hitch, Charles J., Dr., 68, 108, 111

Ho Chi Minh Trail, 78

Holmes, Mike, Gen., 201

Hoover, Herbert, President, 50

Hopkins, Lou, RAdm., 55–57, 59

Horner, Charles A., Gen., 183, 193, 196

House Armed Services Committee, 97, 101, 112, 161, 188

Howse Board, 102, **102**–103, 106, 107

Howze, Hamilton H., Lt. Gen., 102

HUD (heads-up display), 178, 181, 186, 198, 200, 213, 248

Hueber, Fred , Cmdr., 100, 119

Hurlburt Field, (*see* Air Force bases)
Eglin Auxiliary #9, 74, 76, 102, 103, 202
Hussein, Saddam, 193

Ilyushin, Sergei, 40
Immelmann, Max, 15, 77, 221
in-commission rate, 74
Independent Air Force, 17
in-flight refueling probe, 77, 98
Ingalls, David S., Lt. jg, 26, 50
innovation advocate, 142, 184–185, 203–205, 207, 217
Integrated Air Defense (IAD), 78
Integrated Light Attack Avionics System (ILAAS), 90, 129–131, 143–144, 147, 149
integrated electronic navigation and bombing system, 73, 78, 84, 90, 129, 132, 143–144, 146–147, 151, 155–156, 181, 213, 227–228
interdiction, 5, 11, 13, 16–17, 23, 27, 29, 31, 40, 43–45, 65, 67, 70, 79, 82, 84, 94, 109, 123, 146, 165, 179, 185, 192–193, 210, 221, 223–224, 247
"Interim Buy Tactical Fighters," letter, 117
intermediate maintenance, 72
internal bomb bay, 24, 46, 217
Issoudon, France, 21
Iwo Jima, 59

Jackson, 2Lt. Wells R., 74
Jeffrey, Thomas S., Maj. Gen., 157
Jerkins, Harry, Cmdr., 169
Johnson, Harold K., CSA, Gen., 133, 148, 183
Johnson, Kelly, 205
Johnson, Louis, Secretary of Defense, 64
Johnson, Clinton, Lt., 70
Joint Air Force/Army planning, 45, 85, 114
Joint Air Forces/OSD FX Effort ("Fish Study"), 108, 114, 117
Joint Chiefs of Staff, 45, 104–105, 173–174, 188
jointness, 9, 11, 45, 82–84, 123, 136, 138, 140–141, 147, 149, 153–154, 156, 158, 160, 161, 164, 210, 215, 217, 219–220, 229, 248
Jones, David D., Gen., CSAF, CJCS, 209
"Jungle Jim," 74

Kaga, Japanese aircraft carrier, 57
Kaiser, Henry, 60
Kartveli, Alexander, 42
Kasserine Pass, 25

Kay, Avery, Col., 183, 185
Kelly, David, Lt., 170–171, 219
Kelly Field, Texas (*see* Air Force bases)
Kennedy, John F., President, 68, 84, 183, 212
Kennedy administration, 68–69, 74
Khafji, Saudi Arabia, Battle of, 195
Kinney, George C., Gen., 31
Konrad, John W., 98–99, 112
Korean War, 39, 43, 45, 61–64, 69–70, 77, 142, 168, 184
Korth, Fred, Secretary of the Navy, 94
Kosovo, Republic of, 197–199, 214, 248
Kuiper, Richard L., Col., 4, 76

Laird, Melvin R., Secretary of Defense, 159, 161, 187
Landing Zone Albany, 76
Landing Zone, X-Ray, 76
Langley, Samuel Pierpoint, 26
Laning, Captain, 48
Lankford, J. W., 92
LANTIRN (Low Altitude Navigation and Targeting Infrared for Night), 182, 211, 215
Lau, Conrad, 91, 92
Lavelle, John D., Gen., 131, 132
Lafayette Escadrille & Flying Corps, 22
LeMay, Curtis, Gen., 84, 104, 106–107
Leslie, John, Lt., 176
Lewis & Vought Corporation, 98
Lichtermann, Dave, Lt. jg, 168
Leopold, Ray, 185
Light Attack Airplane (VAL) Primer, 92–**93**
light weight fighter (LWF), 190, 203–208, 210, 212–213, 228, 245, 248
Lind, Bill, 185
Lindbergh, Charles, 59, 227
Ling, James, 91
Ling-Temco-Vought (LTV), 91, 97, 112, 117, 179, 248
Litchfield Park, Arizona, 69
Little, Bob, GS-13, 142
Lockett, Frank, Lt., 170
Loh, Michael, Gen., 4, 190, 205–209, 211–212, 217
Long Island City, 98
loss rates, 24, 43, 222
Louisiana Maneuvers, 37
Love, Sol, 91–92, 98–99, 145
Lovett, Robert A., Asst Sec. of War, Secretary of Defense, 36
Low Altitude Bombing System (LABS), 77

Low Altitude Safety & Targeting Enhancement (LASTE), 196–197, 248
low-cost afterburner, 109, 118, 127–128, 131–136, 138
Ludendorff, Erich Friedrich Wilhelm, Gen., 20
"lure and ambush," 76

M-61 cannon, 35, 81, 128, 138–141, 143, 168, 186, 190, 192, 224–225, 227
MacArthur, Douglas, General of the Army, CSA, 45, 163
Mach number, A-7, 99, 206
Mackay Trophy, 33
Mahan, Alfred Thayer, 47
maintenance hours per flight hour, A-7, 99
Manson, Frank, Cmdr., 62
marketing, aircraft companies, 42, 82, 91, 96, 119, 212, 215
Marks, James, Lt. Col., 196
Marne Sector, 22
Marshall, George C., General of the Army, CSA, 37
Martin, Glenn L. Company, 33, 36–37, 39, 48, 51–**52**, 59, 60, 197, 199, 209, 214, 217, 233
massive retaliation, 45, 63, 115
Masson, Didier, 26
Maverick missile, 195, 199
Mayaguez cargo ship, 167, 177
McCain, John, Cmdr. and Senator, 169
McClarren, Charles, Maj., 120, 163
McClellan Committee, 90
McClennan, John, Senator, 85
McClusky, Wade, Cmdr., 56
McDonnell Douglas Corporation, 81, 82, 109, 142, 186–188, 212–216, 248
McNamara, John, Ens., 26
McNamara, Robert, Secretary of Defense, 14, 64, 68–69, 82–85, 87, 89, 95–96, 101–105, 107, 111, 114, 116–118, 128, 132, 135, 138, 140–141, 148–149, 153–154, 157–158, 184–187, 210
McNamara's "List," 95
McSally, Martha, Senator, 201
Medal of Honor, 77
Mersky, Perter, 120, **123**
"Messerschmidt, Capt.," 168
Messines, Battle of, 20
Metz-Frascaty, 15
Mexican Federal Fleet, 26
Meyer, J. C., Gen., 174
Michigan, University of, 91
Midway, Battle of, 12, 36–39, 41, 53, 55–57

175th Tactical Fighter Group (ANG), 197
333d Tactical Fighter Squadron, 191
353d Tactical Fighter Squadron, 164
354th Tactical Fighter Squadron, 167
354th Tactical Fighter Wing, 79, 155, 162, 164–165, 167, 177, 191, 193
355th Tactical Fighter Wing, 191, 167
388th Tactical Fighter Wing, 167, 177
432d Tactical Reconnaissance Wing, 175
442d Tactical Fighter Wing, (Reserve), 197
479th Tactical Fighter Wing, 80
602d Fighter Squadron (Commando), 75–77, 79, 103
4525th Fighter Weapons Wing, 120, 162–163
4554th Tactical Fighter Wing, 164
6441st Tactical Fighter Wing, 80
N. 124, Escadrille Americaine, 22

Air Force Bases
Barksdale AFB, Louisiana, 30, 34
Bentwaters, AB, UK, 191–192
Bien Hoa AB, RVN, 74–76, 103
Bradley Field, Massachusetts, 191
Cannon AFB, New Mexico, 165
Danang AB, RVN, 71
Davis-Monthan AFB, Arizona, 177–178
Edwards AFB, California, 99, 158, 163, 188, 204
Hickam AFB, Hawaii, 30, 32
Hill AFB, Utah, 217
Homestead AFB, Florida, 75
Hurlburt Field, Eglin Auxiliary #9, Florida, 74–76, 102–103, 202
Itazuki AB, Japan, 43
Kelly Field/AFB, Texas, 49–50
Kirtland AFB, New Mexico, 99–100
Korat RTAFB, Thailand, 80, 164–165, 167–168, 177
Langley Field/AFB, Virginia, 29, 30, 127
Luke AFB, Arizona, 120, 162–165
Maxwell AFB, Alabama, 30
McChord AFB, Washington, 75
McClellan AFB, California, 199
McCook Field, Ohio, 31
Misawa AB, Japan, 164
Myrtle Beach AFB, South Carolina, 162, 164, 191
Nakhon Phanom RFAFB, Thailand, 79
Nha Trang AB, RVN, 79
Nellis AFB, Nevada, 9, 80, 106, 184, 191, 197, 202

Pleiku AB, RVN, 79
Qui Nhon AB, RVN, 76
Savannah Army Air Base, Georgia, 30
Ubon RTAFB, Thailand, 81
Udorn RTAFB, Thailand, 70, 76, 79, 81, 175
Wright-Patterson AFB, Ohio, 33, 42, 203–204, 206–207

Naval Air Stations
Cecil Field, NAS, Florida, 57, 100, 119, 220
Cubi Point, Subic Bay, Philippines, 124
China Lake, Naval Air Weapons Center, California, 60, 99, 132, 142–143, 146, 149, 248
Dallas, NAS, Texas, 91, 97–100, 112, 119, 131, 134, 146
El Centro NAS (MCAS), California, 12, 70
Fallon, NAS, Nevada, 9, 12, 170, 220
Kaneohe, NAS/MCB, Hawaii, 55
Lemoore, NAS, California, 8, 100, 119, 120, 168, 170, 216
Miramar, NAS (MCAS), California, 211
North Island, NAS (NASNI), California, 26, 50, 53, 120, 248
Patuxent River, NAS, Naval Air Test Center, Maryland, 99–100, 119, 127
Pensacola, NAS, Florida, 11, 26, 51, 52, 222
Point Mugu, NAS, Naval Air Test Center, Weapons Division, California, 119–120, 248
San Diego, NAS, California (see North Island)
Yorktown Aviation Field, Virginia, 29